POWER IN
SOCIETIES

POWER IN SOCIETIES

Edited by MARVIN E. OLSEN

INDIANA UNIVERSITY

MACMILLAN PUBLISHING CO., INC.
New York
COLLIER MACMILLAN PUBLISHERS
London

MACMILLAN PUBLISHING CO., INC.
866 THIRD AVENUE, NEW YORK, NEW YORK 10022

COLLIER-MACMILLAN CANADA, LTD.

Library of Congress catalog card number: 70-90875

Printing: 10   Year: 9

PREFACE

This collection of sociological writings on the nature, distribution, and use of power in modern societies has two major purposes. The first of these is to delimit and explore what I see as the central theoretical concern of political sociology—the exercise of power in social life. Although the literature in political sociology has been expanding rapidly in recent years, little attention has yet been given to developing this basic theoretical orientation. Through my own essays and the organization of reading selections in this book, I have attempted to meet this challenge, though in a most tentative manner.

The second purpose of the book is to serve as a "learning guide" for sociology students, both undergraduate and graduate, in their study of social power and the organization of modern societies. All of the selections comprising the book (except my essays) have been published previously, and most of them are fairly accessible in the sociological literature. My justification for bringing them together in one volume, therefore, is simply to make them more conveniently available for student use in both scheduled courses and individual study.

More succinctly, the book might be described as a "core readings text" on social power, designed to provide a basic conceptual and theoretical foundation on which a variety of courses in the area of political sociology could be built. My decision to make this book primarily a collection of reading selections rather than a standard textbook was deliberate, on the grounds that upperclassmen and graduate students should be exposed to ideas in their original forms, not as summarized and interpreted by another writer. The book is therefore meant to serve the function of a text, and is not intended to be merely an illustrative supplement to some other work. All of the writings included here make significant contributions to our understanding of social power, and many of them are considered by political sociologists to be of crucial importance. In addition, each section of the book begins with an original essay that attempts to tie together the ideas expressed in the readings that follow. Although the essays thus serve as introductions to the reading selections, they also go beyond these writings to introduce new ideas and propositions.

Most of the laborious clerical work involved in compiling this book has been done by Judith Hadsall, Margaret Marty, Cynthia Griffin, and Virginia Fisher, to whom I owe much gratitude. To the authors of all the reprinted works, whose creative writings made this book possible, I can only express total indebtedness. I am entirely responsible for the selection and editing of these readings, although the students in my sociology of power course during the past several years deserve recognition for their many helpful suggestions and criticisms. Finally, my wife, Katherine Olsen, has given me much help with the chores that typically fall upon authors' spouses—proofreading and index construction—in addition to the patience and encouragement required of a "book widow."

M. E. O.

CONTENTS

INTRODUCTION

Early political philosophers, struggling to explain the bonds of social order that unite men into cohesive organizations, relied heavily on the concept of power and processes of power exertion. Thus, Thomas Hobbes, to whom all modern conflict theorists are indebted, wrote in *Leviathan* that "During the time men live without a common Power to keep them all in awe, they are in that condition which is called warre, as is of every man, against every man."[1] Similarly, John Locke, a forerunner of contemporary consensualist theorists, argued in his *Second Treatise of Civil Government* that "To understand political power right, and derive it from its original, we must consider, what state all men are naturally in, and that is, *a state of perfect freedom* to order their actions, and dispose of their possessions and persons, as they think fit, within the bounds of the law of nature, without asking leave, or depending upon the will of any other man. A *state* also *of equality*, wherein all the power and jurisdiction is reciprocal. . . ."[2]

Twentieth-century sociology has until quite recently largely overlooked this early concern with power, however. For instance, neither Park and Burgess' *Introduction to the Science of Sociology*,[3] which was the standard introductory text in the 1920's and 1930's, nor Ogburn and Nimkoff's *Sociology*,[4] which was probably the most widely used text during the 1940's and 1950's, even list the term "power" in their indexes. Not until the 1960's did social power become a major concern of sociological research and theorizing, and our knowledge of this phenomenon is still woefully inadequate. Much of the revival of interest in power processes has undoubtedly been stimulated by a growing appreciation of Karl Marx as a serious social theorist, but credit must also be given to such contemporary writers as C. Wright Mills, Ralf Dahrendorf, Seymour Martin Lipset, William Kornhauser, Daniel Bell, Gerhard Lenski, Amitai Etzioni, Robert Nisbet, and even Talcott Parsons—all of whom are represented in this volume.

Within the last decade a host of empirical research studies of power structures—primarily in communities and formal associations—have suddenly appeared and attracted considerable attention among sociologists. Concurrently, social theorists have recently proposed that "Every social act is an exercise of power, every social relationship is a power equation, and every social group or system is an organization of power,"[5] and that "The realization of most societal goals, even in situations in which the actor's commitment and knowledge are considerable, requires the application of power."[6] Once the most neglected of sociological phenomena, power is increasingly being seen as a crucial aspect of virtually all social life.

The exercise of social power constitutes the central concern of political sociology,

---

[1] Reprinted in Talcott Parsons, *et al.*, *Theories of Society* (New York: The Free Press of Glencoe, 1961), Vol. I, p. 100.

[2] Reprinted in Parsons, *ibid.*, p. 101.

[3] Robert E. Park and Ernest W. Burgess, *Introduction to the Science of Sociology* (Chicago: The University of Chicago Press, 1921).

[4] William F. Ogburn and Meyer F. Nimkoff, *Sociology* (Boston: Houghton Mifflin Company, 1941).

[5] Amos H. Hawley, "Community Power and Urban Renewal Success," *The American Journal of Sociology*, Vol. 68, January 1963, pp. 422-431.

[6] Amitai Etzioni, *The Active Society* (London: Collier-Macmillan Ltd., 1968), p. 314.

a subdiscipline of sociology that attempts to link it with political science. Topics commonly studied by political sociologists include the state as a social institution in relation to the rest of society, political and social movements, community power systems and decision making, bureaucratic power structures and operations, the role of power in stratification and race relations, political values and attitudes, and political participation through voting and other activities. The common focus of these diverse areas of theorizing and research is social power, as exercised in all organizations from national governments to small groups.

This volume does not attempt to cover the entire field of political sociology, but rather presents a wide selection of both "classical" and contemporary theoretical writings on the nature, distribution, and use of power in societies. Familiarity with this theoretical foundation is a requisite for study and research in all areas of political sociology.

All of the writings included in this book deal with power in social organization, as contrasted with interpersonal interaction—and as the title implies, most of them focus on total societies rather than smaller collectivities. The concept of "social organization," used in a generic sense, refers to all instances of patterned and recurrent social ordering and resulting bounded social entities, plus their associated bodies of cultural ideas.[7] An organizational perspective (sometimes described as "macrosociological") thus sees social power as located within patterns of social relationships and as constituting a property of organized social entities, not individuals. There is a large body of literature in sociology and psychology dealing with interpersonal influence, especially in dyadic and small-group settings, but because most of this writing is social-psychological rather than organizational in perspective, it is not included here.

The decision to focus primarily on total societies, rather than smaller units such as communities or formal associations, was made for two reasons: (1) Most general theories of social power—which are the main concerns of the book—pertain to societies as the most inclusive and complex form of social organization in today's world; power theories relevant to smaller organizations are for the most part simply restatements or modifications of societal theories. (2) Several collections of articles dealing with power in communities and formal associations—many of which are reports of empirical studies—have already been published, but no presently available volume brings together the major theoretical writings on societal power. The section of this book concerned with class and racial power struggles is a partial exception to the over-all societal focus, but even here (a) most of these writings are set in a societal context, and (b) current conditions and events in these two areas are presently having manifold consequences for their encompassing societies.

The seven sections into which the readings are arranged can be thought of as constituting four basic sets: (1) Part I, "Power and Social Organization," contains writings on both the essential nature of social power and the relationship of power to broader processes of social organization. (2) Part II, "Marxian Power Theory,"

---

[7]This conception of social organization is elaborated in Marvin E. Olsen, *The Process of Social Organization* (New York: Holt, Rinehart and Winston Inc., 1968).

Part III, "Elitist Power Theories," and Part IV, "Pluralistic Power Theories," present the three main schools of theoretical thinking about societal power in contemporary political sociology. (3) Part V, "Centralization of Power," and Part VI, "Class and Racial Power Struggles," both deal with major power trends now occurring in many modernized societies.[8] (4) Part VII, "Future Trends in Societal Power," consists of a variety of readings on presently observable power changes that will undoubtedly affect all future "post-industrial" societies, as well as several different models of possible future societies that could result from these changes.

As will be evident in the diverse and often conflicting writings collected in this volume, political sociology cannot at present offer any single, general theory to explain the structuring or exercise of power in societies. Several potential bases for theoretical synthesis can be found within the various schools of theorizing and the writings on power trends, however, if we are willing to put aside our value attachments to particular viewpoints and begin looking for common themes and observations. One noteworthy effort in this direction is Amitai Etzioni's recent writings on "active societies".[9] Nevertheless, these are only initial steps toward the goal of constructing and then testing a general theory of power in societies. That challenge awaits the efforts of future political sociologists—including perhaps some readers of this book.

---

[8]Many, though not all, of the readings in these two sections focus more explicitly on the United States than do any of the other sets of writings. The primary reason for this "bias" is simply that the trends discussed here have been more extensively studied in this society than anywhere else. There is no reason to assume, however, that these same trends could not also occur—and in fact probably are now occurring—in many other modernized nations.

[9]Etzioni, *loc. cit.*

I
POWER AND SOCIAL ORGANIZATION

POWER AS A SOCIAL PROCESS

Marvin E. Olsen

Power exertion is perhaps the least studied and least understood—and yet most fundamental—process in social life. As with energy in the physical world, power pervades all dynamic social phenomena, yet it cannot be directly observed or measured. Because its existence, nature, and strength can only be indirectly inferred from its effects on social activities, both participants and social scientists are often led to overlook its crucial significance.

If by social interaction we mean one actor affecting another, then every instance of interaction and every social relationship involves the exercise of power. And as these activities give rise to broader patterns of social order and delineated social organizations—including total societies—all organized social life becomes infused with power. As expressed by Amos Hawley, "Every social act is an exercise of power, every social relationship is a power equation, and every social group or system is an organization of power. Accordingly, it is possible to transpose any system of social relationships into terms of potential or active power. Perhaps such a transposition is nothing more than the substitution of one terminology for another."[1]

Social power can be viewed analytically as either a consequence or a cause of organized social activities, though in reality both processes occur simultaneously. On the one hand, power does not exist until social actors begin relating to one another in some manner. It is created through social interactions and relationships, as an outgrowth of social ordering. Organized power exertion enables actors to perform collective activities and achieve common goals. On the other hand, power is also a major factor contributing to the creation and perpetuation of social organization. Social relationships and patterns of social order are often established as a direct or indirect result of power being exerted on actors. Although power is neither the sole

---

[1] Amos H. Hawley, "Community Power and Urban Renewal Success," *The American Journal of Sociology*, Vol. 68, January 1963, pp. 422-431.

cause nor the only outcome of the process of social organization, its effects can never be ignored if we wish fully to understand organized social life.

There is no commonly accepted sociological definition of social power, although the essential idea stressed by most writers is that *power is the ability to affect social activities*. Power is not a "thing" possessed by social actors, but rather a dynamic process that occurs in all areas of social life. Two qualifications frequently added to this basic idea are that social power is a generalized rather than a narrowly limited capacity, and that the exercise of power necessitates overcoming resistance. The first qualification is made primarily for analytical convenience, since sociologists are usually concerned with broad and relatively stable patterns of power rather than with every isolated and minute instance of power exertion. The second qualification is semantically redundant, since the idea of affecting social activities logically implies overcoming whatever opposition or limitations may be encountered. Nevertheless, reference to resistance does remind us that the exercise of power is usually a reciprocal process among all participants, and is rarely determined by a single actor no matter how unequal the situation may appear.

Some writers distinguish power from the related concepts of influence and control, usually on the grounds that the effects of power on the recipient are to some extent involuntary, while influence and control are seen as producing a motivational change within affected individuals so that they more or less willingly comply. (In this view, influence involves more-or-less overt persuasion, whereas control rests largely on unconscious norm internalization.) This distinction seems rather arbitrary, though, when we realize that what begins as wholly involuntary compliance may over time shift to willing cooperation, while what seems to be voluntary compliance may be simply a decision to abide by an inescapable directive. A more meaningful use of these terms, therefore, is to keep *power* as the inclusive or generic concept, with *influence* and *control* used to describe the determinateness of possible outcomes as seen from the perspective of the power wielder. At one extreme of this continuum, the effects of mild influence attempts would be quite unpredictable, while the outcomes of total control programs would be largely predetermined.

The actors who exercise social power may be organizations (from small groups to total societies) as well as individuals. Although it is of course true that relationships among organizations are carried out by individuals enacting organizational roles, it is nevertheless the organization as a whole—not the individual spokesmen for the organization—which is wielding power. The representatives of labor and management who meet to bargain on a new contract are able to exert power on each other only because they both represent organized collectivities. Ideally, it should be possible to explain both interpersonal and interorganizational power processes with a single general theory. In practice, however, interpersonal power relationships are most commonly studied by social psychologists using social-psychological concepts and variables, while interorganizational power relationships are investigated by sociologists using somewhat different concepts and variables. The consequence of this scientific bifurcation is two sets of literature on social power that often bear little resemblance to each other. Because this book focuses on power in societies, all of the selections reprinted here are primarily sociological in nature, although some of them do also discuss interpersonal power.

Before he can exert any social power, an actor must have access to *resources* upon which he can draw. These resources may be either tangible goods such as money, land, material possessions, and organizational members, or relatively intangible assets such as knowledge, skills, legitimacy, and organizational unity. In any case, these available resources provide the basis on which the actor's power rests. In contrast to his power, which exists only in his relationships with other actors, his resources can be possessed by him alone.

The amount and kind of an actor's resources provide a potential for power exertion, but the strength of the power he actually exercises in a particular situation is determined by two other factors: resources committed and resistance encountered. An actor who was able and willing to commit all of his limited resources to a relationship might be able to exert considerably more power than an actor with extensive resources which he could not or would not employ. Given a certain level of resource committment, the greater the resistance facing an actor the less power he will be able to wield. Resistance is usually thought of as more-or-less overt opposition by others, but it can also take such forms as time limitations, inadequate channels of communication, and passive indifference by the other actors. In general, the amount of power an actor exercises in a particular relationship is a resultant of the extent and adequacy of his committed resources, multiplied by his skill in converting resources into pressures, minus the degree of resistance encountered.

The actual procedure of converting resources into overt pressures of one kind or another is the heart of the process of power exertion. At the present time, however, sociologists know very little about how this occurs. A few studies of social interaction and small group activities have investigated this process at the interpersonal level using social-psychological variables, but there has been almost no research into the procedures by which organizations carry out the process. It obviously occurs, but how, and what are the crucial determinants of its effectiveness?

In their attempts to clarify further the basic concept of social power, sociologists have vigorously debated four issues that are briefly discussed in the following paragraphs. First, is it useful to classify power as either "potential" or "active"? An actor is sometimes said to have "potential power" when he possesses resources and is capable of employing them if desired. Power is then "active" when these resources are actually converted into actions. This conceptual distinction reminds us that (a) resources must be readily available for use before they become relevant for power exertion, and that (b) an actor can be thought by others to be capable of wielding power even though he does not overtly do so. The first point can more clearly be made, however, simply by adding the term "committed" to "resources." The second point requires more attention, since an actor's potential for exerting power is often assessed by others before he or they act. Such assessments are essentially probabilistic expectations of the actor's willingness to use his available resources and his skill at converting them into actions, based on knowledge of his past performances and the immediate situation. In this latter sense "potential power" is distinct from "committed resources" and is a useful concept for sociological analysis, although another term such as "perceived power" would be desirable, since the accuracy of these assessments is also affected by characteristics (such as values and statuses) of the assessors.

Second, should the concept of social power be limited to activities intended to attain a desired goal, or should it also be applied to activities whose effects on others are unintended and often quite indirect? The resolution of this question usually depends on the phenomenon being investigated in specific studies. For analytical and empirical convenience, the process of power exertion is often limited to purposeful goal-seeking activities and their immediate consequences. But in fact much power wielding is relatively unintended and its effects are indirect and far reaching, so that more encompassing studies must also take these phenomena into consideration.

Third, can social power be viewed as a positive factor in promoting organized social life as well as a negative restriction? Those sociologists who see power as only a negative process often speak of it as "control over others" and deplore its occurrence because of an underlying ideological belief that power is undesirable in social life. In contrast, other writers believe that power can be highly desirable because it enables actors to achieve otherwise unobtainable results. They consequently see social power as a positive process and speak of it as "the ability to attain collective goals." It would seem clear that if sociologists are to study social power objectively, they must at least temporarily put aside all such ideological perspectives and explore both sides of all power processes.

Fourth, is social power being exerted when both (or all) actors are equal in strength? Two separate points are actually being raised here: (1) If the resistance by others to an actor's attempted exercise of power is strong enough to prevent him from having any effect on them, then he is not wielding power in that situation. (2) But if he does succeed in exerting some power on them, it may or may not be balanced by their power actions on him. In a relatively balanced (sometimes called exchange) situation, each actor exerts some amount of power in some actions, so that each one effects the others but in different ways. In a relatively unbalanced situation, meanwhile, most of the power is wielded by one actor, with little reciprocal power being exercised by the others involved. In short, extent of power balancing is a separate question from degree of resistance in any situation.

Beyond these issues concerning the fundamental nature of social power is the problem of classifying power processes into analytical types. Three fairly distinct types or forms of social power are frequently discussed by sociologists: force, dominance, and authority.[2] The major differences among these three types of power lie in the nature of the resources on which they are based.

[2]A fourth type—interpersonal attraction—is often mentioned by social psychologists, but it has not been extensively employed on the organizational level, with the exception of writings on charismatic leaders. For a discussion of three subtypes of interpersonal attraction, see Herbert C. Kelman, "Process of Opinion Change," *Public Opinion Quarterly*, Vol. 25, Spring 1961, pp. 57-78.

To exert *force*, an actor must bring previously uncommitted resources into the situation and either convert them into overt pressures or at least convincingly threaten to do so. He must invest new resources in the relationship beyond those already being employed, and be prepared to use them to back up his demands and overcome resistance. Even if he successfully bluffs the other actors into following his wishes without actually relinquishing his resources, those goods and assets are committed to the power relationship for the duration of its existence, and hence cannot be used elsewhere. Presuming that no actor possesses unlimited available resources, the amount of force that anyone can exert at a given time is therefore also limited—though great disparities may occur among actors in the strengths of the forces they exercise toward one another.

Three commonly mentioned subtypes of force are compensation, deprivation, and persuasion. With compensation (sometimes called "utilitarian power"), the power wielding actor provides others with desired objects or conditions in return for their compliance. Deprivation (sometimes called "coercive power") occurs when the actor applies punishments or withholds expected benefits as a consequence of non-compliance. Persuasion involves the manipulation by the actor of information, emotions, statuses, or norms and values. Each kind of force has a different consequence for the actor using it. Deprivation may be accomplished through threats without actually employing resources or it may require elaborate sanctioning procedures, but in either case the compliance obtained from others is involuntary and hence remains highly unstable and unreliable. Compensation requires relinquishing resources if the relationship is to be maintained, but because the other actors believe that they are also benefiting from the relationship it can be considerably more stable and reliable. Finally, since persuasion often produces relatively permanent motivational changes in the recipients, its effects can be extremely stable and reliable through time, and may continue long after the initial expenditure of resources.

To exert *dominance*, an actor must effectively perform his usual roles and activities within an organization or social system, but he need not draw on additional resources. Functional specialization and interdependence among the members and subunits of an organization tend to make each of them highly vulnerable to the actions of the other participants. As an actor performs his routine roles and activities in the organization, therefore, he often influences or controls the actions of many other interdependent actors, as well as the functioning of the entire organization. To the extent that a member or subunit wields such functional influence or control, dominance is being exerted. The resource base for the exercise of dominance is thus an actor's ability to perform organizational roles and functions and does not depend on his access to any additional goods or assets. In practice he may seek to use his position of dominance to exert force, by drawing on organizational resources for his own use or by threatening to withhold services until his demands are met, but this does not erase the analytical distinction between force and dominance.

Dominance is often observed in such activities as information flows, economic transactions, transportation services, and decision making, although it can occur within any kind of organized activity in which the participants are functionally specialized and interdependent. When studying dominance, sociologists frequently focus on only those few actors at the top or center of the system, since by virtue of their positions they are capable of wielding dominance over a wide range of activities within the organization. Nevertheless, even the lowliest member of the organization can exercise some amount of dominance over others to the extent that they are dependent on him. As all realms of social life in modern societies become increasingly specialized and interdependent, dominance emerges as a crucial type of social power.

To use *authority*, an actor must first be granted legitimacy by those subject to his directions. Either in the past or at the present time they must in some way give him the legitimate right to make decisions concerning them and direct their activities. This grant of legitimacy then becomes the actor's resource base for employing authoritative power, so that we often speak of authority as the exercise of legitimacy. Legitimacy is sometimes given to an actor through direct procedures such as formal votes or informal agreements, but more commonly it is indirectly expressed as one joins an organization, remains a member, and supports the actions of those who claim legitimacy.

Three grounds on which legitimate authority often rest are (a) traditional values, beliefs, norms, and customs, (b) legal prerogatives established through more-or-less rational agreements, and (c) special expertise or knowledge relevant to the situation. To the extent that an actor draws legitimacy from all three sources, as when he is particularly well qualified for a position, obtains it through legal procedures, and adheres to traditional values, his authority is especially strong. Actors with legitimacy, such as organizational leaders, frequently supplement their authority by exercising dominance through their roles and by exerting force—and over time effective use of these other kinds of power can even increase their legitimacy. But for analytical purposes authority must be distinguished from both force and dominance. To repeat, the resource base of authority is voluntarily granted legitimacy, not available additional resources or performance of interdependent roles. Because authority is a highly stable and reliable type of social power, organizational leaders almost invariably seek to protect and extend their legitimacy, no matter how extensively they may also utilize force and dominance in particular situations. They can hardly afford to do otherwise, since without legitimacy their positions are constantly in jeopardy and their ability to provide leadership is severly restricted.

These three categories of social power—force, dominance, and authority—are useful for descriptive purposes, but they tell us nothing about the dynamics of ongoing power processes. Broad patterns of power exertion, or what might be called *power systems* can change in either (or both) of two ways through time. (1) The relative distribution of power among the actors in a system can vary, even though the total amount of power being exercised remains constant. Questions such as "who are the power elites?" or "what is the prevailing balance of power?" or "how did these actors lose power?" all call for *distributive analysis* of power systems. The usual results of this kind of analysis are structural explanations of currently existing power distributions or historical shifts in power arrangements. (2) The total amount of power in the system can increase or decrease, while the relative distribution of power among the actors remains stable. In this case, questions such as "to what extent has the accumulation of resources increased the strength of the whole system?" or "how have poor communications and ineffective leadership reduced the over-all ability of the organization to attain its goals?" require *developmental analysis*. Our focus of attention has now shifted from the component parts to the total organization or system, and our concern is now to relate broad social and cultural trends to the development of over-all patterns of power usage.

Distributive and developmental changes are in no way incompatible, and in fact frequently accompany and reinforce each other. Growth or decline in the total amount of power being exercised often stimulates shifts in power distributions, while a "struggle for power" among actors can strengthen or weaken the power of the whole system. It is nevertheless important that the sociologist differentiate between these two analytical approaches, since they require contrasting initial assumptions. For distributive analysis we must temporarily assume "zero-sum" conditions in which the total amount of power remains constant, so one actor's gain is another's loss. For developmental analysis, however, we assume "positive-sum" conditions in which the total amount of power is constantly varying, so that all actors tend to gain or lose together. Both kinds of power analysis are equally valid and productive of scientific knowledge, and can fruitfully be combined as long as one remains sensitive to whatever assumptions he is making about the nature of social power.

Beyond the conceptual problems discussed thus far in this essay lies the much broader question of the significance of power in social life, and hence its importance for social theory. The prevailing view in contemporary sociology is to treat social power and social integration (especially consensus) as contrasting or alternative perspectives on social organization. It is then argued that for some problems and situations a "power approach" is more fruitful, while for others an "integration approach" will yield greater understanding. Either analytical approach is considered valid, but they are rarely combined in either theory or research. As a result, the attention given to power processes by any sociologist depends largely on his own particular orientation and interests. There is presently no general agreement in sociology on the role of power in social organization, or its relation to other social processes such as conflict and integration.[3]

It is far beyond the scope of this essay to propose a general theory of social organization based on power processes, although in recent years several writers have urged social theorists to turn their attention in this direction. We can at least suggest, however, that *social power in its various forms of force, dominance, and authority may provide a unifying theme around which numerous competing theories*

---

[3]Two notable efforts along these lines are Ralf Dahrendorf, *Class and Class Conflict in Industrial Society* (Stanford, Calif.: Stanford University Press, 1959), and Amitai Etzioni, *The Active Society* (London: Collier—Macmillan Ltd., 1968).

of social organization can be synthesized. Such diverse theoretical schemes as exchange theory, ecological theory, elitist theory, Marxian theory, the normative theories of Durkheim and Sumner, and even Parsonian value theory all incorporate some aspects of power as crucial variables[4]—indeed, power appears to be the only theme common to all of them.

To this proposal we might also add the idea that power and integration do not constitute competing perspectives on social organization, but rather are complementary dynamic processes—along with conflict—within the over-all phenomenon of emergent social organization. Although in reality these various processes are undoubtedly highly interrelated (and perhaps mutually reinforcing), for analytical purposes it may be useful to separate them at least temporarily. As a convenient mnemonic device, we might think of these as the *C* processes: *c*onflict arising from external stresses and internal strains, *c*ohesion being generated by both normative and functional integration processes, *c*ontrol being exercised over social activities through the exertion of force, dominance, and authority, *c*ommunication providing the means through which these processes occur, all of which result in varying degrees of *c*hange or *c*onstancy, the over-all consequence of which is the *c*reation of social organization. The exercise of control—through the use of various kinds of power, but especially legitimate authority—would seem to be the key aspect of this entire phenomenon, since power factors would determine how conflicts were handled and resolved, whether or not functional and normative integration could occur, the flow of communication, and the rates and extent of both constancy and change. In fact, as already suggested by Hawley, perhaps the process of social organization *is* essentially a process of power organization.

The selections comprising the first section of this book deal with the fundamental nature of social power, the processes through which it is generated in social life, and its relevance for understanding social organization. After Amos Hawley's opening statement on the ubiquity of power, the next six articles can be grouped into five sets: (1) Two general discussions of the concept of social power and its components, by Robert Bierstedt and Amitai Etzioni. Bierstedt sees power as the basis of all social organization, primarily in its active forms of force and authority, while Etzioni examines power (primarily force) as the dynamic means by which societies achieve their goals. (2) An article by Robert Dubin on the relationship of functional dominance as a type of power to broader organizational processes, in which he analyzes the ways in which performance of functions within an organization gives an actor dominance over other members.[5] (3) Two essays on authority and its use in social life, by Max Weber and Seymour Martin Lipset. Weber's description of three types of legitimate authority is a classic in political sociology, and Lipset's

---

[4] Summaries of these schools of theoretical thought, as well as references to relevant readings, are given in Marvin E. Olsen, *The Process of Social Organization* (New York: Holt, Rinehart, and Winston, Inc., 1968), Chap. 15.

[5] This paper uses a number of relatively technical concepts and terms, so that a reader without some background in general sociological theory may wish to skip it, but if it can be mastered it offers many stimulating insights into the processes through which functional dominance is generated within social organizations.

more recent writing on relationships between conflict, functional effectiveness, and legitimacy has stimulated much subsequent work. (4) Two theoretical explanations of how power is created in social organization, by Richard Emerson and Talcott Parsons. Emerson proposes what might be called a *dependency theory* of social power which stresses the dependence of one actor on another, whereas Parsons' *trust theory* is based on the analogy of trust invested in organizations to money deposited in banks. (5) The final selection by Ralf Dahrendorf states the traditional view of power and integration as alternative perspectives on social organization, but also discusses processes of interest group formation and conflict as seen from a power perspective. Although these nine writers frequently use differing terms for the same idea, and at some points directly contradict each other, taken together they do give us a comprehensive overview of the nature of power as a social process.

POWER AS AN ATTRIBUTE OF SOCIAL SYSTEMS

Amos H. Hawley

It should be obvious that power in the social sphere, as with energy in the physical, is ubiquitous. It is like energy, too, in that it appears in many forms. Every social act is an exercise of power, every social relationship is a power equation, and every social group or system is an organization of power. Accordingly, it is possible to transpose any system of social relationships into terms of potential or active power. Perhaps such a transposition is nothing more than the substitution of one terminology for another. At the very least, however, it focuses attention on the instruments of control and causes a social system to be viewed as a control mechanism.

The community, for example, may be conceived as an energy system. That is, as a system of relationships among functionally differentiated units the community constitutes a mobilization of power—the capacity to produce results—for dealing with the environment, whether physical or social. Each unit or subsystem—family, church, store, industry—is also an organization of power for the conduct of a function. Both the system and its subsystems tend to approximate a single organization model. Moreover, since the performance of its function by any one part affects in greater or lesser degree the conditions under which other parts carry out their functions, the parent system and each subsystem is an arena in which a more or less continuous interplay of influence occurs. Power, then, is expressed in

SOURCE: Amos H. Hawley, "Community Power and Urban Renewal Success," *The American Journal of Sociology*, Vol. 68, January 1963, pp. 422-423. Reprinted by permission. The present title was supplied by the editor of this volume, and footnotes have been omitted.

two ways: (1) as functional power—that required to execute a function; and (2) as derivative power—that which spills over into external relationships and regulates the interaction between parts. The two modes of manifestation are necessarily connected. The type of function performed determines the kind of derivative influence transmitted to other parts or subsystems. There might also be a quantitative association, though the magnitude of the derivative influence is a consequence not only of the scale to which a function has developed but also of its position in the system. Those subsystems that are most instrumental in relating the system to the environment doubtlessly exert a greater derivative effect than do subsystems one or more steps removed from the key position. Space does not permit a full exposition of a system conception of power. Perhaps enough has been said to indicate that power is a product of a system having developed, that it is lodged only in a system, and that it is most appropriately treated, therefore, as a system property. Whatever power an individual might appear to possess is in effect attached to the office he occupies in a system. He acquires power by attaining to an office and he loses it when he is separated from the office. But the acquiring and losing of power is illusory; the property belongs rather with the office or, better still, to the system in which the office is a specialized function. . . .

AN ANALYSIS OF SOCIAL POWER

Robert Bierstedt

Few problems in sociology are more perplexing than the problem of social power. In the entire lexicon of sociological concepts none is more troublesome than the concept of power. We may say about it in general only what St. Augustine said about time, that we all know perfectly well what it is—until someone asks us. Indeed, Robert M. MacIver has recently been induced to remark that "There is no reasonable adequate study of the nature of social power."[1] The present paper cannot, of course, pretend to be a "reasonable adequate study." It aims at reasonableness rather than adequacy and attempts to articulate the problem as one

SOURCE: Robert Bierstedt, "An Analysis of Social Power," *American Sociological Review*, Vol. 15, December 1950, pp. 730-738. Reprinted by permission. Several footnotes have been omitted, and those remaining have been renumbered.

[1] *The Web of Government* (New York: Macmillan, 1947), p. 458. MacIver goes on to say, "The majority of the works on the theme are devoted either to proclaiming the importance of the role of power, like those of Hobbes, Gumplowicz, Ratzenhofer, Steinmetz, Treitschke, and so forth, or to deploring that role, like Bertrand Russell in his *Power*." *Ibid.* One might make the additional comment that most of the discussions of power place it specifically in a political rather than a sociological context and that in the latter sense the problem has attracted almost no attention.

of central sociological concern, to clarify the meaning of the concept, and to discover the locus and seek the sources of social power itself.

The power structure of society is not an insignificant problem. In any realistic sense it is both a sociological (i.e., a scientific) and a social (i.e., a moral) problem. It has traditionally been a problem in political philosophy. But, like so many other problems of a political character, it has roots which lie deeper than the *polis* and reach into the community itself. It has ramifications which can be discerned only by sociology. Its primitive basis and ultimate locus, as MacIver has emphasized in several of his distinguished books,[2] are to be sought in community and in society, not in government or in the state. It is apparent, furthermore, that not all power is political power and that political power—like economic, financial, industrial, and military power—is only one of several and various kinds of social power. Society itself is shot through with power relations—the power a father exercises over his minor child, a master over his slave, a teacher over his pupils, the victor over the vanquished, the blackmailer over his victim, the warden over his prisoners, the attorney over his own and opposing witnesses, an employer over his employee, a general over his lieutenants, a captain over his crew, a creditor over a debtor, and so on through most of the status relationships of society. Power, in short, is a universal phenomenon in human societies and in all social relationships. . . .

Social power has variously been identified with prestige, with influence, with eminence, with competence or ability, with knowledge (Bacon), with dominance, with rights, with force, and with authority. Since the intension of a term varies, if at all, inversely with its extension—i.e., since the more things a term can be applied to the less precise its meaning—it would seen to be desirable to distinguish power from some at least of these other concepts. Let us first distinguish power from prestige.

The closest association between power and prestige has perhaps been made by E. A. Ross in his classic work on social control. "The immediate cause of the location of power," says Ross, "is prestige." And further,"The class that has the most prestige will have the most power."[3] Now prestige may certainly be construed as one of the sources of social power and as one of the most significant of all the factors which separate man from man and group from group. It is a factor which has as one of its consequences the complex stratification of modern societies, to say nothing of the partial stratification of non-literate societies where the chief and the priest and the medicine-man occupy prestigious positions. But prestige should not be identified with power. They are independent variables. Prestige is frequently unaccompanied by power and when the two occur together power is usually the basis and ground of prestige rather than the reverse. Prestige would seem to be a consequence of power rather than a determinant of it or a necessary component of it. In any event, it is not difficult to illustrate the fact that power and prestige are independent variables, that power can occur without prestige, and prestige without power. . . .

---

[2] See especially *The Modern State* (London: Oxford University Press, 1926), pp. 221-231, and *The Web of Government, op. cit.*, pp. 82-113, *et passim.*

[3] *Social Control* (New York: Macmillan, 1916), p. 78.

Similar observations may be made about the relations of knowledge, skill, competence, ability, and eminence to power. They are all components of, sources of, or synonyms of prestige, but they may be quite unaccompanied by power. When power does accompany them the association is incidental rather than necessary. For these reasons it seems desirable to maintain a distinction between prestige and power.

When we turn to the relationship between influence and power we find a still more intimate connection but, for reasons which possess considerable cogency, it seems desirable also to maintain a distinction between influence and power. The most important reason, perhaps, is that influence is persuasive while power is coercive. We submit voluntarily to influence while power requires submission. The mistress of a king may influence the destiny of a nation, but only because her paramour permits himself to be swayed by her designs. In any ultimate reckoning her influence may be more important than his power, but it is inefficacious unless it is transformed into power. The power of a teacher over his pupils stems not from his superior knowledge (this is competence rather than power) and not from his opinions (this is influence rather than power), but from his ability to apply the sanction of failure, i.e., to withhold academic credit, to the student who does not fulfill his requirements and meet his standards. The competence may be unappreciated and the influence may be ineffective, but the power may not be gainsaid.

Furthermore, influence and power can occur in relative isolation from each other and so also are relatively independent variables. We should say, for example, that Karl Marx has exerted an incalculable influence upon the twentieth century, but this poverty-stricken exile who spent so many of his hours immured in the British Museum was hardly a man of power. Even the assertion that he was a man of influence is an ellipsis. It is the ideas which are influential, not the man. Stalin, on the other hand, is a man of influence only because he is first a man of power. Influence does not require power, and power may dispense with influence. Influence may convert a friend, but power coerces friend and foe alike. Influence attaches to an idea, a doctrine, or a creed, and has its locus in the ideological sphere. Power attaches to a person, a group, or an association, and has its locus in the sociological sphere. . . .

Power is not force and power is not authority, but it is intimately related to both and may be defined in terms of them. We want therefore to propose three definitions and then to examine their implications: (1) power is latent force; (2) force is manifest power; (3) authority is institutionalized power. The first two of these propositions may be considered together. They look, of course, like circular definitions and, as a matter of fact, they are. If an independent meaning can be found for one of these concepts, however, the other may be defined in terms of it and the circularity will disappear. We may therefore suggest an independent definition of the concept of force. Force, in any significant sociological sense of the word, means the application of sanctions. Force, again in the sociological sense, means the reduction or limitation or closure or even total elimination of alternatives to the social action of one person or group by another person or group. "Your money or your life" symbolizes a situation of naked force, the reduction of alternatives to two. The execution of a sentence to hang represents the total elimination of alternatives. One army progressively limits the social action of another until only two alternatives remain for the unsuccessful contender—to surrender or die. Dismissal or demotion of personnal in an association similarly, if much less drastically, represents a closure of alternatives. Now all these are situations of force, or manifest power. Power itself is the predisposition or prior capacity which makes the application of force possible. Only groups which have power can threaten to use force and the threat itself is power. Power is the ability to employ force, not its actual employment, the ability to apply sanctions, not their actual application.[4] Power is the ability to introduce force into a social situation; it is the presentation of force. Unlike force, incidentally, power is always successful; when it is not successful it is not, or ceases to be, power. Power symbolizes the force which *may* be applied in any social situation and supports the authority which *is* applied. Power is thus neither force nor authority but, in a sense, their synthesis.

The implications of these propositions will become clearer if we now discuss the locus of power in society. We may discover it in three areas, (1) in formal organization, (2) in informal organization, and (3) in the unorganized community. The first of these presents a fairly simple problem for analysis. It is in the formal organization of associations that social power is transformed into authority. When social action and interaction proceed wholly in conformity to the norms of the formal organization, power is dissolved without residue into authority. The right to use force is then attached to certain statuses within the association, and this right is what we ordinarily mean by authority.[5] It is thus authority in virtue of which persons in an association exercise command or control over other persons in the same association. It is authority which enables a bishop to transfer a priest from his parish, a priest with his "power of the keys" to absolve a sinner, a commanding officer to assign a post of duty to a subordinate officer, a vice-president to dictate a letter to his secretary, the manager of a baseball team to change his pitcher in the middle of an inning, a factory superintendent to demand that a certain job be completed at a specified time, a policeman to arrest a citizen who has violated a law, and so on through endless examples. Power in these cases is attached to statuses, not to persons, and is wholly institutionalized as authority.

In rigidly organized groups this authority is clearly specified and formally articulated by the norms (rules, statutes, laws) of the association. In less rigidly organized groups penumbral areas appear in which authority is less clearly specified and articulated. Sometimes authority clearly vested in an associational status may not be exercised because it conflicts with a moral norm to which both members and nonmembers of the association adhere in the surrounding community. Sometimes an official may remove a subordinate from office without formal cause and without

---

[4] Sanctions, of course, may be positive or negative, require or prohibit the commission of a social act.

[5] Authority appears frequently in another sense as when, for example, we say that Charles Goren is an authority on bridge or Emily Post on etiquette. Here it carries the implication of superior knowledge or skill or competence and such persons are appealed to as sources of information or as arbiters. In this sense authority is related to influence but not to power.

formal authority because such action, now involving power, finds support in public opinion. Sometimes, on the contrary he may have the authority to discharge a subordinate, but not the power, because the position of the latter is supported informally and "extra-associationally" by the opinion of the community....

It may be observed that the power implied in the exercise of authority does not necessarily convey a connotation of personal superiority. Leo Durocher is not a better pitcher than the player he removes nor, in turn, is he inferior to the umpire who banishes him from the game. A professor may be a "better" scholar and teacher than the dean who dismisses him, a lawyer more learned in the law then the judge who cites him for contempt, a worker a more competent electrician than the foreman who assigns his duties, and so on through thousands of examples. As MacIver has written, "The man who commands may be no wiser, no abler, may be in no sense better than the average of his fellows; sometimes, by any intrinsic standard he is inferior to them. Here is the magic of government."[6] Here indeed is the magic of all social organization.

Social action, as is well known, does not proceed in precise or in absolute conformity to the norms of formal organization. Power spills over the vessels of status which only imperfectly contain it as authority. We arrive, therefore, at a short consideration of informal organization, in which the prestige of statuses gives way to the esteem for persons and in which the social interaction of the members proceeds not only in terms of the explicit norms of the association but also in terms of implicit extra-associational norms whose locus is in the community and which may or may not conflict, at strategic points, with the associational norms. Our previous examples have helped us to anticipate what we have to say about the incidence and practice of power in informal organization. No association is wholly formal, not even the most rigidly organized. Social organization makes possible the orderly social intercourse of people who do not know each other—the crew of a ship and their new captain, the faculty of a university department and a new chairman, the manager of a baseball team and his new recruit, the citizen and the tax collector, the housewife and the plumber, the customer and the clerk. But in any association the members do become acquainted with each other and begin to interact not only "extrinsically" and "categorically," in terms of the statuses they occupy, but also "intrinsically" and "personally," in terms of the roles they play and the personalities they exhibit. Sub-groups arise and begin to exert subtle pressures upon the organization itself, upon the norms which may be breached in the observance thereof, and upon the authority which, however firmly institutionalized, is yet subject to change. These sub-groups may, as cliques and factions, remain within the association or, as sects and splinter groups, break away from it. In any event, no formal organization can remain wholly formal under the exigencies of time and circumstance. Power is seldom completely institutionalized as authority, and then no more than momentarily. If power sustains the structure, opposing power threatens it, and every association is always at the mercy of a majority of its own members....

---

[6] *The Web of Government, op. cit.*, p. 13.

Power appears, then, in associations in two forms, institutionalized as authority in the formal organization and uninstitutionalized as power itself in the informal organization. But this does not exhaust the incidence of power with respect to the associations of society. It must be evident that power is required to inaugurate an association in the first place, to guarantee its continuance, and to enforce its norms. Power supports the fundamental order of society and the social organization within it, wherever there is order. Power stands behind every association and sustains its structure. Without power there is no organization and without power there is no order. The intrusion of the time dimension and the exigencies of circumstance require continual re-adjustments of the structure of every association, not excepting the most inelastically organized, and it is power which sustains it through these transitions.[7] If power provides the initial impetus behind the organization of every association, it also supplies the stability which it maintains throughout its history. Authority itself cannot exist without the immediate support of power and the ultimate sanction of force.

As important as power is, however, as a factor in both the formal and informal organization of associations, it is even more important where it reigns, uninstitutionalized, in the interstices between associations and has its locus in the community itself. Here we find the principal social issues of contemporary society—labor vs. capital, Protestant vs. Catholic, CIO vs. AFL, AMA vs. FSA, Hiss vs. Chambers (for this was not a conflict between individuals), Republican vs. Democrat, the regents of the University of California vs. the faculty, Russia vs. the United States, and countless others throughout the entire fabric of society. It is not the task of our present analysis to examine these conflicts in detail but rather to investigate the role of power wherever it appears. And here we have two logical posibilities—power in the relations of like groups and power in the relations of unlike groups. Examples of the former are commercial companies competing for the same market, fraternal organizations of the same kind competing for members, religious associations competing for adherents, newspapers competing for readers, construction companies bidding for the same contracts, political parties competing for votes, and so on through all the competitive situations of society. Examples of the latter are conflicts between organized labor and organized management, between the legislative and executive branches of government, between different sub-divisions of the same bureaucracy (e.g., Army vs. Navy), between university boards of trustees and an association of university professors, and so on through an equally large number of instances. Power thus appears both in competition and in conflict and has no incidence in groups which neither compete nor conflict, i.e., between groups which do not share a similar social matrix and have no social relations, as for example the American Council of Learned Societies and the American Federation of Labor. Power thus arises only in social opposition of some kind. . . .

If power is one of the imperatives of society it may also be partly a pretense and succeed only because it is inaccurately estimated, or unchallenged. This, of course,

---

[7]If the power of the members, informally exercised, supports an association through changes in structure, it is the structure itself which supports it through changes in personnel.

is a familiar stratagem in war. But it occurs in the majority of power relationships in society. The threat of a strike may succeed when the strike will not. Blackmail may have consequences more dire than the exposure of the secret. The threat of a minority to withdraw from an association may effect it more than an actual withdrawal. The threat of a boycott may achieve the result desired when the boycott itself would fail. . . .

We may, in a comparatively brief conclusion, attempt to locate the sources of power. Power would seem to stem from three sources: (1) numbers of people, (2) social organization, and (3) resources. In a previous paper we have discussed in some detail the role of majorities in both unorganized and organized social groups, and in both the formal and informal aspects of the latter, and arrived at the conclusion, among others, that majorities constitute a residual locus of social power. It is neither necessary nor desirable to review this proposition here, beyond reiterating an emphasis upon the power which resides in numbers. Given the same social organization and the same resources, the larger number can always control the smaller and secure its compliance. If majorities, particularly economic and political majorities, have frequently and for long historical periods suffered oppression, it is because they have not been organized or have lacked resources. The power which resides in numbers is clearly seen in elections of all kinds, where the majority is conceded the right to institutionalize its power as authority—a right which is conceded because it can be taken. This power appears in all associations, even the most autocratic. It is the power of a majority, even in the most formally and inflexibly organized associations, which either threatens or sustains the stability of the associational structure.

As important as numbers are as the primary source of social power, they do not in themselves suffice. As suggested above, majorities may suffer oppression for long historical periods, they may, in short, be powerless or possess only the residual power of inertia. We arrive therefore at the second source of social power—social organization. A well organized and disciplined body of marines or of police can control a much larger number of unorganized individuals. An organized minority can control an unorganized majority. But even here majorities possess so much residual power that there are limits beyond which this kind of control cannot be exercised. These limits appear with the recognition that the majority may organize and thus reverse the control. And an organized majority, as suggested in the paper previously referred to, is the most potent social force on earth.

Of two groups, however, equal or nearly equal in numbers and comparable in organization, the one with access to the greater resources will have the superior power. And so resources constitute the third source of social power. Resources may be of many kinds—money, property, prestige, knowledge, competence, deceit, fraud, secrecy, and, of course, all of the things usually included under the term "natural resources." There are also supernatural resources in the case of religious associations which, as agencies of a celestial government, apply supernatural sanctions as instruments of control. In other words, most of the things we have previously differentiated from power itself may now be re-introduced as among the sources of power. It is easily apparent that, in any power conflict, they can tip the balance when the other sources of power are relatively equal and comparable. But they are not themselves power. Unless utilized by people who are in organized association with one another they are quite devoid of sociological significance.

As a matter of fact, no one of these sources in itself constitutes power, nor does any one of them in combination with either of the others. Power appears only in the combination of all three—numbers, organization, and resources.. . .

POWER AS A SOCIETAL FORCE

Amitai Etzioni

Power Defined. The realization of most societal goals, even in situations in which the actor's commitment and knowledge are considerable, requires the application of power. That is, under most circumstances, societal goals and decisions not supported by at least some degree of some kind of power will not be implemented. Hence, powerless actors are passive actors. The assumption which underlies these statements is that the realization of a societal goal requires introducing a change into societal relations, either in the societal environment or among the member units, and, as a rule, attempts to introduce changes (as distinct from changes that occur "anyhow," which do not constitute the realization of a goal), encounter some resistance. Unless this resistance is reduced, a course of action set will not be a course of action followed. *Power is a capacity to overcome part or all of the resistance, to introduce changes in the face of opposition* (this includes sustaining a course of action or preserving a status quo that would otherwise have been discontinued or altered).

Power is always relational and relative. An actor by himself is not powerful or weak; he may be powerful in relation to some actors in regard to some matters and weak in relation to other actors on other matters. Here, we are interested chiefly in the macroscopic consequences of the application of power; hence, we are concerned with societal power and not with the power of individuals or small groups, although several of the following statements and propositions apply to these units as well.

Power as an Operational Concept. There has been considerable controversy about the definition of power for centuries. Without attempting to review this controversy here or to deal with its many issues, let us briefly indicate our position on the question of whether or not the methodological difficulties involved in the use of the concept can be surmounted. The main methodological objection to the use of the concept of power is that power can be assessed only *post hoc;* we know that *x* has power only after he overcomes the resistance of *y*, and whether or not he can do so—it is said—is unknown until after he has done it. Such *post hoc* analysis has no predictive value. To avoid this difficulty, let us use "power" not for a single

SOURCE: Amitai Etzioni, *The Active Society* (New York: The Free Press, 1968), pp. 314-323, 357-361. Reprinted with permission of The Macmillan Company. Copyright © by The Free Press, a Division of The Macmillan Company, 1968. Footnotes have been omitted.

exercise of it on a single issue over a single subject at one point in time, but rather to refer to a generalized capacity of an actor, in his relations with others, to reduce resistance to the course of action he prefers in a given field (i.e., in the "presence" of other actors) about a set of matters over a period of time. This capacity can be anticipated with a certain degree of probability; on the basis of past instances of the exercise of power, the outcomes of future applications of power can be predicted. Even before an instance of the exercise of power has occurred, we can make probabilistic statements about the expected outcome. These are based on our estimates of the relative assets and the uses made of them by the actors in a given field, which can be studied before power is applied.

All of this is possible once the distinction between assets and power is recognized. Assets are possessions of an actor which *may* be converted into power but are not necessarily so used; hence, there is a systematic difference between the assets of an actor, which may be viewed as a power base or potential, and his actual capacity to reduce the resistance of others, which is the power actually generated. . . . If assets and power are viewed as analytically identical, it is impossible to use the one to formulate predictions about the other.

There are three reasons that the concept of power as a generalized capacity that draws on an asset base but is not identical with it, is particularly useful. First, analysis becomes more realistic. When, for a particular line of action, an affluent actor does not mobilize more than a small fraction of his assets and thus loses to a poorer but more mobilized actor, this, in itself, often leads to a greater mobilization of the affluent actor and, in the long run, to his "victory." Atomistic power analysis, focusing on each instance on the exercise of power, would not be able to account systematically for the interplay between the loss of single campaigns and the winning of the whole drive. Collectivistic power analysis, focusing on differences in assets, may expect the affluent actor to prevail initially. Neither approach would alert the observer to the fact that in situations in which there are only a few rounds and the outcome is irreversible, the poor but highly mobilized actor who generated more power in the critical instance will tend to prevail. This applies, for instance, to movements of revolution or national independence (in systems which are poorly integrated) and to the passing of key legislation (in systems which are better integrated).

The second reason that the concept of power as a generalized capacity is particularly useful concerns the cross-sectoral application of power. Much has been said about the sectoral nature of power—that it cannot be deduced that an actor powerful in one area of societal activity will be powerful in other areas; again, the concept has been declared too fragmented to be fruitful. While we agree that power in one sector (e.g., in economic matters) does not necessarily imply power in others (e.g., in religion), there is nonetheless some halo effect; that is, the very capacity to have one's way in one area generates a degree of superordination in another area. . . . This, we suggest, is in part because power in one sector tends to invoke some power in other sectors (although, as a rule, not commersurate) and in part because power in one sector can be "cashed" in another sector. . . . Thus, an actor whose generalized power is greater will enjoy an advantage over the less powerful actor even in sectors where there is formal equality. The concept of generalized power calls our attention to these power projections.

A third reason that this concept seems useful is that it explains submission even when there is no actual exercise of power. This is because the subjects' considerations—like the application of power—are probabilistic; a small nation or a group of workers refrains from resisting not because it is certain that it will be punished (or, not rewarded) if it were to block the power wielders' course, but because the probility of being treated punitively is higher than it is willing to accept. On the other hand, if the controlling agents cannot exercise sanctions at least occasionally, their power will erode and resistance will rise, as subjective probabilities are adjusted. For all these reasons, in the following discussion "power" means a *generalized* capacity to reduce resistance.

Like energy, power is directly observable only when used. The power of a unit can be predicted by studying its assets, its total structure, and its past performances in this regard. But like the world of physical energy, there is no gain-for-nothing, for power has a cost; assets used to generate it are no longer available to the particular actor. If the asset base is not replenished, the probability of compliance will decline. . . .

Is Power Universal? The concept of power has provoked many debates concerning the socio-political stance it implies. As the concept is used here, the notion of resistance is central. The socio-political world implied is one composed of a plurality of societal actors, many of whom are committed to realizing one or more goals. Scarcity, we assume, prevails in the sense that the total amount of assets available is smaller than that needed to realize all of the goals of all of the actors. (Overcapacity or "affluence" might exist in this or that instrumental realm but is never universal.) Nor are all or even most of the goals of the actors shared or complementary. Hence, while the realization of some goals does not distract from the realization of some others and may even advance them, there is a significant degree of incompatibility among goals (in that the realization of some goals limits the realization of some others) and among means (in that the use of most means for most goals makes these means unavailable for the advancement of any other goal).

From the facts that there is a plurality of actors and of goals and a scarcity of instruments, it follows that societal actors will tend to "resist" each other in the sense of hampering each other's actions. This is not to imply, as has been suggested, that conflict is the prevailing mode of societal relations. Actors often do share some goals and work out a set of priorities among some other goals and a pattern of allocation of scarce instruments. But even if such cooperation and mutual understanding were eventually to encompass the full range of societal action (a situation hard to imagine), the specific pattern of priorities and allocation would still reflect the relative power of the various actors. The agreements reached between an adolescent and his parents, a new nation and a superpower, the poor and City Hall are almost invariably asymmetrical, as indicated both by the respective implementations of divisive (as distinct from complementary and shared) goals and by the respective shares of the scarce instruments and rewards obtained. . . . In cooperative relations, power appears in the ability to eliminate all arrangements which differ from those finally reached. It is true that some concessions are made because of non-rational commitments to shared values—for instance, national pride. Also, in part, the arrangements reached reflect the sides' *estimates* of the outcome of a more explicit use of power. But while the outcomes of negotiations or arbitration rarely reflect only the sides' actual relative power, they usually are significantly affected by it—if not in each round, as the rounds accumulate.

Another reason that power and cooperation are fundamentally related is that patterns of cooperation are not worked out on an *ad hoc* basis or completely voluntarily among the actors concerned; cooperation is often imposed by third parties or is institutionalized and enforced as the result of previous arrangements among the actors. For instance, the degree of cooperation among the republics in Central America in part reflects the power the United States has over them; the degree of cooperation between management and labor is affected by the power the national government has over them as well as by enforceable agreements between them. Power and cooperation are, thus, not a mutually exclusive pair of concepts; cooperation often has a power base, and power is exercised through cooperation.

The tendency to associate power with conflict rather than with cooperation is part of a more general tendency to view power negatively. Hence, it should be emphasized that at least in macroscopic social structures, the realization of many values depends on a "proper" power constellation rather than on the elimination of the role of power. Thus, for instance, democratic processes presuppose a plurality of power centers, each strong enough to compete with the others but not so strong as to be able to undermine the societal framework in which the democratic competition takes place. And in societies in which the law prescribes civil and human rights for its members, the effective safeguard of these rights only in part rests with societal education and in the identification of various members with these values; they need also to be supported by at least a latent capacity for any group of citizens whose rights are denied to exert sufficient power to activate the societal mechanisms necessary to restore their rights. The same holds for "free enterprise" and "free" markets; they may exist between units similiar in economic power but not between oil companies and gasoline stations or between automobile manufacturers and automobile dealers. To put it differently, the power relations among the member-units of a society and between that society and other societies are a major determinant of the degree to which that societal structure will be consonant or in conflict with the values to which the members "individually" and as a collective unit are committed. In short, effective universalism is not to be expected without an appropriate power distribution.

While power and conflict are not Siamese twins, they are intimately connected and frequently appear together. One reason that conflict is a common mode of societal relations rests in the poor societal knowledge most actors have of their potential power as compared to that of other relevant actors. The sources of societal power are many and varied and include such intangible elements as the capacity of a societal unit to mobilize the loyalties of the membership and the efficacy of its organization and elites. Therefore, it is usually difficult for even a detached observer to assess accurately the power of various actors, and when the assessor is himself an actor in the field, the reasons for misjudgment multiply. If the relative power of various societal units were completely measurable, and if there were a supreme judge who could adjust the patterns of priorities of shared projects and the allocation of assets not committed to shared projects—to the changing power assessments—societal conflict would be greatly reduced; a basic function of societal conflict is to substitute for the lack of such measurements and judges. Societal conflict is, therefore, an inherent element of macroscopic processes. It is a major (although by no means the only) expression of power—of the discrepancy between the capacity of an actor to produce change and the readiness of other actors in the field to agree, between the actual distribution of societal power and that which the prevailing stratification structure and political organization of society assume.

Power relations seem to be an inevitable feature of societal structure. It seems that there will always be a plurality of actors, each with a will of his own that is not completely complementary to, or shared by, all other actors, even if they all are members of one community. While the *intensity* of power declines as the scope of shared values and authentic consensus broadens, so long as there is a scarcity of assets and societal actors have a degree of autonomy, some actors will meet with some resistance from some other actors and will use part of their assets to reduce it in order to further their own goals. . . .

To make power a central element of societal analysis is not to assume that other elements—especially goals and values, knowledge and commitment—are less important. On the contrary, we view societal power as a form of the mobilization of societal energy in the service of societal goals. Political elites might seek power for power's sake or, perhaps more accurately, rank the gaining of the instruments of power higher than any other particular goal they seek; but the societal consequences of power lie in the realization of societal goals, whether they be changes in the relations of the societal unit to its environment or the transformation of the societal self. To say that power is a universal feature of society is not to imply that power is omnipotent. A major limitation to power is the values to which actors are committed; actors restrain the use of power under certain circumstances because elites as well as followers *believe* they ought not to use whatever power they command in every situation.

Second, the power of any societal actor, however great, is limited by that of others. Writings in the "power-elite" tradition tend to overestimate the degree to which the power of business or the "military-industrial complex" is autonomous and unchecked. The narrow range of the power of American Presidents is well known, and the limitations of the power of even totalitarian leaders and parties are well documented. Power can be exercised only because—and to the extent that—the power potentials are unevenly distributed among the actors.

Between Power and Coercion. To generate power is not necessarily to rely on force or to be coercive. That there are other sources and means of power—for instance, economic assets—is too obvious to need comment. It is sometimes argued that all other kinds of power "ultimately" rely on force because it is used when economic or moral sanctions fail. While there are cases in which this is true, there are others in which force is not applied even though economic or moral sanctions were not heeded as, for example, in numerous business and interpersonal transactions and relations. Second, even when there is force "in the background," the other sanctions clearly play an autonomous role, for instance, in the likelihood that force will need to be applied.

What is less evident is that although power, by definition, assumes a capacity to reduce resistance, it is not necessarily coercive in the sense of eliminating all or most alternatives to the course imposed on the actors who are subjected to the exercise of power. Of course, power may be coercive; more often, however, power takes effect indirectly by altering the situation. Rather than preventing those subjected to power from following a course of action, it makes the course less attractive (and, by implication, the other alternatives more attractive). Here, the actors still can—if they are willing to pay the higher costs—pursue their original courses. Since few if any acts are without costs (even when these are outweighed by gains), the more common effect of the injection of power into a situation is to alter the costs rather than to destroy the capacity to choose. That is, there is frequently a voluntary element in submission: the unwillingness to pay the cost of not submitting.

Complete coercion occurs when the subjects are, in effect, deprived of the opportunity to choose—e.g., when a parent carries a child away from his toys, or when United States forces physically prevented Cuban exile organizations from raiding Castro's Cuba in 1963 by arresting the leaders and impounding the boats. It has been argued that even in the most coercive situation, the actors have a choice; they can choose to die rather than submit. It is a fact, though, that coercive controls are typically used to foreclose this option, too—to force the subjects to live in jail. The same may be said of collectivities under extreme totalitarian conditions.

There are situations which approximate this extreme case in which, in effect, alternatives are eliminated and the available choices are very skewed—e.g., there are only two alternatives and the penalty of choosing one of them is very high. Therefore, it seems useful to treat the concepts of coercion and noncoercion not as a dichotomy but as points on a continuum. Accordingly, coercion is used to refer to compliance relations in which there is little or no effective choice. Noncoercive compliance includes utilitarian and normative reactions. By this definition, some but by no means all or even most power is coercive, initially or "ultimately."

Another reflection of the liberal tendency to evaluate power negatively, apparent in the inclination to make all power seem coercive, is the focusing upon the illicit uses of power. Actually, power might advance any societal goal, from conserving a status quo to altering it. The notion that evil is imposed by power while goodness flies on its own wings assumes an optimistic view of human nature and societal institutions that has little evidence to support it. The application of power is a principal way of getting things done. Its ethical standing depends in part on the ways in which goals are set and attained; these factors, in turn, depend much more on the distribution of power (what proportion of the members of a unit to which power is applied shares in setting the goals?) and on the amounts and kinds of power used (e.g., the degree of coercion) than on the very fact that power was exercised. *Hence, most societal actors must choose not between getting things done voluntarily or through the exercise of power, or between exercising power or not getting things done, but rather among the varying degrees and kinds of power to apply. . . .*

Assets, Power, and Activation. An exploration of the complicated relations between the assets an actor commands and the power he wields is central for an understanding of the active orientation, because the capacity to act is greatly affected by the possessions of an actor *and* by what he does with these possessions. The common-sense view (and that of some political scientists) tends to estimate the power of an actor by an inventory of his assets. Nations with a large territory, a large population, high production of steel, oil, ship tonnage, or railroad miles are viewed as strong nations. Or, among sub-societies, the rich are viewed as powerful and the poor as weak.

Actually, the amount of assets an actor has determines only the collectivistic context of his power, his power *potential* or base—that is, the amount of assets on which he can draw to support his action. The proportion of these assets he actually uses to generate power is a different, more organizational, more voluntaristic aspect of societal relations. Each actor constantly chooses, although often not consciously, how many of the assets he controls should be *consumed* (used to satisfy immediate needs), *preserved* for later consumption, *invested* to increase his assets, and converted into societal power. Assets are, thus, a relatively "stable" (or structural) aspect of societal relations, while power is more dynamic (or processual).

The relation of power to assets is analogous to the relation of energy to material. The conversion of assets into power is not an abrupt "jump" but rather a process of transformation. Various steps may be taken to activate the assets and bring them closer to a power-yielding state without actually releasing the energy. Such activation occurs, for instance, when a collectivity or society is preparing for a conflict—whether it be a war, a strike, or a period of demonstrations. These preparations are modern analogies to the primitives' war dances. Again, as in thermodynamics or electronics, while societal assets or power potentials may be accumulated and stored or activated in anticipation of future use, there are some costs or "losses" involved since some of the potential energy is "dissipated" and increasingly so as time passes. Thus, arms or means of production grow obsolescent, and morale and leadership not actively engaged tend gradually to erode. . . .

A Classification of Power. The conversion of assets into power generates a variety of sanctions, rewards, and instruments to penalize those who resist, to reward those who assist, to remove those who block, and to provide facilities for those who implement a collectively-set course of action. These sanctions, rewards, and instruments differ in their substance: They are either physical, material, or symbolic. This makes for a threefold classification of assets and power: Power is either coercive (e.g., military forces), utilitarian (e.g., economic sanctions), or persuasive (e.g., propaganda). The classification is exhaustive. Each concrete application of the use of power is either one of the three or is composed of their various combinations. . . .

Utilitarian assets include economic possessions, technical and administrative capabilities, manpower, etc. Utilitarian power is generated when these assets are applied or exchanged in such a fashion as to allow the unit which possesses them to bring other units to support its line of action.

Coercive assets are the weapons, installations, and manpower which the military, the police, or similar agencies use. There is a thin line between utilitarian and coercive assets; civilians may be inducted into the military and factories might be converted to military use. But so long as such a conversion has not occurred, these means will not be viewed as coercive assets. Coercive power (or force) results when one unit uses coercive assets to impose its preferred course of action on others. Note that coercion refers here to the employment of violent means and not to pressure in a more generic sense. Or, to put it differently, coercive power refers to the use of force and not to other means of enforcement.

Persuasive power is exercised through the manipulation of symbols, such as appeals to the values and sentiments of the citizens, in order to mobilize support and to penalize those who deviate (e.g., by excommunicating them). Unlike utilitarian and coercive power, two concepts which are frequently applied, the concept of persuasive power is not widely used and raises several analytic problems which need to be discussed briefly, especially since the relations between assets and power are less evident in regard to persuasion then with respect to the other two categories.

The normative bonds of societal units, the bases of persuasive power, are often perceived as either resting on personal attitudes and interpersonal relations or as having no structural and organizational base at all. Actually, the capacity to persuade is not randomly distributed in social systems. For instance, in societies in which the church is a main source of persuasive power, the power-holders themselves constitute a hierarchy with a variety of goals, in the pursuit of which the hierarchy brings its power to bear. And the secular authorities which have the church's blessing possess access to a source of power that other secular authorities do not. In the Spanish civil war, for example, Franco was granted such support and the Republicans were undermined. Similarly, in democratic societies, access to the mass media is a source of persuasive power that is more available to political incumbents then to the opposition; in totalitarian societies, this source of persuasive power is largely monopolized by the establishment. In short, persuasive power is structured and organized, allocated and applied, in much the same ways as other kinds of power. . . .

The socialization of a people, the values to which they subscribe and the intensity with which they hold them, largely determines the scope and limits of persuasive "assets." At each point in time, we suggest, the values to which actors are committed cannot quickly be changed because these commitments are the result of slow processes. These commitments are assets to those who can appeal to the values and to a power potential not available to those who seek to promote a course of action outside the context of the possible courses of action which these values approve. While commitment to a new value can be developed and then used to support a line of action, this is a much more costly process than appealing to a value that has already been internalized. Hence, the existing distribution of values almost invariably provides an advantage for some lines of action—and of persuasion—over others. The amount of these assets can be measured either in terms of the costs and efforts that were necessary to create and reinforce the relevant commitments (or those which would be required to alter them) or in terms of the scope and amount of action that can be generated by drawing upon them.

The greater the potential appeal of these values and symbols, the larger will be the amount of the persuasive assets of the unit under examination. Persuasive assets are transformed into persuasive power when a member-unit or a system-elite succeeds in demonstrating that a particular course of action which it seeks other units or all member-units to follow is consistent with or an expression of those values and symbols to which the other units are committed.

Power, Influence, and Authority. Influence and power are often used synonymously. We suggest, however, that it is useful to keep these two terms separate in order to express a significant conceptual distinction. An application of *power* changes the actor's situation and/or his conception of his situation—but not his preferences. Resistance is overcome not because the actor subjected to the use of power changes his "will" but because resistance has been made more expensive, prohibitive, or impossible. The exercise of *influence* entails an authentic change in the actor's preferences; given the same situation, he would not choose the same course of action he favored before influence was exercised. While from the power-wielders' viewpoint, the difference between the two might be relatively small (the exercise of influence also consumes assets though it produces fewer or no counter-currents), from the subjects' viewpoint, it is more significant in that influence involves not suspension or suppression of their preferences but a respecification of their commitments.

Of the three kinds of power, persuasive power is the most similar to influence, since both are symbolic and draw on values and sentiments. The difference between them rests in the depth of their effects; persuasion suppresses the actor's preferences without changing them; it, hence, resembles influence on the surface, but there is really an exercise of power beneath. The difference between persuasion and influence is analogous to the difference between propaganda and education. When persuasive power is very effective and influence is superficial, the two are very similar, but, in general, it is not difficult to distinguish one from the other. . . .

Both concepts are related to the concepts of authority and legitimation. *Authority* is defined as legitimate power—that is, power that is used in accord with the subject's values and under conditions he views as proper. But even power that is completely legitimate may still support a course of action that is not desired by the subject and is therefore alienating. This is because the course of action, legitimate or not, is still not an expression of the subject's preferences. Army officers who take their men into battle have the right to do so, a right which the subjects may acknowledge, but this does not necessarily make combat a course of action preferred by the subjects. Illegitimate power is doubly alienating, because the action is both undesirable *and* violates the sense of right and wrong. But if an authorized individual orders the same act, this still would not make the act desirable. Paying taxes to a rejected government, such as a colonial one, after the peoples' consciousness has been aroused by a national independence movement as compared to paying taxes to one's own government when identification with it is high illustrates the difference. Legitimation and satisfaction are not to be confused. On the other nand, when influence is exercised, the act does become desirable even if the influence were illegitimate (although, as a rule, a full measure of influence would require that it be legitimate in terms of the subject's values). . . .

POWER, FUNCTION, AND ORGANIZATION

Robert Dubin

It is the purpose of this paper: (1) to describe some formal properties of a social system called an organization; (2) to analyze functional interdependence within such a system; and (3) to show how the performance of functions in an organization confers power on the functionary. Power of members of a formal organization will be shown to be grounded in the *importance* of the functions they perform in it and the *exclusiveness* with which they perform them. Criteria for determining functional importance will be presented. A simple means for characterizing the exclusiveness facet of power will also be presented.

This discussion is limited to formal organization and the power of functionaries in them. It is believed that, in principle, our analysis will apply to any kind of social system. . . .

In any given operation in an organization there is, in principle, the possibility of specifying all functions necessary for the fulfillment of that operation. We will label the organization a "system," each distinctive operation a "system state," and the functions necessary for the fulfillment of that operation the "state coordinates." We will argue that the importance of any given function for an operation can be measured by the number of different ways the function may be fulfilled, and we will call these different ways the "values" of each function. Finally, we will suggest that the exclusiveness with which functions are performed has a consequence for the influence attaching to the functionaries performing them.

Functional System. A social system, like an organization, can be characterized by the inclusion of all functions, F_1, F_2, F_3, . . ., F_n, performed in it. The function of any behavior is defined as the consequence of that behavior for the social system in which it takes place. This definition follows a long and gallant line of analysis coming out of modern biology, through the anthropologists Radcliffe-Brown and Malinowski, and the sociologists Merton and Parsons, down to the work of the philosopher Nagel. The functions defining a system compose the set of those necessary to maintain the system in all of its states G_k ($k = a, b, c, d, e, . . .$). The boundary of such a system is defined by the inclusive set of functionaries whose

SOURCE: Robert Dubin, "Power, Function, and Organization," *Pacific Sociological Review*, Vol. 6, Spring 1963, pp. 16-22. Reprinted by permission. All footnotes have been omitted.

performance of some function is necessary to maintain the system in at least one of its states.

A state of the system is determined by a particular combination of simultaneously operative functions. We may define a system state as a persisting combination of functions, irrespective of the given values each function may take. (See below the definition of values of a function.) The time interval characterizing "persisting" is variable. A persisting combination of functions may be a recurrent combination or one that appears in a temporal sequence such that particular succeeding states of the system do not occur unless this combination has also occurred.

Such a functional system can be represented by a matrix, as in Figure 1, which is an *F* x *G* table. This matrix displays two salient features of the social system it represents. (1) All functions *ever* operative in the system are shown by the fact that there is at least one + in each column. (2) All states of the system *ever* attained are shown by the fact that there is at least one + in each row.

We will mean by values of a function, like those illustrated in Figure 1, all possible nonzero values that may be assigned to that function. Up to this point we have dichotomized these values into present (+) and absent (0). We may also consider the possibility that every function may have more than one value in any given system state. This may be illustrated by the fact that a given function may be performed by employing several different behaviors, the number of such distinct behaviors being the value for that function. Or, we may consider that for the function called "decision-making," the *number* of alternatives available to a decision-maker is the value of that function in the system state in which he makes a decision.

In measuring the values of a function it is important to distinguish "behavior" from "activity." All behaviors are activities, but not *vice-versa*. The distinction lies in the social significance of the activity. If, and only if, a change in activity is meaningful to others in the system, or to the operation of the system itself, would we speak of two distinct behaviors—the original activity and that to which it

FIGURE 1.
A Functional System

States of System (*G*)	Functions Composing Sytem (*F*)					
	1	2	3	4	5	. . .
a	0 or +	0 or +	0 or +	0 or +	0 or +	0 or +
b	0 or +	0 or +	0 or +	0 or +	0 or +	0 or +
c	0 or +	0 or +	0 or +	0 or +	0 or +	0 or +
d	0 or +	0 or +	0 or +	0 or +	0 or +	0 or +
e	0 or +	0 or +	0 or +	0 or +	0 or +	0 or +
. . .	0 or +	0 or +	0 or +	0 or +	0 or +	0 or +

A zero (0) entry indicates that the function is *not* operative for that state of the system, while a plus (+) entry indicates that the function is operative.

changed. We consider only distinctive behaviors as being tallies in counting up the value of a function. . . .

In general, we conclude that the distinction between behavior and activity is important as one way of making finite the number of values that are associated with each function in a system. Obviously, the usefulness of any method for assigning values to functions depends on there being finite numbers of such values.

A *state coordinate* of a system is a function having a non-zero value. The sub-set of state coordinates at a time *t* specifies the *state of the system* at that time, as we have already suggested above.

Our problem now is to determine two facts about a functional system. *First*, we must know how to rank the importance of functions in the system for each system state. *Second*, we seek to determine the rank order of importance of all functions of the system over all possible states of it. When we have established the connection between functional importance and power, we will then be in a position to assign power to system functionaries in accordance with the relative importance of the functions they perform.

Functional Importance and Power. We will first discuss measures of functional importance in a system. Then attention will turn to the connection between functional importance and power in a system.

1. Criterion of Functional Importance—System State. A function (*F*) has importance for a single state of a system in proportion to the number of values it may take while the system remains in that state.

The first criterion of functional importance tells us that for any given state of the system the rank order of importance of all functions operative in that state is determinate. The order of importance is precisely the rank determined by the number of values each function has in that state.

By this first criterion it is clear that all functions having zero values have *no importance* for that state of the system. The remaining functions having one or more values for the given state are ranked by the number of values they have to determine their importance for that state of the system.

2. Criterion of Functional Importance—System as a Whole. A function (*F*) has importance for a system as a whole in proportion to the number of values it may take, summed for all states of the system.

This second criterion of functional importance tells us that the importance of each function in a system is determinate. It becomes clear, for example, that every function in the system has some importance to it (i.e., has at least one non-zero value in at least one state of the system—a fact that will be of significance shortly in considering the issue of "powerlessness" in a social system). In general, by discovering all the values each function can take for all states of the system, and ranking the functions in accordance with the sum of their values, we get a determinate measure of functional importance of each function relative to all others.

We may illustrate the application of the first two criteria of functional importance with the following hypothetical example. In Figure 2 we suggest a system having three states and four functions. The hypothetical number of values of each function

FIGURE 2
Hypothetical Ranking of Functional Importance In a
System Having Four Functions and Three System States

Function	State A		State B		State C		System as a Whole	
	Number of Values	Rank Order of Importance	Number of Values	Rank Order of Importance	Number of Values	Rank Order of Importance	Number of Values	Rank Order of Importance
F_1	1	2	2	3	3	2	6	2
F_2	0	-	0	—	5	1	5	3
F_3	0	-	3	2	1	3	4	4
F_4	6	1	5	1	0	—	11	1

for each state is shown, which establishes the rank order of importance for that state. There is then summarized the rank order of importance of each function for the system as a whole.

A persistent problem of functional analysis is to determine the order of importance of all operative functions for given states of the system and for the system as a whole. By measuring this importance in terms of the number of different non-zero values each function can take, we have, in principle: (1) a determinate answer to the problem of functional importance, and (2) an obvious lead to an empirical method for making this determination.

Furthermore, we advance beyond merely asserting the presence or absence of a function in a system. We are able to suggest the possible ways in which each function may be operative. Thus, we have a concept beyond "division of labor" to delineate a functional system.

To name the phenomenon of functional importance we coopt the much used term "power." This now means that we are using "power" to denote the amount of influence (functional importance) each function has: (1) in each state of a system, and (2) in the maintenance of the system as a whole.

The import of tying function and power together in this fashion is fivefold.

1. It permits us to extend the concept of function from the simple presence-absence viewpoint so as now to include the more complicated question of how much a function operates in a system. The answer to the "how much" question is called the power of the function in the system.

2. This view of power permits the examination of the phenomenon of joint power of parts of functions in the hierarchy of state coordinates of a system. This, of course, could be extended to the n-tuples of functions using the same criteria of "functional importance" here proposed. Thus in the study of organizations we

should be able to examine the effects of coalition formation, of factions, and of cliques, assigning the measures of their power in the system (in terms of their summed, joint, functional importance).

3. This formulation of the power concept really makes sense out of the notion of fundamental functional requisite of a system. We can now conceive of a "universal" functional requisite of a system as one for which the given function always has a non-zero value for all possible states of the system. . . . It should be clear that a universal function is a system may *not* necessarily be the one of greatest functional importance of the system.

4. It becomes possible to specify a concrete meaning of "power struggle" or "power conflict" in an organization. If two or more functionaries (or groups) are contesting for power, they have two general strategies available. (a) They can maximize the number of different values their functional performance can take, in a given system state, and try to minimize the number of different values their opponent's functional performance can take. The difference between the number of own values and the number of opponent's values is the balance of power in the particular system state. For example, at the end of a chess game "checkmate" is the condition of zero value for the loser—no moves remain for his king. (b) They can shift the system from a state in which opponent has more power to a state where their own power is greater. For instance, highway engineers can increase their power over a construction decision *vis-a-vis* fiscal officials by shifting the grounds of decision from availability of funds to the engineering feasibility of the proposed project. This increases the number of alternatives for decision ("values" of their function) while at the same time minimizing or eliminating the function of fiscal officers with respect to the engineering grounds for decision.

5. We have already suggested that in the system as a whole the performance of any of its necessary functions becomes an act of power. All *functionaries*, therefore, have some power in the system. This is a fact seldom recognized in the studies of so-called "power elites" where the implicit assumption made is that only the designated elites have power and other members of the system do not. The only meaningful sense in which "powerlessness" can be treated from our standpoint is the situation of "attachment to" a social organization rather than participation in it.

In summary, we have suggested a way to measure "power in" a system that differs from the two usual conceptualizations. The "power to" approach essentially concludes that a social actor, by his presence in a system, can choose the conditions of the next state of the system in spite of any stance taken by all other functionaries in the system. Thus Weber's dictum: "Power (Macht) is the probability that one actor within a social relationship will be in a position to carry out his own will despite resistence, regardless of the basis on which this probability rests," fits this formulation. French's formulation is similar: ". . . the power of *A* over *B* (with respect to a given opinion) is equal to the maximum force which *A* can induce on *B* minus the maximum resisting force which *B* can mobilize in the opposite direction." His position does not specify the content of the forces marshaled for or against the course of action. By casting the analysis in terms of functions we are able to do this.

The "power of" approach is usually an attempt to assess the number of states of an organization in which a given functionary or group of functionaries are operative. Thus Mills' discussion of the power elite and Hunter's of community power structure attempt to count states of a system, like a community, and assign power to participants in accordance with the number of states in which they function. Our proposal makes the measurement of the "power of" more precise by demonstrating a way of counting the relative degree to which each function contributes to the state of a system.

There are many important operational problems in developing the kinds of empirical counts necessary to measure the operation of functions in a system. Briefly, the following are obvious.

1. To what extent are all possible values of a function in a given state of a system visible to the investigator? This may be a serious observational problem. In a biological system, for example, where the function of temperature control is operative, it is usually feasible to determine experimentally the range and number of possible values within which the function operates to maintain the system in a viable state. In a social system, where experimentation is less readily possible, prolonged direct observation may be the most feasible way to record the range of possible values. Here "natural experiments" are often crucial in establishing the extreme values of given functions, making inferences possible about the intermediate values.

2. How can the investigator determine the joint impact of several functions on a state of a system? In general, in social systems, the division of labor is seldom so minute that each functionary has one and only one function to perform in each state of the system. Indeed, it is much more characteristic that "bundles" of functions constitute the job of most organizational functionaries. This becomes obvious in the examination of job descriptions which are usually limited to the most visible functions and seldom contain the less visible ones. Thus, a close observation of what people are doing individually and in dependent groups, in given states of an organization, usually reveals the joint operations of functions.

A major problem for functionalists dealing with social systems has been the basic assumption of the all-or-none character of functional activation in given states of a system. This has been equivalent to taking a matrix, like Figure 1, and scoring with a binary system of presence or absence, zero or plus. From this standpoint it is not possible to make a distinction among functions operating in a given state of a system according to their importance to the system.

When, however, we do as here suggested and assign importance in a system to functions in accordance to the number of possible values each function can take, we clearly have a meaningful way of distinguishing differences among operating functions. These differences become the first measure of the power of each function *in the system*. This is the measure of *functional importance* to the system. In the next section we will deal with the second measure of power, exclusiveness of functional performance.

Power and Functional Exclusiveness. The second general measure of power in a social system revolves around a personnel issue. If we now focus attention on the functional agent and not the function we can ask: "Does the number of functionaries capable of performing a given function make any difference in the amount of power of any single functionary? Our answer is: "Yes, it makes a difference."

3. *Criterion of Functional Exclusiveness.* For *any given level* of functional importance in an organization, the power residing in a functionary is inversely proportional to the number of other functionaries in the organization capable of performing the function.

The criterion of functional exclusiveness is a measure of the replaceability of any given functionary by another in the system. It will be noted that this criterion is operative for any level of functional importance, and *only within that level.* Thus, the sole file clerk in a small office would have a maximum of power equivalent to her functional importance in the organization as a whole, while the president would have maximum power at his much higher level of functional importance, precisely because each is the only organization member capable of executing immediately his respective functions.

The particular form chosen for expressing the impact on power of functional exclusiveness produces results that intuitively accord with experience. This is the only justification for choosing the inverse relationship. For example, if we find the value of a function performed by a unique and irreplaceable individual to be 30, then the value becomes 15 where there are two possible performers, 10 when three can execute the functions, and 3 where there are ten interchangeable functionaries. The big drop in amount of power due to functional exclusiveness is, of course, between sole jurisdiction over a function and any sharing of it. Once there is some interchangeability among functionaries, and particularly after there are as few as five available substitutes for the performance of a function, power is materially reduced for a given level of functional importance.

We can visualize the effects on power of functional importance and functional exclusiveness in Figure 3. The left-hand scale records the level of functional importance and the horizontal scale the amount of functional exclusiveness. Their combined effect on power is read from the right-hand scale.

If this suggested relationship between functional exclusiveness and the amount of power at any given level of functional importance can be empirically demonstrated, we have a model for comprehending the nature of one form of individual competition in organizations. We would argue that the rewards of individual competition are very great when the winner takes all, but the power payoff deteriorates very rapidly where there can be multiple winners. Exclusiveness in functioning has primary incentive value in an organization only at the one pole and loses its payoff values very rapidly on moving away from that pole. Obviously, other incentives, like striving for assignment of greater functional importance, take over as mechanisms for insuring individual competition in organizations when the exclusiveness of functional performance ceases to provide incentive for behavior. . . .

If the "assignment problem" of organizations includes the possibility that allocations of functions may be used as a mechanism for controlling accumulation

FIGURE 3
Generalized Relationship of Functional Importance and
Functional Exclusiveness to Power

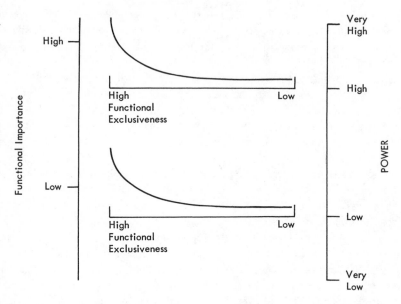

of power, then it follows that exclusiveness of functioning, and the power deriving from it, can be controlled through the number of functionaries assigned to functional performance. This may prove costly in a payroll sense to the organization over the short run. It may, on the other hand, prove economical in the long run because of reduced power of any single organization member to make system transforming errors, or forestall adequate decision execution. Indeed, one could argue from this that the committee system of decision-making, although costly of time and energy of participants, may be organizationally economical. It reduces the opportunity for accumulating power by any single functionary over decision-making along the "exclusiveness" axis.

Functioning Organizations and Power. The arguments of this paper have been simple ones. Power *in* a social system derives from the importance of functions to the development or maintenance of states of the system, and the exclusiveness with which these functions are executed by system agents. We have suggested two general criteria for measuring *functional importance*. An intuitively useful way of measuring the impact of *functional exclusiveness* on the power of functionaries has also been proposed. . . . [This article concludes with a detailed discussion of four distinctive cases in which the mathematics of measuring power in organizations is worked out. Interested readers should consult the original source for this discussion of how to apply measures of organization power.—Ed.]

THE TYPES OF AUTHORITY AND IMPERATIVE CO-ORDINATION

Max Weber

I. The Basis of Legitimacy. "Imperative co-ordination" was defined above as the probability that certain specific commands (or all commands) from a given source will be obeyed by a given group of persons. It thus does not include every mode of exercising "power" or "influence" over other persons. The motives of obedience to commands in this sense can rest on considerations varying over a wide range from case to case; all the way from simple habituation to the most purely rational calculation of advantage. A criterion of every true relation of imperative control, however, is a certain minimum of voluntary submission; thus an interest (based on ulterior motives or genuine acceptance) in obedience.

Not every case of imperative co-ordination makes use of economic means; *still less* does it always have economic objectives. But normally (not always) the imperative co-ordination of the action of a considerable number of men requires control of a staff of persons. It is necessary that a definite, supposedly reliable group of persons will be primarily oriented to the execution of the supreme authority's general policy and specific commands.

The members of the administrative staff may be bound to obedience to their superior (or superiors) by custom, by affectual ties, by a purely material complex of interests, or by ideal (*wertrational*) motives. *Purely* material interests and calculations of advantage as the basis of solidarity between the chief and his administrative staff result, in this as in other connections in a relatively unstable situation. Normally other elements, affectual and ideal, supplement such interests. In certain exceptional, temporary cases the former may be alone decisive. In everyday routine life these relationships, like others, are governed by custom and in addition, material calculation of advantage. But these factors, custom and personal advantage, purely affectual or ideal motives of solidarity, do not, even taken together, form a sufficiently reliable basis for a system of imperative co-ordination. In addition there is normally a further element, the belief in legitimacy.

It is an induction from experience that no system of authority voluntarily limits itself to the appeal to material or affectual or ideal motives as a basis for guaranteeing its continuance. In addition every such system attempts to establish and to cultivate the belief in its "legitimacy." But according to the kind of legitimacy which is claimed, the type of obedience, the kind of administrative staff developed to guarantee it, and the mode of exercising authority, will all differ

SOURCE: Max Weber, *The Theory of Social and Economic Organization*, translated by A. M. Henderson and Talcott Parsons (Glencoe: The Free Press, 1947), pp. 324-325, 328-330, 341-342, 358-362. Reprinted with permission of The Macmillan Company, copyright 1947 by Talcott Parsons. All footnotes and several of Weber's subheadings have been omitted.

fundamentally. Equally fundamental is the variation in effect. Hence, it is useful to classify the types of authority according to the kind of claim to legitimacy typically made by each. . . .

There are three pure types of legitimate authority. The validity of their claims to legitimacy may be based on:

1. Rational grounds—resting on a belief in the "legality" of patterns of normative rules and the right of those elevated to authority under such rules to issue commands (legal authority).

2. Traditional grounds—resting on an established belief in the sanctity of immemorial traditions and the legitimacy of the status of those exercising authority under them (traditional authority); or finally,

3. Charismatic grounds—resting on devotion to the specific and exceptional sanctity, heroism or exemplary character of an individual person, and of the normative patterns or order revealed or ordained by him (charismatic authority).

In the case of legal authority, obedience is owed to the legally established impersonal order. It extends to the persons exercising the authority of office under it only by virtue of the formal legality of their commands and only within the scope of authority of the office. In the case of traditional authority, obedience is owed to the *person* of the chief who occupies the traditionally sanctioned position of authority and who is (within its sphere) bound by tradition. But here the obligation of obedience is not based on the impersonal order, but is a matter of personal loyalty within the area of accustomed obligations. In the case of charismatic authority, it is the charismatically qualified leader as such who is obeyed by virtue of personal trust in him and his revelation, his heroism or his exemplary qualities so far as they fall within the scope of the individual's belief in his charisma. . . .

II. Legal Authority with a Bureaucratic Administrative Staff. The effectiveness of legal authority rests on the acceptance of the validity of the following mutually inter-dependent ideas:

1. That any given legal norm may be established by agreement or by imposition, on grounds of expediency or rational values or both, with a claim to obedience at least on the part of the members of the corporate group. This is, however, usually extended to include all persons within the sphere of authority or of power in question—which in the case of territorial bodies is the territorial area—who stand in certain social relationships or carry out forms of social action which in the order governing the corporate group have been declared to be relevant.

2. That every body of law consists essentially in a consistent system of abstract rules which have normally been intentionally established. Furthermore, administration of law is held to consist in the application of these rules to particular cases; the administrative process in the rational pursuit of the interests which are specified in the order governing the corporate group within the limits laid down by legal precepts and following principles which are capable of generalized formulation and are approved in the order governing the group, or at least not disapproved in it.

3. That thus the typical person in authority occupies an "office." In the action associated with his status, including the commands he issues to others, he is subject

to an impersonal order to which his actions are oriented. This is true not only for persons exercising legal authority who are in the usual sense "officials," but, for instance, for the elected president of a state.

4. That the person who obeys authority does so, as it is usually stated, only in his capacity as a "member" of the corporate group and what he obeys is only "the law." He may in this connection be the member of an association, of a territorial commune, of a church, or a citizen of a state.

5. In conformity with point 3, it is held that the members of the corporate group, in so far as they obey a person in authority, do not owe this obedience to him as an individual, but to the impersonal order. Hence, it follows that there is an obligation to obedience only within the sphere of the rationally delimited authority which, in terms of the order, has been conferred upon him. . . .

III. Traditional Authority. A system of imperative co-ordination will be called "traditional" if legitimacy is claimed for it and believed in on the basis of the sanctity of the order and the attendant powers of control as they have been handed down from the past, "have always existed." The person or persons exercising authority are designated according to traditionally transmitted rules. The object of obedience is the personal authority of the individual which he enjoys by virtue of his traditional status. The organized group exercising authority is, in the simplest case, primarily based on relations of personal loyalty, cultivated through a common process of education. The person exercising authority is not a "superior," but a personal "chief."

His administrative staff does not consist primarily of officials, but of personal retainers. Those subject to authority are not "members" of an association, but are either his traditional "comrades" or his "subjects." What determines the relations of the administrative staff to the chief is not the impersonal obligation of office, but personal loyalty to the chief.

Obedience is not owed to enacted rules, but to the person who occupies a position of authority by tradition or who has been chosen for such a position on a traditional basis. His commands are legitimized in one of two ways: (1) partly in terms of traditions which themselves directly determine the content of the command and the objects and extent of authority. In so far as this is true, to overstep the traditional limitations would endanger his traditional status by under-mining acceptance of his legitimacy. (2) In part, it is a matter of the chief's free personal decision, in that tradition leaves a certain sphere open for this. This sphere of traditional prerogative rests primarily on the fact that the obligations of obedience on the basis of personal loyalty are essentially unlimited. There is thus a double sphere: on the one hand, of action which is bound to specific tradition; on the other hand, of that which is free of any specific rules.

In the latter sphere, the chief is free to confer "grace" on the basis of his personal pleasure or displeasure, his personal likes and dislikes, quite arbitrarily, particularly in return for gifts which often become a source of regular income. So far as his action follows principles at all, these are principles of substantive ethical common sense, of justice, or of utilitarian expediency. They are not, however, as in the case of legal authority, formal principles. The exercise of authority is normally oriented to the question of what the chief and his administrative staff will normally permit, in view of the traditional obedience of the subjects and what will or will not arouse their resistance. When resistance occurs, it is directed against the person of the chief or of a member of his staff. The accusation is that he has failed to observe the traditional limits of his authority. Opposition is not directed against the system as such.

It is impossible in the pure type of traditional authority for law or administrative rules to be deliberately created by legislation. What is actually new is thus claimed to have always been in force but only recently to have become known through the wisdom of the promulgator. The only documents which can play a part in the orientation of legal administration are the documents of tradition; namely, precedents.

IV. Charismatic Authority. The term "charisma" will be applied to a certain quality of an individual personality by virtue of which he is set apart from ordinary men and treated as endowed with supernatural, superhuman, or at least specifically exceptional powers or qualities. These are such as are not accessible to the ordinary person, but are regarded as of divine origin or as exemplary, and on the basis of them the individual concerned is treated as a leader. In primitive circumstances this peculiar kind of deference is paid to prophets, to people with a reputation for therapeutic or legal wisdom, to leaders in the hunt, and heroes in war. It is very often thought of as resting on magical powers. How the quality in question would be ultimately judged from any ethical, aesthetic, or other such point of view is naturally entirely indifferent for purposes of definition. What is alone important is how the individual is actually regarded by those subject to charismatic authority, by his "followers" or "disciples". . . .

1. It is recognition on the part of those subject to authority which is decisive for the validity of charisma. This is freely given and guaranteed by what is held to be a "sign" or proof, originally always a miracle, and consists in devotion to the corresponding revelation, hero worship, or absolute trust in the leader. But where charisma is genuine, it is not this which is the basis of the claim to legitimacy. This basis lies rather in the conception that it is the *duty* of those who have been called to charismatic mission to recognize its quality and to act accordingly. Psychologically this "recognition" is a matter of complete personal devotion to the possessor of the quality, arising out of enthusiasm, or of despair and hope. . . .

2. If proof of his charismatic qualification fails him for long, the leader endowed with charisma tends to think his god or his magical or heroic powers have deserted him. If he is for long unsuccessful, above all if his leadership fails to benefit his followers, it is likely that his charismatic authority will disappear. This is the genuine charismatic meaning of the "gift of grace." . . .

3. The corporate group which is subject to charismatic authority is based on an emotional form of communal relationship. The administrative staff of a charismatic leader does not consist of "officials"; at least its members are not technically trained. It is not chosen on the basis of social privilege nor from the point of view of domestic or personal dependency. It is rather chosen in terms of the charismatic

qualities of its members. The prophet has his disciples; the war lord his selected henchmen; the leader, generally, his followers. There is no such thing as "appointment" or "dismissal," no career, no promotion. There is only a "call" at the instance of the leader on the basis of the charismatic qualification of those he summons. There is no hierarchy; the leader merely intervenes in general or in individual cases when he considers the members of his staff inadequate to a task with which they have been entrusted. There is no such thing as a definite sphere of authority and of competence, and no appropriation of official powers on the basis of social privileges. There may, however, be territorial or functional limits to charismatic powers and to the individual's "mission." There is no such thing as a salary or a benefice. Disciples or followers tend to live primarily in a communistic relationship with their leader on means which have been provided by voluntary gift. There are no established administrative organs. In their place are agents who have been provided with charismatic authority by their chief or who possess charisma of their own. There is no system of formal rules, of abstract legal principles, and hence no process of judicial decision oriented to them. But equally there is no legal wisdom oriented to judicial precedent. Formally concrete judgments are newly created from case to case and are originally regarded as divine judgments and revelations. . . .

Charismatic authority is thus specifically outside the realm of everyday routine and the profane sphere. In this respect, it is sharply opposed both to rational, and particularly bureaucratic, authority, and to traditional authority, whether in its patriarchal, patrimonial, or any other form. Both rational and traditional authority are specifically forms of everyday routine control of action; when the charismatic type is the direct antitheses of this. Bureaucratic authority is specifically rational in the sense of being bound to intellectually analyzable rules; while charismatic authority is specifically irrational in the sense of being foreign to all rules. Traditional authority is bound to the precedents handed down from the past and to this extent is also oriented to rules. Within the sphere of its claims, charismatic authority repudiates the past, and is in this sense a specifically revolutionary force. . . .

SOCIAL CONFLICT, LEGITIMACY, AND DEMOCRACY

Seymour Martin Lipset

Legitimacy and Effectiveness. The stability of any given democracy depends not only on economic development but also upon the effectiveness and the legitimacy of its political system. Effectiveness means actual performance, the extent to which the system satisfies the basic functions of government as most of the population and such powerful groups within it as big business or the armed forces see them. Legitimacy involves the capacity of the system to engender and maintain the belief that the existing political institutions are the most appropriate ones for the society. The extent to which contemporary democratic political systems are legitimate depends in large measure upon the ways in which the key issues which have historically divided the society have been resolved.

While effectiveness is primarily instrumental, legitimacy is evaluative. Groups regard a political system as legitimate or illegitimate according to the way in which its values fit with theirs. . . . Legitimacy, in and of itself, may be associated with many forms of political organization, including oppressive ones. Feudal societies, before the advent of industrialism, undoubtedly enjoyed the basic loyalty of most of their members. Crises of legitimacy are primarily a recent historical phenomenon, following the rise of sharp cleavages among groups which are able, because of mass communication, to organize around different values than those previously considered to be the only acceptable ones.

A crisis of legitimacy is a crisis of change. Therefore, its roots must be sought in the character of change in modern society. Crises of legitimacy occur during a transition to a new social structure, if (1) the *status* of major conservative institutions is threatened during the period of structural change; (2) all the major groups in the society do not have access to the political system in the transitional period, or at least as soon as they develop political demands. After a new social structure is established, if the new system is unable to sustain the expectations of major groups (on the grounds of "effectiveness") for a long enough period to develop legitimacy upon the new basis, a new crisis may develop.

Tocqueville gives a graphic description of the first general type of loss of legitimacy, referring mainly to countries which moved from aristocratic monarchies to democratic republics: ". . . epochs sometimes occur in the life of a nation when the old customs of a people are changed, public morality is destroyed, religious belief shaken, and the spell of tradition broken . . . ." The citizens then have "neither the instinctive patriotism of a monarchy nor the reflecting patriotism of a republic; . . . they have stopped between the two in the midst of confusion and distress."[1]

If, however, the status of major conservative groups and symbols is not threatened during this transitional period, even though they lose most of their power, democracy seems to be much more secure. And thus we have the absurd fact that ten out of the twelve stable European and English-speaking democracies are monarchies. Great Britain, Sweden, Norway, Denmark, the Netherlands, Belgium, Luxembourg, Australia, Canada, and New Zealand are kingdoms, or dominions of a monarch, while the only republics which meet the conditions of stable democratic procedures are the United States and Switzerland, plus Uruguay in Latin America.

SOURCE: From Seymour Martin Lipset, *Political Man* (New York: Doubleday & Co., Inc., 1960), pp. 64-71, 74, 76-79. Copyright © 1960 by Seymour Martin Lipset. Reprinted by permission of Doubleday & Company, Inc. Most footnotes have been omitted, and those remaining have been renumbered.

[1]Alexis de Tocqueville, *Democracy in America*, Vol. I (New York: Alfred A. Knopf, Vintage ed., 1945), pp. 251-52.

The preservation of the monarchy has apparently retained for these nations the loyalty of the aristocratic, traditionalist, and clerical sectors of the population which resented increased democratization and equalitarianism. And by accepting the lower strata and not resisting to the point where revolution might be necessary, the conservative orders won or retained the loyalty of the new "citizens." In countries where monarchy was overthrown by revolution, and orderly succession was broken, forces aligned with the throne have sometimes continued to refuse legitimacy to republican successors down to the fifth generation or more.... Thus one main source of legitimacy lies in the continuity of important traditional integrative institutions during a transitional period in which new institutions are emerging.

The second general type of loss of legitimacy is related to the ways in which different societies handle the "entry into politics" crisis–the decision as to when new social groups shall obtain access to the political process. In the nineteenth century these new groups were primarily industrial workers; in the twentieth, colonial elites and peasant peoples. Whenever new groups become politically active (e.g., when the workers first seek access to economic and political power through economic organization and the suffrage, when the *bourgeoisie* demand access to and participation in government, when colonial elites insist on control over their own system), easy access to the *legitimate* political institutions tends to win the loyalty of the new groups to the system, and they in turn can permit the old dominating strata to maintain their own status. In nations like Germany where access was denied for prolonged periods, first to the *bourgeoisie* and later to the workers, and where force was used to restrict access, the lower strata were alienated from the system and adopted extremist ideologies which, in turn, kept the more established groups from accepting the workers' political movement as a legitimate alternative.

Political systems which deny new strata access to power except by revolution also inhibit the growth of legitimacy by introducing millennial hopes into the political arena. Groups which have to push their way into the body politic by force are apt to overexaggerate the possibilities which political participation affords. Consequently, democratic regimes born under such stress not only face the difficulty of being regarded as illegitimate by groups loyal to the *ancien régime* but may also be rejected by those whose millennial hopes are not fulfilled by the change. France, where right-wing clericalists have viewed the Republic as illegitimate and sections of the lower strata have found their expectations far from satisfied, is an example. And today many of the newly independent nations of Asia and Africa face the thorny problem of winning the loyalties of the masses to democratic states which can do little to meet the utopian objectives set by nationalist movements during the period of colonialism and the transitional struggle to independence.

In general, even when the political system is reasonably effective, if at any time the status of major conservative groups is threatened, or if access to politics is denied to emerging groups at crucial periods, the system's legitimacy will remain in question. On the other hand, a breakdown of effectiveness, repeatedly or for a long period, will endanger even a legitimate system's ability.

A major test of legitimacy is the extent to which given nations have developed a common "secular political culture," mainly national rituals and holidays. The

United States has developed a common homogeneous culture in the veneration accorded the Founding Fathers, Abraham Lincoln, Theodore Roosevelt, and their principles. These common elements, to which all American politicians appeal, are not present in all democratic societies. In some European countries, the left and the right have a different set of symbols and different historical heroes. . . .

Knowledge concerning the relative degree of legitimacy of a nation's political institutions is of key importance in any attempt to analyze the stability of these institutions when faced with a crisis of effectiveness. The relationship between different degrees of legitimacy and effectiveness in specific political systems may be presented in the form of a fourfold table, with examples of countries characterized by the various possible combinations:

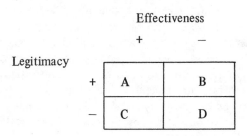

Effectiveness

Legitimacy

	+	−
+	A	B
−	C	D

Societies which fall in box A, which are, that is, high on the scale of both legitimacy and effectiveness, have stable political systems, like the United States, Sweden, and Britain.[2] Ineffective and illegitimate regimes, which fall in box D, are by definition unstable and break down, unless they are dictatorships maintaining themselves by force, like the governments of Hungary and eastern Germany today.

The political experiences of different countries in the early 1930s illustrate the effect of other combinations. In the late 1920s, neither the German nor the Austrian republic was held legitimate by large and powerful segments of its population. Nevertheless, both remained reasonably effective. In terms of the table, they fell in box C. When the effectiveness of various governments broke down in the 1930s, those societies which were high on the scale of legitimacy remained democratic, while such countries as Germany, Austria, and Spain lost their freedom, and France narrowly escaped a similar fate. Or to put the changes in terms of the table, countries which shifted from A to B remained democratic, while those which shifted from C to D broke down. The military defeat of 1940 underlined French democracy's low position on the scale of legitimacy. It was the sole defeated democracy which furnished large-scale support for a Quisling regime.

Situations like these demonstrate the usefulness of this type of analysis. From a short-range point of view, a highly effective but illegitimate system, such as a

---

[2]The race problem in the American South does constitute one basic challenge to the legitimacy of the system, and at one time did cause a breakdown of the national order. This conflict has reduced the commitment of many white southerners to the democratic game down to the present. . . .

well-governed colony, is more unstable than regimes which are relatively low in effectiveness and high in legitimacy. The social stability of a nation like Thailand, despite its periodic *coups d' etat*, stands out in sharp contrast to the situation in neighboring former colonial nations. On the other hand, prolonged effectiveness over a number of generations may give legitimacy to a political system. In the modern world, such effectiveness means primarily constant economic development. Those nations which have adapted more successfully to the requirements of an industrial system have the fewest internal political strains, and have either preserved their traditional legitimacy or developed strong new symbols. . . .

Legitimacy and Conflict. Inherent in all democratic systems is the constant threat that the group conflicts which are democracy's life-blood may solidify to the point where they threaten to disintegrate the society. Hence conditions which serve to moderate the intensity of partisan battle are among the key requisites of democratic government.

Since the existence of a moderate state of conflict is in fact another way of defining a legitimate democracy, it is not surprising that the principal factors determining such an optimum state are closely related to those which produce legitimacy viewed in terms of continuities of symbols and statuses. The character and content of the major issues have emerged in Western nations: first, the place of the church and/or various religions within the nation; second, the admission of the lower strata, particularly the workers, to full political and economic "citizenship" through universal suffrage and the right to bargain collectively; and third, the continuing struggle over the distribution of the national income.

The significant question here is: Were these issues dealt with one by one, with each more or less solved before the next arose; or did the problems accumulate, so that traditional sources of cleavage mixed with newer ones? Resolving tensions one at a time contributes to a stable political system; carrying over issues from one historical period to another makes for a political atmosphere characterized by bitterness and frustration rather than tolerance and compromise. Men and parties come to differ with each other, not simply on ways of settling current problems, but on fundamental and opposed outlooks. This means that they see the political victory of their opponents as a major moral threat, and the whole system, as a result, lacks effective value-integration. . . .

Where a number of historic cleavages intermix and create the basis for ideological politics, democracy will be unstable and weak, for by definition such politics does not include the concept of tolerance. . . .

Wherever the social structure operates so as to isolate *naturally* individuals or groups with the same political outlook from contact with those who hold different views, the isolated individuals or groups tend to back political extremists. It has been repeatedly noted, for example, that workers in so-called "isolated" industries—miners, sailors, fishermen, lumbermen, sheepshearers, and longshoremen—who live in communities predominately inhabited by others in the same occupation usually give overwhelming support to the more left-wing platforms. Such districts tend to vote Communist or socialist by large majorities, sometimes to the point of having what is essentially a "one-party" system. The political intolerance of farm-based groups in times of crisis may be another illustration of this same pattern, since farmers, like workers in isolated industries, have a more homogeneous political environment than do those employed in most urban occupations. . . .

The available evidence. suggests that the chances for stable democracy are enhanced to the extent that groups and individuals have a number of crosscutting, politically relevant affiliations. To the degree that a significant proportion of the population is pulled among conflicting forces, its members have an interest in reducing the intensity of political conflict. As Robert Dahl and Talcott Parsons have pointed out, such groups and individuals also have an interest in protecting the rights of political minorities.

A stable democracy requires relatively moderate tension among its contending political forces. And political moderation is facilitated by the system's capacity to resolve key dividing issues before new ones arise. If the issues of religion, citizenship, and "collective bargaining" are allowed to accumulate, they reinforce each other, and the more reinforced and correlated the sources of cleavage, the less likelihood for political tolerance. Similarly, the greater the isolation from heterogeneous political stimuli, the more the background factors "pile up" in one direction, the greater the chances that the group or individual will have an extremist perspective. These two relationships, one on the level of partisan issues, the other on the level of party support, are joined by the fact that parties reflecting accumulated unresolved issues will further seek to isolate their followers from conflicting stimuli. The best conditions for political cosmopolitanism are again those of economic development—the growth of urbanization, education, communications media, and increased wealth. Most of the obviously isolated occupations—mining, lumbering, agriculture—are precisely those whose relative share of the labor force declines sharply with industrialization.·

Thus the factors involved in modernization or economic development are linked to those which establish legitimacy and tolerance. But it should always be remembered that correlations are only statements about relative degrees of congruence, and that another condition for political action is that the correlation never be so clear-cut that men feel they cannot change the direction of affairs by their actions. . . .

POWER-DEPENDENCE RELATIONS

Richard M. Emerson

Judging from the frequent occurrence of such words as *power, influence, dominance and submission, status and authority,* the importance of power is widely recognized, yet considerable confusion exists concerning these concepts. There is an extensive literature pertaining to power, on both theoretical and empirical levels, and in small group as well as large community contexts. Unfortunately, this already large and rapidly growing body of research has not achieved the cumulative character desired. Our *integrated* knowledge of power does not significantly surpass the conceptions left by Max Weber.[1]

This suggests that there is a place at this moment for a systematic treatment of social power. The underdeveloped state of this area is further suggested by what appears, to this author, to be a recurrent flaw in common conceptions of social power; a flaw which helps to block adequate theoretical development as well as meaningful research. That flaw is the implicit treatment of power as though it were an attribute of a person or group ("X is an influential person." "Y is a powerful group." etc.). Given this conception, the natural research question becomes "Who in community X are the power holders?". The project then proceeds to rank-order persons by some criterion of power, and this ordering is called the *power-structure.* This is a highly questionable representation of a "structure," based upon a questionable assumption of *generalized power.*[2]

It is commonly observed that some person X dominates Y, while being subservient in relations with Z. Furthermore, these power relations are frequently intransitive! Hence, to say that "X has power" is vacant, unless we specify "over whom." In making these necessary qualifications we force ourselves to face up to the obvious: power is a property of the social relation; it is not an attribute of the actor.[3]

In this paper an attempt is made to construct a simple theory of the power aspects of social relations. Attention is focused upon characteristics of the relationship as such, with little or no regard for particular features of the persons or groups engaged in such relations. Personal traits, skills or possessions (such as wealth) which might be relevant to power in one relation are infinitely variable across the set of possible relations, and hence have no place in a general theory.

The Power-Dependence Relation. While the theory presented here is anchored most intimately in small group research, it is meant to apply to more complex community relations as well. In an effort to make these conceptions potentially as

SOURCE: Richard M. Emerson, "Power-Dependence Relations," *American Sociological Review,* Vol. 27, February 1962, pp. 31-37, 39-41. Reprinted by permission. Several footnotes have been omitted, and those that remain have been renumbered.

[1] Max Weber, in *The Theory of Social and Economic Organization,* (New York: Oxford University Press, 1947), presents what is still a classic formulation of power, authority and legitimacy. However, it is characteristic of Weber that he constructs a typology rather than an organized theory of power.

[2] The notion of "generalized power" which is not restricted to specific social relations, if taken literally, is probably meaningless. Power may indeed be generalized, across a finite set of relations in a power network, but this notion, too, requires very careful analysis. Are you dealing with some kind of halo effect (reputations if you wish), or are the range and boundary of generalized power anchored in the power structure itself? These are questions which must be asked and answered.

[3] Just as power is often treated as though it were a property of the person, so leadership, conformity, etc., are frequently referred to the personal traits of "leaders," "conformers" and so on, as if they were distinguishable types of people. In a sociological perspective such behavior should be explicitly treated as an attribute of a relation rather than a person.

broadly applicable as possible, we shall speak of relations among *actors*, where an actor can be either a person or a group. Unless otherwise indicated, any relation discussed might be a person-person, group-person or group-group relation.

Social relations commonly entail *ties of mutual dependence* between the parties. A *depends* upon B if he aspires to goals or gratifications whose achievement is facilitated by appropriate actions on B's part. By virtue of mutual dependency, it is more or less imperative to each party that he be able to control or influence the other's conduct. At the same time, these ties of mutual dependence imply that each party is in a position, to some degree, to grant or deny, facilitate or hinder, the other's gratification. Thus, it would appear that the power to control or influence the other resides in control over the things he values, which may range all the way from oil resources to ego-support, depending upon the relation in question. In short, *power resides implicitly in the other's dependency*. When this is recognized, the analysis will of necessity revolve largely around the concept of dependence.[4]

Two variables appear to function jointly in fixing the dependence of one actor upon another. Since the precise nature of this joint function is an empirical question, our proposition can do no more than specify the directional relationships involved:

Dependence (*Dab*). The dependence of actor A upon actor B is (1) directly proportional to A's *motivational investment* in goals mediated by B, and (2) inversely proportional to the *availability* to those goals to A outside of the A-B relation.

In this proposition "goal" is used in the broadest possible sense to refer to gratifications consciously sought as well as rewards unconsciously obtained through the relationship. The "availability" of such goals outside of the relation refers to alternative avenues of goal-achievement, most notably other social relations. The costs associated with such alternatives must be included in any assessment of dependency.

If the dependence of one party provides the basis for the power of the other, that power must be defined as a potential influence:

Power (*Pab*). The power of actor A over actor B is the amount of resistance on the part of B which can be potentially overcome by A.

Two points must be made clear about this definition. First, the power defined here will not be, of necessity, observable in every interactive episode between A and B, yet we suggest that it exists nonetheless as a potential, to be explored, tested, and occasionally employed by the participants. Pab will be empirically manifest only *if* A makes some demand, and only *if* this demand runs counter to B's desires (resistance to be overcome). Any operational definition must make reference to *change* in the conduct of B attributable to demands made by A.

Second, we define power as the "resistance" which can be overcome, without restricting it to any one domain of action. Thus, if A is dependent upon B for love and respect, B might then draw A into criminal activity which he would normally

---

[4]The relation between power and dependence is given similar emphasis in the systematic treatment by J. Thibaut and H. H. Kelley, *The Social Psychology of Groups* (New York: John Wiley and Sons, 1959).

resist. The reader might object to this formulation, arguing that social power is in fact restricted to certain channels. If so, the reader is apparently concerned with "legitimized power" embedded in a social structure. . . .

The premise we began with can now be stated as Pab = Dba; the power of A over B is equal to, and based upon, the dependence of B upon A. Recognizing the reciprocity of social relations, we can represent a power-dependence relation as a pair of equations:

$$Pab = Dba$$
$$Pba = Dab.$$

Before proceeding further we should emphasize that these formulations have been so worded in the hope that they will apply across a wide range of social life. At a glance our conception of dependence contains two variables remarkably like supply and demand ("availability" and "motivational investment," respectively). We prefer the term *dependency* over these economic terms because it facilitates broader application, for all we need to do to shift these ideas from one area of application to another is change the motivational basis of dependency. We can speak of the economic dependence of a home builder upon a loan agency as varying directly with his desire for the home, and hence capital, and inversely with the "availability" of capital from other agencies. Similarly, a child may be dependent upon another child based upon motivation toward the pleasures of collective play, the availability of alternative playmates, etc. The same generic power-dependence relation is involved in each case. The dependency side of the equation may show itself in "friendship" among playmates, in "filial love" between parent and child, in "respect for treaties" among nations. On the other side of the equation, I am sure no one doubts that mothers, lovers, children, and nations enjoy the power to influence their respective partners, within the limit set by the partner's dependence upon them. . . .

Balance and Imbalance. The notion of reciprocity in power-dependency relations raises the question of equality or inequality of power in the relation. If the power of A over B (Pab) is confronted by equal opposing power of B over A, is power then neutralized or cancelled out? We suggest that in such a balanced condition, power is in no way removed from the relationship. A pattern of "dominance" might not emerge in the interaction among these actors, but that does not imply that power is inoperative in either or both directions. A *balanced* relation and an *unbalanced* relation are represented respectively as follows:

Pab = Dba	Pab = Dba
‖ ‖	v v
Pba = Dab	Pba = Dab

Consider two social relations, both of which are balanced, but at *different levels* of dependence. . . . A moment's thought will reveal the utility of the argument that balance does not neutralize power, for each party may continue to exert profound control over the other. It might even be meaningful to talk about the parties being controlled by the relation itself.

Rather than cancelling out considerations of power, reciprocal power provides the basis for studying three more features of power-relations: first, a power advantage can be defined as Pab minus Pba, which can be either positive or negative (a power disadvantage); second, the *cohesion* of a relationship can be defined as the average of Dab and Dba, though this definition can be refined; and finally, it opens the door to the study of *balancing operations* as structrual changes in power-dependence relations which tend to reduce power advantage.

Discussion of balancing tendencies should begin with a concrete illustration. In the unbalanced relation represented symbolically above, A is the more powerful party because B is the more dependent of the two. Let actor B be a rather "unpopular" girl, with puritanical upbringing, who wants desperately to date; and let A be a young man who occasionally takes her out, while dating other girls as well. (The reader can satisfy himself about A's power advantage in this illustration by referring to the formulations above.) Assume further that A "discovers" this power advantage, and, in exploring for the limits of his power, makes sexual advances. In this simplified illustration, these advances should encounter resistance in B's puritanical values. Thus, when a power advantage is *used*, the weaker member will achieve one value at the expense of other values.

In this illustration the tensions involved in an unbalanced relation need not be long endured. They can be reduced in either of two ways: (1) the girl might reduce the psychic costs involved in continuing the relation by redefining her moral values, with appropriate rationalizations and shifts in reference group attachments; or (2) she might renounce the value of dating, develop career aspirations, etc., thus reducing A's power. Notice that the first solution does *not* of necessity alter the unbalanced relation. The weaker member has sidestepped one painful demand but she is still vulnerable to new demands. By contrast, the second solution alters the power relation itself. In general, it appears that an unbalanced relation is unstable for it encourages the use of power which in turn sets in motion processes which we will call (a) cost reduction and (b) balancing operations.

Cost Reduction. The "cost" referred to here amounts to the "resistance" to be overcome in our definition of power—the cost involved for one party in meeting the demands made by the other. The process of cost reduction in power-dependence relations shows itself in many varied forms. In the courting relation above it took the form of alteration in moral attitudes on the part of a girl who wanted to be popular; in industry it is commonly seen as the impetus for improved plant efficiency and technology in reducing the cost of production. What we call the "mark of oppression" in the character structure of members of low social castes (the submissive and "painless" loss of freedom) might well involve the same power processes, as does the "internalization of parental codes" in the socialization process. . . .

In general, *cost reduction* is a process involving change in values (personal, social, economic) which reduces the pains incurred in meeting the demands of a powerful other. It must be emphasized, however, that these adjustments do not necessarily alter the balance or imbalance of the relation, and, as a result, they must be distinguished from the more fundamental *balancing operations* described below. It must be recognized that cost reducing tendencies will take place even under conditions of balance, and while this is obvious in economic transactions, it is equally true of other social relations, where the "costs" involved are anchored in modifiable attitudes and values. . . . We suggest that cost reducing tendencies generally will function to deepen and stabilize social relations over and above the condition of balance.

Balancing Operations. The remainder of this paper will deal with balancing processes which operate through changes in the variables which define the structure of the power-dependence relation as such. The formal notation adopted here suggests *exactly four generic types* of balancing operations. In the unbalanced relation

$$Pab = Dba$$
$$v \qquad v$$
$$Pba = Dab,$$

balance can be restored either by an increase in Dab or by a decrease in Dba. If we recall that *dependence* is a joint function of two variables, the following alterations will move the relation toward a state of balance:

1. If B reduces motivational investment in goals mediated by A.
2. If B cultivates alternative sources for gratification of those goals.
3. If A increases motivational investment in goals mediated by B.
4. If A is denied alternative sources for achieving those goals.

While these four types of balancing operation are dictated by the logic of the scheme, we suggest that each corresponds to well known social processes. The first operation yields balance through motivational withdrawal by B, the weaker member. The second involves the cultivation of alternative social relations by B. The third is based upon "giving status" to A, and the fourth involves coalition and group formation. . . .

In the interest of simplicity and clarity, we will illustrate each of the four generic types of balancing operations in relations among children in the context of play. Consider two children equally motivated toward the pleasures of contributing to such play. These children, A and B, form a balanced relation if we assume further that each has the other as his only playmate, and the give-and-take of their interactions might well be imagined, involving the emergence of such equalitarian rules as "taking turns," etc. Suppose now that a third child C, moves into the neighborhood and makes the acquaintance of A, but *not* B. The A-B relation will be thrown out of balance by virtue of A's decreased dependence upon B. The reader should convince himself of this fact by referring back to the proposition on dependence. Without any of these parties necessarily "understanding" what is going on, we would predict that A would slowly come to dominate B in the pattern of their interactions. On more frequent occasions B will find himself deprived of the pleasures A can offer, thus slowly coming to sense his own dependency more acutely. By the same token A will more frequently find B saying "yes" instead of "no" to his proposals, and he will gain increased awareness of his power over B. The growing self-images of these children will surely reflect and perpetuate this pattern.

Operation Number One: Withdrawal. We now have the powerful A making demands of the dependent B. One of the processes through which the tensions in the unbalanced A-B relation can be reduced is *motivational withdrawal* on the part of B, for this will reduce Dba and Pab. In this illustration, child B might lose some of his interest in collective play under the impact of frustrations and demands imposed by A. Such a withdrawal from the play relation would presumably come about if the other three balancing operations were blocked by the circumstances peculiar to the situation. The same operation was illustrated above in the case of the girl who might renounce the value of dating. It would seem to be involved in the dampened level of aspiration associated with the "mark of oppression" referred to above.

In general, the denial of dependency involved in this balancing operation will have the effect of moving actors away from relations which are unbalanced to their disadvantage. The actor's motivational orientations and commitments toward different areas of activity will intimately reflect this process.

Operation Number Two: Extension of Power Network. Withdrawal as a balancing operation entails subjective alterations in the weaker actor. The second operation takes place through alterations in a structure we shall call a *power network*, defined as two or more *connected* power-dependence relations. As we have seen in our illustration, when the C-A relation is connected through A with the A-B relation, forming a simple linear network C-A-B, the properties of A-B are altered. In this example, a previously balanced A-B relation is thrown out of balance, giving A a power advantage. This points up the general fact that while each relation in a network will involve interactions which appear to be independent of other relations in the network (e.g., A and B are seen to play together in the absence of C; C and A in the absence of B), the internal features of one relation are nonetheless a function of the entire network. Any adequate conception of a "power structure" must be based upon this fact.

In this illustration the form of the network throws both relations within it out of balance, thus stimulating one or several of the balancing operations under discussion. If balancing operation number two takes place, *the network* will be extended by the formation of new relationships. The tensions of imbalance in the A-B and A-C relations will make B and C "ready" to form new friendships (1) with additional children D and E, thus lengthening a linear network, or (2) with each other, thus "closing" the network. It is important to notice that the lengthened network balances some relations, but not the network as a whole, while the closed network is completely balanced under the limiting assumptions of this illustration. Thus, we might offer as a corollary to operation number two: Power networks tend to achieve closure.

If the reader is dissatisfied with this illustration in children's play relations, let A be the loan agent mentioned earlier, and B, C, . . .,N be home builders or others dependent upon A for capital. This is the familiar monopoly situation with the imbalance commonly attributed to it. As a network, it is a set of relations connected only at A. Just as the children were "ready" to accept new friends, so the community of actors B, C, . . .,N is ready to receive new loan agencies.

Balancing operation number two involves in all cases the *diffusion* of dependency into new relations in a network. . . .

It is convenient at this juncture to take up balancing operation number four, leaving number three to the last.

Operation Number Four: Coalition Formation. Let us continue with the same illustration. When the B-C relation forms, closing the C-A-B network in the process of balancing, we have what appears to be a coalition of the two weaker against the one stronger. This, however, is not technically the case, for A is not involved in the B-C interactions; he simply exists as an alternative playmate for both B and C.

The proper representation of coalitions in a triad would be (AB)-C, (AC)-B, or (BC)-A. That is, a triadic network reduces to a coalition only if two members unite as a single actor in the process of dealing directly with the third. The difference involved here may be very small in behavioral terms, and the distinction may seem overly refined, but it goes to the heart of an important conceptual problem (the difference between a closed "network" and a "group"), and it rests upon the fact that two very different balancing operations are involved. The C-A-B network is balanced through the addition of a third relation (C-B) in operation number two, but it is still just a power network. In operation number four it achieves balance through collapsing the two-relational network into one group-person relation with the emergence of a "collective actor." Operation number two reduces the power of the stronger actor, while number four increases the power of weaker actors through collectivization. If the rewards mediated by A are such that they can be jointly enjoyed by B and C, then the tensions of imbalance in the A-B and A-C relations can be resolved in the (BC)-A coalition.

In a general way, Marx was asking for balancing operation number four in his call to "Workers of the world," and the collectivization of labor can be taken as an illustration of this balancing tendency as an historic process. Among the balancing operations described here, coalition formation is the one most commonly recognized as a power process. However, the more general significance of this balancing operation seems to have escaped notice, for the typical coalition is only one of the many forms this same operation takes. . . .

Operation Number Three: Emergence of Status. One important feature of group structure remains to be discussed: status and status hierarchies. It is interesting that the one remaining balancing operation provided in this theory takes us naturally to the emergence of status ordering. Operation number three increases the weaker member's power to control the formerly more powerful member through increasing the latter's motivational investment in the relation. This is normally accomplished through giving him status recognition in one or more of its many forms, from ego-gratification to monetary differentials. The ego-rewards, such as prestige, loom large in this process because they are highly valued by many recipients while given at low cost to the giver.

The discussion of status hierarchies forces us to consider *intra*-group relations, and how this can be done in a theory which treats the group in the singular as *an* actor. . . . Every intra-group relation involves at once every member of the group. Thus, in a group with members A, B, C, and D, the relations A-B, A-C, etc. do not exist. Any interactions between A and B, for example, lie outside of the social system in question unless one or both of these persons "represents" the group in his actions, as in the coalition pattern discussed at length above. The relations which do exist are (ABCD)-A, (ABCD)-B, (ABCD)-C and (ABCD)-D as a minimum, plus whatever relation of the (ABCD)-(AB) type may be involved in the peculiar structure of the group in question. Thus, in a group of N members we have theoretical reason for dealing with N *group-member* relations rather than considering all of the

$$\frac{N(N-1)}{2}$$

possible member-member relations. Each of these group-member relations can now be expressed in the familiar equations for a power-dependence relation:

$$Pgm_i = Dm_ig$$
$$Pm_ig = Dgm_i.$$

To account for the emergence of a status hierarchy within a group of N members, we start with a set of N group-member relations of this type and consider balancing operations in these relations.

Let us imagine a five-member group and proceed on three assumptions: (1) *status* involves differential valuation of members (or roles) by the group, and this valuation is equivalent to, or an expression of, Dgm_i; (2) a member who is highly valued in other *similar* groups he belongs to or might freely join; and (3) all five members have the same motivational investment in the group at the outset. Assumptions two and three are empirical, and when they are true they imply that Dgm and Dmg are inversely related across the N group-member relations. This in turn implies a state of imbalance of a very precarious nature so far as group stability is concerned. The least dependent member of a group will be the first to break from the group, and these members are precisely the most valued members. It is this situation which balancing operation number three alleviates through "giving status" to the highly valued members, thus gaining the power to keep and control those members. . . .

Among the factors involved in status ordering, this theory focuses attention upon the extreme importance of the availability factor in dependency as a determinant of status position and the values employed in status ordering. In considering Dgm (the relative value or importance the group attaches to member roles) it is notably difficult to rely upon a functional explanation. Is the pitcher more highly valued than the center fielder because he is functionally more important or because good pitchers are harder to find? Is the physicist valued over the plumber because of a "more important" functional contribution to the social system, or because physicists are more difficult to replace, more costly to obtain, etc.? The latter considerations involve the availability factor. We suggest here that the *values* people use in ordering roles or persons express the dependence of the system upon those roles, and that the *availability* factor in dependency plays the decisive part in historically shaping those values.[5] . . .

Conclusion. The theory put forth in this paper is in large part contained implicitly in the ties of mutual dependence which bind actors together in social systems. Its principal value seems to be its ability to pull together a wide variety of social events, ranging from the internalization of parental codes to society-wide movements, like the collectivization of labor, in terms of a few very simple principles. Most important, the concepts involved are subject to operational formulation. Two experiments testing certain propositions discussed above led to the following results:

1. Conformity (Pgm) varies directly with motivational investment in the group;
2. Conformity varies inversely with acceptance in alternative groups;
3. Conformity is high at both status extremes in groups with membership turnover . . .;
4. Highly valued members of a group are strong conformers *only if* they are valued by other groups as well. (This supports the notion that special status rewards are used to hold the highly valued member who does not depend heavily upon the group, and that in granting him such rewards power is obtained over him.);
5. Coalitions form among the weak to control the strong (balancing operation number three);
6. The greatest rewards within a coalition are given to the less dependent member of the coalition (balancing operation number three, analogous to "status giving").

Once the basic ideas in this theory have been adequately validated and refined, both theoretical and empirical work must be extended in two main directions. First, the interaction process should be studied to locate carefully the factors leading to *perceived* power and dependecy in self and others, and the conditions under which power, as a potential, will be employed in action. Secondly, and, in the long run, more important, will be study of *power networks* more complex than those referred to here, leading to more adequate understanding of complex power structures. The theory presented here does no more than provide the basic underpinning to the study of complex networks.

---

[5] "Motivational investment" and "availability," which jointly determine dependency at any point in time, are functionally related through time. This is implied in our balancing operations. While these two variables can be readily distinguished in the case of Dmg, they are too intimately fused in Dgm to be clearly separated. The values by which a group sees a given role as "important" at time two evolve from felt scarcity in that role and similar roles at time one.

THE MONOPOLY OF FORCE AND THE "POWER BANK"

Talcott Parsons

We have suggested that force plays a part in power systems parallel to that of gold in monetary systems. Only in one special instance is the commodity value of gold the "real basis" of the value of the dollar. Similarly, only in one special aspect is the command of physical force in a power system the "real basis" of the authority of government or the leadership of private collectivities, as the case may be. In the economic case, it is the credit system, built up primarily through the institution of banking but through several other types of mechanisms, that "frees" monetary exchange from the limitations of metallic money. The "ultimate" basis of the value of its money then is the productivity of the economy.

We now suggest that there is a directly parallel set of phenomena in power systems. The primary functions of power are to facilitate the mobilization of instrumental resources like money and services and of support and the influence on which it partially depends. To repeat, this mobilization occurs through the promotion of binding obligations, the bindingness of which is symbolized by the willingness of those with power to resort to negative sanctions in case of noncompliance, sanctions that can be arranged in a rough order of severity from the threat of mild disadvantage to the drastic use of force. We have repeatedly insisted, however, that the problem of the motivation of compliance under normal conditions must not be confused with the problem of what sanctions will and will not be used in what order of severity and under what circumstances, when noncompliance occurs or is threatened. What motivation alter has for accepting or avoiding the sanctions is still a third question.

A particularly cogent set of reasons for making these distinctions lies in the existence and prominence in advanced political systems of a political analogy of the bank, which we may call, in appropriate quotation marks, the "power bank." The hallmark of the money bank is the fact that the dollars, as we noted, do double duty, remaining at the disposal of depositors while they are also at the disposal of borrowers. In the case of power, commitments to the performance of binding obligations are the analog of dollars and may be said to do double duty.

This point can be illustrated most clearly by the example of an electoral system, public or private. Members, in their capacity as voters, may be said to have entrusted power ("deposited" it) to elected leadership, power that they reserve the right to withdraw, if not on demand, at least at the next election. Some of this power is indeed immediately returned in the form of decisions that directly satisfy constituency interests. This return is reflected in party references to the record of benefits accruing to various categories of constituents during a term of office. In

SOURCE: Talcott Parsons, "Some Reflections on the Place of Force in Social Processes," in *Harry Eckstein*, ed., *Internal War* (New York: The Free Press, 1964), pp. 57-65. Reprinted with permission of The Macmillan Company. © by The Free Press of Glencoe, a Division of The Macmillan Company, 1963.

many political systems, private as well as public, however, this return does not exhaust the activities of leadership. The leadership also "invests" a portion of its power in making commitments in what it conceives to be a larger collective interest, commitments that are in fact not in response to the immediate demands of constituent interest groups. Above all, these commitments tie up resources that in some sense "belong" to the constitutency beyond the periods when the leadership is formally in control of them.

In the case of governments, the honoring of obligations assumed by opposing parties in previous administrations, frequently in foreign affairs but often domestically, is an indication of this phenomenon. For example, although the appropriations are made, for the most part, formally on an annual basis, money spent by the United States government in the fields of scientific research and training has in fact become, to a considerable extent, a permanent obligation, in spite of the legal authority of Congress to cut it off with a single vote. A good private example is the ploughing back of profits by corporations without detailed authorization by the stockholders, although the latter have the formal rights to stop it and take the money as dividends.

The essential point is that a "power bank," like a money bank, is, if it is functioning well, "insolvent" at any given moment with respect to its formal obligations, in the sense that it cannot fulfill all its legitimate obligations if there is insistence on their fulfillment too rapidly. Even relatively mild pressure to exceed the accustomed rate of fulfillment will force adoption of a rigid priority system and the rapid liquidation of some commitments that are otherwise highly desirable. Extreme pressure will tend to bring about a serious breakdown of the power system. When a vicious circle of "deflationary" pressure of this type gets under way, the tendency is to bring the role of negative sanctions increasingly to the fore and to resort to threats of sanctions of increasing severity. The "constitutional" powers can be quickly exhausted. At the end of the road lies the resort to force in the interest of what particular groups conceive to be their rights. The monopoly of force in the hands of government presents special problems that will be discussed presently.

This general set of considerations constitutes what we believe to be the basis of at least one of the most important objections to the very commonly held "zero-sum" conception of the nature of power. If power were equatable with physical force or even "based on" it in a sense other than the one we have discussed, it might be more plausible to hold that the power controlled by some units in the system was necessarily subtracted from a fixed total, the balance of which was controlled by the others.

That there is a distributive aspect of power is almost obvious and is clearly implied by our comparison with money. We wish, however, to extend the parallel to the point where we postulate a set of mechanisms of expansion and contraction of the total as a function of forces operating on the level of the system as a whole, which is parallel to the phenomenon of credit in the case of money. We think that these considerations are highly relevant to the problems of the place of force and constitute some of the reasons why the complexity of the relations between power and force that we have outlined is so important.

It should also be clear from this argument that we think that the basic phenomena of power systems are dependent on the institutionalization of what ordinarily is called authority. That is to say that, for cases of the exercise of authority—in which we include the vote—compliance is both legitimately and "normally" to be expected. It is, however, in the case of normatively regulated action that conformity with normative expectations sometimes, indeed often, fails. . . .

We have already laid stress on the tendency to develop a monopoly of the control of force in the hands of government. It is vital to our argument that this concentration cannot, except for a limiting type, be the case with power. A monopoly of the use of power in governmental hands would be a definition of the ideal type of a totalitarian regime. It has been one of our most important contentions that power should be regarded as a circulating medium that operates throughout the society wherever organizations in the sense of collectivities exist. Of course, in this sense, the big organizations like governments, productive enterprises, and trade unions stand out conspicuously, but in principle, families, even friendship cliques, and many other groups also have some power. In the aggregate, the power of small units may be very great, although, of course, the question of effective organization always arises.

Among those societies with highly developed organization, the modern Western, and rather particularly the American type, is characterized by pluralism. Although the scale of organization is large, there are many, even among large organizations, that are more or less independent of one another. It is important not to make absolute independence in itself a criterion of pluralism. There is, moreover, a shading from the very large through many intermediate grades to the very small. Government is by no means monolithic, splintered as it is by the separation of powers, federalism (in the United States), local independence, and the internal complexity of such an immensely ramified organization as the federal executive branch. The same is true, in varying degrees, of many large private organizations.

In any complex society, more conspicuously in the more pluralistic ones, what may be called the "power structure" rests in a state of more or less stable and probably significantly shifting equilibrium. Processes of circulation operate continuously, through exchanges of commitments of resources and of opportunities for their utilization, through giving and withdrawing support for various collective goals, and through the decisions that signify commitment—not only of mobile resources, but of organizations themselves.

There is, finally, the very important point that individual persons have *plural* memberships in and commitments to collectivities. Although unevenly spread throughout a population, this plurality increases with higher differentiation of the general social structure. An increased spread of memberships implies, as one price of enhanced effectiveness, an increased potential for conflict among them or, put in obverse form, an increasingly delicate equilibrium among such loyalties.

This equilibrium both among collectivities and among loyalties to memberships—which, it should be remembered, cut across each other—is dependent on the maintenance of a level of "confidence," a factor very similar to the confidence that operates in monetary systems. In the latter, it involves the expectation of probabilities, not only of the fulfillment of contractual obligations and of relinquishing them. In the political case, it is confidence in the probability of what we have called compliance. This confidence centers on the fulfillment of obligations already assumed through collectivity memberships, but in a parallel to the economic case, it extends also to rates of expected acceptance of new obligations–through entry of the younger generations into the labor force and hence into employment, for example. . . .

Disturbances of this equilibrium may originate in any of a number of places–specificity of origin is not an important consideration here. The question is whether or not the immediate consequence of a disturbance is "deflationary" in the sense of its effect on the system of expectations of which the power structure is made. One general condition favorable to such deflationary influence is, of course, an over-extension of power commitments, analogous to inflation in the economic sense. This problem presents a very important field of inquiry that unfortunately cannot be followed up here; that such conditions exist will simply be taken as given.

In our present context, a deflationary influence is one that leads to a demand for a binding decision or exercise of power, to which the demander has some kind of right but which is out of line with the normal expectations of operation of the system. That some units will encounter emergency conditions, as some depositors unexpectedly must withdraw their balances, is to be taken for granted. Whether the rate of imposition of such demands is abnormal is a matter for statistical estimate, unless the individual case is of overwhelming quantitative magnitude in terms of claims either on resources or on support.

Any such disturbance may, of course, be met. On the other hand, if it is not met or if the difficulty of meeting it creates a question of the capacity of the system to meet its general obligations, it *may* (not necessarily must) motivate other units to present demands they would not otherwise have presented *at this time.*

If such a process once gets under way, it may enter into a vicious-circle pattern. That is, each assertion of demands for collective decision, for satisfaction of interests that would not ordinarily have been presented, will stimulate other units to assert their demands. There can then develop a *cumulative* pressure on the relevant collectivities. The general type of response will then be twofold. First, an increasingly stringent scale of priorities of what can and cannot be done will be set up; second, increasingly severe negative sanctions for noncompliance with collective decisions will be imposed.

With respect to the first tendency, the most important point to note is the presumption that most if not all of the demands made on collective leadership are legitimate and that, in general, their presumptive legitimacy is not dependent on specific conditions of timing and other constraints–if the analogy to the bank depositors holds up. This circumstance, once "confidence" has been sufficiently impaired, is bound to increase the pressure, since there is no formal way to make newly imposed priorities seem legitimate other than the process of "legal" pronouncement, which may or may not match the normative "sentiments" of the important groups.

With respect to the second tendency, we have already asserted that increasing severity of sanctions leads in the direction of resort to force. If pressure to fulfill demands becomes sufficiently severe and the objective possibility of fulfilling them sufficiently low, then it seems inevitable that the most vociferous insisters, who at the same time are low on the priority scale, will have to be threatened with force to deter them. Here again it must be remembered that we are positing a situation where it is objectively impossible to fulfill all the legitimate demands within a short time but where, at the same time, this incapacity is also felt to be legitimate.

The most common responses to increasing severity of sanctions are two. One is to seek security through "digging in" in a protected position, the protection of which may involve independent command of force but may also take the form of command of other resources of the most various kinds. This reaction is the withdrawal from dependence on the ramified power system, which is analogous to economic withdrawal into gold or into "real" assets—a feature of economic deflation that, interestingly, is shared with inflationary situations. The other general response is the active, aggressive attempt to *enforce* demands against the inclinations of the collective leadership. This response clearly leads in the direction of seeking capacity to implement countersanctions of severity equal to or exceeding that of those commanded by the collective leadership. Force plays a central part in any such system of countersanctions, but it should be remembered that it does not stand alone. . . .

SOCIAL STRUCTURE, GROUP INTERESTS, AND CONFLICT GROUPS

Ralf Dahrendorf

Integration and Values Versus Coercion and Interests: The Two Faces of Society. Throughout the history of Western political thought, two views of society have stood in conflict. Both these views are intended to explain what has been, and will probably continue to be, the most puzzling problem of social philosophy: how is it that human societies cohere? There is one large and distinguished school of thought according to which social order results from a general agreement of values. . .which outweighs all possible or actual differences of opinion and interest. There is another equally distinguished school of thought which holds that coherence and order in society are founded on force and constraint, on the domination of some and the subjection of others. To be sure, these views are not at all points mutually

SOURCE: Excerpted from *Class and Class Conflict in Industrial Society* by Ralf Dahrendorf with the permission of the publishers, Stanford University Press and Routledge & Kegan Paul, Ltd., London.© 1959 by the Board of Trustees of the Leland Stanford Junior University. Several footnotes have been omitted, and those remaining have been renumbered.

exclusive. The Utopian (as we shall call those who insist on coherence by consensus) does not deny the existence of differences of interest; nor does the Rationalist (who believes in coherence by constraint and domination) ignore such agreements of value as are required for the very establishment of force. But Utopian and Rationalist alike advance claims of primacy for their respective standpoints. For the Utopian, differences of interest are subordinated to agreements of value, and for the Rationalist these agreements are but a thin, and as such ineffective, coating of the primary reality of differences that have to be precariously reconciled by constraint. . . .

The sociological Utopian does not claim that order *is based on* a general consensus of values, but that it *can be conceived of in terms of* such consensus, and that, if it is conceived of in these terms, certain propositions follow which are subject to the test of specific observations. Analogously, for the sociological Rationalist the assumption of the coercive nature of social order is a heuristic principle rather than a judgment of fact. But this obvious reservation does not prevent the Utopians and the Rationalists of sociology from engaging in disputes which are hardly less intense (if often rather less imaginative and ingenious) than those of their philosophical antecedents. . . .

Generally speaking, it seems to me that two (meta-) theories can and must be distinguished in contemporary sociology. One of these, the *integration theory of society*, conceives of social structure in terms of a functionally integrated system held in equilibrium by certain patterned and recurrent processes. The other one, the *coercion theory of society*, views social structure as a form of organization held together by force and constraint and reaching continuously beyond itself in the sense of producing within itself the forces that maintain it in an unending process of change. Like their philosophical counterparts, these theories are mutually exclusive. But—if I may be permitted a paradoxical formulation that will be explained presently—in sociology (as opposed to philosophy) a decision which accepts one of these theories and rejects the other is neither necessary nor desirable. There are sociological problems for the explanation of which the integration theory of society provides adequate assumptions; there are other problems which can be explained only in terms of the coercion theory of society; there are, finally, problems for which both theories appear adequate. For sociological analysis society is Janus-headed, and its two faces are equivalent aspects of the same reality.

In recent years, the integration theory of society has clearly dominated sociological thinking. In my opinion, this prevalence of one partial view has had many unfortunate consequences. However, it has also had at least one agreeable consequence, in that the very one-sidedness of this theory gave rise to critical objections which enable us today to put this theory in its proper place. . . .

For purposes of exposition it seems useful to reduce each of the two faces of society to a small number of basic tenets, even if this involves some degree of oversimplification as well as overstatement. The integration theory of society, as displayed by the work of Parsons and other structural-functionalists, is founded on a number of assumptions of the following type:

1. Every society is a relatively persistent, stable structure of elements.

2. Every society is a well-integrated structure of elements.

3. Every element in a society has a function, i.e., renders a contribution to its maintenance as a system.

4. Every functioning social structure is based on a consensus of values among its members.

In varying forms, these elements of (1) stability, (2) integration, (3) functional coordination, and (4) consensus recur in all structural-functional approaches to the study of social structure. They are, to be sure, usually accompanied by protestations to the effect that stability, integration, functional coordination, and consensus are only "relatively" generalized. Moreover, these assumptions are not metaphysical propositions about the essence of society; they are merely assumptions for purposes of scientific analysis. As such, however, they constitute a coherent view of the social process[1] which enables us to comprehend many problems of social reality. . . .

What I have called the coercion theory of society can also be reduced to a small number of basic tenets, although here again these assumptions oversimplify and overstate the case:

1. Every society is at every point subject to processes of change; social change is ubiquitous.

2. Every society displays at every point dissensus and conflict; social conflict is ubiquitous.

3. Every element in a society renders a contribution to its disintegration and change.

4. Every society is based on the coercion of some of its members by others. . . .

I need hardly add that, like the integration model, the coercion theory of society constitutes but a set of assumptions for purposes of scientific analysis and implies no claim for philosophical validity—although, like its counterpart, this model also provides a coherent image of social organization.

Now, I would claim that, in a sociological context, neither of these models can be conceived as exclusively valid or applicable. They constitute complementary, rather than alternative, aspects of the structure of total societies as well as of every element of this structure. We have to choose between them only for the explanation of specific problems; but in the conceptual arsenal of sociological analysis they exist side by side. Whatever criticism one may have of the advocates of one or the other of these models can therefore be directed only against claims for the exclusive validity of either.[2] Strictly speaking, both models are "valid" or, rather, useful and necessary for sociological analysis. We cannot conceive of society unless we realize the dialectics of stability and change, integration and conflict, function and motive force, consensus and coercion. . . .

It is evidently virtually impossible to think of society in terms of either model

---

[1] It is important to emphasize that "stability" as a tenet of the integration theory of society does not mean that societies are "static." It means, rather, that such processes as do occur (and the structural-functional approach is essentially concerned with processes) serve to maintain the patterns of the system as a whole. . . .

[2] This, it seems to me, is the only—if fundamental—legitimate criticism that can be raised against Parsons' work on this general level. . . .

without positing its opposite number at the same time. There can be no conflict, unless this conflict occurs within a context of meaning, i.e., some kind of coherent "system." No conflict is conceivable between French housewives and Chilean chess players, because these groups are not united by, or perhaps "integrated into," a common frame of reference. Analogously, the notion of integration makes little sense unless it presupposes the existence of different elements that are integrated. . . . Using one or the other model is therefore a matter of emphasis rather than of fundamental difference; and there are, as we shall see, many points at which a theory of group conflict has to have recourse to the integration theory of social structure.

Inevitably, the question will be raised, also, whether a unified theory of society that includes the tenets of both the integration and the coercion models of society is not at least conceivable—for as to its desirability there can be little doubt. Is there, or can there be, a general point of view that synthesizes the unsolved dialectics of integration and coercion? So far as I can see, there is no such general model; as to its possibility, I have to reserve judgment. It seems at least conceivable that unification of theory is not feasible at a point which has puzzled thinkers ever since the beginning of Western philosophy.

For the explanation of the formation of conflict groups out of conditions of social structure, we shall employ a model that emphasizes the ugly face of society. In the following sections. . .I shall try to show how, on the assumption of the coercive nature of social structure, relations of authority become productive of clashes of role interest which under certain conditions lead to the formation of organized antagonistic groups within limited social organizations as well as within total societies. . . .

Power and Authority. From the point of view of the integration theory of social structure, units of social analysis ("social systems") are essentially voluntary associations of people who share certain values and set up institutions in order to ensure the smooth functioning of cooperation. From the point of view of coercion theory, however, the units of social analysis present an altogether different picture. Here, it is not voluntary cooperation or general consensus but enforced constraint that makes social organizations cohere. In institutional terms, this means that in every social organization some positions are entrusted with a right to exercise control over other positions in order to ensure effective coercion; it means, in other words, that there is a differential distribution of power and authority. One of the central theses of this study consists in the assumption that this differential distribution of authority invariably becomes the determining factor of systematic social conflicts of a type that is germane to class conflicts in the traditional (Marxian) sense of this term. The structural origin of such group conflicts must be sought in the arrangement of social roles endowed with expectations of domination or subjection. Wherever there are such roles, group conflicts of the type in question are to be expected. Differentiation of groups engaged in such conflicts follows the lines of differentiation of roles that are relevant from the point of view of the exercise of authority. Identification of variously equipped authority roles is the first task of conflict analysis;[3] conceptually and empirically all further steps of analysis follow from the investigation of distributions of power and authority. . . .

In the present study we are concerned exclusively with relations of authority, for these alone are part of social structure and therefore permit the systematic derivation of group conflicts from the organization of total societies and associations within them. The significance of such group conflicts rests with the fact that they are not the product of structurally fortuitous relations of power but come forth wherever authority is exercised—and that means in all societies under all historical conditions. (1) Authority relations are always relations of super – and subordination. (2) Where there are authority relations, the superordinate element is socially expected to control, by orders and commands, warnings and prohibitions, the behavior of the subordinate element. (3) Such expectations attach to relatively permanent social positions rather than to the character of individuals; they are in this sense legitimate. (4) By virtue of this fact, they always involve specification of the persons subject to control and of the spheres within which control is permissible.[4] Authority, as distinct from power, is never a relation of generalized control over others. (5) Authority being a legitimate relation, noncompliance with authoritative commands can be sanctioned; it is indeed one of the functions of the legal system (and of course of quasi-legal customs and norms) to support the effective exercise of legitimate authority.

Alongside the term "authority," we shall employ (and have employed) in this study the terms "domination" and "subjection." These will be used synonymously with the rather clumsy expressions "endowed with authority" or "participating in the exercise of authority" (domination), and "deprived of authority" or "excluded from the exercise of authority" (subjection).

It seems desirable for purposes of conflict analysis to specify the relevant unit of social organization in analogy to the concept of social system in the analysis of integration. To speak of specification here is perhaps misleading. "Social system" is a very general concept applicable to all types of organization; and we shall want to employ an equally general concept which differs from that of social system by emphasizing a different aspect of the same organizations. It seems to me that Max Weber's category "imperatively coordinated association" (*Herrschaftsverband*) serves this purpose despite its clumsiness.

In conflict analysis we are concerned *inter alia* with the generation of conflict groups by the authority relations obtaining in imperatively coordinated associations.

---

[3] To facilitate communication, I shall employ in this study a number of abbreviations. These must not however be misunderstood. Thus, "conflict analysis" in this context stands for "analysis of group conflicts of the class type, class being understood in the traditional sense." At no point do I want to imply a claim for a generalized theory of social conflict.

[4] This element of the definition of authority is crucial. It implies that the manager who tries to control people outside his firm, or the private lives of people inside his firm, trespasses the borderline between authority and power. Although he has authority over people in his firm, his control assumes the form of power as soon as it goes beyond the specified persons and spheres of legitimate control. This type of trespassing is of course frequent in every authority relation; and an empirical phenomenon well worth investigating is to what extent the fusion of authority and power tends to intensify group conflicts.

Since imperative coordination, or authority, is a type of social relation present in every conceivable social organization, it will be sufficient to describe such organizations simply as associations. . . . In looking at social organizations not in terms of their integration and coherence but from the point of view of their structure of coercion and constraint, we regard them as (imperatively coordinated) associations rather than as social systems. Because social organizations are also associations, they generate conflicts of interest and become the birthplace of conflict groups. . . .

Authority relations exist wherever there are people whose actions are subject to legitimate and sanctioned prescriptions that originate outside them but within social structure. This formulation, by leaving open who exercises what kind of authority, leaves little doubt as to the omnipresence of some kind of authority somehow exercised. For it is evident that there are many forms and types of authority in historical societies. There are differences of a considerable order of magnitude between the relations of the citizen of classical Athens and his slaves, the feudal landlord and his villeins and serfs, the nineteenth-century capitalist and his workers, the secretary of a totalitarian state party and its members, the appointed manager of a modern enterprise and its employees, or the elected prime minister of a democratic country and the electorate. No attempt will be made in this study to develop a typology of authority. But it is assumed throughout that the existence of domination and subjection is a common feature of all possible types of authority and, indeed, of all possible types of association and organization.

The notion of power and authority employed in the present study represents what Parsons in a critical review of C. W. Mills' book on the American power elite calls the "zero-sum" concept of authority. . . .[5] Like all other elements of social structure, authority has two faces—those, so to speak, of Mills and of Parsons—and on the highest level of abstraction it is illegitimate to emphasize either of these to the exclusion of the other. Authority is certainly not *only* productive of conflict; but neither is it *only* (or even primarily) "a facility for the performance of function in and on behalf of the society as a system." If we are concentrating in this study on what Parsons would call the "negative functions" of authority, we do so because this aspect is more appropriate and useful for the analysis of structurally generated systematic social conflicts.

In referring to the ugly face of authority as a "zero-sum" concept, Parsons brings out one further aspect of this category which is essential for our considerations. By zero-sum, Parsons evidently means that from the point of view of the disruptive "functions" of authority there are two groups or aggregates of persons, of which one possesses authority to the extent to which the other one is deprived of it.[6] This implies—for us, if not for Parsons—that in terms of the coercion theory of society

---

[5]C. W. Mills, *The Power Elite* (New York: Oxford University Press, 1956).

[6]There is one implication of the expression "zero-sum" which would be contrary to my thesis. Mathematically, it would be possible for both groups to have no authority in the sense of a complete absence of authority. I have argued above that under all conditions the authority of one aggregate is, so to speak, greater than zero, and that of the other aggregate correspondingly smaller than zero. The presence of authority, and its unequal distribution, are universal features of social structure.

we can always observe a dichotomy of positions in imperatively coordinated associations with respect to the distribution of authority. Parsons, in his critique of Mills, compares the distribution of authority to the distribution of wealth. It seems to me that this comparison is misleading. However unequally wealth may be distributed, there always is a continuum of possession ranging from the lowest to the highest rank. Wealth is not and cannot be conceived as a zero-sum concept. With respect to authority, however, a clear line can at least in theory be drawn between those who participate in its exercise in given associations and those who are subject to the authoritative commands of others. . . . Authority has not remained unaffected by the modern process of division of labor. But even here, groups or aggregates can be identified which do not participate in the exercise of authority other than by complying with given commands or prohibitions. Contrary to all criteria of social stratification, authority does not permit the construction of a scale. So-called hierarchies of authority (as displayed, for example, in organization charts) are in fact hierarchies of the "plus-side" of authority, i.e., of the differentiation of domination; but there is, in every association, also a "minus-side" consisting of those who are subjected to authority rather than participate in its exercise.

In two respects this analysis has to be specified, if not supplemented. First, for the individual incumbent of roles, domination in one association does not necessarily involve domination in all others to which he belongs, and subjection, conversely, in one association does not mean subjection in all. The dichotomy of positions of authority holds for specific associations only. . . . Although empirically a certain correlation of the authority positions of individuals in different associations seems likely, it is by no means general and is in any case a matter of specific empirical conditions. It is at least possible, if not probable, that if individuals in a given society are ranked according to the sum total of their authority positions in all associations, the resulting pattern will not be a dichotomy but rather like scales of stratification according to income or prestige. For this reason it is necessary to emphasize that in the sociological analysis of group conflict the unit of analysis is always a specific association and the dichotomy of positions within it.

As with respect to the set of roles associated with an individual, total societies, also, do not usually present an unambiguously dichotomic authority structure. There are a large number of imperatively coordinated associations in any given society. Within every one of them we can distinguish the aggregates of those who dominate and those who are subjected. But since domination in industry does not necessarily involve domination in the state, or a church, or other associations, total societies can present the picture of a plurality of competing dominant (and, conversely, subjected) aggregates. This, again, is a problem for the analysis of specific historical societies and must not be confounded with the clearer lines of differentiation within any one association. Within the latter, the distribution of authority always sums up to zero, i.e., there always is a division involving domination and subjection. . . . [7]

---

[7] Inevitably, the qualifications introduced in the two preceding paragraphs are rather vague if stated merely in the abstract. They are, however, of the utmost importance for empirical

While its "disruptive" or conflict-generating consequences are not the only aspect of authority, they are the one relevant in terms of the coercion model of society. Within the frame of reference of this model, (1) the distribution of authority in associations is the ultimate "cause" of the formation of conflict groups, and (2), being dichotomous, it is, in any given association, the cause of the formation of two, and only two, conflict groups. . . .

Latent and Manifest Interests. The analytical process of conflict group formation can be described in terms of a model. Throughout, the categories employed in this model will be used in terms of the coercion theory of social structure. With this restriction in mind, the thesis that conflict groups are based on the dichotomous distribution of authority in imperatively coordinated associations can be conceived of as the basic assumption of the model. To this assumption we now add the proposition that differentially equipped authority positions in associations involve, for their incumbents, conflicting interests. The occupants of positions of domination and the occupants of positions of subjection hold, by virtue of these positions, certain interests which are contradictory in substance and direction. . . .

For purposes of the sociological analysis of conflict groups and group conflicts, it is necessary to assume certain structurally generated orientations of the actions of incumbents of defined positions. By analogy to conscious ("subjective") orientations of action, it appears justifiable to describe these as "interests." It has to be emphasized, however, that by so doing no assumption is implied about the substance of these interests or the consciousness and articulate orientation of the occupants of the positions in question. . . .[8]

The substance of socially structured "objective" interests can be described only in highly formal terms: they are interests in the maintenance or modification of a *status quo*. Our model of conflict group formation involves the proposition that of the two aggregates of authority positions to be distinguished in every association, one—that of domination—is characterized by an interest in the maintenance of a social structure that for them conveys authority, whereas the other—that of subjection—involves an interest in changing a social condition that deprives its incumbents of authority. The two interests are in conflict.

Max Weber has convincingly demonstrated that the problem of maintaining or changing given structures of authority can be expressed, both conceptually and empirically, in terms of the basis of legitimacy of relations of authority. From our assumption of an at least latent conflict of interests in every imperatively coordinated association, it follows that the legitimacy of authority must always be precarious. There always is one aggregate of positions and their incumbents which represents the institutionalized doubt in the legitimacy of the *status quo* of the

---

analysis. By strictly postulating imperatively coordinated associations as units of conflict analysis, we are able to consider, e.g., the relations between industry and society as an empirical problem which allows of varying solutions in different historical contexts. Similarly we can, by this emphasis, regard subjection (and consequent deprivation) in several associations as a condition strengthening and intensifying conflict, but by no means necessary in historical situations. . . .

[8]This statement will be qualified below by the distinction of "latent" and "manifest interests." Strictly speaking, it holds for latent interests only.

distribution of authority. In this sense, the proposition that there are "objective" interests in changing any given structure of authority might also be expressed in terms of the potential illegitimacy of all relations of authority. Empirically, group conflict is probably most easily accessible to analysis if it be understood as a conflict about the legitimacy of relations of authority. In every association, the interests of the ruling group are the values that constitute the ideology of the legitimacy of its rule, whereas the interests of the subjected group constitute a threat to this ideology and the social relations it covers. . . .

I suggest that the category of interest in the coercion theory of society must be understood in strict analogy to that of role expectation. The "objective" interests under discussion are in fact role interests, i.e., expected orientations of behavior associated with authority roles in imperatively coordinated associations. Again, the individual incumbent of roles may or may not internalize these expectations. But in our context he behaves in an "adapted" or "adjusted" manner if he contributes to the conflict of contradictory interests rather than to the integration of a social system. The individual who assumes a position in an association finds these role interests with his position, just as he finds certain role expectations from the point of view of the social system. For different purposes of sociological analysis, different aspects of its basic unit—the position-role—are relevant; roles, too, have two faces. In our context they figure primarily as sets of expected interests within imperatively coordinated associations.

For certain purposes of the theory of conflict group formation, it will prove useful to replace the concept of role interests by another one which makes its relation to the incumbents of authority positions even more apparent. Role interests are, from the point of view of the "player" of roles, *latent interests*, i.e., undercurrents of his behavior which are predetermined for him for the duration of his incumbency of a role, and which are independent of his conscious orientations. As such they can, under conditions to be specified presently, become conscious goals which we shall correspondingly call *manifest interests*. By contrast to latent interests, manifest interests are psychological realities. . . . The specific substance of manifest interests can be determined only in the context of given social conditions; but they always constitute a formulation of the issues of structurally generated group conflicts of the type in question. In this sense, manifest interests are the program of organized groups. . . .

Quasi-Groups and Interest Groups. So far our discussion has left undecided the question as to what kind of aggregates conflict groups are. . . . In describing these groupings, the categories of quasi-group and interest group are essential.

We have postulated two conflicting orientations of latent interests as characteristic of the role structure of imperatively coordinated associations. By implication, this means, of course, that the authority positions equipped with expected interests as well as their incumbents have at least one attribute in common. In a significant sense, the occupants of identical authority positions, i.e., either of positions of domination or of positions of subjection, find themselves in a common situation. Being united by a common, potentially permanent, characteristic, they are more than mere masses or incoherent quantities. At the same time, the incumbents of like authority positions in an association do not in any sociologically tenable sense constitute a group.... For groups, a feeling of belongingness is as constitutive as a minimum of organization; but both are explicitly not demanded by the concept of latent interests. The aggregates of incumbents of positions with identical role interests are at best a potential group.... We shall use for this particular type of social grouping the term *quasi-group*....

The constituent element of the type of quasi-groups with which we are here concerned is the community of certain latent interests. Latent interests are not psychological phenomena; quasi-groups based on them might therefore be called a mere theoretical construction. They are "theoretical phenomena," i.e., units constructed for the purpose of explaining problems of social conflict.... Only by doubtful analogy can we speak of "members" of such aggregates or quasi-groups. Thus it transcends the legitimate possibilities of theory construction to postulate common modes of behavior for these "members."

On the other hand, common modes of behavior are characteristic of *interest groups* recruited from larger quasi-groups. Interest groups are groups in the strict sense of the sociological term; and they are the real agents of group conflict. They have a structure, a form of organization, a program or goal, and a personnel of members.... Interest groups are always "secondary groups"; their members are in contact with each other only by virtue of their membership or by way of their elected or appointed representatives....

The statement that conflict groups are interest groups is meaningful, but incomplete. The category of interest group is a general category; virtually any secondary group can be regarded as an interest group—a chess club as well as an occupational association, a football team as well as a political party or a trade union. The specific difference of the quasi-groups and interest groups with which we are concerned in this study accrues from their origin in the authority structure of associations or, to put it differently, from the formal characteristic of their underlying (latent or manifest) interests as interests related to the legitimacy of relations of domination and subjection. This limitation clearly excludes the chess club, the football team, and the occupational association, while it leaves us to consider groupings such as trade unions and political parties. Whenever we refer in the subsequent analysis to quasi-groups and interest groups without specifically stating this limitation, this is merely an abbreviated way of referring to conflict groups as they emerge from the authority structure of associations....

II
MARXIAN POWER THEORY

MARX AS A POWER THEORIST

Marvin E. Olsen

Political philosophers from Plato onward have written extensively about the exercise of power, but Karl Marx must be singled out as the principal intellectual father of contemporary political sociology. Whereas most political philosophers prior to him had in one way or another linked their discussions of power to the state, seeing government and related organizations (such as the military) as the main foci of power in society, Marx broke sharply with this tradition. He argued instead that power originates primarily in economic production, that it permeates and influences all aspects of society, that the main wielders of social power are social classes, and that government is essentially a servant of the dominant social class. Marx thus expanded the concept of power from a specifically political phenomenon to a ubiquitous social process and offered a theory of societal development based on the exercise of power.[1]

This essay has two purposes: first, to sketch the highlights of Marx's basic theory, as an overview of the readings which follow; and second, to suggest directions in which his provocative insights might be broadened into a more encompassing power theory of social organization.[2]

---

[1] The only writer who might seriously challenge Marx as a founder of political sociology was Alexis de Tocqueville. He also treated power as a pervasive social process extending far beyond the political state, but he did not provide a systematic theory of power with the scope or consistency of Marx's ideas, and hence has not had an impact comparable to that of Marx or later writers. Quite belatedly, many political sociologists are today "rediscovering" Tocqueville and giving much closer attention to his works.

[2] This discussion of Marx is drawn from several sources, including: T.B. Bottomore and Maximilien Rubel, *Karl Marx: Selected Writings in Sociology and Social Philosophy* (London: C. A. Watts & Co., Ltd., 1956); Ralf Dahrendorf, *Class and Class Conflict in Industrial Society* (Stanford, Calif.: Stanford University Press, 1959); Karl Marx, *Capital* (Moscow: Foreign Languages Publishing House, 1954); C. Wright Mills, *The Marxists* (New York: Dell Publishing Co., 1962); Joseph Schumpeter, *Capitalism, Socialism, and Democracy* (New York: Harper & Row, Publishers, 1962); and Irving M. Zeitlin, *Marxism: A Re-Interpretation,* (Princeton, N.J.: D. Van Nostrand Co., Inc., 1967).

Marx's ideas on the nature of society can be divided into three major components: a sociological perspective—primacy of economically generated power; a philosophy of history—dialectic social change; and a connecting thesis—social classes in continual conflict.

Intensive study of Western European societies, in both their feudalistic and industrialized stages, led Marx to adopt the fundamental postulate that *all Western societies rest on a foundation of economic production*. Since men must first produce goods and services if they are to survive or attain goals, the nature and effectiveness of the productive process will inevitably influence—though never totally determine—all other aspects of social and cultural life. Any real society will contain many diverse "modes of production," but for analytical purposes, Marx argued, we need examine only the dominant mode of a given era. In feudal societies this is agriculture, whereas in industrialized societies it is manufacturing.

Within a society's dominant mode of production, the "forces of production," or technological and physical aspects of economic activity, are important in determining how effectively surplus resources (that is, wealth) can be produced. But economic technology does not determine how these resources will be used and distributed in society. Especially crucial for social organization, therefore, is a second aspect of the economy, which Marx called the "social relations of production." By this he meant the relationships of various segments of the population to the economy—who owns or controls the major means of production, and who doesn't. Whoever controls the dominant mode of economic production in a society will determine how the existing technology will be utilized and how the resulting resources will be distributed, with the consequence that these persons will exercise power throughout the total society.

This theoretical perspective gave Marx a key to understanding the power dynamics of all societies, but it did not explain long-term trends in human history. For this he turned to the idea of dialectic social change. From the philosopher Hegel he took the dialectic model of a prevailing thesis giving rise to a conflicting antithesis, both of which eventually merge into a new synthesis, which in turn forms the thesis of a new dialectic. But he applied this process to social conditions rather than to philosophical ideas, on the grounds that ideas have meaning only in relation to the social conditions from which they arise. In his words, he "stood Hegel on his feet."

The dialectic process was for Marx not an inherent tendency within human society, but rather an analytical tool with which to explain the broad sweep of human history—at least in Western Europe. In other words, *dialectic change is never inevitable, but when major social changes do occur they tend to follow the dialectic process*. Because the component sectors of a society are in continual conflict for control over the means of economic production (and hence for power and wealth), all societies contain within themselves potential "seeds" of change. Whether or not these "seeds" actually "blossom" into radical social changes remains a problematic question for both the participants and scientific observers, however. Theoretically, all societies can be expected to develop from the thesis of feudalism through the antithesis of capitalism to the synthesis of socialism. Empirically, though, this process is contingent on many intervening factors, including the amount of control the ruling elites exercise over the rest of the society, the degree of organization existing among the nonelites, and the effectiveness of the leaders advocating social change. For this reason, Marx saw himself first of all as a spokesman for the masses in industrial society, urging them to become aware of their common situation, to organize themselves, and to take action to overthrow the ruling owners of industry. Only in this manner could capitalism be destroyed and the process of dialectic change be carried to fruition.

If Marx had ended his analysis at this point he would have left two major questions unanswered. First, what are the segments of a society which compete for control of the means of production and how do they relate to one another? Second, why won't socialism become the thesis for further dialectic change? He answered both of these questions by bridging the theoretical gap between his sociological perspective and his philosophy of history with the thesis of conflicting social classes. This thesis consists of a definition of classes, an analysis of the nature of capitalism, and an argument for class conflict and revolution. He defined a social class as a population of people within a society who stand in a common relation to the major means of economic production, and who therefore exercise similar amounts of power in society and are in continual conflict with other classes. He analyzed the capitalistic economic system in great depth to discover why it produced the extreme exploitation of workers he observed in all industrialized societies. And he concluded that dialectic social change would end only if social classes were completely abolished and radically new types of society were established.

Marx believed that for analytical purposes the industrialized societies of Europe (which at that time were all thoroughly capitalistic) could be seen as consisting of two major social classes: the bourgeoisie who owned the means of production (the factories), and the proletariat who were forced to sell their labor to the industrialists. He clearly recognized the existence of other classes as well, such as agricultural peasants, small merchants, and professionals and intellectuals, but he contended that they were not analytically important because they were either rapidly disappearing or were slowly being driven from their "middle class" positions into the proletariat. Using current nineteenth-century economic theory, Marx argued that the dominant bourgeoisie were forced by the intrinsic laws of capitalism to exploit their workers by paying them less than the value of their labor. If capitalists did not exploit their workers they made no profit and soon went out of business. Hence the inherent economic injustice of industrial capitalism. Although much of Marx's technical economic analysis has been rejected by contemporary economists, there is abundant historical evidence that early industrialists did in fact severely exploit their workers to increase their profits. We realize today, furthermore, that the exploitation and other conditions Marx witnessed are common problems of the basic process of industrialization, whatever its form.

The proletariat in industrial societies constitutes a "class-in-itself," as determined by its subordinate relationship to the means of production. But before it can become a "class-for-itself" and take action to alter its social condition, it must develop class consciousness and class organization. The bourgeoisie make their fatal mistake, Marx contended, when they begin to drive the old middle class, especially intellectuals, into the industrial proletariat by forcing them to sell their services on the labor market. These intellectuals can provide the leadership that the workers have previously lacked, promote class consciousness and organization among the workers, and initiate revolutionary social change of the entire society.

The resulting social change might conceivably be quite gradual, but Marx insisted that in practice this is highly unlikely. From his observations of the historical shift from feudalism to capitalism, he concluded that the dominant class will never voluntarily surrender its control over society, but instead will use all its power— especially that of the government and the military—to resist change. Hence *if the proletariat is ever to gain control of the means of production from the bourgeoisie, it must do so through violent class conflict*, or total revolution.

Following this revolution, the leaders of the proletariat will face the demanding tasks of completely reordering society by putting all productive activities under public ownership and of teaching the workers to assume the wide responsibilities which are now theirs. In this interim period it will therefore be necessary to create a temporary "dictatorship of the proletariat" headed by the revolutionary leaders. Marx firmly believed, however, that eventually a truly "classless society" could be achieved, in which there would be no more economic exploitation, in which the state as an enforcer of social control would no longer be necessary and hence would largely wither away, and in which the full possibilities of creative human life would be enjoyed by all. The final stage of dialectic social change would thus be reached under socialism, when true "human history" would begin.

His reasoning in support of this belief went as follows: In a fully communistic society control over the means of economic production would be shared by everyone, so that by definition there would be no more social classes. If no social classes, then no more class exploitation and class conflict. Hence no remaining bases for dialectic social change. A morally perfect society will then have been attained on earth, in which all people participate and benefit equally. Individual and collective social responsibility, not power and exploitation, will now form the basis of organized social life.

In sum, by defining social classes in terms of their differing relationships to the means of economic production and by maintaining that public control over the means of production will end class exploitation, conflict, and dialectic change, Marx neatly joined his sociological perspective and his philosophy of history into a unified theory of society as he then knew it.

Putting aside whatever moral evaluations we might want to make about Marx's ideal "classless society," we are faced with the question of what sociological insights did he suggest that may be useful in understanding social organization? Included in any such inventory of Marx's sociological contributions would be these five ideas:

1. The fundamental importance of economic production in providing resources necessary for all other kinds of social activities within a society. Although the economy may not directly affect numerous spheres of social life, it does provide a foundation on which all other social organization rests. We do not have to be "economic determinists" to appreciate the extensive indirect influence of economic activities throughout a society.

2. A conception of society as consisting of numerous subparts—whether they be social classes or any other organized entities—which are functionally interrelated but which also possess considerable autonomy to pursue their own goals, and which therefore come into frequent conflict with each other. From this perspective a society is not a completely unified and harmonious whole, nor do requirements and goals of the total society normally take precedence over those of its subparts. Intrasocietal conflict, not integration, is the "normal" state of human affairs, and the attainment of harmony and unity is at best an imperfectly achieved goal.

3. A broad view of human history as a continual process of social change toward increasingly complex—and demanding—forms of social organization. Whether or not the dialectic model provides the most useful analytical tool with which to examine societal change is an unresolved empirical question, but the fact that human history is a story of constant conflict and change cannot be denied.

4. The crucial significance of powerful elites in shaping and controlling virtually all societies. The size, composition, and power of such elites has of course varied from one society to another and also through time, but all known societies beyond the bare subsistence level have contained elites who exercised various kinds of power over others. At this point in history we do not know whether power concentration is inherent in all social organization or whether the current slow trend toward increased equality for all can be carried to full realization. But quite clearly neither the historian nor the sociologist can ignore the actions of elites in their studies of all past and present societies.

5. Finally and perhaps most important of all, Marx's writings provide the beginnings of a general power theory of social organization. His stress on relationships to the means of production as the primary determinant of social structure, together with his analyses of the ways in which elites have historically controlled their societies, suggests that we should look to the exercise of power as the principal cause of social ordering in society. Marx did not elaborate a general power theory of social organization in precise detail, but he did convincingly demonstrate the relevance of such a theory for understanding human society. The unfinished task now confronting contemporary social scientists is to expand, refine, and formalize power theory so that it can be adequately tested in empirical research.

A necessary first step in constructing a general power theory of social organization is to extend Marx's ideas along several dimensions. *Three directions in which theoretical extensions might be made are in the types of power considered, the resource bases available for generating power, and the possible patterns of actual power wielding.* First, many sociologists have argued that Marx gave too much attention to force (especially violence), and neglected other kinds of power such as dominance and authority. Indeed, it may be that as societies become "modernized" and "civilized" they tend to substitute functional dominance and legitimate authority for at least the more oppressive forms of force as bases of social order.[3]

---

[3]The thesis of increased reliance on functional dominance in highly developed organizations has been presented by Amos H. Hawley, "Human Ecology," *International Encyclopedia of the Social Sciences*, David L. Sills, ed. (New York: The Macmillan Company and the Free Press),

Second, it can also be argued that Marx's concern with ownership of the means of economic production as the major resource base for social power is too limited to fit contemporary developed societies. While not denying the importance of this source of power, we must also consider such resource bases as access to political decision making, information flows through the mass media, scientific research and applied engineering, and police and military organizations. Third, we need not limit our analysis of actual power patterns to "downward" exertion from a single source. A highly organized society might in fact contain a diverse variety of power patterns with influence and control flowing in all directions. Max Weber's ideal type of hierarchial bureaucracy further contributed to the assumption that a centralized hierarchy of power is the most efficient and rational form of social organization, so that only recently have many social scientists begun to explore other possible patterns of power. In the past few years, however, numerous writings have examined power decentralization and polyarchy.[4]

By expanding the scope of power theory in these directions our theoretical perspective becomes considerably more inclusive and complex than Marx's scheme. But have we not at the same time lost much of the predictive capability of Marxian theory? Have we sacrificed a limited but useful theory for a broader but much more vague theoretical perspective? This criticism undoubtedly has some validity, so that if we leave our "power perspective" at this point we may have given up more than we have gained in theoretical insight. Clearly needed now are attempts to formulate a rigorous and precise power theory of social organization that takes into account these necessary extensions. One possible direction which such theory construction might take is suggested by contemporary ecological theory.[5]

A central theorem of social ecology is that the parts of an organization that control the flow of necessary resources from the environment into the organization—its "key functionaries"—exercise dominance over all other parts with which they are functionally interrelated. In a loosely structured (or relatively "open") organization many parts are in direct contact with the environment, so that no one part wields much dominance. When an organization becomes more tightly unified (or "closed"), however, most of these parts are cut off from the environment, leaving only one or a very few key functionaries which mediate all resource procurement. All other parts of the organization then become dependent on the remaining key functionaries for their necessary resources, and at the same time are complexly interrelated with one another. Within such a highly interdependent system each part continues to exercise some dominance, but the strength of its power is inversely related to its functional distance from the key functionaries.

Without too much distortion, Marx's emphasis on control over production—and more generally on the economic foundation of society—can be translated into these

---

Vol. 4, pp. 328-337. The importance of legitimate authority in modern organizations has been stressed by Ralf Dahrendorf, *Class and Class Conflict in Industrial Society* (Stanford, Calif.: Stanford University Press, 1959), Chap. 5.

[4] As an example of this literature, see Robert A. Dahl and Charles E. Lindblom, *Politics, Economics, and Welfare* (New York: Harper and Row, 1953).

[5] The following discussion is drawn largely from Amos H. Hawley, "Human Ecology," *loc. cit.*

ecological terms of key functionaries exercising dominance throughout society. In all past and present human societies, scarcity of economic resources has been a crucial factor imposing limitations on all other social activities. Hence the economy has tended to dominate all other parts of the society, and those actors who controlled it have been in a position to exercise dominance throughout social life. But what might happen in a society if the economy became so efficient and effective that economic scarcity were no longer a major problem? No society has yet approached such a condition of economic abundance, but recent trends in highly industrialized nations such as the United States indicate that this is not impossible.

The ecological scheme can easily be extended to cover this kind of "post-industrial society."[6] Under conditions of total economic abundance the economy and those who operated it would no longer be the key functionaries with dominant power in society—as long as the economy continued to operate without interruption. Other scarce resources might then assume critical importance, giving those who controlled them dominant power. One possible scarce resource could be scientific and technical knowledge and trained manpower, since all segments of society (including the economy) would presumably be highly dependent on educated specialists and the knowledge and skills they possessed. In this case, the crucial sphere of activity for the society would become education, especially higher education. Scientists, professors, and teachers would then become the key functionaries with dominant social power in society. In Marx's terms, there could be a new ruling class, determined by relationships to informational and educational production.

This kind of ecological theorizing suffers from many of the same limitations of Marxian theory and is open to numerous criticisms. It substitutes dominance for force as the principal type of power in society, and completely ignores legitimate authority. It also considers only one major resource base for generating power, although this need not be economic production. And it continues to utilize a single pattern of power exertion, from the "top" of a functional hierarchy downward. Nevertheless, it does provide stimulating ideas for extending Marxian theory into "post-industrial societies." The challenge now facing sociologists is to carry these theoretical explorations even further, towards the formulation and testing of a truly encompassing yet rigorous power theory of social organization.

The readings comprising this section represent the various major themes in Marxian theory, as well as two critiques of Marx as a sociologist. A brief but often quoted statement by Marx presents the idea that an economic foundation underlies all societies, and the first part of the Communist Manifesto by Marx and Friedrich Engels stresses the importance of class organization and conflict in promoting dialectical social change throughout history. C. Wright Mills then summarizes the main ideas of Marxian theory in a series of seventeen propositions, many of which

---

[6]Although he does not use ecological theory, Daniel Bell has suggested most of the following ideas in his "Notes on the Post-Industrial Society," *The Public Interest*, No. 6 (Winter 1967), pp. 24-35, and No. 7 (Spring 1967), pp. 102-118.

contain the concept of power. Finally, Joseph Schumpeter evaluates Marx's contributions to sociological thought, giving special attention to his theory of social classes.

THE MATERIALISTIC CONCEPTION OF HISTORY

Karl Marx

In the social production which men carry on they enter into definite relations that are indispensable and independent of their will; these relations of production correspond to a definite stage of development of their material forces of production. The sum total of these relations of production constitutes the economic structure of society—the real foundation, on which rises a legal and political superstructure and to which correspond definite forms of social consciousness. The mode of production in material life determines the social, political and intellectual life processes in general. It is not the consciousness of men that determines their being, but, on the contrary, their social being that determines their consciousness. At a certain stage of their development, the material forces of production in society come in conflict with the existing relations of production, or—what is but a legal expression for the same thing—with the property relations within which they have been at work before. From forms of development of the forces of production these relations turn into their fetters. Then begins an epoch of social revolution. With the change of the economic foundation the entire immense superstructure is more or less rapidly transformed. In considering such transformations a distinction should always be made between the material transformation of the economic conditions of production which can be determined with the precision of natural science, and the legal, political, religious, aesthetic or philosophic—in short, ideological forms in which men become conscious of this conflict and fight it out. Just as our opinion of an individual is not based on what he thinks of himself, so can we not judge of such a period of transformation by its own consciousness; on the contrary this consciousness must be explained rather from the contradictions of material life, from the existing conflict between the social forces of production and the relations of production. No social order ever disappears before all the productive forces for which there is room in it have been developed; and new higher relations of production never appear before the material conditions of their existence have matured in the womb of the old society itself. Therefore, mankind always sets itself only such tasks as it can solve; since, looking at the matter more closely, we will always find that the task itself arises only when the material conditions necessary

SOURCE: Karl Marx, Preface to *A Contribution to the Critique of Political Economy* (Chicago: Charles H. Kerr and Co., 1904), pp. 11-12.

for its solution already exist or are at least in the process of formation. In broad outlines we can designate the Asiatic, the ancient, the feudal, and the modern bourgeois modes of production as so many epochs in the progress of the economic formation of society. The bourgeois relations of production are the last antagonistic form of the social process of production—antagonistic not in the sense of individual antagonism, but of one arising from the social conditions of life of the individuals; at the same time the productive forces developing in the womb of bourgeois society create the material conditions for the solution of that antagonism. This social formation constitutes, therefore, the closing chapter of the prehistoric stage of human society.

MANIFESTO OF THE COMMUNIST PARTY

Karl Marx and Friedrich Engels

Bourgeois and Proletarians[1]. The history of all hitherto existing society is the history of class struggles.

Freeman and slave, patrician and plebeian, lord and serf, guildmaster and journeyman, in a word, oppressor and oppressed stood in constant opposition to one another, carried on an uninterrupted, now hidden, now open fight, a fight that each time ended, either in a revolutionary reconstitution of society at large, or in the common ruin of the contending classes.

In the earlier epochs of history, we find almost everywhere a complicated arrangement of society into various orders, a manifold gradation of social rank. In ancient Rome we have patricians, knights, plebeians, slaves; in the Middle Ages, feudal lords, vassals, guild-masters, journeymen, apprentices, serfs; in almost all of these classes, again, subordinate gradations.

The modern bourgeois society that has sprouted from the ruins of feudal society has not done away with class antagonisms. It has but established new classes, new conditions of oppression, new forms of struggle in place of the old ones.

Our epoch, the epoch of the bourgeoisie, possesses, however, this distinctive feature: It has simplified the class antagonisms. Society as a whole is more and more splitting up into two great hostile camps, into two great classes directly facing each other—bourgeoisie and proletariat.

SOURCE: Karl Marx and Friedrich Engels, *Manifesto of the Communist Party*, Part I. Most footnotes have been omitted, and those remaining have been renumbered.

[1] By bourgeoisie is meant the class of modern capitalists, owners of the means of social production and employers of wage labour. By proletariat, the class of modern wage labourers who, having no means of production of their own, are reduced to selling their labour power in order to live. [*Note by F. Engels to the English edition of 1888.*]

From the serfs of the Middle Ages sprang the chartered burghers of the earliest towns. From these burgesses the first elements of the bourgeoisie were developed.

The discovery of America, the rounding of the Cape, opened up fresh ground for the rising bourgeoisie. The East-Indian and Chinese markets, the colonisation of America, trade with the colonies, the increase in the means of exchange and in commodities generally, gave to commerce, to navigation, to industry, an impulse never before known, and thereby, to the revolutionary element in the tottering feudal society, a rapid development.

The feudal system of industry, in which industrial production was monopolised by closed guilds, now no longer sufficed for the growing wants of the new markets. The manufacturing system took its place. The guildmasters were pushed aside by the manufacturing middle class; division of labour between the different corporate guilds vanished in the face of division of labor in each single workshop.

Meantime the markets kept ever growing, the demand ever rising. Even manufacture no longer sufficed. Thereupon, steam and machinery revolutionised industrial production. The place of manufacture was taken by the giant, modern industry, the place of the industrial middle class by industrial millionaires, the leaders of whole industrial armies, the modern bourgeois.

Modern industry has established the world market, for which the discovery of America paved the way. This market has given an immense development to commerce, to navigation, to communication by land. This development has, in its turn, reacted on the extension of industry; and in proportion as industry, commerce, navigation, railways extended, in the same proportion the bourgeoisie developed, increased its capital, and pushed into the background every class handed down from the Middle Ages.

We see, therefore, how the modern bourgeoisie is itself the product of a long course of development, of a series of revolutions in the modes of production and of exchange.

Each step in the development of the bourgeoisie was accompanied by a corresponding political advance of that class. An oppressed class under the sway of the feudal nobility, an armed and self-governing association in the mediaeval commune[2]; here independent urban republic (as in Italy and Germany), there taxable "third estate" of the monarchy (as in France); afterwards, in the period of manufacture proper, serving either the semi-feudal or the absolute monarchy as a counterpoise against the nobility, and, in fact, corner-stone of the great monarchies in general—the bourgeoisie has at last, since the establishment of modern industry and of the world market, conquered for itself, in the modern representative state, exclusive political sway. The executive of the modern state is but a committee for managing the common affairs of the whole bourgeoisie.

The bourgeoisie, historically, has played a most revolutionary role in history.

---

[2] This was the name given their urban communities by the townsmen of Italy and France, after they had purchased or conquered their initial rights of self-government from their feudal lords. [*Note by F. Engels to the German edition of 1890.*]

The bourgeoisie, wherever it has got the upper hand, has put an end to all feudal, patriarchal, idyllic relations. It has pitilessly torn asunder the motley feudal ties that bound man to his "natural superiors," and has left no other nexus between man and man than naked self-interest, than callous "cash payment." It has drowned the most heavenly ecstasies of religious fervour, of chivalrous enthusiasm, of philistine sentimentalism, in the icy water of egotistical calculation. It has resolved personal worth into exchange value, and in place of the numberless indefeasible chartered freedoms, has set up that single, unconscionable freedom—Free Trade. In one word, for exploitation, veiled by religious and political illusions, it has substituted naked, shameless, direct, brutal exploitation.

The bourgeoisie has stripped of its halo every occupation hitherto honoured and looked up to with reverent awe. It has converted the physician, the lawyer, the priest, the poet, the man of science, into its paid wage labourers.

The bourgeoisie has torn away from the family its sentimental veil, and has reduced the family relation to a mere money relation.

The bourgeoisie has disclosed how it came to pass that the brutal display of vigour in the Middle Ages, which reactionaries so much admire, found its fitting complement in the most slothful indolence. It has been the first to show what man's activity can bring about. It has accomplished wonders far surpassing Egyptian pyramids, Roman aqueducts, and Gothic cathedrals; it has conducted expeditions that put in the shade all former exoduses of nations and crusades.

The bourgeoisie cannot exist without constantly revolutionising the instruments of production, and thereby the relations of production, and with them the whole relations of society. Conservation of the old modes of production in unaltered form, was, on the contrary, the first condition of existence for all earlier industrial classes. Constant revolutionising of production, uninterrupted disturbance of all social conditions, everlasting uncertainty and agitation distinguish the bourgeois epoch from all earlier ones. All fixed, fast frozen relations, with their train of ancient and venerable prejudices and opinions, are swept away, all newformed ones become antiquated before they can ossify. All that is solid melts into air, all that is holy is profaned, and man is at last compelled to face with sober senses his real conditions of life and his relations with his kind.

The need of a constantly expanding market for its products chases the bourgeoisie over the whole surface of the globe. It must nestle everywhere, settle everywhere, establish connections everywhere.

The bourgeoisie has through its exploitation of the world market given a cosmopolitan character to production and consumption in every country. To the great chagrin of reactionaries, it has drawn from under the feet of industry the national ground on which it stood. All old-established national industries have been destroyed or are daily being destroyed. They are dislodged by new industries, whose introduction becomes a life and death question for all civilised nations, by industries that no longer work up indigenous raw material, but raw material drawn from the remotest zones; industries whose products are consumed, not only at home, but in every quarter of the globe. In place of the old wants, satisfied by the production of the country, we find new wants, requiring for their satisfaction the products of distant lands and climes. In place of the old local and national seclusion and self-sufficiency, we have intercourse in every direction, universal inter-dependence of nations. And as in material, so also in intellectual production. The intellectual creations of individual nations become common property. National one-sidedness and narrow-mindedness become more and more impossible, and from the numerous national and local literatures there arises a world literature.

The bourgeoisie, by the rapid improvement of all instruments of production, by the immensely facilitated means of communication, draws all, even the most barbarian, nations into civilisation. The cheap prices of its commodities are the heavy artillery with which it batters down all Chinese walls, with which it forces the barbarians' intensely obstinate hatred of foreigners to capitulate. It compels all nations, on pain of extinction, to adopt the bourgeois mode of production; it compels them to introduce what it calls civilisation into their midst, i.e., to become bourgeois themselves. In one word, it creates a world after its own image.

The bourgeois has subjected the country to the rule of the towns. It has created enormous cities, has greatly increased the urban population as compared with the rural, and has thus rescued a considerable part of the population from the idiocy of rural life. Just as it has made the country dependent on the towns, so it has made barbarian and semi-barbarian countries dependent on the civilised ones, nations of peasants on nations of bourgeois, the East on the West.

The bourgeoisie keeps more and more doing away with the scattered state of the population, of the means of production, and of property. It has agglomerated population, centralised means of production, and has concentrated property in a few hands. The necessary consequence of this was political centralisation. Independent, or but loosely connected provinces, with separate interests, laws, governments and systems of taxation, became lumped together into one nation, with one government, one code of laws, one national class interest, one frontier and one customs tariff.

The bourgeoisie, during its rule of scarce one hundred years, has created more massive and more colossal productive forces than have all preceding generations together. Subjection of nature's forces to man, machinery, application of chemistry to industry and agriculture, steam navigation, railways, electric telegraphs, clearing of whole continents for cultivation, canalisation of rivers, whole populations conjured out of the ground—what earlier century had even a presentiment that such productive forces slumbered in the lap of social labour?

We see then: the means of production and of exchange, on whose foundation the bourgeoisie built itself up, were generated in feudal society. At a certain stage in the development of these means of production and of exchange, the conditions under which feudal society produced and exchanged, the feudal organisation of agriculture and manufacturing industry, in one word, the feudal relations of property became no longer compatible with the already developed productive forces; they became so many fetters. They had to be burst asunder; they were burst asunder.

Into their place stepped free competition, accompanied by a social and political constitution adapted to it, and by the economic and political sway of the bourgeois class.

A similar movement is going on before our own eyes. Modern bourgeois society with its relations of production, of exchange and of property, a society that has conjured up such gigantic means of production and of exchange, is like the sorcerer who is no longer able to control the powers of the nether world whom he has called up by his spells. For many a decade past the history of industry and commerce is but the history of the revolt of modern productive forces against modern conditions of production, against the property relations that are the conditions for the existence of the bourgeoisie and of its rule. It is enough to mention the commercial crises that by their periodical return put the existence of the entire bourgeois society on its trial, each time more threateningly. In these crises a great part not only of the existing products, but also of the previously created productive forces, are periodically destroyed. In these crises there breaks out an epidemic that, in all earlier epochs, would have seemed an absurdity—the epidemic of overproduction. Society suddenly finds itself put back into a state of momentary barbarism; it appears as if a famine, a universal war of devastation had cut off the supply of every means of subsistence; industry and commerce seem to be destroyed. And why? Because there is too much civilisation, too much means of subsistence, too much industry, too much commerce. The productive forces at the disposal of society no longer tend to further the development of the conditions of bourgeois property; on the contrary, they have become too powerful for these conditions, by which they are fettered, and so soon as they overcome these fetters, they bring disorder into the whole of bourgeois society, endanger the existence of bourgeois property. The conditions of bourgeois society are too narrow to comprise the wealth created by them. And how does the bourgeoisie get over these crises? On the one hand, by enforced destruction of a mass of productive forces; on the other, by the conquest of new markets, and by the more thorough exploitation of the old ones. That is to say, by paving the way for more extensive and more destructive crises, and by diminishing the means whereby crises are prevented.

The weapons with which the bourgeoisie felled feudalism to the ground are now turned against the bourgeoisie itself.

But not only has the bourgeoisie forged the weapons that bring death to itself; it has also called into existence the men who are to wield those weapons—the modern working class—the proletarians.

In proportion as the bourgeoisie, i.e., capital, is developed, in the same proportion is the proletariat, the modern working class, developed—a class of labourers, who live only so long as they find work, and who find work only so long as their labour increases capital. These labourers, who must sell themselves piecemeal, are a commodity, like every other article of commerce, and are consequently exposed to all the vicissitudes of competition, to all the fluctuations of the market.

Owing to the extensive use of machinery and to division of labour, the work of the proletarians has lost all individual character, and, consequently, all charm for the workman. He becomes an appendage of the machine, and it is only the most simple, most monotonous, and most easily acquired knack, that is required of him. Hence, the cost of production of a workman is restricted, almost entirely, to the means of subsistence that he requires for his maintenance, and for the propagation of his race. But the price of a commodity, and therefore also of labour power, is equal to its cost of production. In proportion, therefore, as the repulsiveness of the work increases, the wage decreases. Nay more, in proportion as the use of machinery and division of labour increases, in the same proportion the burden of toil also increases, whether by prolongation of the working hours, by increase of the work exacted in a given time, or by increased speed of the machinery, etc.

Modern industry has converted the little workshop of the patriarchal master into the great factory of the industrial capitalist. Masses of labourers, crowded into the factory, are organised like soldiers. As privates of the industrial army they are placed under the command of a perfect hierarchy of officers and sergeants. Not only are they slaves of the bourgeois class, and of the bourgeois state; they are daily and hourly enslaved by the machine, by the overlooker, and, above all, by the individual bourgeois manufacturer himself. The more openly this despotism proclaims gain to be its end and aim, the more petty, the more hateful and the more embittering it is.

The less the skill and exertion of strength implied in manual labour, in other words, the more modern industry becomes developed, the more is the labour of men superseded by that of women. Differences of age and sex have no longer any distinctive social validity for the working class. All are instruments of labour, more or less expensive to use, according to their age and sex.

No sooner is the exploitation of the labourer by the manufacturer, so far at an end, that he receives his wages in cash, than he is set upon by the other portions of the bourgeoisie, the landlord, the shopkeeper, the pawnbroker, etc.

The lower strata of the middle class—the small tradespeople, shopkeepers, and retired tradesmen generally, the handicraftsmen and peasants—all these sink gradually into the proletariat, partly because their diminutive capital does not suffice for the scale on which modern industry is carried on, and is swamped in the competition with the large capitalists, partly because their specialised skill is rendered worthless by new methods of production. Thus the proletariat is recruited from all classes of the population.

The proletariat goes through various stages of development. With its birth begins its struggle with the bourgeoisie. At first the contest is carried on by individual labourers, then by the work people of a factory, then by the operatives of one trade, in one locality, against the individual bourgeois who directly exploits them. They direct their attacks not against the bourgeois conditions of production, but against the instruments of production themselves; they destroy imported wares that compete with their labour, they smash to pieces machinery, they set factories ablaze, they seek to restore by force the vanished status of the workman of the Middle Ages.

At this stage the labourers still form an incoherent mass scattered over the whole country, and broken up by their mutual competition. If anywhere they unite to form more compact bodies, this is not yet the consequence of their own active union, but of the union of the bourgeoisie, which class, in order to attain its own political ends, is compelled to set the whole proletariat in motion, and is moreover yet, for a time, able to do so. At this stage, therefore, the proletarians do not fight their enemies, but the enemies of their enemies, the remnants of absolute monarchy, the landowners, the non-industrial bourgeois, the petty bourgeoisie. Thus the whole historical movement is concentrated in the hands of the bourgeoisie; every victory so obtained is a victory for the bourgeoisie.

But with the development of industry the proletariat not only increases in number; it becomes concentrated in greater masses, its strength grows, and it feels that strength more. The various interests and conditions of life within the ranks of the proletariat are more and more equalised, in proportion as machinery obliterates all distinctions of labour, and nearly everywhere reduces wages to the same low level. The growing competition among the bourgeois, and the resulting commercial crises, make the wages of the workers ever more fluctuating. The unceasing improvement of machinery, every more rapidly developing, makes their livelihood more and more precarious; the collisions between individual workmen and individual bourgeois take more and more the character of collisions between two classes. Thereupon the workers begin to form combinations (trades unions) against the bourgeois; they club together in order to keep up the rate of wages; they found permanent associations in order to make provisions beforehand for these occasional revolts. Here and there the contest breaks out into riots.

Now and then the workers are victorious, but only for a time. The real fruit of their battles lies, not in the immediate result, but in the ever expanding union of the workers. This union is helped on by the improved means of communication that are created by modern industry, and that place the workers of different localities in contact with one another. It was just this contact that was needed to centralise the numerous local struggles, all of the same character, into one national struggle between classes. But every class struggle is a political struggle. And that union, to attain which the burghers of the Middle Ages, with their miserable highways, required centuries, the modern proletarians, thanks to railways, achieve in a few years.

This organization of the proletarians into a class, and consequently into a political party, is continually being upset again by the competition between the workers themselves. But it ever rises up again, stronger, firmer, mightier. It compels legislative recognition of particular interests of the workers, by taking advantage of the divisions among the bourgeoisie itself. Thus the ten-hours' bill in England was carried.

Altogether, collisions between the classes of the old society further in many ways the course of development of the proletariat. The bourgeoisie finds itself involved in a constant battle. At first with the aristocracy; later on, with those portions of the bourgeoisie itself, whose interests have become antagonistic to the progress of industry; at all times with the bourgeoisie of foreign countries. In all these battles it sees itself compelled to appeal to the proletariat, to ask for its help, and thus, to drag it into the political arena. The bourgeoisie itself, therefore, supplies the proletariat with its own elements of political and general education, in other words, it furnishes the proletariat with weapons for fighting the bourgeoisie.

Further, as we have already seen, entire sections of the ruling classes are, by the advance of industry, precipitated into the proletariat, or are at least threatened in their conditions of existence. These also supply the proletariat with fresh elements of enlightenment and progress.

Finally, in times when the class struggle nears the decisive hour, the process of dissolution going on within the ruling class, in fact within the whole range of old society, assumes such a violent, glaring character, that a small section of the ruling class cuts itself adrift, and joins the revolutionary class, the class that holds the future in its hands. Just as, therefore, at an earlier period, a section of the nobility went over to the bourgeoisie, so now a portion of the bourgeoisie goes over to the proletariat, and in particular, a portion of the bourgeois ideologists, who have raised themselves to the level of comprehending theoretically the historical movement as a whole.

Of all the classes that stand face to face with the bourgeoisie today, the proletariat alone is a really revolutionary class. The other classes decay and finally disappear in the face of modern industry; the proletariat is its special and essential product. The lower middle class, the small manufacturer, the shopkeeper, the artisan, the peasant, all these fight against the bourgeoisie, to save from extinction their existence as fractions of the middle class. They are therefore not revolutionary, but conservative. Nay more, they are reactionary, for they try to roll back the wheel of history. If by chance they are revolutionary, they are so only in view of their impending transfer into the proletariat; they thus defend not their present, but their future interests; they desert their own standpoint to place themselves at that of the proletariat.

The "dangerous class," the social scum, that passively rotting mass thrown off by the lowest layers of old society, may, here and there, be swept into the movement by a proletarian revolution; its conditions of life, however, prepare it far more for the part of a bribed tool of reactionary intrigue.

In the conditions of the proletariat, those of old society at large are already virtually swamped. The proletarian is without property; his relation to his wife and children has no longer anything in common with the bourgeois family relations; modern industrial labour, modern subjection to capital, the same in England as in France, in America as in Germany, has stripped him of every trace of national character. Law, morality, religion, are to him so many bourgeois prejudices, behind which lurk in ambush just as many bourgeois interests.

All the preceding classes that got the upper hand, sought to fortify their already acquired status by subjecting society at large to their conditions of appropriation. The proletarians cannot become masters of the productive forces of society, except by abolishing their own previous mode of appropriation, and thereby also every other previous mode of appropriation. They have nothing of their own to secure and to fortify; their mission is to destroy all previous securities for, and insurances of, individual property.

All previous historical movements were movements of minorities, or in the interest of minorities. The proletarian movement is the self-conscious independent movement of the immense majority, in the interest of the immense majority. The proletariat, the lowest stratum of our present society, cannot stir, cannot raise itself up, without the whole superincumbent strata of official society being sprung into the air.

Though not in substance, yet in form, the struggle of the proletariat with the bourgeoisie is at first a national struggle. The proletariat of each country must, of course, first of all settle matters with its own bourgeoisie.

In depicting the most general phases of the development of the proletariat, we traced the more or less veiled civil war, raging within existing society, up to the point where that war breaks out into open revolution, and where the violent overthrow of the bourgeoisie lays the foundation for the ways of the proletariat.

Hitherto, every form of society has been based, as we have already seen, on the antagonism of oppressing and oppressed classes. But in order to oppress a class, certain conditions must be assured to it under which it can, at least, continue its slavish existence. The serf, in the period of serfdom, raised himself to membership in the commune, just as the petty bourgeois, under the yoke of feudal absolutism, managed to develop into a bourgeois. The modern labourer, on the contrary, instead of rising with the progress of industry, sinks deeper and deeper below the conditions of existence of his own class. He becomes a pauper, and pauperism develops more rapidly than population and wealth. And here it becomes evident, that the bourgeoisie is unfit any longer to be the ruling class in society, and to impose its conditions of existence upon society as an over-riding law. It is unfit to rule because it is incompetent to assure an existence to its slave within his slavery, because it cannot help letting him sink into such a state, that it has to feed him, instead of being fed by him. Society can no longer live under this bourgeoisie, in other words, its existence is no longer compatible with society.

The essential condition for the existence and for the sway of the bourgeois class, is the formation and augmentation of capital; the condition for capital is wage labour. Wage labour rests exclusively on competition between the labourers. The advance of industry, whose involuntary promoter is the bourgeoisie, replaces the isolation of the labourers, due to competition, by their revolutionary combination, due to association. The development of modern industry, therefore, cuts from under its feet the very foundation on which the bourgeoisie produces and appropriates products. What the bourgeoisie therefore produces, above all, are its own grave-diggers. Its fall and the victory of the proletariat are equally inevitable. . . .

INVENTORY OF MARX'S IDEAS

C. Wright Mills

The distinctive character of Marx's "scientific socialism," I think, lies in this: his images of the ideal society are connected with the actual workings of the society in which he lived. Out of his projections of the tendencies he discerns in society as it

SOURCE: From *The Marxists* by C. Wright Mills. Copyright 1962 by C. Wright Mills. Reprinted by permission of Brandt & Brandt. A few footnotes have been omitted, and those remaining have been renumbered.

is actually developing he makes up his image of the future society (the post-capitalist society that he wants to come about). That is why he refuses, at least in his maturity, to *proclaim* ideals. Morally, of course, he condemns. Sociologically, he points to the results of that which he condemns. Politically, he directs attention to the agency of historical change—the proletariat—and he argues, with facts and figures, theories and slogans, that this developing connection between human agency and implicit goal is the most important trend in capitalist society. For by the development of this agency within it, capitalist society itself will be overthrown and socialism installed. The historical creation of the proletariat is the central thrust within the capitalist realm of necessity. That thrust is driving capitalism toward the revolutionary leap into the socialist epoch, into the realm of freedom.

This connection of ideal or goal with agency is at once a moral and an intellectual strategy. It sets Marx off from those he characterized as utopian socialists. This connection between built-in agency and socialist ideal is the political pivot around which turn the decisive features of his model of society and many specific theories of historical trend going on within it. It also provides a focus in social theory for the moral discontent registered in socialist aspirations; and on occasion, a new focus for liberal ideals as well. And it leads—as we shall presently see—to the direct ambiguities of marxian doctrine: this connection between ideal and agency has been at the bottom of the continual second thoughts, metaphysical squabbles, and major revisions by marxists who have come after Marx.

To explain the economic and psychological mechanics by which this built-in historical agency is developed, and how this development inevitably leads to the overthrow of capitalism—these are the organizing points of classic marxism. To explain delays in this development and find ways to facilitate and speed it up, or patiently to wait for it—these are the points from which subsequent varieties of marxism depart.

The remarkable coherence of Marx's system, the close correlation of its elements is in large measure a reflection of the consistency with which he holds in view the central thrust toward the development of the proletariat and its act of revolution. If we keep this in mind, we will not violate marxism as a whole. We must now attempt to set forth, for the moment without criticism, a brief inventory of the most important conceptions and propositions of classic marxism.

1. The economic basis of a society determines its social structure as a whole, as well as the psychology of the people within it.

Political, religious, and legal institutions as well as the ideas, the images, the ideologies by means of which men understand the world in which they live, their place within it, and themselves—all these are reflections of the economic basis of society.

This proposition rests upon the master distinction within Marx's materialist model of society: the economic base (variously referred to as the mode of economic production, the substructure, the economic foundation) is distinguished from the rest of the society (called the superstructure or institutional and ideological forms). In the economic base, Marx includes the forces and the relations of production. In capitalism the latter means essentially the institution of private property and the consequent class relations between those who do and those who do not own it. The forces of production, a more complex conception, include both material and social elements: (a) natural resources, such as land and minerals, so far as they are used as objects of labor; (b) physical equipment such as tools, machines, technology; (c) science and engineering, the skills of men who invent or improve this equipment; (d) those who do work with these skills and tools; (e) their division of labor, insofar as this social organization increases their productivity.

2. *The dynamic of historical change is the conflict between the forces of production and the relations of production.*

In earlier phases of capitalism, the relations of production facilitate the development of the forces of production. One cannot find a more handsome celebration of the work of capitalists in industrialization than in the pages of Marx's *Capital*. But in due course the capitalist organization of industry—the relations of production—come to fetter the forces of production; they come into objective contradiction with them. "Contradiction" I take to mean a problem that is inherent in and cannot be solved without modifying, or "moving beyond," the basic structure of the society in which it occurs. For Marx, "the basic structure" means the capitalist economy.

Continuous technological development and its full use for production conflicts with the interest of the property owners. The capitalists prohibit the utilization of new inventions, buying them up to avoid the loss of their investment in existing facilities. They are interested in increased productivity and in technical progress only as profits can thereby be maintained or increased. Thus capital itself is "the real historical barrier of capital production."

3. *The class struggle between owners and workers is a social, political and psychological reflection of objective economic conflicts.*

These conflicts lead to different reactions among the members of the different classes of bourgeois society. The "objective" contradiction within the capitalist economy, in brief, has its "subjective" counterpart in the class struggle within capitalist society. In this struggle the wageworkers represent the expanding forces of production and the owners represent the maintenance of the established relations of production (property relations mainly) and with them, the exploitation of the unpropertied class.

History is thus an objective sequence, a dialectic, a series of contradictions and of their resolutions. History is also a struggle between classes. These two ways of thinking are, within marxism, quite consistent. For Marx held that the revolution will result from the developing material forces of production as they come into conflict with the relations of production; this revolution will be realized by the struggle of the classes, a struggle caused by the objective, economic contradiction.

The point may be put more abstractly, in line with the "dialectical" method. In Marx's view, continual change—and change into its opposite—is inherent in all reality, and so in capitalist society. The dialectical method is a way of understanding the history of a social structure by examining its conflicts rather than its harmonies. In brief, and in ordinary language, the "laws of dialectics" are as follows: (a) if things change enough, they become different, qualitatively, from what they were to begin with; (b) one thing grows out of another and then comes into conflict with it; (c) history thus proceeds by a series of conflicts and resolutions rather than merely by minute and gradual changes.

4. Property as a source of income is the objective criterion of class: within capitalism the two basic classes are the owners and the workers.

Marx left unfinished his categories of social stratification. A few definitions and remarks are available in *Capital* along with his class analysis of historical events and remarks made in his more abstracted model of capitalist society. From all these, his conceptions and theories appear to be as follows:

The basic criterion of class is the relation of men to the means of production, an objective criterion having primarily to do with economic and legal fact. Those who own the means of production are bourgeoisie, those whom they hire for wages are proletariat. So defined, these terms point to aggregates of people, not to social organizations or psychological matters.

In this objective sense, Marx writes in *The German Ideology*, "the class ... achieves an independent existence over and against individuals, so that the latter find their condition of existence predestined and hence have their position in life and their personal development assigned to them by their class, become subsumed under it."

This statement can be made empirically, as Max Weber later did, in a way that does not violate Marx's meaning. The chances for an individual to achieve that which he values, and even the values themselves, are dependent upon the objective, economic class-position he occupies. At least for statistical aggregates, this is so, irrespective of any psychological opinions or attitudes.

5. Class struggle rather than harmony—"natural" or otherwise—is the normal and inevitable condition in capitalist society.

Marx's denial of any theory of natural harmony is an affirmation that in capitalist society conflicts of interest are basic. By "basic" we are to understand: irremediable within the system: if one interest is fulfilled, the other cannot be. For Marx and for most marxists, the general and basic conflict of interest comes from the division between propertied and non-propertied classes. Whether these classes are aware of it or not, there is an inevitable conflict of interest between them, defined by the relation of each to the means of production. A contradiction of their basic interests prevails.

6. Within capitalist society, the workers cannot escape their exploited conditions and their revolutionary destiny by winning legal or political rights and privileges; unions and mass labor parties are useful as training grounds for revolution, but are not a guarantee of socialism.

Middle-class democracy is always and necessarily based upon economic inequalities and exploitation. Hence Marx continually warns against reformist illusions, and exposes them by reference to the objective contradiction between productive forces and productive relations. There is only one way out: the wageworkers must themselves, by their successful struggle as a property-less class against the property-owning class, resolve the objective contradiction. They themselves must liberate the constructive forces of production by overturning the entire superstructure that is rooted in the capitalist relations of production. The productive forces, now fettered by capitalist rigidity, will then go forward at an enormously accelerated rate of progress.

7. Exploitation is built into capitalism as an economic system, thus increasing the chances for revolution.

Whatever his wages may be, under capitalism the worker is economically exploited. That is the practical meaning of Marx's doctrine of "surplus value." Only human labor, for Marx, can create value. But by the application of his labor power, the worker produces a greater value than he is paid for by the capitalist for whom he works. The "surplus value" thus created is appropriated by the capitalist class, and so the worker under capitalism is exploited.

8. The class structure becomes more and more polarized, thus increasing the chance for revolution.

The composition of capitalist society will undergo these changes: (a) the bourgeoisie or middle class will decrease in numbers; (b) the wageworkers will increase in numbers; (c) all other "intermediary classes" will fade out of the political picture, as the society is polarized between bourgeoisie and proletariat. In general, by "intermediary" classes Marx means the petty bourgeoisie, those of small property; and not white collar employees.

9. The material misery of the workers will increase, as will their alienation.

The increasing misery of the wageworkers refers not only to the physical misery of their life conditions but also to the psychological deprivation arising from their alienation. It is essential to keep these separate, and to remember that for Marx the latter seemed the more important, that alienation could exist and deepen even if material standards of living were improved. However, he expected that the workers will increasingly suffer in both respects, although many latter-day marxists stress the psychological deprivation, the alienation of men at work.

It is to misunderstand Marx, I believe, to equate alienation with whatever is measured as "work dissatisfaction" by industrial psychologists in the USA today. Behind Marx's difficult conception of alienation there is the ideal of the human meaning he believes work ought to have and which he believes it will come to have in a socialist society.

According to Marx, wage work under capitalism is an activity by which men acquire the things they need. It is an activity undertaken for ulterior ends and not in itself a satisfying activity. Men are alienated from the process of their work itself, it is external to them, imposed by social conditions. It is not a source of self-fulfillment but rather a miserable denial of self. They do not "develop freely" their physical and mental energies by their work, but exhaust themselves physically and debase themselves mentally.

Moreover, in work the laborer gives over to the owner the control of his activity: "It is not his work, but work for someone else . . . in work he does not belong to himself but to another person." At work, men are homeless; only during leisure do they feel at home.

Finally, work results in the creation of private property; the product of the work belongs to another. The worker empties himself into this product; the more he works the greater his product, but it is not his. Private property, accordingly, causes him to be alienated. Thus the alienation of labor and the system of private property are reciprocal.

Alienation, working together with economic exploitation, leads to increasing misery—and so in due course, to the formation of the proletariat as a class-for-itself.

10. The wageworkers—a class-in-itself—will be transformed into the proletariat, a class-for-itself.

The first phase—a class-in-itself—refers to the objective fact of the class as an aggregate, defined by its position in the economy.

The second—a class-for-itself—refers to the members of this class when they have become aware of their identity as a class, aware of their common situation, and of their role in changing or in preserving capitalist society. Such class consciousness is not included in the objective definition of the term "class"; it is an expectation, not a definition. It is something that, according to Marx, is going to develop among the members of the classes. How it will develop he does not make as clear as why it will, for according to his analysis of their condition, as the interests of the two classes are in objective and irremediable conflict, their members will eventually become aware of their special interests and will pursue them.

Ideas and ideology are determined (as stated in proposition 1) by the economic bases of a society. The class consciousness of the proletariat will follow this rule. The ideas men come to have are generally determined by the stage of history in which they live, and by the class position they occupy within it. There is not, however, a universal and certainly not an immediate one-to-one correlation. The ideas of the ruling class in a given society are generally the ruling ideas of that epoch. Men who are not in this ruling class but who accept its definitions of reality and of their own interests are "falsely conscious." But in due course, true class consciousness will be realized among the proletariat.

The workers will become increasingly class conscious and increasingly international in their outlook. These economic and psychological developments occur as a result of the institutional and technical development of capitalism itself. In this process, the proletariat will abandon nationalist allegiances and take up loyalties to their own class, regardless of nationality. Like the relations of production, nationalism fetters their true interest which is to release the forces of production.

11. The opportunity for revolution exists only when objective conditions and subjective readiness coincide.

Neither the objective conditions for successful revolution nor revolutionary urges within the proletariat, in Marx's view, continuously increase. Both ebb and flow with the development of objective conditions and the resulting political and psychological ones. Sometimes Marx emphasizes the subjective factor of revolutionary class war, sometimes the underlying objective developments. Thus in 1850:

"Under the conditions of this general prosperity, when the productive forces of bourgeois society develop as abundantly as is at all possible within the existing bourgeois conditions, there can be no question of a real revolution. Such a revolution is only possible in those periods when the two factors, the modern productive forces and the bourgeois forms of production, come to contradict one another."

The proletariat must do the job by its own revolutionary action as a proletariat, but can succeed only under the correct objective conditions. Sooner or later, the will and the conditions will coincide. Many trends, already indicated, facilitate this. In addition, another rule points toward the proletarian revolution:

12. The functional indispensability of a class in the economic system leads to its political supremacy in the society as a whole.

This unstated premise of Marx is the underlying assumption, I believe, of the marxist theory of power. On this premise the capitalists have replaced the nobles, and capitalism has succeeded feudalism. In a similar manner, reasoned Marx, the proletariat will replace the bourgeoisie, and socialism replace capitalism. Old rulers who were once functionally indispensable are so no longer. In the course of capitalist development the bourgeoisie, like the feudal nobles before them, have become parasitical. They cannot help this. It is their destiny. And so they are doomed.

13. In all class societies the state is the coercive instrument of the owning classes.

This of course follows from the theory of power, just stated, and from the conception of the superstructure as economically determined. The state is seen as an instrument of one class and, in advanced capitalism, of a class that is in economic decline. The class of which the state is the coercive instrument is no longer economically progressive, no longer functionally indispensable, and yet it still holds power. It must, therefore, act increasingly by coercion.

14. Capitalism is involved in one economic crisis after another. These crises are getting worse. So capitalism moves into its final crisis—and the revolution of the proletariat.

As the proletariat are subjectively readied, the objective mechanics of capitalism moves the system into increasingly severe crises. The economic contradictions that beset it insure increasing crisis. This cannot be halted until the base of capitalism is abolished, for crisis is inherent in the nature of this system.

15. The post-capitalist society will first pass through a transitional stage—that of the dictatorship of the proletariat; then it will move into a higher phase in which true communism will prevail.

No one, Marx held, can say exactly what the nature of post-capitalist society will be. Only utopians and dreamers draw up detailed blueprints of the future. Just as he does not like to proclaim ideals, so Marx dislikes to go into explicit detail about the future. Either kind of discussion seems to him "idealistic" in the sense of "irrelevant" or "unrealistic." Nonetheless it is possible to find in the relevant texts, mainly his *Critique of the Gotha Program*, Marx's image of the future society:

The transitional stage may be equated with the revolution. The appropriating class will itself be expropriated, the owners' state will be broken up, the productive facilities transferred to society in order to permit a rational planning of the economy. In this first stage, society will be administered and defended against its enemies by a dictatorship of the revolutionary proletariat. This will probably be something like what he supposed the Paris Commune of 1871 to have been. Still "stamped with the birth-marks of the old society, the newborn society will be limited in many ways by inheritances from the old, capitalist society."

But history will not end there. A higher phase—that of communism—will develop; it will be characterized, first, by the fact that the proletariat as a revolutionary class (not just an aggregate of wageworkers) will form "the immense majority" of the population. The proletariat will be the nation; and so in the nation there will be no class distinctions and no class struggle. More than that, specialization of labor itself, as known under capitalism, with all its deformation of men, will not exist. The inherited opposition of manual and mental labor, the conflict between town and country, will disappear.

Second, the state will wither away, for the only function of the state is to hold down the exploited class. Since the proletariat will be virtually the total population, and thus cease to be a proletariat, they will need no state. Anarchy of production will be replaced by rational and systematic planning of the whole. Only in its second phase, when it has eliminated the remaining vestiges of capitalism and developed its own economic base, will society proceed on principles quite distinct from those of capitalism. Only then will men cease to govern men. Man will administer things. Public authority will replace state power. Only then will the ruling principle of communist society be: "From each according to his abilities, to each according to his needs."

16. Although men make their own history, given the circumstances of the economic foundation, the way they make it and the direction it takes are determined. The course of history is structurally limited to the point of being inevitable.

I have noted that in Marx's historical model of society the agency of change is intrinsically connected with socialist ideals. His major propositions and expectations have to do with the development of its historic agency, and with the revolutionary results of that development. Two general questions of interpretation arise when we confront this central view: (a) In general, does Marx believe in historical inevitability? (b) In connection with the mechanics of the central thrust, does he hold that the economic factor is the determining factor in capital society? These questions have been much argued over, as well they might be; for later marxists, notably Lenin, they have been of leading political urgency. Major party strategy has been debated in terms of different answers to them.

My answer to both questions is Yes. Classic marxism contains only one general theory of how men make history. Only in such terms as it provides do all the specific conceptions and theories of Marx make sense. That theory of history-making, very briefly, is as follows:

". . .each person follows his own consciously desired end, and it is precisely the resultant of these many wills operating in different directions and of their manifold effects upon the outer world that constitute history . . . the many individual wills active in history for the most part produce results quite other than those they intended—often quite the opposite: their motives [of individuals] therefore in relation to the total result are likewise only of secondary significance. On the other hand, the further question arises: what driving forces in turn stand behind these motives? What are the historical causes which translate themselves into these motives in the brains of these actors?"[1]

In the historical development of marxism, as we shall later see, there is always the tension between history as inevitable and history as made by the wills of men. It will not do, I think, to lessen that tension by "re-interpreting" or "explaining" what Marx plainly wrote on the theme. Politicians who must justify decisions by reference to founding doctrine may need to do that. We do not. It is better to try to keep the record straight, and to designate departures from classic marxism as departures.

Aside from the documentary evidence, I believe that Marx is a determinist for the following reasons:

(a) The question of the historical agency is clearly bound up with the problem of historical inevitability and with the ideal of socialism. However ambiguous assorted quotations may make the point seem, classic marxism does differ from utopian socialism and from liberalism precisely on this point. It may be that in arguing against utopian socialism and against liberalism Marx stresses the idea of inevitability. Be that as it may, I am less concerned with *why* he held this view than with the fact that he did.

(b) Marx's refusal to preach ideals and his reluctance to discuss the society of the future makes no sense otherwise. Because he did believe in the historical inevitability, as he saw it, he can treat socialism not as an ideal, a program, a choice of means, or as a matter of or for political decision. He can treat it as a matter for scientific investigation.

(c) He did not try to persuade men of any new moral goals, because he believed that the proletariat would inevitably come to them. "In the last analysis," social existence determines consciousness. Historical developments will implant these goals into the consciousness of men, and men will then act upon them. The individual has little choice. If his consciousness is not altogether determined, his choice is severely limited and pressed upon him by virtue of his class position and all the influences and limitations to which this leads.

(d) Historically, the idea of Progress has been fully incorporated into the very ethos of marxism. Marx re-seats this idea—in the development of the proletariat. This becomes the gauge for moral judgments of progress and retrogression. Generally in his temper and in his theories of the master trends of capitalism in decline Marx is quite optimistic.

17. The social structure, as noted in proposition number 1, is determined by its economic foundations; accordingly, the course of its history is determined by changes in these economic foundations.

I have held this point until the end, because it is a point of great controversy. There is a tendency among some marxists to attempt to "defend" Marx's economic determinism by qualifying it. They do this in the manner of Engels' later remarks (made in letters) about the interplay of various factors, or by opposing to it a vague

---

[1] F. Engels, *Ludwig Feuerbach* (New York, 1935), pp. 58-59.

sociological pluralism, by which everything interacts with everything and no causal sequence is ever quite determinable. Neither line of argument, even when put in the abstruse terms of "dialectical materialism," seems very convincing or helpful. Moreover, to dilute the theory in these ways is to transform it from a definite theory, which may or may not be adequate, into equivocation, a mere indication of a problem.

Marx stated clearly the doctrine of economic determinism. It is reflected in his choice of vocabulary; it is assumed by, and fits into, his work as a whole—in particular his theory of power, his conception of the state, his rather simple notions of class and his use of these notions (including the proletariat as the agency of history-making). We may of course assume with Engels that he allows a degree of free-play among the several factors that interact, and also that he provides a flexible time-schedule in which economic causes do their work. But in the end—and usually the end is not so very far off—economic causes are "the basic," the ultimate, the general, the innovative causes of historical change.

To Marx "economic determinism" does *not* mean that the desire for money or the pursuit of wealth, or calculation of economic gain is the master force of biography or of history. In fact, it does not pertain directly to *motives* of any sort. It has to do with the social—the class—context under which motives themselves arise and function in biography and in history. The *causes* of which Marx writes are causes that lie behind the motives which propel men to act. We must understand this in the terms of his model of history-making: "Marx examines the causal nature of the resultants of individual wills, without examining the latter in themselves; he investigates the laws underlying *social* phenomena, paying no attention to their relation with the phenomena of the individual consciousness."[2]

Such are the bare outlines of classic marxism. In summary, it consists of a model of maturing capitalist society and of theories about the way this society and the men within it are changing. In this society, the productive facilities are owned privately and used to make private profit; the rest of the population works for wages given by those who own. It is a society that is changing because its forces of production come into increasing conflict with the organization of its economy by the owners and by their state.

At bottom, developments of its economic basis—in particular its economic contradictions—are making for changes in all its institutions and ideologies. Increasingly resulting in crisis, increasingly deepening the exploitation of men by men, these contradictions are causing the development of the historical agency which upon maturity is destined to overturn capitalism itself. That agency is the proletariat, a class which within capitalism is being transformed from a mere aggregate of wageworkers into a unified and conscious class-for-itself, aware of its common interests, and alert to the revolutionary way of realizing them.

The objective or institutional conflicts are a fact of capitalist life, but may not yet be reflected fully as the class struggle of owners and workers. Now a minority, concerned only with their immediate interests, the workers are growing more and

---

[2] Nikolai Bukharin, *Economic Theory of the Leisure Class* (New York, 1927), p. 40.

more exploited, more alienated, more miserable, and more organized; in their ranks what men are interested in is coming to coincide with what is to men's interest; and the workers are becoming more numerous. They are coming to be "the self-conscious independent movement of the immense majority" in pursuit of their real and long-run interests. They are coming to true self-consciousness because of self-consciousness itself is being changed by the relations of production men enter into independent of their will. And having become self-conscious, they cannot pursue their interests, they cannot raise themselves up, "without the whole super-incumbent strata of official society being sprung into the air."[3]

That is why when the time is ripe, when capitalism is mature and the proletariat ready, the revolution of the proletariat by the most politically alert sector of the proletariat is going to occur. Then bourgeois institutions and all their works will be smashed. In turn, the post-capitalist society of socialism will evolve into the communist realm of freedom.

Comprehending every feature of man's activities, human and inhuman, Marx's conception is bitterly filled with sheer intellect and with brilliant leaps of the mind; it is at once analysis, prophecy, orientation, history, program. It is "the most formidable, sustained and elaborate indictment ever delivered against an entire social order, against its rulers, its supporters, its ideologists, its willing slaves, against all whose lives are bound up with its survival."[4]

No sooner were its outlines stated than it began to be revised by other men who were caught up in the torment of history-making. Then the intellectual beauty of its structure, the political passion of its central thrust began to be blunted by the will of political actors and the recalcitrance of historical events.

MARX THE SOCIOLOGIST

Joseph A. Schumpeter

Marx the sociologist brought to bear on his task an equipment which consisted primarily of an extensive command over historical and contemporaneous fact. His knowledge of the latter was always somewhat antiquated, for he was the most bookish of men and therefore fundamental materials, as distinguished from the material of the newspapers, always reached him with a lag. But hardly any historical

---

[3] Karl Löwith, *Meaning in History* (Chicago, 1950), p. 41.

[4] Isaiah Berlin, *Karl Marx* (New York, 1959), p. 21.

SOURCE: Abridged from pp. 10-20 in *Capitalism, Socialism, and Democracy,* third edition, by Joseph A. Schumpeter. Copyright 1942, 1947 by Joseph A Schumpeter. Copyright 1950 by Harper & Row Publishers, Incorporated. Reprinted by permission of Harper & Row, Publishers, and George Allen & Unwin Ltd. Footnotes have been omitted.

work of his time that was of any general importance or scope escaped him, although much of the monographic literature did. While we cannot extol the completeness of his information in this field as much as we shall his erudition in the field of economic theory, he was yet able to illustrate his social visions not only by large historical frescoes but also by many details most of which were as regards reliability rather above than below the standards of other sociologists of his time. These facts he embraced with a glance that pierced through the random irregularities of the surface down to the grandiose logic of things historical. In this there was not merely passion. There was not merely analytic impulse. There were both. And the outcome of his attempt to formulate that logic, the so-called Economic Interpretation of History, is doubtless one of the greatest individual achievements of sociology to this day. Before it, the question sinks into insignificance whether or not this achievement was entirely original and how far credit has in part to be given to predecessors, German and French.

The economic interpretation of history does *not* mean that men are, consciously or unconsciously, wholly or primarily, actuated by economic motives. On the contrary, the explanation of the role and mechanism of non-economic motives and the analysis of the way in which social reality mirrors itself in the individual psyches is an essential element of the theory and one of its most significant contributions. Marx did not hold that religions, metaphysics, schools of art, ethical ideas and political volitions were either reducible to economic *motives* or of no importance. He only tried to unveil the economic *conditions* which shape them and which account for their rise and fall. The whole of Max Weber's facts and arguments fits perfectly into Marx's system. Social groups and classes and the ways in which these groups or classes explain to themselves their own existence, location and behavior were of course what interested him most. He poured the vials of his most bilious wrath on the historians who took those attitudes and their verbalizations (the ideologies or, as Pareto would have said, *derivations*) at their face value and who tried to interpret social reality by means of them. But if ideas or values were not for him the prime movers of the social process, neither were they mere smoke. If I may use the analogy, they had in the social engine the role of transmission belts. We cannot touch upon that most interesting post-war development of these principles which would afford the best instance by which to explain this, the Sociology of Knowledge. But it was necessary to say this much because Marx has been persistently misunderstood in this respect. Even his friend Engels, at the open grave of Marx, defined the theory in question as meaning precisely that individuals and groups are swayed primarily by economic motives, which in some important respects is wrong and for the rest piteously trivial.

While we are about it, we may as well defend Marx against another misunderstanding: the *economic* interpretation of history has often been called the *materialistic* interpretation. It has been called so by Marx himself. This phrase greatly increased its popularity with some, and its unpopularity with other people. But it is entirely meaningless. Marx's philosophy is no more materialistic than is Hegel's, and his theory of history is not more materialistic than is any other attempt to account for the historic process by the means at the command of empirical science. It should be clear that this is logically compatible with any metaphysical or religious belief—exactly as any physical picture of the world is. Medieval theology itself supplies methods by which it is possible to establish this compatibility.

What the theory really says may be put into two propositions: (1) The forms or conditions of production are the fundamental determinant of social structures which in turn breed attitudes, actions and civilizations. Marx illustrates his meaning by the famous statement that the "hand-mill" creates feudal, and the "steam-mill," capitalist societies. This stresses the technological element to a dangerous extent, but may be accepted on the understanding that mere technology is not all of it. Popularizing a little and recognizing that by doing so we lose much of the meaning, we may say that it is our daily work which forms our minds, and that it is our location within the productive process which determines our outlook on things—or the sides of things we see—and the social elbowroom at the command of each of us. (2) The forms of production themselves have a logic of their own; that is to say, they change according to necessities inherent in them so as to produce their successors merely by their own working. To illustrate by the same Marxian example: the system characterized by the "hand-mill" creates an economic and social situation in which the adoption of the mechanical method of milling becomes a practical necessity that individuals or groups are powerless to alter. The rise and working of the "steam-mill" in turn creates new social functions and locations, new groups and views, which develop and interact in such a way as to outgrow their own frame. Here, then, we have the propeller which is responsible first of all for economic and, in consequence of this, for any other social change a propeller the action of which does not itself require any impetus external to it.

Both propositions undoubtedly contain a large amount of truth and are, as we shall find at several turns of our way, invaluable working hypotheses. Most of the current objections completely fail, all those for instance which in refutation point to the influence of ethical or religious factors, or the one already raised by Eduard Bernstein, which with delightful simplicity asserts that "men have heads" and can hence act as they choose. After what has been said above, it is hardly necessary to dwell on the weakness of such arguments: of course men "choose" their course of action which is not directly enforced by the objective data of the environment; but they choose from standpoints, views and propensities that do not form another set of independent data but are themselves molded by the objective set.

Nevertheless, the question arises whether the economic interpretation of history is more than a convenient approximation which must be expected to work less satisfactorily in some cases than it does in others. An obvious qualification occurs at the outset. Social structures, types and attitudes are coins that do not readily melt. Once they are formed they persist, possibly for centuries, and since different structures and types display different degrees of this ability to survive, we almost always find that actual group and national behavior more or less departs from what we should expect it to be if we tried to infer it from the dominant forms of the productive process. Though this applies quite generally, it is most clearly seen when a highly durable structure transfers itself bodily from one country to another. The social situation created in Sicily by the Norman conquest will illustrate my meaning. Such facts Marx did not overlook but he hardly realized all their implications.

A related case is of more ominous significance. Consider the emergence of the feudal type of landlordism in the kingdom of the Franks during the sixth and seventh centuries. This was certainly a most important event that shaped the structure of society for many ages and *also influenced conditions of production, wants and technology included.* But its simplest explanation is to be found in the function of military leadership previously filled by the families and individuals who (retaining that function however) became feudal landlords after the definitive conquest of the new territory. This does not fit the Marxian schema at all well and could easily be so construed as to point in a different direction. Facts of this nature can no doubt also be brought into the fold by means of auxiliary hypotheses but the necessity of inserting such hypotheses is usually the beginning of the end of a theory.

Many other difficulties that arise in the course of attempts at historical interpretation by means of the Marxian schema could be met by admitting some measure of interaction between the sphere of production and other spheres of social life. But the glamour of fundamental truth that surrounds it depends precisely on the strictness and simplicity of the one-way relation which it asserts. If this be called in question, the economic interpretation of history will have to take its place among other propositions of a similar kind—as one of many partial truths—or else to give way to another that does tell more fundamental truth. However, neither its rank as an achievement nor its handiness as a working hypothesis is impaired thereby.

To the faithful, of course, it is simply the master key to all the secrets of human history. And if we sometimes feel inclined to smile at rather naive applications of it, we should remember what sort of arguments it replaced. Even the crippled sister of the economic interpretation of history, the Marxian Theory of Social Classes, moves into a more favorable light as soon as we bear this in mind.

Again, it is in the first place an important contribution that we have to record. Economists have been strangely slow in recognizing the phenomenon of social classes. Of course they always classified the agents whose interplay produced the processes they dealt with. But these classes were simply sets of individuals that displayed some common character: thus, some people were classed as landlords or workmen because they owned land or sold the services of their labor. Social classes, however, are not the creatures of the classifying observer but live entities that exist as such. And their existence entails consequences that are entirely missed by a schema which looks upon society as if it were an amorphous assemblage of individuals or families. It is fairly open to question precisely how important the phenomenon of social classes is for research in the field of purely economic theory. That it is very important for many practical applications and for all the broader aspects of the social process in general is beyond doubt.

Roughly speaking, we may say that the social classes made their entrance in the famous statement contained in the *Communist Manifesto* that the history of society is the history of class struggles. Of course, this is to put the claim at its highest. But even if we tone it down to the proposition that historical events may often be interpreted in terms of class interests and class attitudes and that existing class structures are always an important factor in historical interpretation, enough remains to entitle us to speak of a conception nearly as valuable as was the economic interpretation of history itself. . . .

Curiously enough, Marx has never, as far as we know, worked out systematically what it is plain was one of the pivots of his thought. It is possible that he deferred the task until it was too late, precisely because his thinking ran so much in terms of class concepts that he did not feel it necessary to bother about definitive statement at all. It is equally possible that some points about it remained unsettled in his own mind, and that his way toward a full-fledged theory of classes was barred by certain difficulties he had created for himself by insisting on a purely economic and over-simplified conception of the phenomenon. He himself and his disciples both offered applications of this under-developed theory to particular patterns of which his own *History of the Class Struggles in France* is the outstanding example. Beyond that no real progress has been achieved. The theory of his chief associate, Engels, was of the division of labor type and essentially un-Marxian in its implications. Barring this we have only the sidelights and *apercus*—some of them of striking force and brilliance—that are strewn all over the writings of the master, particularly in *Das Kapital* and the *Communist Manifesto*.

The task of piecing together such fragments is delicate and cannot be attempted here. The basic idea is clear enough, however. The stratifying principle consists in the ownership, or the exclusion from ownership, of means of production such as factory buildings, machinery, raw materials and the consumers' goods that enter into the workman's budget. We have thus, fundamentally, two and only two classes, those owners, the capitalists, and those have-nots who are compelled to sell their labor, the laboring class or proletariat. The existence of intermediate groups, such as are formed by farmers or artisans who employ labor but also do manual work, by clerks and by the professions is of course not denied; but they are treated as anomalies which tend to disappear in the course of the capitalist process. The two fundamental classes are, by virtue of the logic of their position and quite independently of any individual volition, essentially antagonistic to each other. Rifts within each class and collisions between subgroups occur and may even have historically decisive importance. But in the last analysis, such rifts or collisions are incidental. The one antagonism that is not incidental but inherent in the basic design of capitalist society is founded upon the private control over the means to produce: the very nature of the relation between the capitalist class and the proletariat is strife—class war.

As we shall see presently, Marx tries to show how in that class war capitalists destroy each other and eventually will destroy the capitalist system too. He also tries to show how the ownership of capital leads to further accumulation. But this way of arguing as well as the very definition that makes the ownership of something the constituent characteristic of a social class only serves to increase the importance of the question of "primitive accumulation," that is to say, of the question how capitalists came to be capitalists in the first instance or how they acquired that stock of goods which according to the Marxian doctrine was necessary in order to enable them to start exploiting. On this question Marx is much less explicit. He contemptuously rejects the bourgeois nursery tale (*Kinderfibel*) that some people rather than others became, and are still becoming every day, capitalists by superior intelligence and energy in working and saving. Now he was well advised to sneer at that story about the good boys. For to call for a guffaw is no doubt an excellent method of disposing of an uncomfortable truth, as every politician knows to his profit. Nobody who looks at historical and contemporaneous fact with anything like an unbiased mind can fail to observe that this children's tale, while far from telling the whole truth, yet tells a good deal of it. Supernormal intelligence and energy account for industrial success and in particular for the *founding* of industrial positions in nine cases out of ten. And precisely in the initial stages of capitalism and of every individual industrial career, saving was and is an important element in the process though not quite as explained in classic economics. It is true that one does not ordinarily attain the status of capitalist (industrial employer) by saving from a wage or salary in order to equip one's factory by means of the fund thus assembled. The bulk of accumulation comes from profits and hence presupposed profits—this is in fact the *sound* reason for distinguishing saving from accumulating. The means required in order to start enterprise are typically provided by borrowing other people's savings, the presence of which in many small puddles is easy to explain, or [by] the deposits which banks create for the use of the would-be entrepreneur. Nevertheless, the latter does save as a rule: the function of his saving is to raise him above the necessity of submitting to daily drudgery for the sake of his daily bread and to give him breathing space in order to look around, to develop his plans and to secure cooperation. As a matter of economic theory, therefore, Marx had a real case—though he overstated it—when he denied to saving the role that the classical authors attributed to it. Only his inference does not follow. And the guffaw is hardly more justified than it would be if the classical theory were correct.

The guffaw did its work, however, and helped to clear the road for Marx's alternative theory of primitive accumulation. But this alternative theory is not as definite as we might wish. Force-robbery-subjugation of the masses facilitating their spoliation and the results of the pillage in turn facilitating subjugation—this was all right of course and admirably tallied with ideas common among intellectuals of all types, in our day still more than in the day of Marx. But evidently it does not solve the problem, which is to explain how some people acquired the power to subjugate and to rob. . . .

Now at least the semblance of a solution is afforded by the historical quality of all the major theories of Marx. For him, it is essential for the *logic* of capitalism, and not only a matter of *fact*, that it grew out of a feudal state of society. Of course the same question about the causes and the mechanism of social stratification arises also in this case, but Marx substantially accepted the bourgeois view that feudalism was a reign of force in which subjugation and exploitation of the masses were already accomplished facts. The class theory devised primarily for the conditions of capitalist society was extended to its feudal predecessor—as was much of the conceptual apparatus of the economic theory of capitalism—and some of the most thorny problems were stowed away in the feudal compound to reappear in a settled state, in the form of data, in the analysis of the capitalist pattern. The feudal exploiter was simply replaced by the capitalist exploiter. In those cases in which feudal lords actually turned into industrialists, this alone would solve what is thus left of the problem. Historical evidence lends a certain amount of support to this view: many feudal lords, particularly in Germany, in fact did erect and run factories, often providing the financial means from their feudal rents and the labor from the agricultural population (not necessarily but sometimes their serfs). In all other cases the material available to stop the gap is distinctly inferior. The only frank way of expressing the situation is that from a Marxian standpoint there is no satisfactory explanation, that is to say, no explanation without resorting to non-Marxian elements suggestive of non-Marxian conclusions.

This, however, vitiates the theory at both its historical and its logical source. Since most of the methods of primitive accumulation also account for later accumulation—primitive accumulation, as it were, continues throughout the capitalist era—it is not possible to say that Marx's theory of social classes is all right *except* for the difficulties about processes in a distant past. But it is perhaps superfluous to insist on the shortcomings of a theory which not even in the most favorable instances goes anywhere near the heart of the phenomenon it undertakes to explain, and which never should have been taken seriously. These instances are to be found mainly in that epoch of capitalist evolution which derived its character from the prevalence of the medium-sized owner-managed firm. Beyond the range of that type, class positions, though in most cases reflected in more or less corresponding economic positions, are more often the cause than the consequence of the latter: business achievement is obviously not everywhere the only avenue to social eminence and only where it is can ownership of means of production casually determine a group's position in the social structure. Even then, however, it is as reasonable to make that ownership the defining element as it would be to define a soldier as a man who happens to have a gun. The water-tight division between people who (together with their descedants) are supposed to be proletarians once for all is not only, as has often been pointed out, utterly unrealistic but it misses the salient point about social classes—the incessant rise and fall of individual families into and out of the upper strata. The facts I am alluding to are all obvious and indisputable. If they do not show on the Marxian canvas, the reason can only be in their un-Marxian implications.

It is not superflous, however, to consider the role which that theory plays within Marx's structure and to ask ourselves what analytic intention—as distinguished from its use as a piece of equipment for the agitator—he meant it to serve.

On the one hand, we must bear in mind that for Marx the theory of Social Classes and the Economic Interpretation of History were not what they are for us, viz., two independent doctrines. With Marx, the former implements the latter in a particular way and thus restricts—makes more definite—the *modus operandi* of the conditions or forms of production. These determine the social structure and, through the social structure, all manifestations of civilization and the whole march of cultural and political history. But the social structure is, for all non-socialist epochs, defined in terms of classes—those two classes—which are the true dramatis personae and at the same time the only *immediate* creatures of the logic of the capitalist system of production which affects everything else through them. This explains why Marx was forced to make his classes purely economic phenomena, and even phenomena that were economic in a very narrow sense: he thereby cut himself off from a deeper view of them, but in the precise spot of his analytic schema in which he placed them he had no choice but to do so.

On the other hand, Marx wished to define capitalism by the same trait that also defines his class division. A little reflection will convince the reader that this is not a necessary or natural thing to do. In fact it was a bold stroke of analytic strategy which linked the fate of the class phenomenon with the fate of capitalism in such a way that socialism, which in reality has nothing to do with the presence or absence of social classes, became, by definition, the only possible kind of classless society, excepting primitive groups. This ingenious tautology could not equally well have been secured by any definitions of classes *and* of capitalism other than those chosen by Marx—the definition by private ownership of means of production. Hence there had to be just two classes, owners and non-owners, and hence all other principles of division, much more plausible ones among them, had to be severely neglected or discounted or else reduced to that one.

The exaggeration of the definiteness and importance of the dividing line between the capitalist class in that sense and the proleteriat was surpassed only by the exaggeration of the antagonism between them. . . . In social life, antagonism and synagogism are of course both ubiquitous and in fact inseparable except in the rarest of cases. . . . Again, however, he had no choice, not because he wanted to arrive at revolutionary results—these he could have derived just as well from dozens of other possible schemata—but because of the requirements of his own analysis. *If* class struggle was the subject matter of history and also the means of bringing about the socialist dawn, and *if* there had to be just those two classes, than their relation had to be antagonistic on principle or else the force in his system of social dynamics would have been lost. . . .

This particular theory of social classes is the analytic tool which, by linking the economic interpretation of history with the concepts of the profit economy, marshals all social facts, makes all phenomena confocal. It is therefore not simply a theory of an individual phenomenon which is to explain that phenomenon and nothing else. It has an organic function which is really much more important to the Marxian system than the measure of success with which it solves its immediate problem. This function must be seen if we are to understand how an analyst of the power of Marx could ever have borne with its shortcomings. . . .

III

ELITIST POWER THEORIES

ELITIST THEORY AS A RESPONSE TO MARX

Marvin E. Olsen

Many of the ideas of elitist theory can be found in the writings of Plato and of Machiavelli, but all of the major figures in this school of thought—especially Vilfredo Pareto, Gaetano Mosca, and Robert Michels—can best be understood as writing in response to Marx. Their common concern was to show that concentration of power in a small group of elites is inevitable in modern societies, thus negating Marx's vision of evolutionary social change toward a classless society of power equality. At the same time, however, they held that some change can occur through gradual circulation of elites without class conflict and total revolution. Neither Mosca not Michels were personally happy with these conclusions, but they felt obliged as social theorists to take what they believed was a realistic view of the exercise of power in society, in contradiction to Marx's admittedly idealistic vision.

We shall not attempt here to elaborate all of the ideas of each of these writers or their modern counterparts; these are made quite clear in the readings that follow. Our concern instead will be to summarize the main themes of this body of power theory, to mention a number of unresolved questions raised by the elitists, and to suggest possible directions for further elaboration of elitist theory.

The principal argument of Pareto, Mosca, and Michels was that *in all societies past the bare subsistence level there has been—and hence presumably will be in the future—one or a few small sets of dominant, ruling elites.*[1] Regardless of the formal nature of the government—authoritarian, monarchal, or democratic—if we examine the true distribution of power we inevitably find oligarchy of the few over the many. The masses cannot and do not govern themselves. Elites employ whatever

---

[1]This discussion of these three elitist theorists is drawn primarily from the following sources: Vilfredo Pareto, *Sociological Writings*, edited by S. E. Finer, translated by Derick Mifton (New York: Fredrick A. Praeger, 1966); Gaetano Mosca, *The Ruling Class*, edited by Arthur Livingston, translated by Hannah D. Kahn (New York: McGraw-Hill Book Company, Inc., 1939); and Robert Michels, *Political Parties*, translated by Eden and Cedar Paul (New York: The Free Press, 1966).

social and cultural means are at their disposal to maintain their power and rule society, including such methods as control of the government or the economy, use of police and military forces, absorption (or cooptation) of threatening challengers, manipulation of mass communications and education, and creation of legitimizing myths and values. Hence, these elites frequently influence many aspects of social life, and partially or largely shape the structure and activities of the total society. For analytical purposes, to explain the actions of the ruling elites is to explain the predominant features of their entire society.

The elites are always a small minority of the total population, but they are well organized and highly cohesive, and are thus able to make maximum effective use of the resources they control. Elitist theorists differ in their descriptions of organizational patterns among elites, but they have suggested that in a highly developed society there might be several different categories of elites, including "ruling elites" who directly exercise power, one or more sets of "subelites" who execute elite decisions and policies and who thus maintain the elites in power (as well as provide a constant supply of new personnel), numerous groups of "counterelites" who occasionally challenge the rulers and seek to overthrow them (but who are most commonly absorbed into the ruling class without seriously disturbing its power), and perhaps even several layers of "semielites" between the rulers and the masses who provide necessary resources, channels of communication, and protection for the rulers.

No matter how complex this structure of interrelated elite groups, however, the social distance between all of them and the rest of the population is so great as to constitute a virtually unscalable barrier. The elites exercise power, whereas the "masses" do not. Hence, for ease of analysis most elitist theories have worked with what is essentially a "two-class" model of society. In this respect they have been similar to Marx, with one important exception. Whereas for Marx the subject class could organize and overthrow the dominant class, elitists have seen the "masses" as always being unorganized and incapable of collective action. Hence, it might be more accurate to speak of elitist theory as based on a simple "one-class" model.

The elitist theorists do offer a broader explanation of the underlying bases of social power than that proposed by Marx, however. For them, *control of the means of economic production is just one possible resource for exercising power, rather than the only one.* But they disagree sharply in their analyses of these variable power bases and in their explanations of why ruling elites are inevitable in society. They have employed both psychological and sociological arguments, although the balance tends to shift from Pareto to Mosca to Michels.

Pareto's explanation of elites was derived from his general theory of society as a system of primarily "nonlogical" activities shaped by psychological "sentiments" or "residues." Individuals who display certain kinds of sentiments tend to gain positions of power as a result of their personal characteristics, especially if their sentiments are compatible with existing social, economic, and political conditions. Pareto's writings suggest interesting questions about relationships between personality characteristics of leaders and prevailing patterns of social organization, but his theoretical rationale for the existence of elites cannot stand by itself if we reject his basic theory of sentiments.

Mosca's arguments for the inevitability of elites are a mixture of psychological and sociological propositions, which he failed to synthesize into a consistent thesis. On the whole, he maintained, elites tend to be superior individuals in such qualities as ambition, personal drive, capacity for hard work, strength of will, and self-confidence. As a result of a continual struggle for social preeminence (status or prestige), some individuals rise to positions of power over others. But the competition is not equal for all, since one's family background significantly influences one's final achievements. In particular, children from elitist families have tremendous advantages over others because of the education and training they receive, the resources they inherit, and the social opportunities open to them. Hence elite families tend to be self-perpetuating through many generations. In addition, however, Mosca also proposed that in the long run elites will be representative of the dominant social, economic, political, religous, cultural, and other organized "interests" or "forces" in society. As these underlying interests and forces slowly change, so will the elites. This idea is essentially an expansion of Marx's emphasis on relations to the means of production, broadened to include other sources of power besides control of the economy.

Michels' observations, finally, were the most empirical and the most sociological in nature. They can be divided into three main categories: "structural," "operational," and "practical." His structural arguments were based on the fact that virtually all organizations, from labor unions to total societies, tend to have a hierarchial structure in which authority and other forms of power are exercised downward from the top. Even though final authority may be vested in the membership as a whole, the necessity for leadership and over-all coordination makes popular voting and similar procedures mere rituals. Instead of being servants of the members, leaders become in fact the legitimate rulers. Operationally, leaders have many other advantages over ordinary members in the exercise of power. They acquire special skills and experience in running the organizations that nonleaders lack. Over time they build up extensive webs of relationships and personal influence throughout the organization, as well as perceived legitimacy for wielding power. They are usually much better organized than other members, and can block or coopt potential challengers. And they control organizational resources such as finances, communication media, and disciplinary agencies, all of which they can use to their own benefit. Often they even come to be seen by others as indispensable if the organization is to achieve its goals. Finally, in a very practical sense, there may be no realistic alternative to oligarchy. On the one hand, leaders frequently seek to perpetuate themselves or their chosen heirs in office as long as possible, so as to protect their own power and privileges and to ensure that their policies are carried out. On the other hand, most ordinary members tend to be uninterested in assuming the responsibilities of leadership and indifferent or apathetic toward problems of the whole organization. They desire and welcome leadership from above that will relieve them of the burdens of collective decision making, and quite willingly submit to the dictates of leaders.

Many of the specific points made by these three writers are undoubtedly open to debate, and their ideas are not entirely consistent with one another. Nevertheless, taken as a whole they provide a compelling argument for the inevitability of elites in all societies. In the words of Michels' famous "iron law of oligarchy," "whoever says organization, says oligarchy."[2]

Despite their diverse lines of reasoning, Pareto, Mosca, and Michels therefore all concluded that in real social life it would always be impossible to attain Marx's ideal of a "classless society" in which all persons were economically and politically equal. Since concentration of power in society is based on more than just ownership of the means of production, control over the economy can change without seriously disrupting or destroying elite power. Both Pareto and Mosca went to great lengths to demonstrate that *when social change does occur it tends to be cyclical rather than evolutionary in nature*, with one set of elites merely replacing another. The organization and composition of elite groups can thus vary through time in broad cycles, but societies are always ruled by powerful elites. Moreover, most people accept the "myths" or "political formulas" propounded by elites to justify their actions and legitimize their power, so that the "masses" usually have no desire to revolt against the ruling class. A "proletarian revolution" is therefore highly unlikely, but even if it should occur it would only result in the substitution of one oligarchy for another.

Several crucial theoretical questions about elites were raised by Pareto, Mosca, and Michels that neither they nor subsequent writers have resolved. We shall briefly examine five of these issues. First, to the extent that powerful elites have existed in most societies, can their presence and actions be explained best by psychological or sociological theory, or by some combination of both? Most sociologists understandably prefer Michels' kind of sociological reasoning to Pareto's scheme of psychological "sentiments," while viewing Mosca as an insightful but not very systematic observer. Patterns of social ordering, they insist, always provide the structural framework that makes possible concentration of power in elite positions and within which elites act. But cannot contemporary social psychology go beyond Pareto to provide more useful knowledge about links between individual actions and social structure in the exercise of power? Some work has recently been done along these lines, though most of it has been limited to small groups. What is clearly needed before we can settle the debate about the inevitability of power concentration is a convergence of theorizing and research from both analytical perspectives.

Second, is elite power based ultimately on the skillful use of force and fraud, or is it a functional necessity in complex social organizations? This question cuts across the sociological-psychological distinction mentioned above, and is perhaps the main theoretical issue in the study of elites. Themes of force and fraud pervade the writings of Pareto, Mosca, and Michels—as well as Marx—but beneath the surface in all cases (especially Michels) are implicit functional arguments. Given such facts as requirements for rapid decision making and over-all coordination, the benefits of centralized communications and planning, and apathy among the "masses," is not

---

[2]Robert Michels, *op. cit.*, p. 365.

concentration of power in the hands of small numbers of elites a functional necessity in contemporary societies and other organizations? Much current social scientific thinking takes this direction, but in recent years it has received a fair amount of criticism. Do the facts warrant the conclusion, or are there perhaps other means of achieving over-all communication, coordination, control, and planning that do not depend on domination by powerful elites? In short, although rule by elites is exceedingly common, must it be seen as inevitable in all modern societies?

The third unresolved question concerns the two-class (or one-class) analytical model that most elitist theorists have at least partially accepted. Despite increasing awareness of the importance of subelites and counterelites, the major distinction between elites and "masses" still remains. Do the empirical facts justify the use of some form of this model, or is it blinding us to the realities of contemporary social life? A two-class model does not perhaps greatly distort social reality if the preponderance of power in a society is derived from one major kind of resource (such as ownership of land in a feudal society) and hence forms a single dimension, and if all power wielders are fairly unified. But as resource bases multiply, as power becomes multidimensional, and as powerful actors become divided into numerous conflicting groups, a more complex model is obviously needed. No adequate multidimensional and multiclass model has yet been fully developed in sociology, however.

Fourth, does the idea of "circulation of elites"—either from counterelites or occasionally from the masses—provide an adequate explanation of social change? And should such circulation of individuals even be termed social change? Marx would have emphatically said "no"! Rejecting this explanation of change does not of course necessitate our accepting Marx's insistence on violent conflict and revolution as a complete explanation, but certainly many sweeping historical changes have involved open conflict between classes. There is no logical reason why a more inclusive theory of social change could not incorporate both of these views as well as many other variables, but such a theory does not yet exist.

Finally, must elitist theory carry the overtones of political conservatism and the negative evaluation of conflict and change that are often read into the writings of Pareto, Mosca, and Michels? Although it is unfair to describe these theorists as advocates of such value positions, their ideas certainly do not encourage hopes for realizing power equality as envisioned by Marx. If one tries hard enough it is probably possible to find justification for any ideological position in any analysis of social power, but the conclusions of the elitist have been happily accepted by many would-be autocrats and dictators, and have been the despair of radical reformers. This question is closely tied to the three previous ones, since functional arguments for the necessity of elites, use of a two-class model, and a circulation explanation of change do support conservative ideological views of power, whereas a "force and fraud" argument, a multidimensional model, and a conflict theory of change do encourage a more radical perspective. If some of these latter ideas can be incorporated into elitist theory, it may then be possible to rid it of at least any explicit ideological bias.

Numerous sociologists—three of whom are represented in this section—are today exploring elitist theory, seeking to extract its most useful ideas and expand them into a more comprehensive explanation of the exercise of power in modern societies. The following paragraphs sketch several of the themes they have discussed.

They frequently begin by pointing out that basic terms such as "elites" and "ruling classes" have not been adequately clarified. If we use "elites" as a generic concept referring to all actors in a society who exercise significant power of any kind, it then becomes extremely inclusive, serving to alert sociologists to the process of power exertion but not directing them to any specific aspects of power. This broad concept of "elites" can be made more precise, however, if we recognize that all modern societies—even those with autocratic governments—contain not just one dimension of power (as implied by Marx) but rather a wide array of fairly distinct power dimensions. *Each of these spheres of power activities, of which the national government is only one, can then have its own set of relatively specialized elites*—which Suzanne Keller calls "strategic elites."[3] Nonelites in one area may be elites or subelites in another area, so there need not be any vast, unorganized, completely powerless "masses" in the society. There may be a tendency for the various sets of strategic elites to have overlapping memberships and to cooperate with each other—the nature and extent of this in any society is a question for empirical research—but there is not likely be a single, closed oligarchy that dominates the entire society.

The term "political elites" can then be reserved for those persons who actively control the government, through either decision-making or key administrative positions. The classical elitist theorists were certainly correct in observing that some form of centralized government is indispensable in modern societies and that this will necessarily create a set of political elites. Their error lay in assuming that these political elites must invariably also constitute the elites in all other spheres of activity. To the extent that a society does contain many separate dimensions of power, there can be other sets of strategic elites in industry, science, education, religion, communications, medicine, law, the arts, and so on. Collectively, they might be referred to as the "ruling class" in a society.

Below the dominant elites and their immediate subelites in each sector of society there might also exist an "active stratum," composed of all those people who participate actively and at least occasionally exercise some influence in this area, but who do not occupy major positions of power. In politics this category could be termed the "political activists" or "political stratum," and would include everyone active in political affairs, from local officials and party leaders on up. Similar strata of active, influential participants could presumably be identified in all other structures of power. Since there is no theoretical reason why all members of a society might not be active and influential in at least one sphere of activity, this expanded version of elitist theory could take everyone into account.

These conceptual clarifications enable us to offer a resolution of the continuing debate between the "elitist" and "class" theories of power organization. We have

[3] Suzanne Keller, *Beyond the Ruling Class* (New York: Random House, 1963).

already broadened the idea of elites beyond politics, to include all dimensions of power in society. In a similar manner we can also broaden the idea of class beyond economics, applying it to any grouping of social actors who share common access to some resource base and hence exercise roughly equivalent kinds and amounts of power, and who are organized around their mutual interests. Given multiple dimensions of power in society, we can then expect to find numerous sets of classes on these various dimension, as well as separate bodies of strategic elites.

We bring together the ideas of classes and elites by suggesting that each class (and each set of interrelated classes on a single dimension) could have its own elites, subelites, and activists. In other words, *a class (or set of classes) provides the membership, resource, and organizational bases on which its elite positions rest and from which its elites derive their power.* The greater the resources of a particular class, of course, the more power its elites could exert throughout the society. Social classes would not be the only sources of elites in a society, since many other kinds of organizational networks would also contain their own power-wielding elites. But classes and class leaders would be examined by sociologists as major parts of the total societal power system, especially when studying social change. To the extent that social classes cut across other more specialized organizations, class-based elites could become quite powerful, but the existence of numerous separate, conflicting classes and class dimensions could prevent any one group of these elites from dominating the entire society.

Beyond demonstrating the inevitability of elites in all societies, many elitist theorists have been primarily concerned with describing the structure and composition of these elite groups—that is, how are they organized and who are their members? These are important questions, but they tell us little about the dynamic processes of power wielding by elites. A complete theory of elite power must also answer such questions as "How do elites gain and retain their positions?" and "Through what means do elites in various sectors of society exercise power?" and "What are the consequences of these power actions for the society?" The specific details of these processes will of course vary from one situation to another, but it should be possible to identify common patterns and trends.

For instance, Piet Thoenes has recently suggested that there is today a tendency in many spheres of modern societies toward a fusion of decision-making and administrative activities.[4] Positions of power and responsibility, he argues, are increasingly being taken over by technical experts who claim the right to exercise legitimate authority on the grounds that they possess special competence within their areas of specialization. To some extent this is perhaps a desirable trend, since many technical issues and problems can be resolved satisfactorily without opening them to public debate. But as more and more kinds of activities and issues become defined as "technical" rather than "political" in nature, are not all nonexperts slowly being excluded from participation in decision-making? In other words, are we not now in the process of creating many new sets of elites who derive their power

---

[4]Piet Thoenes, *The Elite in the Welfare State*, edited by J.A. Banks, translated by J.E. Bingham (New York: The Free Press, 1966).

from possession of special knowledge and skills and whose decisions cannot be challenged by nonspecialists? And if this process were carried to its extreme, might not the total society eventually become a highly efficient autocracy ruled by specialized technical experts? Thoenes' analysis can be challenged on several grounds, but it is an excellent example of a current attempt to apply elitist theory to contemporary dynamic social trends.

A final topic of heated debate among present-day elitists is whether or not the existence of powerful elites in many areas of society negates any possibility of realizing political democracy. The debate actually goes clear back to Plato and was discussed extensively by Mosca and Michels, but it still remains a central issue for elitist theorists. Both Mosca and Michels personally favored a representative form of political democracy, and maintained that it could be compatible with the existence of elites. The main target of their attack was the Marxian ideal of complete political equality, or "rule by the masses." As we have already seen, they insisted that centralized government was absolutely necessary in modern society and that this invariably created one or more sets of political elites. The only alternative in their view was mob rule, which they thoroughly rejected. Workable democracy could be preserved despite powerful political elites, Mosca believed, if there were equality of educational and other opportunities for all, if recruitment into the political elites were open and competitive, if counterelites were free to challenge the ruling political elites for power, and if there were a strong legal system of "juridical defense" to protect individual rights. Under these conditions there would be continual "circulation of elites" and viable checks upon the powers of political elites.

Present-day demands for extension of at least some forms of political equality to all persons through "participatory democracy" raise serious questions about Mosca's thesis, however. Is it not possible to involve more people in more areas of political decision-making without sacrificing the desired benefits of a dynamic central government that promotes public programs for the welfare of all? One possible resolution of this dilemma lies in the continual growth of numerous independent sets of strategic elites and activists in diverse areas of social activity, each of which would have its own autonomous resource base for exercising power. This goal underlies the pluralistic conception of society, although that conception may require expansion toward what we shall describe in a later essay as a "systemic" model of post-industrial societies.

The following reading selections on elitist theory can be divided into two sets: The first set consists of writings by Vilfredo Pareto, Gaetano Mosca, and Robert Michels, in which they state the basic tenets of classical elitist theory. Comprising the second set are selections by the contemporary sociologists Raymond Aron, T. B. Bottomore, and Piet Thoenes. They explore the applicability of elitist theory to modern societies and discuss the theoretical issues sketched in this essay.

ELITES AND FORCE

Vilfredo Pareto

Social Elites and Their Circulation. Whether certain theorists like it or not, the fact is that human society is not a homogeneous thing, that individuals are physically, morally, and intellectually different. Here we are interested in things as they actually are. Of that fact, therefore, we have to take account. And we must also take account of another fact: that the social classes are not entirely distinct, even in countries where a caste system prevails; and that in modern civilized countries circulation among the various classes is exceedingly rapid. . . .

Suppose we begin by giving a theoretical definition of the thing we are dealing with, making it as exact as possible, and then go on to see what practical considerations we can replace it with to get a first approximation. Let us for the moment completely disregard considerations as to the good or bad, useful or harmful, praiseworthy or reprehensible character of the various traits in individuals, and confine ourselves to degrees—to whether, in other words, the trait in a given case be slight, average, intense, or more exactly, to the index that may be assigned to each individual with reference to the degree, or intensity, in him of the trait in question.

Let us assume that in every branch of human activity each individual is given an index which stands as a sign of his capacity, very much the way grades are given in the various subjects in examinations in school. The highest type of lawyer, for instance, will be given 10. The man who does not get a client will be given 1—reserving zero for the man who is an out-and-out idiot. To the man who has made his millions—honestly or dishonestly as the case may be—we will give 10. To the man who has earned his thousands we will give 6; to such as just manage to keep out of the poor-house, 1, keeping zero for those who get in. To the woman "in politics," such as the Aspasia of Pericles, the Maintenon of Louis XIV, the Pompadour of Louis XV, who has managed to infatuate a man of power and play a part in the man's career, we shall give some higher number, such as 8 or 9; to the strumpet who merely satisfies the senses of such a man and exerts no influence on public affairs, we shall give zero. To a clever rascal who knows how to fool people and still keep clear of the penitentiary, we shall give 8, 9, or 10, according to the number of geese he has plucked and the amount of money he has been able to get out of them. To the sneak-thief who snatches a piece of silver from a restaurant table and runs away into the arms of a policeman, we shall give 1. To a poet like Carducci we shall give 8 or 9 according to our tastes; to a scribbler who puts people to rout with his sonnets we shall give zero. For chess-players we can get very precise

SOURCE: Vilfredo Pareto, *The Mind and Society,* trans. by A. Bongiorno and A. Livingston, ed. by A. Livingston, four volumes (New York: Harcourt, Brace, and Co., 1935), pp. 1419-1427, 1429-1432, 1512-1518, 1525-1527. Reprinted with the permission of The Pareto Fund. Most footnotes and references have been omitted, and those remaining have been renumbered.

indices, noting what matches, and how many, they have won. And so on for all the branches of human activity. . . .

In short, we are here as usual resorting to scientific analysis, which distinguishes one problem from another and studies each one separately. As usual, again, we are replacing imperceptible variations in absolutely exact numbers with the sharp variations corresponding to groupings by class, just as in examinations those who are passed are sharply and arbitrarily distinguished from those who are "failed," and just as in the matter of physical age we distinguish children from young people, the young from the aged.

So let us make a class of the people who have the highest indices in their branch of activity, and to that class give the name of *élite*.

For the particular investigation with which we are engaged, a study of the social equilibrium, it will help if we further divide that class into two classes: a *governing élite*, comprising individuals who directly or indirectly play some considerable part in government, and a *non-governing élite*, comprising the rest.[1]

A chess champion is certainly a member of the *élite*, but it is no less certain that his merits as a chess-player do not open the doors to political influence for him; and hence unless he has other qualities to win him that distinction, he is not a member of the governing *élite*. Mistresses of absolute monarchs have oftentimes been members of the *élite*, either because of their beauty or because of their intellectual endowments; but only a few of them, who have had, in addition, the particular talents required by politics, have played any part in government.

So we get two strata in a population: (1) A lower stratum, the *non-élite*, with whose possible influence on government we are not just here concerned; then (2) a higher stratum, *the élite*, which is divided into two: (a) a governing *élite*; (b) a non-governing *élite*.

In the concrete, there are no examinations whereby each person is assigned to his proper place in these various classes. That deficiency is made up for by other means, by various sorts of labels that serve the purpose after a fashion. Such labels are the rule even where there are examinations. The label "lawyer" is affixed to a man who is supposed to know something about the law and often does, though sometimes again he is an ignoramus. So, the governing *élite* contains individuals who wear labels appropriate to political offices of a certain altitude—ministers, Senators, Deputies, chief justices, generals, colonels, and so on—making the apposite exceptions for those who have found their way into that exalted company without possessing qualities corresponding to the labels they wear.

Such exceptions are much more numerous than the exceptions among lawyers, physicians, engineers, millionaires (who have made their own money), artists of

---

[1]Kolabinska, *La circulation des élites en France*, p. 5: "The outstanding idea in the term *'élite'* is 'superiority.' That is the only one I keep. I disregard secondary connotations of appreciation or as to the utility of such superiority. I am not interested here in what is desirable. I am making a simple study of what is. In a broad sense I mean by the *élite* in a society people who possess in marked degree qualities of intelligence, character, skill, capacity, of whatever kind. . . . On the other hand I entirely avoid any sort of judgment on the merits and utility of such classes. . . ."

distinction, and so on; for the reason, among others, that in these latter departments of human activity the labels are won directly by each individual, whereas in the *élite* some of the labels—the label of wealth, for instance—are hereditary. In former times there were hereditary labels in the governing *élite* also—in our day hardly more than the label of king remains in that status; but if direct inheritance has disappeared, inheritance is still powerful indirectly; and an individual who has inherited a sizable patrimony can easily be named Senator in certain countries, or can get himself elected to the parliament by buying votes or, on occasion, by wheedling voters with assurances that he is a democrat of democrats, a Socialist, an Anarchist. Wealth, family, or social connexions also help in many other cases to win the label of the *élite* in general, or of the governing *élite* in particular, for persons who otherwise hold no claim upon it.

In societies where the social unit is the family the label worn by the head of the family also benefits all other members. In Rome, the man who became Emperor generally raised his freedmen to the higher class, and oftentimes, in fact, to the governing *élite*. For that matter, now more, now fewer, of the freedmen taking part in the Roman government possessed qualities good or bad that justified their wearing the labels which they had won through imperial bounty. In our societies, the social unit is the individual; but the place that the individual occupies in society also benefits his wife, his children, his connexions, his friends. . . .

Furthermore, the manner in which the various groups in a population intermix has to be considered. In moving from one group to another an individual generally brings with him certain inclinations, sentiments, attitudes, that he has acquired in the group from which he comes, and that circumstance cannot be ignored.

To this mixing, in the particular case in which only two groups, the *élite* and the non-*élite*, are envisaged, the term "circulation of élites" has been applied[2]—in French, *circulation des élites* [or in more general terms "class-circulation"].

In conclusion we must pay special attention (1), in the case of one single group, to the proportions between the total of the group and the number of individuals who are nominally members of it but do not possess the qualities requisite for effective membership; and then (2), in the case of various groups, to the ways in which transitions from one group to the other occur, and to the intensity of that movement—that is to say, to the velocity of the circulation.

Velocity in circulation has to be considered not only absolutely but also in relation to the supply of and the demand for certain social elements. A country that is always at peace does not require many soldiers in its governing class, and the production of generals may be overexuberant as compared with the demand. But when a country is in a state of continuous warfare many soldiers are necessary, and though production remains at the same level it may not meet the demand. That, we

---

[2] [And most inappropriately, for, in this sense, the phrase never meant more than circulation within the *élite*. Furthermore, the *élite* is not the only class to be considered, and the principles that apply to circulation within the *élite* apply to circulation within such lower classes as one may choose for one purpose or another to consider.—A.L.]

might note in passing, has been one of the causes for the collapse of many aristocracies.[3] . . .

Higher Class and Lower Class in General.   The least we can do is to divide society into two strata: a higher stratum, which usually contains the rulers, and a lower stratum, which usually contains the ruled. That fact is so obvious that it has always forced itself even upon the most casual observation, and so for the circulation of individuals between the two strata. Even Plato had an inkling of class-circulation and tried to regulate it artificially. The "new man," the upstart, the *parvenu,* has always been a subject of interest, and literature has analyzed him unendingly. Here, then we are merely giving a more exact form to things that have long been perceived more or less vaguely. . . .

The upper stratum of society, the *élite,* nominally contains certain groups of peoples, not always very sharply defined, that are called aristocracies. There are cases in which the majority of individuals belonging to such aristocracies actually possess the qualities requisite for remaining there; and then again there are cases where considerable numbers of the individuals making up the class do not possess those requisites. Such people may occupy more or less important places in the governing *élite* or they may be barred from it.

In the beginning, military, religious, and commercial aristocracies and plutocracies—with a few exceptions not worth considering—must have constituted parts of the governing *élite* and sometimes have made up the whole of it. The victorious warrior, the prosperous merchant, the opulent plutocrat, were men of such parts, each in his own field, as to be superior to the average individual. Under those circumstances the label corresponded to an actual capacity. But as time goes by, considerable, sometimes very considerable, differences arise between the capacity and the label; while on the other hand, certain aristocracies originally figuring prominently in the rising *élite* end by constituting an insignificant element in it. That has happened especially to military aristocracies.

Aristocracies do not last. Whatever the causes, it is an incontestable fact that after a certain length of time they pass away. History is a graveyard of aristocracies. The Athenian "People" was an aristocracy as compared with the remainder of a population of resident aliens and slaves. It vanished without leaving any descent. The various aristocracies of Rome vanished in their time. So did the aristocracies of the Barbarians. Where, in France, are the descendants of the Frankish conquerors? The genealogies of the English nobility have been very exactly kept; and they show that very few families still remain to claim descent from the comrades of William the Conqueror. The rest have vanished. In Germany the aristocracy of the present

---

[3]Kolabinska, *op. cit.,* p. 10: "Inadequate recruiting in the *élite* does not result from a mere numerical proportion between new members and old. Account has to be taken of the number of persons who possess the qualities required for membership in the governing *élite* but are refused admittance; or else, in an opposite direction, the number of new members the *élite* might require but does not get. In the first case, the production of persons possessing unusual qualities as regards education may far surpass the number of such persons that the *élite* can accommodate, and then we get what has been called an 'intellectual proletariat.' "

day is very largely made up of descendants of vassals of the lords of old. The populations of European countries have increased enormously during the past few centuries. It is as certain as certain can be that the aristocracies have not increased in proportion.

They decay not in numbers only. They decay also in quality, in the sense that they lose their vigour, that there is a decline in the proportions of the residues which enabled them to win their power and hold it. The governing class is restored not only in numbers, but—and that is the more important thing—in quality, by families rising from the lower classes and bringing with them the vigour and the proportions of residues necessary for keeping themselves in power. It is also restored by the loss of its more degenerate members.

If one of those movements comes to an end, or worse still, if they both come to an end, the governing class crashes to ruin and often sweeps the whole of a nation along with it. Potent cause of disturbance in the equilibrium is the accumulation of superior elements in the lower classes and, conversely, of inferior elements in the higher classes. If human aristocracies were like thorough-breds among animals, which reproduce themselves over long periods of time with approximately the same traits, the history of the human race would be something altogether different from the history we know.

In virtue of class-circulation, the governing *élite* is always in a state of slow and continuous transformation. It flows on like a river, never being today what it was yesterday. From time to time sudden and violent disturbances occur. There is a flood—the river overflows its banks. Afterwards, the new governing *élite* again resumes its slow transformation. The flood has subsided, the river is again flowing normally in its wonted bed.

Revolutions come about through accumulations in the higher strata of society—either because of a slowing-down in class-circulation, or from other causes—of decadent elements no longer possessing the residues suitable for keeping them in power, and shrinking from the use of force; while meantime in the lower strata of society elements of superior quality are coming to the fore, possessing residues suitable for exercising the functions of government and willing enough to use force.

In general, in revolutions the members of the lower strata are captained by leaders from the higher strata, because the latter possess the intellectual qualities required for outlining a tactic, while lacking the combative residue supplied by the individuals from the lower strata.

Violent movements take place by fits and starts, and effects therefore do not follow immediately on their causes. After a governing class, or a nation, has maintained itself for long periods of time on force and acquired great wealth, it may subsist for some time still without using force, buying off its adversaries and paying not only in gold, but also in terms of the dignity and respect that it had formerly enjoyed and which constitute, as it were, a capital. In the first stages of decline, power is maintained by bargainings and concessions, and people are so deceived into thinking that the policy can be carried on indefinitely. So the decadent Roman Empire bought peace of the Barbarians with money and honours.

So Louis XVI, in France, squandering in a very short time an ancestral inheritance of love, respect, and almost religious reverence for the monarchy, managed, by making repeated concessions, to be the King of the Revolution. So the English aristocracy managed to prolong its term of power in the second half of the nineteenth century down to the dawn of its decadence, which was heralded by the "Parliament Bill" in the first years of the twentieth. . . .

The Use of Force in Society. To ask whether or not force ought to be used in a society, whether the use of force is or is not beneficial, is to ask a question that has no meaning; for force is used by those who wish to preserve certain uniformities and by those who wish to overstep them; and the violence of the ones stands in contrast and in conflict with the violence of the others. In truth, if a partisan of a governing class disavows the use of force, he means that he disavows the use of force by insurgents trying to escape from the norms of the given uniformity. On the other hand, if he says he approves of the use of force, what he really means is that he approves of the use of force by the public authority to constrain insurgents to conformity. Conversely, if a partisan of the subject class says he detests the use of force in society, what he really detests is the use of force by constituted authorities in forcing dissidents to conform; and if, instead, he lauds the use of force, he is thinking of the use of force by those who would break away from certain social uniformities.

Nor is there any particular meaning in the question as to whether the use of violence to enforce existing uniformities is beneficial to society, or whether it is beneficial to use force in order to overstep them; for the various uniformities have to be distinguished to see which of them are beneficial and which deleterious to society. . . . So, to solve the problem as to the use of force, it is not enough to solve the other problem as to the utility, in general, of certain types of social organization; it is essential also and chiefly to compute all the advantages and all the drawbacks, direct and indirect. Such a course leads to the solution of a scientific problem; but it may not be and oftentimes is not the course that leads to an increase in social utility. . . .

What now are the correlations that subsist between this method of applying force and other social facts? We note, as usual, a sequence of actions and reactions, in which the use of force appears now as cause, now as effect. As regards the governing class, one gets, in the main, five groups of facts to consider: (1) A mere handful of citizens, so long as they are willing to use violence, can force their will upon public officials who are not inclined to meet violence with equal violence. If the reluctance of the officials to resort to force is primarily motivated by humanitarian sentiments, that result ensues very readily; but if they refrain from violence because they deem it wiser to use some other means, the effect is often the following: (2) To prevent or resist violence, the governing class resorts to "diplomacy," fraud, corruption—governmental authority passes, in a word, from the lions to the foxes. The governing class bows its head under the threat of violence, but it surrenders only in appearance, trying to turn the flank of the obstacle it cannot demolish in frontal attack. In the long run that sort of procedure comes to exercise a far-reaching influence on the selection of the governing class, which is now recruited only from the foxes, while the lions are blackballed. The individual who best knows the arts of sapping the strength of the foes of "graft" and of winning back by fraud and deceit what seemed to have been surrendered under pressure of force, is now leader of leaders. The man who has bursts of rebellion, and does not know how to crook his spine at the proper times and places, is the worst of leaders, and his presence is tolerated among them only if other distinguished endowments offset that defect. (3) So it comes about that the residues of the combination-instinct (Class I) are intensified in the governing class, and the residues of group-persistence (Class II) debilitated; for the combination-residues supply, precisely, the artistry and resourcefulness required for evolving ingenious expedients as substitutes for open resistance, while the residues of group-persistence stimulate open resistance, since a strong sentiment of group-persistence cures the spine of all tendencies to curvature. (4) Policies of the governing class are not planned too far ahead in time. Predominance of the combination instincts and enfeeblement of the sentiments of group-persistence result in making the governing class more satisfied with the present and less thoughtful of the future. The individual comes to prevail, and by far, over family, community, nation. Material interests and interests of the present or a near future come to prevail over the ideal interests of community or nation and interests of the distant future. The impulse is to enjoy the present without too much thought for the morrow. (5) Some of these phenomena become observable in international relations as well. Wars become essentially economic. Efforts are made to avoid conflicts with the powerful and the sword is rattled only before the weak. Wars are regarded more than anything else as speculations. A country is often unwittingly edged towards war by nursings of economic conflicts which, it is expected, will never get out of control and turn into armed conflicts. Not seldom, however, a war will be forced upon a country by peoples who are not so far advanced in the evolution that leads to the predominance of Class I residues.

As regards the subject class, we get the following relations, which correspond in part to the preceding: (1) When the subject class contains a number of individuals disposed to use force and with capable leaders to guide them, the governing class is, in many cases, overthrown and another takes its place. That is easily the case where governing classes are inspired by humanitarian sentiments primarily, and very very easily if they do not find ways to assimilate the exceptional individuals who come to the front in the subject classes. A humanitarian aristocracy that is closed or stiffly exclusive represents the maximum of insecurity. (2) It is far more difficult to overthrow a governing class that is adept in the shrewd use of chicanery, fraud, corruption; and in the highest degree difficult to overthrow such a class when it successfully assimilates most of the individuals in the subject class who show those same talents, are adept in those same arts, and might therefore become the leaders of such plebeians as are disposed to use violence. Thus left without leadership, without talent, disorganized, the subject class is almost always powerless to set up any lasting regime. (3) So the combination-residues (Class I) become to some extent enfeebled in the subject class. But that phenomenon is in no way comparable to the corresponding reinforcement of those same residues in the governing class; for the governing class being composed, as it is, of a much smaller number of individuals, changes considerably in character from the addition to it or withdrawal from it of relatively small numbers of individuals; whereas shifts of identical numbers produce but slight effects in the enormously greater total of the subject class. For that matter the subject class is still left with many individuals possessed of combination-instincts that are applied not to politics or activities connected with politics but to arts and trades independent of polities. That circumstance lends stability to societies, for the governing class is required to absorb only a small number of new individuals in order to keep the subject class deprived of leadership. However, in the long run the differences in temperament between the governing class and the subject class become gradually accentuated, the combination-instincts tending to predominate in the ruling class, and instincts of group-persistence in the subject class. When that difference becomes sufficiently great, revolution occurs. (4) Revolution often transfers power to a new governing class, which exhibits a reinforcement in its instincts of group-persistence and so adds to its designs of present enjoyment aspirations towards ideal enjoyments presumably attainable at some future time—scepticism in part gives way to faith. (5) These considerations must to some extent be applied to international relations. If the combination-instincts are reinforced in a given country beyond a certain limit, as compared with the instincts of group-persistence, that country may be easily vanquished in war by another country in which that change in relative proportions has not occurred. The potency of an ideal as a pilot to victory is observable in both civil and international strife. People who lose the habit of applying force, who acquire the habit of considering policy from a commercial standpoint and of judging it only in terms of profit and loss, can readily be induced to purchase peace; and it may well be that such a transaction taken by itself is a good one, for war might have cost more money than the price of peace. Yet experience shows that in the long run, and taken in connexion with the things that inevitably go with it, such practice leads a country to ruin. The combination-instincts rarely come to prevail in the whole of a population. More commonly that situation arises in the upper strata of society, there being few if any traces of it in the lower and more populous classes. So when a war breaks out one gazes in amazement on the energies that are suddenly manifested by the masses at large, something that could in no way have been foreseen by studying the upper classes only. . . .

Ruling-class theories, when the requirement of logic is not too keenly felt, appeal simply to sentiments of veneration for holders of power, or for abstractions such as "the state," and to sentiments of disapprobation for individuals who try to disturb or subvert existing orders. Then when it is deemed advisable to satisfy the need of logic, the effort is to create a confusion between the violation of an established uniformity for the individual's exclusive profit and a violation designed to further some collective interest or some new uniformity. The aim in such a derivation is to carry over to the social or political act the reprobation that is generally visited upon common crime. Frequent in our day are reasonings in some way connected with the theology of Progress. Not a few of our modern governments have revolutionary origins. How condemn the revolutions that might be tried against them without repudiating the forefathers? That is attended to by invoking a new divine right:

Insurrection was legitimate enough against governments of the past, where authority was based on force; it is not legitimate against modern governments, where the authority is based on "reason." Or else: Insurrection was legitimate against kings and oligarchies; it is never legitimate against "the People." Or again: Rebellion is justifiable where there is no universal suffrage, but not where that panacea is the law of the land. Or again: Revolt is useless and therefore reprehensible in all countries where "the People" are able to express their "will." Then finally—just to give some little satisfaction to their Graces, the Metaphysicists: Insurrection cannot be tolerated where a "state of law" exists. . . .

Again as usual, no one of these derivations has any exact meaning. All governments use force, and all assert that they are founded on reason. In the fact, whether universal suffrage prevails or not, it is always an oligarchy that governs, finding ways to give to the "will of the people" that expression which the few desire, from the "royal law" that bestowed the *imperium* on the Roman Emperors down to the votes of a legislative majority elected in one way or another, from the plebiscite that gave the empire to Napoleon III down to the universal suffrage that is shrewdly bought, steered, and manipulated by our "speculators." Who is this new god called Universal Suffrage? He is no more exactly definable, no less shrouded in mystery, no less beyond the pale of reality, than the hosts of other divinities; nor are there fewer and less patent contradictions in his theology than in theirs. Worshippers of Universal Suffrage are not led by their god. It is they who lead him—and by the nose, determining the sanctity of "majority rule," they resist "majority rule" by obstructionist tactics, even though they form but small minorities, and burning incense to the goddess Reason, they in no wise disdain, in certain cases, alliances with Chicanery, Fraud, and Corruption.

Substantially such derivations express the sentiments felt by people who have climbed into the saddle and are willing to stay there—along with the far more general sentiment that social stability is a good thing. If, the moment a group, large or small, ceased to be satisfied with certain norms established in the community of which it is a part, it flew to arms to abolish them, organized society would fall to pieces. Social stability is so beneficial a thing that to maintain it it is well worth while to enlist the aid of fantastic ideals and this or that theology—among the others, the theology of universal suffrage—and be resigned to putting up with certain actual disadvantages. Before it becomes advisable to disturb the public peace, such disadvantages must have grown very very serious; and since human beings are effectively guided not by the sceptical reasonings of science but by "living faiths" expressed in ideals, theories such as the divine right of kings, the legitimacy of oligarchies, of "the people," of "majorities," of legislative assemblies, and other such things, may be useful within certain limits, and have in fact proved to be, however absurd they may be from the scientific standpoint.

Theories designed to justify the use of force by the governed are almost always combined with theories condemning the use of force by the public authority. A few dreamers reject the use of force in general, on whatever side; but their theories either have no influence at all or else serve merely to weaken resistance on the part of people in power, so clearing the field for violence on the part of the governed. . . .

THE RULING CLASS

Gaetano Mosca

Among the constant facts and tendencies that are to be found in all political organisms, one is so obvious that it is apparent to the most casual eye. In all societies—from societies that are very meagerly developed and have barely attained the dawnings of civilization, down to the most advanced and powerful societies— two classes of people appear—a class that rules and a class that is ruled. The first class, always the less numerous, performs all political functions, monopolizes power and enjoys the advantages that power brings, whereas the second, the more numerous class, is directed and controlled by the first, in a manner that is now more or less legal, now more or less arbitrary and violent, and supplies the first, in appearance at least, with material means of subsistence and with the instrumentalities that are essential to the vitality of the political organism.

In practical life we all recognize the existence of this ruling class (or political class, as we have elsewhere chosen to define it). We all know that, in our own country, whichever it may be, the management of public affairs is in the hands of a minority of influential persons, to which management, willingly or unwillingly, the majority defer. We know that the same thing goes on in neighboring countries, and in fact we should be put to it to conceive of a real world otherwise organized—a world in which all men would be directly subject to a single person without relationships of superiority or subordination, or in which all men would share equally in the direction of political affairs. If we reason otherwise in theory, that is due partly to the exaggerated importance that we attach to two political facts that loom far larger in appearance than they are in reality.

The first of these facts—and one has only to open one's eyes to see it—is that in every political organism there is one individual who is chief among the leaders of the ruling class as a whole and stands, as we say, at the helm of the state. That person is not always the person who holds supreme power according to law. At times, alongside of the hereditary king or emperor there is a prime minister or a major-domo who wields an actual power that is greater than the sovereign's. At other times, in place of the elected president the influential politician who has procured the president's election will govern. Under special circumstances there may be, instead of a single person, two or three who discharge the functions of supreme control.

The second fact, too, is readily discernible. Whatever the type of political organization, pressures arising from the discontent of the masses who are governed, from the passions by which they are swayed, exert a certain amount of influence on the policies of the ruling, the political, class.

SOURCE: Modified from *The Ruling Class,* by Gaetano Mosca, pp. 50, 51, 53, 56, 57, 59-68, 70-72, 80, 81, 83-85, 103, 105-107, 116-119, 121-123, 125, 126, 130, 139, 141-147. Copyright, 1939, McGraw-Hill, Inc. Used with permission of McGraw-Hill Book Company. Footnotes have been omitted.

But the man who is at the head of the state would certainly not be able to govern without the support of a numerous class to enforce respect for his orders and to have them carried out; and granting that he can make one individual, or indeed many individuals, in the ruling class feel the weight of his power, he certainly cannot be at odds with the class as a whole or do away with it. Even if that were possible, he would at once be forced to create another class, without the support of which action on his part would be completely paralyzed. On the other hand, granting that the discontent of the masses might succeed in deposing a ruling class, inevitably, as we shall later show, there would have to be another organized minority within the masses themselves to discharge the functions of a ruling class. Otherwise all organization, and the whole social structure, would be destroyed.

From the point of view of scientific research the real superiority of the concept of the ruling, or political, class lies in the fact that the varying structure of ruling classes has a preponderant importance in determining the political type, and also the level of civilization, of the different peoples. . . .

We think it may be desirable, nevertheless, to reply at this point to an objection which might very readily be made to our point of view. If it is easy to understand that a single individual cannot command a group without finding within the group a minority to support him, it is rather difficult to grant, as a constant and natural fact, that minorities rule majorities, rather than majorities minorities. But that is one of the points—so numerous in all the other sciences—where the first impression one has of things is contrary to what they are in reality. In reality the dominion of an organized minority, obeying a single impulse, over the unorganized majority, is inevitable. The power of any minority is irresistible as against each single individual in the majority, who stands alone before the totality of the organized minority. At the same time, the minority is organized for the very reason that it is a minority. A hundred men acting uniformly in concert, with a common understanding, will triumph over a thousand men who are not in accord and can therefore be dealt with one by one. Meanwhile it will be easier for the former to act in concert and have a mutual understanding simply because they are a hundred and not a thousand. It follows that the larger the political community, the smaller will the proportion of the governing minority to the governed majority be, and the more difficult will it be for the majority to organize for reaction against the minority.

However, in addition to the great advantage accruing to them from the fact of being organized, ruling minorities are usually so constituted that the individuals who make them up are distinguished from the mass of the governed by qualities that give them a certain material, intellectual or even moral superiority; or else they are the heirs of individuals who possessed such qualities. In other words, members of a ruling minority regularly have some attribute, real or apparent, which is highly esteemed and very influential in the society in which they live. . . .

Everywhere—in Russia and Poland, in India and medieval Europe—the ruling warrior classes acquire almost exclusive ownership of the land. Land, as we have seen, is the chief source of production and wealth in countries that are not very far advanced in civilization. But as civilization progresses, revenue from land increases proportionately. With the growth of population there is, at least in certain periods, an increase in rent, in the Ricardian sense of the term, largely because great centers of consumption arise—such at all times have been the great capitals and other large cities, ancient and modern. Eventually, if other circumstances permit, a very important social transformation occurs. Wealth rather than military valor comes to be the characteristic feature of the dominant class: the people who rule are the rich rather than the brave.

The condition that in the main is required for this transformation is that social organization shall have concentrated and become perfected to such an extent that the protection offered by public authority is considerably more effective than the protection offered by private force. In other words, private property must be so well protected by the practical and real efficacy of the laws as to render the power of the proprietor himself superfluous. This comes about through a series of gradual alterations in the social structure whereby a type of political organization, which we shall call the "feudal state," is transformed into an essentially different type, which we shall term the "bureaucratic state.". . .

Once this transformation has taken place, wealth produces political power just as political power has been producing wealth. In a society already somewhat mature—where, therefore, individual power is curbed by the collective power—if the powerful are as a rule the rich, to be rich is to become powerful. And, in truth, when fighting with the mailed fist is prohibited whereas fighting with pounds and pence is sanctioned, the better posts are inevitably won by those who are better supplied with pounds and pence. . . .

In societies in which religious beliefs are strong and ministers of the faith form a special class a priestly aristocracy almost always arises and gains possession of a more or less important share of the wealth and the political power. Conspicuous examples of that situation would be ancient Egypt (during certain periods), Brahman India and medieval Europe. Oftentimes the priests not only perform religious functions. They possess legal and scientific knowledge and constitute the class of highest intellectual culture. Consciously or unconsciously, priestly hierarchies often show a tendency to monopolize learning and hamper the dissemination of the methods and procedures that make the acquisition of knowledge possible and easy. . . .

Specialized knowledge and really scientific culture, purged of any sacred or religious aura, become important political forces only in a highly advanced stage of civilization, and only then do they give access to membership in the ruling class to those who possess them. But in this case too, it is not so much learning in itself that has political value as the practical applications that may be made of learning to the profit of the public or the state. . . .

There are examples in abundance where we see that longstanding practice in directing the military and civil organization of a community creates and develops in the higher reaches of the ruling class a real art of governing which is something better than crude empiricism and better than anything that mere individual experience could suggest. In such circumstances aristocracies of functionaries arise, such as the Roman senate, the Venetian nobility and to a certain extent the English aristocracy. . . . However, even if the art of governing has now and again enjoyed prestige with certain classes of persons who have long held possession of political functions, knowledge of it has never served as an ordinary criterion for admitting to public offices persons who were barred from them by social station. The degree of mastery of the art of governing that a person possesses is, moreover, apart from exceptional cases, a very difficult thing to determine if the person has given no practical demonstration that he possesses it.

In some countries we find hereditary castes. In such cases the governing class is explicitly restricted to a given number of families, and birth is the one criterion that determines entry into the class or exclusion from it. Examples are exceedingly common. There is practically no country of long-standing civilization that has not had a hereditary aristocracy at one period or another in its history. . . .

In this connection two preliminary observations are in point. In the first place, all ruling classes tend to become hereditary in fact if not in law. All political forces seem to possess a quality that in physics used to be called the force of inertia. They have a tendency, that is, to remain at the point and in the state in which they find themselves. Wealth and military valor are easily maintained in certain families by moral tradition and by heredity. Qualification for important office—the habit of, and to an extent the capacity for, dealing with affairs of consequence—is much more readily acquired when one has had a certain familiarity with them from childhood. Even when academic degrees, scientific training, special aptitudes as tested by examinations and competitions, open the way to public office, there is no eliminating that special advantage in favor of certain individuals which the French call the advantage of *positions déjà prises.* In actual fact, though examinations and competitions may theoretically be open to all, the majority never have the resources for meeting the expense of long preparation, and many others are without the connections and kinships that set an individual promptly on the right road, enabling him to avoid the groping and blunders that are inevitable when one enters an unfamiliar environment without any guidance or support.

The democratic principle of election by broad-based suffrage would seem at first glance to be in conflict with the tendency toward stability which, according to our theory, ruling classes show. But it must be noted that candidates who are successful in democratic elections are almost always the ones who possess the political forces above enumerated, which are very often hereditary. In the English, French and Italian parliaments we frequently see the sons, grandsons, brothers, nephews and sons-in-law of members and deputies, ex-members and ex-deputies.

In the second place, when we see a hereditary caste established in a country and monpolizing political power, we may be sure that such a status de jure was preceded by a similar status de facto. Before proclaiming their exclusive and hereditary right to power the families or castes in question must have held the scepter of command in a firm grasp, completely monopolizing all the political forces of that country at that period. Otherwise such a claim on their part would only have aroused the bitterest protests and provoked the bitterest struggles.

Hereditary aristocracies often come to vaunt supernatural origins, or at least origins different from, and superior to, those of the governed classes. Such claims are explained by a highly significant social fact, namely that every governing class tends to justify its actual exercise of power by resting it on some universal moral principle. This same sort of claim has come forward in our time in scientific trappings. A number of writers, developing and amplifying Darwin's theories, contend that upper classes represent a higher level in social evolution and are therefore superior to lower classes by organic structure. . . .

Now history very definitely shows the special abilities as well as the special defects—both very marked—which have been displayed by aristocracies that have either remained absolutely closed or have made entry into their circles difficult. The ancient Roman patriciate and the English and German nobilities of modern times give a ready idea of the type we refer to. Yet in dealing with this fact, and with the theories that tend to exaggerate its significance, we can always raise the same objection—that the individuals who belong to the aristocracies in question owe their special qualities not so much to the blood that flows in their veins as to their very particular upbringing, which has brought out certain intellectual and moral tendencies in them in preference to others.

Among all the factors that figure in social superiority, intellectual superiority is the one with which heredity has least to do. The children of men of highest mentality often have very mediocre talents. That is why hereditary aristocracies have never defended their rule on the basis of intellectual superiority alone, but rather on the basis of their superiorities in character and wealth.

It is argued, in rebuttal, that education and environment may serve to explain superiorities in strictly intellectual capacities but not differences of a moral order—will power, courage, pride, energy. The truth is that social position, family tradition, the habits of the class in which we live, contribute more than is commonly supposed to the greater or lesser development of the qualities mentioned. . . .

Courage in battle, impetuousness in attack, endurance in resistance—such are the qualities that have long and often been vaunted as a monopoly of the higher classes. Certainly there may be vast natural and—if we may say so—innate differences between one individual and another in these respects; but more than anything else traditions and environmental influences are the things that keep them high, low or just average, in any large group of human beings. . . .

What we see is that as soon as there is a shift in the balance of political forces—when, that is, a need is felt that capacities different from the old should assert themselves in the management of the state, when the old capacities, therefore, lose some of their importance or changes in their distribution occur—then the manner in which the ruling class is constituted changes also. If a new source of wealth develops in a society, if the practical importance of knowledge grows, if an old religion declines or a new one is born, if a new current of ideas spreads, then, simultaneously, far-reaching dislocations occur in the ruling class. One might say, indeed, that the whole history of civilized mankind comes down to a conflict between the tendency of dominant elements to monopolize political power and transmit possession of it by inheritance, and the tendency toward a dislocation of old forces and in insurgence of new forces; and this conflict produces an unending ferment of endosmosis and exosmosis between the upper classes and certain portions of the lower. Ruling classes decline inevitably when they cease to find scope for the capacities through which they rose to power, when they can no longer render the social services which they once rendered, or when their talents and the services they render lose in importance in the social environment in which they live. . . .

The ruling class may also be vanquished and destroyed in whole or in part by foreign invasions, or, when the circumstances just mentioned arise, it may be driven from power by the advent of new social elements who are strong in fresh political forces. Then, naturally, there comes a period of renovation, or, if one prefer, of revolution, during which individual energies have free play and certain individuals, more passionate, more energetic, more intrepid or merely shrewder than others, force their way from the bottom of the social ladder to the topmost rungs.

Once such a movement has set in, it cannot be stopped immediately. The example of individuals who have started from nowhere and reached prominent positions fires new ambitions, new greeds, new energies, and this molecular rejuvenation of the ruling class continues vigorously until a long period of social stability slows it down again. We need hardly mention examples of nations in such periods of renovation. . . .

Suppose now that a society gradually passes from its feverish state to calm. Since the human being's psychological tendencies are always the same, those who belong to the ruling class will begin to acquire a group spirit. They will become more and more exclusive and learn better and better the art of monopolizing to their advantage the qualities and capacities that are essential to acquiring power and holding it. Then, at last, the force that is essentially conservative appears—the force of habit. Many people become resigned to a lowly station, while the members of certain privileged families or classes grow convinced that they have almost an absolute right to high station and command. . . .

Feudal and Bureaucratic Systems. As we have just seen, in fairly populous societies that have attained a certain level of civilization, ruling classes do not justify their power exclusively by de facto possession of it, but try to find a moral and legal basis for it, representing it as the logical and necessary consequence of doctrines and beliefs that are generally recognized and accepted. . . .

This legal and moral basis, or principle, on which the power of the political class rests, is what we have elsewhere called, and shall continue here to call, the "political formula.". . . The political formula can hardly be the same in two or more different societies; and fundamental or even notable similarities between two or more political formulas appear only where the peoples professing them have the same type of civilization (or—to use an expression which we shall shortly define—belong to the same social type). According to the level of civilization in the peoples among whom they are current, the various political formulas may be based either upon supernatural beliefs or upon concepts which, if they do not correspond to positive realities, at least appear to be rational. We shall not say that they correspond in either case to scientific truths. A conscientious observer would be obliged to confess that, if no one has ever seen the authentic document by which the Lord empowered certain privileged persons or families to rule his people on his behalf, neither can it be maintained that a popular election, however liberal the suffrage may be, is ordinarily the expression of the will of a people, or even of the will of the majority of a people.

And yet that does not mean that political formulas are mere quackeries aptly invented to trick the masses into obedience. Anyone who viewed them in that light would fall into grave error. The truth is that they answer a real need in man's social nature; and this need, so universally felt, of governing and knowing that one is governed not on the basis of mere material or intellectual force, but on the basis of a moral principle, has beyond any doubt a practical and a real importance. . . .

Mankind is divided into social groups each of which is set apart from other groups by beliefs, sentiments, habits and interests that are peculiar to it. The individuals who belong to one such group are held together by a consciousness of common brotherhood and held apart from other groups by passions and tendencies that are more or less antagonistic and mutually repellent. As we have already indicated, the political formulas must be based upon the special beliefs and the strongest sentiments of the social group in which it is current, or at least upon the beliefs and sentiments of the particular portion of that group which holds political preeminence.

This phenomenon—the existence of social groups each of which has characteristics peculiar to itself and often presumes absolute superiority over other groups. . .—has been recognized and studied by many writers, and particularly by modern scholars, in dealing with the principle of nationality. . . . Actually, moreover, in the formation of the group, or social type, many other elements besides a more or less certain racial affinity figure—for example, community of language, of religion, of interests, and the recurring relationships that result from geographical situation. It is not necessary that all these factors be present at one and the same time, for community of history—a life that is lived for centuries in common, with identical or similar experiences, engendering similar moral and intellectual habits, similar passions and memories—often becomes the chief element in the development of a conscious social type.

Before we proceed any further, it might be wise to linger briefly on the two types into which, in our opinion, all political organisms may be classified, the feudal and the bureaucratic.

This classification, it should be noted, is not based upon essential, unchanging criteria. It is not our view that there is any psychological law peculiar to either one of the two types and therefore alien to the other. It seems to us, rather, that the two types are just different manifestations, different phases, of a single constant tendency whereby human societies become less simple, or, if one will, more complicated in political organization, as they grow in size and are perfected in civilization. Level of civilization is, on the whole, more important in this regard than size, since, in actual fact, a literally huge state may once have been feudally organized. At bottom, therefore, a bureaucratic state is just a feudal state that has advanced and developed in organization and so grown more complex; and a feudal state may derive from a once bureaucratized society that has decayed in civilization and reverted to a simpler, more primitive form of political organization, perhaps falling to pieces in the process.

By "feudal state" we mean that type of political organization in which all the executive functions of society—the economic, the judicial, the administrative, the military—are exercised simultaneously by the same individuals, while at the same time the state is made up of small social aggregates, each of which possesses all the organs that are required for self-sufficiency. The Europe of the Middle Ages offers the most familiar example of this type of organization—that is why we have chosen to designate it by the term "feudal"; but as one reads the histories of other peoples or scans the accounts of travelers of our own day one readily perceives that the type is widespread. . . .

In the bureaucratic state not all the executive functions need to be concentrated in the bureaucracy and exercised by it. One might even declare that so far in history that has never been the case. The main characteristic of this type of social organization lies, we believe, in the fact that, wherever it exists, the central power conscripts a considerable portion of the social wealth by taxation and uses it first to maintain a military establishment and then to support a more or less extensive number of public services. The greater the number of officials who perform public duties and receive their salaries from the central government or from its local agencies, the more bureaucratic a society becomes.

In a bureaucratic state there is always a greater specialization in the functions of government than in a feudal state. The first and most elementary division of capacities is the withdrawal of administrative and judiciary powers from the military element. The bureaucratic state, furthermore, assures a far greater discipline in all grades of political, administrative and military service. . . . The personal qualities of the supreme head exert relatively little influence on the destinies of a bureaucratic state. A society that is bureaucratically organized may retain its freedom even if it repudiates an old political formula and adopts a new one, or even if it subjects its social type to very far-reaching modifications. . . .

Bureaucratic organization need not necessarily be centralized, in the sense commonly given to that expression. Often bureaucratization is compatible with a very liberal provincial autonomy, as in China, where the eighteen strictly Chinese provinces preserved broad autonomous privileges and the capital city of each province looked after almost all provincial affairs.

States of European civilization—even the most decentralized of them—are all bureaucratized. As we have already indicated, the chief characteristic of a bureaucratic organization is that its military functions, and other public services in numbers more or less large, are exercised by salaried employees. Whether salaries are paid exclusively by the central government or in part by local bodies more or less under the control of the central government is a detail that is not as important as it is often supposed to be . . . . But when vast human organisms, spreading over huge territories and comprising millions and millions of individuals, are involved, nothing short of bureaucratic organization seems capable of uniting under a single impulse the immense treasures of economic power and moral and intellectual energy with which a ruling class can in a measure modify conditions within a society and make its influence effective and powerful beyond its own frontiers. Under a feudal organization the authority which a given member of the ruling class exerts over individuals of the subject class, few or many, may be more direct, oppressive, and arbitrary. Under a bureaucratic organization society is influenced less by the given individual leader than by the ruling class as a whole . . . .

Ruling Class and Social Type. We have just seen that every social type has a tendency to concentrate into a single political organism. We must now add that the political organism, in expanding, almost always aims at spreading its own social type, and often succeeds in doing so. . . .

When a state is made up of a mixture of social types, the ruling class should be recruited almost entirely from the dominant type; and if that rule is not observed, because the dominant type is too weak either in numbers or in moral and intellectual energies, then the country may be looked upon as a sick country that stands on the brink of serious political upheavals. . . .

When a number of differing social types are mixed together in one state, a directing, if not strictly a ruling, class almost inevitably develops within the types that are in subjection. Sometimes this class is the first to be absorbed by the ruling type. . . . The case where several social types coexist in guises more or less masked within a single political organism may be noted in countries that present all the appearances of strong social unity. This situation arises whenever the political formula, on which the ruling class in a given society bases its dominion, is not accessible to the lower classes, or when the complex of beliefs and moral and philosophical principles that underlie the formula have not sunk deeply enough into the consciousness of the more populous and less well educated strata of society. The same thing occurs when there is any considerable difference between the customs, culture and habits of the ruling class and those of the governed classes. . . .

As a rule it is the very ancient political formulas, complexes of beliefs and sentiments which have the sanction of the ages, that succeed in making their way into the lowest strata of human societies. On the other hand, when rapid flows of ideas agitate the higher classes, or the more active intellectual centers, which are generally located in large cities, the lower classes and the outlying districts of a state are likely to be left behind, and differing social types tend to form inside the society. . . .

Psychological and intellectual isolation on the part of the lower classes, as well as too noticeable differences in beliefs and education between the various social classes, give rise to social phenomena that are very interesting to the student of the political sciences, dangerous as they may be to the societies in which they occur.

In the first place, as a consequence of their isolation, within the lower classes another ruling class, or directing minority, necessarily forms, and often this new class is antagonistic to the class that holds possession of the legal government. When this class of plebeian leaders is well organized it may seriously embarrass an official government. . . .

In the second place, whenever and wherever a section of the ruling class tries to overthrow the legal government, whether because of conversion to a new political formula or for some other reason, it always seeks the support of the lower classes, and these readily follow its lead when they are hostile or indifferent to the established order. This alliance is so often struck that the plebs becomes an essential instrument in almost all upheavals and revolutions, and to the same alliance also is due the fact that we so often find men from the higher social levels leading popular movements. Yet the opposite phenomenon also appears at times. The portion of the ruling class that is holding power and resisting the revolutionary current may find its main support in the lower classes, which still cling loyally to old ideas and to the old social type. . . .

But the most dangerous among the consequences that may result from differences in social type between the various social classes, and from the reciprocal isolation of classes that necessarily follows in their wake, is a decline in energy in the upper classes, which grow poorer and poorer in bold and aggressive characters and richer and richer in "soft," remissive individuals. We have seen that that development is practically impossible in a state of the feudal type. In a society that is broken up into virtually independent fragments the heads of the individual groups have to be energetic, resourceful men. Their supremacy in large measure depends on their own physical or moral strength, which, moreover, they are continually exercising in struggles with their immediate neighbors. As social organization progresses and the governing class begins to reap the benefits of an improved bureaucratic machine, its superiority in culture and wealth, and especially its better organization and firmer cohesion, may compensate to some extent for the lack of individual energy; and so it may come about that considerable portions of the governing class, especially the circles that give the society its intellectual tone and direction, lose the habit of dealing with people of the lower classes and commanding them directly. . . .

A ruling class is the more prone to fall into errors of this kind the more closed it is, actually if not legally, to elements rising from the lower classes. In the lower classes the hard necessities of life, the unending and carking scramble for bread, the lack of literary culture, keep the primordial instincts of struggle and the unfailing ruggedness of human nature, alive. In any case, whether or not the factor of intellectual and moral isolation is reinforced by this factor of, so to say, personal isolation, certain it is that when the ruling class has degenerated in the manner described, it loses its ability to provide against its own dangers and against those of the society that has the misfortune to be guided by it. So the state crashes at the first appreciable shock from the outside foe. Those who govern are unable to deal with the least flurry; and the changes that a strong and intelligent ruling class would have carried out at a negligible cost in wealth, blood and human dignity take on the proportions of a social cataclysm. . . .

Juridical Defense. In a society that has attained any degree of civilization at all, the struggle between individuals is not a struggle for existence but a struggle for preeminence. But even ignoring that, we find altogether paradoxical the principle that is proclaimed by these self-styled positivists, to the effect that within every social group those individuals who are most moral and therefore most highly endowed with altruistic sentiments are the ones who are destined to survive (in our terms, to attain the highest social rankings). . . .

It follows that, in all societies, so-called evolution, the selection of the best, ought to eventuate in a perpetuation and multiplication of individuals of average morality, who are, in literal fact, the best adapted to what is called the struggle for existence.

Survival, or, as we consider it more accurate to say, preeminence, ought preferably to await those characters who, in whatever sort of social environment, represent a moral mean of the most highly refined gold. And yet the evolutionary theory does not seem to become acceptable even with that basic emendation, since it assumes in any event that the moral element is always the main factor in the success or failure of an individual in achieving the aims that he sets out to achieve in life. In practice things do not work out that way at all. To say nothing of the influence of chance, which is far greater than is commonly supposed, the possession in greater or lesser degree of certain intellectual qualities, such as readiness of perception and keenness of observation, figures very considerably in the decision as to whether a man is to reach the higher ranks in his society or is to stay in the lower. But there is the very great influence also of other qualities, which depend upon the individual's temperament, without being, strictly speaking, either intellectual or moral—such qualities as tenacity of purpose, self-confidence and, above all, *activity*. If we set out to judge whether an individual will or will not get on in life—whatever the type of society—we find that we cannot use any single criterion, to be sure, but that if we would keep an eye on the main factor, we must watch and see whether he is *active*, and whether he knows how to make good use of his activity.

Apart from brief periods of violent revolution, personal qualities are always less important, as regards attaining the highest positions in life, than birth or family. In any type of society, whether ostensibly democratic or otherwise, being born to a high station is one of the best claims a person can have to staying there. Families that have occupied the highest levels in the social scale for a number of generations often lack the qualities that are best fitted to carry a man from the bottom to the top, while they possess very different qualities in abundance. Except in unusual cases that are due to careful education, old aristocratic families are not distinguished for activity. . . .

We can accept as true only one portion of the selectionist theory. One may safely grant that, other things being equal, in a struggle between two societies that society will triumph in which the individual members are on the average better equipped in moral sense and therefore more united, more trustful of each other and more capable of self-sacrifice. But that exception hurts the evolutionary thesis as a whole more than it helps it. If, in a given society, a higher average of moral sense cannot be explained by any survival of the best individuals, then, granting that the higher average is there, it can be ascribed only to the better organization of the society—to causes, in other words, that are historical in nature and that are the worst enemies of those who try to explain social pheonomena primarily by changes in the individual organism or in the individual "psyche.". . .

In societies of ancient culture that have for centuries enjoyed sound political organizations, the repression of immoral impulses—what some criminologists call the "inhibition" that curbs impulses—is unquestionably stronger and acquires all the force of inveterate habit. By a long and slow process of elaboration such societies gradually develop the institutions that enable a universal morality to curb the expression of individual immorality in a certain number of public and private relationships. When they are not under the sway of interests and passions, almost all individuals come to understand that a given act is not consistent with the sentiments of justice that prevail in the society in which they live. . . .

So in a highly developed civilization not only do moral instincts—and for that matter selfish passions—become more refined, more conscious, more perfect. In a society in which political organization has made great progress, moral discipline is itself unquestionably greater, and the too selfish acts that are inhibited, or obstructed, by the reciprocal surveillance and restraint of the individuals who compose the society are more numerous and more clearly defined. . . .

The social mechanisms that regulate this disciplining of the moral sense constitute what we call "juridical defense" (respect for law, government by law). These mechanisms are not equally perfect in all societies. It may happen that a society that has advanced further than some other in the arts and sciences remain conspicuously inferior to that other in this respect. And it may also happen that juridical defense weakens and becomes less efficient in societies that are traversing periods of scientific and economic progress. . . .

The political organization proper, the organization that establishes the character of the relations between the governing class and the governed and between the various levels and various sections of the ruling class, is the factor that contributes more than any other to determining the degree of perfection that juridical defense, or government by law, can attain in a given people. The existence of an honest government, a government that is based on integrity and justice, a government that is truly liberal in Guicciardini's sense of the term, is the best guarantee that one can have that the rights commonly known as private will be effectively upheld—in other words, that property will be protected. . . .

If a political organism is to progress in the direction of attaining greater and greater improvement in juridical defense, the prime and most essential requisite is that the secular and ecclesiastical powers shall be separated, or, better, that the principle on which the exercise of temporal authority is based shall have nothing sacred and immutable about it. When power rests on a system of ideas and beliefs outside of which it is felt that there can be neither truth nor justice, it is almost impossible that its acts should be debated and moderated in practice. Social progress can hardly reach a point where, in such a case, the different powers will harmonize with each other and check each other effectively enough to prevent absolute control by the individual, or individuals, who stand at the head of the social order. . . .

Next after the separation of secular and ecclesiastical authority, the most essential requisites for a more or less advanced type of juridicial defense are to be found in the way in which wealth is distributed in a society and in the way in which military forces are organized. Here again a distinction must be drawn between nations that are still in their feudal period and nations that have already developed a bureaucratic organization.

In the feudal state, wealth and military power are ordinarily concentrated in the hands of the ruling class—wealth consisting largely in the ownership of land, as is uniformly the case in rudimentary stages of civilization. Even in a feudal society this state of affairs presents many drawbacks, but in that type of society it never has the effects it has in more highly perfected types of social organization. The head of a feudal state will be able to wrong any one of his barons, but he will never be absolute master of them all. They have at their disposal a certain amount of public force, if one may so speak, and will always be able to exercise de facto a right of resistance which, in bureaucratic states, once it is recognized, is written into the constitutions and the code books of public law. The individual barons, in their turn, find that there is a limit to the tyranny which they can exercise over the masses of their subjects. Unreasonableness on their part may provoke a desperate unrest which may easily become rebellion. So it turns out that in all truly feudal countries the rule of the masters may be violent and arbitrary by fits and starts, but on the whole it is considerably limited by customs. . . .

But when the class that monopolizes wealth and arms embodies its power in a centralized bureaucracy and an irresistible standing army, we get despotism in its worst form—namely, a barbarous and primitive system of government that has the instruments of an advanced civilization at its disposal, a yoke of iron which is applied by rough and reckless hands and which is very hard to break, since it has been steeled and tempered by practiced artisans. . . .

There is no use either in cherishing illusions as to the practical consequences of a system in which political power and control of economic production and distribution are irrevocably delegated to, or conferred upon, the same persons. In so far as the state absorbs and distributes a larger and larger portion of the public wealth, the leaders of the ruling class come to possess greater and greater facilities for influencing and commanding their subordinates, and more and more easily evade control by anybody. . . . If, then, all the instruments of production pass into the hands of the government, the officials who control and apportion production become the arbiters of the fortunes and welfare of all, and we get a more powerful oligarchy, a more all-embracing "racket," than has ever been seen in a society of advanced civilization. If all moral and material advantages depend on those who hold power, there is no baseness that will not be resorted to in order to please them; just as there is no act of chicanery or violence that will not be resorted to in order to attain power, in other words, in order to belong to the number of those who hand out the cake rather than to the larger number of those who have to rest content with the slices that are doled out to them.

A society is best placed to develop a relatively perfect political organization when it contains a large class of people whose economic position is virtually independent of those who hold supreme power and who have sufficient means to be able to devote a portion of their time to perfecting their culture and acquiring that interest in the public weal—that aristocratic spirit, we are almost tempted to say—which alone can induce people to serve their country with no other satisfactions than those that come from individual pride and self-respect. In all countries that ever have been, or now are, in the lead as regards juridical defense—or liberty, as it is commonly called—such a class has been prominent. . . .

As civilization grows, the number of the moral and material influences which are capable of becoming social forces increases. For example, property in money, as the fruit of industry and commerce, comes into being alongside of real property. Education progresses. Occupations based on scientific knowledge gain in importance.

So a new social class forms which, up to a certain point, counterbalances the material prestige of the rich and the moral prestige of the clergy. Not only that. Mutual toleration results from advanced culture, and toleration enables different religions and different political currents to exist side by side, balancing and checking one another. Specialization of public functions enables many different influences to express themselves in government and to participate in the control of the state. At the same time public discussion of the acts of the rulers becomes possible. Freedom of the press, so-called, is a very recent instrument of juridical defense. . . .

And yet, in order to gain an influence proportionate to its real importance every political force has to be organized, and before it can be well organized, a number of factors, important among them time and tradition, are indispensable. That is why, in one country or another at one time or another, we see an actual disproportion between the importance that a class has acquired in society and the direct influence it exerts in the government of the country. One thinks at once of the French bourgeoisie before 1789, or of the English middle classes before 1832. There is almost always some one political force, furthermore, that manifests an invincible tendency to overreach or absorb the others, and so to destroy a juridical equilibrium that has gradually been established. That is true both of political forces of a material character, such as wealth and military power, and of forces of a moral character, such as the great currents of religion or thought. Each of such currents claims to monopolize truth and justice, and all types of exclusivism and bigotry, whether Christian or Mohammedan, whether sacred or rationalistic, whether inspired by the infallibility of the pope or by the infallibility of democracy, are equally pernicious from this point of view. Every country, every epoch, has its own peculiar current of ideas and beliefs, which being the strongest current, bears down upon the political mechanism and tends to subvert it. . . .

A number of moral forces have long striven to upset the juridical equilibrium in Europe: the Church, social democracy, nationalism. In spite of its strong organization the Church may be considered the least violent and menacing of them all, and it will continue to be so unless danger of proletarian revolution forces the upper classes to turn again to religious beliefs which they have now abandoned or profess but tepidly. Among material forces, a force that is able very easily to override all the powers of the state and sometimes to violate, let alone the norms of justice and equity, the literal text of the law, is mobile wealth—it is money or at least that portion of money which is powerfully organized. The great development of banking systems and of credit, the growth of large corporations, which often control the communication systems of vast territories and entire states, the great enlargement of public debts, have in the last hundred years created new structures, new elements of political importance, so that some of the greatest states in the Old World and the New have already had occasion to learn from experience how overbearing and how all-pervasive their influence can be.

The relative ease with which money, or mobile wealth, can be organized and the possibility of concentrating control of large amounts of money in the hands of a few individuals help to explain its growing preponderance in power. In this phenomenon we have one of the many examples of an organized minority prevailing over a disorganized majority. A very small number of individuals can control all the banks of issue in a country or all the companies engaged in transportation by land or sea. They can own and control great stock companies and industrial corporations which deal in commodities that are indispensable to national defense, such as iron and steel. They can carry out public works for which not even the finances of the richest governments would be adequate. With hundreds of millions at their disposal, such individuals possess the most varied resources for threatening or cajoling other interests however far-reaching, and for intimidating and corrupting public officials, ministries, legislative bodies, newspapers. Meantime, that portion—and undoubtedly it is the larger portion—of the national capital which is invested in the hosts and hosts of small or medium-sized industries, or scattered about in many hands in the form of savings in amounts more or less large, has no power whatever to react. Be it noted that the far larger part of the capital of banks and industrial corporations usually belongs to small and medium-sized stockholders, who not only remain completely passive but are often the first victims of their leaders, who succeed in founding great fortunes and building up powerful public influence on the losses they inflict on others. . . .

When a system of political organization is based upon a single absolute principle, so that the whole political class is organized after a single pattern, it is difficult for all social forces to participate in public life, and more difficult still for any one force to counterbalance another. That is as true when power is in the hands of elected officials who are said to be chosen by the people as it is when power is entrusted exclusively to employees who are assumed to be appointed by a prince. The checks which bureaucracy and democracy can enforce upon themselves and which are applied through the agency of other bureaucrats or elected officials are always inadequate. In practice they never wholly achieve their purposes. . . .

THE IRON LAW OF OLIGARCHY

Robert Michels

Impossibility of Direct Government by the Masses. The practical ideal of democracy consists in the self-government of the masses in conformity with the decision of popular assemblies. But while this system limits the extension of the principle of delegation, it fails to provide any guarantee against the formation of an oligarchical camerilla. Undoubtedly it deprives the natural leaders of their quality as functionaries, for this quality is transferred to the people themselves. The crowd, however, is

SOURCE: Robert Michels, *Political Parties,* translated by Eden and Cedar Paul (New York: *The Free Press,* 1962), pp. 64-68, 70-74, 76-77, 81, 85-88, 92, 107-109, 111-112, 117, 120-122, 124, 126-127, 167-170, 342, 346-348, 353-354, 364-365, 367-368, 371. Reprinted with permission of the Macmillan Company. Copyright © 1962 by The Crowell & Collier Publishing Company. Footnotes have been omitted.

always subject to suggestion, being readily influenced by the eloquence of great popular orators; moreover, direct government by the people, admitting of no serious discussions or thoughtful deliberations, greatly facilitates *coups de main* of all kinds by men who are exceptionally bold, energetic, and adroit.

It is easier to dominate a large crowd than a small audience. The adhesion of the crowd is tumultuous, summary, and unconditional. Once the suggestions have taken effect, the crowd does not readily tolerate contradiction from a small minority, and still less from isolated individuals. A great multitude assembled within a small area is unquestionably more accessible to panic alarms, to unreflective enthusiasm, and the like, than is a small meeting, whose members can quietly discuss matters among themselves.

It is a fact of everyday experience that enormous public meetings commonly carry resolutions by acclamation or by general assent, whilst these same assemblies, if divided into small sections, say of fifty persons each, would be much more guarded in their assent. . . .

The most formidable argument against the sovereignty of the masses is, however, derived from the mechanical and technical impossibility of its realization.

The sovereign masses are altogether incapable of undertaking the most necessary resolutions. The impotence of direct democracy, like the power of indirect democracy, is a direct outcome of the influence of number. In a polemic against Proudhon (1849), Louis Blanc asks whether it is possible for thirty-four millions of human beings (the population of France at that time) to carry on their affairs without accepting what the pettiest man of business finds necessary, the inter-mediation of representatives. He answers his own question by saying that one who declares direct action on this scale to be possible is a fool, and that one who denies its possibility need not be an absolute opponent of the idea of the state. The same question and the same answer could be repeated today in respect of party organization. Above all in the great industrial centers, where the labor party sometimes numbers its adherents by tens of thousands, it is impossible to carry on the affairs of this gigantic body without a system of representation. . . .

It is obvious that such a gigantic number of persons belonging to a unitary organization cannot do any practical work upon a system of direct discussion. The regular holding of deliberative assemblies of a thousand members encounters the gravest difficulties in respect of room and distance; while from the topographical point of view such an assembly would become altogether impossible if the members numbered ten thousand. . . .

Hence the need for delegation, for the system in which delegates represent the mass and carry out its will. Even in groups sincerely animated with the democratic spirit, current business, the preparation and the carrying out of the most important actions, is necessarily left in the hands of individuals. . . .

Originally the chief is merely the servant of the mass. The organization is based upon the absolute equality of all its members. Equality is here understood in its most general sense, as an equality of like men. . . .

This generic conception of equality is, however, gradually replaced by the idea of equality among comrades belonging to the same organization, all of whose members enjoy the same rights. The democratic principle aims at guaranteeing to all an equal influence and an equal participation in the regulation of the common interests. All are electors, and all are eligible for office. The fundamental postulate of the *Declaration des Droits de l'Homme* finds here its theoretical application. All the offices are filled by election. The officials, executive organs of the general will, play a merely subordinate part, are always dependent upon the collectivity, and can be deprived of their office at any moment. The mass of the party is omnipotent.

At the outset, the attempt is made to depart as little as possible from pure democracy by subordinating the delegates altogether to the will of the mass, by tieing them hand and foot. In the early days of the movement of the Italian agricultural workers, the chief of the league required a majority of four-fifths of the votes to secure election. When disputes arose with the employers about wages, the representative of the organization, before undertaking any negotiations, had to be furnished with a written authority, authorized by the signature of every member of the corporation. All the accounts of the body were open to the examination of the members, at any time. . . . It is obvious that democracy in this sense is applicable only on a very small scale. In the infancy of the English labor movement, in many of the trade unions, the delegates were either appointed in rotation from among all the members, or were chosen by lot. Gradually, however, the delegates' duties became more complicated; some individual ability becomes essential, a certain oratorical gift, and a considerable amount of objective knowledge. It thus becomes impossible to trust to blind chance, to the fortune of alphabetic succession, or to the order of priority, in the choice of a delegation whose members must possess certain peculiar personal aptitudes if they are to discharge their mission to the general advantage.

Such were the methods which prevailed in the early days of the labor movement to enable the masses to participate in party and trade-union administration. Today they are falling into disuse, and in the development of the modern political aggregate there is a tendency to shorten and stereotype the process which transforms the led into a leader—a process which has hitherto developed by the natural course of events. Here and there voices make themselves heard demanding a sort of official consecration for the leaders, insisting that it is necessary to constitute a class of professional politicians, of approved and registered experts in political life. . . .

Even today, the candidates for the secretaryship of a trade union are subject to examination as to their knowledge of legal matters and their capacity as letter-writers. The socialist organizations engaged in political action also directly undertake the training of their own officials. . . .

It is undeniable that all these educational institutions for the officials of the party and of the labor organizations tend, above all, towards the artificial creation of an *elite* of the working class, of a caste of cadets composed of persons who aspire to the command of the proletarian rank and file. Without wishing it, there is thus effected a continuous enlargement of the gulf which divides the leaders from the masses.

The technical specialization that inevitably results from all extensive organization renders necessary what is called expert leadership. Consequently the power of determination comes to be considered one of the specific attributes of leadership, and is gradually withdrawn form the masses to be concentrated in the hands of the leaders alone. Thus the leaders, who were at first no more than the executive organs of the collective will, soon emancipate themselves from the mass and become independent of its control.

Organization implies the tendency to oligarchy. In every organization, whether it be a political party, a professional union, or any other association of the kind, the aristocratic tendency manifests itself very clearly. The mechanism of the organization, while conferring a solidity of structure, induces serious changes in the organized mass, completely inverting the respective position of the leaders and the led. As a result of organization, every party or professional union becomes divided into a minority of directors and a majority of directed.

It has been remarked that in the lower stages of civilization tyranny is dominant. Democracy cannot come into existence until there is attained a subsequent and more highly developed stage of social life. Freedoms and privileges, and among these latter the privilege of taking part in the direction of public affairs, are at first restricted to the few. Recent times have been characterized by the gradual extension of these privileges to a widening circle. This is what we know as the era of democracy. But if we pass from the sphere of the state to the sphere of party, we may observe that as democracy continues to develop, a backwash sets in. With the advance of organization, democracy tends to decline. Democratic evolution has a parabolic course. At the present time, at any rate as far as party life in concerned, democracy is in the descending phase. It may be enunciated as a general rule that the increase in the power of the leaders is directly proportional with the extension of the organization. In the various parties and labor organizations of different countries the influence of the leaders is mainly determined (apart from racial and individual grounds) by the varying development of organization. Where organization is stronger, we find that there is a lesser degree of applied democracy.

Every solidly constructed organization, whether it be a democratic state, a political party, or a league of proletarians for the resistance of economic opression, presents a soil eminently favorable for the differentiation of organs and of functions. The more extended and the more ramified the official apparatus of the organization, the greater the number of its members, the fuller its treasury, and the more widely circulated its press, the less efficient becomes the direct control exercised by the rank and file, and the more is this control replaced by the increasing power of committees. . . .

As organization develops, not only do the tasks of the administration become more difficult and more complicated, but, further, its duties become enlarged and specialized to such a degree that it is no longer possible to take them all in at a single glance. In a rapidly progressive movement, it is not only the growth in the number of duties, but also the higher quality of these, which imposes a more extensive differentiation of function. Nominally, and according to the letter of the rules, all the acts of the leaders are subject to the ever vigilant criticism of the rank and file. In theory the leader is merely an employee bound by the instruction he receives. He has to carry out the orders of the mass, of which he is no more than the executive organ. But in actual fact, as the organization increases in size, this control becomes purely fictitious. The members have to give up the idea of themselves conducting or even supervising the whole administration, and are compelled to hand these tasks over to trustworthy persons specially nominated for the purpose, to salaried officials. The rank and file must content themselves with summary reports, and with the appointment of occasional special committees of inquiry. Yet this does not derive from any special change in the rules of the organization. It is by very necessity that a simple employee gradually becomes a "leader," acquiring a freedom of action which he ought not to possess. The chief then becomes accustomed to dispatch important business on his own responsibility, and to decide various questions relating to the life of the party without any attempt to consult the rank and file. It is obvious that democratic control thus undergoes a progressive diminution, and is ultimately reduced to an infinitesimal minimum. In all the socialist parties there is a continual increase in the number of functions withdrawn from the electoral assemblies and transferred to the executive committees. In this way there is constructed a powerful and complicated edifice. The principle of division of labor coming more and more into operation, executive authority undergoes division and subdivision. There is thus constituted a rigorously defined and hierarchical bureaucracy. In the catechism of party duties, the strict observance of hierarchical rules becomes the first article. The hierarchy comes into existence as the outcome of technical conditions, and its constitution is an essential postulate of the regular functioning of the party machine.

It is indisputable that the oligarchical and bureaucratic tendency of party organization is a matter of technical and practical necessity. It is the inevitable product of the very principle of organization. Not even the most radical wing of the various socialist parties raises any objection to this retrogressive evolution, the contention being that democracy is only a form of organization and that where it ceases to be possible to harmonize democracy with organization, it is better to abandon the former than the latter. . . .

In all times, in all phases of development, in all branches of human activity, there have been leaders. It is true that certain socialists, above all the orthodox Marxists of Germany, seek to convince us that socialism knows nothing of "leaders," that the party has "employees" merely, being a democratic party, and the existence of leaders being incompatible with democracy. But a false assertion such as this cannot override a sociological law. Its only result is, in fact, to strengthen the rule of the leaders, for it serves to conceal from the mass a danger which really threatens democracy.

For technical and administrative reasons, no less than for tactical reasons, a strong organization needs an equally strong leadership. As long as an organization is loosely constructed and vague in its outlines, no professional leadership can arise. . . . The more solid the structure of an organization becomes in the course of the evolution of the modern political party, the more marked becomes the tendency to replace the emergency leader by the professional leader. Every party organization which has attained to a considerable degree of complication demands that there should be a certain number of persons who devote all their activities to the work of the party. The mass provides these by delegations, and the delegates, regularly appointed, become permanent representatives of the mass for the direction of its affairs.

For democracy, however, the first appearance of professional leadership marks the beginning of the end, and this, above all, on account of the logical impossibility of the "representative" system, whether in parliamentary life or in party delegation. Jean Jacques Rousseau may be considered as the founder of this aspect of the criticism of democracy. He defines popular government as "the exercise of the general will" and draws from this the logical inference that "it can never be alienated from itself, and the sovereign—who is nothing but a collective concept— can only be represented by himself. Consequently the instant a people gives itself to representatives, it is no longer free." A mass which delegates its sovereignty, that is to say transfers its sovereignty to the hands of a few individuals, abdicates its sovereign functions. For the will of the people is not transferable, nor even the will of the single individuals. . . .

This criticism of the representative system is applicable above all in our own days, in which political life continually assumes more complex forms. As this complexity increases, it becomes more and more absurd to attempt to "represent" a hetero- geneous mass in all the innumerable problems which arise out of the increasing differentiation of our political and economic life. To represent, in this sense, comes to mean that the purely individual desire masquerades and is accepted as the will of the mass. In certain isolated cases, where the questions involved are extremely simple, and where the delegated authority is of brief duration, representation is possible. But permanent representation will always be tantamount to the exercise of dominion by the representatives over the represented. . . .

Psychological Causes of Leadership. One who holds the office of delegate acquires a moral right to that office, and delegates remain in office unless removed by extraordinary circumstances or in obedience to rules observed with exceptional strictness. An election made for a definite purpose becomes a life incumbency. Custom becomes a right. One who has for a certain time held the office of delegate ends by regarding that office as his own property. If refused reinstatement, he threatens reprisals (the threat of resignation being the least serious among these) which will tend to sow confusion among his comrades, and this confusion will continue until he is victorious.

Resignation of office, in so far as it is not a mere expression of discouragement or protest (such as disinclination to accept a candidature in an unpromising constitu- ency), is in most cases a means for the retention and fortification of leadership. Even in political organizations greater than party, the leaders often employ this stratagem, thus disarming their adversaries by a deference which does not lack a specious democratic color. The opponent is forced to exhibit in return an even greater deference, and this above all when the leader who makes use of the method is really indispensable, or is considered indispensable by the mass. . . .

There is no exaggeration in the assertion that among the citizens who enjoy political rights the number of those who have a lively interest in public affairs is insignificant. In the majority of human beings the sense of an intimate relationship between the good of the individual and the good of the collectivity is but little developed. Most people are altogether devoid of understanding of the actions and reactions between that organism we call the state and their private interests, their prosperity, and their life. . . .

In the life of modern democratic parties we may observe signs of similar indifference. It is only a minority which participates in party decisions, and sometimes that minority is ludicrously small. The most important resolutions taken by the most democratic of all parties, the socialist party, always emanate from a handful of the members. It is true that the renouncement of the exercise of democratic rights is voluntary; except in those cases, which are common enough, where the active participation of the organized mass in party life is prevented by geographical or topographical conditions. Speaking generally, it is the urban part of the organization which decides everything; the duties of the members living in country districts and in remote provincial towns are greatly restricted; they are expected to pay their subscriptions and to vote during elections in favor of the candidates selected by the organization of the great town. . . .

The same thing happens in party life as happens in the state. In both, the demand for monetary supplies is upon a coercive foundation, but the electoral system has no established sanction. An electoral right exists, but no electoral duty. Until this duty is superimposed upon the right, it appears probable that s small minority only will continue to avail itself of the right which the majority voluntarily renounces, and that the minority will always dictate laws for the indifferent and apathetic mass. The consequence is that, in the political groupings of democracy, the participation in party life has an echeloned aspect. The extensive base consists of the great mass of electors; upon this is superposed the enormously smaller mass of enrolled members of the local branch of the party, numbering perhaps one-tenth or even as few as one-thirtieth of the electors; above this, again, comes the much smaller number of the members who regularly attend meetings; next comes the group of officials of the party; and highest of all, consisting in part of the same individuals as the last group, come the half-dozen or so members of the executive committee. Effective power is here in inverse ratio to the number of those who exercise it. . . .

Though it grumbles occasionally, the majority is really delighted to find persons who will take the trouble to look after its affairs. In the mass, and even in the organized mass of the labor parties, there is an immense need for direction and guidance. This need is accompanied by a genuine cult for the leaders, who are regarded as heroes. . . .

The mass is sincerely grateful to its leaders, regarding gratitude as a sacred duty. As a rule, this sentiment of gratitude is displayed in the continual re-election of the leaders who have deserved well of the party, so that leadership commonly becomes perpetual. It is the general feeling of the mass that it would be "ungrateful" if they failed to confirm in his functions every leader of long service. . . .

Intellectual Factors. In the infancy of the socialist party, when the organization is still weak, when its membership is scanty, and when its principal aim is to diffuse a knowledge of the elementary principles of socialism, professional leaders are less numerous than are leaders whose work in this department is no more than an accessory occupation. But with the further progress of the organization, new needs continually arise, at once within the party and in respect of its relationships with the outer world. Thus the moment inevitably comes when neither the idealism and enthusiasm of the intellectuals, nor yet the goodwill with which the proletarians devote their free time on Sundays to the work of the party, suffice any longer to meet the requirements of the case. The provisional must then give place to the permanent, and dilettantism must yield to professionalism.

With the appearance of professional leadership, there ensues a great accentuation of the cultural differences between the leaders and the led. Long experience has shown that among the factors which secure the dominion of minorities over majorities—money and its equivalents (economic superiority), tradition and hereditary transmission (historical superiority)—the first place must be given to the formal instruction of the leaders (so-called intellectual superiority). Now the most superficial observation shows that in the parties of the proletariat the leaders are, in matters of education, greatly superior to the led. . . .

Whilst their occupation and the needs of daily life render it impossible for the masses to attain to a profound knowledge of the social machinery, and above all of the working of the political machine, the leader of working-class origin is enabled, thanks to his new situation, to make himself intimately familiar with all the technical details of public life, and thus to increase his superiority over the rank and file. In proportion as the profession of politician becomes a more complicated one, and in proportion as the rules of social legislation become more numerous, it is necessary for one who would understand politics to possess wider experience and more extensive knowledge. Thus the gulf between the leaders and the rest of the party becomes ever wider, until the moment arrives in which the leaders lose all true sense of solidarity with the class from which they have sprung, and there ensues a new class-division between ex-proletarian captains and proletarian common soldiers. When the workers choose leaders for themselves, they are with their own hands creating new masters whose principal means of dominion is found in their better instructed minds. . . .

The democratic masses are thus compelled to submit to a restriction of their own wills when they are forced to give their leaders an authority which is in the long run destructive to the very principle of democracy. The leader's principal source of power is found in his indispensability. One who is indispensable has in his power all the lords and masters of the earth. The history of the working-class parties continually furnishes instances in which the leader has been in flagrant contradiction with the fundamental principles of the movement, but in which the rank and file have not been able to make up their minds to draw the logical consequences of this conflict, because they feel that they cannot get along without the leader, and cannot dispense with the qualities he has acquired in virtue of the very position to which they have themselves elevated him, and because they do not see their way to find an adequate substitute. . . .

The incompetence of the masses is almost universal throughout the domains of political life, and this constitutes the most solid foundation of the power of the leaders. The incompetence furnishes the leaders with a practical and to some extent with a moral justification. Since the rank and file are incapable of looking after their own interests, it is necessary that they should have experts to attend to their affairs. From this point of view it cannot be always considered a bad thing that the leaders should really lead. The free election of leaders by the rank and file presupposes that the latter possess the competence requisite for the recognition and appreciation of the competence of the leaders. . . .

The Stability of Leadership. Long tenure of office involves dangers for democracy. For this reason those organizations which are anxious to retain their democratic essence make it a rule that all the offices at their disposal shall be conferred for brief periods only. If we take into account the number of offices to be filled by universal suffrage and the frequency of elections, the American citizen is the one who enjoys the largest measure of democracy. In the United States, not only the legislative bodies, but all the higher administrative and judicial officials are elected by popular vote. It has been calculated that every American citizen must on an average exercise his function as a voter twenty-two times a year. The members of the socialist parties in the various countries must today exercise similarly extensive electoral activities: nomination of candidates for parliament, county councils, and municipalities; nomination of delegates to local and national party congresses; election of committees; re-election of the same; and so on, *da capo*. In almost all the socialist parties and trade unions the officers are elected for a brief term, and must be reelected at least every two years. The longer the tenure of office, the greater becomes the influence of the leader over the masses and the greater therefore his independence. Consequently a frequent repetition of election is an elementary precaution on the part of democracy against the virus of oligarchy.

Since in the democratic parties the leaders owe their position to election by the mass, and are exposed to the chance of being dispossessed at no distant date, when forced to seek re-election, it would seem at first sight as if the democratic working of these parties were indeed secured. A persevering and logical application of democratic principles should in fact get rid of all personal considerations and of all attachment to tradition. Just as in the political life of constitutional states the ministry must consist of members of that party which possesses a parliamentary majority, so also in the socialist party the principal offices ought always to be filled by the partisans of those tendencies which have prevailed at the congresses. Thus the old party dignitaries ought always to yield before youthful forces, before those who have acquired that numerical preponderance which is represented by at least half of the membership plus one. It must, moreover, be a natural endeavor not to leave the same comrades too long in occupation of important offices, lest the holders of these should stick in their grooves, and should come to regard themselves as God-given leaders. But in those parties which are solidly organized, the actual state of affairs is far from corresponding to this theory. The sentiment of tradition, in cooperation with an instinctive need for stability, has as its result that the leadership represents always the past rather than the present. Leadership is indefinitely retained, not because it is the tangible expression of the relationships between the forces existing in the party at any given moment, but simply because it is already constituted. It is through gregarious idleness, or, if we may employ the euphemism, it is in virtue of the law of inertia, that the leaders are so often confirmed in their office as long as they like. These tendencies are particularly evident in the German social democracy, where the leaders are practically irremovable. . . .

It is in this manner that the leaders of an eminently democratic party, nominated by indirect suffrage, prolong throughout their lives the powers with which they have once been invested. The reelection demanded by the rules becomes a pure formality. The temporary commission becomes a permanent one, and the tenure of office an established right. The democratic leaders are more firmly established in their seats than were ever the leaders of an aristocratic body. Their term of office comes greatly to exceed the mean duration of ministerial life in monarchical states. . . .

There is an additional motive in operation. In the working-class organization, whether founded for political or for economic ends, just as much as in the life of the state, it is indispensable that the official should remain in office for a considerable time, so that he may familiarize himself with the work he has to do, may gain practical experience, for he cannot become a useful official until he has been given time to work himself into his new office. Moreover, he will not devote himself zealously to his task, he will not feel himself thoroughly at one with the aim he is intended to pursue, if he is likely to be dismissed at any moment; he needs the sense of security provided by the thought that nothing but circumstances of an unforeseen and altogether extraordinary character will deprive him of his position. Appointment to office for short terms is democratic, but is quite unpractical alike on technical and psychological grounds. Since it fails to arouse in the employee a proper sense of responsibility, it throws the door open to administrative anarchy. . . .

In proportion as the chiefs become detached from the mass they show themselves more and more inclined, when gaps in their own ranks have to be filled, to effect this, not by way of popular election, but by cooptation, and also to increase their own effectives wherever possible, by creating new posts upon their own initiative. There arises in the leaders a tendency to isolate themselves, to form a sort of cartel, and to surround themselves, as it were, with a wall, within which they will admit those only who are of their own way of thinking. Instead of allowing their successors to be appointed by the choice of the rank and file, the leaders do all in their power to choose these successors for themselves, and to fill up gaps in their own ranks directly or indirectly by the exercise of their own volition. . . .

In the nomination of candidates for election we find, in addition, another grave oligarchical phenomenon, nepotism. The choice of the candidates almost always depends upon a little clique, consisting of the local leaders and their assistants, which suggests suitable names to the rank and file. In many cases the constituency comes to be regarded as a family property. . . .

The Struggle Between the Leaders and the Masses. Those who defend the arbitrary acts committed by the democracy, point out that the masses have at their disposal means whereby they can react against the violation of their rights. These means consist in the right of controlling and dismissing their leaders. Unquestionably this defense possesses a certain theoretical value, and the authoritarian inclinations of the leaders are in some degree attenuated by these possibilities. In states with a democratic tendency and under a parliamentary regime, to obtain the fall of a detested minister it suffices, in theory, that the people should be weary of him. In the same way, once more in theory, the ill-humor and the opposition of a socialist group or of an election committee is enough to effect the recall of a deputy's mandate, and in the same way the hostility of the majority at the annual congress of trade unions should be enough to secure the dismissal of a secretary. In practice, however, the exercise of this theoretical right is interfered with by the working of the whole series of conservative tendencies to which allusion has previously been made, so that the supremacy of the autonomous and sovereign masses is rendered purely illusory. . . .

With the institution of leadership there simultaneously begins, owing to the long tenure of office, the transformation of the leaders into a closed caste. . . .

Democracy and the Iron Law of Oligarchy. The only scientific doctrine which can boast of ability to make an effective reply to all the theories, old or new, affirming the immanent necessity for the perennial existence of the "political class" in the Marxist doctrine. In this doctrine the state is identified with the ruling class — an identification from which Bakunin, Marx's pupil, drew the extreme consequences. The state is merely the executive committee of the ruling class, or, to quote the expression of a recent neo-Marxist, the state is merely a "trade-union formed to defend the interest of the powers-that-be." It is obvious that this theory greatly resembles the conservative theory of Gaetano Mosca. . . .

The Marxist theory of the state, when conjoined with a faith in the revolutionary energy of the working class and the democratic effects of the socialization of the means of production, leads logically to the idea of a new social order which to the school of Mosca appears utopian. According to the Marxists the capitalist mode of production transforms the great majority of the population into proletarians, and thus digs its own grave. As soon as it has attained maturity, the proletariat will seize political power, and will immediately transform private property into state property. "In this way it will eliminate itself, for it will thus put an end to all social differences, and consequently to all class antagonisms. In other words, the proletariat will annul the state, *qua* state. Capitalist society, divided into classes, has need of the state as an organization of the ruling class, . . . whose purpose it is to maintain the capitalist system of production in its own interest and in order to effect the continued exploitation of the proletariat. Thus to put an end to the state is synonymous with putting an end to the existence of the dominant class." But the new collectivist society, the society without classes, which is to be established upon the ruins of the ancient state, will also need elective elements. . . . It is none the less true that social wealth cannot be satisfactorily administered in any other manner than by the creation of an extensive bureaucracy. In this way we are led by an inevitable logic to the flat denial of the possibility of a state without classes. The administration of an immeasurable large capital, above all when this capital is collective property, confers upon the administrator influence at least equal to that possessed by the private owner of capital. Consequently the critics in advance of the Marxist social order ask whether the instinct which today leads the members of the possessing classes to transmit to their children the wealth which they (the parents) have amassed, will not exist also in the administrators of the public wealth of the socialist state, and whether these administrators will not utilize their immense influence in order to secure for their children the succession to the offices which they themselves hold. . . .

The sociological phenomena whose general characteristics have been discussed in this chapter and in preceding ones offer numerous vulnerable points to the scientific opponents of democracy. These phenomena would seem to prove beyond dispute that society cannot exist without a "dominant" or "political" class, and that the ruling class, while its elements are subject to a frequent partial renewal, nevertheless constitutes the only factor of sufficiently durable efficacy in the history of human development. According to this view, the government, or, if the phrase be preferred, the state, cannot be anything other than the organization of a minority. It is the aim of this minority to impose upon the rest of society a "legal order," which is the outcome of the exigencies of dominion and of the exploitation of the mass of helots effected by the ruling minority, and can never be truly representative of the majority. The majority is thus permanently incapable of self-government. Even when the discontent of the masses culminates in a successful attempt to deprive the bourgeoisie of power, this is after all, so Mosca contends, effected only in appearance; always and necessarily there springs from the masses a new organized minority which rasies itself to the rank of a governing class. Thus the majority of human beings, in a condition of eternal tutelage, are predestined by tragic necessity to submit to the dominion of a small minority, and must be content to constitute the pedestal of an oligarchy. . . .

Final Considerations. Leadership is a necessary phenomenon in every form of social life. Consequently it is not the task of science to inquire whether this phenomenon is good or evil, or predominantly one or the other. But there is great scientific value in the demonstration that every system of leadership is incompatible with the most essential postulates of democracy. We are now aware that the law of the historic necessity of oligarchy is primarily based upon a series of facts of experience. Like all other scientific laws, sociological laws are derived from empirical observation. In order, however, to deprive our axiom of its purely descriptive character, and to confer upon it that status of analytical explanation which can alone transform a formula into law, it does not suffice to contemplate from a unitary outlook those phenomena which may be empirically established; we must also study the determining causes of these phenomena. Such has been our task.

Now, *if* we leave out of consideration the tendency of the leaders to organize themselves and to consolidate their interests, and if we leave also out of consideration the gratitude of the led towards the leaders, and the general immobility and passivity of the masses, we are led to conclude that the principal cause of oligarchy in the democratic parties is to be found in the technical indispensability of leadership.

The process which has begun in consequence of the differentiation of functions in the party is completed by a complex of qualities which the leaders acquire through their detachment from the mass. At the outset, leaders arise SPONTANEOUSLY; their functions are ACCESSORY and GRATUITOUS. Soon, however, they become PROFESSIONAL leaders, and in this second stage of development they are STABLE and IRREMOVABLE.

It follows that the explanation of the oligarchical phenomenon which thus results is partly PSYCHOLOGICAL; oligarchy derives, that is to say, from the psychical transformations which the leading personalities in the parties undergo in the course of their lives. But also, and still more, oligarchy depends upon what we may term the PSYCHOLOGY OF ORGANIZATION ITSELF, that is to say, upon the tactical and technical necessities which result from the consolidation of every disciplined political aggregate. Reduced to its most concise expression, the fundamental sociological law of political parties (the term "political" being here used in its most comprehensive significance) may be formulated in the following terms: "It is organization which gives birth to the dominion of the elected over the electors, of the mandataries over the mandators, of the delegates over the delegators. Who says organization, says oligarchy."

Every party organization represents an oligarchical power grounded upon a democratic basis. We find everywhere that the power of the elected leaders over the electing masses is almost unlimited. The oligarchical structure of the building suffocates the basic democratic principle. . . .

From this chain of reasoning and from these scientific convictions it would be erroneous to conclude that we should renounce all endeavors to ascertain the limits which may be imposed upon the powers exercised over the individual by oligarchies (state, dominant class, party, etc.). It would be an error to abandon the desperate enterprise of endeavoring to discover a social order which will render possible the complete realization of the idea of popular sovereignty. In the present work, as the writer said at the outset, it has not been his aim to indicate new paths. But it seemed necessary to lay considerable stress upon the pessimist aspect of democracy which is forced on us by historical study. We had to inquire whether, and within what limits, democracy must remain purely ideal, possessing no other value than that of a moral criterion which renders it possible to appreciate the varying degrees of that oligarchy which is immanent in every social regime. In other words, we have had to inquire if, and in what degree, democracy is an ideal which we can never hope to realize in practice. . . .

Democracy is a treasure which no one will ever discover by deliberate search. But in continuing our search, in laboring indefatigably to discover the undiscoverable, we shall perform a work which will have fertile results in the democratic sense. We have seen, indeed, that within the bosom of the democratic working-class party are born the very tendencies to counteract which that party came into existence. Thanks to the diversity and to the unequal worth of the elements of the party, these tendencies often give rise to manifestations which border on tyranny. . . .

The democratic currents of history resemble successive waves. They break ever on the same shoal. They are ever renewed. This enduring spectacle is simultaneously encouraging and depressing. When democracies have gained a certain stage of development, they undergo a gradual transformation, adopting the aristocratic spirit, and in many cases also the aristocratic forms, against which at the outset they struggled so fiercely. Now new accusers arise to denounce the traitors; after an era of glorious combats and of inglorious power, they end by fusing with the old dominant class, whereupon once more they are in their turn attacked by fresh opponents who appeal to the name of democracy. It is probable that this cruel game will continue without end.

SOCIAL CLASS, POLITICAL CLASS, RULING CLASS

Raymond Aron

The first theoreticians of sociology, at the beginning of the 19th century, Saint-Simon, Auguste Comte, Alexis de Tocqueville, and Karl Marx, stressed the contrast between the *ancien régime* and modern society, the post-Revolutionary society. Pre-Revolutionary society was composed of orders or estates. Before 1789 the French were not born free and equal; they did not all have the same rights; they were not all subject to the same obligations. Social heterogeneity was considered normal—heterogeneity not only of occupation, of income, and of living conditions but also of juridical status. Whatever social mobility there was, classes appeared hereditary; the juridical status of the noble like that of the non-noble was determined at birth. The French Revolution generated a society whose principles were fundamentally different. All the members of society became theoretically subject to the same legislation and, although limitations on the right of suffrage and the distinction between active and passive citizens were maintained in Western Europe for much of the last century, the accepted ideology recognized and proclaimed the universal extension of citizenship. Juridically homogeneous, composed of citizens with equal rights, modern society was nevertheless divided into groups (I purposely employ the vaguest term) which were ordered into a more or less clear hierarchy, with members of each group sharing enough traits to be discernible from members of other groups. Sociologists were in search of the right interpretation of the difference between the society of the *ancien regime* and modern society; they wanted to clarify the relationship between the estates of yesterday and the social groups of today.

One of the first interpretations could be found in the celebrated parable of Saint-Simon: suppose the elite[1] of diplomats, counselors of state, ministers,

---

SOURCE: Raymond Aron, "Social Class, Political Class, Ruling Class," trans. by Reinhard Bendix and Seymour M. Lipset. Reprinted by permission from the *European Journal of Sociology*, Vol. I, 1960, pp. 260-281. Several footnotes have been omitted.

[1]By "elite" I here refer to the minority which, in each of the enumerated professions, has succeeded best and occupies the highest positions.

parliamentarians and generals were suddenly eliminated by a catastrophe—society would not be mortally harmed. The same quantity of riches would be produced and the living conditions of the majority would not be seriously affected. On the other hand, suppose the elite of bankers, industrialists, engineers and technicians were eliminated, then society would be paralyzed because the production of wealth would cease or be slowed down greatly. This famous text's central theme is the contrast between industrial society and politico-military society. The former is the sub-structure, the latter is nothing more than the super-structure (if we translate the Saint-Simonian distinction into Marxian terminology). The two schools— Saint-Simonian and positivist on the one hand, and Marxian on the other—give a different interpretation of the conflicts within industrial society itself. Without denying the conflicts of interests between employers and employees, Saint-Simon and Auguste Comte consider them to be secondary: the interests of the two groups are fundamentally the same but are opposed to the interests of the survivors of the theological and military age. On the other hand, according to Karl Marx, the conflict between wage-earners and capitalists, between the workers and the owners of the means of production, is decisive. They form two classes and it is their struggle that is the mainspring of historical change and, finally, of the socialist revolution.

Marxism is, so to speak, an interpretation of the society of the *ancien regime* made in the light of modern society, and of modern society made in the light of the society of the *ancien regime*. Neither juridical equality nor even political equality has substantially modified the condition of the masses. The workers are not "liberated" just because they vote once every four years. The *social groups* of modern society are not less distinct nor do they form less of a hierarchy than the pre-Revolutionary orders. And if they are comparable to these orders, in spite of juridical equality among individuals, do they not retrospectively throw light upon the true origin, that is, upon the base of the structure of the *ancien regime*? The upper class (from now on let us employ this term in place of the term "social group") is always that which possesses the means of production—yesterday the land, today the land or the factories. The capitalists of our day are the equivalents of the feudal barons, and in their day the latter were the equivalents of the capitalists. Marx does not deny the unique character of modern society as formulated by the Saint-Simonians, but he does deny the essential solidarity of the producers as affirmed by economists, Saint-Simonians, and positivists. It is only after the socialist revolution that social classes—those of the *ancien regime* as well as those of modern society—will be eliminated and the promise offered by the prodigious development of productive capacities will be fulfilled.

This interpretation of two societies—pre-Revolutionary and post-Revolutionary—by the same scheme brings with it a parallel between the advent of the bourgeoisie and the rise of the proletariat. As the capitalist relations of production were formed in the midst of the feudal society, so socialist relations of production will form in the midst of capitalist society and the socialist revolution will give the power to the proletariat as the bourgeois revolution has given the political power to the bourgeoisie who were already holding the real social power. But this very comparison immediately illustrates the paradox, or, rather, the internal contradiction, of Marxian interpretation.

Let us consider the world of labor. Within every complex society one distinguishes among different groups according to the occupation practiced (farmers, merchants, craftsmen) and within each of these groups there is a hierarchy by property, success, luck, and income. The feudal lord and the capitalist financier or industrialist have in common the ownership of the means of production. But the function provided by the feudal lord was military; once the security of the peasants was assured, the peasants no longer needed the lord. They only needed the equivalent of a landowner in the large farm area where collective activity required managers or lawyers. In the factories or mills those who can organize or manage are obviously indispensable, although they need not be the owners. In other words, elimination of capitalists cannot mean elimination of managers; it only means the elimination of owners and the taking over of managerial functions by nonowners. . . .

Where is the difference between the managerial group in an industrial society without private ownership of the instruments of production and the same stratum in a system in which individual ownership of the means of production exists? That is the major question which arises à *propos* of the concept of the proletariat as the dominant class.

Furthermore, in pre-Revolutionary society, the bourgeoisie constituted a privileged minority. Before the Revolution they occupied positions of command and prestige. The Revolution gave them the political power formerly exercised by the king and, in part, by the nobles. But in gaining power, the bourgeoisie remained the same. However, the proletariat must delegate power to "representatives"; the representatives cease being proletarians the day they begin directing a factory, a corporation or a ministry. The bourgeoisie in power remain the bourgeoisie. Proletarians in power are no longer proletarians.

Alexis de Tocqueville, whose thoughts were no less focussed upon the comparison between the *ancien regime* and modern society than Comte's or Marx's, also considered the social classes as the principal actors of history. In *l'Ancien Régime et la Révolution* he wrote this revealing statement: "I speak of classes, they alone should concern the historian."[2] . . .

The existence of the State, the machinery of State—civil and military—creates difficulty for this interpretation of social and political history in terms of classes. Louis-Napoléon and his original retinue of Parisian bohemians take possession of the French State. Which class is in power? The peasant-proprietors who have voted *en masse* for the nephew of the great emperor? The high-bourgeoisie of capitalists whose interests will be safeguarded and protected by the imperial regime? Or are class relationships expressed in the imperial regime? Would similar relationships have been possible in a different type of regime; what would have been the consequences of a bourgeois republic?

Tocqueville would have been able to answer all these questions. Although he saw the classes as the principal actors of history, the State or the government is not

---

[2]Vol. II, Chap. XII, p. 179 (edited by J. P. Mayer).

explained entirely by classes and their struggles. Governments can be said to be representative, but neither the mode of representation nor the constitutional rules are determined strictly by the social context. Modern societies all uphold equality, but they may be liberal or despotic.

Marx observed the enormous machinery of State and the conquest of this by a clique of adventurers. He refused to derive from these facts the lesson which they contain; he refused to acknowledge the absence of a direct connection between political conflicts and social struggles. The operation of the state apparatus is never independent of the social classes but yet is not adequately explained by the power of only one class. Having dogmatically affirmed that the State is the instrument of exploitation in the service of the dominant class, Marx observed as an historian the relative autonomy of the political order. But he refused to recognize it explicitly. He sought refuge in utopia when he envisaged the proletarian revolution. The true revolution would not consist of conquering the State as is done by all revolutions which maintain a society of classes and the domination—exploitation of the masses by the bourgeoisie. The true revolution would destroy the machinery of the State.

Such a revolutionary utopia offers an easy target for the realistic theorists who think in terms of a ruling class.

The modern theoreticians of elites or oligarchies, G. Mosca, V. Pareto, R. Michels, are in part the legitimate descendants of classical political philosophy. But at the same time they are critics of parliamentarian democracy and socialist utopia. These political philosophers have never doubted the inequality of men's intellectual capacities or the inequality of citizens in wealth and power. To them, the problem was not to eliminate natural or social inequalities, but to assure the accession of the most worthy to the positions of responsibility, and, at the same time, to establish reciprocal relations—of authority and obedience, of benevolence and confidence—between the governors and the governed. Machiavelli had suggested that these relations were not always what they ought to be in the eyes of the moralists, and that the means most generally employed by rulers—force and deception—are reprehensible and necessary. But even if we put aside the pessimism of Machiavelli, the classic conception ran the risk of seeming cynical from the very moment it was used against democratic or socialist ideology. To say that all the parties, including those who claim to speak in the name of democracy and who conform to the obligations of a democratic constitution, are in fact led by a small number of men, a more or less permanent first estate, is to restore the iron law of oligarchy, a law which only appears deceiving or scandalous to democrats inclined to believe that the power *of* the people is exercised *by* the people.

What is true for the party is all the more true for a regime regardless of the way the rulers are recruited. No matter how it operates—in theory or practice— government is always in the hands of a small number of men. In this respect the supposedly democratic regimes are no different from despotic or authoritarian governments. The formulas may change, that is to say, the ideas or principles in whose name minorities rule, but the fact of oligarchy remains. In the first part of his life, G. Mosca indefatigably *unmasked* the liberal and bourgeois democracies by bringing to light the power of politicians, and beyond that, the intrigues and pressures of the leaders of finance and industry, all of which lay behind the letter of the law and appeals to the people. V. Pareto pursued the same enterprise in a still more polemical tone. Although he stated his agreement with Karl Marx concerning the class struggle, he predicted that the future proletarian revolution would simply be one more example of revolution made by a minority for its own gain. Marx agreed with the oligarchical interpretation of all revolutions except for the future socialist revolution. It was easy and tempting to refuse to agree that this exception was possible and to put the future revolution in the same category as the large number of its predecessors.

To designate these oligarchies, which Mosca distinguished mostly by their respective *formulas* and which Pareto characterized by their psychosocial attitudes (violence or cunning, revolutionary syndicalists or plutocrats), three terms have been used: *elite, political class,* and *ruling class.* It may appear that to distinguish among these three terms is not very important: after all, sociologists may legitimately use any terms which please them, provided that they define them exactly. But hesitation in choosing among the concepts reflects an ambiguity related to reality. . . .

I use the term *elite* in the broadest sense: all those who in diverse activities are high in the hierarchy, who occupy any important privileged positions, whether in terms of wealth or of prestige. The term *political class* should be reserved for the much more narrow minority who actually exercise the political functions of government. The *ruling class* would be situated between the *elite* and the *political class*: it includes those privileged people who, without exercising actual political functions, influence those who govern and those who obey, either because of the moral authority which they hold, or because of the economic or financial power they possess.

Of these three terms, elite[3] is the one which I like least, because it has equivocal implications. Is it possible or useful to group as an entity all those who have succeeded, including the kings of the underworld? In certain occupations, such as those of craftsmen, ability is not recognized outside of a small circle, and confers neither power nor fame. To pinpoint the circle within which success insures entry to the elite is not easy nor, for that matter, is it useful. Basically this word serves no purpose other than to recall the iron law of oligarchy, and the inequality of talent and success (success is not always proportional to talent).

On the other hand, the two terms, "political class" and "ruling class" pose an important problem, that of the relations between the minority which actually exercises political power and the larger minority which exercises authority or has prestige in society at large, but is not involved in the government activities. Every regime has a political class whether its political system is democratic or Soviet. A society can not be said to have a ruling class if the heads of its industry, its trade-unions, and political parties, consider each other as enemies, when they have no feeling of solidarity. . . .

---

[3]On the other hand, I do not object to the use of the term "elite" used in the plural, as an equivalent of that which I call the leading categories.

It is clear that a small number governs always and everywhere; but who is this small number? What are the methods of recruitment, the organization, the formulas? How is authority exercised? What are the relations of the political class with the other groups who are privileged and have power and prestige?

These questions are all the more unavoidable as social differentiation has intensified in the course of the past century since these first sociological doctrines were proclaimed, while during the same period, claims to equality for all have become more resolute. Today, equality before the law is no longer challenged in philosophical terms, and the universal right of political participation through a general suffrage is no longer disputed. All members of society are citizens. But in a "civil society," to use Hegel's expression, each citizen has an occupation. The functions of administration at the city, regional or national level, like the political functions (often elective), are exercised by men who are or become professionals. The political class is not hereditary in the East or in the West. In the East as in the West, the holders of state authority have *connections* (it remains to specify what these are) with the economically powerful and with those high in intellectual or spiritual prestige. We must analyze the various social categories which can belong to the ruling class—or again as I have explained before—the various sorts of elites, if we wish to compare societies with respect to their political class or ruling class.

Four antitheses—temporal power and spiritual power, civil power and military power, political power and administrative power, political power and economic power—illustrate the modern differentiation of the functions of control, the increase in the number of social groups actually capable of exercising the functions of control or of substantially influencing those who exercise it.

In all societies, those who establish the hierarchy of values, form the ways of thinking, and determine the content of beliefs, constitute what Auguste Comte called the spiritual power. In our day the spiritual power is shared among or disputed by three kinds of men: the priests, survivors of the spiritual power which the founder of positivism called theological; the intellectuals, writers or scholars; and the party ideologists. A look at the regimes, Soviet and Western, is sufficient to point up a fundamental difference in the structural relations of their leading groups. According to the Soviet formula, it is party ideologists who proclaim the supreme truth and teach what is sacred. Priests officially enjoy little prestige and intellectuals must subscribe to the ideological truth, more or less modified according to the time and the man.

Power in modern societies wants to be civilian in its origin and legitimacy since it bases its "title to rule," its legitimacy on popular endorsement. But it is only effective if it obtains the obedience of the commanders of the army and of the police. In fact, in our age, many regimes owe their power to the action of the army. There are many politicians who first wore the uniform and owe all or part of their moral authority and prestige to their military past.

The modern State is first of all an administrative State. Citizens, as the economic subjects, are permanently subject to the rules of officials who fix the laws of competition between individuals and determine the consequences of the laws in each circumstance. This administrative power is in a sense "de-personalized" and sometimes deprived of its political character: officials command in the capacity of officials and citizens obey the laws and the anonymous representatives of the State. But high administrators belong to the governing minority because they influence the decisions of politicians. The administrative power influences the distribution of the social product which constitutes one of the stakes in the struggle between social groups.

In the West, politicians are differentiated from administrators, although, in certain states, ministers are chosen from among the officials. They are more or less "professionals," depending upon whether or not politics is their primary career and sole source of income. They are, however, always "differentiated" in the sense that their activity, as representatives or as ministers, is inserted into a network of obligations, rights, and specific actions.

The network of these political actions is tied to other networks of social actions, more specifically to the network which can be called economic. Two categories of privileged persons, holders of two sorts of power, emerge from the economic system: *managers of collective labor*, owners of the means of production, directors, engineers, and *leaders of the masses*, heads of workers' unions, and eventually heads of political parties, anxious to organize an occupational group (the industrial workers) on the basis of a class affiliation.

These leading figures are present in any modern society, whether it is a Soviet regime or a Western regime. The relationships provided by the formula or imposed by the law or custom between the various types of privileged persons—holders of moral or legal authority, of actual economic or social power—I call the *structure of the ruling class* or of the power leaders. The Western type of regime is distinguished not only by differentiation among the heads of various power structures, but also by a free dialogue among them. The Soviet type of regime is defined by a lesser degree of differentiation and, especially, by a lesser degree of freedom of dialogue or opposition between priests and intellectuals, between intellectuals and ideologues, ideologues and heads of the party, heads of the party and government. Managers of enterprises do not constitute a category distinct from the state officials. The leaders of the masses, at the factory level, officers of local unions, are more concerned with keeping the masses in line than with expressing their grievances and are recruited because of their abilities to fulfill this function.

A regime of the Soviet type, in distinction to a regime of the Western type, tends to re-establish the confusion between the concepts of society and state. Modern western systems create or accentuate the distinction by differentiating political functions from others. They tolerate legitimate conflict among professional and political organizations which are independent of each other. Furthermore, in the East, from the enterprise to the central office of the ministry, managers are State officials, whereas in the West, those responsible for the management of the economy are divided into multiple categories (owner, nonowner, manager, state official). In the East, the heads of the party are at the same time government executives, leaders of the masses, and official ideologues. In the West, the government continually has to face a more or less independent opposition, union officials, and writers, scholars, and ideologues who never cease disputing the true and the false, the sacred and the scandalous. The voices of the temporary holders of government office are not able to dominate the tumult of debate or propaganda.

These remarks do not aim at developing a theory of the ruling class in the East or West, but only at indicating the kind of problems which are posed by the study of *modern oligarchies* or, if one prefers, the study of the *oligarchical fact within modern societies*. Social differentiation has not spared the *oligarchs* but it has led to two extreme types: the regrouping of leading categories beneath the temporal and spiritual authority of the leaders of a single party, and the disintegration of the ruling class into a sort of permanent cold war (or peaceful coexistence) among the leading groups. Most Western regimes are situated between these two extremes. Great Britain seems to me to be the best example of a country whose regime is Western but which still possesses a ruling class: the higher echelons in the world of affairs, of the university, of the press, church, and of politics find themselves in the same clubs; they often have family ties, they are aware of the community they constitute, they consist in a relatively defined way of the higher interests of England. This class is open to talented persons, it absorbs individuals of lowly origin and does not reject those of high status origin who have assumed the leadership of popular movements of protest. These summits of different groups constitute a ruling class to the extent that the political class and the social elite overlap. . . .

The relations between these leading strata and the social classes must be clarified. All the evidence indicates that these relations differ according to the type of society and the type of regime. We will only treat them here in the context of modern industrial society as it has flourished in the 20th century in the United States, in the Soviet Union, and in Western Europe.

The mass of the population is divided into occupations—agriculture, industry, and services—which economic progress has multiplied and differentiated. The income of each depends essentially upon the place occupied in the processes of production, the place being defined either by the relation to the ownership of the means of production, or by the qualifications needed for the work involved, or by these two criteria together. A Soviet type society only allows for the second criterion since it radically eliminated private ownership of the means of production. The social organization which appears basic to individuals is the system of production and exchanges, the family community is no longer a unit of production, and the religious or ideological communities, in most cases, no longer supplies the means of subsistence. "Civil society". . . in Hegel's sense, envelops the whole of society and constitutes, as it were, the substructure. Does it give rise to classes in conflict, one of which—the exploited class—has as a mission the revolutionary overthrow of the established regime? Neither in the Soviet Union, nor in the United States, is the working class revolutionary. In other words, it does not seem to think or act as if its objective or ambition were the overthrow of the economic or political regime. Neither is it in power; it has not been transformed into a "universal class" in the East or in the West. It seems revolutionary only in France and in Italy where large numbers of workers vote in favor of a regime of the Soviet type within a society of the Western type.

The industrial workers—Russian or American—are integrated into a certain administrative and technical organization. Empirical study establishes the magnitude of the differences in income within the working class. What is the differential in wages between the unskilled laborer and the skilled laborer? Do the workers as a class have the same way of living, the same convictions; do they have the consciousness of kind to constitute a social or historical unit with its own mission? In other words, when it is a question of class—and we take the example of the working class because, according to all the authors, it presents the most defined characteristics of a class—one poses two questions: To what extent does the class exist *objectively*? To what extent does it have an awareness of itself and what is the content— conservative, reformist, or revolutionary—of this awareness?

The first question may be posed both with respect to the Soviet working class and the American working class. The second question is not posed or does not allow an empirically determined answer with respect to the Soviet working class, because the authority structure forbids dealing with the question. Let us place ourselves within a modern industrial enterprise: the workers are subject to an authority which is not democratic in its origin (nomination, not election) or in its mode of exercise (commanding, not discussing). If the union members are allowed to do so, they will present with greater or lesser vehemence, economic (higher salaries, fringe benefits) or political (participation in plant decisions) demands. If the unionized workers are directed by secretaries named by or subject to the ruling Communist party, certain demands will not be made. The very existence of an interest of a specific class, possibly opposed to the interest of the directors of the enterprise, would be denied.

Let us now place ourselves on a more general level, that of industrial workers generally. The same opposition is found even more distinctly here. Class awareness, the idea of a common vocation depends more on propaganda and on organization than on the degree of objective community (to what extent are the workers the same or different from the other members of the society in general?). Workers cannot gain an awareness of themselves as a class if the economic and political regime forbids independent organizations, or to put it another way, if the structure of relations among the leading strata prevents dialogue among the intellectuals, the leaders of the masses, and the politicians.

The relations of classes are not unilaterally determined by the interactions within the leading strata. If one compares the various Western societies, it would be unreasonable to attribute the revolutionary attitude of the working class, in France or in Italy, only to the actions of the leaders. Do the leaders determine the attitude of the masses or are they carried along by the masses? The answer must be made according to the circumstances, and it is rarely categorical in one sense or another. We wish to show that the "class-relationships" only become clear in an industrial society on the condition that socio-economic organizations outside of the machinery of the single party of the State are tolerated. What the comparison between the Soviet universe and the Western world reveals is that the structure of the ruling groups, and not class-relationships, determines the essence of the economic-political regimes.

It is true that social groups are formed differently according to whether or not private ownership of the instruments of production, of the land, or of the machines is tolerated. Distribution of wages and level and style of living of groups are influenced by the status of property, and still more by the mode of regulation (market or planning). But the major differences come from the structure of the power groups, the relations established by the regime between the society and the State. It is enough for a regime of the Soviet type to establish itself, that a Communist party, alone or with the aid of the Red Army, should take power. It is not, then, the state of the productive forces but the state of the political forces—that is the military—which is the main cause of the varying characteristics of each type of society, the cause of the rise or fall of one type of society or another.

Let us compare the results of these analyses with the sociological doctrines discussed earlier and with the interpretations—more or less justified or polemical—which each regime gives of itself and of others.

The reality of the Soviet regime does not have much in common with the myth of the "universal class" and of the "power of the proletariat." Power is exercised by the party which represents the proletariat but which is obviously no longer directed by proletarians. Certainly a Communist type revolution radically eliminates the survivors of the former privileged classes (nobles and bourgeois property-owners); the members of the power groups of the new society emerge from the popular masses and, in theory, the regime facilitates success by the best endowed, attenuating but not excluding the transmission of privileges within families through its abolition of private property and of the accumulation of familial wealth.

Some merits of such a regime are, on the one hand, those which it attributes to itself, but, on the other, some are exactly opposite to those which the official ideology proclaims. The struggle of groups for the division of the national product, the clash between workers and property owners disappears as the doctrine suggests. Society ceases to be the theater of a permanent cold war. But peace is re-established, not by abolishing the occasions for, or the stakes of, the conflicts, but by preventing the organization of class armies and propaganda for class war. Saint-Simonians and Marxists both consider as basic, the cooperation of all producers—both managers and employees, since they have the same fundamental interests. But the Saint-Simonians did not believe that it was necessary to destroy private ownership of the instruments of production in order for all the producers to recognize their solidarity. Marxists, on the contrary, have argued that there would be a class struggle as long as there is a distinction between capitalists and proletarians. They eliminated the private ownership of the instruments of production, the capitalist class; then in accord with their doctrine, they proclaimed that there were no longer classes or that the classes were no longer antagonists. Finally, so that reality could not make a lie of their doctrine, they gave a monopoly of power to their party and its ideology. The representatives of all groups in society who must express themselves through the party, using its vocabulary, vie with each other in their affirmation of the disappearance of classes and class-struggle.

The Soviet regime is a reaction against the tendency, characteristic of the Western societies, of differentiation of functions and the dispersion of power groups. It re-establishes the unit of a ruling class, the spiritual and political unity of those in positions to lead, which in the West has been threatened by the dialogue among the politicians, intellectuals, and leaders of the masses. In this sense, it is the opposite of what it claims to be; it accentuates the oligarchical fact which it denies, it confirms the cynicism of Pareto, it represents the victory of a minority which calls upon the voice of history or the proletariat in the same way that other minorities have called upon the voice of God or of the People. The elite theory of a Pareto is better adapted to the interpretation of revolutions which claim to follow Marx than is Marxism. The revolutionary efficacy of the State has been gloriously illustrated by those who say that the State is only the instrument of the economically privileged class. It is easy for those who hold the military power to quickly assure themselves of economic authority and political power.

But the Westerner, "unmasking" the Soviet reality with the aid of the conceptions of a Pareto, would be wrong to belittle the historical accomplishments of the adverse regime. For it has actually put an end to class struggle, not, it is true, by substituting a miraculous harmony of interests in place of the contradictions of yesterday, but by first proclaiming and then refusing to doubt that such harmony exists from now on. The monopoly of a party and of an ideology, the submission by the intellectuals and the mass leaders to the orders of the leader of the party, contribute to the restoration of a ruling class. Now, the Western regimes are menaced less by the total power of monopolists than by the disintegration of the *social consensus*, by the rivalry among the major power groups.

Soviet polemicists and Western critics who believe themselves to be the heirs of Marx, "unmask" Western type democracy by exposing the sinister role of monopolists or of power elites. The existence of oligarchy once again, is not in question. But the characteristic trait of the oligarchy, within Western societies, is not the hidden power of a group of men (the heads of industry or of the army); rather it is the absence of a common will, of a common conception among the power strata who fight each other according to the rules of the game of the democratic polity. The much greater danger is that the struggle among the power groups does not necessarily give the ordinary citizen a sense of freedom. Even if the functioning of the economy and the conduct of diplomacy in the United States are not controlled, directed, or thought up by one man or by any one conscious team, the citizen does not acquire, for all that, the conviction that he is capable of influencing the course of events or the policies of industry or of the army. The mythology of hidden power elites succeeds because it expresses the impotence felt by the majority and it designates those responsible, those who "really" have power. The sense of impotence is made no less authentic by the fact that the "power elite" does not exist, or that it is everyone and no one at the same time. . . .

The scientific and political controversy over the concepts of social class and ruling class has at its origin one specific trait of modern societies, the separation of social power and of political authority, the differentiation of functions, in particular, of political functions. The sociologists of the last century all recognized this separation of the society and the State. . ., all admitted that the development of industrial society contributed to the re-establishment of unity, the surviving parts of feudalism and of the *ancien regime* gradually disappeared and the State became the authentic expression of modern society. But none of the great sociologists on the continent had a clear idea of what the modern State would be, of what would be the true expression of modern society. Some saw it taken over by the producers, others heralded the dying out of the State after the victory of the proletariat, others questioned the respective probabilities for representative regimes or for despotism.

One of the principal causes of these uncertainties was the very ambiguity of the notion of class which was applied to privileged minorities—noble and bourgeois—and to the masses—peasants and workers. The privileged classes of the *ancien regime* were minorities who held social power (by landownership), military force (they exercised judicial and administrative functions). Before the Revolution the noble class had lost a large part of its economic power and almost all of its judicial and administrative functions. Different men exercised these functions, and these men depended more and more upon the machinery of State. But the pre-Revolutionary nobility continued to furnish the model of the "dominant class" of industrial society, a minority which is socially privileged and which actually exercises power in society and the State. This picture is inadequate for modern society which is characterized by a differentiation of functions that forbids property owners and managers of the means of production to themselves even if army officers or political executives. As this confusion between the reality of power and the way in which the summits of different structures operate, is too difficult for modern men to understand, the ideologists invented the myth of clandestine elites who have omnipotence through their ability to infiltrate the state.

Reality is at once simpler and more complex. Authority relations within modern societies are essentially multiple because the worker, the citizen, the taxpayer, the motorist are each subject to a separate set of regulations—technical, administrative, legal, political. The men who direct these organizations, who preside over these apparatuses, are inevitably different. On the basis of these facts, the diversity of power groups is the first relevant datum, the relations among these upper strata have a specific character in each regime. The Western regimes tolerate dialogue among these groups, the Soviet regimes confer a party and authority monopoly on a party and ideology. The separation between society and State is reduced, the competition among the power groups attenuated. . . .

The diversity of leading strata is inseparable from the nature of modern societies, but these strata may constitute a ruling class when they are made such in a single party system or when, in a competitive party system, they preserve the sense of a common interest in the regime and in the State, when they continue to be recruited for the most part from a narrow and, as it were, an aristocratic group. The two notions of leading strata and of ruling class can and ought to be used in scientific analyses without an ideological intention. In the eyes of certain people, they pass as politically oriented, but this is wrong. It is true that such concepts "unmask" the mythical confusion of the proletariat with the ruling class of the Soviet societies, and the hypothetical confusion of economic and political power in democratic societies. But they also unmask the *naiveté* of democratic ideology, *a la* Lincoln, "by the people and for the people." Otherwise the concepts do not settle the real problems in the East and West, of the agreement or divorce between the sentiments and interests of the large number on the one hand, and the action of the dominant minorities on the other. One may still argue that a ruling class, unified by the discipline of a party, is more efficient for the welfare of a society than is free competition among minorities.

ELITES AND SOCIETY

T. B. Bottomore

The Elite: Concept and Ideology. Both Mosca and Pareto . . . were concerned with elites in the sense of groups of people who either exercised directly, or were in a position to influence very strongly the exercise of, political power. At the same time, they recognized that the "governing elite" or "political class" is itself composed of distinct social groups. Pareto observed that the "upper stratum of society, the *elite*, nominally contains certain groups of people, not always very sharply defined, that are called aristocracies," and he went on to refer to "military, religious, and commercial aristocracies and plutocracies."[1] The point was made more sharply in a study of elites in France by a pupil of Pareto, Marie Kolabinska, who discussed explicitly the movement of individuals between the different sub-groups of the governing elite, and set out to examine in some detail the history of four such groups: the rich, the nobles, the armed aristocracy and the clergy.[2] Nevertheless, Pareto is always inclined to emphasize more strongly the division between *the* governing elite and the non-elite, and it is Mosca who examines more thoroughly the composition of the elite itself, especially in the modern democratic societies. Thus he refers to "the various party organizations into which the political class is divided," and which have to compete for the votes of the more numerous classes; and later on he remarks that "it cannot be denied that the representative system [of government] provides a way for many different social forces to participate in the political system and, therefore, to balance and limit the influence of other social forces and the influence of bureaucracy in particular." This last passage also reveals a considerable divergence between Pareto and Mosca in their interpretation of the development of political systems. Pareto always emphasizes the universality of the distinction between governing elite and masses, and he reserves his most scathing comments for the modern notions of "democracy," "humanitarianism" and "progress." Mosca, on the other hand, is prepared to recognize, and in a qualified way to approve, the distinctive features of modern democracy; in his first

---

SOURCE: From *Elites and Society* by T. B. Bottomore (London: C. A. Watts & Co., Ltd., and New York: Basic Books, Inc.© 1964 by T. B. Bottomore.) pp. 4-14, 30-38. Reprinted by permission. Most footnotes have been omitted, and those remaining have been renumbered.
    [1] V. Pareto, *The Mind and Society*, III, pp. 1429-30.
    [2] Marie Kolabinska, *La circulation des élites en France*, p. 7.

book, it is true, he observes that in a parliamentary democracy, "the representative is not elected by the voters but, as a rule, has himself elected by them . . . or . . . his friends have him elected"; but in his later works he concedes that the majority may, through its representatives, have a certain control over government policy. As Meisel notes, it is only in his criticism of Marx that Mosca makes a sharp disjunction between masses and minorities; for the most part he presents a more subtle and complex theory in which the political class itself is influenced and restrained by a variety of "social forces" (representing numerous different interests in society), and also by the moral unity of the society as a whole which is expressed in the rule of law. In Mosca's theory, an elite does not simply rule by force and fraud, but "represents," in some sense, the interests and purposes of important and influential groups in the society.

There is another element, too, in Mosca's theory which modifies its original stark outlines. In modern times, the elite is not simply raised high above the rest of society; it is intimately connected with society through a sub-elite, a much larger group which comprises, to all intents and purposes, the whole "new middle class" of civil servants, managers and white collar workers, scientists and engineers, scholars and intellectuals. This group does not only supply recruits to the elite (the ruling class in the narrow sense); it is itself a vital element in the government of society, and Mosca observes that "the stability of any political organism depends on the level of morality, intelligence and activity that this second stratum has attained." It is not unreasonable, then, to claim, as did Gramsci, that Mosca's "political class . . . is a puzzle. One does not exactly understand what Mosca means, so fluctuating and elastic is the notion. Sometimes he seems to think of the middle class, sometimes of men of property in general, and then again of those who call themselves 'the educated.' But on other occasions Mosca apparently has in mind the 'political personnel'.". . .[3]

The conceptual scheme which Mosca and Pareto have handed down thus comprises the following common notions: in every society there is, and must be, a minority which rules over the rest of society; this minority—the "political class" or "governing elite," composed of those who occupy the posts of political command and, more vaguely, those who can directly influence political decisions—undergoes changes in its membership over a period of time, ordinarily by the recruitment of new individual members from the lower strata of society, sometimes by the incorporation of new social groups, and occasionally by the complete replacement of the established elite by a "counter-elite," as occurs in revolutions. . . . From this point, the conceptions of Pareto and Mosca diverge. Pareto insists more strongly upon the separation between rulers and ruled in every society, and dismisses the view that a democratic political system differs from any other in this respect. He explains the circulation of elites in mainly psychological terms, making use of the idea of residues (sentiments) which he has set out at great length in the earlier parts of *The Mind and Society*. Mosca, on the other hand, is much more aware of the heterogeneity of the elite, the higher stratum of the political class, itself; of the

---

[3] Antonio Gramsci, *Note sul Machiavelli.*

interests or social forces which are represented in it; and, in the case of modern societies, of its intimate bonds with the rest of society, principally through the lower stratum of the political class, the "new middle class." Thus Mosca also allows that there is a difference between modern democracies and other types of polity, and to some extent he recognizes that there is interaction between the ruling minority and the majority, instead of a simple dominance by the former over the latter. Finally, Mosca explains the circulation of elites sociologically as well as psychologically, in so far as he accounts for the rise of new elites (or of new elements in the elite) in part by the emergence of social forces which represent new interests (e.g., technological or economic interests) in the society.

Later studies of elites have followed Pareto and Mosca, especially the latter, closely in their concern with problems of political power. Thus H. D. Lasswell, both in his early writings which were commended by Mosca himself, and more recently in the Hoover Institute Studies on elites, has devoted himself particularly to the study of the political elite, which he defines in the following terms: "The political elite comprises the power holders of a body politic. The power holders include the leadership and the social formations from which leaders typically come, and to which accountability is maintained, during a given period."[4] The difference from the conceptions of Pareto and Mosca is that the *political elite* is here distinguished from other elites which are less closely associated with the exercise of power, although they may have a considerable social influence, and that the idea of "social formations" (including social classes) from which elites are typically recruited is reintroduced into a scheme of thought from which, especially in Pareto's theory, it had been expelled. As we shall see in a moment, the idea of elites was originally conceived in opposition to the idea of social classes. A similar development is apparent in the writings of Raymond Aron, who has also been chiefly concerned with the elite in the sense of a governing minority, but has attempted to establish a relation between the elite and social classes,[5] has insisted upon the plurality of elites in modern societies and has examined the social influence of the intellectual elite, which does not ordinarily form part of the system of political power.

The fresh distinctions and refinements which have been made in the concept of the elite call for a more discriminating terminology than has been employed hitherto. The term "elite(s)" is now generally applied, in fact, to functional, mainly occupational, groups which have high status (for whatever reason) in a society; and henceforward I shall use it, without qualification, in this sense. The study of such elites is fruitful in several ways: the size of the elites, the number of different elites, their relations with each other and with the groups that wield political power, are among the most important facts which have to be considered in distinguishing between different types of society and in accounting for changes in social structure;

---

[4]Lasswell, in H.D. Lasswell, D. Lerner, and C.E. Rothwell, *The Comparative Study of Elites.*
[5]Raymond Aron, "Social Structure and the Ruling Class, Part I," *British Journal of Sociology,* I (I), 1950. "The problem of combining in a synthesis 'class' sociology and 'elite' sociology ... can be reduced to the following question: 'What is the relation between social differentiation and political hierarchy in modern societies?'"

so, too, is the closed or open character of the elites, or in other words, the nature of the recruitment of their members and the degree of social mobility which this implies. If the general term "elite" is to be applied to these functional groups, we shall need another term for the minority which rules a society, which is not a functional group in exactly the same sense, and which is in any case of such great social importance that it deserves to be given a distinctive name. I shall use here Mosca's term, the "political class," to refer to all those groups which exercise political power or influence, and are directly engaged in struggles for political leadership; and I shall distinguish within the political class a smaller group, the political elite, which comprises those individuals who actually exercise political power in a society at any given time. The extent of the political elite is, therefore, relatively easy to determine: it will include members of the government and of the high administration, military leaders, and, in some cases, politically influential families of an aristocracy or royal house and leaders of powerful economic enterprises. It is less easy to set the boundaries of the political class; it will, of course, include the political elite, but it may also include "counter-elites" comprising the leaders of political parties which are out of office, and representatives of new social interests or classes (e.g., trade union leaders), as well as groups of businessmen, and intellectuals who are active in politics. The political class, therefore, is composed of a number of groups which may be engaged in varying degrees of co-operation, competition or conflict with each other.

The concept of the political elite was presented by Mosca and Pareto as a key term in a new social science, but it had another aspect which is scarcely less apparent in their writings; namely, that it formed part of a political doctrine which was opposed to, or critical of, modern democracy, and still more opposed to modern socialism. C. J. Friedrich has drawn attention to the fact that the nineteenth-century European doctrines of rule by an elite of superior individuals—doctrines which encompassed Carlyle's philosophy of the hero and Nietzsche's vision of the superman as well as the more prosaic studies of Mosca, Pareto and Burckhardt—were "all offspring of a society containing as yet many feudal remnants," and that these doctrines represented so many different attempts to revive ancient ideas of social hierarchy and to erect obstacles to the spread of democratic notions.[6] The social environment of such doctrines is defined still more narrowly by G. Lukacs, who suggests that the problem of political leadership was raised by sociologists precisely in those countries which had not succeeded in establishing a genuine bourgeois democracy (i.e., in which the feudal elements were especially strong); and he points to Max Weber's concept of "charisma" (in Germany) and Pareto's concept of "elites" (in Italy) as similar and typical manifestations of this preoccupation.[7]

The opposition between the idea of elites and the idea of democracy may be expressed in two forms: first, that the insistence in the elite theories upon the inequality of individual endowment runs counter to a fundamental strand in

---

[6]Carl J. Friedrich, *The New Image of the Common Man.*
[7]G. Lukács, *Die Zerstörung der Vernunft.*

democratic political thought, which is inclined rather to emphasize an underlying equality of individuals; and secondly, that the notion of a governing minority contradicts the democratic theory of majority rule. But this opposition need not be by any means so rigorous and extreme as appears at first sight. If democracy is regarded as being primarily a political system, it may well be argued, as many have done, that "government *by* the people" (i.e., the effective rule of the majority) is impossible in practice, and that the significance of political democracy is primarily that the positions of power in society are open in principle to everyone, that there is competition for power, and that the holders of power at any time are accountable to the electorate. Schumpeter presented such a view of democracy, which has since been widely accepted, when he defined the democratic method as "that institutional arrangement for arriving at political decisions in which individuals acquire the power to decide by means of competitive struggle for the people's vote."[8] Similarly, Karl Mannheim, who at an earlier stage had seen in the views of the elite theorists an irrational justification of "direct action," and of unconditional subordination to a leader,[9] came later to regard such theories as being compatible with democracy: ". . . the actual shaping of policy is in the hands of elites; but this does not mean to say that the society is not democratic. For it is sufficient for democracy that the individual citizens, though prevented from taking a direct part in government all the time, have at least the *possibility* of making their aspirations felt at certain intervals."[10]

Moreover, it can equally well be argued that, even if democracy is regarded as comprising more than a political system, it is still compatible with elite theories; for the idea of equality which democracy as a form of society may be held to imply can easily be re-interpreted as "equality of opportunity." Democracy will then be treated as a type of society in which the elites—economic and cultural, as well as political—are "open" in principle, and are in fact recruited from different social strata on the basis of individual merit. This conception of the place of elites in a democracy is actually suggested by the theory of the circulation of elites, and it is stated explicitly in Mosca's writings.

It needs to be emphasized at this point that both the conceptions I have discussed—that of political competition, and that of equality of opportunity—can be presented as corollaries of liberal, or *laissez-faire*, economic theory. Schumpeter was quite aware of this: "This concept (of competition for political leadership) presents similar difficulties as the concept of competition in the economic sphere, with which it may be usefully compared"[11]; and a more recent writer has stated the connection still more forcefully: ". . . the theory of elites is, essentially, only a refinement of social *laissez-faire*. The doctrine of opportunity in education is a mere silhouette of the doctrine of economic individualism, with its emphasis on competition and 'getting-on.' "[12] In one sense, therefore, the elite theories of Pareto and

---

[8] J. A. Schumpeter, *Capitalism, Socialism and Democracy.*
[9] Karl Mannheim, *Ideology and Utopia* (1929, English trans. 1936), p. 119.
[10] *Idem, Essays on the Sociology of Culture.*
[11] J. A. Schumpeter, *op. cit.*, p. 271.
[12] Raymond Williams, *Culture and Society* (Penguin Books edn.), p. 236.

Mosca were not (and those of their successors are not now) opposed to the general idea of democracy. Their original and main antagonist was, in fact, socialism, and especially Marxist socialism. As Mosca wrote: "In the world in which we are living socialism will be arrested only if a realistic political science succeeds in demolishing the metaphysical and optimistic methods that prevail at present in social studies. . ." This "realistic science," which Pareto, Weber, Michels and others in different ways helped to further, was intended above all to refute Marx's theory of social classes on two essential points: first, to show that the Marxist conception of a "ruling *class*" is erroneous, by demonstrating the continual circulation of elites, which prevents in most societies, and especially in modern industrial societies, the formation of a stable and closed ruling class; and secondly, to show that a classless society is impossible, since in every society there is, and must be, a minority which actually rules. As Meisel so aptly comments: " 'Elite' was originally a middle class notion. . . . (In the Marxist theory) . . . the proletariat is to be the ultimate class which will usher in the classless society. Not so. Rather, the history of all societies, past and future, is the history of its ruling classes . . . there will always be a ruling class, and therefore exploitation. This is the anti-socialist, specifically anti-Marxist, bent of the elitist theory as it unfolds in the last decade of the nineteenth century."[13] The elitist theories also oppose socialist doctrines in a more general way, by substituting for the notion of a class which rules by virtue of economic or military power, the notion of an elite which rules because of the superior qualities of its members. As Kolabinska says, ". . . the principal notion conveyed by the term 'elite' is that of superiority. . . ."[14]

These reflections upon the ideological elements in elite theories provoke some further questions. It is possible, as I have suggested, to reconcile the idea of elites with democratic social theories; yet the early exponents of elite theories were undoubtedly hostile to democracy (although Mosca changed his views somewhat after his experience of Fascist rule in Italy, and became a cautious defender of some aspects of democratic government), and the hostility is still more marked in the case of those, such as Carlyle and Nietzsche, who presented social myths rather than scientific theories of politics. How is this to be explained? There is, first, the fact that these nineteenth-century thinkers conceived democracy in a different way, as a stage in the "revolt of the masses" leading with apparent necessity towards socialism. In criticizing democracy, therefore, they were, in an indirect way, combating socialism itself. It should be noticed, further, that the elite theorists themselves have had an important influence in producing the new definitions of democracy, such as that of Schumpeter, which are then held up as being compatible with the notion of elites. . . .

Another characteristic of the elite theories has been reproduced in many recent social theories which are directed against socialism; it is that, while these theories criticize the determinism which they find especially in Marxism, they themselves tend to establish an equally strict kind of determinism. The fundamental argument of the elite theorists is not merely that every known society has been divided into

---

[13] J. H. Meisel, *The Myth of the Ruling Class*, p. 10.
[14] M. Kolabinska, *op. cit.*, p. 5.

two strata—a ruling minority and a majority which is ruled—but that all societies *must* be so divided. In what respect is this less deterministic than Marxism? For whether men are obliged to attain the classless society or are necessarily prevented from ever attaining it, are they not equally unfree? It may be objected that the cases are not alike: that the elite theorists are only excluding one form of society as impossible, while leaving open other possibilities (and Mosca claimed that in the social sciences it is easier to foresee *what is never going to happen*, than to foresee exactly what will happen); whereas the Marxists are predicting that a particular form of society will necessarily come into existence. But one might equally well say that the elite theorists—and especially Pareto—are claiming that one type of political society is universal and necessary, and that the Marxists deny the universal validity of this "law of elites and masses" and assert man's liberty to imagine and create new forms of society. In short, there is in both theories an element of social determinism which may be more or less strongly emphasized.

From the Ruling Class to the Power Elite. The concepts of "ruling class" and "governing elite" are used in descriptions and explanations of political happenings, and their value must be judged by the extent to which they make possible reasonable answers to important questions about political systems. Do the rulers of society constitute a social group? Is it a cohesive or divided, an open or closed group? How are its members selected? What is the basis of their power? Is this power unrestricted or is it limited by that of other groups in society? Are there significant and regular differences between societies in these respects, and if so, how are they to be explained?

The two concepts are alike in emphasizing the division between rulers and ruled as one of the most important facts of social structure. But they state the division in different ways: the concept of a "governing elite" contrasts the organized, ruling minority with the unorganized majority, or masses, while the concept of a "ruling class" contrasts the dominant class with subject classes, which may themselves be organized, or be creating organizations. From these different conceptions arise differences in the way of conceiving the relations between rulers and ruled. In the Marxist theory, which employs the concept of a ruling class, the conflict between classes becomes the principal force producing changes of social structure; but in the elite theories—in spite of the fact that Pareto praised highly Marx's conception of class struggle, which he described as "profoundly true,"[15]—the relations between the organized minority and the unorganized majority are necessarily represented as more passive, and the resulting problem of how to explain the rise and fall of ruling elites, if it is confronted at all, has to be dealt with either by postulating a recurrent decadence in the elite (Pareto) or by introducing the idea of the rise of new "social forces" among the masses (Mosca) which brings the theory close to Marxism.

A further difference between the two concepts lies in the extent to which they make possible explanations of the cohesion of the ruling minority. The "governing elite," defined as those who occupy the positions of command in a society, is merely assumed to be a cohesive group, unless other considerations, such as their membership of the wealthy class, or their aristocratic family origins are introduced

[15] Pareto, *Les systèmes socialistes*, II, p. 405.

(as they are consistently by Mosca, and occasionally by Pareto). But the "ruling class," defined as the class which owns the major instruments of economic production in a society, is shown to be a cohesive social group; first, because its members have definite economic interests in common, and, more importantly, because it is engaged permanently in a conflict with other classes in society, through which its self-awareness and solidarity are continually enhanced. Furthermore, this concept states in a precise form what is the basis of the minority's ruling position, namely its economic dominance, while the concept of the "governing elite" says little about the bases of the power which the elite possesses, except in so far as it incorporates elements from the Marxist theory of classes. In Mills' study of the "power elite," there is an attempt to explain the power position of the three principal elites taken separately—that of the business executives by the growth in size and complexity of business corporations; that of the military chiefs by the growing scale and expense of the weapons of war, determined by technology and the state of international conflict; and that of the national political leaders, in a somewhat less satisfactory way, by the decline of the legislature, of local politics and of voluntary organizations—but the unity of the power elite as a single group, and the basis of *its* power, are not explained. Why is there *one* power elite and not *three*?

The superiority of the concept of "ruling class" lies in its greater fertility and suggestiveness and in its value in the construction of theories. But I have pointed our earlier some of its defects, and it is now necessary to consider whether these can be overcome. The most important step in this direction would be to give up the Marxist view of the concept as a description of a real phenomenon which is to be observed in all societies in the same general form, and to regard it instead as an "ideal type," in the sense which Max Weber gave to this term. If we treat the concept in this way we can proceed to ask how closely the relationships in a particular society approach the ideal type of a ruling class and subject classes; and so employ the concept, properly, as a tool of thought and investigation. It is then possible to see clearly that the idea of a "ruling class" originated in the study of a particular historical situation—the end of feudalism and the beginnings of modern capitalism—and to consider how far, and in what respects, other situations diverge from this ideal type, as a result of the absence or weakness of class formation, the influence of factors other than the ownership of property in the creation of classes, and the conflict between different forms of power.

There are two sorts of situation in which we can see especially plainly a divergence from the ideal type of a ruling class. One is that in which, although there is an "upper class"—that is to say, a clearly demarcated social group which has in its possession a large part of the property of society and receives a disproportionately large share of the national income, and which has created on the basis of these economic advantages a distinctive culture and way of life—this class does not enjoy undisputed or unrestricted political power, in the sense that it is able to maintain easily its property rights or to transmit them unimpaired from generation to generation. This kind of situation has been discerned by many observers particularly in the modern democracies, in which, as I noted earlier, there is a potential opposition between the ownership of wealth and productive resources by a small upper class, and the possession of political power, through the franchise, by the mass of the population. . . .

In order to determine whether in such a case there is a "ruling class" it is necessary first to examine the degree in which the upper class has been successful in perpetuating its ownership of property. We shall have to note, on one side, that in the democratic countries during the present century a considerable number of restrictions have been placed upon the use of private property, and that there has probably been some reduction in the inequalities of wealth and income, as a result of progressive taxation, and of the growth of publicly owned property and publicly administered social services. On the other side we must note that the decline in the proportion of private wealth owned by the upper class has been modest and very slow, and that the redistribution of income through taxation has not proceeded very far. . . . The upper class in Britain has been able to resist with considerable success the attacks upon its economic interests, and that in this sense of having the power to defend its interests it has maintained itself during the present century as a ruling class. The situation in the other democratic countries, with the exception of the Scandinavian countries, does not differ greatly from that in Britain; in all of them, right-wing governments have been in power during most of the present century and the redistribution of wealth and income has occurred slowly, if at all. One must be sceptical, therefore, of the view that the extension of voting rights to the mass of the population can establish at once—or has in fact established in the short period of time in which modern democracies have existed—popular rule, and eliminate the power of a ruling class. What seems to have taken place in the democratic countries up to the present time is not so much a reduction in the power of the upper class as a decline in the radicalism of the working class.

The second type of situation in which there is a divergence from the "ruling class—subject classes" model is that in which the ruling group is not a class in Marx's sense. One instance is provided by those societies in which a stratum of intellectuals or bureaucrats may be said to wield supreme power—in China under the rule of the *literati* or in India under the rule of the Brahmins. Another instance is to be found in the present-day Communist countries where power is concentrated in the leaders of a political party. In these cases, however, we need to examine carefully how far the ruling stratum is clearly distinguishable from a ruling class. . . .

The possession of the means of administration may be, as Max Weber argued, an alternative to the possession of means of economic production, as a basis of political power. This distinction is perhaps more obvious in the case of the present-day Communist countries, in which there is no private ownership of the means of production, and in which the officials of the ruling party and the state control the economy. Wittfogel has attempted, in a very ingenious way, to assimilate this type of political power to the general category of "oriental despotism"[16] but I think the differences are too great—the existence of private ownership of land and other resources, and the intimate bonds between the officials

---

[16] Karl Wittfogel, *Oriental Despotism*.

and the property-owning classes in one case, and the specific characteristics of rule by a political party in the other—for this attempt to be successful. The political system of the Communist countries seems to approach the pure type of a "power elite," that is, a group which, having come to power with the support or acquiescence of particular classes in the population, maintains itself in power chiefly by virtue of being an organized minority confronting the unorganized majority; wheras in the case of ancient China or India we have to deal with a system which combines the features of a ruling class and a power elite.

There is another element in the position of a ruling class, which has already been mentioned and which needs to be examined more fully in its bearing upon those situations in which the existence of such a class is doubtful. Since the power of a ruling class arises from its ownership of property, and since this property can easily be transmitted from generation to generation, the class has an enduring character. It is constituted by a group of families which remain as its component elements over long periods of time through the transmission of the family property. Its composition is not entirely immutable, for new families may enter it and old families may decline, but the greater part of its members continue from generation to generation. Only when there are rapid changes in the whole system of production and property ownership does the composition of the ruling class change significantly; and in that case we can say that one ruling class has been replaced by another. If, however, we were to find, in a particular society or type of society, that the movement of individuals and families between the different social levels was so continuous and so extensive that no group of families was able to maintain itself for any length of time in a situation of economic and political pre-eminence, then we should have to say that in such a society there was no ruling class. It is, in fact, this "circulation of elites" (in the terminology of the elite theorists) or "social mobility" (in the language of more recent sociological studies) that has been fixed upon by a number of writers as a second important characteristic of modern industrial societies—the first being universal suffrage—which must qualify severely, if it does not altogether exclude, the assertion that there is a ruling class in these societies. By this means we may arrive at the view, which was formulated by Karl Mannheim among others,[17] that the development of industrial societies can properly be depicted as a movement from a class system to a system of elites, from a social hierarchy based upon the inheritance of property to one based upon merit and achievement.

This confrontation between the concepts of "ruling class" and "political elite" shows, I think, that, while on one level they may be totally opposed, as elements in wide-ranging theories which interpret political life, and especially the future possibilities of political organization, in very different ways, on another level they may be seen as complementary concepts, which refer to different types of political system or to different aspects of the same political system. With their help we can attempt to distinguish between societies in which there is a ruling class, and at the same time elites which represent particular aspects of its interests; societies in which there is no ruling class, but a political elite which founds its power upon the control

[17]See especially, *Man and Society*, Part II, Chapt. II.

of the administration, or upon military force, rather than upon property ownership and inheritance; and societies in which there exists a multiplicity of elites among which no cohesive and enduring group of powerful individuals or families seems to be discoverable at all.

THE ELITE IN THE WELFARE STATE

Piet Thoenes

Consequent upon an unbroken series of technical improvements in the process of production, a remarkable shift of emphasis has taken place in economic thought and action over the past two hundred years. Classical economics was primarily a doctrine of scarcity. It was concerned with the production and consumption of goods which had value; that is to say of goods, of which the community in general did not have enough. . . .

There would be little point here in undertaking a detailed description of the course of the Industrial Revolution. But the core of the process of thought that emerged from it in regard to classical economics, in so far as it concerns us here, boils down to the following. Human needs are unlimited; it follows from this that there exists an unlimited demand for goods. The means available for the satisfying of this unlimited need are scarce. Therefore, it is inconceivable that the demand will fall short of the capacity for production; for this reason attention is centered primarily upon the expansion of production capacity.

It is, moreover, the price mechanism which selects and indicates which needs remain satisfied and which unsatisfied, and thus determines how the scarce means of production are to be put to use. But in choosing this as a basic principle—a principle which was obvious in those days when poverty was a natural phenomenon—classical economics was not the slightest bit concerned about the possibility of over-production, but rather with the possibility of a falling-off in the total demand.

In fact, despite the warnings of the theoreticians, the belief in these rules of the game of classical economics continued until the world crisis of 1929 convinced the most conservative of employers, in the harshest of fashions, that times had changed.

The Keynesian system which came into play after this has two characteristics which differ fundamentally from the old system. In the first place the economic system does not function automatically; it needs a guardian. The government has a

SOURCE: Piet Thoenes, *The Elite in the Welfare State,* ed. by J. A. Banks, Trans. by J. E. Bingham (New York: The Free Press, 1966), pp. 141-146, 151-152, 154-168. Reprinted with permission of The Macmillan Co.© by *The Free Press,* New York, 1966. Footnotes have been omitted.

central task in the system. Thinking is structured in terms of a national economy. So long as all goes well, the government's strategy is to stand aside; but it is determined to keep its finger on the pulse of economic process by means of detailed statistical information. If anything should go awry it intervenes, by changing the bank rate, by price control, by exercising an influence over consumption, or by wage restraint.

Secondly, the tricky point is no longer the encouragement of production capacity, but guaranteeing the disposal of the turnover. A stable core of consumers with purchasing power and the will to buy is the backbone of the system. The social consequences of this are obvious. The old class structure is disappearing, inasmuch as this has been correctly described by the Dutch sociologist, van Heek, as a society which consists primarily of groups which are socially unequal because they have different economic strength whenever their interests clash in the labour or goods market, owing to their position in a system in which private ownership preponderates. . . .

Two elements are now important for the view of the Welfare State. Within the framework of classical economics a system of production has been instituted which guarantees a flow of goods, and which guarantees in principle a subsistence for everyone, certainly as far as volume is concerned; and in the Welfare State, the government is an important authority who must see to it that consumers do indeed receive these goods. . . . If the government does not see to it that the consumers are able and willing to buy in sufficient quantity, a crisis threatens in the production sector. Welfare, which is brought about under government supervision, is not simply a blessing on its own account; it is the necessary condition for the survival of the capitalist system.

The liberal period was characterized—as were all the preceding ones—by poignant contrasts between rich and poor. In a world of poverty the poor were a natural phenomenon. But when the capitalist methods of production seemed capable of producing a flow of goods of hitherto unheard-of proportions, people began to wonder whether this flow could be directed in such a way that poverty might be abolished, perhaps not even as a relative phenomenon, but absolutely. . . .

At first economic theory gave only slight encouragement to the notion of the extension of welfare. The classical argument was that poverty was the best possible stimulus for hard work, and that the will to work was ultimately the source of production. A second argument was that wages must remain low in order to keep the whole monetary field wide open for investment. In this way economic theories provided the arguments for political strife. Many of the less well-off did not appear to be quite so fully convinced of the logic of this system. Armed with a dissenting theory, the Marxist, and later the planning-type socialist, campaigned for a more egalitarian distribution of wealth.

In view of this antagonism, the liberal period can be said to have been characterized in so far as welfare is concerned, by a struggle that was fought out in the political arena between a group which held the existing situation to be more or less the correct one, and another group which held it not to be the correct one, and never likely to be.

However, owing to the altered situation as regards the approach to economic affairs in the Welfare State, this opposition of views has been deprived of its theoretical basis. On the one hand, it is now plain to the owner of the means of production that a reasonable increase in the amount of pay (as the expansion of welfare might be called) leads to an increase in his turnover. In fact he is no longer keen on the poor worker but on the wealthy one. On the other hand, the trade union leader is rather touchy about the argument that too great a wage outlay limits opportunities for investment, and which can therefore be a cause of endemic unemployment in the event of automation or a population explosion. This is not to say that the argument over the degree or the nature of the expansion of welfare is closed, but it has for the time been shifted to the technical field of optimal choice. The interests of both groups are no longer in opposition; in fact they are to a great extent moving along parallel lines.

The struggle has been reduced to a discussion between technical experts. Any antagonism which there may still be, is no longer to do with an argument about the nature of the system, but rather about the adaptation of a system which is accepted by all. . . .

In the liberal period a government, or the representatives of the people could, in principle, take decisions of a political nature because of their recognized political qualities. Although they often had personal contacts with the economic machine they were not supposed to consult it at all when they were making their decisions. Armaments, birth control, provision of education, medical care, were considered in the light of their political, cultural or social consequences.

In the Welfare State the government has taken upon itself such far-reaching responsibility for the proper functioning of what appears to be such a delicately poised economic machine, that considerations prompted by this fact must to a great degree determine its political decisions. What effect will disarmament have upon the system of full employment? What does birth control mean in terms of the labour market? How will the raising of the school-leaving age affect industrial training? What bearing has medical care on the retirement age of old people entitled to State pensions?

The obvious consequence of this accumulation of problems is that political government is becoming greatly restricted in view of the requirements of an agreed economic system; and contemporary evaluation of this economic system veers away from political judgments, because there are no important groups hostile to the system, and because governmental decisions have to be taken within this system on grounds of sound professional knowledge. In this way there has come into being a technical machine within the State, which few people are inclined to attempt to control from outside. Indeed, to control it at all is very difficult.

Moreover, it is so extensive and has such wide ramifications that its technical requirements have an influence on decisions in a number of other sectors. In so far as there is still a tension between what is and what should be, any debate about it will be confused, because here, too, decisions are made in accordance with the all-powerful technical system of control of consumption so essential for the maintenance of production. . . .

New Tensions. The argument of the preceding pages is that there were certain classical issues of social conflict in the liberal period, some of which were solved in the liberal period itself, others of which achieved their solution by means of the Welfare State, and the remainder moved from the politico-sociological plane to the socio-psychological. Does this mean that the Welfare State has sailed into more or less *a-historical* waters? From a sociological point of view, has a stage of rest and stability—a homeostatic period—been reached? . . . Has the Welfare State itself given to rise to any new tensions that could contribute towards its development? . . .

In turning to the political sphere for observations on the likelihood that the Welfare State has created new tensions, it is important to begin by drawing a distinction between administrative and governmental decisions, for this is precisely where the political image of the Welfare State has undergone a metamorphosis.

In theory a governmental decision represents a pronouncement regarding a choice between two aims. In a situation of limited means—and a political situation is one of limited means—preference is given to the achievement of a specific aim or set of aims over and above the accomplishment of other possibilities. An administrative decision, on the other hand, serves to indicate the means which are to be adopted for the purpose of carrying out aims which have already been agreed on. The administrative decision follows a section of policy that has been agreed on. The administrative decision follows a section of policy that has been previously arrived at, or of governmental choice. In theory the correctness of the administrative decision is subject to check. The better it furthers the carrying out of decisions taken by the government, the better a decision it is.

If we think along these lines, the difference between governmental and administrative decisions can be taken to be the difference between the choice of aims and the choice of means. It is not always easy to say whether a specific concrete decision will have to be characterized as a governmental decision or as an administrative decision. The way in which this can be settled depends on the place which this decision takes within a wider series of decisions. . . .

Whether a decision is to be regarded as a governmental or an administrative one depends on where the decision comes within a series of decisions which follow on one from another. As soon as any decision is seen to have a more important one placed one degree above it, it takes on a more administrative character. In principle it can be regarded as a development from a governmental decision already taken earlier. In the light of the differing degrees of importance, the whole matter of decisions takes on a more technical character. The nature of a decision is really derived from the interpretation which is set on the next higher decision above it. The higher the level of the governmental decision, the longer is the chain of administrative decision depending from it. . . .

The classical liberal view paid homage to the idea that life develops best when each individual is pursuing his own interests. In this connection the State had a significant role. It preserved the *status quo*, and controlled relationships with other nations. But the internal development of society was something in which the government had no right to meddle, except in cases of emergency. Looked at in this way, the liberal period could be expected to be marked by a lack of political activity in regard to the internal make-up of social life.

Yet it soon becomes clear, if cognizance is taken of the way in which development actually occurred, that this was in no wise the case. Throughout the whole of the liberal period Government and Parliament seemed to be continually busy slowing down, speeding up, controlling; and while the machine was functioning it was being reviewed and fitted for new requirements. It can roughly be said that during the first half of its existence the liberal state had its hands full, carrying out its proposed aims and squaring accounts with the institutions of a preceding age. It was very much engrossed in the destruction of its own principles and with preparing the ground for what was later to be the Welfare State.

Of course, as a result it had a great number of administrative regulations; but above the upper limit of administrative regulations there still remained plenty of scope for interesting political discussion. The administrative apparatus was still comparatively unobtrusive; and this raises the question of whether the democratic machinery as it was developed in the liberal period can function satisfactorily within the setting of the Welfare State. It certainly can in those sectors in which the switch-over has led to no fundamental changes. For instance, it was formerly possible in matters of foreign policy and it can be equally so in the Welfare State. But what is the situation as regards internal social development?

It seems fairly clear straight away that, in this situation, as far as democratic action is concerned, there is a great deal that has yet to be won. Universal suffrage and the enormous increase of population have created an incomparably larger potential supply of people interested in politics. At the same time, in economic and social affairs the State has taken unto itself a number of great responsibilities which at an earlier date it had delegated. But if we examine these two arguments more closely there is reason for some doubt.

Firstly, then, as to the greater interest in politics. To gauge this empirically still remains a very uncertain task. . . . Is it unreasonable to suppose that political interest is declining in proportion to the decrease in the number of minor matters over which a tension between what is and what ought to be happens to manifest itself? In view of the analysis in the foregoing paragraphs the latter now appears to be very much the case.

Which of the matters of social interest that used to bother the consciences of past times still do so today? Although mention has certainly been made, in the previous paragraph, to an element of tension, yet it is not really so much a matter of tension *within* the political sphere, but rather a tension at its roots. Whatever is the point of an institutionalized democracy, if those who have the right to vote can scarcely manage to display any interest in what is laid before them for their judgment?. . .

Here the second point at issue demands attention. What are the topics of discussion which are laid before the public in the Welfare State? Is it not simply the case that, in a controlled society more than ever, the essential factors which determine the character of that society are influenced by the State, and because they are matters of State concern they have come within the sphere of politics? Surely this must lead automatically to a revival of political debate?

There is no doubt about the fact that the government in the Welfare State regards itself as being responsible for a great number of activities in the economic, social and cultural fields, which previously were assumed to be domain of natural development, or of private institutions. It becomes more and more obvious that the task of the government involves very considerable intervention. But it is worthy of note that those decisions which now have to be taken are changing in character. Whereas they previously came into the category of governmental decisions, they have now become much more administrative ones. . . .

Decisions which are now looked upon as nothing but administrative were not so regarded in the early days of the Welfare State. At that time lively political discussion could be carried on concerning the required methods or rate of change from the liberal society into something different, but as soon as the main decisions about this had been made and people began to think along new lines, political discussion fell behind and technical discussion came to the fore. . . .

If, for example, the idea is accepted that care of the aged is a generally desirable ethical postulate, and if the idea is also accepted at the same time that private initiative in this respect ought to be replaced by a large measure of government control, political debate is automatically closed. The amount of monetary allowance, the method of the redistribution of incomes, however important they may be to those directly concerned, are nevertheless nothing more than administrative decisions. The moment the Welfare State has adopted a series of basic ethical and socio-economic principles acceptable to all parties, then, to be sure, all further government regulations on this matter can be regarded merely as rules, as technical details of a political programme which all have agreed upon.

So the role of parliament and of public opinion no longer lies in the domain of choice-making, but rather in that of the custodianship of the choice which has already been made—quite literally a custodianship. If there ever was a caretaker element in the functions of a political machine, it is much more the case with the Welfare State than it was in the liberal state. On the one hand the community basis has been so greatly broadened and on the other hand the level of administrative decision has been so much raised, that the scope for political decisions of any consequence, apart from those belonging to the period of installation, is severely limited.

In view of this it would appear that the significance of the democratic political system for the Welfare State needs to be re-emphasized and re-analysed. For present purposes it is suggested that this entails two basic propositions, derived from fundamental convictions, first that we are *en route* towards the realization of a certain type of society, and, secondly, that the road presents numerous occasions for political choice and that therefore there must be an electorate which will make the correct choice. From the very beginning the ideals of ever-increasing rationality and of material and intellectual progress have stood out like mileposts along the road, but what is now obvious is that the Welfare State is becoming much more remarkable in its desire to preserve an existing principle than for its concern for one that is on the move. . . . The choice has been made, and all the electorate is called upon to do is to confirm the choice. Its representatives are under control and their main task in this respect is the guardianship of what follows on that which has already been decided. . . .

There are, of course, certain well-organized opposition groups who, on principle, still set themselves against the expansion of the programme. In the universities, for example, there have been a few diehards or a few hotheads to whose way of thinking the programme offers, in essence, either too much or too little. In the literary world interest has been roused by the plausible pen of a few scientific fiction authors; but in point of fact this has not constituted any sort of threat. Extremism of the left or of the right does not play any significant part in the Welfare State. Religious bodies do not offer any real opposition. The trade unions and the socialist parties offer at most technical criticism. Employers, and the Liberal and Conservative Parties are stalwart supporters of the programme. In a situation of this sort, the keeping of a strict watch is rather superfluous. Why should anyone guard what nobody wants to make away with? If there are any dangers, they threaten from outside and abroad. Indeed, anyone who criticizes the system from within runs the risk of being dubbed a mischief-maker and of being blamed for causing vigilance *vis-à-vis* the outside world to slacken. Hence it does not look as if the sphere of internal politics is going to continue to be the one in which democratic political activity will celebrate any great triumphs. Possibly the older generation can still manage to carry on the old tensions left over from the liberal period. How far these are going to appeal to the younger generation and spur them on to political enthusiasm still remains to be seen.

There is no mistaking it; the fact that in the Welfare State a great number of decisions of an administrative character by-pass the government machine does not mean that they are low-level decisions. No doubt such decisions do occur, but that is not the problem that concerns us here. The noteworthy thing is that a specific problem in the liberal period could be a government problem and therefore of political interest, whereas now the same matter is the logical outcome of decisions previously made, and has taken on a predominantly administrative character.

For instance, consider a proposal for the raising of the school-leaving age. In the liberal period this might have been defended by a right-wing socialist member, on account of the fact that the proletariat also had a right to share in progress. A left-wing socialist member might have rejected it, for as far as he was concerned its only result would have been two extra years' indoctrination with the dogmas of an objectionable system. A rural conservative might have rejected it on the grounds that too much learning made it difficult for young people to accept the traditional set-up; an urban liberal might have accepted it because it was going to supply him with more skilled workers; and so on. All these standpoints are conceivable but the main thing is that certain outlooks on life can supply the background for the formation of opinions.

Such a discussion as this is not really impossible within a Welfare State, although the desire for education is so great that it would be hardly decent to raise one's voice against such a proposal. Yet there are no doubt a number of other aspects which will be brought out by people—all experts to a man. What will be the consequences as regards opportunities for employment? Can the raising of the school-leaving age, just like the reduction of working hours, pick up the slack on the labour market which has been brought about by automation? For which professions is a longer schooling an advantage as a preparatory training? What sort of effect is it going to have on the already agreed long-term plan for industrialization? What extra capital expenditure does the scheme involve, and does it in fact bring capital expenditure to a level still within the bounds of possibility and necessity?. . .

What this argument amounts to is that a number of problems have been taken out of the sphere of political debate because, more than in the past, they have become problems which, within the system which has been agreed upon, inevitably come to be settled on their technical merits. In regard to this change of task within the machinery of state, we can speak of a dysfunction. Politicians have to pass judgment about matters on which they are not altogether expert. Officials take decisions of a political nature, but they have not been trained to recognize these as such.

However, a still more troublesome problem is that it is becoming so difficult to ascertain to what extent the system really does require to have certain matters dealt with as technical ones. Presumably there are regulations which even in these new circumstances have definite political aspects but they are nevertheless dealt with simply by being either accepted or rejected without sufficient reference to the requirements of the system. People have to be absolutely conversant with the political and economic machinery of the Welfare State before being able to claim the right to pronounce with authority on its elasticity and capacity for change. Whether room will be permitted for political "deviations" depends on their certainty. In other words, the concession of political priorities has become a matter of technical knowledge within the socio-economic system now in force. To a greater degree than ever, it is not political principles but rather administrative or technico-professional knowledge that can tip the scales.

In this way recommendations are made more and more by experts. Experts are the skilled technicians of the system. In view of the fact that their position and their influence are from the start the outcome of the system, their recommendations (which after all are in principle technical ones) will seldom run contrary to the system itself. And so, generally speaking, reliance on an expert involves a lessening of the authority of the political control body. . . .

In a democratic system, those who are responsible for the task of governing are called upon to be trustworthy and able. In this connection "trustworthy" means that their appointment is the outcome of the electors' wish to have a specific programme realized or preserved. The need for trustworthiness becomes more urgent in proportion to the increase (and less so if there should be a decrease) in the tempting alternatives which present themselves to the leaders of the government. "Able" in this context means that members of the government are endowed with the capacity to carry out the programme to which they have devoted themselves. One of the weaknesses of democracy is that it has been forced, in various circumstances, to have a specific policy carried out by a man of only second-rate ability, because the ablest did not fulfil the requirements of the party line. . . .

For that matter, the democratic system has always rendered homage to the idea that a number of important posts in the government actually called for the possession of more ability than of trustworthiness. The waterways, the railways, the post office, the mines, and indeed even the army, are much better served by a sound technical administration than by a management with political responsibilities. As far as the needs of such services were concerned, there was, so to speak, no need for democracy ever to have been invented.

Now in the Welfare State this phenomenon, originally of but marginal importance, suddenly comes right to the centre of the stage. Economic affairs, social affairs, finance, agriculture, social services are all less than before political ministries and more than ever technical ones, on account of the fact that they work within the socio-economic system of the Welfare State. Government assessment through parliamentary debate has adapted itself to this situation. There is no argument about the extent to which the welfare is concerned in its own development. There is no hesitation in agreeing that the Welfare State is being augmented. It is possible to have different opinions as to priorities and tempo, but these remain matters for technical debate. Has the time come for a round of pay increases? Must capital expenditure be slowed down a little? Is there sufficient scope for a somewhat freer wage-structure?

This, then, is where a new situation of tension arises. Just as it is dangerous to allow political decisions to be taken by administrators so it is ridiculous to allow administrative decisions to be taken by politicians. The whole machinery of control of internal government only makes sense as a democratic machine when it really is dealing with matters of political choice. If this should no longer be the case, democracy would be a waste of time and would mean the employment of *trustworthy* people in cases where it would be possible to employ *skilled* people....

The democratic way of doing things derives its significance from the conviction that social progress must rest on its participants' choice of government. Yet if a situation should arise in which this progress seems to be, politically speaking, held up, there is no necessity for any government decision to be taken. Thus the structure of democracy no longer suits the new situation.

The stubborn retention of democratic ritual in a situation where it is no longer called for, has the result that the democratic process is threatened with becoming undignified, even where it still retains some sense. Moreover, as regards the functioning of the Welfare State, a new form of government begins to develop as an undercurrent.... What we must particularly bear in mind when we are studying this issue is the question of whether the Welfare State, as a matter of fact, does not have any real political problems as such, or whether it continues to have them, but in the disguise of technical topics. This is a fundamental question of our time.

IV
PLURALISTIC POWER THEORIES

SOCIAL PLURALISM AS A BASIS FOR DEMOCRACY

Marvin E. Olsen

Since the beginning of this century, Marxian and elitist theorists have argued bitterly about the nature of social power, its distribution and use in society, and possibilities for future changes. But on one crucial point they have always been in complete agreement: In all known societies past the bare subsistence level power has been highly centralized in the hands of a small portion of the population. These wielders of power, whether they be the members of a dominant social class or a set of ruling elites, frequently exercise considerable control over many spheres of social activity, and indirectly influence much of the structure and functioning of their societies. Perhaps it may be possible some day to alter this situation radically in many societies, or perhaps such changes will never occur, but power exertion in all modern societies is seen as intensely centralized at the present time.

In marked contrast, the theory of social pluralism rejects this central tenet of the Marxists and the elitists, on both empirical and theoretical grounds. Empirically, social pluralists maintain that in many contemporary societies—especially those that are relatively "democratic"[1] —social power tends to be relatively decentralized, or at least not extensively centralized. There is considerable variation among social pluralists in the degrees of power decentralization they see existing in different societies, but they all agree that the Marxian-elitist picture of extreme centralization is far overdrawn.

Theoretically, these writers make two related arguments: First, it is possible for modern societies to achieve considerable power decentralization through extensive pluralism without undergoing a radical Marxian revolution. And second, widespread pluralism in a society is a necessary prerequisite for democratic decision-making and

---

[1] This term is used here in its popular meaning, without any attempt at precise definition, as a convenient way of referring to those North American, Western European, and scattered Asiatic nations commonly thought of as political democracies.

government. In short, social pluralism decentralizes power throughout a society and thus provides the social foundation required for effective political democracy.

Our concerns in this essay are to sketch the pluralistic societal model, in both its structural and functional aspects, and to raise a few questions about the adequacy of pluralism for supporting democratic decision-making on the societal level. Two points of caution must be observed, however. Since this pluralistic model is essentially an "ideal type," we should not expect any actual society to resemble it completely. Furthermore, this discussion of pluralism is focused on total societies, not smaller organizations. The pluralistic model has also been applied, with a few minor modifications, to communities and formal associations, but its strengths and weaknesses are often quite different in these kinds of settings.

The idea of a division of power within the political system, as a means of preventing tyranny, has been discussed by political philosophers since antiquity. Aristotle pointed out the benefits to be gained from differentiating various governmental activities, and Montesquieu in the eighteenth century stressed the desireability of embodying legislative, executive, and judicial functions in separate bodies. In addition, the federal type of government divides political power along geographic lines, with the national state sharing sovereignty with one or more levels of local government.

The pluralistic model goes far beyond the political system, however, to encompass the entire society. James Madison's *The Federalist, No. 10* sketched the main features of this broader conception of pluralism and suggested it's importance for political democracy. But it was Alexis de Tocqueville, writing in the 1830's, who first gave clear expression to the idea of social pluralism as a model for a whole society. Tocqueville saw mass equality, created by the breakdown or absence of traditional hierarchies of feudal authority, as providing fertile ground for the emergence of a "tyranny of the majority" that would be totally destructive of individual freedom. Although he held no personal sympathies for traditional aristocracy, he recognized that it did give a society political stability by imposing several levels of authority and decision-making between the ruling monarch and the people. These made it possible for the king to rule adequately (if not in the interests of the people) by providing established channels for communication and power exertion. In a society of mass equality that lacked such intermediate levels of organization, however, everyone would be at the immediate mercy of either constantly shifting majorities or organized minorities.

Tocqueville's proposed "functional alternative" for traditional aristocracy in modern democratic societies was a multitude of private, voluntary, autonomous, special-interest associations. A well-organized network of such voluntary associations, he argued, would not only provide an effective substitute for the nobility in promoting social stability, but would also give all citizens effective means of influencing political decisions. "If men are to remain civilized, or to become so, the art of associating together must grow and improve, in the same ratio to which the equality of conditions is increased."[2]

---

[2] Alexis de Tocqueville, *Democracy in America*, Vol. II (New York: Schocken Books, 1961), p. 133.

Tocqueville's proposal has today become the central proposition of the pluralistic societal model. *A highly pluralistic society would thus contain a vast proliferation of autonomous groups, associations, and other organizations.* Such organizations are often described as "intermediate" because of their location between individual citizens and the national government. They are private organizations, controlled by their members and possessing their own power resources, and hence operate relatively independently of the state—although they may be subject to limited governmental regulation. Some of them, such as political parties and lobbies, may regularly act as parts of the political system, but most of them will be "parapolitical," entering the political arena only when their particular concerns are involved. Each intermediate organization will be relatively specialized in its activities and goals, so that all of them will become functionally interdependent and interrelated. Nevertheless, each remains an autonomous organization in relation both to the state and to all other organizations. Finally, membership is voluntary, so that ideally a person might belong to as many different organizations as he wished, depending on his interests and available time. The resulting overlapping of individual memberships among organizations would not curtail organizational autonomy, however.

From a more dynamic perspective, *a pluralistic society is characterized by continual and extensive flows of information and influence among all its constituent parts.* These flows occur through the intermediate organizations, which act as mediators between individual citizens and the societal government.[3] They serve their individual members by: (a) providing numerous channels for acquiring information about public issues and activities; (b) enabling persons with similar interests and concerns to generate power resources by organizing for collective action; (c) giving these persons established means through which they can gain access to and exert influence upon governmental decision-makers; (d) supporting spokesmen and leaders who can effectively challenge the actions and positions of the political rulers; and (e) protecting individuals from manipulation by political elites through mass propaganda and state-manipulated associations.

At the same time, intermediate organizations also benefit governmental leaders by: (a) giving them numerous sources of information about public interests, concerns, and activities throughout the society; (b) providing institutionalized channels through which they can act to maintain adequate social order, control deviant actions, and carry out public programs of all types; and (c) insulating them for direct dependence on mass public opinion and mass movements, thus enabling them to take socially necessary but unpopular actions without fear of riots or other uprisings.

Finally, these "mediating" voluntary organizations benefit the entire society by: (a) keeping the government at least moderately responsive to the wishes of the total population; (b) making it possible to resolve conflicts through negotiation and

---

[3]These mediating functions of intermediate organizations are extensively discussed by William Kornhauser in *The Politics of Mass Society* (New York: The Free Press, 1959). See also Robert A. Dahl and Charles E. Lindblom, *Politics, Economics, and Welfare* (New York: Harper and Row, 1953) Chap. 11.

compromise rather than violent confrontation; (c) preventing any single individual or small group from dominating the entire society; (d) promoting relative social stability through time; and (e) encouraging gradual but continual social change. In sum, by bringing all members of the society (including political elites) within an established web of interdependent social organization, a pluralistic social structure makes possible effective political democracy.

If intermediate organizations are to perform these mediating functions adequately, however, they must meet two crucial criteria: They must be small enough and close enough to their members so that individuals can directly influence organizational decisions and activities, but at the same time they must be large enough and well enough organized to be capable of exerting at least some social power on other organizations and on the government. At first glance these requirements may appear to be contradictory, but they can be satisfied if the society contains several levels of organizations. Individuals might first form small clubs, committees, and similar groups according to their particular interests, locations, or other factors. Several such groups might in turn comprise larger organizations concerned with somewhat broader goals. These associations might then merge into national and even international organizations with extensive ranges of activities. The resulting over-all organizational network has now become large and powerful enough to influence the national government directly while simultaneously maintaining social links with each individual member. Through the combined efforts of many such organizational webs, the power of the political rulers can ultimately be controlled by the citizens, and governmental actions can be continually directed toward the needs of the entire society.

All of these features of a pluralistic society undoubtedly seem highly desirable, but isn't there also a very real possibility that the entire process might break down as each organization sought its own special goals with complete disregard for the interests of other organizations or the total society? Could not a pluralistic society quickly disintegrate into a maze of self-oriented, hostile organizations in constant conflict, if not open warfare, with one another? To answer this criticism, pluralistic theorists have insisted that *numerous integrative conditions must also be present in a society if pluralism is to operate effectively*. These include crosscutting or overlapping memberships that prevent individuals from becoming too strongly attached to any one organization, functional interdependence and interlocking relationships and activities among the various organizations, established procedures through which organizations can express their views and exert influence, high levels of general public education, widespread mass communications, common acceptance of the legitimacy of the existing political and legal orders, and a set of basic overarching societal values and norms. Given these conditions, they argue, a society should be able to enjoy the benefits of social pluralism while also remaining adequately integrated.

Of all these necessary integrative conditions, the requirement for some degree of value consensus is most often criticized. Is not the pluralistic model, these critics ask, merely an extention into the socio-political realm of traditional laissez-faire economic theory—which was long ago discarded by economists as far too simplistic to explain modern economies? Just as laissez-faire economics depended on the "invisible hand" of the marketplace to keep the system operating smoothly, does not the theory of social pluralism assume the existence of a "natural harmony of interests"—to borrow a phrase from utilitarian philosophy—among all parts of the society? In other words, is not the vague reference to "value consensus" actually concealing the much broader but still necessary assumptions of an absence of strong conflicting values, deep social cleavages, uncompromising ideologies, and extremist politics?[4]

Only if these highly restricting assumptions are met, claim the critics, will diverse activities by competing, self-oriented, special-interest organizations result in promotion of the general welfare and maintenance of societal unity. Lacking these conditions, pluralism may paralyze or destroy a society, since membership in intermediate associations never insures commitment by individuals to the total society and its goals. As a pluralistic society changes through time, some of its intermediate organizations are bound to see themselves as being adversely affected or deprived, while others will develop new aspirations and goals. In both cases, these organizations are likely to decide that the existing social and political orders are inadequate, and reject them in favor of extremist ideologies, violent conflict, and attempts at radical social change. The result would be considerable disintegration of societal unity, if not total anarchy.

Two other shortcomings of the pluralistic model are also worthy of attention. First, to the extent that social pluralism relies upon and promotes extensive functional specialization and interdependence among intermediate organizations, does it not thereby increase the necessity for societal-wide but highly centralized coordination, regulation, and control of all social activities? It would thus appear that an unanticipated but perhaps inevitable outgrowth of social pluralism is power centralization—which takes us right back to the arguments of the elitists, and seems to negate the possibility of political democracy that was the original justification for pluralism. This dilemma can be circumvented only if we can devise means of achieving unified coordination, regulation, and planning throughout a society that do not necessitate the imposition of centralized authoritarian control. A possible solution to this problem will be suggested in the final essay on the systemic societal model, but for the time being we simply note that this is a critical deficiency in the pluralistic model that has not yet been resolved.

The second shortcoming, which also remains unanswered, pertains to the practicality of the pluralistic model in modern societies. In contemporary industrialized-urbanized-bureaucratized nations the state tends to predominate over all other parts of the society, overshadowing every other type of organization in power exertion and scope of activities. Given this situation, can private, voluntary associations with limited resources and interests ever effectively influence the national government, no matter how large or well organized they may be? In relation to the state, do not all intermediate organizations become relatively powerless on the societal level, capable

---

[4]Joseph Gusfield, "Mass Society and Extremist Politics," *American Sociological Review*, Vol. 27 (February 1962), pp. 19-30.

of acting only as peripheral spectators in the arena of national affairs? And if this is so, what hope is there for political democracy in modern societies?

Political leaders may of course dutifully listen while spokesmen of various intermediate organizations plead their special interests, and may even grant minor concessions to these organizations to keep them satisfied. But more commonly, it is argued, skillful political elites merely "play off" one special-interest association against another in a complex "balancing act" that nullifies the influence attempts of them all. Moreover, the political rulers may then subtly coopt these intermediate organizations and use them as agents for carrying out elite policies.[5] In short, is social pluralism at all workable in modern nation-states? This question again relates back to the "iron law of oligarchy" of elitist theory, and appears to make the possibilities of power decentralization and political democracy even less tenable in contemporary societies. To overcome this limitation, we must discover organizational procedures for limiting the scope of the national government and simultaneously creating intermediate organizations that can exercise significant amounts of power in society. The systemic societal model also attempts to meet this challenge.

The conception of "contervailing power" developed in economic theory by John Kenneth Galbraith offers a partial answer to many of these criticisms of pluralism, and significantly alters the basic pluralistic model.[6] The idea of countervailing power was devised to describe the economies of contemporary "capitalistic" societies such as the United States, in which many spheres of economic activity are largely dominated by a few huge corporations, and to which the classical model of a laissez-faire competitive market is no longer applicable. In the competitive-market scheme, as in the usual pluralistic model, power-wielding is controlled by competition among a large number of relatively small and independent units, all of which operate on the "same side" of the market. For instance, if one retail store attempts to increase its profits by raising its prices far above the prevailing levels, it will presumably be forced back into line by other stores that will undersell it. Similarly, in the standard pluralistic model, if one voluntary association seeks to gain more than its "fair share" of benefits from the government, it will be undercut by other competing associations that demand less and offer more public utility in return.

In a countervailing-power market, in contrast, the power of huge corporations is limited not by their few competitors—who frequently offer almost identical products at similar prices—but rather by organized forces operating on the "opposite side" of the market. These might include labor unions, consumer-oriented chain stores (or consumer cooperatives), and governmental regulatory agencies. Some of the ways in which they typically exercise countervailing power are described by Galbraith in the selection reprinted here. When this process is generalized to the entire society and incorporated in the pluralistic model, each broad sphere of social activities—such as medicine or education or communications or economic production or governmental administration—becomes a highly organized functional network

---

[5] This criticism of the pluralistic model is drawn from C. Wright Mills, *The Power Elite* (New York: Oxford University Press, 1956), Chap. 11.

[6] John Kenneth Galbraith, *American Capitalism* (Boston: Houghton Mifflin Company, 1956).

or system. Each of these networks (including the national government) is then controlled primarily by other functional networks exercising countervailing power against it, rather than by a proliferation of relatively small voluntary associations attempting futilely to influence political rulers. Similarly, the organizations comprising each functional network would themselves be limited in their activities by the countervailing power of other opposing organizations in the system. In this manner, the pluralistic societal model can utilize the idea of countervailing power to provide an organizational base for effective power decentralization—and perhaps viable political democracy.

The four readings comprising this section span the historical development of the theory of social pluralism: Alexis de Tocqueville suggests the basic idea of intermediate voluntary associations throughout society. Robert A. Nisbet contrasts eighteenth-century ideals of mass popular democracy with traditional patterns of aristocratic authority and shows how the conception of social pluralism developed as a compromise (or synthesis) of these conflicting political theories. Gerhard De Gré focuses on the consequences of various kinds of social structures for individual freedom and argues that pluralism offers more freedom to individuals than does either loosely organized, segmented society or a highly centralized, oligarchial society. John Kenneth Galbraith, finally, explains his notion of countervailing power and shows how it operates in the American economy.

INFLUENCE OF DEMOCRACY ON THE FEELINGS OF THE AMERICANS

Alexis de Tocqueville

Why Democratic Nations Show a More Ardent and Enduring Love of Equality Than of Liberty. The first and most intense passion which is engendered by the equality of condition is, I need hardly say, the love of that same equality. My readers will therefore not be surprised that I speak of it before all others. . . .

The principle of equality may be established in civil society, without prevailing in the political world. Equal rights may exist of indulging in the same pleasures, of entering the same professions, of frequenting the same places—in a word, of living in the same manner and seeking wealth by the same means, although all men do not take an equal share in the government.

A kind of equality may even be established in the political world, though there should be no political freedom there. A man may be the equal of all his countrymen save one, who is the master of all without distinction, and who selects equally from among them all the agents of his power.

SOURCE: Alexis de Tocqueville, *Democracy in America*, trans. by Henry Reeves (New York: Schocken Books, 1961), Vol. II, Book 2, pp. 113-133, 138-143.

Several other combinations might be easily imagined, by which very great equality would be united to institutions more or less free, or even to institutions wholly without freedom.

Although men cannot become absolutely equal unless they be entirely free, and consequently equality, pushed to its furthest extent, may be confounded with freedom, yet there is good reason for distinguishing the one from the other. The taste which men have for liberty, and that which they feel for equality, are, in fact, two different things; and I am not afraid to add, that, amongst democratic nations, they are two unequal things. . . .

Freedom has appeared in the world at different times and under various forms; it has not been exclusively bound to any social condition, and it is not confined to democracies. Freedom cannot, therefore, form the distinguishing characteristic of democratic ages. The peculiar and preponderating fact which marks those ages as its own is the equality of conditions; the ruling passion of men in those periods is the love of this equality. Ask not what singular charm the men of democratic ages find in being equal, or what special reasons they may have for clinging so tenaciously to equality rather than to the other advantages which society holds out to them: equality is the distinguishing characteristic of the age they live in; that, of itself, is enough to explain that they prefer it to all the rest. . . .

That political freedom may compromise in its excesses the tranquillity, the property, the lives of individuals, is obvious to the narrowest and most unthinking minds. But, on the contrary, none but attentive and clear-sighted men perceive the perils with which equality threatens us, and they commonly avoid pointing them out. They know that the calamities they apprehend are remote, and flatter themselves that they will only fall upon future generations, for which the present generation takes but little thought. The evils which freedom sometimes brings with it are immediate; they are apparent to all, and all are more or less affected by them. The evils which extreme equality may produce are slowly disclosed; they creep gradually into the social frame; they are only seen at intervals, and at the moment at which they become most violent, habit already causes them to be no longer felt.

The advantages which freedom brings are only shown by length of time; and it is always easy to mistake the cause in which they originate. The advantages of equality are instantaneous, and they may constantly be traced from their source. . . .

I think that democratic communities have a natural taste for freedom: left to themselves, they will seek it, cherish it, and view any privation of it with regret. But for equality, their passion is ardent, insatiable, incessant, invincible: they call for equality in freedom; and if they cannot obtain that, they still call for equality in slavery. They will endure poverty, servitude, barbarism—but they will not endure aristocracy.

This is true at all times, and especially true in our own. All men and all powers seeking to cope with this irresistible passion will be overthrown and destroyed by it. In our age, freedom cannot be established without it, and despotism itself cannot reign without its support.

Of Individualism in Democratic Countries. I have shown how it is that in ages of equality every man seeks for his opinions within himself: I am now about to show

how it is that, in the same ages, all his feelings are turned towards himself alone. *Individualism* is a novel expression, to which a novel idea has given birth. Our fathers were only acquainted with egotism. Egotism is a passionate and exaggerated love of self, which leads a man to connect everything with his own person, and to prefer himself to everything in the world. Individualism is a mature and calm feeling, which disposes each member of the community to sever himself from the mass of his fellow-creatures; and to draw apart with his family and his friends; so that, after he has thus formed a little circle of his own, he willingly leaves society at large to itself. Egotism originates in blind instinct: individualism proceeds from erroneous judgment more than from depraved feelings; it originates as much in the deficiencies of the mind as in the perversity of the heart.

Egotism blights the germ of all virtue: individualism, at first, only saps the virtues of public life; but, in the long run, it attacks and destroys all others, and is at length absorbed in downright egotism. Egotism is a vice as old as the world, which does not belong to one form of society more than to another: individualism is of democratic origin, and it threatens to spread in the same ratio as the equality of conditions.

Amongst aristocratic nations, as families remain for centuries in the same condition, often on the same spot, all generations become as it were contemporaneous. A man almost always knows his forefathers, and respects them: he thinks he already sees his remote descendants, and he loves them. He willingly imposes duties on himself towards the former and the latter; and he will frequently sacrifice his personal gratifications to those who went before and to those who will come after him.

Aristocratic institutions have, moreover, the effect of closely binding every man to several of his fellow-citizens. As the classes of an aristocratic people are strongly marked and permanent, each of them is regarded by its own members as a sort of lesser country, more tangible and more cherished than the country at large. As in aristocratic communities all the citizens occupy fixed positions, one above the other, the result is that each of them always sees a man above himself whose patronage is necessary to him, and below himself another man whose co-operation he may claim.

Men living in aristocratic ages are therefore almost always closely attached to something placed out of their own sphere, and they are often disposed to forget themselves. It is true that in those ages the notion of human fellowship is faint, and that men seldom think of sacrificing themselves for mankind; but they often sacrifice themselves for other men. In democratic ages, on the contrary, when the duties of each individual to the race are much more clear, devoted service to any one man becomes more rare; the bond of human affection is extended, but it is relaxed.

Amongst democratic nations new families are constantly springing up, others are constantly falling away, and all that remain change their condition; the woof of time is every instant broken, and the track of generations effaced. Those who went before are soon forgotten; of those who will come after no one has any idea: the interest of man is confined to those in close propinquity to himself.

As each class approximates to other classes, and intermingles with them, its members become indifferent and as strangers to one another. Aristocracy had made a chain of all the members of the community, from the peasant to the king: democracy breaks that chain, and severs every link of it.

As social conditions become more equal, the number of persons increases who, although they are neither rich enough nor powerful enough to exercise any great influence over their fellow-creatures, have nevertheless acquired or retained sufficient education and fortune to satisfy their own wants. They owe nothing to any man, they expect nothing from any man; they acquire the habit of always considering themselves as standing alone, and they are apt to imagine that their whole destiny is in their own hands.

Thus not only does democracy make every man forget his ancestors, but it hides his descendants, and separates his contemporaries, from him; it throws him back for ever upon himself alone, and threatens in the end to confine him entirely within the solitude of his own heart.

Individualism Stronger at the Close of a Democratic Revolution Than at Other Periods. The period when the construction of democratic society upon the ruins of an aristocracy has just been completed, is especially that at which this separation of men from one another, and the egotism resulting from it, most forcibly strike the observation. Democratic communities not only contain a large number of independent citizens, but they are constantly filled with men who, having entered but yesterday upon their independent condition, are intoxicated with their new power. They entertain a presumptuous confidence in their strength, and as they do not suppose that they can henceforward ever have occasion to claim the assistance of their fellow-creatures, they do not scruple to show that they care for nobody but themselves.

An aristocracy seldom yields without a protracted struggle, in the course of which implacable animosities are kindled between the different classes of society. These passions survive the victory, and traces of them may be observed in the midst of the democratic confusion which ensues.

Those members of the community who were at the top of the late gradations of rank cannot immediately forget their former greatness; they will long regard themselves as aliens in the midst of the newly composed society. They look upon all those whom this state of society has made their equals as oppressors, whose destiny can excite no sympathy; they have lost sight of their former equals, and feel no longer bound by a common interest to their fate: each of them, standing aloof, thinks that he is reduced to care for himself alone. Those, on the contrary, who were formerly at the foot of the social scale, and who have been brought up to the common level by a sudden revolution, cannot enjoy their newly acquired independence without secret uneasiness; and if they meet with some of their former superiors on the same footing as themselves, they stand aloof from them with an expression of triumph and of fear.

It is, then, commonly at the outset of democratic society that citizens are most disposed to live apart. Democracy leads men not to draw near to their fellow-creatures; but democratic revolutions lead them to shun each other, and perpetuate in a state of equality the animosities which the state of inequality engendered.

The great advantage of the Americans is that they have arrived at a state of democracy without having to endure a democratic revolution; and that they are born equal, instead of becoming so.

That the Americans Combat the Effects of Individualism by Free Institutions. Despotism, which is of a very timorous nature, is never more secure of continuance than when it can keep men asunder; and all its influence is commonly exerted for that purpose. No vice of the human heart is so acceptable to it as egotism: a despot easily forgives his subjects for not loving him, provided they do not love each other. He does not ask them to assist him in governing the state; it is enough that they do not aspire to govern it themselves. He stigmatizes as turbulent and unruly spirits those who would combine their exertions to promote the prosperity of the community; and, perverting the natural meaning of words, he applauds as good citizens those who have no sympathy for any but themselves.

Thus the vices which despotism engenders are precisely those which equality fosters. These two things mutually and perniciously complete and assist each other. Equality places men side by side, unconnected by any common tie; despotism raises barriers to keep them asunder: the former predisposes them not to consider their fellow-creatures, the latter makes general indifference a sort of public virtue.

Despotism then, which is at all times dangerous, is more particularly to be feared in democratic ages. It is easy to see that in those same ages men stand most in need of freedom. When the members of a community are forced to attend to public affairs, they are necessarily drawn from the circle of their own interests, and snatched at times from self-observation. As soon as a man begins to treat of public affairs in public, he begins to perceive that he is not so independent of his fellow-men as he had at first imagined, and, that, in order to obtain their support, he must often lend them his co-operation. . . .

The Americans have combated by free institutions the tendency of equality to keep men asunder, and they subdued it. The legislators of America did not suppose that a general representation of the whole nation would suffice to ward off a disorder at once so natural to the frame of democratic society, and so fatal: they also thought that it would be well to infuse political life into each portion of the territory, in order to multiply to an infinite extent opportunities of acting in concert, for all the members of the community, and to make them constantly feel their mutual dependence on each other. The plan was a wise one. The general affairs of a country only engage the attention of leading politicians, who assemble from time to time in the same places; and as they often lose sight of each other afterwards, no lasting ties are established between them. But if the object be to have the local affairs of a district conducted by the men who reside there, the same persons are always in contact, and they are, in a manner, forced to be acquainted, and to adapt themselves to one another.

It is difficult to draw a man out of his own circle to interest him in the destiny of the state, because he does not clearly understand what influence the destiny of the state can have upon his own lot. But if it be proposed to make a road cross the end of his estate, he will see at a glance that there is a connection between this small public affair and his greatest private affairs; and he will discover, without its being shown to him, the close tie which unites private to general interest. Thus, far more may be done by entrusting to the citizens the administration of minor affairs than by surrendering to them the control of important ones, towards interesting them in the public welfare, and convincing them that they constantly stand in need one of the other in order to provide for it. A brilliant achievement may win for you the favour of a people at one stroke; but to earn the love and respect of the population which surrounds you, a long succession of little services rendered and of obscure good deeds—a constant habit of kindness, and an established reputation for disinterestedness—will be required. Local freedom, then, which leads a great number of citizens to value the affection of their neighbours and of their kindred, perpetually brings men together, and forces them to help one another, in spite of the propensities which sever them.

In the United States the more opulent citizens take great care not to stand aloof from the people; on the contrary, they constantly keep on easy terms with the lower classes: they listen to them, they speak to them every day. They know that the rich in democracies always stand in need of the poor; and that in democratic ages you attach a poor man to you more by your manner than by benefits conferred. The magnitude of such benefits, which sets off the difference of conditions, causes a secret irritation to those who reap advantage from them; but the charm of simplicity of manners is almost irresistible: their affability carries men away, and even their want of polish is not always displeasing. This truth does not take root at once in the minds of the rich. They generally resist it as long as the democratic revolution lasts, and they do not acknowledge it immediately after that revolution is accomplished. They are very ready to do good to the people, but they still choose to keep them at arm's length; they think that is sufficient, but they are mistaken. They might spend fortunes thus without warming the hearts of the population around them; that population does not ask them for the sacrifice of their money, but of their pride. . . .

Of the Use Which the Americans Make of Public Associations in Civil Life. If each citizen did not learn, in proportion as he individually becomes more feeble and consequently more incapable of preserving his freedom single-handed, to combine with his fellow-citizens for the purpose of defending it, it is clear that tyranny would unavoidably increase together with equality.

Those associations only which are formed in civil life, without reference to political objects, are here adverted to. The political associations which exist in the United States are only a single feature in the midst of the immense assemblage of associations in that country. Americans of all ages, all conditions, and all dispositions, constantly form associations. They have not only commercial and manufacturing companies, in which all take part, but associations of a thousand other kinds—religious, moral, serious, futile, extensive or restricted, enormous or diminutive. The Americans make associations to give entertainments, to found establishments for education, to build inns, to construct churches, to diffuse books, to send missionaries to the antipodes; and in this manner they found hospitals, prisons, and schools. If it be proposed to advance some truth, or to foster some feeling by the encouragement of a great example, they form a society. Wherever, at the head of some new undertaking, you see the Government in France, or a man of rank in England, in the United States you will be sure to find an association. . . .

Thus the most democratic country on the face of the earth is that in which men have in our time carried to the highest perfection the art of pursuing in common the object of their common desires, and have applied this new science to the greatest number of purposes. Is this the result of accident? Or is there in reality any necessary connexion between the principle of association and that of equality?

Aristocratic communities always contain, amongst a multitude of persons who by themselves are powerless, a small number of powerful and wealthy citizens, each of whom can achieve great undertakings single-handed. In aristocratic societies men do not need to combine in order to act, because they are strongly held together. Every wealthy and powerful citizen constitutes the head of a permanent and compulsory association, composed of all those who are dependent upon him, or whom he makes subservient to the execution of his designs.

Amongst democratic nations, on the contrary, all the citizens are independent and feeble; they can do hardly anything by themselves, and none of them can oblige his fellow-men to lend him their assistance. They all, therefore, fall into a state of incapacity, if they do not learn voluntarily to help each other. If men living in democratic countries had no right and no inclination to associate for political purposes, their independence would be in great jeopardy; but they might long preserve their wealth and their cultivation: whereas if they never acquired the habit of forming associations in ordinary life, civilization itself would be endangered. A people amongst which individuals should lose the power of achieving great things single-handed, without acquiring the means of producing them by united exertions, would soon relapse into barbarism.

Unhappily, the same social condition which renders associations so necessary to democratic nations, renders their formation more difficult amongst those nations than amongst all others. When several members of an aristocracy agree to combine, they easily succeed in doing so: as each of them brings great strength to the partnership, the number of its members may be very limited; and when the members of an association are limited in number, they may easily become mutually acquainted, understand each other, and establish fixed regulations. The same opportunities do not occur amongst democratic nations, where the associated members must always be very numerous for their association to have any power. . . .

A Government might perform the part of some of the largest American companies; and several States, members of the Union, have already attempted it; but what political power could ever carry on the vast multitude of lesser undertakings which the American citizens perform every day, with the assistance of the principle of association? It is easy to foresee that the time is drawing near when man will be less and less able to produce, of himself alone, the commonest necessaries of life. The task of the governing power will therefore perpetually increase, and its very efforts will extend it every day. The more it stands in the place of associations, the more will individuals, losing the notion of combining together, require its assistance: these are causes and effects which unceasingly engender each other. Will the administration of the country ultimately assume the management of all the manufactures, which no single citizen is able to carry on?. . . . The morals and the intelligence of a democratic people would be as much endangered as its business and manufactures, if the government ever wholly usurped the place of private companies.

Feelings and opinions are recruited, the heart is enlarged, and the human mind is developed by no other means than by the reciprocal influence of men upon each other. I have shown that these influences are almost null in democratic countries; they must therefore be artificially created, and this can only be accomplished by associations.

When the members of an aristocratic community adopt a new opinion, or conceive a new sentiment, they give it a station, as it were, beside themselves, upon the lofty platform where they stand; and opinions or sentiments so conspicuous to the eyes of the multitude are easily introduced into the minds or hearts of all around. In democratic countries the governing power alone is naturally in a condition to act in this manner; but it is easy to see that its action is always inadequate, and often dangerous. A government can no more be competent to keep alive and to renew the circulation of opinions and feelings amongst a great people, than to manage all the speculations of productive industry. No sooner does a government attempt to go beyond its political sphere and to enter upon this new track, than it exercises, even unintentionally, an insupportable tyranny; for a government can only dictate strict rules, the opinions which it favours are rigidly enforced, and it is never easy to discriminate between its advice and its commands. Worse still will be the case if the government really believes itself interested in preventing all circulation of ideas; it will then stand motionless, and oppressed by the heaviness of voluntary torpor. Governments therefore should not be the only active powers: associations ought, in democratic nations, to stand in lieu of those powerful private individuals whom the equality of conditions has swept away.

As soon as several of the inhabitants of the United States have taken up an opinion or a feeling which they wish to promote in the world, they look out for mutual assistance; and as soon as they have found each other out, they combine. From that moment they are no longer isolated men, but a power seen from afar, whose actions serve for an example, and whose language is listened to. . . .

In democratic countries the science of association is the mother of science; the progress of all the rest depends upon the progress it has made.

Amongst the laws which rule human societies there is one which seems to be more precise and clear than all others. If men are to remain civilized, or to become so, the art of associating together must grow and improve, in the same ratio in which the equality of conditions is increased. . . .

THE CONTEXTS OF DEMOCRACY

Robert A. Nisbet

Definitions of democracy are as varied as the interests of persons and generations. Democracy is made identical with intellectual freedom, with economic justice, with social welfare, with tolerance, with piety, moral integrity, the dignity of man, and general civilized decency. As a word, democracy has come to be a kind of terminological catch-all for the historic virtues of civilization even as the word totalitarianism has become a catch-all for its evils. But the understanding of political democracy, its excellences and capacities, is served no better by this indiscriminating approach than is the understanding of totalitarianism.

Democracy may be associated with any and all of the virtues listed above, but it is, fundamentally, a theory and structure of *political power*. The historical root of democracy, as distinguished from liberalism which is historically a theory of *immunity* from power, is the proposition that the legitimacy of all political power arises from, and only from, the consent of the governed, the *people*. Lincoln's famous definition of democracy as government of, by, and for the people cannot be improved upon either as a moral ideal or as a historical description. And it is as right and as institutionally relevant today as it was in Lincoln's day.

But with respect to the "people," as with the "individual," everything depends upon the practical, cultural contexts in which we choose to regard the people. The "people," no less than the "individual," is an abstraction, subject not merely to varying verbal usages but also to historically changing political demands and moral imperatives.

We may regard the people as simply a numerical aggregate of individuals regarded for political and administrative purposes as discrete and socially separated, an aggregate given form and meaning only by the nature of the State and its laws. Or, alternatively, we may regard the people as indistinguishable from a culture, its members as inseparable from the families, unions, churches, professions, and traditions that actually compose a culture.

The difference between the two ways of considering the people is vast, and it is decisive in any political theory of democracy. The "will" of the people is one thing, substantively, when it is conceived in purely political terms as arising from a vast aggregate of socially separated, politically integrated *individuals*. It is something very different when it is conceived in terms of the social unities and cultural traditions in which political, like all other, judgments are actually formed and reinforced.

In the first view of the people, a conception of political democracy must inevitably rest heavily upon the State and its formal agencies of function and control. Units of administration become, necessarily, atomistic individuals, conceived

---

SOURCE: Abridged from *Community and Power*, (*The Quest for Community*), pp. 248-270, 274-279, by Robert A. Nisbet. Copyright 1953 by Oxford University Press, Inc. Used by permission of the publisher and author.

abstractly and divorced from the cultural contexts. When the people are regarded in this way, the principal problem of democratic theory and administration becomes not the larger problem of distribution of function and authority in *society* but, rather, the discovery of means by which the human being is brought ever closer to the people *in their political wholeness* and, in practical terms, to the formal administrative structure of the State. By omitting reference to the other authority-wielding and need-gratifying associations in society, by focusing on the abstract political mass, this view of the people becomes administratively committed at the outset to a potentially totalitarian view of the State.

But if we take the second view of the people, the State emerges as but *one* of the associations of man's existence. Equally important to a democratic theory founded on this perspective is the whole plurality of other associations in society. The intermediary associations and the spontaneous social groups which compose society, rather than atomized political particles, become the prime units of theoretical and practical consideration. The major objective of political democracy becomes that of making harmonious and effective the varied group allegiances which exist in society, not sterilizing them in the interest of a monistic political community.

Historically, we find both conceptions of the people in the writings of democratic philosophers and statesmen. But it is the second, the pluralist, conception that is more relevant to the actual history of democracy, especially in the United States, England, the Scandinavian countries, and Switzerland. And, as I shall emphasize in this chapter, it is the reaffirmation of this conception that seems to me absolutely indispensable to the success of liberal democracy at the present time.

It would be naive, however, to fail to see the powerful influence that is now exerted everywhere by the first, the unitary, view of the people and democracy. It is highly important that we examine this unitary tradition of democracy, for the difference between it and the pluralist tradition may well determine our effort to maintain liberal democracy under the pressure of the powerful quest for community in the present age.

II. The unitary view of democracy, like the ideology of the political community with which it is so closely allied, arose in France during the latter part of the eighteenth century. As a theory it was constructed in light of prevailing rationalist conceptions of man and society, and as an attack upon the still largely feudal social structure. It was based foremost upon the premise that the authorities and responsibilities wielded historically by kings, nobles, and churchmen belonged by nature to the people and should, as a matter of practical policy, be transferred to the people. But the French rationalists used the term people in a way that was remarkably abstract and as divorced from circumstance as some of their other terms.

The image of the people that governed the minds of men like Rousseau and Condorcet and was to spread in revolutionary fashion throughout the world in the nineteenth century was an image derived not from history or experience but from the same kind of conceptualization that had produced the fateful conception of the General Will. Just as the "real" will of the people was distinguished by Rousseau and his disciples from the attitudes and beliefs actually held at any given time by the people, so, in this rationalist view, the "people" had to be distinguished from the actual plurality of persons which experience revealed. If right government was to be made a reality by the rationalists, the "people" had to be separated from existing institutions and beliefs and brought into the single association of the people's State.

Just as the rationalist made the realization of individuality contingent upon the individual's release from his primary contexts of association, so he made the realization of the "people's will" dependent on the release of the whole people—abstractly regarded—from traditional institutions and authorities. And just as the rationalist conceptually endowed the individual with social instincts and drives independent of any social organization, so he endowed the people itself with a natural harmony and stability that would give it all the necessary requisites of persistence and continuity. What we may notice in the case of the rationalist's construct of the people, as in his construct of the individual, is the unconscious transfer of virtues, stabilities, and motivations from a *historical social organization* to an entity regarded as naturally independent of all historical change and social pressure.

Here, of course, philosophy of Progress was marvelously comforting. For the very essence of the idea of secular progress was its premise that history is inherently organizational in direction, leading always, and without the need of man's guiding hand, to ever higher conditions of civilization. The consequences of institutional dislocation, of the ruthless separating of the people from cherished values and memberships, could be disregarded. History would supply its own correctives. It was only necessary to be certain that the *obstacles* to progress—classes, religious institutions, family solidarities, gilds, and so forth—were removed.

Inevitably the principal strategy of unitary democracy came to be fixed, like the strategies of nationalism and military socialism, in terms of the sterilization of old social loyalties, the emancipation of the people from local and regional authorities, and the construction of a scene in which the individual would be the sole unit, and the State the sole association, of society. Hence, the rising stress on large-scale bureaucracy: to provide new agencies representative of the *whole* people for the discharge of powers and responsibilities formerly resident in classes, parishes, and families. Hence, the increasing adiministrative centralization of society: to reduce in number and influence the intermediate social authorities. Hence the growing stress upon standardization: to increase the number of cultural qualities shared by the people as a whole and to diminish those shared only be fractions of the population. Hence, also, the drive toward political collectivism: to bring into full light the pre-existent harmony which the rationalists never doubted made a natural unity of the people.

State and individual were the two elements of the unitary theory of democracy. The abstract individual was conceived as the sole bearer of rights and responsibilities. The State, conceived in the image of people who lay incorruptible beneath the superstructure of society, would be the area of fraternity and secular rehabilitation. All that lay between these two elements—gilds, churches, professions, classes, unions of all kinds—were suspect for their fettering influence upon the individual and their divisive consequences to the people's State.

This, in its essentials, is the unitary tradition of democracy. It is, despite its exalted motives, almost indistinguishable from the ideology of the absolute political community. This is the tradition that provides so much of the historic relation between democracy and nationalism, between democracy and collectivism, between democracy and that whole tendency toward cultural standardization which has periodically alienated some of the most liberal of minds. This is the tradition that offers so many of the catchwords and deceptive slogans of contemporary Communism in its typical forms of the "People's States." This is the tradition that led Proudhon to define democracy, bitterly, as the State magnified to the nth power, and Tocqueville to see in it, for all his reluctant admiration for democracy, the seeds of despotism greater than anything before provided by history. . . .

Given the mounting evils of the new industrialism, the appearance of new structures of economic power beyond anything seen before, and the widening incidence of economic insecurity, the techniques of administrative centralization were tempting indeed to men of good will. As against the possibilities of redress and security inherent in voluntary association, in the church, and in the local community, those of the State seemed not merely greater but infinitely more swift in possible attainment. Increasingly, American liberalism became committed to the State as the major area of social rehabilitation and to administrative centralization as the means. Imperceptibly the historic emphasis upon localism was succeeded by nationalism, pluralism by monism, and decentralization by centralization.

Today, it is the widening appeal of the collectivist, unitary ideal of democracy, set in conditions of social dislocation and moral alienation, stimulated by the demands of mass warfare, that makes the problem of power so ominous in the Western democracies.

III. We may see in the administrative techniques of unitary democracy certain justifications of a historical nature. Given a society overpowered by inherited traditions, traditions manifestly inimical to both technical advancement and human rights; given a society that is nearly stationary from the hold of ecclesiastical, class, or kinship ties, and overrich to the point of chaos in local and regional diversity, the techniques of administrative uniformity and centralization can have a pragmatic value that is unquestionable. Such, in considerable degree, was the European society of the eighteenth century. Such, in even larger degree, is the society of, say, contemporary India.

Plainly, however, we are not, in the United States, living in that kind of society. Ours is a society characterized increasingly, as we have seen, by the sterilization of group differences—local, class, regional, and associative—which lie outside the administrative framework of the State. And ours is a State characterized by ever-rising centralization of function and authority. Both characteristics—social atomization and political centralization—are the unmistakable attributes of the beginnings of mass society. And because of these social and political realities the requirements of liberal democracy are profoundly different from what they were a century or two ago. . . .

While we seek constantly to make democracy more secure in the world by diplomatic agreements and national security legislation, we do not often remind ourselves that the most powerful resources of democracy lie in the cultural *allegiances* of citizens, and that these allegiances are nourished psychologically in the smaller, internal areas of family, local community, and association.

These are the areas that contain the images of the larger society, the areas within which human beings are able to define, and render meaningful, democratic values. When the small areas of association become sterile psychologically, as the result of loss of institutional significance, we find ourselves resorting to ever-increasing dosages of indoctrination from above, and indoctrination that often becomes totalitarian in significance. We find ourselves with a society that suffers increasingly from, to use the expressive words of Lamennais, apoplexy at the center and anemia at the extremities. To be sure, liberals strive earnestly to maintain the rights and equalities of individuals before the rising structure of legislative and executive political power. They appeal to the courts, but not even the American judicial system can remain for very long untouched by the drive toward political uniformity and centralization. They appeal to the rights of man but, except in a religious sense which few liberals take seriously, there are no rights of man that do not proceed from the society in which human beings live. In any event, it is the liberal concentration of interest upon the *individual*, rather than upon the associations in which the individual exists, that serves, paradoxical as it may seem, to intensify the processes that lead straight to increased governmental power. . . .

Individual *versus* State is as false an antithesis today as it ever was. The State grows on what it gives to the individual as it does on what it takes from competing social relationships—family, labor union, profession, local community, and church. And the individual cannot but find a kind of vicarious strength in what is granted to the State. For is he not himself a part of the State? Is he not a fraction of the sovereign? And is he not but adding to his political status as citizen what he subtracts from his economic, religious, and cultural statuses in society?

He is; and in this fractional political majesty the individual finds not only compensation for the frustrations and insecurities to which he is heir in mass society but also the intoxicating sense of collective freedom.

To find the essence of freedom in the fact of the ultimate political sovereignty of the people, in the existence of mass electorates, in the individual's constitutionally guaranteed participation every two or four years in the election of his public servants, is tempting in the modern world. For it is supported by the premise, so alluring to the reformer and the disinherited alike, that political power, however great and far-reaching it may be, if it is but continuously and sensitively in touch with mass wish and acquiescence, ceases to be power in the ordinary sense. It becomes collective self-determination, collective freedom. Power becomes, in this view, marvelously neutralized and immaterialized.

"Our contemporaries," Tocqueville observed a century ago, "are constantly excited by two conflicting passions: they want to be led and they wish to remain free. As they cannot destroy either the one or the other of these contrary propensities, they strive to satisfy them both at once. They devise a sole, tutelary, and all-powerful form of government elected by the people. They combine the principle of centralization and that of popular sovereignty; this gives them respite: they console themselves for being in tutelage by the reflection that they have chosen their own guardians. Every man allows himself to be in leading strings, because he sees that it is not a person or class of persons, but the people at large who hold the end of the chain. . . .

"I admit that by this means room is left for the intervention of individuals in the more important affairs: but it is not the less suppressed in the smaller and more private ones. It must not be forgotten that it is especially dangerous to enslave men in the minor details of life. For my own part, I should be inclined to think freedom less necessary in the great things than in the little ones, if it were possible to be secure of the one without possessing the other.[1]

It is especially dangerous to enslave men in the minor details of life. Could any insight be more relevant to the contemporary problem of power in Western society? Too often in our intellectual defenses of freedom, in our sermons and manifestoes for democracy, we have fixed attention only on the more obvious historical threats to popular freedom: kings, military dictators, popes, and financial titans. We have tended to miss the subtler but infinitely more potent threats bound up with diminution of authorities and allegiances in the smaller areas of association and with the centralization and standardization of power that takes place in the name of, and on behalf of, the *people*.

Here, of course, it is always persuasive to argue that modern increases in the administrative authority of the State have been generally associated with the enhancement of mass welfare. But this is no answer to the problem of power. As Jefferson shrewdly pointed out, the State with the power to do things *for* people has the power to do things *to* them. In plain fact the latter power increases almost geometrically in proportion to the former.

Nor is it an answer to the problem of power to argue that political power in the democracies is achieved in the name of the people and through actions of representatives of the people. For we have learned from European experience that it is not primarily the source of power that is at issue but the nature of the power and the degree of unity and unconditionality which it holds over human beings.

The collective political power of the people has increased enormously during the past century. So have available means of political participation by the common man: the referendum, the direct primary, the recall, the continuous abolition of restrictions on voting, and other even more direct means of participation. Yet, along with these increases in popular democracy, it must be observed that there has been a general leveling of local, regional, and associative differences, a nationalization of culture and taste, a collectivization of mind, and a continuous increase in the real powers of government over management, labor, education, religion, and social welfare. Democracy, far from heightening human autonomy and cultural freedom, seems rather to have aided in the process of mechanization that has weakened them. It must be repeated again, however, that this is not the inevitable consequence of the democratic ideal of power vested residually in the people. It is the consequence of the systems of public administration which we have grafted onto the democratic ideal.

---

[1]*Democracy in America*, Reeve translation edited by Phillips Bradley (New York, 1945), Vol. 2, pp. 319-20.

IV. In this development of unitary democracy, of bureaucratic centralization, contemporary mass warfare has, of course, a profoundly contributory significance. "War is the health of the State," Randolph Bourne once declared. It is the health of the State as it is the disease, or rather the starvation, of other areas of social function and authority. . . . Even Tocqueville, with all his fear of centralization, was moved to write: "I do not deny that a centralized social power may be able to execute great undertakings with facility in a given time and on a particular point. This is especially true of war, in which success depends much more on the means of transferring all the resources of a nation to one single point than on the extent of these resources. Hence it is chiefly in war that nations desire, and frequently need, to increase the powers of the central government. All men of military genius are fond of centralization, which increases their strength; and all men of centralizing genius are fond of war which compels nations to combine all their powers in the hands of the government.[2]

It is precisely this military imperative of governmental centralization that makes continued warfare, or preparation for war, have so deadly an effect on all other institutions in society. For it is difficult to perform the administrative measures necessary to political and military centralization without drawing in drastic fashion from the functions, the authorities, and the allegiances that normally fall to such institutions as religion, profession, labor union, school, and local community. . . . Given the quickening effects of war on social dislocation and cultural sterilization, it is not strange that the State should become, in time of war, the major refuge of men. Democracy cannot but become ever more unitary, omnicompetent, centralized.

To the imperatives of modern war must be added two other supports of the unitary, collectivist view of democracy. These are two intellectual perspectives, idols of the mind, as Francis Bacon might have called them. The first is the veneration, nurtured by countless centuries of discord, for *unity*. The second is the seemingly ineradicable faith, derived from ancient, medieval, and modern ideas of change, in *historical necessity*.

With respect to the first, it is hard to avoid the fact that unity has had, historically, a symbolic appeal greater than any possessed by the values of plurality and diversity. From the earliest Greek metaphysicians down to the present, the greatest single objective of philosophy has been that of converting plurality into unity, "chaos" into intellectual order. Mind itself has been interpreted in terms that suggest monistic sovereignty by so many philosophers. The deep religious appeal of unity in experience, the craving of all human beings for an inner sense of order, and the age-old rationalist desire to transmute the flux and diversity of experiences into symmetrical schemes of meaning have all, in one way or another, contributed to the modern veneration for unity and uniformity in society.

The worship of unity offers no problems so long as it is confined to areas of aesthetics, religion, and metaphysics. But when transferred, under the stress of social dislocations, to the area of politics, it frequently becomes sinister. For then it tends

---

[2] *Ibid.*, pp. 300-301.

to become absorbed, as an ideal, by existent structures of administrative power. The philosophical quest for unity and certainty becomes, as it were, a kind of apologetics for political standardization and centralization. It is assumed that the spiritual unity which every human being inwardly prizes can be achieved only by an environment made ever more uniform institutionally. In the present age, certainly, he who cries Unity will inevitably have more listeners than he who cries, so irrelevantly it must seem, Plurality and Diversity.

The second intellectual perspective reinforcing the unitary view of democracy is that of historical necessity. The tendency of the human mind to convert the empirical order of changes and events in history into a logical, *necessary* order gives strong support to the view that centralization and political collectivism are somehow in the ordained direction of the future even as they have been the apparent logical development of the past.

The greatest intellectual and moral offense the modern intellectual can be found guilty of is that of seeming to think or act outside what is commonly held to be the linear progress of civilization.... In practical terms, we are dealing with a habit of mind that seizes selectively upon *certain* aspects of the present age, e.g. political omnicompetence and administrative centralization, and invests these not just with the ordinary attributes of goodness or rightness, but with that far greater virtue of *necessity*.

We tend thus to subordinate our planning to an imaginary course of evolution in society. In the perspective of Progress the data of the past are necessarily ruled out of practical consideration for present planning purposes simply because, within this perspective, the past can only be likened to the infancy or youth of an organism that is now in maturity and looking toward endless intensification of maturity. History is conceived as a continuous movement, a flow, a unified process, a development, with a beginning, a middle, and a logical, ethical end....

The supremacy of Marxism in the modern history of socialism comes in large part from the tactical success Marx and Engels had in investing the ethical ideal of socialism with historical necessity. Other socialists had held up their ideal as something to be described in detail, planned for, and worked for. When Marx scorned such efforts as being utopian and unhistorical and insisted that the future must develop inexorably out of the present, he not only prevented any further consideration of what he contemptuously called "kitchen recipes" but also placed the ideal of socialism firmly in the context of existent trends toward national collectivism and administrative centralization. For Marx, socialism was a stage of society that must develop dialectically out of the *significant* present. Pluralism, localism, voluntary association—all of these to Marx were mere survivals of medievalism. What was *real* in the present was industrialism, collectivism, and administrative centralization.

What is true of Marxian socialism has been true of a great deal of modern political and economic philosophy.... The modern facts of political mechanism, centralization, and collectivism are seen in the perspective of inevitable development in modern history. They seem to be the very direction of history itself. Present differences of political opinion hence usually resolve themselves into differences about who shall guide this developing reality and how little or how much should be administered it in the way of fuel. Any sharp alternative has the disadvantage of running up against the widely flung facts of uniformity and centralization, and the additional disadvantage of seeming to be filiated with historical conditions of the past which give it a manifestly "unprogressive" character.

The imperatives of war, the veneration of unity and uniformity, and the faith in historical necessity, with its corollary of irreversible historical processes—these, then, are the most powerful supports for the unitary perspective of democracy at the present time. Given these, together with the constant diminution in the significance of the non-political areas of kinship, religion, and other forms of association, the task of centralization and omnicompetence is not too difficult even in the presence of liberal values. Given these conditions and perspectives, the transition from liberal democracy to totalitarianism will not seem too arduous or unpleasant. It will indeed be scarcely noticed, save by the "utopians," the "reactionaries," and similar eccentrics.

V. Admittedly, there is a degree of unity without which any culture, like any musical composition, would become chaotic. And there is indeed a degree of centralization of authority apart from which no structure—political government, church, or labor union—could operate. So much is true. Yet, given the society in which we now live, it is difficult not to conclude that the requirements of liberal democracy are very different from those which seemed so necessary to men of good will a century ago.

The problem of freedom and authority can no longer be given even the semblance of solution by appeals to the talisman of popular sovereignty. For, despite the unquestioned moral rightness of the proposition that all legitimate political power must flow from the people, we are living in an age in which *all* forms of government, totalitarianism as well as liberal democracy, seek to root their authority in the soil of popular acquiescence. The greatest discovery in nineteenth-century politics, as we have seen, was the principle that the real power of a State may actually be enhanced, not diminished, by widening its base to include the whole of a population. The exploitation of this revolutionary principle of power reaches its highest development in the total State where no effort is spared to drive the functions and symbols of political authority as deeply as possible into the minds and wills of all the people, thus making State power a part of human personality, a projection of the self.

Popular sovereignty, then, is not enough. As a moral principle it must remain our point of departure, but if democracy is to remain liberal democracy, if it is not to become transmuted into the State of the masses, with its power converted into a monolith, we must face the crucial problems of the relation of political authority to all the other forms of authority in society. The reinforcement of these and their constitutional relationship to the political authority of the State become, in the present century, the major problem of democracy. Because of our single-minded concentration upon the individual as the sole unit of society and upon the State as the sole source of legitimate power, we have tended to overlook the fact that freedom thrives in cultural diversity, in local and regional differentiation, in associative pluralism, and, above all, in the *diversification of power*.

Basically, all of these are reducible, I believe, to the single massive problem of the relation of political government to the plurality of cultural associations which form the intermediate authorities of society. These are many: religious, economic, professional, local, recreational. academic, and so forth. Each of them is a structure, often large, of authorities and functions. Each of them is an organization of human purposes and allegiances related to some distinctive institutional end. Each of them is, apart from the checks provided by the existence of other and competing forms of association, potentially omnicompetent in its relation to its members. And whether it is the economic corporation, the huge labor union, or the profession, each offers, in its own way, innumerable problems of freedom and control in society. There is no unalterable guarantee of freedom in any one of them.

Nevertheless, it is the continued existence of this array of intermediate powers in society, of this plurality of "private sovereignties," that constitutes, above anything else, the greatest single barrier to the conversion of democracy from its liberal form to its totalitarian form. It is the fact of *diversity* of appeal that is foremost in this social constitution. Apart from its setting in a competitive framework, any one of these large-scale intermediate authorities is capable of expanding its own control over members to a point that exceeds the requirements of freedom. But the most notable characteristic of this whole array of social authorities in European history has been the ceaseless competition for human allegiance that goes on among them. . . .

VI. . . .Modern liberalism unfortunately has tended on the whole to step from the cherished individual of the nineteenth century to the myth of the all-benign State in the twentieth. While it has seldom been intolerant of intermediate associations, it has made little effort to formulate a theory of liberal democracy that includes them, that makes them indispensable to free, representative government. In general, modern democratic thought has settled single-mindedly upon the same elements that are crucial to the political community: the abstract individual and the State.

Yet, any careful historical examination reveals the roots political democracy has had in practice in social groups and cultural communities. Man does not live merely as one of a vast aggregate of arithmetically equal, socially undifferentiated, individuals. He does not live his life merely in terms of the procedures and techniques of the administrative State—not, at least, in a free society. As a concrete *person* he is inseparable from the plurality of social allegiances and memberships which characterize his social organization and from the diversities of belief and habit which form a culture.

Most of the tendencies in contemporary society toward the erosion of cultural differences and the standardization of cultural tastes, beliefs, and activities, which are so often charged, mistakenly, against technology and science, are the product, actually, of a centralization of authority and function and a desecration of local and cultural associations. . . .

Only through its intermediate relationships and authorities has any State ever achieved the balance between organization and personal freedom that is the condition of a creative and enduring culture. These relationships begin with the family and with the small informal social groups which spring up around common interests and cultural needs. Their number extends to the larger associations of society, to the churches, business associations, labor unions, universities, and professions. They are the real sources of liberal democracy. . . .

Only in their social interdependences are men given to resist the tyranny that always threatens to arise out of any political government, democratic or other. Where the individual stands alone in the face of the State he is helpless. "Despotism," wrote Tocqueville, "is never more secure of continuance then when it can keep men asunder; and all its influence is commonly exerted for that purpose." The desire for freedom arises only out of men's reverence for exterior and competing values. Genuine freedom is not based upon the negative psychology of release. Its roots are in positive acts of dedication to ends and values. Freedom presupposes the autonomous existence of values that men wish to be free to follow and live up to. Such values are social in the precise sense that they arise out of, and are nurtured by, the voluntary associations which men form.

VII. But neither social values nor autonomous social relationships can thrive apart from their possession of meaningful functions and authorities. We end this chapter on the theme with which it began: the centrality of the problem of power, its distribution in society, and its control. Man may be a social animal, but he does not devote himself in any serious way to groups and associations that are no longer clearly related to the larger structure of function and authority in society.

What has been so apparent in the modern history of the family will be no less apparent in the future histories of profession, university, labor union, and all other forms of association in our culture. Deprive these entities of their distinctive functions through increasing nationalization of service and welfare, divest them of the authorities over their members through increasing centralization of political power in society, and these associations, like the extended family, the church, and the local community, must shrink immeasurably in their potential contributions to culture.

Modern philosophies of freedom have tended to emphasize, as we have seen, either the individual's *release* from power of every kind—generally, through an appeal to natural rights—or the individual's *participation* in some single structure of authority like the General Will, which replaces all other structures.

But from the point of view of the real, the historical roots of liberal democracy, freedom has rested neither upon release nor upon collectivization but upon the *diversification* and the *decentralization* of power in society. In the division of authority and the multiplication of its sources lie the most enduring conditions of freedom. "The only safeguard against power," warned Montesquieu, "is rival power." He was echoed by Lord Acton more than a century later, who declared that "Liberty depends upon the division of power."

Freedom, it has been well said, lies in the interstices of authority. This is indeed, I believe, the real reconciliation of the demands of order and the demands of freedom. Authority, any society, any association, must have. It is simply the structure of the association. But the sole possibility of personal freedom and cultural autonomy lies in the maintenance of a plurality of authorities in any society. Each of these may be tight enough as an individual system to provide a context of security for its members. So long as there are other and competing authorities, so long as man has even the theoretical possibility of removing himself from any that for him has grown oppressive and of placing himself within the framework of some other associative authority, it cannot be said that his freedom has suffered.

It is in these terms, I think, that the role of political government becomes clear in the democracies. Not to sterilize the normal authorities of associations, as does the total State through a pre-emption of function, a deprivation of authority, and a monopolization of allegiance, but to reinforce these associations, to provide, administratively, a means whereby the normal competition of group differences is held within bounds and an environment of law within which no single authority, religious or economic, shall attain a repressive and monopolistic influence—this is the role of government in a democracy....

VIII. We cannot be reminded too often that the stifling effects of centralization upon society are as evident in large-scale private industry as they are in political government. Big government and big business have developed together in Western society, and each has depended on the other. To these two has been added more recently a third force in society—big labor. In all three spheres, and, for that matter in our universities, charities, and various other activities, there is a strong tendency to organize administration in terms of the ideas of power inherited from the seventeenth and eighteenth centuries.

But there is a point beyond which centralized administration cannot go if the meaning and urgency of the ends of any association are to be kept alive in the minds of the individuals who comprise the association....

It will be recognized at once that planning and administration in terms of decentralization, localism, and associative autonomy is far more difficult than administration carried on under the myth of territorial masses of discrete individual atoms. Not only does it go against the tendency of the whole history of modern economic, educational, and political administration, but, on its own terms, it raises problems of organization that are immense....

The necessity of decentralization is by no means confined to the structure of the political State, great as the need there may be. Decentralization is just as necessary in the operation of the other great associations of modern society—the industrial corporation, the labor union, the large church, the profession, and the great university. More than a little of the diminution in the psychological and cultural influence of these associations in recent times results from their failure to remain responsive to the small areas of association within them. This is the consequence of the same kind of centralization and collectivization we see in politics. The fault lies in the common failure to unite the broad purposes of the larger associations with the small, informal relationships composing them.

The labor union, the legal or medical association, or the church will become as centralized and as remote as the national State itself unless these great organizations are rooted in the smaller relationships which give meaning to the ends of the large associations. To conceive of a great labor union, industrial enterprise, or church as an association of *individual* members is but to intensify the processes of atomization which such associations can and should counteract. No large association will remain an object of personal allegiance, no matter how crucial its goals may be, unless it is constantly sensitive to the existence of the informal but potent relationships of which it is really composed. It has surely become evident by this time that the most successful and allegiance-evoking business enterprises and cultural associations in modern life are those that regard themselves as associations of *groups*, not of raw individuals. To recognize the existence of informal social relationships, to keep central purposes constantly alive in these small groups, and to work toward the increased spontaneity and autonomy of these groups is, I believe, the cardinal responsibility of the great private association.

Only thus will the large formal associations remain important agencies of order and freedom in democracy. Only thus will they succeed in arresting and banishing the augmenting processes of insecurity and moral isolation which now paralyze individual wills and strike at the roots of stable culture.

There is a vast difference between the type of planning—whether in the large State, industry, or the school—that seeks to enmesh the individual in a custodial network of detailed rules for his security and society's stability, and the type of planning that is concerned with the creation of a political and economic *context* within which the spontaneous associations of men are the primary sources of freedom and order. The latter type of planning is compatible with competition, diversity, rivalry, and the normative conflicts that are necessary to cultural creativity. The former type is not. . . .

The liberal values of autonomy and freedom of personal choice are indispensable to a genuinely free society, but we shall achieve and maintain these only by vesting them in the conditions in which liberal democracy will thrive—diversity of culture, plurality of association, and division of authority.

FREEDOM AND SOCIAL STRUCTURE

Gerard DeGré

The problem of freedom is an old one, but for free men its importance is such that it can bear periodical reexamination. The term itself is ambiguous, for it has been used in many senses, not only by the philosophers but by practical statesmen as well. The discussion of freedom has often been involved with the idea of free will; at other times it has referred more concretely to freedom of action within society. The questions connected with free will and determinism are primarily problems for metaphysics and ethics and, in the main, only normative answers can be given to them. The conditions

SOURCE: Gerard DeGré, "Freedom and Social Structure," *American Sociological Review*, Vol. 11, October 1964, pp. 529-536. Reprinted by permission. Several footnotes have been omitted, and those remaining have been renumbered.

which are conducive to freedom of social action, however, are more amenable to historical and sociological investigation, and it is this relationship which will provide the basis for discussion.

From the sociological standpoint the problem of freedom is primarily a problem of social structure. This means that it is a legitimate task for the sociologist to inquire into the socio-historical conditions, particularly the structure of power relationships present in various types of societies, which are most closely correlated with freedom of social action. A thorough study would, of course, require an intensive historical research into the fluctuation of freedom under the impact of changing forms of political, economic, and social organization. But even a preliminary presentation of the question requires some working definition of freedom that will lend itself to some degree of objectivity of treatment. The problem therefore resolves itself into two main topics for analysis: the nature of freedom, and the consideration of the forms of social structure which are conducive to freedom.

It may be said that the amount of freedom that an individual possesses is measured by the number of things he can do without interference from others. In this sense his freedom is a function of someone else's freedom, for this other person's concrete freedoms may be such that they tend to inhibit the freedom of action of the first individual. If Van Wyck has the freedom to levy assessments on the produce of Jones, then Jones does not have the freedom to dispose of the product of his labor as he sees fit. If Jones joins with Smith and Muller and Larski, then he may be able to limit and institutionalize the amount of assessments so that the economic relationship to Van Wyck becomes much more predictable. It then becomes much more possible for Smith to plan his course of economic action. The freedom of any concrete individual or group, therefore, would appear to be a *resultant* of his or their position *vis à vis* other persons or groups. This paper will attempt to show that freedom flourishes most when the relationships of groups are in a relative equilibrium determined by a reciprocity and accommodation necessitated by each group having to take into account in its action the interests, values and power of other groups. This is true according to the degree to which the various groups are relatively equal to one another, thereby insuring the improbability of any one group attaining a monopoly of control over the rest.

Freedom may be defined in terms of the *probability* that specific groups or individuals can formulate their ends of conduct and initiate a course of action with a minimum degree of constraint from other persons, and with a high degree of predictability of the consequences of their acts within the institutional and associational structure of the community. In other words, it is determined by the degree to which persons, distributively or collectively, can plan a course of action without arbitrary and unpredictable interference. The essence of freedom, therefore, is its *rationality*, in the sense that it is defined according to the *predictability* of the probable expectations tied up with a course of action.

It must not be forgotten, however, that predictability in itself does not exhaust completely the meaning of freedom. For although the essential rationality of freedom implies the ability of the agent to plan his actions with reference to his probable expectations; the range of action may be severely limited by the institutional structure of society, so that even if the agent can count on the relative stability of the stateways and *mores*, his action may be inhibited by the socio-juridical structure of a narrow, authoritarian state. The rationality of freedom implies, therefore, not only the relative predictability of the future; it implies, as well, the ability to plan and act with a minimum degree of external constraint. Both of these aspects of freedom are implied in the popular definition in terms of the degree to which "man is the master of his own destiny."

II. Man, as a political animal, lives his life in groups, and the concrete freedoms which he enjoys derive their sustenance and vitality from the backing of his group *vis à vis* other groups. The romantic, highly individualized conception of freedom, so popular in the literature of the nineteenth century, and useful as it may be in motivating individual thought and action; fails, nevertheless, to provide a realistic theory of freedom which can do justice to the sociological and historical roots of social action. Romanticism provides an ideal of freedom rather than an explanation or analysis. In its emphasis on the ideal of personal autonomy, Romanticism brushes aside the problem of the situational determination of freedom. . . .

A sociological theory of freedom, therefore, must take as its starting point the *socius*, that is, the individual as a member of a group, class, or social type, rather than the abstract individual-as-such that forms the nucleus of Romanticism.

Studies in the field of the sociology of knowledge[1] have demonstrated that the idea of freedom is itself conditioned by the group membership of the individual. For the conservative, freedom usually means the freedom to exercise his prerogatives and to conduct his affairs with a minimum of interference from the state or other organized groups. Although at first glance this conception might not seem to run contrary to our general definition of freedom, in practice it tends to violate social freedom to the degree to which it refuses to recognize the claims of other groups to free action. In other words, it recognizes freedom only *for its own class*, and endeavors to keep other social strata subordinated to its will.

The revolutionist, on the other hand, defines freedom primarily in terms of freedom from the restrictions and prerogatives of a strongly intrenched dominant class, and, in its revolutionary fervor, calls for the destruction of that class. This is as true of the ascendant bourgeoisie in its struggle against the feudal aristocracy as it is of the revolutionary proletariat of our day.

A little reflection makes it clear that both of these groups are operating with a *particularistic* conception of freedom, for they both define freedom in terms of their own class interest. The unreconstructed conservative and the reactionary admit freedom as a good only for their own group, and wish to deny it to others just as soon as they feel that their class interests are threatened. The revolutionist, in reaction to this situation, wishes to deny the very basis of freedom to the dominant group, that is, their continued existence.

A *pluralistic* or *total* definition of freedom must take into account the interests and

---

[1]Cf. Karl Mannheim, *Ideology and Utopia* (New York: Harcourt, Brace & Co., 1936, esp. pp. 244-246). Also Manheim's "Das Konservative Denken", "*Archiv fur Sozialwissenschaft und Sozialpolitik*," vol. 57, pp. 90. ff.

aspirations of all societal groupings: economic, political and cultural. Because of this, the methodological standpoint of an objective social philosophy must be *moderate*, in spite of the personal political predilections of the investigator.

If the degree of freedom is dependent upon the relative absence of external constraint, it will be correlated also with those societal conditions which tend to limit the power of social groups in relationship to one another. The problem of freedom, therefore, is primarily a problem of the group structure of society.[2] ...

Within a specific socio-historical situation, the existing system of power relationships will determine the degree of freedom which is present. The system of power relationships itself is the resultant of the relative power of the component groups of a society. The social freedom of any individual, in turn, is largely dependent upon the relative freedom of the group of which he is a member.

Inasmuch as the freedom of the individual is rooted in the social situation of his group, and derives efficacy and stability through the backing of his group in the social field of action, the problem of inter-group relations is definitive in determining the conditions of freedom.

III. What types of social intergroup structures are to be analyzed? The strictly political classifications are misleading, for they refer primarily to forms of government rather than types of society. The Aristotelean classification into monarchy, aristocracy and democracy is not of much help, for specific freedoms have flourished under all three forms. Economic classifications, as well, are often irrelevant, for commercial, industrial and agricultural communities exhibit varying degrees of freedom. A socio-economic classification is perhaps more to the point, but even the categories: feudal, bourgeois-capitalist, proletarian-socialist, fascist, etc., fail when viewed in historical perspective, for all of these types may take a totalitarian form whenever one of the constituent social groups achieves a relative monopoly of control and power. This does not mean that political or economic forms are irrelevant to freedom, for certain historical correlations can be demonstrated to exist, but only that the social basis of freedom is broader than its economic or political base.

Our classification of societal types must therefore be *sociological*, rather than economic or political. A sociological classification of inter-group structures has its basis, as has been indicated, in the group structure as such. This means that the typology is to be constructed on the most general level of analysis, i.e., on the basis of the inter-group relations within the total system of social relationships.

Emile Durkheim in his *Division of Labor in Society*[3] has suggested one such classification which we may take as our starting point. He divides societies into those based on *mechanical* solidarity and those based on *organic* solidarity. According to his system, mechanical social structures are those which are characterized by such features as homogeneity, little or no division of labor, a minimum degree of individuality and a maximum degree of social constraint. These conditions exist primarily in primitive

---

[2] This definition is derived from Max Weber's definition of social relation given in his *Wirtschaft und Gesellschaft*. (Translated by José Medina Echavarria under the title *Economia y Sociedad*, Mexico, D.F.: Fondo de Cultura Economica, 1944, 4 vols., Vol. I, sect. 3, pp. 24-26).

[3] Emile Durkheim, *The Division of Labor in Society*, transl. by George Simpson (New York: Macmillan Co., 1933).

societies where differentiation of groups, individuals and social functions is at a minimum. Since practically no differentiation is present, there is little diversification of group interests, values or attitudes. Such societies, to use a biological analogy, may be said to be *amorphous*.

A later differentiation, which occurs when institutions begin to crystallize out of the division of society according to a more clear cut differentiation of the religious from the secular, the economic from the recreational, etc., is the *segmental* society. The division here, however, is still primarily *institutional* rather than *associational*. There is as yet little differentiation into functional groups, the division is rather on the basis of different collective interests of the community.

As individuals begin to specialize according to institutional interests, and start to perform more specialized economic functions, definite groups with specific group interests begin to emerge. The greater the degree of specialization which is reached, the larger becomes the amount of interdependence of the specialized segments, and the more diverse become the interests and attitudes of the component groups. In this way the *organic* society emerges, characterized by a high degree of group differentiation, multiplication of interests, specialization of function, increasing interdependence and wide *heterogeneity*. Because of the diversification of interests and values which is concomitant with this increasing heterogeneity, the amount of collective constraint decreases, since the unanimity of attitudes which prevailed in amorphous societies is no longer present, and the divergent social group must learn to accommodate themselves to one another.

According to Durkheim, this transition from primitive amorphous societies through segmental to organic social structures is an evolutionary process intimately correlated with the division of labor and an increasing specialization of function. This development has as its consequence the multiplication of societal groups as well as the increasing individualization of their members. Inasmuch as freedom is closely correlated with group structure, Durkheim's theory of group differentiation as a general historical process provides a preliminary orientation to our problem of constructing a typology of social structures.

We have seen that the multiplication of groups caused by the division of labor in an organic society has as its consequence an increasing need for accommodation between the divergent social groups. As long as no specific group obtains a monopoly of power, the various groups can protect the interests of their constituent individuals. On the other hand, as soon as one particular group begins to achieve a relative monopoly of power, the concrete freedoms of the members of other groups begin to decline proportionately. This is true, apparently, no matter which group obtains a dominant position to the extent that it no longer needs to take into account the interests and values of other groups.

During some periods of history it has been the priesthood that has achieved an almost complete monopoly of politico-hierocratic power: Egypt, Medieval Christendom, Zwingli's Geneva, Cotton Mather's New England. At other times, the land-owning aristocracy arrogated to itself an almost complete control over the machinery of the state. In its turn, the ascendant bourgeoisie has been able to control the Legislatures to the virtual exclusion of other social classes. Proletarian governments have rooted out the vestiges of any opposition, not only from other class alignments, but from within their own "classless" stratum as well. In Fascist societies it has been the government party machine and bureaucracy itself which has achieved the greatest monopoly of force and control the world has ever seen.

In most of these cases political dominance has been achieved through the disproportionate degree of economic control of certain groups as compared to the other groups within a society. The source of the initial advantage may have been due originally to conquest, e.g., early feudalism. Sometimes it has been the result of greater technical competence as in the case of Rome. Perhaps in most cases it has been due to the fact that certain groups were strategically situated historically to take full advantage of a changing economic situation, and the lack of enterprise, interest or imagination of other more firmly intrenched strata; e.g., the bankers and merchants of Renaissance Florence *vis à vis* the old Florentine aristocracy.[4]

Although it would be difficult to overestimate the importance of economic control in determining the structure of power relationships, this should not blind us to the relevance of ideological and political factors as well. The fact that certain political doctrines may be considered extremely useful by particular groups in furthering their own ends does not mean necessarily that the parties expressing these doctrines are the "tools" of these groups. The political party, rather, may be their accomplices and eventually their masters. A case to the point is Nazi Germany where the National Socialist party eventually achieved dominance over the economic interests which originally backed them in their ascent to power. At other times, ecclesiastical, military, ideological or charismatic groups have attained strategic positions in the distribution of power relationships which enabled them to dominate politically the historical situation in spite of a relatively secondary economic position.

Inasmuch as the amount of power of any specific group is restricted by the social pressure which other groups can bring against it, it follows that a hyper-individualized or atomized society is in greater danger of falling under the dominance of the first organized group that comes along than is a society where various units of possible resistance already exist. A society split into too large a number of tiny conflicting groups, as well, will find it difficult to organize a significant opposition in case of need. On the other hand, when one or two groups have obtained control of the social structure, the resulting oligarchy is in a position to dominate the majority for its own purposes. The optimum condition for freedom, therefore, lies somewhere midway between totalitarianism at one extreme and atomized individualism at the other.

IV. In order to visualize the relationship between freedom and social structure just described, a graphic device may prove useful. The optimum condition for freedom may be represented by the high point of a bell-shaped curve; the decline of the probability of freedom in the directions of both atomism and totalitarianism is indicated by the declining slopes to the left and right of the medial distribution. (Fig. I)

In this statistical analogy the horizontal ordinate represents a continuum from a completely disorganized social structure (atomism) to the absolutely regimented

---

[4] Alfred von Martin, *Sociology of the Renaissance* (New York: Oxford University Press, 1944).

society (totalitarianism). The intervening steps represent degrees of group organization and concentration. The vertical ordinate represents the varying degrees of probability that free institutions will be present in relationship to the underlying social inter-group structure.

FIGURE I.
Variations of Freedom in Relation to Systems
of Power Relationships.

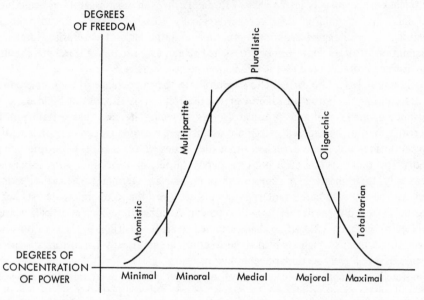

Thus the minimal degree of group integration (extreme individualism) is correlated with a low degree of freedom and would be illustrative of Hobbs' "war of all against all." This provides the first type of our projected classification, and may be designated as *atomistic*. Historical types tending to fall within this area of the curve are anarchy, frontier democracy, and the magic-ridden, cut-throat competitive economy of Dobu.[5]

The minoral degree of societal integration is characterized by the shattering of society into a multitude of small competing groups, resulting in a relatively low degree of social stability which in turn can pave the way for dictatorship and the monolithic state. It is characterized by a multiplication of small groups: many autonomous economic organizations, a large number of competing sects, a multi-party system where no one party can achieve a parliamentary majority or significant minority, and a society lacking a basic consensus concerning its ends, institutions or organization. In the world-political sphere we have the example of the Holy Roman Empire and the Italian City States which were at the mercy of unified national powers. Societal types

---

[5] Ruth Benedict, *Patterns of Culture* (New York: Houghton Mifflin Co., 1934).

are more difficult to find, although in certain respects the French political scene during the thirties approximated this condition . . . [of] a *multipartite* system. . . .

The high, medial segment of the curve represents the optimum condition for the development and maintenance of freedom. It is the *pluralist* society characterized by the presence of large, well integrated groups representing significant divisions of interests and values. The various groups are limited in their power by the fact that the interests of other groups must be taken into account. The power of the state is limited by the power of organized public opinion and large special interest groups; the pressure exercised by business interests is counterbalanced by the forces of organized labor; both management and labor must take into account the interests of an integrated consumers' movement and other public agencies; no one religious group possesses a monopoly of spiritual values, and the various religious groups learn to accommodate themselves to one another; religious thought is denied absolute sovereignty over ideas by the presence of independent secular thought maintained by a free press, free universities, free literary movements, learned societies and organized scientific research. In the sphere of production, a pluralist society might allow for the operation of more than one form of economic organization: not only corporations and single entrepreneurships, but worker owned cooperatives and state organized collectives as well. Probably no community has ever achieved the optimum degree of pluralist organization, but the United States of America, Great Britain and Sweden may be considered as illustrative of societies tending to approximate the conditions of a pluralist society. The problem of the citizenry of these states is to extend the equilibrating democratic forces which tend to secure the pluralistic conditions of freedom, while combating the twin dangers of monolithic totalitarianism and atomistic individualism. In this connection it must be stressed that a consensus must exist amongst the various groups concerning the relative desirability and validity of the underlying institutional structure. This consensus exists to the degree to which the groups are convinced that they can realize their aims within the framework of the society as a going order. Without this basic agreement, the pluralist society degenerates into a conflict society of warring strata, classes, organizations and pressure groups.

The ancient term, *oligarchy*, may be retained to designate the declining slope of our hypothetical curve. The chief index is the increasing concentration of power into the hands of specific vested interests; irrespective of whether these interests are aristocratic, bourgeois, military, proletarian, ecclesiastic or bureaucratic. It is inevitable, perhaps, that this tendency will manifest itself at critical historical junctures and revolutionary periods. The role of the moderate (if he keeps his head) during these periods is to provide a critical oasis during the transition, while adapting himself realistically to the logic of events and the pattern of history. This means that the role of the moderate is a progressive rather than a reactionary one; but that, at the same time, he cannot share the fanaticism of the extreme left any more than he can that of the extreme right, and still be the carrier of general human and cultural values: the dignity of man, individual responsibility, judicial impartiality, the preference of persuasion to force; in a word, all of the *values* which make him prefer freedom to domination. In normal times, the moderate or pluralist will tend to support those social strata which have not as yet achieved relative equality of status within the society.

Located at the bottom of our declining slope is the *totalitarian* society. It is totalitarian precisely because it has systematically destroyed all independent groups and autonomous opinion. It resembles the atomistic society in that the individual again operates without the backing of any group of his own. It differs from the atomistic society, however, in the fact that this time the atomized individual faces the full power of an omnipotent Leviathan state. Because of this it might be preferable to label the process as "massification" rather than "atomization." For while "atomization" takes place more or less spontaneously, "massification" is the product of the deliberate policy of the totalitarian state to destroy all possible social groups which could some day challenge its authority.

The purpose of constructing the hypothetical curve was to provide a frame of reference within which the relationship of freedom and social structure might be shown as a continuum. The curve, obviously, does not represent an experimentally derived frequency distribution. It might be described as an "ideal-typical" curve, arbitrarily divided into five segments, each segment representing a formal "pure type" of social structure. On the basis of this ideal typical distribution it is then possible to define societal types more precisely, and to locate roughly on the curve historically given social structures. The curve serves as a reminder, as well, that freedom is a matter of degree, rather than an "all-or-none" affair, and that it is correlated with the structure of group relationships present in society.

THE THEORY OF COUNTERVAILING POWER

John Kenneth Galbraith

On the night of November 2, 1907, the elder Morgan played solitaire in his library while panic gripped Wall Street. Then, when the other bankers had divided up the cost of saving the tottering Trust Company of America, he presided at the signing of the agreement, authorized the purchase of the Tennessee Coal & Iron Company by the Steel Corporation to encourage the market, cleared the transaction with President Roosevelt and the panic was over. There, as legend has preserved and doubtless improved the story, was a man with power a self-respecting man could fear.

A mere two decades later, in the crash of 1929, it was evident that the Wall Street bankers were as helpless as everyone else. Their effort in the autumn of that year to check the collapse in the market is now recalled as an amusing anecdote. . . .

SOURCE: John Kenneth Galbraith, *American Capitalism* (Boston: Houghton Mifflin Company, 1952), pp. 108-123, 126-128, 130-134. Reprinted by permission. Several footnotes have been omitted and those remaining have been renumbered.

As the banker, as a symbol of economic power, passed into the shadows his place was taken by the giant industrial corporation. The substitute was much more plausible. The association of power with the banker had always depended on the somewhat tenuous belief in a "money trust"—on the notion that the means for financing the initiation and expansion of business enterprises was concentrated in the hands of a few men. The ancestry of this idea was in Marx's doctrine of finance capital; it was not susceptible to statistical or other empirical verification at least in the United States.

By contrast, the fact that a substantial proportion of all production was concentrated in the hands of a relatively small number of huge firms was readily verified. That three or four giant firms in an industry might exercise power analogous to that of a monopoly, and not different in consequences, was an idea that had come to have the most respectable of ancestry in classical economics. So as the J. P. Morgan Company left the stage, it was replaced by the two hundred largest corporations—giant devils in company strength. Here was economic power identified by the greatest and most conservative tradition in economic theory. Here was power to control the prices the citizen paid, the wages he received, and which interposed the most formidable of obstacles of size and experience to the aspiring firm. What more might it accomplish were it to turn its vast resources to corrupting politics and controlling access to public opinion?

Yet, as was so dramatically revealed to be the case with the omnipotence of the banker in 1929, there are considerable gaps between the myth and the fact. The comparative importance of a small number of great corporations in the American economy cannot be denied except by those who have a singular immunity to statistical evidence or striking capacity to manipulate it. In principle the American is controlled, livelihood and soul, by the large corporation; in practice he seems not to be completely enslaved. . . .

II. As with social efficiency, and its neglect of technical dynamics, the paradox of the unexercised power of the large corporation begins with an important oversight in the underlying economic theory. In the competitive model—the economy of many sellers each with a small share of the total market—the restraint on the private exercise of economic power was provided by other firms on the same side of the market. It was the eagerness of competitors to sell, not the complaints of buyers, that saved the latter from spoliation. It was assumed, no doubt accurately, that the nineteenth-century textile manufacturer who overcharged for his product would promptly lose his market to another manufacturer who did not. If all manufacturers found themselves in a position where they could exploit a strong demand, and mark up their prices accordingly, there would soon be an inflow of new competitors. The resulting increase in supply would bring prices and profits back to normal.

As with the seller who was tempted to use his economic power against the customer, so with the buyer who was tempted to use it against his labor or suppliers. The men who paid less than prevailing wage would lose his labor force to those who paid the worker his full (marginal) contribution to the earnings of the firm. In all cases the incentive to socially desirable behavior was provided by the competitor. It was to the same side of the market—the restraint of sellers by other sellers and of buyers by other buyers, in other words to competition—that economists cameto look for the self-regulatory mechanism of the economy.

They also came to look to competition exclusively and in formal theory still do. The notion that there might be another regulatory mechanism in the economy has been almost completely excluded from economic thought. Thus, with the wide-spread disappearance of competition in its classical form and its replacement by the small group of firms if not in overt, at least in conventional or tacit collusion, it was easy to suppose that since competition had disappeared, all effective restraint on private power had disappeared. . . .

In fact, new restraints on private power did appear to replace competition. They were nurtured by the same process of concentration which impaired or destroyed competition. But they appeared not on the same side of the market but on the opposite side, not with competitors but with customers or suppliers. It will be convenient to have a name for this counterpart of competition and I shall call it *countervailing power.*[1]

To begin with a broad and somewhat too dogmatically stated proposition, private economic power is held in check by the countervailing power of those who are subject to it. The first begets the second. The long trend toward concentration of industrial enterprise in the hands of a relatively few firms has brought into existence not only strong sellers, as economists have supposed, but also strong buyers as they have failed to see. The two develop together, not in precise step but in such manner that there can be no doubt that the one is in reponse to the other.

The fact that a seller enjoys a measure of monopoly power, and is reaping a measure of monopoly return as a result, means that there is an inducement to those firms from whom he buys or those to whom he sells to develop the power with which they can defend themselves against exploitation. It means also that there is a reward to them, in the form of a share of the gains of their opponents' market power, if they are able to do so. In this way the existence of market power creates an incentive to the organization of another position of power that neutralizes it.

The contention I am here making is a formidable one. It comes to this: Competition which, at least since the time of Adam Smith, has been viewed as the autonomous regulator of economic activity and as the only available regulatory mechanism apart from the state, has, in fact, been superseded. Not entirely, to be sure. I should like to be explicit on this point. Competition still plays a role. There are still important markets where the power of the firm as (say) a seller is checked or circumscribed by those who provide a similar or a substitute product or service. This, in the broadest sense that can be meaningful, is the meaning of competition. The role of the buyer on the other side of such markets is essentially a passive one. It consists in looking for, perhaps asking for, and responding to the best bargain. The active restraint is provided by the competitor who offers, or threatens to offer, a better bargain. However, this is not the only or even the typical restraint on the

---

[1] I have been tempted to coin a new word for this which would have the same convenience as the term competition and had I done so my choice would have been "countervailence." However, the phrase "countervailing power" is more descriptive and does not have the raw sound of any newly fabricated word.

exercise of economic power. In the typical modern market of few sellers, the active restraint is provided not by competitors but from the other side of the market by strong buyers. Given the convention against price competition, it is the role of the competitor that becomes passive in these markets.

It was always one of the basic presuppositions of competition that market power exercised in its absence would invite the competitors who would eliminate such exercise of power. The profits of a monopoly position inspired competitors to try for a share. In other words competition was regarded as a *self-generating* regulatory force. The doubt whether this was in fact so after a market had been pre-empted by a few large sellers, after entry of new firms had become difficult and after existing firms had accepted a convention against price competition, was what destroyed the faith in competition as a regulatory mechanism. Countervailing power is also a self-generating force and this is a matter of great importance. Something, although not very much, could be claimed for the regulatory role of the strong buyer in relation to the market power of sellers, did it happen that, as an accident of economic development, such strong buyers were frequently juxtaposed to strong sellers. However the tendency of power to be organized in response to a given position of power is the vital characteristic of the phenomenon I am here identifying. As noted, power on one side of a market creates both the need for, and the prospect of reward to, the exercise of countervailing power from the other side. This means that, as a common rule, we can rely on countervailing power to appear as a curb on economic power. There are also, it should be added, circumstances in which it does not appear or is effectively prevented from appearing. To these I shall return. . . .

In the market of small numbers or oligopoly, the practical barriers to entry and the convention against price competition have eliminated the self-generating capacity of competition. The self-generating tendency of countervailing power, by contrast, is readily assimilated to the common sense of the situation and its existence, once we have learned to look for it, is readily subject to empirical observation.

Market power can be exercised by strong buyers against weak sellers as well as by strong sellers against weak buyers. In the competitive model, competition acted as a restraint on both kinds of exercise of power. This is also the case with countervailing power. In turning to its practical manifestations, it will be convenient, in fact, to begin with a case where it is exercised by weak sellers against strong buyers.

III. The operation of countervailing power is to be seen with the greatest clarity in the labor market where it is also most fully developed. Because of his comparative immobility, the individual worker has long been highly vulnerable to private economic power. The customer of any particular steel mill, at the turn of the century, could always take himself elsewhere if he felt he was being over-charged. Or he could exercise his sovereign privilege of not buying steel at all. The worker had no comparable freedom if he felt he was being underpaid. Normally he could not move and he had to have work. Not often has the power of one man over another been used more callously than in the American labor market after the rise of the large corporation. As late as the early twenties, the steel industry worked a twelve-hour day and seventy-two-hour week with an incredible twenty-four-hour stint every fortnight when the shift changed.

No such power is exercised today and for the reason that its earlier exercise stimulated the counteraction that brought it to an end. In the ultimate sense it was the power of the steel industry, not the organizing abilities of John L. Lewis and Philip Murray, that brought the United Steel Workers into being. The economic power that the worker faced in the sale of his labor—the competition of many sellers dealing with few buyers—made it necessary that he organize for his own protection. There were rewards to the power of the steel companies in which, when he had successfully developed countervailing power, he could share.

As a general though not invariable rule one finds the strongest unions in the United States where markets are served by strong corporations. And it is not an accident that the large automobile, steel, electrical, rubber, farm-machinery and non-ferrous metal-mining and smelting companies all bargain with powerful unions. Not only has the strength of the corporations in these industries made it necessary for workers to develop the protection of countervailing power; it has provided unions with the opportunity for getting something more as well. If successful they could share in the fruits of the corporation's market power. By contrast there is not a single union of any consequence in American agriculture, the country's closest approach to the competitive model. The reason lies not in the difficulties in organization; these are considerable, but greater difficulties in organization have been overcome. The reason is that the farmer has not possessed any power over his labor force, and at least until recent times has not had any rewards from market power which it was worth the while of a union to seek. As an interesting verification of the point, in the Great Valley of California, the large farmers of that area have had considerable power vis-à-vis their labor force. Almost uniquely in the United States, that region has been marked by persistent attempts at organization by farm workers.

Elsewhere in industries which approach the competition of the model one typically finds weaker or less comprehensive unions. The textile industry, boot and shoe manufacture, lumbering and other forest industries in most parts of the country, and smaller wholesale and retail enterprises, are all cases in point. I do not, of course, advance the theory of countervailing power as a monolithic explanation of trade-union organization. No such complex social phenomenon is likely to have any single, simple explanation. American trade unions developed in the face of the implacable hostility, not alone of employers, but often of the community as well. In this environment organization of the skilled crafts was much easier than the average, which undoubtedly explains the earlier appearance of durable unions here. . . . Nevertheless, as an explanation of the incidence of trade-union strength in the American economy, the theory of countervailing power clearly fits the broad contours of experience. There is, I venture, no other so satisfactory explanation of the great dynamic of labor organization in the modern capitalist community and none which so sensibly integrates the union into the theory of that society.

IV. The labor market serves admirably to illustrate the incentives to the development of countervailing power and it is of great importance in this market. However, its development, in response to positions of market power, is pervasive in the economy. As a regulatory device one of its most important manifestations is in the relation of the large retailer to the firms from which it buys. The way in which countervailing power operates in these markets is worth examining in some detail.

One of the seemingly harmless simplifications of formal economic theory has been the assumption that producers of consumers' goods sell their products directly to consumers. All business units are held, for this reason, to have broadly parallel interests. Each buys labor and materials, combines them and passes them along to the public at prices that, over some period of time, maximize returns. It is recognized that this is, indeed, a simplification; courses in marketing in the universities deal with what is excluded by this assumption. Yet it has long been supposed that the assumption does no appreciable violence to reality.

Did the real world correspond to the assumed one, the lot of the consumer would be an unhappy one. In fact goods pass to consumers by way of retailers and other intermediaries and this is a circumstance of first importance. Retailers are required by their situation to develop countervailing power on the consumer's behalf. . . .

Retailing remains one of the industries to which entry is characteristically free. It takes small capital and no very rare talent to set up as a seller of goods. Through history there have always been an ample supply of men with both and with access to something to sell. The small man can provide convenience and intimacy of service and can give an attention to detail, all of which allow him to co-exist with larger competitors.

The advantage of the larger competitor ordinarily lies in its lower prices. It lives constantly under the threat of an erosion of its business by the more rapid growth of rivals and by the appearance of new firms. This loss of volume, in turn, destroys the chance for the lower costs and lower prices on which the firm depends. This means that the larger retailer is extraordinarily sensitive to higher prices by its suppliers. It means also that it is strongly rewarded if it can develop the market power which permits it to force lower prices.

The opportunity to exercise such power exists only when the suppliers are enjoying something that can be taken away; i.e., when they are enjoying the fruits of market power from which they can be separated. Thus, as in the labor market, we find the mass retailer, from a position across the market, with both a protective and a profit incentive to develop countervailing power when the firm with which it is doing business is in possession of market power. . . .

Countervailing power in the retail business is identified with the large and powerful retail enterprises. Its practical manifestation, over the last half-century, has been the rise of the food chains, the variety chains, the mail-order houses (now graduated into chain stores), the department-store chains, and the co-operative buying organizations of the surviving independent department and food stores.

This development was the countervailing response to previously established positions of power. The gains from invading these positions have been considerable and in some instances even spectacular. The rubber tire industry is a fairly commonplace example of oligopoly. Four large firms are dominant in the market. In the thirties, Sears, Roebuck & Co. was able, by exploiting its role as a large and indispensable customer, to procure tires from Goodyear Tire & Rubber Company at a price from twenty-nine to forty per cent lower than the going market. These it resold to thrifty motorists for from a fifth to a quarter less than the same tires carrying the regular Goodyear brand.

As a partial consequence of the failure of the government to recognize the role of countervailing power many hundreds of pages of court records have detailed the exercise of this power by the Great Atlantic & Pacific Tea Company. There is little doubt that this firm, at least in its uninhibited days, used the countervailing power it had developed with considerable artistry. In 1937, a survey by the company indicated that, for an investment of $175,000, it could supply itself with corn flakes. Assuming that it charged itself the price it was then paying to one of the three companies manufacturing this delicacy, it could earn a modest sixty-eight per cent on the outlay. Armed with this information, and the threat to go into the business which its power could readily make effective, it had no difficulty in bringing down the price by approximately ten per cent. Such gains from the exercise of countervailing power, it will be clear, could only occur where there is an exercise of original market power with which to contend. The A & P could have reaped no comparable gains in buying staple products from the farmer. Committed as he is to the competition of the competitive model, the farmer has no gains to surrender. Provided, as he is, with the opportunity of selling all he produces at the impersonally determined market price, he has not the slightest incentive to make a special price to A & P at least beyond that which might in some circumstances be associated with the simple economies of bulk sale.

The examples of the exercise of countervailing power by Sears, Roebuck and A & P just cited show how this power is deployed in its most dramatic form. The day-to-day exercise of the buyer's power is a good deal less spectacular but also a good deal more significant. At the end of virtually every channel by which consumers' goods reach the public there is, in practice, a layer of powerful buyers. In the food market there are the great food chains; in clothing there are the department stores, the chain department stores and the department store buying organizations; in appliances there are Sears, Roebuck and Montgomery Ward and the department stores; these latter firms are also important outlets for furniture and other house furnishings; the drug and cosmetic manufacturer has to seek part of his market through the large drug chains and the department stores; a vast miscellany of consumers' goods pass to the public through Woolworth's, Kresge's and other variety chains.

The buyers of all these firms deal directly with the manufacturer and there are few of the latter who, in setting prices, do not have to reckon with the attitude and reaction of their powerful customers. The retail buyers have a variety of weapons at their disposal to use against the market power of their suppliers. Their ultimate sanction is to develop their own source of supply as the food chains, Sears, Roebuck and Montgomery Ward have extensively done. They can also concentrate their entire patronage on a single supplier and, in return for a lower price, give him security in his volume and relieve him of selling and advertising costs. This policy has been widely followed and there have also been numerous complaints of the leverage it gives the retailer on his source of supply. . . .

There are producers of consumers' goods who have protected themselves from exercise of countervailing power. Some, like the automobile and the oil industry, have done so by integrating their distribution through to the consumer—a strategy which attests the importance of the use of countervailing power by retailers. Others have found it possible to maintain dominance over an organization of small and dependent and therefore fairly powerless dealers. It seems probable that in a few industries, tobacco manufacture for example, the members are ordinarily strong enough and have sufficient solidarity to withstand any pressure applied to them by the most powerful buyer. However, even the tobacco manufacturers, under conditions that were especially favorable to the exercise of countervailing power in the thirties, were forced to make liberal price concessions, in the form of advertising allowances, to the A & P and possibly also to other large customers. When the comprehensive representation of large retailers in the various fields of consumers' goods distribution is considered, it is reasonable to conclude—the reader is warned that this is an important generalization—that most positions of market power in the production of consumers' goods are covered by positions of countervailing power. . . .

Countervailing power also manifests itself, although less visibly, in producers' goods markets. For many years the power of the automobile companies, as purchasers of steel, has sharply curbed the power of the steel mills as sellers. Detroit is the only city where the historic basing-point system was not used to price steel. Under the basing-point system, all producers regardless of location quoted the same price at any particular point of delivery. This obviously minimized the opportunity of a strong buyer to play one seller off against the other. The large firms in the automobile industry had developed the countervailing power which enabled them to do precisely this. They were not disposed to tolerate any limitations on their exercise of such power. . . .

The more normal operation of countervailing power in producers' goods markets has, as its point of departure, the relatively small number of customers which firms in these industries typically have. Where the cigarette or soap manufacturer numbers his retail outlets by the hundreds of thousands and his final consumers by the millions, the machinery or equipment manufacturer counts his customers by the hundreds or thousands and, very often, his important ones by the dozen. But here, as elsewhere, the market pays a premium to those who develop power as buyers that is equivalent to the market power of those from whom they buy. The reverse is true where weak sellers do business with strong buyers. . . .

V. The development of countervailing power requires a certain minimum opportunity and capacity for organization, corporate or otherwise. If the large retail buying organizations had not developed the countervailing power which they have used, by proxy, on behalf of the individual consumer, consumers would have been faced with the need to organize the equivalent of the retailer's power. This would have been a formidable task but it has been accomplished in Scandinavia where the consumer's co-operative, instead of the chain store, is the dominant instrument of countervailing power in consumers' goods markets. There has been a similar though less comprehensive development in England and Scotland. In the Scandinavian countries the co-operatives have long been regarded explicitly as instruments for bringing power to bear on the cartels; i.e., for exercise of countervailing power. This is readily conceded by many who have greatest difficulty in seeing private mass buyers in the same role. But the fact that consumer co-operatives are not of any great importance in the United States is to be explained, not by any inherent incapacity of the American for such organization, but because the chain stores pre-empted the gains of countervailing power first. The counterpart of the Swedish Kooperative Forbundet or the British Co-operative Wholesale Societies has not appeared in the United States simply because it could not compete with the A & P and other large food chains. The meaning of this, which incidentally has been lost on devotees of the theology of co-operation, is that the chain stores are approximately as efficient in the exercise of countervailing power as a co-operative would be. In parts of the American economy where proprietary mass buyers have not made their appearance, notably in the purchase of farm supplies, individuals (who are also individualists) have shown as much capacity to organize as the Scandinavians and the British and have similarly obtained the protection and rewards of countervailing power. The Grange League Federation, the Eastern States Farmers' Exchange and the Illinois Farm Supply Company, co-operatives with annual sales running to multi-million-dollar figures, are among the illustrations of the point.

However, it must not be assumed that it is easy for great numbers of individuals to coalesce and organize countervailing power. In less developed communities, Puerto Rico for example, one finds people fully exposed to the exactions of strategically situated importers, merchants and wholesalers and without the apparent capacity to develop countervailing power in their own behalf. Anyone, incidentally, who doubts the force of the countervailing power exercised by large retailer-buying organizations would do well to consider the revolution which the entry of the large chain stores would work in an economy like that of Puerto Rico and also how such an intrusion would be resented and perhaps resisted by importers and merchants now able to exercise their market power with impunity against the thousands of small, independent and inefficient retailers who are their present outlets.

In the light of the difficulty in organizing countervailing power, it is not surprising that the assistance of government has repeatedly been sought in this task. Without the phenomenon itself being fully recognized, the provision of state assistance to the development of countervailing power has become a major function of government—perhaps *the* major domestic function of government. Much of the domestic legislation of the last twenty years, that of the New Deal episode in particular, only becomes fully comprehensible when it is viewed in this light. . . .

VI. I come now to the major limitation on the operation of countervailing power—a matter of much importance in our time. Countervailing power is not exercised uniformly under all conditions of demand. It does not function at all as a restraint on market power when there is inflation or inflationary pressure on markets. . . .

Countervailing power, as fully noted in the earlier parts of this chapter, is organized either by buyers or by sellers in response to a stronger position across the market. But strength, i.e., relative strength, obviously depends on the state of aggregate demand. When demand is strong, especially when it is at inflationary levels, the bargaining position of poorly organized or even of unorganized workers is favorable. When demand is weak the bargaining position of the strongest union deteriorates to some extent. The situation is similar where countervailing power is exercised by a buyer. A scarcity of demand is a prerequisite to his bringing power to bear on suppliers. If buyers are plentiful—if supply is small in relation to current demand—sellers are under no compulsion to surrender to the bargaining power of any particular customer. They have alternatives.[2]

Broadly speaking, positions of countervailing power have been developed in a context of limited—or, more accurately, of not unlimited demand. This is partly because such periods have had a much higher incidence in history than the episodes of unlimited or inflationary demand. It is partly because periods of drastically restricted demand, by providing exceptional opportunity for aggression by the strong against the weak, have also provided an exceptional incentive to building countervailing power. Much of the structure of organization on which countervailing power depends traces its origins to such periods.

The depression years of the thirties, needless to say, were a particularly fruitful period in this respect. Accordingly, and in sharp contrast with most other types of business, these years were very favorable to the development of the chain stores and also of various group buying enterprises. . . . By contrast, during the years of strong demand and short supply of World War II, the chain stores lost ground, relatively, to independents. As this strong demand in relation to supply destroyed their capacity to exercise countervailing power, their advantage disappeared. . . .

The depression years also provided a notable inducement to the trade union movement. With prosperity in the forties and fifties labor organization too lost its momentum. Finally, to the depression years we owe nearly all of the modern arrangements for exercise of countervailing power by and on behalf of the farmers.

Given this structural accommodation by the economy to limited demand, the appearance of unlimited demand is somewhat devastating. There is everywhere a shift of bargaining power to sellers. The balance of force appropriate to limited demand is everywhere upset. The market power of strong sellers, until now offset by that of strong buyers, is enhanced. The countervailing power of weak sellers is suddenly and adventitiously reinforced.

These effects can again be seen with greatest clarity in the labor market. Here they also have their most portentous consequences. In industries where strong firms bargain with strong unions, the management of the former has what has come to be considered a normal resistance to wage increases when demand is not pressing upon capacity. To yield is to increase unit costs. The firm cannot with impunity pass along these higher costs to its customers. There may be a question as to whether other firms in the industry will follow suit; there will always be a question of the effect of the higher prices on sales. If the demand for the products is in any measure elastic the consequence of the higher prices will be a loss of volume. This, with its effect on employment in the industry, is something of which modern union leadership, as well as management, is usually conscious. Thus the trial of strength between union and management associated with collective bargaining is, essentially although not exclu-

---

[2] The everyday business distinction between a "buyers" and a "sellers" market and the frequency of its use reflect the importance which participants in actual markets attach to the ebb and flow of countervailing power. That this distinction has no standing in formal economics follows from the fact that countervailing power has not been recognized by economists. . . .

sively, over the division of profits. When demand is limited, we have, in other words, an essentially healthy manifestation of countervailing power. . . .

Under conditions of strong demand, however, collective bargaining takes on a radically different form. Then management is no longer constrained to resist union demands on the grounds that higher prices will be reflected in shrinking volume. There is now an adequate supply of eager buyers. The firm that first surrenders to the union need not worry lest it be either the first or the only one to increase prices. There are buyers for all. No one has occasion, as the result of price increases, to worry about a general shrinkage in volume. A strong demand means an inelastic demand. On the other hand, there are grave disadvantages for management in resisting the union. Since profits are not at stake, any time lost as the result of a strike is a dead loss. Worker morale and the actual loss of part of the working force to employers who offer better wages must be reckoned with. Thus when demand is sufficiently strong to press upon the capacity of industry generally to supply it, there is no real conflict of interest between union and employer. Or to put it differently, all bargaining strength shifts to the side of the union. The latter becomes simply an engine for increasing prices, for it is to the mutual advantage of union and employer to effect a coalition and to pass the costs of their agreement on in higher prices. Other buyers along the line, who under other circumstances might have exercised their countervailing power against the price increases, are similarly inhibited. Thus under inflationary pressure of demand, the whole structure of countervailing power in the economy is dissolved. . . .

V
CENTRALIZATION OF POWER

POWER CENTRALIZATION AS A SOCIAL PROCESS

Marvin E. Olsen

To resolve the theoretical debate among proponents of Marxian, elitist, and pluralistic explanations of power exertion, sociologists must eventually conduct extensive empirical studies of the use and distribution of social power in numerous societies. Very little research of this nature has yet been attempted, however, and much of what has been done has been severely criticized on both methodological and theoretical grounds.[1] Furthermore, it has been limited almost exclusively to the United States. The reading selections comprising this section are typical of the current literature in this area, but they cannot be considered definitive studies of power distribution in the contemporary United States. Much research obviously remains to be done, both in this society and elsewhere.

If such studies are to be theoretically relevant, however, they must be cast within a meaningful analytical framework. Part of this task involves clarifying the nature of social power and its relationship to the broader phenomenon of social organization, but equally necessary is elaboration of the process of power centralization. A crucial point of contention between pluralistic theory and both the Marxian and elitist theories is the degree of power centralization in modern societies. Before this question can be empirically resolved, however, sociologists must achieve some common agreement on the meaning of power centralization as a social process. This essay, therefore, is an attempt to specify the nature of power centralization within societies.

If the exercise of social power were evenly distributed throughout all parts of a society, then no particular segment could exert controlling force, dominance, or authority for any period of time. In any particular situation one actor might wield more power than others, but this person or organization would not maintain power

---

[1] In addition to C. Wright Mills' *The Power Elite* (New York: Oxford University Press, 1956), two other recent and highly criticized studies of this nature have been Floyd Hunter's *Top Leadership, USA* (Chapel Hill, N.C.: University of North Carolina Press, 1959), and G. William Domhoff, *Who Rules America?* (Englewood Cliffs, N.J.: Prentice-Hall, 1967).

superiority on other occasions. In contrast, *with centralization of power more and more collective activities are influenced or controlled by a small set of actors—* whom we shall for convenience call elites. With total centralization—as described by the totalitarian model of society to be described in a later section—all power in a society would be exercised by one set of elites who could fully control all social actions and organizations in the society. But there can also be many degrees of power centralization that fall short of total control.

As elites expand the scope of their influence and consolidate their control, they frequently seek to imbed their power in established patterns of social organization. As long as their ability to exercise power depends on their own personal skills and knowledge or on their stockpile of resources for exerting coercive force, their power will remain unstable and capricious. But if they can transfer the basis of their power exertion from transitory actions to established social positions, their influence and control will become stable and relatively permanent. Three common means of accomplishing this transition are (a) creating organized channels for transmitting compensatory and persuasive (as opposed to coercive) force, (b) acquiring functional dominance over vital social processes such as economic markets, and (c) gaining legitimate authority with which others voluntarily comply. To the extent that these efforts are successful, *centralization involves consolidation of power wielding within a relatively small number of stable organizational positions.* Different individuals may now move in and out of these elite positions without markedly altering the extensive influence and control exercised by whomever occupies the positions at any given time.

Those positions that exert power throughout large portions of a society are, moreover, commonly clustered together in one or a few interrelated organizational networks—such as the political system. In the twentieth century we are so accustomed to thinking of the national government as the focus of centralized power in society that it may require more than a moment's reflection to realize that this need not always be so. In a theocracy, for instance, the dominant church might be the focus of power centralization, whereas in a society undergoing rapid industrialization the owners and managers of basic industries might constitute the predominant power elites. And it is conceivable that in the future, power centralization within "post-industrial" societies might increasingly be focused in some other kind of organization—such as universities.[2] In any case, however, the process of power centralization normally occurs within established patterns of social organization.

How concentrated must power become in a society before we can speak of societal-wide power centralization? In one sense this is a meaningless question, since if we envision power centralization as an ongoing social process that can vary widely in extent from one situation to another, then we should ask "to what degree is the exercise of power centralized in this society at this time?" In a less formal sense, though, the question is often raised and debated by those seeking to compare one society with another or to examine historical trends. For instance, some writers are

---

[2] Daniel Bell, "Notes on the Post-Industrial Society," *The Public Interest*, No. 6, Winter 1967, pp. 24-35, and No. 7, Spring 1967, pp. 102-118.

willing to speak of relative power decentralization if there are several sets of separate and competing elites, even though most other individuals still exercise little or no influence.[3] In contrast, other writers would describe this situation as one of relative power centralization, and reserve the label of decentralization for conditions that more nearly approximated equality of power wielding among all actors.[4] The common result of these terminological differences is much unnecessary and confusing haggling over words.

As à means of clarifying communication, we might think of a continuum ranging from complete power equality among all actors at one end to complete power centralization in one position at the opposite end. For precise scientific analysis, we should obviously quantify this continuum (say from 0.0 to 1.0) and then place any given society at a specific point on the continuum on the basis of objective measurement. Since we cannot even approximate this procedure now, however, a feasible compromise might be to describe verbally several positions along the continuum, and then attempt to classify societies into the resulting categories. Thus we might describe a particular society as (a) highly decentralized (no identifiable foci of power), (b) moderately decentralized (scattered minor foci of power), (c) balanced (numerous significant foci of power, but all actors exercising some power), (d) moderately centralized (several major but competing foci of power), or (e) highly centralized (one or a very few dominant foci of power). This scheme is admittedly quite crude, but it does at least encourage us to think of power centralization as a variable phenomenon, while discouraging uncompromising arguments over whether a society is either "centralized" or "decentralized."

The two schematic figures most commonly used to represent moderate or high degrees of power centralization are a triangle and a circle. With a triangle, power is assumed to be centralized at the apex and to be exercised downward through successive organizational levels. With a circle, power wielding is assumed to be focused at the center and to radiate outward in all directions toward the periphery. Although both figures illustrate power centralization, they convey very different connotations of how power is exercised by elites. A triangle suggests that actors occupying positions at the apex of the structure use power to control social activities throughout the society in a rather direct or authoritarian manner. This scheme also allows only one set of "top elites" for the entire society, and hence conveys an impression of extreme power centralization. A circle, in contrast, implies that incumbents of positions located near the center of the structure perform necessary coordinating and regulating functions for the society in a more indirect or nonarbitrary manner. And if we divide the circle into several wedge-shaped sections, each representing a different sector of society, we can then portray the center as a small circle of interrelated elite positions located in the various sectors, rather than as a single position. For these reasons, the circle analogy offers more conceptual flexibility than does a triangle, and is perhaps more applicable to all but totally centralized (or totalitarian) societies.

As a dynamic process, *centralization of power can occur either through redistribu-*

---

[3] Robert A. Dahl, *Who Governs?* (New Haven, Conn.: Yale University Press, 1961).
[4] Robert Presthus, *Men at the Top* (New York: Oxford University Press, 1964).

tion of existing patterns of influence and control or through creation of new resources for power exertion—or in both ways simultaneously. If the total amount of power being exerted in a society remains relatively constant over a period of time, then consolidation of power in the hands of a few elites will mean loss of power by other actors. This would be the case, for example, if all local governments in a society were abolished and their activities taken over by the national government. If the total amount of power being exercised in the society were to increase through time, however then considerable centralization could occur without depriving nonelites of whatever power they currently wielded. To continue the above example, if the national government were to gain access to large quantities of new resources through state-directed industrialization or military conquest, its ability to wield power throughout the society would increase even if it left local governments intact. Both processes do occur, often in combination, but the latter phenomenon of growth has undoubtedly predominated as loosely unified agricultural societies have developed into modern industrialized nations. To the extent that over-all growth has prevailed over redistribution of power, severe internal conflicts have probably been minimized, since nonelites have not become powerless in an absolute sense even if they may have become proportionately less powerful in comparison with elites.

The historical process of power centralization within modern societies can be explained in both empirical and theoretical terms. The empirical explanation points to a variety of other social, political, and economic trends that together seem almost inevitably to produce some degree of power centralization. These developments include political unification of previously autonomous or semiautonomous local political entities, intensive industrialization with its concurrent emergence of gigantic business organizations and extensive economic markets, creation of modern mass communication and transportation systems, growth of large cities and the resulting urbanization of an entire society, and wide-spread formation of huge bureaucratic organizations in government and many other areas from religion to education. Without going into elaborate details here, we can easily see that all of these factors tend to push a society in the direction of ever-increasing power centralization—though to some extent these trends may in turn be further stimulated by the exercise of centralized power.

The theoretical explanation of power centralization within societies is derived from the theory of functional integration. Very briefly, this theory states that if a society is to remain unified in the face of growing role diversification and specialization (or division of labor), it must create elaborate mechanisms for coordinating, regulating, and controlling social activities.[5] The more highly specialized the various parts of a society, the more interdependent they tend to become on one another through extensive exchange relationships. But such a complex

---

[5]The theory of functional integration is based on Emile Durkheim's idea of "organic solidarity," as presented in *The Division of Labor in Society*, translated by George Simpson (New York: The Free Press, 1933). For a more extensive discussion of contemporary functional integration theory, see Marvin E. Olsen, *The Process of Social Organization* (New York: Holt, Rinehart, and Winston, 1968), Chap. 11.

network of interdependent exchange relationships can operate effectively only if it is coordinated and directed by some kind of over-all centralized authority. This central agency performs such activities as facilitating communication among all the involved parts, establishing and enforcing uniform operating rules and procedures, handling serious conflicts and disruptions, and ensuring that no one part gains enough power to exploit the entire system for its own benefit. As a result of these activities, power commonly tends to become increasingly centralized in this coordinating agency—which in modern nations is usually the national government.

Notice, however, that the theory does not say that power must inevitably be centralized in a single set of elites, but only that over-all coordination is necessary to maintain societal integration. At least two other alternatives are also possible: (a) the society could disintegrate into a number of relatively autonomous smaller units, or (b) each type of activity in the society might be coordinated by a separate agency that dealt only with a limited sphere of events, thus permitting numerous foci of power. Nor must we assume that performance of centralized regulation and coordination functions necessarily leads to consolidation of decision making and control. It may be possible to separate decentralized decision making from centralized coordination, as will be suggested in the systemic societal model described in the final section of this book.

If a process of power centralization is occurring to at least some extent within a society, does this necessarily mean that decentralized organization—and presumably political democracy—will automatically decline? Many contemporary social critics have assumed so, and have loudly bemoaned the numerous trends toward increased centralization that they have observed in their societies. But perhaps their assumption is at least partially false, on both counts.

First, the assumption that power centralization always negates any possibility of decentralized social organization rests on a confusion between organizational fragmentation and decentralization. If social activities are fragmented they are broken into many small, unrelated clusters. In contrast, decentralized activities are organized into a coherent whole whose parts each possess considerable functional autonomy. As social activities become ordered into stable patterns of social organization, social actors and actions that were once fragmented into numerous smaller clusters tend to come together to form a single, unified organizational entity. One common result of this process of social organization is the creation of new power resources and increased exercise of power throughout the organization by central elites, as derived from their positions of functional dominance and their legitimate authority. In short, the process of social organization often creates centralized social power in the place of fragmented, powerless social anarchy.

Organizational decentralization, and corresponding decentralized power, can only be achieved, however, after some minimal unified organization and centralized power have previously been created. Put differently, partially autonomous organizational parts cannot exert decentralized power in the organization until that organization has been created and its parts have become interrelated. In some cases, these parts may acquire their resources and power from central elites, so that power decentralization would involve redistribution of the total power being exerted in the organization, thus reversing the previous centralization process. Under conditions of continual organizational growth, however, this reversal need not occur, and central elites can keep on increasing their ability to exert power at the same time that decentralized power is expanding throughout the component parts. We then encounter the seeming paradox of simultaneous power centralization and decentralization—as a result of extensive growth in social organization and power resources.

The second assumption of the social critics—that power centralization necessarily weakens or destroys political democracy—can also be challenged, regardless of whether or not there are accompanying processes of decentralization. The crucial factor here is our conception of political democracy. If by "democracy" we mean only the classical idea of all members of a society coming together and reaching common decisions through debate and voting, then power centralization does indeed quickly prohibit democratic politics. Centralized power is an outgrowth of extensive, complex, unified social organization, which is not conducive to "mass-popular" democracy. The elitist theorists have fully convinced us of that. But there is an alternative meaning of political democracy, as expressed by numerous political philosophers: effective participation by all citizens of a society in political decision-making processes. The key phrase here is "effective participation," which implies that the people exert influence on political elites and political decisions, even though they may not formally make the final decisions. This notion of democracy, which underlies the pluralistic model of society, is fully compatible with at least moderate amounts of power centralization in complex societies—though it would still be negated by complete totalitarian centralization.

To achieve this kind of meaningful political democracy in a partially centralized society, however, several other conditions must also be met: (a) there must be established means through which individuals can exert influence on political elites, (b) incumbents of central elite positions must be chosen through open competition on the basis of merit, (c) full opportunities to acquire requisite paticipatory and leadership skills (e.g., education) must be available to all, (d) basic sustenance needs of the people must be adequately met, leaving them some free time, energy, and resources for political activities, (e) there must be an elaborate communication system to provide all people with necessary information, and (f) rights of individuals and minorities must be strenuously protected through a strong legal system. Viable political democracy is thus not an easy goal to achieve or maintain in any society, no matter what the distribution of power. But democracy is possible in contemporary, complex, moderately centralized nations—if the above social conditions can be created.

Concern with the centralization of power in society is not unique to the present era, as seen in the first reading selection from Alexis de Tocqueville; in the 1830's he clearly foresaw the possibility that ever increasing power centralization might well accompany the spread of social and economic equality in a society such as the United States. The rest of the articles in this section all center around the contention by C. Wright Mills that the United States is currently experiencing extensive power centralization and a concurrent loss of political democracy, resulting in a dominant "power elite." Two different selections from Mills' writings present this argument. Both Daniel Bell and Talcott Parsons then criticize Mills' thesis, but from different perspectives. Bell cites numerous historical trends and current developments that tend to contradict Mills, whereas Parsons attacks the logic and theory of Mills' argument. David Riesman briefly sketches his own conception of the contemporary U.S. power structure, which at first appears to differ sharply from that of Mills. In the final paper, however, William Kornhauser skillfully demonstrates that there are more similarities than differences between Mills' and Riesman's ideas, and suggests that both of them hold rather limited conceptions of social power and power centralization.

INFLUENCE OF DEMOCRATIC OPINIONS AND SENTIMENTS ON POLITICAL SOCIETY

Alexis de Tocqueville

That Equality Naturally Gives Men a Taste for Free Institutions. The principle of equality, which makes men independent of each other, gives them a habit and a taste for following, in their private actions, no other guide but their own will. This complete independence, which they constantly enjoy towards their equals and in the intercourse of private life, tends to make them look upon all authority with a jealous eye, and speedily suggests to them the notion and the love of political freedom. Men living at such times have a natural bias to free institutions. . . .

Of all the political effects produced by the equality of conditions, this love of independence is the first to strike the observing, and to alarm the timid; nor can it be said that their alarm is wholly misplaced, for anarchy has a more formidable aspect in democratic countries than elsewhere. As the citizens have no direct influence on each other, as soon as the supreme power of the nation fails, which kept them all in their several stations, it would seem that disorder must instantly reach its utmost pitch, and that, every man drawing aside in a different direction, the fabric of society must at once crumble away.

I am however persuaded that anarchy is not the principal evil which democratic ages have to fear, but the least. For the principle of equality begets two tendencies; the one leads men straight to independence, and may suddenly drive them into anarchy; the other conducts them by a longer, more secret, but more certain road, to servitude. Nations readily discern the former tendency, and are prepared to resist it; they are led away by the latter, without perceiving its drift; hence it is peculiarly important to point it out. . . .

That the Notions of Democratic Nations on Government Are Naturally Favourable to the Concentration of Power. The notion of secondary powers, placed between

SOURCE: Alexis de Tocqueville, *Democracy in America* trans. by Henry Reeve (New York: Schocken Books, 1961), Vol. II, Book 4, pp. 343-355, 378-386.

the sovereign and his subjects, occurred naturally to the imagination of aristocratic nations, because those communities contained individuals or families raised above the common level, and apparently destined to command by their birth, their education, and their wealth. This same notion is naturally wanting in the minds of men in democratic ages, for converse reasons; it can only be introduced artificially, it can only be kept there with difficulty; whereas they conceive, as it were without thinking upon the subject, the notion of a sole and central power which governs the whole community by its direct influence. Moreover in politics, as well as in philosophy and in religion, the intellect of democratic nations is peculiarly open to simple and general notions. Complicated systems are repugnant to it, and its favourite conception is that of a great nation composed of citizens all resembling the same pattern, and all governed by a single power.

The very next notion to that of a sole and central power, which presents itself to the minds of men in the ages of equality, is the notion of uniformity of legislation. As every man sees that he differs but little from those about him, he cannot understand why a rule which is applicable to one man should not be equally applicable to all others. Hence the slightest privileges are repugnant to his reason; the faintest dissimilarities in the political institutions of the same people offend him, and uniformity of legislation appears to him to be the first condition of good government.

I find, on the contrary, that this same notion of a uniform rule, equally binding on all the members of the community, was almost unknown to the human mind in aristocratic ages; it was either never entertained, or it was rejected. . . .

As the conditions of men become equal amongst a people, individuals seem of less importance, and society of greater dimensions; or rather, every citizen, being assimilated to all the rest, is lost in the crowd, and nothing stands conspicuous but the great and imposing image of the people at large. This naturally gives the men of democratic periods a lofty opinion of the privileges of society, and a very humble notion of the rights of individuals; they are ready to admit that the interests of the former are everything, and those of the latter nothing. They are willing to acknowledge that the power which represents the community has far more information and wisdom than any of the members of that community; and that it is the duty, as well as the right, of that power to guide as well as govern each private citizen. . . .

The Americans hold that in every state the supreme power ought to emanate from the people; but when once that power is constituted, they can conceive, as it were, no limits to it, and they are ready to admit that it has the right to do whatever it pleases. They have not the slightest notion of peculiar privileges granted to cities, families, or persons: their minds appear never to have foreseen that it might be possible not to apply with strict uniformity the same laws to every part, and to all the inhabitants.

These same opinions are more and more diffused in Europe; they even insinuate themselves amongst those nations which most vehemently reject the principle of the sovereignty of the people. Such nations assign a different origin to the supreme power, but they ascribe to that power the same characteristics. Amongst them all, the idea of intermediate powers is weakened and obliterated: The idea of rights inherent in certain individuals is rapidly disappearing from the minds of men; the idea of the omnipotence and sole authority of society at large rises to fill its place. These ideas take root and spread in proportion as social conditions become more equal, and men more alike; they are engendered by equality, and in turn they hasten the progress of equality. . . .

That the Sentiments of Democratic Nations Accord With Their Opinions in Leading Them to Concentrate Political Power. If it be true that, in ages of equality, men readily adopt the notion of a great central power, it cannot be doubted on the other hand that their habits and sentiments predispose them to recognize such a power and to give it their support. . . .

As the men who inhabit democratic countries have no superiors, no inferiors, and no habitual or necessary partners in their undertakings, they readily fall back upon themselves and consider themselves as beings apart. . . . Hence such men can never, without an effort, tear themselves from their private affairs to engage in public business; their natural bias leads them to abandon the latter to the sole visible and permanent representative of the interests of the community, that is to say, to the State. Not only are they naturally wanting in a taste for public business, but the have frequently no time to attend to it. Private life is so busy in democratic periods, so excited, so full of wishes and of work, that hardly any energy or leisure remains to each individual for public life. . . .

The love of public tranquillity is frequently the only passion which these nations retain, and it becomes more active and powerful amongst them in proportion as all other passions droop and die. This naturally disposes the members of the community constantly to give or to surrender additional rights to the central power, which alone seems to be interested in defending them by the same means that it uses to defend itself.

As in ages of equality no man is compelled to lend his assistance to his fellow-men, and none has any right to expect much support from them, every one is at once independent and powerless. These two conditions, which must never be either separately considered or confounded together, inspire the citizen of a democratic country with very contrary propensities. His independence fills him with self-reliance and pride amongst his equals; his debility makes him feel from time to time the want of some outward assistance, which he cannot expect from any of them, because they are all impotent and unsympathizing. In this predicament he naturally turns his eyes to that imposing power which alone rises above the level of universal depression. . . .

The hatred which men bear to privilege increases in proportion as privileges become more scarce and less considerable, so that democratic passions would seem to burn most fiercely at the very time when they have least fuel. . . . When all conditions are unequal, no inequality is so great as to offend the eye; whereas the slightest dissimilarity is odious in the midst of general uniformity: the more complete is this uniformity, the more insupportable does the sight of such a difference become. Hence it is natural that the love of equality should constantly increase together with equality itself, and that it should grow by what it feeds upon.

This never-dying ever-kindling hatred, which sets a democratic people against the smallest privileges, is peculiarly favourable to the gradual concentration of all political rights in the hands of the representative of the State alone. The sovereign, being necessarily and incontestably above all the citizens, excites not their envy, and each of them thinks that he strips his equals of the prerogative which he concedes to the crown.

The man of a democratic age is extremely reluctant to obey his neighbour who is his equal; he refuses to acknowledge in such a person ability superior to his own; he mistrusts his justice, and is jealous of his power; he fears and he condemns him; and he loves continually to remind him of the common dependence in which both of them stand to the same master.

Every central power which follows its natural tendencies courts and encourages the principle of equality; for equality singularly facilitates, extends, and secures the influence of a central power.

In like manner it may be said that every central government worships uniformity: uniformity relieves it from inquiry into an infinite number of small details which must be attended to if rules were to be adapted to men, instead of indiscriminately subjecting men to rules: thus the government likes what the citizens like, and naturally hates what they hate. These common sentiments, which, in democratic nations, constantly unite the sovereign and every member of the community in one and the same conviction, establish a secret and lasting sympathy between them. The faults of the government are pardoned for the sake of its tastes; public confidence is only reluctantly withdrawn in the midst even of its excesses and its errors, and it is restored at the first call. Democratic nations often hate those in whose hands the central power is vested; but they always love that power itself.

Thus, by two separate paths, I have reached the same conclusion. I have shown that the principle of equality suggests to men the notion of a sole, uniform, and strong government: I have now shown that the principle of equality imparts to them a taste for it. To governments of this kind the nations of our age are therefore tending. They are drawn thither by the natural inclination of mind and heart; and in order to reach that result, it is enough that they do not check themselves in their course.

I am of opinion, that, in the democratic ages which are opening upon us, individual independence and local liberties will ever be the produce of artificial contrivance; that centralization will be the natural form of government. . . .

What Sort of Despotism Democratic Nations Have to Fear. No sovereign ever lived in former ages so absolute or so powerful as to undertake to administer by his own agency, and without the assistance of intermediate powers, all the parts of a great empire: none ever attempted to subject all his subjects indiscriminately to strict uniformity of regulation, and personally to tutor and direct every member of the community. The notion of such an undertaking never occurred to the human mind; and if any man had conceived it, the want of information, the imperfection of the administrative system, and above all, the natural obstacles caused by the inequality of conditions, would speedily have checked the execution of so vast a design. . . .

But it would seem that if despotism were to be extablished amongst the democratic nations of our days, it might assume a different character; it would be more extensive and more mild; it would degrade men without tormenting them. I do not question that in an age of instruction and equality like our own, sovereigns might more easily succeed in collecting all political power into their own hands, and might interfere more habitually and decidedly within the circle of private interests, than any sovereign of antiquity could ever do. But this same principle of equality which facilitates despotism, tempers its rigour. We have seen how the manners of society become more humane and gentle in proportion as men become more equal and alike. When no member of the community has much power or much wealth, tyranny is, as it were, without opportunities and a field of action. As all fortunes are scanty, the passions of men are naturally circumscribed—their imagination limited, their pleasures simple. This universal moderation moderates the sovereign himself, and checks within certain limits the inordinate stretch of his desires. . . .

I think then that the species of oppression by which democratic nations are menaced is unlike anything which ever before existed in the world: our contemporaries will find no prototype of it in their memories. I am trying myself to choose an expression which will accurately convey the whole of the idea I have formed of it, but in vain; the old words despotism and tyranny are inappropriate: the thing itself is new; and since I cannot name it, I must attempt to define it.

I seek to trace the novel features under which despotism may appear in the world. The first thing that strikes the observation is an innumerable multitude of men all equal and alike, incessantly endeavouring to procure the petty and paltry pleasures with which they glut their lives. Each of them, living apart, is as a stranger to the fate of all the rest—his children and his private friends constitute to him the whole of mankind; as for the rest of his fellow-citizens, he is close to them, but he sees them not; he touches them, but he feels them not; he exists but in himself and for himself alone; and if his kindred still remain to him, he may be said at any rate to have lost his country.

Above this race of men stands an immense and tutelary power, which takes upon itself alone to secure their gratifications, and to watch over their fate. That power is absolute, minute, regular, provident, and mild. It would be like the authority of a parent, if, like that authority, its object was to prepare men for manhood; but it seeks on the contrary to keep them in perpetual childhood: it is well content that the people should rejoice, provided they think of nothing but rejoicing. For their happiness such a government willingly labours, but it chooses to be the sole agent and the only arbiter of that happiness: it provides for their security, foresees and supplies their necessitites, facilitates their pleasures, manages their principal concerns, directs their industry, regulates the descent of property, and subdivides their inheritances—what remains, but to spare them all the care of thinking and all the trouble of living?

Thus it every day renders the exercise of the free agency of man less useful and less frequent; it circumscribes the will within a narrower range, and gradually robs a man of all the uses of himself. The principle of equality has prepared men for these things: it has predisposed men to endure them, and oftentimes to look on them as benefits.

After having thus successively taken each member of the community in its powerful grasp, and fashioned them at will, the supreme power then extends its arm over the whole community. It covers the surface of society with a network of small complicated rules, minute and uniform, through which the most original minds and the most energetic characters cannot penetrate, to rise above the crowd. The will of man is not shattered, but softened, bent, and guided: men are seldom forced by it to act, but they are constantly restrained from acting: such a power does not destroy, but it prevents existence; it does not tyrannize, but it compresses, enervates, extinguishes, and stupefies a people, till each nation is reduced to be nothing better than a flock of timid and industrious animals, of which the government is the shepherd.

I have always thought that servitude of the regular, quiet, and gentle kind which I have just described, might be combined more easily than is commonly believed with some of the outward forms of freedom; and that it might even establish itself under the wing of the sovereignty of the people.

Our contemporaries are constantly excited by two conflicting passions; they want to be led, and they wish to remain free: as they cannot destroy either one or the other of these contrary propensities, they strive to satisfy them both at once. They devise a sole, tutelary, and all-powerful form of government, but elected by the people. They combine the principle of centralization and that of popular sovereignty; this gives them a respite: they console themselves for being in tutelage by the reflection that they have chosen their own guardians. Every man allows himself to be put in leading-strings, because he sees that it is not a person or a class of persons, but the people at large that holds the end of his chain.

By this system the people shake off their state of dependence just long enough to select their master, and then relapse into it again. A great many persons at the present day are quite contented with this sort of compromise between administrative despotism and the sovereignty of the people; and they think they have done enough for the protection of individual freedom when they have surrendered it to the power of the nation at large. This does not satisfy me: the nature of him I am to obey signifies less to me than the fact of extorted obedience.

I do not however deny that a constitution of this kind appears to me to be infinitely preferable to one, which, after having concentrated all the powers of government, should vest them in the hands of an irresponsible person or body of persons. Of all the forms which democratic despotism could assume, the latter would assuredly be the worst.

When the sovereign is elective, or narrowly watched by a legislature which is really elective and independent, the oppression which he exercises over individuals is sometimes greater, but it is always less degrading; because every man, when he is oppressed and disarmed, may still imagine, that whilst he yields obedience it is to himself he yields it, and that it is to one of his own inclinations that all the rest give way. In like manner I can understand that when the sovereign represents the nation, and is dependent upon the people, the rights and the power of which every citizen is deprived, not only serve the head of the state, but the state itself; and that private persons derive some return from the sacrifice of their independence which they have made to the public. To create a representation of the people in every centralized country is, therefore, to diminish the evil which extreme centralization may produce, but not to get rid of it.

I admit that by this means room is left for the intervention of individuals in the more important affairs; but it is not the less suppressed in the smaller and more private ones. It must not be forgotten that it is especially dangerous to enslave men in the minor details of life. For my own part, I should be inclined to think freedom less necessary in great things than in little ones, if it were possible to be secure of the one without possessing the other.

Subjection in minor affairs breaks out every day, and is felt by the whole community indiscriminately. It does not drive men to resistance, but it crosses them at every turn, till they are led to surrender the exercise of their will. Thus their spirit is gradually broken and their character enervated; whereas that obedience, which is exacted on a few important but rare occasions, only exhibits servitude at certain intervals, and throws the burden of it upon a small number of men. It is in vain to summon a people, which has been rendered so dependent on the central power, to choose from time to time the representatives of that power; this rare and brief exercise of their free choice, however important it may be, will not prevent them from gradually losing the faculties of thinking, feeling, and acting for themselves, and thus gradually falling below the level of humanity.

I add that they will soon become incapable of exercising the great and only privilege which remains to them. The democratic nations which have introduced freedom into their political constitution, at the very time when they were augmenting the despotism of their administrative constitution, have been led into strange paradoxes. To manage those minor affairs in which good sense is all that is wanted—the people are held to be unequal to the task; but when the government of the country is at stake, the people are invested with immense powers; they are alternately made the playthings of their ruler, and his masters—more than kings, and less than men. After having exhausted all the different modes of election, without finding one to suit their purpose, they are still amazed, and still bent on seeking further; as if the evil they remark did not originate in the constitution of the country far more than in that of the electoral body.

It is, indeed, difficult to conceive how men who have entirely given up the habit of self-government should succeed in making a proper choice of those by whom they are to be governed; and no one will ever believe that a liberal wise, and energetic government can spring from the suffrages of a subservient people. . . .

I believe that it is easier to establish an absolute and despotic government amongst a people in which the conditions of society are equal, than amongst any other; and I think that if such a government were once established amongst such a people, it would not only oppress men, but would eventually strip each of them of several of the highest qualities of humanity. Despotism therefore appears to me peculiarly to be dreaded in democratic ages. . . .

It results from the very constitution of democratic nations and from their necessities, that the power of government amongst them must be more uniform, more centralized, more extensive, more searching, and more efficient than in other countries. Society at large is naturally stronger and more active, individuals more subordinate and weak; the former does more, the latter less; and this is inevitably the case.

It is not therefore to be expected that the range of private independence will ever be as extensive in democratic as in aristocratic countries;—nor is this to be desired; for, amongst aristocratic nations, the mass is often sacrificed to the individual, and the prosperity of the greater number to the greatness of the few. It is both necessary and desirable that the government of a democratic people should be active and powerful: and our object should not be to render it weak or indolent, but solely to prevent it from abusing its aptitude and its strength. . . .

THE POWER ELITE

C. Wright Mills

Except for the unsuccessful Civil War, changes in the power system of the United States have not involved important challenges to its basic legitimations. Even when they have been decisive enough to be called "revolutions," they have not involved the "resort to the guns of a cruiser, the dispersal of an elected assembly by bayonets, or the mechanisms of a police state."[1] Nor have they involved, in any decisive way, any ideological struggle to control masses. Changes in the American structure of power have generally come about by institutional shifts in the relative positions of the political, the economic, and the military orders. From this point of view, and broadly speaking, the American power elite has gone through four epochs, and is now well into a fifth.

I. 1. During the first—roughly from the Revolution through the administration of John Adams—the social and economic, the political and the military institutions were more or less unified in a simple and direct way: the individual men of these several elites moved easily from one role to another at the top of each of the major institutional orders. Many of them were many-sided men who could take the part of legislator and merchant, frontiersman and soldier, scholar and surveyor.[2]

SOURCE: C. Wright Mills, *The Power Elite* (New York: Oxford University Press, 1956), pp. 269-287. Reprinted by permission. Several footnotes have been omitted, and those remaining have been renumbered.

[1] Elmer Davis, *But We Were Born Free* (Indianapolis: Bobbs-Merrill, 1953), p. 187.

[2] For points used to characterize the first and second of these phases, I have drawn from Robert Lamb, "Political Elites and the Process of Economic Development," in *The Progress of Underdeveloped Areas*, edited by Bert Hoselitz (Chicago: The University of Chicago Press, 1952).

Until the downfall of the Congressional caucus of 1824, political institutions seemed quite central; political decisions, of great importance; many politicians, considered national statesmen of note. "Society, as I first remember it," Henry Cabot Lodge once said, speaking of the Boston of his early boyhood, "was based on the old families; Doctor Holmes defines them in the 'Autocrat' as the families which had held high position in the colony, the province and during the Revolution and the early decades of the United States. They represented several generations of education and standing in the community.... They had ancestors who had filled the pulpits, sat upon the bench, and taken part in the government under the crown; who had fought in the Revolution, helped to make the State and National constitutions and served in the army or navy; who had been members of the House or Senate in the early days of the Republic, and who had won success as merchants, manufacturers, lawyers, or men of letters."[3]

Such men of affairs, who—as I have noted—were the backbone of Mrs. John Jay's social list of 1787, definitely included political figures of note. The important fact about these early days is that social life, economic institutions, military establishment, and political order coincided, and men who were high politicians also played key roles in the economy and, with their families, were among those of the reputable who made up local society. In fact, this first period is marked by the leadership of men whose status does not rest exclusively upon their political position, although their political activities are important and the prestige of politicians high. And this prestige seems attached to the men who occupy Congressional position as well as the cabinet. The elite are political men of education and of administrative experience, and, as Lord Bryce noted, possess a certain "largeness of view and dignity of character."[4]

2. During the early nineteenth century—which followed Jefferson's political philosophy, but, in due course, Hamilton's economic principles—the economic and political and military orders fitted loosely into the great scatter of the American social structure. The broadening of the economic order which came to be seated in the individual property owner was dramatized by Jefferson's purchase of the Louisiana Territory and by the formation of the Democratic-Republican party as successor to the Federalists.

In this society, the "elite" became a plurality of top groups, each in turn quite loosely made up. They overlapped to be sure, but again quite loosely so. One definite key to the period, and certainly to our images of it, is the fact that the Jacksonian Revolution was much more of a status revolution than either an economic or a political one. The metropolitan 400 could not truly flourish in the face of the status tides of Jacksonian democracy; alongside it was a political elite in charge of the new party system. No set of men controlled centralized means of power; no small clique dominated economic, much less political, affairs. The

---

[3]Henry Cabot Lodge, *Early Memoirs*, cited by Dixon Wecter, *The Saga of American Society* (New York: Scribner's, 1937), p. 206.

[4]Lord James Bryce, *The American Commonwealth* (New York: Macmillan, 1918), vol. 1, pp. 84-5....

economic order was ascendant over both social status and political power; within the economic order, a quite sizable proportion of all the economic men were among those who decided. For this was the period—roughly from Jefferson to Lincoln—when the elite was at most a loose coalition. The period ended, of course, with the decisive split of southern and northern types.

Official commentators like to contrast the ascendancy in totalitarian countries of a tightly organized clique with the American system of power. Such comments, however, are easier to sustain if one compares mid-twentieth-century Russia with mid-nineteenth-century America, which is what is often done by Tocqueville-quoting Americans making the contrast. But that was an America of a century ago, and in the century that has passed, the American elite have not remained as patrioteer essayists have described them to us. The "loose cliques" now head institutions of a scale and power not then existing and, especially since World War I, the loose cliques have tightened up. We are well beyond the era of romantic pluralism.

3. The supremacy of corporate economic power began, in a formal way, with the Congressional elections of 1866, and was consolidated by the Supreme Court decision of 1886 which declared that the Fourteenth Amendment protected the corporation. That period witnessed the transfer of the center of initiative from government to corporation. Until the First World War (which gave us an advanced showing of certain features of our own period) this was an age of raids on the government by the economic elite, an age of simple corruption, when Senators and judges were simply bought up. Here, once upon a time, in the era of McKinley and Morgan, far removed from the undocumented complexities of our own time, many now believe, was the golden era of the American ruling class.

The military order of this period, as in the second, was subordinate to the political, which in turn was subordinate to the economic. The military was thus off to the side of the main driving forces of United States history. Political institutions in the United States have never formed a centralized and autonomous domain of power; they have been enlarged and centralized only reluctantly in slow response to the public consequence of the corporate economy.

In the post-Civil War era, that economy was the dynamic; the "trusts" — as policies and events make amply clear—could readily use the relatively weak governmental apparatus for their own ends. That both state and federal governments were decisively limited in their power to regulate, in fact meant that they were themselves regulatable by the larger moneyed interests. Their powers were scattered and unorganized; the powers of the industrial and financial corporations concentrated and interlocked. The Morgan interests alone held 341 directorships in 112 corporations with an aggregate capitalization of over $22 billion—over three times the assessed value of all real and personal property in New England. With revenues greater and employees more numerous than those of many states, corporations controlled parties, bought laws, and kept Congressmen of the "neutral" state. And as private economic power overshadowed public political power, so the economic elite overshadowed the political.

Yet even between 1896 and 1919, events of importance tended to assume a political form, foreshadowing the shape of power which after the partial boom of the 'twenties was to prevail in the New Deal. Perhaps there has never been any period in American history so politically transparent as the Progressive era of President-makers and Muckrakers.

4. The New Deal did *not* reverse the political and economic relations of the third era, but it did create within the political arena, as well as in the corporate world itself, competing centers of power that challenged those of the corporate directors. As the New Deal directorate gained political power, the economic elite, which in the third period had fought against the growth of "government" while raiding it for crafty privileges, belatedly attempted to join it on the higher levels. When they did so they found themselves confronting other interests and men, for the places of decision were crowded. In due course, they did come to control and to use for their own purposes the New Deal institutions whose creation they had so bitterly denounced.

But during the 'thirties, the political order was still an instrument of small propertied farmers and businessmen, although they were weakened, having lost their last chance for real ascendancy in the Progressive era. The struggle between big and small property flared up again, however, in the political realm of the New Deal era, and to this struggle there was added, as we have seen, the new struggle of organized labor and the unorganized unemployed. This new force flourished under political tutelage, but nevertheless, for the first time in United States history, social legislation and lower-class issues became important features of the reform movement.

In the decade of the 'thirties, a set of shifting balances involving newly instituted farm measures and newly organized labor unions—along with big business—made up the political and administrative drama of power. These farm, labor, and business groups, moreover, were more or less contained within the framework of an enlarging governmental structure, whose political directorship made decisions in a definitely political manner. These groups pressured, and in pressuring against one another and against the governmental and party system, they helped to shape it. But it could not be said that any of them for any considerable length of time used that government unilaterally as their instrument. That is why the 'thirties was a *political* decade: the power of business was not replaced, but it was contested and supplemented: it became one major power within a structure of power that was chiefly run by political men, and not by economic or military men turned political.

The earlier and middle Roosevelt administrations can best be understood as a desperate search for ways and means, within the existing capitalist system, of reducing the staggering and ominous army of the unemployed. In these years, the New Deal as a system of power was essentially a balance of pressure groups and interest blocs. The political top adjusted many conflicts, gave way to this demand, sidetracked that one, was the unilateral servant of none, and so evened it all out into such going policy line as prevailed from one minor crisis to another. Policies were the result of a political act of balance at the top. Of course, the balancing act that Roosevelt performed did not affect the fundamental institutions of capitalism as a type of economy. By his policies, he subsidized the defaults of the capitalist economy, which had simply broken down; and by his rhetoric, he balanced its political disgrace, putting "economic royalists" in the political doghouse.

The "welfare state," created to sustain the balance and to carry out the subsidy, differed from the "laissez-faire" state: "If the state was believed neutral in the days of T.R. because its leaders claimed to sanction favors for no one," Richard Hofstadter has remarked, "the state under F.D.R. could be called neutral only in the sense that it offered favors to everyone."[5] The new state of the corporate commissars differs from the old welfare state. In fact, the later Roosevelt years—beginning with the entrance of the United States into overt acts of war and preparations for World War II—cannot be understood entirely in terms of an adroit equipoise of political power.

II. We study history, it has been said, to rid ourselves of it, and the history of the power elite is a clear case for which this maxim is correct. Like the tempo of American life in general, the long-term trends of the power structure have been greatly speeded up since World War II, and certain newer trends within and between the dominant institutions have also set the shape of the power elite and given historically specific meaning to its fifth epoch:

1. In so far as the structural clue to the power elite today lies in the political order, that clue is the decline of politics as genuine and public debate of alternative decisions—with nationally responsible and policy-coherent parties and with autonomous organizations connecting the lower and middle levels of power with the top levels of decision. America is now in considerable part more a formal political democracy than a democratic social structure, and even the formal political mechanics are weak.

The long-time tendency of business and government to become more intricately and deeply involved with each other has, in the fifth epoch, reached a new point of explicitness. The two cannot now be seen clearly as two distinct worlds. It is in terms of the executive agencies of the state that the rapprochement has proceeded most decisively. The growth of the executive branch of the government, with its agencies that patrol the complex economy, does not mean merely the "enlargement of government" as some sort of autonomous bureaucracy: it has meant the ascendancy of the corporation's man as a political eminence.

During the New Deal the corporate chieftains joined the political directorate; as of World War II they have come to dominate it. Long interlocked with government, now they have moved into quite full direction of the economy of the war effort and of the postwar era. This shift of the corporation executives into the political directorate has accelerated the long-term relegation of the professional politicians in the Congress to the middle levels of power.

2. In so far as the structural clue to the power elite today lies in the enlarged and military state, that clue becomes evident in the military ascendancy. The warlords have gained decisive political relevance, and the military structure of America is now in considerable part a political structure. The seemingly permanent military threat places a premium on the military and upon their control of men, material, money, and power; virtually all political and economic actions are now judged in terms of

---

[5] Richard Hofstadter, *The Age of Reform* (New York: Knopf, 1955), p. 305.

military definitions of reality: the higher warlords have ascended to a firm position within the power elite of the fifth epoch.

In part at least this has resulted from one simple historical fact, pivotal for the years since 1939: the focus of elite attention has been shifted from domestic problems, centered in the 'thirties around slump, to international problems, centered in the 'forties and 'fifties around war. Since the governing apparatus of the United States has by long historic usage been adapted to and shaped by domestic clash and balance, it has not, from any angle, had suitable agencies and traditions for the handling of international problems. Such formal democratic mechanics as had arisen in the century and a half of national development prior to 1941, had not been extended to the American handling of international affairs. It is, in considerable part, in this vacuum that the power elite has grown.

3. In so far as the structural clue to the power elite today lies in the economic order, that clue is the fact that the economy is at once a permanent-war economy and a private-corporation economy. American capitalism is now in considerable part a military capitalism, and the most important relation of the big corporation to the state rests on the coincidence of interests between military and corporate needs, as defined by warlords and corporate rich. Within the elite as a whole, this coincidence of interest between the high military and the corporate chieftains strengthens both of them and further subordinates the role of the merely political men. Not politicians, but corporate executives, sit with the military and plan the organization of war effort.

The shape and meaning of the power elite today can be understood only when these three sets of structural trends are seen at their point of coincidence: the military capitalism of private corporations exists in a weakened and formal democratic system containing a military order already quite political in outlook and demeanor. Accordingly, at the top of this structure, the power elite has been shaped by the coincidence of interest between those who control the major means of production and those who control the newly enlarged means of violence; from the decline of the professional   politician and the rise to explicit political command of the corporate chieftains and the professional warlords; from the absence of any genuine civil service of skill and integrity, independent of vested interests.

The power elite is composed of political, economic, and military men, but this instituted elite is frequently in some tension: it comes together only on certain coinciding points and only on certain occasions of "crisis." In the long peace of the nineteenth century, the military were not in the high councils of state, not of the political directorate, and neither were the economic men—they made raids upon the state but they did not join its directorate. During the 'thirties, the political man was ascendant. Now the military and the corporate men are in top positions.

Of the three types of circle that compose the power elite today, it is the military that has benefited the most in its enhanced power, although the corporate circles have also become more explicitly intrenched in the more public decision-making circles. It is the professional politician that has lost the most, so much that in examining the events and decisions, one is tempted to speak of a political vacuum in which the corporate rich and the high warlord, in their coinciding interests, rule.

It should not be said that the three "take turns" in carrying the initiative, for the mechanics of the power elite are not often as deliberate as that would imply. At times, of course, it is—as when political men, thinking they can borrow the prestige of generals, find that they must pay for it, or, as when during big slumps, economic men feel the need of a politician at once safe and possessing vote appeal. Today all three are involved in virtually all widely ramifying decisions. Which of the three types seems to lead depends upon "the tasks of the period" as they, the elite, define them. Just now, these tasks center upon "defense" and international affairs. Accordingly, as we have seen, the military are ascendant in two senses: as personnel and as justifying ideology. That is why, just now, we can most easily specify the unity and the shape of the power elite in terms of the military ascendancy.

But we must always be historically specific and open to complexities. The simple Marxian view makes the big economic man the *real* holder of power; the simple liberal view makes the big political man the chief of the power system; and there are some who would view the warlords as virtual dictators. Each of these is an oversimplified view. It is to avoid them that we use the term "power elite" rather than, for example, "ruling class"[6]

In so far as the power elite has come to wide public attention, it has done so in terms of the "military clique." The power elite does, in fact, take its current shape from the decisive entrance into it of the military. Their presence and their ideology are its major legitimations, whenever the power elite feels the need to provide any. But what is called the "Washington military clique" is not composed merely of military men, and it does not prevail merely in Washington. Its members exist all over the country, and it is a coalition of generals in the roles of corporation executives, of politicians masquerading as admirals, of corporation executives acting like politicians, of civil servants who become majors, of vice-admirals who are also the assistants to a cabinet officer, who is himself, by the way, really a member of the managerial elite.

Neither the idea of a "ruling class" nor of a simple monolithic rise of "bureaucratic politicians" nor of a "military clique" is adequate. The power elite today involves the often uneasy coincidence of economic, military, and political power.

---

[6] "Ruling class" is a badly loaded phrase. "Class" is an economic term; "rule" a political one. The phrase, "ruling class," thus contains the theory that an economic class rules politically. That short-cut theory may or may not at times be true, but we do not want to carry that one rather simple theory about in the terms that we use to define our problems; we wish to state the theories explicitly, using terms of more precise and unilateral meaning. Specifically, the phrase "ruling class," in its common political connotations, does not allow enough autonomy to the political order and its agents, and it says nothing about the military as such. It should be clear to the reader by now that we do not accept as adequate the simple view that high economic men unilaterally make all decisions of national consequence. We hold that such a simple view of "economic determinisim" must be elaborated by "political determinism" and "military determinism"; that the higher agents of each of these three domains now often have a noticeable degree of autonomy; and that only in the often intricate ways of coalition do they make up and carry through the most important decisions. Those are the major reasons we prefer "power elite" to "ruling class" as a characterizing phrase for the higher circles when we consider them in terms of power.

III. Even if our understanding were limited to these structural trends, we should have grounds for believing the power elite a useful, indeed indispensable, concept for the interpretation of what is going on at the topside of modern American society. But we are not, of course, so limited: our conception of the power elite does not need to rest only upon the correspondence of the institutional hierarchies involved, or upon the many points at which their shifting interests coincide. The power elite, as we conceive it, also rests upon the similarity of its personnel, and their personal and official relations with one another, upon their social and psychological affinities. In order to grasp the personal and social basis of the power elite's unity, we have first to remind ourselves of the facts of origin, career, and style of life of each of the types of circle whose members compose the power elite.

The power elite is *not* an aristocracy, which is to say that it is not a political ruling group based upon a nobility of hereditary origin. It has no compact basis in a small circle of great families whose members can and do consistently occupy the top positions in the several higher circles which overlap as the power elite. But such nobility is only one possible basis of common origin. That it does not exist for the American elite does not mean that members of this elite derive socially from the full range of strata composing American society. They derive in substantial proportions from the upper classes, both new and old, of local society and the metropolitan 400. The bulk of the very rich, the corporate executives, the political outsiders, the high military, derive from, at most, the upper third of the income and occupational pyramids. Their fathers were at least of the professional and business strata, and very frequently higher than that. They are native-born Americans of native parents, primarily from urban areas, and, with the exceptions of the politicians among them, overwhelmingly from the East. They are mainly Protestants, especially Episcopalian or Presbyterian. In general, the higher the position, the greater the proportion of men within it who have derived from and who maintain connections with the upper classes. The generally similar origins of the members of the power elite are underlined and carried further by the fact of their increasingly common educational routine. Overwhelmingly college graduates, substantial proportions have attended Ivy League colleges, although the education of the higher military, of course, differs from that of other members of the power elite.

But what do these apparently simple facts about the social composition of the higher circles really mean? In particular, what do they mean for any attempt to understand the degree of unity, and the direction of policy and interest that may prevail among these several circles? Perhaps it is best to put this question in a deceptively simple way: in terms of origin and career, who or what do these men at the top represent?

Of course, if they are elected politicians, they are supposed to represent those who elected them; and, if they are appointed, they are supposed to represent, indirectly, those who elected their appointers. But this is recognized as something of an abstraction, as a rhetorical formula by which all men of power in almost all systems of government nowadays justify their power of decision. At times it may be true, both in the sense of their motives and in the sense of who benefits from their decisions. Yet it would not be wise in any power system merely to assume it.

The fact that members of the power elite come from near the top of the nation's class and status levels does not mean that they are necessarily "representative" of the top levels only. And if they were, as social types, representative of a cross-section of the population, that would not mean that a balanced democracy of interest and power would automatically be the going political fact.

We cannot infer the direction of policy merely from the social origins and careers of the policy-makers. The social and economic backgrounds of the men of power do not tell us all that we need to know in order to understand the distribution of social power. For: (1) Men from high places may be ideological representative of the poor and humble. (2) Men of humble origin, brightly self-made, may energetically serve the most vested and inherited interests. Moreover (3), not all men who effectively represent the interests of a stratum need in any way belong to it or personally benefit by policies that further its interests. Among the politicians, in short, there are sympathetic *agents* of given groups, conscious and unconscious, paid and unpaid. Finally (4), among the top decision-makers we find men who have been chosen for their positions because of their "expert knowledge." These are some of the obvious reasons why the social origins and careers of the power elite do not enable us to infer the class interests and policy directions of a modern system of power.

Do the high social origin and careers of the top men mean nothing, then, about the distribution of power? By no means. They simply remind us that we must be careful of any simple and direct inference from origin and career to political character and policy, not that we must ignore them in our attempt at political understanding. They simply mean that we must analyze the political psychology and the actual decisions of the political directorate as well as its social composition. And they mean, above all, that we should control, as we have done here, any inference we make from the origin and careers of the political actors by close understanding of the institutional landscape in which they act out their drama. Otherwise we should be guilty of a rather simple-minded biographical theory of society and history.

Just as we cannot rest the notion of the power elite solely upon the institutional mechanics that lead to its formation, so we cannot rest the notion solely upon the facts of the origin and career of its personnel. We need both, and we have both—as well as other bases, among them that of the status intermingling.

But it is not only the similarities of social origin, religious affiliation, nativity, and education that are important to the psychological and social affinities of the members of the power elite. Even if their recruitment and formal training were more heterogeneous than they are, these men would still be of quite homogeneous social type. For the most important set of facts about a circle of men is the criteria of admission, of praise, of honor, of promotion that prevails among them; if these are similar within a circle, then they will tend as personalities to become similar. The circles that compose the power elite do tend to have such codes and criteria in common. The co-optation of the social types to which these common values lead is often more important than any statistics of common origin and career that we might have at hand.

There is a kind of reciprocal attraction among the fraternity of the successful—not between each and every member of the circles of the high and mighty, but between enough of them to insure a certain unity. On the slight side, it is a sort of tacit, mutual admiration; in the strongest tie-ins, it proceeds by intermarriage. And there are all grades and types of connection between these extremes. Some overlaps certainly occur by means of cliques and clubs, churches and schools.

If social origin and formal education in common tend to make the members of the power elite more readily understood and trusted by one another, their continued association further cements what they feel they have in common. Members of the several higher circles know one another as personal friends and even as neighbors; they mingle with one another on the golf course, in the gentleman's clubs, at resorts, on transcontinental airplanes, and on ocean liners. They meet at the estates of mutual friends, face each other in front of the TV camera, or serve on the same philanthropic committee; and many are sure to cross one another's path in the columns of newspapers, if not in the exact cafes from which many of these columns originate. As we have seen, of "The New 400" of cafe society, one chronicler has named forty-one members of the very rich, ninety-three political leaders, and seventy-nine chief executives of corporations.

"I did not know, I could not have dreamed," Whittaker Chambers has written, "of the immense scope and power of Hiss' political alliances and his social connections, which cut across all party lines and ran from the Supreme Court to the Religious Society of Friends, from governors of states and instructors in college faculties to the staff members of liberal magazines. In the decade since I had last seen him, he had used his career, and, in particular, his identification with the cause of peace through his part in organizing the United Nations, to put down roots that made him one with the matted forest floor of American upper class, enlightened middle class, liberal and official life. His roots could not be disturbed without disturbing all the roots on all sides of him."[7]

The sphere of status has reflected the epochs of the power elite. In the third epoch, for example, who could compete with big money? And in the fourth, with big politicians, or even the bright young men of the New Deal? And in the fifth, who can compete with the generals and the admirals and the corporate officials now so sympathetically portrayed on the stage, in the novel, and on the screen? Can one imagine *Executive Suite* as a successful motion picture in 1935? or *The Caine Mutiny*?

The multiplicity of high-prestige organizations to which the elite usually belong is revealed by even casual examination of the obituaries of the big businessman, the high-prestige lawyer, the top general and admiral, the key senator: usually, high-prestige church, business associations, plus high-prestige clubs, and often plus

---

[7]Whittaker Chambers, *Witness* (New York: Random House, 1952), p. 550.

military rank. In the course of their lifetimes, the university president, the New York Stock Exchange chairman, the head of the bank, the old West Pointer—mingle in the status sphere, within which they easily renew old friendships and draw upon them in an effort to understand through the experience of trusted others those contexts of power and decision in which they have not personally moved.

In these diverse contexts, prestige accumulates in each of the higher circles, and the members of each borrow status from one another. Their self-images are fed by these accumulations and these borrowings, and accordingly, however segmental a given man's role may seem, he comes to feel himself a "diffuse" or "generalized" man of the higher circles a "broad-gauge" man. Perhaps such inside experience is one feature of what is meant by "judgment."

The key organizations, perhaps, are the major corporations themselves, for on the boards of directors we find a heavy overlapping among the members of these several elites. On the lighter side, again in the summer and winter resorts, we find that, in an intricate series of overlapping circles; in the course of time, each meets each or knows somebody who knows somebody who knows that one.

The higher members of the military, economic, and political orders are able readily to take over one another's point of view, always in a sympathetic way, and often in a knowledgeable way as well. They define one another as among those who count, and who, accordingly, must be taken into account. Each of them as a member of the power elite comes to incorporate into his own integrity, his own honor, his own conscience, the viewpoint, the expectations, the values of the others. If there are no common ideals and standards among them that are based upon an explicitly aristocratic culture, that does not mean that they do not feel responsibility to one another.

All the structural coincidence of their interests as well as the intricate, psychological facts of their origins and their education, their careers and their associations make possible the psychological affinities that prevail among them, affinities that make it possible for them to say of one another: He is, of course, one of us. And all this points to the basic, psychological meaning of class consciousness. Nowhere in America is there as great a "class consciousness" as among the elite; nowhere is it organized as effectively as among the power elite. For by class consciousness, as a psychological fact, one means that the individual member of a "class" accepts only those accepted by his circle as among those who are significant to his own image of self.

Within the higher circles of the power elite, factions do exist; there are conflicts of policy; individual ambitions do clash. There are still enough divisions of importance within the Republican party, and even between Republicans and Democrats, to make for different methods of operation. But more powerful than these divisions are the internal discipline and the community of interests that bind the power elite together, even across the boundaries of nations at war.

IV. Yet we must give due weight to the other side of the case which may not question the facts but only our interpretation of them. There is a set of objections that will inevitably be made to our whole conception of the power elite, but which has essentially to do with only the psychology of its members. It might well be put by liberals or by conservatives in some such way as this:

"To talk of a power elite—isn't this to characterize men by their origins and associations? Isn't such characterization both unfair and untrue? Don't men modify themselves, especailly Americans such as these, as they rise in stature to meet the demands of their jobs? Don't they arrive at a view and a line of policy that represents, so far as they in their human weaknesses can know, the interests of the nation as a whole? Aren't they merely honorable men who are doing their duty?"

What are we to reply to these objections?

1. We are sure that they are honorable men. But what is honor? Honor can only mean living up to a code that one believes to be honorable. There is no one code upon which we are all agreed. That is why, if we are civilized men, we do not kill off all of those with whom we disagree. The question is not: are these honorable men? The question is; what are their codes of honor? The answer to that question is that they are the codes of their circles, of those to whose opinions they defer. How could it be otherwise? That is one meaning of the important truism that all men are human and that all men are social creatures. As for sincerity, it can only be disproved, never proved.

2. To the question of their adaptability—which means their capacity to transcend the codes of conduct which, in their life's work and experience, they have acquired—we must answer: simply no, they cannot, at least not in the handful of years most of them have left. To expect that is to assume that they are indeed strange and expedient: such flexibility would in fact involve a violation of what we may rightly call their character and their integrity. By the way, may it not be precisely because of the lack of such character and integrity that earlier types of American politicians have not represented as great a threat as do these men of character?

It would be an insult to the effective training of the military, and to their indoctrination as well, to suppose that military officials shed their military character and outlook upon changing from uniform to mufti. This background is more important perhaps in the military case than in that of the corporate executives, for the training of the career is deeper and more total.

"Lack of imagination," Gerald W. Johnson has noted, "is not to be confused with lack of principle. On the contrary, an unimaginative man is often a man of the highest principles. The trouble is that his principles conform to Cornford's famous definition: 'A principle is a rule of inaction giving valid general reasons for not doing in a specific instance what to unprincipled instinct would seem to be right.' "[8]

Would it not be ridiculous, for example, to believe seriously that, in psychological fact, Charles Erwin Wilson represented anyone or any interest other than those of the corporate world? This is not because he is dishonest; on the contrary, it is because he is probably a man of solid integrity—as sound as a dollar. He is what he is and he cannot very well be anything else. He is a member of the professional corporation elite, just as are his colleagues, in the government and out of it; he rep-

---

[8]Gerald W. Johnson, "The Superficial Aspect," *New Republic*, 25 October 1954, p. 7.

resents the wealth of the higher corporate world; he represents its power; and he believes sincerely in his oft-quoted remark that "what is good for the United States is good for the General Motors Corporation and vice versa."

The revealing point about the pitiful hearings on the confirmation of such men for political posts is not the cynicism toward the law and toward the lawmakers on the middle levels of power which they display, nor their reluctance to dispose of their personal stock. The interesting point is how impossible it is for such men to divest themselves of their engagement with the corporate world in general and with their own corporations in particular. Not only their money, but their friends, their interests, their training—their lives in short—are deeply involved in this world. The disposal of stock is, of course, merely a purifying ritual. The point is not so much financial or personal interests in a given corporation, but identification with the corporate world. To ask a man suddenly to divest himself of these interests and sensibilities is almost like asking a man to become a woman.

3. To the question of their patriotism, of their desire to serve the nation as a whole, we must answer first that, like codes of honor, feelings of patriotism and views of what is to the whole nation's good, are not ultimate facts but matters upon which there exists a great variety of opinion. Furthermore, patriotic opinions too are rooted in and are sustained by what a man has become by virtue of how and with whom he has lived. This is no simple mechanical determination of individual character by social conditions; it is an intricate process, well established in the major tradition of modern social study. One can only wonder why more social scientists do not use it systematically in speculating about politics.

4. The elite cannot be truly thought of as men who are merely doing their duty. They are the ones who determine their duty, as well as the duties of those beneath them. They are not merely following orders: they give the orders. They are not merely "bureaucrats": they command bureaucracies. They may try to disguise these facts from others and from themselves by appeals to traditions of which they imagine themselves the instruments, but there are many traditions, and they must choose which ones they will serve. They face decisions for which there simply are no traditions.

Now, to what do these several answers add up? To the fact that we cannot reason about public events and historical trends merely from knowledge about the motives and character of the men or the small groups who sit in the seats of the high and mighty. This fact, in turn, does not mean that we should be intimidated by accusations that in taking up our problem in the way we have, we are impugning the honor, the integrity, or the ability of those who are in high office. For it is not, in the first instance, a question of individual character; and if, in further instances, we find that it is, we should not hesitate to say so plainly. In the meantime, we must judge men of power by the standards of power, by what they do as decision-makers, and not by who they are or what they may do in private life. Our interest is not in that: we are interested in their policies and in the *consequences* of their conduct of office. We must remember that these men of the power elite now occupy the strategic places in the structure of American society; that they command the dominant institutions of a dominant nation; that, as a set of men, they are in a position to make decisions with terrible consequences for the underlying populations of the world. . . .

THE STRUCTURE OF POWER IN AMERICAN SOCIETY

C. Wright Mills

Power has to do with whatever decisions men make about the arrangements under which they live, and about the events which make up the history of their times. Events that are beyond human decision do happen; social arrangements do change without benefit of explicit decision. But in so far as such decisions are made, the problem of who is involved in making them is the basic problem of power. In so far as they could be made but are not, the problem becomes who fails to make them? . . .

How large a role any explicit decisions do play in the making of history is itself an historical problem. For how large that role may be depends very much upon the means of power that are available at any given time in any given society. In some societies, the innumerable actions of innumerable men modify their milieux, and so gradually modify the structure itself. These modifications—the course of history—go on behind the backs of men. History is drift, although in total "men make it." Thus, innumerable entrepreneurs and innumerable consumers by ten-thousand decisions per minute may shape and re-shape the free-market economy. Perhaps this was the chief kind of limitation Marx had in mind when he wrote, in *The 18th Brumaire*, that "Men make their own history, but they do not make it just as they please; they do not make it under circumstances chosen by themselves."

But in other societies—certainly in the United States and in the Soviet Union today—a few men may be so placed within the structure that by their decisions they modify the milieux of many other men, and in fact nowadays the structural conditions under which most men live. Such elites of power also make history under circumstances not chosen altogether by themselves, yet compared with other men, and compared with other periods of world history, these circumstances do indeed seem less limiting.

I should contend that "men are free to make history," but that some men are indeed much freer than others. For such freedom requires access to the means of decision and of power by which history can now be made. It has not always been so made; but in the later phases of the modern epoch it is. It is with reference to this epoch that I am contending that if men do not make history, they tend increasingly to become the utensils of history-makers.

The history of modern society may readily be understood as the story of the

SOURCE: C. Wright Mills, "The Structure of Power in American Society," *The British Journal of Sociology*, Vol. 9, March 1958, pp. 29-41. Reprinted by permission.

enlargement and the centralization of the means of power—in economic, in political, and in military institutions. The rise of industrial society has involved these developments in the means of economic production. The rise of the nation state has involved these developments in the means of violence and in those of political administration. . . .

II. The power to make decisions of national and international consequence is now so clearly seated in political, military, and economic institutions that other areas of society seem off to the side and, on occasion, readily subordinated to these. The scattered institutions of religion, education and family are increasingly shaped by the big three, in which history-making decisions now regularly occur. . . . There is no longer, on the one hand, an economy, and, on the other, a political order, containing a military establishment unimportant to politics and to money-making. There is a political economy numerously linked with military order and decision. This triangle of power is now a structural fact, and it is the key to any understanding of the higher circles in America today. For as each of these domains has coincided with the others, as decisions in each have become broader, the leading men of each—the high military, the corporation executives, the political directorate—have tended to come together to form the power elite of America.

The political order, once composed of several dozen states with a weak federal-center, has become an executive apparatus which has taken up into itself many powers previously scattered, legislative as well as administrative, and which now reach into all parts of the social structure. The long-time tendency of business and government to become more closely connected has since World War II reached a new point of explicitness. Neither can now be seen clearly as a distinct world. The growth of executive government does not mean merely the "enlargement of government" as some kind of autonomous bureaucracy: under American conditions, it has meant the ascendancy of the corporation man into political eminence. Already during the New Deal, such men had joined the political directorate; as of World War II they came to dominate it. Long involved with government, now they have moved into quite full direction of the economy of the war effort and of the post-war era.

The economy, once a great scatter of small productive units in somewhat automatic balance, has become internally dominated by a few hundred corporations, administratively and politically interrelated, which together hold the keys to economic decision. This economy is at once a permanent-war economy and a private-corporation economy. The most important relations of the corporation to the state now rest on the coincidence between military and corporate interests, as defined by the military and the corporate rich, and accepted by politicians and public. Within the elite as a whole, this coincidence of military domain and corporate realm strengthens both of them and further subordinates the merely political man. Not the party politician, but the corporation executive, is now more likely to sit with the military to answer the question: what is to be done?

The military order, once a slim establishment in a context of civilian distrust, has become the largest and most expensive feature of government; behind smiling public relations, it has all the grim and clumsy efficiency of a great and sprawling bureaucracy. The high military have gained decisive political and economic relevance.

The seemingly permanent military threat places a premium upon them and virtually all political and economic actions are now judged in terms of military definitions of reality: the higher military have ascended to a firm position within the power elite of our time. . . .

1. To understand the unity of this power elite, we must pay attention to the psychology of its several members in their respective milieux. In so far as the power elite is composed of men of similar origin and education, of similar career and style of life, their unity may be said to rest upon the fact that they are of similar social type, and to lead to the fact of their easy intermingling. This kind of unity reaches its frothier apex in the sharing of that prestige which is to be had in the world of the celebrity. It achieves a more solid culmination in the fact of the interchangeability of positions between the three dominant institutional orders. It is revealed by considerable traffic of personnel within and between these three, as well as by the rise of specialized go-betweens as in the new style high-level lobbying.

2. Behind such psychological and social unity are the structure and the mechanics of those institutional hierarchies over which the political directorate, the corporate rich, and the high military now preside. How each of these hierarchies is shaped and what relations it has with the others determine in large part the relations of their rulers. Were these hierarchies scattered and disjointed, then their respective elites might tend to be scattered and disjointed; but if they have many interconnections and points of coinciding interest, then their elites tend to form a coherent kind of grouping. The unity of the elite is not a simple reflection of the unity of institutions; but men and institutions are always related; that is why we must understand the elite today in connection with such institutional trends as the development of a permanent-war establishment, alongside a privately incorporated economy, inside a virtual political vacuum. For the men at the top have been selected and formed by such institutional trends.

3. Their unity, however, does not rest solely upon psychological similarity and social intermingling, nor entirely upon the structural blending or commanding positions and common interests. At times it is the unity of a more explicit co-ordination.

To say that these higher circles are increasingly co-ordinated, that this is *one* basis of their unity, and that at times—as during open war—such co-ordination is quite wilful, is not to say that the co-ordination is total or continuous, or even that it is very surefooted. Much less is it to say that the power elite has emerged as the realization of a plot. Its rise cannot be adequately explained in any psychological terms. . . .

III. There are of course other interpretations of the American system of power. The most usual is that it is a moving balance of many competing interests. The image of balance, at least in America, is derived from the idea of the economic market: in the nineteenth century, the balance was thought to occur between a great scatter of individuals and enterprises; in the twentieth century, it is thought to occur between great interest blocs. In both views, the politician is the key man of power because he is the broker of many conflicting powers.

I believe that the balance and the compromise in American society—the "counter-vailing powers" and the "veto groups," of parties and associations, of strata and unions—must now be seen as having mainly to do with the middle levels of power. It is these middle levels that the political journalist and the scholar of politics are most likely to understand and to write about—if only because being mainly middle class themselves, they are closer to them. Moreover these levels provide the noisy content of most "political" news and gossip; the images of these levels are more or less in accord with the folklore of how democracy works; and, if the master-image of balance is accepted, many intellectuals, especially in their current patrioteering, are readily able to satisfy such political optimism as they wish to feel. Accordingly, liberal interpretations of what is happening in the United States are now virtually the only interpretations that are widely distributed.

But to believe that the power system reflects a balancing society is, I think, to confuse the present era with earlier times, and to confuse its top and bottom with its middle levels.

By the top levels, as distinguished from the middle, I intend to refer, first of all, to the scope of the decisions that are made. At the top today, these decisions have to do with all the issues of war and peace. They have also to do with slump and poverty which are now so very much problems of international scope. I intend also to refer to whether or not the groups that struggle politically have a chance to gain the positions from which such top decisions are made, and indeed whether their members do usually hope for such top national command. Most of the competing interests which make up the clang and clash of American politics are strictly concerned with their slice of the existing pie. Labor unions, for example, certainly have no policies of an international sort other than those which given unions adopt for the strict economic protection of their members. Neither do farm organizations. The actions of such middle-level powers may indeed have consequence for top-level policy; certainly at times they hamper these policies. But they are not truly concerned with them, which means of course that their influence tends to be quite irresponsible.

The facts of the middle levels may in part be understood in terms of the rise of the power elite. The expanded and centralized and interlocked hierarchies over which the power elite preside have encroached upon the old balance and relegated it to the middle level. But there are also independent developments of the middle levels. These, it seems to me, are better understood as an affair of entrenched and provincial demands than as a center of national decision. As such, the middle level often seems much more of a stalemate than a moving balance.

1. The middle level of politics is not a forum in which there are debated the big decisions of national and international life. Such debate is not carried on by nationally responsible parties representing and clarifying alternative policies. There are no such parties in the United States. More and more, fundamental issues never come to any point or decision before Congress, much less before the electorate in party campaigns. . . .

The American political campaign distracts attention from national and international issues, but that is not to say that there are no issues in these campaigns. In each district and state, issues are set up and watched by organized interests of sovereign local importance. The professional politician is of course a party politician, and the two parties are semi-feudal organizations: they trade patronage and other favors for votes and for protection. The differences between them, so far as national issues are concerned, are very narrow and very mixed up. Often each seems to be fifty parties, one to each state; and accordingly, the politician as campaigner and as Congressman is not concerned with national party lines, if any are discernible. Often he is not subject to any effective national party discipline. He speaks for the interests of his own constituency, and he is concerned with national issues only in so far as they affect the interests effectively organized there, and hence his chances of reelection. That is why, when he does speak of national matters, the result is so often such an empty rhetoric. Seated in his sovereign locality, the politician is not at the national summit. He is on and of the middle levels of power.

2. Politics is not an arena in which free and independent organizations truly connect the lower and middle levels of society with the top levels of decision. Such organizations are not an effective and major part of American life today. As more people are drawn into the political arena, their associations become mass in scale, and the power of the individual becomes dependent upon them; to the extent that they are effective, they have become larger, and to that extent they have become less accessible to the influence of the individual. This is a central fact about associations in any mass society; it is of most consequence for political parties and for trade unions.

In the 'thirties, it often seemed that labor would become an insurgent power independent of corporation and state. Organized labor was then emerging for the first time on an American scale, and the only political sense of direction it needed was the slogan, "organize the unorganized." Now without the mandate of the slump, labor remains without political direction. Instead of economic and political struggles it has become deeply entangled in administrative routines with both corporation and state. One of its major functions, as a vested interest of the new society, is the regulation of such irregular tendencies as may occur among the rank and file.

There is nothing, it seems to me, in the make-up of the current labor leadership to allow us to expect that it can or that it will lead, rather than merely react. In so far as it fights at all it fights over a share of the goods of a single way of life and not over that way of life itself. The typical labor leader in the U.S.A. today is better understood as an adaptive creature of the main business drift than as an independent actor in a truly national context.

3. The idea that this society is a balance of powers requires us to assume that the units in balance are of more or less equal power and that they are truly independent of one another. These assumptions have rested, it seems clear, upon the historical importance of a large and independent middle class. In the latter nineteenth century and during the Progressive Era, such a class of farmers and small businessmen fought politically—and lost—their last struggle for a paramount role in national decision. Even then, their aspirations seemed bound to their own imagined past.

This old, independent middle class has of course declined. On the most generous count, it is now 40 per cent of the total middle class (at most 20 per cent of the total labor force). Moreover, it has become politically as well as economically dependent upon the state, most notably in the case of the subsidized farmer.

The *new* middle class of white-collar employees is certainly not the political pivot of any balancing society. It is in no way politically unified. Its unions, such as they are, often serve merely to incorporate it as hanger-on of the labor interest. For a considerable period, the old middle class *was* an independent base of power; the new middle class cannot be. Political freedom and economic security *were* anchored in small and independent properties; they are not anchored in the worlds of the white-collar job. Scattered property holders were economically united by more or less free markets; the jobs of the new middle class are integrated by corporate authority. Economically, the white-collar classes are in the same condition as wage workers; politically, they are in a worse condition, for they are not organized. They are no vanguard of historic change; they are at best a rearguard of the welfare state.

The agrarian revolt of the 'nineties, the small-business revolt that has been more or less continuous since the 'eighties, the labor revolt of the 'thirties—each of these has failed as an independent movement which could countervail against the powers that be; they have failed as politically autonomous third parties. But they have succeeded as parochial interests seated in particular districts, in local divisions of the two parties, and in Congress. What they would become, in short, are well-established features of the *middle* levels of balancing power, on which we may now observe all those strata and interests which in the course of American history have been defeated in their bids for top power or which have never made such bids.

Fifty years ago many observers thought of the American state as a mask behind which an invisible government operated. But nowadays, much of what was called the old lobby, visible or invisible, is part of the quite visible government. The "governmentalization of the lobby" has proceeded in both the legislative and the executive domain, as well as between them. The executive bureaucracy becomes not only the center of decision but also the arena within which major conflicts of power are resolved or denied resolution. "Administration" replaces electoral politics; the maneuvering of cliques (which include leading Senators as well as civil servants) replaces the open clash of parties.

The shift of corporation men into the political directorate has accelerated the decline of the politicians in the Congress to the middle levels of power; the formation of the power elite rests in part upon this relegation. It rests also upon the semi-organized stalemate of the interest of sovereign localities, into which the legislative function has so largely fallen; upon the virtually complete absence of a civil service that is a politically neutral but politically relevant depository of brainpower and executive skill; and it rests upon the increased official secrecy behind which great decisions are made without benefit of public or even of Congressional debate.

IV. There is one last belief upon which liberal observers everywhere base their interpretations and rest their hopes. That is the idea of the public and the associated idea of public opinion. Conservative thinkers, since the French Revolution, have of course Viewed With Alarm the rise of the public, which they have usually called the masses, or something to that effect. "The populace is sovereign," wrote Gustave Le Bon, "and the tide of barbarism mounts." But surely those who have supposed the masses to be well on their way to triumph are mistaken. In our time, the influence of publics or of masses within political life is in fact decreasing, and such influence as on occasion they do have tends, to an unknown but increasing degree, to be guided by the means of mass communication.

In a society of publics, discussion is the ascendant means of communication, and the mass media, if they exist, simply enlarge and animate this discussion, linking one face-to-face public with the discussions of another. In a mass society, the dominant type of communication is the formal media, and the publics become mere markets for these media: the "public" of a radio program consists of all those exposed to it. When we try to look upon the United States today as a society of publics, we realize that it has moved a considerable distance along the road to the mass society.

In official circles, the very term, "the public", has come to have a phantom meaning, which dramatically reveals its eclipse. The deciding elite can identify some of those who clamour publicly as "Labor," others as "Business," still others as "Farmer." But these are not the public. "The public" consists of the unidentified and the non-partisan in a world of defined and partisan interests. In this faint echo of the classic notion, the public is composed of those remnants of the old and new middle classes whose interests are not explicitly defined, organized, or clamorous. In a curious adaptation, "the public" often becomes, in administrative fact, "the disengaged expert," who, although ever so well informed, has never taken a clear-cut and public stand on controversial issues. He is the "public" member of the board, the commission, the committee. What "the public" stands for, accordingly, is often a vagueness of policy (called "open-mindedness"), a lack of involvement in public affairs (know as "reasonableness"), and a professional disinterest (known as "tolerance").

All this is indeed far removed from the eighteenth-century idea of the public of public opinion. That idea parallels the economic idea of the magical market. Here is the market composed of freely competing entrepreneurs; there is the public composed of circles of people in discussion. As price is the result of anonymous, equally weighted, bargaining individuals, so public opinion is the result of each man's having thought things out for himself and then contributing his voice to the great chorus. To be sure, some may have more influence on the state of opinion than others, but no one group monopolizes the discussion, or by itself determines the opinions that prevail.

In this classic image, the people are presented with problems. They discuss them. They formulate viewpoints. These viewpoints are organized, and they compete. One viewpoint "wins out." Then the people act out this view, or their representatives are instructed to act it out, and this they promptly do.

Such are the images of democracy which are still used as working justifications of power in America. We must now recognize this description as more a fairy tale than a useful approximation. The issues that now shape man's fate are neither raised nor decided by any public at large. The idea of a society that is at bottom composed of publics is not a matter of fact; it is the proclamation of an ideal, and as well the assertion of a legitimation masquerading as fact.

I cannot here describe the several great forces within American society as well as elsewhere which have been at work in the debilitation of the public. I want only to remind you that publics, like free associations, can be deliberately and suddenly smashed, or they can more slowly wither away. But whether smashed in a week or withered in a generation, the demise of the public must be seen in connection with the rise of centralized organizations, with all their new means of power, including those of the mass media of distraction. These, we now know, often seem to expropriate the rationality and the will of the terrorized or—as the case may be—the voluntarily indifferent society of masses. In the more democratic process of indifference the remnants of such publics as remain may only occasionally be intimidated by fanatics in search of "disloyalty." But regardless of that, they lose their will for decisions because they do not possess the instruments for decision; they lose their sense of political belonging because they do not belong; they lose their political will because they see no way to realize it.

The political structure of a modern democratic state requires that such a public as is projected by democratic theorists not only exist but that it be the very forum within which a politics of real issues is enacted.

It requires a civil service that is firmly linked with the world of knowledge and sensibility, and which is composed of skilled men who, in their careers and in their aspirations, are truly independent of any private, which is to say, corporation, interests.

It requires nationally responsible parties which debate openly and clearly the issues which the nation, and indeed the world, now so rigidly confronts.

It requires an intelligentsia, inside as well as outside the universities, who carry on the bid discourse of the western world, and whose work is relevant to and influential among parties and movements and publics.

And it certainly requires, as a fact of power, that there be free associations standing between families and smaller communities and publics, on the one hand, and the state, the military, the corporation, on the other. For unless these do exist, there are no vehicles for reasoned opinion, no instruments for the rational exertion of public will.

Such democratic formations are not now ascendant in the power structure of the United States, and accordingly the men of decision are not men selected and formed by careers within such associations and by their performance before such publics. The top of modern American society is increasingly unified, and often seems wilfully co-ordinated: at the top there has emerged an elite whose power probably exceeds that of any small group of men in world history. The middle levels are often a drifting set of stalemated forces: the middle does not link the bottom with the top. The bottom of this society is politically fragmented, and even as a passive fact, increasingly powerless: at the bottom there is emerging a mass society.

These developments, I believe, can be correctly understood neither in terms of the liberal nor the Marxian interpretation of politics and history. Both of these ways of thought arose as guidelines to reflection about a type of society which does not now exist in the United States. We confront there a new kind of social structure, which embodies elements and tendencies of all modern society, but in which they assumed a more naked and flamboyant prominence.

That does not mean that we must give up the ideals of these classic political expectations. I believe that both have been concerned with the problem of rationality and of freedom: liberalism, with freedom and rationality as supreme facts about the individual; Marxism, as supreme facts about man's role in the political making of history. What I have said here, I suppose, may be taken as an attempt to make evident why the ideas of freedom and of rationality now so often seem so ambiguous in the new society of the United States of America.

IS THERE A RULING CLASS IN AMERICA?

Daniel Bell

The Terms. *Elite.* Throughout [Mills'] book, the term elite is used in a variety of ways. Sometimes the term denotes "membership in clique-like sets of people," or "the morality of certain personality types," or "statistics of selected values" such as wealth, political position, etc.... He says that he defines elites primarily on the basis of "institutional position." But what does this mean?

Institutions, Domains, etc. Behind men and behind events, linking the two, says Mills, are the major institutions of society: The military, the political, and the economic. But, actually, the military, the economic, the political, as Mills uses these terms, are not institutions but sectors, or what Weber calls *orders*, or vertical hierarchies—each with their enclosed strata—in society. To say that this sector, or order, is more important than that—that in some societies, for example, the religious orders are more important than the political—is to give us large-scale boundaries of knowledge. But surely we want and need more than that....

Power. Throughout the book, there is a curious lack of definition of the word power. Only twice, really, does one find a set of limits to the word:

By the powerful we mean, of course, those who are able to realize their will, even if others resist it (p. 9).

All politics is a struggle for power: the ultimate kind of power is violence (p. 171)....

Power in Mills' terms is domination. But we do not need an elaborate discussion to see that this view of power avoids more problems than it answers, and particularly once one moves away from the outer boundary of *power as violence* to *institutionalized power*, with which Mills is concerned. For in society, particularly constitutional regimes, and *within* associations, where violence is not the rule, we are in the realm of norms, values, traditions, legitimacy, consensus, leadership, and identification—all the modes and mechanisms of command and authority, their acceptance or denial, which shape action in the day-to-day world, *without violence.* And these aspects of power Mills has eschewed.

The Command Posts. It is rather striking, too, given Mills' image of power, and politics, as violence, that the metaphor to describe the people of power is a military one. We can take this as a clue to Mills' implicit scheme. But, being little more than a

SOURCE: Daniel Bell, *The End of Ideology* (Glencoe: The Free Press, 1960), pp. 46-51, 57-67. Reprinted with permission of The Macmillan Company.© 1960 by The Free Press, a Corporation.

metaphor, it tells us almost nothing about *who* has the power. The men who hold power, he says, are those who run the *organizations* or domains which have power. But how do we know they have power, or what power they have? Mills simply takes as postulates: (1) the organization or institution has power; (2) *position in it gives power.* How do we know? Actually, we can only know if power exists by what people *do* with their power.

What powers people have, what decisions they make, how they make them, what factors they have to take into account in making them—all these enter into the question of whether position *can* be transferred into power. But Mills has said: "The idea of the power elite implies nothing about the process of decision-making as such—it is an attempt to delimit the social areas within which that process, *whatever its character*, goes on. It is a conception of who is involved in the process" (p. 21). Thus, we find ourselves stymied. *Who* depends upon position? But position, as I have argued, is only meaningful if one can define the character of the decisions made with such power. And this problem Mills eschews. . . .

The Big Decisions. The power elite comes into its own on the "big decisions." In fact, this is an implicit definition of the power of the elite: only they can effect the "big decisions." Those who talk of a new social balance, or pluralism, or the rise of labor, are talking, if at all correctly, says Mills, about the "middle levels" of power. They fail to see the big decisions.

But, curiously, except in a few instances, Mills fails to specify what the big decisions are. The few, never analyzed with regard to how the decisions were actually made or who made them, are five in number: the steps leading to intervention in World War II; the decision to drop the atom bomb over Hiroshima and Nagasaki; the declaration of war in Korea; the indecisions over Quemoy and Matsu in 1955; the hesitation regarding intervention in Indochina when Dien Bien Phu was on the verge of falling.

It is quite striking (and it is in line with Mills' conception of politics) that all the decisions he singles out as the "big decisions" are connected with *violence.* These are, it is true, the ultimate decisions a society can make: the commitment or refusal to go to war. And in this regard Mills is right. They *are* big decisions. But what is equally striking in his almost cursory discussion of these decisions is the failure to see that they are not made by the power elite. They are the decisions which, in our system, are vested constitutionally in the individual who must bear the responsibility for the choices—the president. And, rather than being a usurpation of the power of the people, so to speak, this is one of the few instances in the Constitution where such responsibility is specifically defined and where accountability is clear. . . .

To say that the leaders of a country have a constitutional responsibility to make crucial decisions is a fairly commonplace statement. To say that the power elite makes such decisions is to invest the statement with a weight and emotional charge that is quite impressive, but of little meaning.

The Question of Interests. So far we have been accepting the terms "command posts" and "power elite" in Mills' own usage. But now a difficulty enters: the question not only of *who* constitutes the power elite but how *cohesive* they are. Although Mills contends that he does not believe in a conspiracy theory, his loose account of the centralization of power among the elite comes suspiciously close to it. . . .

Yet we can only evaluate the meaning of any centralization of power on the basis of what people do with their power. What *unites* them? What *divides* them? And this involves a definition of *interests*. To say, as Mills does: *"All* means of power tend to become *ends* to an elite that is in command of them. And that is why we may define the power elite in terms of power—as those who occupy the command posts" (p. 23)—is circular.

What does it mean to say that power is an end in itself for the power elite? If the elite is cohesive and is facing another power group, the maintenance of power may be an end in itself. But is the elite cohesive? We do not know without first coming back to the question of interests. And the nature of interests implies a selection of values by a group, or part of a group, over against others, and this leads to a definition of particular privileges, and so on.

Certainly, one cannot have a power elite, or a ruling class, without *community of interests.* Mills implies one: the interest of the elite is in the maintenance of the capitalist system as a *system.* But this is never really discussed or analyzed in terms of the meaning of capitalism, the impact of political controls on the society, or the changes in capitalism in the last twenty-five years.

But even if the interest be as broad as Mills implies, one still has the responsibility of identifying the conditions for the maintenance of the system, and the issues and interests involved. Further, one has to see whether there is or has been a *continuity of interests*, in order to chart the cohesiveness or the rise and fall of particular groups.

One of the main arguments about the importance of the *command posts* is the growing centralization of power, which would imply something about the nature of interests. Yet there is almost no sustained discussion of the forces leading to centralization. These are somewhat assumed, and hover over the book, but are never made explicit. Yet only a sustained discussion of these tendencies would, it seems to me, uncover the *locales* of power and their shifts. For example: the role of technology and increasing capital costs as major factors in the size of enterprise; forces in the federalization of power, such as the need for regulation and planning on a national scale because of increased communication, complexity of living, social and military services, and the managing of the economy; the role of foreign affairs. Curiously, Soviet Russia is not even mentioned in the book, although so much of our posture has been dictated by Russian behavior.

Since his focus is on *who* has power, Mills spends considerable effort in tracing the social origins of the men at the top. But, in a disclaimer toward the end of the book (pp. 280-287) he says that the conception of the power elite does not rest upon common social origins (a theme which underlies, say, Schumpeter's notion of the rise and fall of classes) or upon personal friendship, but (although the presumption is not made explicit) upon their "institutional position." But such a statement begs the most important question of all: *the mechanisms of co-ordination among the power holders.* One can say obliquely, as Mills does, that they "meet each other," but this tells us little. If there are "built-in" situations whereby each position merges into another, what are they? One can say, as Mills does, that the new requirements of government require increased recruitment to policy positions from outside groups. But then, what groups—and what do they do? . . .

The Continuity of Power. If in his analysis of politics Mills draws from Pareto, in his image of economic power he becomes a "vulgar" Marxist. Mills notes:

The recent social history of American capitalism does not reveal any distinct break in the continuity of the higher capitalist class. . . . Over the last half-century in the economy as in the political order, there has been a remarkable *continuity of interests*, vested in the *types* of higher economic men who guard and advance them. . . .(p. 147). . .

In his summation of economic control, Mills paints an even more extraordinary picture:

The top corporations are not a set of splendidly isolated giants. They have been knitted together by explicit associations within their respective industries and regions and in supra-associations such as the NAM. These associations organize a unity among the managerial elite and other members of the corporate rich. They translate narrow economic powers into industry-wide and class-wide power; and they use these powers, first, on the economic front, for example, with reference to labor and its organizations; and second, on the political front, for example in their large role in the political sphere. And they infuse into the ranks of smaller businessmen the views of big business (p. 122).

This is a breath-taking statement. . . . That there is some co-ordination is obvious; but unity of this scope—and smoothness—is almost fanciful. Mills cites no evidence for these assertions. The facts, actually, point to the other direction. Trade associations in the United States have declined; they were primarily important during wartime as a means of representing industry on government boards. The NAM has become increasingly feckless, and there has been a decline in member interest and contributions. And industry has divided on a wide variety of issues including labor policy (e.g., the large steel and auto companies have been attacked by General Electric and other firms for accepting s.u.b.—supplementary unemployment benefits).

Mills speaks of "their large role in the political sphere." But against whom are the members of the power elite united, and what kinds of issues unite them in the political sphere? I can think of only one issue on which the top corporations would be united: tax policy. In almost all others, they divide. They are divided somewhat on labor. There are major clashes in areas of self-interest, such as those between railroads, truckers, and the railroads and the airlines; or between coal and oil, and coal and natural gas interests. Except in a vague, ideological sense, there are relatively few political issues on which the managerial elite is united.

The problem of *who unites with whom on what* is an empirical one, and this consideration is missing from Mills' work. If such co-ordination as Mills depicts does exist, a further question is raised as to how it comes about. We know, for example, that as a consequence of bureaucratization, career lines within corporations become lengthened and, as a consequence, there is shorter tenure of office for those who reach the top. Within a ten-year period, A.T.&T. has had three executive officers, all of whom had spent thirty to forty years *within* the corporation. If men spend so much time *within* their corporate shells, how do members of the "elite" get acquainted?

In this preoccupation with elite manipulation, Mills becomes indifferent to the problems of what constitutes problems of power in the everyday life of the country. This is quite evident in the way he summarily dismisses all other questions, short of the "big decisions," as "middle level" and, presumably, without much *real* meaning. *Yet are these not the stuff of politics*, the issues which divide men and create the interest conflicts that involve people in a sense of ongoing reality: labor issues, race problems, tax policy, and the like? Is this not the meaning of power to people as it touches their lives?

The use of the term elite poses another question about the utility of its limits for discussing powers. Why use the word *elite* rather than *decision-makers* or even *rulers*? To talk of *decision-making*, one would have to discuss policy formulation, pressures, etc. To talk of *rule*, one would have to discuss the nature of rule. But if one talks of an elite, one need only discuss institutional position, and one can do so only if, as Mills assumes, the fundamental nature of the system is unchanged, so that one's position is to chart the circulation at the top. The argument that the fundamental nature of the system—i.e., that of basic legitimations, of continuity of the capitalist class—is unchanged in a curious one, for if power has become so centralized and synchronized, as Mills now assumes, is this not a fundamental change in the system?

Yet, even if one wants to talk in terms of elites, there have been key shifts in power in American society: the breakup of family capitalism (and this is linked to a series of shifts in power in Western society as a whole), but most importantly—and obviously—the decisive role of the political arena.

From Economics to Politics. In the decade before World War I, the growing power of the trusts, the direct influence of the bankers in the economy, the ideological rise of socialism all tended to focus attention on the class system as the hidden but actually decisive element in shaping society and social change. . . .

But later historiography has considerably modified this crude chiaroscuro and has drawn in many subtle tones between the black and the white. . . .

This is not to deny the existence of classes or the nature of a class system. *But one cannot, unless the society is highly stratified, use the class structure for direct political analysis.* A class system defines the *mode* of gaining wealth and privilege in a society. (This mode can be land [real property], corporate title ["fictitious" property], skill [technical or managerial], mercenaries [*condottieri*], or direct political allocation [party, bureaucracy, or army], and this class system has to be legitimated, in legal forms, in order to assure its continuity. Often this wealth and privilege carries with it power and prestige, but there is no direct correlation.) But most important, whatever the mode, class analysis does not tell us directly *who* exercises the power, nor does it tell us much about the competition within that mode for power. Unless that mode and its legitimations are directly challenged, one rarely sees a class acting as a class in unified fashion. Once a specific mode is established, competition for privilege within the system is high, and various and different interests develop. The growing complexity of society necessarily multiplies those interests, regional or functional, and in an open society the political arena—unless there is a conflict to overthrow the system—is a place where different interests fight it out for advantage. That is why, usually, the prism of "class" is too crude to follow the swift play of diverse political groups. . . .

At one point in later American history, the dominant business class—the plutocracy, rather than any landed squirearchy—came close to imprinting a clear mark on American politics. By the turn of the twentieth century the growing industrial class had scored a smashing economic victory. With that victory came some efforts to dissolve the structure of group interests by developing a pervasive political ideology which could also serve the emergent national feeling. One such attempt was the doctrine of imperialism in the "manifest destiny" of Beveridge and the "Americanism" of Franklin Giddings. This was alien to a heterogeneous people, or at least premature. The second and more successful effort was in the identification of capitalism with democracy. The early commercial class had feared democracy as a *political* instrument whereby the "swinish multitude" (Burke) would prepare the way for a radical despotism. The ideology of victorious industrial capitalism defined democracy almost completely in agreeable *economic* terms, as liberty of contract.

If the dominant business class was unable to exercise direct political control of the society, it could establish its ideological hegemony. While in the period from 1880 to 1912 the middle class (small farmers and businessmen, and many professionals) had supported the sporadic anti-trust and antimonopoly outbursts, such opinions and movements were dissolved by the subsequent two decades of war, prosperity, and propaganda.

This unity burst with the bubble of prosperity because the ideologists of free enterprise, rugged or otherwise, did not understand the realities of the "socialized" economy that had come into being. They had failed to grasp the degree to which this market economy imposes a particular type of dependency upon everyone. . . .

The public face of the New Deal was a set of sweeping social reforms, and, quite naively, some writers, and, indeed, Roosevelt himself, have called the New Deal an assertion of human rights over property rights. But such terms carry little meaning, either philosophically or pragmatically. Are "support prices" for farmers a property right or a human right? In effect, what the New Deal did was to *legitimate* the idea of *group* rights, and the claim of groups, as groups, rather than individuals, for governmental support. Thus unions won the right to bargain collectively and, through the union shop, to enforce a group decision over individuals; the aged won pensions, the farmers gained subsidies; the veterans received benefits; the minority groups received legal protections, etc. None of these items, in themselves, were unique. Together, they added up to an extraordinary social change. Similarly, the government has always had some role in directing the economy. But the permanently enlarged role, dictated on the one hand by the necessity to maintain full employment, and, on the other, by the expanded military establishment, created a vastly different set of powers in Washington than ever before in our history. . . .

In the emergence of the political economy a new kind of decision-making has taken place. In the market society, peoples' wants are registered by their "dollar votes," as part of the automatic interaction of supply and demand. The sum total of individual dollars-and-cents decisions, operating independently of each other, added up, as Bentham thought, to a social decision, e.g., the general consensus. Thus, when decisions on the allocation of resources operated through the market, dollars, not ideology, determined what was to be produced. In this sense, economics was the key to social power, and politics its pale reflection.

But politics, operating through the government, has more and more become the means of registering a social and economic decision. Here, instead of acting independently as in a market, the individual is forced to work through particular collectivities to enforce his will. Since in a managed economy, "politics," not dollars, determines major production, the intervention of the government not only sharpens pressure-group identifications but forces each to adopt an ideolgy which can justify its claims and which can square with some concept of "national interest."

The Types of Decisions. Ultimately, if one wants to discuss power, it is more fruitful to discuss it in terms of *types of decisions* rather than elites. And curiously, Mills, I would argue, ultimately agrees, for the real heart of the book is a polemic against those who say that decisions are made democratically in the United States. Mills writes:

More and more of the fundamental issues never came to any point of decision before Congress . . . much less before the electorate (p. 255).

Insofar as the structural clue to the power elite today lies in the political order, that clue is the decline of politics as genuine and public debates of alternative decisions . . . America is now in considerable part more a formal political democracy (p. 224).

Now, to some extent this is true, but not, it seems to me, with the invidious aspect with which Mills invests the judgment.

In many instances, even the "interested public" feels itself "trapped," so to speak, by its inability to affect events. Much of this arises out of the *security* nature of problems, so that issues are often fought out in a bureaucratic labyrinth. The decision on the H-bomb was one such issue. Here we had groups of scientists versus a section of the military, particularly SAC. Unless one assumes that everyone ever involved in decision-making is a member of the power elite—which is circular—*we have to locate the source of such decisions, for these are the central problems of a sociology of power.*

But another, equally important reason for being unable to affect events is the onset of what one can only call, inaptly, "technical decision making": the fact that once a policy decision is made, or once a technological change comes to the fore, or once some long crescive change has become manifest, a number of other consequences, if one is being "functionally rational," almost inevitably follow. Thus, shifts of power become "technical" concomitants of such "decisions," and a sociology of power must identify the kinds of consequences which follow the different kinds of decisions. . . .

To ignore the problems of this type of "imperative" decision-making is, it seems to me, to ignore the stuff of politics as well as the new nature of power in contemporary society. The theory of the "power elite" implies a unity of purpose and community of interest among the elite that is not proven or demonstrated. It is simply asserted.

THE DISTRIBUTION OF POWER IN AMERICAN SOCIETY

Talcott Parsons

Mills' central theme is the contention—in contrast to what he refers to as the traditional view of the political pluralism of American society—that there has developed to an unprecedented degree, in the last generation or so, a concentration of power in the hands of a small, relatively tightly integrated group of people. These are defined as the people occupying the institutional "command posts" of the society, the places where the decisions are made that have the greatest immediate and direct influence on the course of events in the society and on the shaping of its future and that of the rest of the world, so far as that future is dependent on what happens in the United States. Mills argues that the power of this group has grown disproportionately to the growth in size and power of the society as a whole.

The "command posts" in question are centered in large-scale organizations, which are certainly a prominent feature of American society. The power elite are in general those who occupy the decision-making positions in these large organizations. Mills identifies these in only two basic areas, business and government—although for his purposes the field of government is subdivided into the military and the political sectors; indeed, he almost tends to treat the military as independent of the rest of government. He clearly is thinking of the centralized type of organization where a few "top executives" exercise the main immediate decision-making power, in contrast to the democratic association with a somewhat more decentralized structure of authority and influence. It seems to be largely on this ground that he contends that the executive branch of the federal government has gained a pronounced ascendancy over the legislative. He relegates Congress—even the most influential group of Senators—to what he calls the "middle level" of the power structure; such people do not belong to the "power elite". . . .

Generally, Mills is rather vague on the relations between the power elite and other elements which in some sense enjoy rather high prestige. He emphasizes the prominence of lawyers among the "political directorate," but there is no clear analysis of the role of professional groups in the occupational structure generally; one presumes that except for a few lawyers who are successful in politics or business, and perhaps some engineers, professional people do not belong to the power elite. Similarly he emphasizes that members of the power elite have more than the average amount of education, and in particular he stresses the proportion who have been to select private schools and to "Ivy League" colleges. In general, he is greatly concerned about the fact that the power elite are not "representative" of the population as a whole in the sense of constituting a random sample by socio-economic origin, by education, by ethnic group, etc. . . .

Of the three main subgroups, Mills treats the "political directorate" as by far the

SOURCE: *From Structure and Process in Modern Societies* by Talcott Parsons, pp. 201-222 and 225. Reprinted with permission of The Macmillan Company. © 1960 by The Free Press.

weakest. It has, according to him, been greatly infiltrated by the business element, so that it can scarcely be treated as independent. Hence virtually the only element independent of what might be called the business oligarchy is the military—and this, he holds, is coming increasingly to fuse with the business group, or at least to form a close community of interest with it.

The pluralistic components of our older political traditions, Mills feels, are rooted primarily in local groupings—partly, of course, through the constitutional provisions which establish federalism and make Congressional representation dependent on local constituencies. But the operations of the big organizations have become national in scope, and often international. Hence structures rooted in localism have simply been pushed into a secondary position.

But at the same time Mills contends that the structural base of authentic localism has been progressively atrophied through the development of what he calls the "mass society." The most conspicuous phenomena of the mass society are the prevalence and characteristics of the media of mass communication, which tend to serve as instruments of power elite out of the reach of locally based "publics" and influential elements in them. . . .

Mills repeatedly disavows any intention of presenting a "conspiratorial" interpretation of American social and political development. He stresses the institutional positions occupied by his elite rather than their personalities and conspiratorial activities. Nevertheless he often comes very close to this implication because of his special theory that a peculiar irresponsibility attaches to the elite and their actions. By this he seems to mean the absence or relative ineffectiveness of formal legal restraints or of a system of "checks and balances" of the sort which has traditionally been associated with our political system. His contention, thus, is that the power elite has been freed from the historic restraints of our society and uses its power in terms of what he calls a "higher immorality"—a conception which is not very clearly explained.

Finally, it should be mentioned that in this, as in some of his previous writings, Mills' general tone toward both men and institutions is sharply caustic. *The Power Elite* certainly purports to be an exposition and an explanation of what has been happening in American society, but it is equally an indictment. There is no pretense of even trying to maintain a scientific neutrality; the book is a fiery and sarcastic attack on the pretensions of the "higher circles" in America, either to competence in exercise of their responsibilities, or to moral legitimation of their position. . . .

II. In my opinion, two salient sets of processes have been going on in American society during the past half-century, the combination of which encompasses the main facts which are essential to our problem. The first of these is the dynamic of a maturing industrial society, including not only the highly industrialized economy itself but its setting in the society as a whole—notably, its political system and class structure (in a wider sense of the term "class" than Mills')—and the repercussions of the industrial development on the rest of the society. The second concerns the altered position of the United States in world society, which is a consequence in part of our own economic growth, in part of a variety of exogenous changes, including the relative decline of the Western European powers, the rise of Soviet Russia, and the break-up of the "colonial" organization of much of the non-white world. The enormous enhancement of American power and responsibility in the world has taken place in a relatively short time and was bound to have profound repercussions on the characteristics of our own society. Our old political isolation has disappeared and given way to the deepest of involvements.

My first thesis is that these two processes *both* work in the direction of increasing the relative importance of government in our society and, with it, of political power. But their impact has been all the greater because of the extent to which the United States has been an almost specifically non-political society. This has been evidenced above all in the institutions and tradition of political decentralization already mentioned, one aspect of which is the localism which Mills discusses. A second, however, has been a cultural tradition which has emphasized economic values—an emphasis on enterprise and production in an activist sense, not a merely passive hedonistic valuation of the enjoyment of material well-being. Moreover, the virtually unimpeded process of settlement of a continent in political isolation from the main system of world powers has favored maintenance of this emphasis to a greater extent than would otherwise have readily been possible.

At some points in his discussion, Mills seems to look back to the Jeffersonian picture of a system of economic production consisting mainly of small farmers and artisans, with presumably a small mercantile class mediating between them and consumers. Clearly this is not a situation compatible with high industrial development, in either of two respects. First, the order of decentralization of production, where the standard unit is a family-size one, is incompatible with either the organization or the technology necessary for high industrialism. Second, the "Jeffersonian" economy is not one in which economic production is differentiated from other social functions in specialized organizations; instead, the typical productive unit is at the same time a kinship unit and a unit of citizenship in the community. . . .

Leadership is an essential function in all social systems which, with their increase of scale and their functional differentiation, tend to become more specialized. I think we can, within considerable limits, regard the emergence of the large firm with operations on a nation-wide basis as a "normal" outcome of the process of growth and differentiation of the economy. Similarly, the rise to prominence within the firm of specialized executive functions is also a normal outcome of a process of growth in size and in structural differentiation. The question then arises whether the process of concentration of firms, and of executive power within firms, has "gone too far" because it has been greatly influenced by factors extraneous to the process of economic development itself.

Mills makes the assertion that the size of the large firm has exceeded the limits of economic efficiency. He presents no evidence, and I think most competent persons would regard this as an exceedingly difficult question. There is, however, one line of evidence not cited by Mills which has a bearing on it. It is true that the absolute size of firms has steadily increased—General Motors today is larger than any firm of the 1920's. But the *relative* share of the largest firms in the production of the economy has remained essentially stable for more than a generation, a fact which points to some kind of equilibrium condition with respect to the degree of concentration in the system as a whole. . . .

Generally speaking, Mills' argument is that the power of the very rich and the corporate rich *within* the economy, is inordinately great and, by virtue of the factor of cumulative advantage, is becoming continually greater. At the very least, I think, it can be said that his case is not proved and that there is equally good, if not better, evidence for an alternative view, particularly with reference to the trend.

First, I am not able to accept Mills' close identification of the very rich (i.e., the holders of "great fortunes") with the "corporate rich" (the primary holders of executive power in business organizations) as a single class in any very useful sense. Certainly, in the "heroic age" of American Capitalism, from the Civil War to just after the turn of the century, the dominant figures were the entrepreneurs who, mainly as the founders of great enterprises and as the bankers and promoters concerned with mergers and reorganizations and the like, came to control these great organizations. But the dominant sociological fact of the outcome of that era was that these owning groups did not, as a group, succeed in consolidating their position precisely *within* their own enterprises and in the economy. It is a notorious fact that the *very* large enterprise, still largely under family control through property holdings, is much more the exception than the rule. Instead, the control has passed—by no means fully, but for the most part—to professional career executives, who have not reached their positions through the exercise of *property* rights but through some sort of process of appointment and promotion. . . .

There are, above all, two ways in which Mills' treatment obscures the importance and nature of this shift. First, he continues to speak of power *within* the economy as based on property. To a considerable degree, of course, this is legally true, since the legal control of enterprise rests with stockholders. But, as Berle and Means first made abundantly clear, very generally it is not substantively true. In the old-style family enterprise, still predominant in the small-business sector of the economy, the functions of management and ownership are fused in the same people. In the larger enterprise they have by and large become differentiated. The fact that executives receive large salaries and bonuses is not to be twisted into an assumption that they control, so far as they do, through their property rights. Paradoxical as it may seem, a relatively backward industrial economy like that of France is far more *property*-based than is the case with the United States. In general, property holdings have not, of course, been expropriated, except for their diminution through inheritance and income taxes, which are not as negligible as Mills maintains. What has happened is that their relation to the *power* structure of the economy has been greatly altered. Mills almost entirely passes over this change.

The second problem concerns the process of recruitment in the higher occupational reaches of the economy. It is entirely clear that the process operates in the higher reaches overwhelmingly by appointment, i.e., the decisions of superiors as individuals or in small groups as to who should occupy certain positions. It is also true that the process is relatively unformalized—e.g., there are no competitive examinations and few, if any, formal qualifications of training. But from these facts Mills concludes, and again and again reiterates, that executive competence has very little, if anything, to do with the selection, that it is an overwhelmingly arbitrary process of choosing those who are congenial to the selectors, presumably because they can be counted upon to be "yes men." At the very least this contention is unproved, and I seriously doubt its correctness. There are certainly many difficulties and imperfections in the selection process. But I think it almost certain that higher levels of competence are selected than would on the average be the case through kinship ascription, and that, as such processes go, the levels selected are relatively high. . . .

So far I have been speaking about the nature and power position of the elite *within* the economy. The general tenor of my argument has been that, given the nature of an industrial society, a relatively well-defined elite or leadership group *should be expected to develop* in the business world; it is out of the question that power should be diffused equally among an indefinite number of very small units, as the ideal of pure competition and a good deal of the ideology of business itself would have it. . . .

The problem of an elite within the economy must, however, be clearly distinguished from that of an elite in the society as a whole and the power position occupied by such an elite. There are two main orders of questions bearing on the transition from one to the other. Though a thorough consideration of this transition would lead into very far-reaching questions, for present purposes one can be treated rather briefly. Mills gives us the impression that "eliteness" in any society, including our own, is overwhelmingly a question of the power that an individual or a group can command. By this, he means. . . influence on the "big" decisions directly affecting what happens in the society in the short run. But there are many elements in the society which are relatively powerless in this sense, but nevertheless of the greatest functional importance. Our society has almost divested kinship units as such of important power in this sense. But this does not mean at all that the family has ceased to be important. Closely linked with this is the question of the feminine role. Women qua women by and large do not have a position of power comparable to that of men; but this is not to say that they are unimportant—otherwise how can we account for the extent of our national preoccupations with questions of sexuality? Finally, there is a *distinct* difference between the rank-order of occupations—which, relative to other role-types, are closely involved with decision-making in a society like ours—by power and by prestige. The most striking case is the relatively high position of the professions relative to executive roles in business, as revealed by the famous North-Hatt data. Physicians as a group do not exercise great power, but there is no reason to question their very high prestige, which has been demonstrated in study after study.

The second main context, however, directly concerns the question of power. In a complex society the primary locus of power lies in the political system. There are many subtle analytical problems involved in the delineation of this system and its functions in the society which cannot be gone into here; this formula will have to suffice. Two questions are, however, primary for our purposes: the degree of differentiation of the political system from other systems; and its own internal structure. These two problems, it will be noted, parallel those raised with reference to the economy.

For historical reasons, it seems clear that the development of the American political system, since the breakdown of the first synthesis associated with the "founders of the Republic," has lagged behind that of the economy. This is a function primarily of the two factors already noted—the economic emphasis inherent in our system of values, and the relative lack of urgency of certain political problems because of our especially protected and favored national position. Relative to the economic structure, which had by that time grown enormously, the political was at its weakest in the period from the Civil War to the end of the century; this situation is sketched by Mills in broadly correct terms. Since then, both internal exigencies and the exigencies of our international position have been stimuli for major changes.

Internally, beyond the more elementary provisions for law and order and essential minimum services—much of this, of course, on a local basis—the main focus of the development of our political system has been *control* of economic organization and processes, and coping with some of the social consequences of economic growth and industrialization. The process started well before the turn of the century with the Interstate Commerce legislation and the Anti-Trust Act and continued through the New Deal era, not steadily but with waves of new measures and levels of political control.

A major problem in relation to Mills' analysis is whether this is "genuine" control. His view seems to be that at times it has been, but that on balance it is the business power-holders who control government, not vice versa. . . . In my opinion this is a misinterpretation. If genuine and, in some sense, effective controls had not been imposed, I find it impossible to understand the bitter and continuing opposition on the part of business to the measures which have been taken. Even some of those most completely taken for granted now, like the Federal Reserve system, were bitterly fought at the time. It therefore seems to me to be the sounder interpretation that there has been a genuine growth of autonomous governmental power—apart from the military aspect, which will be discussed presently—and that one major aspect of this has been relatively effective control of the business system. This control and the growth of "big government" have been generally accepted in the society as a whole. The participation of big-business men in governmental processes is by no means to be interpreted as a simple index of their power to dominate government in their own interests, as Mills often seems to maintain.

To me, another indication of Mills' biased view of the governmental situation is his almost complete failure even to mention the political parties, or to analyze their differences. . . . So Mills is practically forced to the view that the alleged control operates above and beyond the party system. This seems to be connected with his relegation of the legislative branch to the "middle level" of power. I have strong reservations about this, but also it must not be forgotten that the presidency is the biggest prize of all in party politics, and it is its importance which forms the primary integrating focus of our particular type of party system. Surely the presidency is not simply the football of an inner clique which manipulates the executive branch independently of the party.

Mills, of course, recognizes that the aftermath of two world wars, the rise of Communist power, and the relative decline of the older Western Great Powers provide the occasion for the increasing prominence of the military group in our governmental system. Before these changes—and, indeed, to a remarkable extent, as late as the 1950's—the military played a far smaller role in this country than in any other society of comparable scale and organizational and technological development. Part of the change may be interpreted as simply the redressing of a balance. But it seems to me correct to say that for the last ten years there has been a special situation attributable to the extremely unsettled condition of the world at large and to the difficulties entailed for the American system, given its background, in meeting the problem on its own terms. There is thus a sense in which it is true that the higher military officers have tended to fill a vacuum in the field of national decision-making. There are two main points to be made about Mills' treatment of the matter. First, more in this field than perhaps any other, Mills' discussion is marred by a hasty tendency to generalize from very recent short-run developments to the long-run prospects of the structure of the society. Even here he fails to mention that in certain crucial questions the recommendations of the military have been overruled by civilian authority. . . .

Related to the position of the higher military officers is what Mills calls the "military metaphysic," meaning the definition of international problems in terms of the primacy of military force. That there has been such a tendency, and that it has gone beyond the objective requirements of the situation, seem to be unquestionable. But I very much doubt whether it is as absolute as many of Mills' statements make it appear, and a swing in another direction is discernible. This seems to be another case of Mills' tendency to make large generalizations about major trends from short-run experience.

Finally, let us say a word about what Mills calls the "political directorate"—that is, the non-military component in the groups most influential in the affairs of government and politics. Again I think there is a certain correctness in his contention that a definite weakness exists here, and that the high participation both of business and of military elements in the exercise of power is related to this. But a difficulty arises in terms of the perspective on American society which I have been emphasizing throughout. Both the non-political stress in American social structure and values generally, and the recency and intensity of the pressures to build up this aspect of our structure would lead one to predict that it would be a major focus of strain. American society has not developed a well-integrated political-government elite, in the sense that it has developed a relatively well-integrated business-executive group. For this reason responsibility has been carried— imperfectly, of course—by a very miscellaneous group which includes members of the business and military groups, as would be expected, but also "politicians," in the usual sense of people making an at least partial career out of elective office and the influencing of elections; professional people, particularly lawyers but also economists, political scientists, and even natural scientists. . . ; journalists; and, a very important element, upper-class people in more than the purely economic sense that Mills employs, of whom Franklin Roosevelt was one and Adlai Stevenson, though also a lawyer, is another. In my opinion, the structure of the American political leadership group is far from a settled thing. It certainly is not settled in terms of the long-run dominance of a business-military coalition.

Mills holds that the United States has no higher civil service at all, in the European sense, and seems to imply that we should have. There is relative truth in his empirical contention, though I think he tends to underestimate the real influence of "non-political" government officials on longer-run policy. Good examples are the Department of Agriculture and the Reclamation Service of the Department of the Interior—and now, increasingly, the Public Health Service. I think that this is even true of the Foreign Service. . . .

At least it seems highly probable that, in the nature of the case, the tendency will be toward a strengthening of the element of professional governmental officials who are essentially independent both of short-run "politics" and of elements extraneous to the structure of government and its responsibilities. In fact, the military officer is a special case of this type, and though his role is not stabilized, it presumably must come to be more important than it traditionally has been. However, it is questionable how far the specific models of civil service organization either of Britain or of Continental Europe—particularly, certain of their special connections with the class structure and the educational system—are appropriate to American conditions. . . .

Above all, I do not think that Mills has made a convincing case for his contention that the power structure impinging directly on American government is in process of crystallizing into a top business-military coalition with a much weaker political "junior partner" whose main function presumably is, by manipulation of the mass media and the political process in the narrower sense, to keep the great majority of Americans from protesting too loudly or even from awakening to what allegedly is "really" going on. On a number of counts which have been reviewed, there is a case on a short-run basis for part of his interpretation. But I think that the kinds of factors brought out in the previous discussion make it extremely dubious that even the partial correctness of his interpretation of a current situation will prove to be a sound indicator of what is to be expected over such longer periods as a generation or more.

My conviction on this point is strengthened by a variety of other considerations which, for reasons of space, cannot be discussed here, but may be mentioned. First, I am extremely skeptical of Mills' interpretation of what he calls the "mass society," which includes the structural position of the great majority of the American population. In this he ignores both kinship and friendship, and the whole mass of associational activities and relationships. One example is the spread of church membership—which I suppose Mills would dismiss as simply an escape from the boredom of white-collar life, but in my opinion is of considerable positive significance.

Another very important complex which Mills either treats cavalierly or ignores completely involves education at the various levels, and with it the enormous development, over a century, of science and learning and the professions resting upon them. It is true that the people rooted in these areas of the social structure are not prominent in the power elite, and are even subject to some conflicts with it; but they would not be expected to be prominent in this way—their functions in the society are different. Nonetheless, they must be taken very seriously into account in a diagnosis of what has been happening to the society as a whole. One of the most important sets of facts concerns the ways in which the services of technical professional groups have come to penetrate the structures both of business and of government, a circumstance which over a period of time has greatly enhanced the role of the universities as custodians of learning and sources of trained personnel.

Finally, there is one special case of a professional group whose role Mills treats with serious inadequacy—namely, lawyers. First, he dismisses the judicial branch of government as just "trailing along," with the implication that with a slight lag it simply does the bidding of the "real" holders of power. This seems to be a most biased appraisal of the role of the courts. Not to speak of the longer-run record, the initiative taken by the courts in the matter of racial segregation and in the reassertion of civil liberties after the miasma of McCarthyism does not appear to me to be compatible with Mills' views. Similar considerations seem to apply to various aspects of the role of the private legal profession, notably with respect to the *control* of processes in the business world. Mills tends to assume that the relation between law and business is an overwhelmingly one-way relation; lawyers are there to serve the interests of businessmen and essentially have no independent influence. This, I think, is an illusion stemming largely from Mills' preoccupation with a certain kind of power. His implicit reasoning seems to be that since lawyers have less power than businessmen, they do not really "count."

III. The last problem I wish to raise, therefore, concerns Mills' conception of power and its use as a category of social analysis. Unfortunately, the concept of power is not a settled one in the social sciences, either in political science or in sociology. Mills, however, adopts one main version of the concept without attempting to justify it. This is what may be called the "zero-sum" concept; power, that is to say, is power *over* others. The power A has in a system is, necessarily and by definition, at the expense of B. This conception of power then is generalized to the whole conception of the political process when Mills says that "Politics is a struggle for power." ...

The essential point at present is that, to Mills, power is not a facility for the performance of function in, and on behalf of, the society as a system, but is interpreted exclusively as a facility for getting what one group, the holders of power, wants by preventing another group, the "outs," from getting what it wants.

What this conception does is to elevate a secondary and derived aspect of a total phenomenon into the central place. A comparison may help to make this clear. There is obviously a distributive aspect of wealth and it is in a sense true that the wealth of one person or group by definition cannot also be possessed by another group. Thus the *distribution* of wealth is, in the nature of the case, a focus of conflicts of interest in a society. But what of the positive functions of wealth and of the conditions of its production? It has become fully established that the wealth available for distribution can only come about through the processes of production, and that these processes require the "co-operation" or integration of a variety of different agencies—what economists call the "factors of production." Wealth, in turn, is a generalized class of facilities available to units of the soceity—individuals and various types and levels of collectivities—for whatever uses may be important to them. But even apart from the question of what share each gets, the fact that there should be wealth to divide, and how much, cannot be taken for granted as given except within a very limited context.

Very similar things can be said about power in a political sense. Power is a generalized facility or resource in the society. It has to be divided or allocated, but it also has to be produced and it has collective as well as distributive functions. It is the capacity to mobilize the resources of the society for the attainment of goals for which a general "public" commitment has been made, or may be made. It is mobilization, above all, of the action of persons and groups, which is *binding* on them by virtue of their position in the society. Thus within a much larger complex Mills concentrates almost exclusively on the distributive aspect of power. He is interested only in *who* has power and what *sectoral* interests he is serving with his power, not in how power comes to be generated or in what communal rather than sectorial interests are served.

The result is a highly selective treatment of the whole complex of the power problem. There is, in the first place, a tendency to exaggerate the empirical importance of power by alleging that it is only power which "really" determines what happens in a society. Against this, I would place the view that power is only one of several cognate factors in the determination of social events. This bias of Mills is particularly evident in his tendency to foreshorten social processes and emphasize overwhelmingly short-run factors. There is, secondly, the tendency to think of power as presumptively illegitimate; if people exercise considerable power, it must be because they have somehow usurped it where they had no right and they intend to use it to the detriment of others. This comes out most conspicuously in Mills' imputation of irresponsibility to his "power elite" and the allegation, vaguely conceived and presented with very little evidence, that they are characterized by a "higher immorality" . . . .

Back of all this lies, I am sure, an only partly manifest "metaphysical" position which Mills shares with Veblen and a long line of indicters of modern industrial society. I would call it a utopian conception of an ideal society in which power does not play a part at all.

This is a philosophical and ethical background which is common both to utopian liberalism and socialism in one society and to a good deal of "capitalist" ideology. They have in common an underlying "individualism" of a certain type. This is not primarily individualism in the sense that the welfare and rights of the individual constitute fundamental moral values, but rather that *both* individual and collective rights are alleged to be promoted only by *minimizing* the positive organization of social groups. Social organization as such is presumptively bad because, on a limited, short-run basis, it always and necessarily limits the freedom of the individual to do exactly what he may happen to want. The question of the deeper and longer-run dependence of the goals and capacities of individuals themselves on social organization is simply shoved into the background. From this point of view, both power in the individual enterprise and power in the larger society are presumptively evil in themselves, because they represent the primary visible focus of the capacity of somebody to see to it that somebody else acts or does not act in certain ways, whether at the moment he wants to or not. . . .

Hence, in my opinion, many of the difficulties of Mills' analysis of a crucial problem in American society arise from his failure to transcend the dilemmas inherent in much of the individualistic tradition in American and, more broadly, in Western thought. It seems to me that he is clearly and, in the degree to which he pushes this position, unjustifiably anti-capitalist. He is partly pro-liberal and probably even more pro-socialist. But in the American scene a choice between these old alternatives of ideological orientation is no longer enough. It is necessary not only to criticize existing conditions from the older philosophical or ideological points of view, but to take serious stock of the ideological assumptions underlying the bulk of American political discussion of such problems as power.

WHO HAS THE POWER?

David Riesman

In terms of class, or elite theory, the first decades of American politics can be described as a period of conscious leadership by a mercantile-aristocratic group subject to occasional check, even displacement, by farmers and artisans who usually left politics alone. We might think of the latter as veto groups, and in that sense we can view the period between the end of the Civil War and 1900 as an exceptional period when the old veto groups were in retreat and the new ones had not yet found themselves. Yet, though the analogy between today and a hundred years ago is helpful, it conceals important differences in the mood and structure of the veto groups. Perhaps the most important change is the numerical elaboration and complexity of the latter and the fact that they not only exercise the residual veto of the farmer and artisan groups in the earlier period but also are constantly pressing their claims on the social and political sphere. These veto groups are lobbies, and also more than lobbies. . . .

The Veto Groups. The lobby in the old days actually ministered to the clear leadership, privilege, and imperative of the business ruling class. Today we have substituted for that leadership a series of groups, each of which has struggled for and finally attained a power to stop things conceivably inimical to its interests and, within far narrower limits, to start things. The movie-censoring groups, the farm groups and the labor and professional groups, the major ethnic groups and major regional groups, have in many instances succeeded in maneuvering themselves into a position in which they are able to neutralize those who might attack them. The very increase in the number of these groups, and in the kinds of interests "practical" and "fictional" they are protecting, marks therefore, a decisive change from the lobbies of an earlier day.

SOURCE: David Riesman, with Nathan Glazer and Revel Denney, *The Lonely Crowd* (New Haven: Yale University Press, 1951), pp. 242-248, 252, 254. Copyright ©1950 by Yale University Press. Reprinted by permission. Footnotes have been omitted.

There is a change in method, too, in the way the groups are organized, the way they handle each other, and the way they handle the public, that is, the unorganized.

These veto groups are neither leader-groups nor led-groups. The only leaders of national scope left in the United States today are those who can placate the veto groups. The only followers left in the United States today are those unorganized and sometimes disorganized unfortunates who have not yet invented their group.

Within the veto groups, there is, of course, the same struggle of antagonistic cooperators for top places that goes on in other bureaucratic setups. Among the veto groups competition is monopolistic; rules of fairness and fellowship dictate how far one can go. Despite the rules there are, of course, occasional "price wars," like the jurisdictional disputes of labor unions or Jewish defense groups; these are ended by negotiation, the division of territory, and the formation of a roof organization for the previously split constituency. These big monopolies, taken as a single group, are in devastating competition with the not yet grouped, much as the fair-trade economy competes against the free-trade economy. These latter scattered followers find what protection they can in the interstices around the group-minded.

Each of the veto groups in this pattern is capable of an aggressive move, but the move is sharply limited in its range by the way in which the various groups have already cut up the sphere of politics and arrayed certain massive expectations behind each cut. Both within the groups and in the situation created by their presence, the political mood tends to become one of other-directed tolerance. The vetos so bind action that it is hard for the moralizers to conceive of a program that might in any large way alter the relations between political and personal life or between political and economic life. In the amorphous power structure created by the veto groups it is hard to distinguish rulers from the ruled, those to be aided from those to be opposed, those on your side from those on the other side. This very pattern encourages the inside-dopester who can unravel the personal linkages, and discourages the enthusiast or indignant who wants to install the good or fend off the bad. Probably, most of all it encourages the new-style indifferent who feels and is often told that his and everyone else's affairs are in the hands of the experts and that laymen, though they should "participate," should not really be too inquisitive or aroused.

By their very nature the veto groups exist as defense groups, not as leadership groups. If it is true that they do "have the power," they have it by virtue of a necessary mutual tolerance in which each of these groups allows all the other groups to dominate its agenda of attention. More and more they mirror each other in their style of political action, including their interest in public relations and their emphasis on internal harmony of feelings. There is a tendency for organizations as differently oriented as, say, the Young Socialists and the 4-H Club, to adopt similar psychological methods of salesmanship to obtain and solidify their recruits. . . .

Various groups have discovered that they can go quite far in the amorphous power situation in America without being stopped. Our society is behaviorally open enough to permit a considerable community of gangsters a comfortable living under a variety of partisan political regimes. In their lack of concern for public relations these men are belated businessmen. So are some labor leaders who have discovered their power to hold up the economy, though in most situations what is surprising is the moderation of labor demands—a moderation based on psychological restraints rather than any power that could effectively be interposed. Likewise, it is sometimes possible for an aggressive group, while not belonging to the entrenched veto-power teams, to push a bill through a legislature. Thus, the original Social Security Act went through Congress, so far as I can discover, because it was pushed by a devoted but tiny cohort; the large veto groups including organized labor were neither very much for it nor very much against it.

For similar reasons those veto groups are in many political situations strongest whose own memberships are composed of veto groups, especially veto groups of one. The best example of this is the individual farmer who, after one of the farm lobbies has made a deal for him, can still hold out for more. The farm lobby's concern for the reaction of other veto groups, such as labor unions, cuts little ice with the individual farmer. This fact may strengthen the lobby in a negotiation: it can use its internal public relations problems as a counter in bargaining, very much as does a diplomat who tells a foreign minister that he must consider how Senator McKellar will react. For, no matter what the other-directedness of the lobby's leaders, they cannot bind their membership to carry out a public relations approach. Many labor unions have a similar power because they cannot control their memberships who, if not satisfied with a deal made by the union, can walk off or sabotage a job.

In contrast, those veto groups are often weaker whose other-directed orientation can dominate their memberships. Large corporations are vulnerable to a call from the White House because, save for a residual indignant like Sewell Avery, their officials are themselves other-directed and because, once the word from the chief goes out, the factory superintendents, no matter how boiling mad, have to fall into line with the new policy by the very nature of the centralized organization for which they work: they can sabotage top management on minor matters but not, say, on wage rates or tax accounting. As against this, the American Catholic Church possesses immense veto-group power because it combines a certain amount of centralized command—and a public picture of a still greater amount—with a highly decentralized priesthood and a membership organization of wide-ranging ethnic, social, and political loyalties; this structure permits great flexibility in bargaining.

These qualifications, however, do not change the fact that the veto groups, taken together, constitute a new buffer region between the old, altered, and thinning extremes of those who were once leaders and led. It is both the attenuation of leaders and led, and the other-oriented doings of these buffers, that help to give many moralizers a sense of vacuum in American political life. In the economy the monopolies, with their potential for delaying technological progress, are more than held at bay by the leverage of the remaining free sectors and by the inevitable—and inevitably fierce—competition among groups of monopolies for the consumer-dollar vote. In politics a similar form of monopolistic competition goes on as the veto groups in certain situations compete for the unorganized or try to steal a march on one another. But as is obvious, the dollar vote is a far more sensitive instrument than the ballot-box vote, despite efforts, for example by proportional representation, to make the latter more flexible. And while some of the unorganized sectors in politics might like to prod the veto groups in the way the free-trade economy prods the fair-trade economy, they lack the dynamite of technological invention. Thus, such progress as there is in national politics seems slow in comparison with the urgent needs of the present day and in comparison with the hopes, or the fears, of the remaining moralizers. . . .

There are, of course, still some veto groups that have more power than others and some individuals who have more power than others. But the determination of who these are has to be made all over again for our time: we cannot be satisfied with the answers given by Marx, Mosca, Michels, Pareto, Weber, Veblen, or Burnham, though we can learn from all of them. Paradoxically, it may be that while the mesas of the veto groups have replaced the mountain peaks of class in the United States, power has nevertheless become more concentrated in another respect, namely in the decline of the older separations of power, both constitutional and social-psychological. Most of the constitutional separations—executive, legislative, and judicial; upper chamber and lower chamber; federal and state—are of diminishing importance. So are the social-psychological separations that formerly buttressed the political ones: the separations between those who sought power through wealth and wealth through power; between those locally oriented and those nationally oriented; between those who looked to business models and those who looked to agrarian ones. . . .

Rather, power on the national scene must be viewed in terms of issues. It is possible that, where an issue involves only two or three veto groups, themselves tiny minorities, the official or unofficial broker among the groups can be quite powerful—but only on that issue. However, where the issue involves the country as a whole, no individual or group leadership is likely to be very effective, because the entrenched veto groups cannot be budged: unlike a party that may be defeated at the polls, or a class that may be replaced by another class, the veto groups are always "in". . . .

"POWER ELITE" OR "VETO GROUPS"?

William Kornhauser

In the 50's two books appeared purporting to describe the structure of power in present-day America. They reached opposite conclusions: where C. Wright Mills found a "power elite," David Riesman found "veto groups." Both books have enjoyed a wide response, which has tended to divide along ideological lines. It would appear that *The Power Elite* has been most favorably received by radical intellectuals, and *The Lonely Crowd* has found its main response among liberals. Mills and Riesman have not been oblivious to their differences. Mills is quite explicit on the matter: Riesman is a

SOURCE: Willian Kornhauser, " 'Power Elite' or 'Veto Groups'?" in Seymour Martin Lipset and Leo Lowenthal, eds., *Culture and Social Character* (Glencoe: The Free Press, 1961), pp. 252-267. Reprinted with permission of the Macmillan Company © by The Free Press, a Corporation 1959.

"romantic pluralist" who refuses to see the forest of American power inequalities for the trees of short-run and discrete balances of power among the diverse groups. (244)[1] Riesman has been less explicitly polemical, but he might have had Mills in mind when he spoke of those intellectuals "who feel themselves very much out of power and who are frightened of those who they think have the power," and who "prefer to be scared by the power structures they conjure up than to face the possibility that the power structure they believe exists has largely evaporated." (257-258)[2]

I wish to intervene in this controversy just long enough to do two things: (1) locate as precisely as possible the items upon which Riesman and Mills disagree; and (2) formulate certain underlying issues in the analysis of power that have to be met before such specific disagreements as those Riesman and Mills can profitably be resolved.

We may compare Mills and Riesman on power in America along five dimensions:

1. Structure of power: how power is distributed among the major segments of present-day American society.

2. Changes in the structure of power: how the distribution of power has changed in the course of American history.

3. Operation of the structure of power: the means whereby power is exercised in American society.

4. Bases of the structure of power: how social and psychological factors shape and sustain the existing distribution of power.

5. Consequences of the structure of power: how the existing distribution of power affects American society.

Structure of Power. It is symptomatic of their underlying differences that Mills entitles his major consideration of power simply "the power elite," whereas Riesman has entitled one of his discussions "who has the power?" Mills is quite certain about the location of power, and so indicates by the assertive form of his title. Riesman perceives a much more amorphous and indeterminate power situation, and conveys this view in the interrogative form of his title. These contrasting images of American power may be diagrammed as two different pyramids of power. Mills' pyramid of power contains three levels:

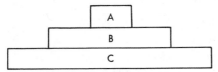

The apex of the pyramid (A) is the "power elite": a unified power group composed of the top government executives, military officials, and corporation directors. The second level (B) comprises the "middle levels of power": a diversified and balanced plurality of interest groups, perhaps most visibly at work in the halls of Congress. The third level (C) is the "mass society": the powerless mass of unorganized and atomized people who are controlled from above.

---

[1] Page references in the text for remarks by C. Wright Mills refer to *The Power Elite* (New York: Oxford University Press, 1956).

[2] Page references in the text for remarks by David Riesman refer to *The Lonely Crowd* (New York: Doubleday Anchor, 1953).

Riesman's pyramid of power contains only two major levels:

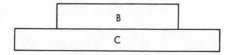

The two levels roughly correspond to Mills' second and third levels, and have been labeled accordingly. The obvious difference between the two pyramids is the presence of a peak in the one case and its absence in the other. Riesman sees no "power elite," in the sense of a single unified power group at the top of the structure, and this in the simplest terms contrasts his image of power in America with that of Mills. The upper level of Riesman's pyramid (B) consists of "veto groups": a diversified and balanced plurality of interest groups, each of which is primarily concerned with protecting its jurisdiction by blocking efforts of other groups that seem to threaten that jurisdiction. There is no decisive ruling group here, but rather an amorphous structure of power centering in the interplay among these interest groups. The lower level of the pyramid (C) comprises the more or less unorganized public, which is sought as an ally (rather than dominated) by the interest groups in their maneuvers against actual or threatened encroachments on the jurisdiction each claims for itself.

Changes in the Structure of Power. Riesman and Mills agree that the American power structure has gone through four major epochs. They disagree on the present and prospective future in the following historical terms: Mills judges the present to represent a fifth epoch, whereas Riesman judges it to be a continuation of the fourth.

The first period, according to Mills and Riesman, extended roughly from the founding of the republic to the Jacksonian era. During this period, Riesman believes America possessed a clearly demarcated ruling group, composed of a "landed-gentry and mercantalist-money leadership." (239) According to Mills, "the important fact about these early days is that social life, economic institutions, military establishment, and political order coincided, and men who were high politicians also played key roles in the economy and, with their families, were among those of the reputable who made up local society." (270)

The second period extended roughly from the decline of Federalist leadership to the Civil War. During this period power became more widely dispersed, and it was no longer possible to identify a sharply defined ruling group. "In this society, " Mills writes, "the 'elite' became a plurality of top groups, each in turn quite loosely made up." (270) Riesman notes that farmer and artisan groups became influential, and "occasionally, as with Jackson, moved into a more positive command." (240)

The third period began after the Civil War and extended through McKinley's administration in Riesman's view (240) and until the New Deal according to Mills. (271) They agree that the era of McKinley marked the high point of the unilateral supremacy of corporate economic power. During this period, power once more became concentrated, but unlike the Federalist period and also unlike subsequent periods, the higher circles of economic institutions were dominant.

The fourth period took definite shape in the 1930's. In Riesman's view this period marked the ascendancy of the "veto groups," and rule by coalitions rather than by a unified power group. Mills judges it to have been so only in the early and middle Roosevelt administrations: "In these years, the New Deal as a system of power was essentially a balance of pressure groups and interest blocs." (273)

Up to World War II, then, Mills and Riesman view the historical development of power relations in America along strikingly similar lines. Their sharply contrasting portrayal of present-day American power relations begins with their diverging assessments of the period beginning about 1940. Mills envisions World War II and its aftermath as marking a new era in American power relations. With war as the major problem, there arises a new power group composed of corporate, governmental, and military directors.

The formation of the power elite, as we may now know it, occurred during World War II and its aftermath. In the course of the organization of the nation for that war, and the consequent stabilization of the war-like posture, certain types of man have been selected and formed, and in the course of these institutional and psychological developments, new opportunities and intentions have arisen among them.[3]

Where Mills sees the ascendancy of a power elite, Riesman sees the opposite tendency toward the dispersal of power among a plurality of organized interests:

There has been in the last fifty years a change in the configuration of power in America, in which a single hierarchy with a ruling class at its head has been replaced by a number of "veto groups" among which power is dispersed. (239)

The shifting nature of the lobby provides us with an important clue as to the difference between the present American political scene and that of the age of McKinley. The ruling class of businessmen could relatively easily (though perhaps mistakenly) decide where their interests lay and what editors, lawyers, and legislators might be paid to advance them. The lobby ministered to the clear leadership, privilege, and imperative of the business ruling class. Today we have substituted for that leadership a series of groups, each of which has struggled for and finally attained a power to stop things conceivably inimical to its interests and, within far narrower limits, to start things. (246-247)

In short, both Mills and Riesman view the current scene from an historical perspective; but where one finds a hitherto unknown *concentration* of power, the other finds an emerging *indeterminacy* of power.

Operation of the Structure of Power. Mills believes the power elite sets all important public policies, especially foreign policy. Riesman, on the other hand, does not believe that the same group or coalition of groups sets all major policies, but rather that the question of who exercises power varies with the issue at stake: most groups are inoperative on most issues, and all groups are operative primarily on those issues that vitally impinge on their central interests. This is to say that there are as many power structures as there are distinctive spheres of policy. (256)

As to the modes of operation, both Mills and Riesman point to increasing *manipulation*, rather than command or persuasion, as the favored form of power play. Mills emphasizes the secrecy behind which important policy-determination occurs.

---

[3]C. Wright Mills, "The Power Elite," in A. Kornhauser (ed.), *Problems of Power in American Society* (Detroit: Wayne University Press, 1957), p. 161.

Riesman stresses not so much manipulation under the guise of secrecy as manipulation under the guise of mutual tolerance for one another's interests and beliefs. Manipulation occurs, according to Riesman, because each group is trying to hide its concern with power in order not to antagonize other groups. Power relations tend to take the form of "monopolistic competition": "rules of fairness and fellowship [rather than the impersonal forces of competition] dictate how far one can go." (247) Thus both believe the play of power takes place to a considerable extent backstage; but Mills judges this power play to be under the direction of one group, while Riesman sees it as controlled by a mood and structure of accommodation among many groups.

Mills maintains that the mass media of communication are important instruments of manipulation: the media lull people to sleep, so to speak, by suppressing political topics and by emphasizing "entertainment." Riesman alleges that the mass media give more attention to politics and problems of public policy than their audiences actually want, and thereby convey the false impression that there is more interest in public affairs than really exists in America at the present time. Where Mills judges the mass media of communication to be powerful political instruments in American society (315-316), Riesman argues that they have relatively little significance in this respect. (228-231)

Bases of the Structure of Power. Power tends to be patterned according to the structure of interest in a society. Power is shared among those whose interests coincide, and divides along lines where interests diverge. To Mills, the power elite is a reflection and solidification of a *coincidence of interests* among the ascendant institutional orders. The power elite rests on the "many interconnections and points of coinciding interests" of the corporations, political institutions, and military services. (19) For Riesman, on the other hand, there is an amorphous power structure, which reflects a *diversity of interests* among the major organized groups. The power structure of veto groups rests on the divergent interests of political parties, business groups, labor organizations, farm blocs, and a myriad of other organized groups. (247)

But power is not a simple reflex of interests alone. It also rests on the capabilities and opportunities for cooperation among those who have similar interests, and for confrontation among those with opposing interests. Mills argues in some detail that the power elite rests not merely on the coincidence of interests among major institutions but also on the "psychological similarity and social intermingling" of their higher circles. (19) By virtue of similar social origins (old family, upper-class background), religious affiliations (Episcopalian and Presbyterian), education (Ivy League college or military academy), and the like, those who head up the major institutions share codes and values as well as material interests. This makes for easy communication, especially when many of these people already know one another, or at least know many people in common. They share a common way of life, and therefore possess both the will and the opportunity to integrate their lines of action as representatives of key institutions. At times this integration involves "explicit co-ordination," as during war. (19-20) So much for the bases of power at the apex of the structure.

At the middle and lower levels of power, Mills emphasizes the lack of independence and concerted purpose among those who occupy similar social positions. In his book on the middle classes,[4] Mills purports to show the weakness of white-collar people that results from their lack of economic independence and political direction. The white-collar worker simply follows the more powerful group of the moment. In his book on labor leaders,[5] Mills located the alleged political impotence of organized labor in its dependence on government. Finally, the public is conceived as composed of atomized and submissive individuals who are incapable of engaging in effective communication and political action. (302 ff.)

Riesman believes that power "is founded, in large measure, on interpersonal expectations and attitudes." (253) He asserts that in addition to the diversity of interest underlying the pattern of power in America there is the psycho-cultural fact of widespread feelings of weakness and dependence at the top as well as at the bottom of the power structure: "If businessmen feel weak and dependent they do in actuality become weaker and more dependent, no matter what material resources may be ascribed to them." (253) In other words, the amorphousness of power in America rests in part on widespread feelings of weakness and dependence. These feelings are found among those whose position in the social structure provides resources that they could exploit, as well as among those whose position provides less access to the means of power. In fact, Riesman is concerned to show that people at all levels of the social structure tend to feel weaker than their objective position warrants.

The theory of types of conformity that provides the foundation of so much of Riesman's writings enters into his analysis of power at this point. The "other-directed" orientation in culture and character helps to sustain the amorphousness of power. The other-directed person in politics is the "inside-dopester," the person who possesses political competence but avoids political commitment. This is the dominant type in the veto groups, since other-direction is prevalent in the strata from which their leaders are drawn. "Both within the [veto] groups and in the situation created by their presence, the political mood tends to become one of other-directed tolerance." (248) However, Riesman does not make the basis of power solely psychological. . . .

Riesman and Mills agree that there is widespread apathy in American society, but they disagree on the social distribution of political apathy. Mills locates the apathetic primarily among the lower social strata, whereas Riesman finds extensive apathy in higher as well as lower strata. Part of the difference may rest on what criteria of apathy are used. Mills conceives of apathy as the lack of political meaning in one's life, the failure to think of personal interests in political terms, so that what happens in politics does not appear to be related to personal troubles.[6] Riesman extends the notion of apathy to include the politically uninformed as well as the politically uncommitted.[7] Thus political indignation undisciplined by political understanding is not a genuine political orientation. Riesman judges political apathy to be an important *basis* for amorphous power relations. Mills, on the other hand, treats political apathy primarily as a *result* of the concentration of power.

---

[4] *White Collar* (New York: Oxford University Press, 1951).
[5] *The New Men of Power* (New York: Harcourt, Brace and Company, 1948).
[6] *White Collar* p. 327.
[7] David Riesman and Nathan Glazer, "Criteria for Political Apathy," in Alvin W. Gouldner (ed.), *Studies in Leadership* (New York: Harper & Brothers, 1950).

Consequences of the Structure of Power. Four parallel sets of consequences of the structure of power for American society may be inferred from the writings of Mills and Riesman. The first concerns the impact of the power structure on the interests of certain groups or classes in American society. Mills asserts that the existing power arrangements enhance the interests of the major institutions whose directors constitute the power elite. (276 ff.) Riesman asserts the contrary: no one group or class is decisively favored over others by the culminated decisions on public issues. (257)

The second set of consequences concerns the impact of the structure of power on the quality of politics in American society. Here Mills and Riesman are in closer agreement. Mills maintains that the concentration of power in a small circle, and the use of manipulation as the favored manner of exercising power, lead to the decline of politics as public debate. People are decreasingly capable of grasping political issues, and of relating them to personal interests.[8] Riesman also believes that politics has declined in meaning for large numbers of people. This is not due simply to the ascendancy of "veto groups," although they do foster "the tolerant mood of other-direction and hasten the retreat of the inner-directed indignants." (251) More important, the increasing complexity and remoteness of politics make political self-interest obscure and aggravate feelings of impotence even when self-interest is clear.[9]

The third set of consequences of the American power structure concerns its impact on the quality of power relations themselves. Mills contends that the concentration of power has taken place without a corresponding shift in the bases of legitimacy of power: power is still supposed to reside in the public and its elected representatives, whereas in reality it resides in the hands of those who direct the key bureaucracies. As a consequence, men of power are neither responsible nor accountable for their power. (316-317) Riesman also implies that there is a growing discrepancy between the facts of power and the images of power, but for the opposite reason from Mills: power is more widely dispersed than is generally believed. (257-258)

Finally, a fourth set of consequences concerns the impact of the power structure on democratic leadership. If power tends to be lodged in a small group that is not accountable for its power, and if politics no longer involves genuine public debate, then there will be a *severe weakening of democratic institutions*, if not of leadership (the power elite exercises leadership in one sense of the term, in that it makes decisions on basic policy for the nation). Mills claims that power in America has become so concentrated that it increasingly resembles the Soviet system of power. . . .

If, on the other hand, power tends to be dispersed among groups that are primarily concerned to protect and defend their interests rather than to advance general policies and their own leadership, and if at the same time politics has declined as a sphere of duty and self-interest, then there will be a *severe weakening of leadership*. Thus Riesman believes that "power in America seems to [be] situational and mercurial; it resists attempts to locate it." (257) This "indeterminacy and amorphousness" of power inhibits the development of leadership: "Where the issue involves the country as

---

[8] *White Collar*, pp. 342-350.
[9] "Criteria for Political Apathy," p. 520.

a whole, no individual or group leadership is likely to be very effective, because the entrenched veto groups cannot be budged." (257) "Veto groups exist as defense groups, not as leadership groups." (248) Yet Riesman does not claim that the decline of leadership directly threatens American democracy, at least in the short run: the dispersion of power among a diversity of balancing "veto groups," operates to support democratic institutions even as it inhibits effective leadership. The long run prospects of a leaderless democracy are of course less promising.

Two Portraits of the American Power Structure

	Mills	Riesman
Levels	a. Unified power elite	a. No dominant power elite
	b. Diversified and balanced plurality of interest groups	b. Diversified and balanced plurality of interest groups
	c. Mass of unorganized people who have practically no power over elite	c. Mass of unorganized people who have some power over interest groups
Changes	a. Increasing concentration of power	a. Increasing dispersion of power
Operation	a. One group determines all major policies	a. Who determines policy shifts with the issue
	b. Manipulation of people at the bottom by group at the top	b. Monopolistic competition among organized groups
Bases	a. Coincidence of interests among major institutions (economic, military, governmental)	a. Diversity of interests among major organized groups
		b. Sense of weakness and dependence among those in higher as well as lower status
Consequences	a. Enhancement of interests of corporations, armed forces, and executive branch of government	a. No one group or class is forced significantly over others
	b. Decline of politics as public debate	b. Decline of politics as duty and self-interest
	c. Decline of responsible and accountable power— loss of democracy	c. Decline of capacity for effective leadership

In the second part of this paper, I wish to raise certain critical questions about Riesman's and Mills' images of power. One set of questions seeks to probe more deeply the basic area of disagreement in their views. A second set of questions concerns their major areas of agreement.

Power usually is analyzed according to its distribution among the several units of a system. Most power analysts construe the structure of power as a *hierarchy*—a rank-order of units according to their amount of power. The assumption often is made that there is only one such structure, and that all units may be ranked vis-à-vis one another. Units higher in the hierarchy have power over units lower in the structure, so there is a one-way flow of power. Mills tends to adopt this image of the structure of power.

Riesman rejects this conception of the power structure as mere hierarchy:

...The image of power in contemporary America presented [in *The Lonely Crowd*] departs from current discussions of power which are usually based on a search for a ruling class. (260)

Riesman is not just denying the existence of a power elite in contemporary American society; he is also affirming the need to consider other aspects of power than only its unequal distribution. He is especially concerned to analyze common responses to power:

If the leaders have lost the power, why have the led not gained it? What is there about the other-directed man and his life situation which prevents the transfer? In terms of situation, it seems that the pattern of monopolistic competition of the veto groups resists individual attempts at power aggrandizement. In terms of character, the other-directed man simply does not seek power, perhaps, rather, he avoids and evades it. (275)

Whereas Mills emphasizes the *differences* between units according to their power, Riesman emphasizes their *similarities* in this respect. In the first view, some units are seen as dominated by other units, while in the second view, all units are seen as subject to constraints that shape and limit their use of power *in similar directions*.

The problem of power is not simply the differential capacity to make decisions, so that those who have power bind those who do not. Constraints also operate on those who are in decision-making positions, for if these are the places where acts of great consequence occur, so are they the targets for social pressures. These pressures become translated into restrictions on the alternatives among which decision-makers can choose. Power may be meaningfully measured by ascertaining the range of alternatives that decision-makers can realistically consider. To identify those who make decisions is not to say how many lines of action are open to them, or how much freedom of choice they enjoy.

A major advance in the study of power is made by going beyond a formal conception of power, in which those who have the authority to make decisions are assumed to possess the effective means of power and the will to use it. Nor can it be assumed that those not in authority lack the power to determine public policy. The identification of effective sources of power requires analysis of how *decision-*

makers are themselves subject to various kinds of constraint. Major sources of constraint include (1) opposing elites and active publics; and (2) cultural values and associated psychological receptivities and resistances to power. A comparison of Mills and Riesman with respect to these categories of constraint reveals the major area of disagreement between them.

Mills implies that both sources of constraint are by and large inoperative on the highest levels of power. (1) There is little opposition among the top power-holders. Since they are not in opposition to one another, they do not constrain one another. Instead, they are unified and mutually supportive. Furthermore, there are few publics to constrain the elite. Groups capable of effective participation in broad policy determination have been replaced by atomized masses that are powerless to affect policy, since they lack the social bases for association and communication. Instead, people in large numbers are manipulated through organizations and media controlled by the elite. (2) Older values and codes no longer grip elites, nor have they been replaced by new values and codes that could regulate the exercise of power. Top men of power are not constrained either by an inner moral sense or by feelings of dependence on others. The widespread permissiveness toward the use of expedient means to achieve success produces "the higher immorality," that is to say, elites that are irresponsible in the use of power.

In sharp contrast to Mills, Riesman attaches great importance to both kinds of constraints on decision-makers. (1) There is a plethora of organized groups, "each of which has struggled for and finally attained a power to stop things conceivably inimical to its interests." (247) Furthermore, there is extensive opportunity for large numbers of people to influence decision-makers, because the latter are constrained by their competitive relations with one another to bid for support in the electoral arena and more diffusely in the realm of public relations. (2) The cultural emphasis on "mutual tolerance" and social conformity places a premium on "getting along" with others at the expense of taking strong stands. People are psychologically disposed to avoid long-term commitments as a result of their strong feelings of dependence on their immediate peers. "Other-directed" persons seek approval rather than power.

In general, the decisive consideration in respect to the restraint of power is the presence of multiple centers of power. Where there are many power groups, not only are they mutually constrained; they also are dependent on popular support, and therefore responsive to public demands. Now, there are many readily observable cases of institutionalized opposition among power groups in American society. In the economic sphere, collective bargaining between management and labor is conflict of this kind; and to the extent that "countervailing power" among a few large firms has been replacing competition among many small firms in the market place, there is a *de facto* situation of opposition among economic elites. In the political sphere, there is a strong two-party system and more or less stable factionalism within both parties, opposition among interest blocs in state and national legislatures, rivalry among executive agencies of government and the military services, and so forth.

Mills relegates these conflicting groups to the middle levels of power. Political parties and interest groups, both inside and outside of government, are not important units in the structure of power, according to Mills. It would seem that he takes this position primarily with an eye to the sphere of foreign policy, where only a few people finally make the big decisions. But he fails to put his argument to a decisive or meaningful test: he does not examine the pattern of decisions to show that foreign policy not only is made *by* a few people (this, after all, is a constitutional fact), but that it is made *for their particular interests*. Mills' major premise seems to be that all decisions are taken by and for special interests; there is no action oriented toward the general interests of the whole community. Furthermore, Mills seems to argue that because only a very few people occupy key decision-making *positions*, they are free to decide on whatever best suits their particular interests. But the degree of *autonomy* of decision-makers cannot be inferred from the number of decision-makers, nor from the *scope* of their decisions. It is determined by the character of decision-making, especially the dependence of decision-makers on certain kinds of *procedure* and *support*.

Just as Mills is presenting a distorted image of power in America when he fails to consider the pressures on those in high positions, so Riesman presents a biased picture by not giving sufficient attention to *power differentials* among the various groups in society. When Riesman implies that if power is dispersed, then it must be relatively equal among groups and interests, with no points of concentration, he is making an unwarranted inference. . . .

If Riesman greatly exaggerates the extent to which organized interests possess equal power, nevertheless he poses an important problem that Mills brushes aside. For Riesman goes beyond merely noting the existence of opposition among "veto groups" to suggest that they operate to smother one another's initiative and leadership. It is one thing for interest groups to constrain one another; it is something else again when they produce stalemate. Riesman has pointed to a critical problem for pluralist society: the danger that power may become fragmented among so many competing groups that effective general leadership cannot emerge.

On Mills' side, it is indisputable that American political institutions have undergone extensive centralization and bureaucratization. This is above all an *institutional* change wrought by the greatly expanded scale of events and decisions in the contemporary world. But centralization cannot be equated with a power elite. There can be highly centralized institutions and at the same time a fragmentation of power among a multiplicity of relatively independent public and private agencies. Thus Riesman would appear to be correct that the substance of power lies in the hands of many large organizations, and these organizations are not unified or coordinated in any firm fashion. If they were, surely Mills would have been able to identify the major mechanisms that could produce this result. That he has failed to do so is the most convincing evidence for their nonexistence.

To complete this analysis, we need only remind ourselves of the fundamental area of agreement between our two critics of American power relations. Both stress *the absence of effective political action* at all levels of the political order, in particular among the citizenry. For all of their differences, Mills and Riesman agree that there has been a decline in effective political participation, or at least a failure of political participation to measure up to the requirements of contemporary events and decisions. This failure has not been compensated by an increase in effective political action at the center: certainly Riesman's "veto groups" are not capable of defining and realizing the community's general aspirations; nor is Mills' "power elite" such a political agency. Both are asserting the inadequacy of political associations, including public opinion, party leadership, Congress, and the Presidency, even as they see the slippage of power in different directions. In consequence, neither is sanguine about the capacity of the American political system to provide responsible leadership, especially in international affairs.

If there is truth in this indictment, it also may have its sources in the very images of power that pervade Mills' and Riesman's thought. They are both inclined toward a negative response to power; and neither shows a willingness to confront the idea of a political system and the ends of power in it. Riesman reflects the liberal suspicion of power, as when he writes "we have come to realize that men who compete primarily for wealth are relatively harmless as compared with men who compete primarily for power." That such assertions as this may very well be true is beside the point. For certainly negative consequences of power can subsist alongside of positive ones. At times Riesman seems to recognize the need for people to seek and use power if they as individuals and the society as a whole are to develop to the fullest of their capacities. But his dominant orientation toward power remains highly individualistic and negative.

Mills is more extreme than Riesman on this matter, since he never asks what is socially required in the way of resources of power and uses of power, but instead is preoccupied with the magnitude of those resources and the (allegedly) destructive expropriation of them by and for the higher circles of major institutions. It is a very limited notion of power that construes it only in terms of coercion and conflict among particular interests. Societies require arrangements whereby resources of power can be effectively used and supplemented for public goals. This is a requirement for government, but the use of this term should not obscure that fact that government either commands power or lacks effectiveness. Mills does not concern himself with the *ends* of power, nor with the conditions for their attainment. He has no conception of the bases of political order, and no theory of the functions of government and politics. He suggests nothing that could prevent his "power elite" from developing into a full-blown totalitarianism. The logic of Mills' position finally reduces to a contest between anarchy and tyranny.

The problem of power seems to bring out the clinician in each of us. We quickly fasten on the pathology of power, whether we label the symptoms as "inside-dopesterism" (Riesman) or as "the higher immorality" (Mills). As a result, we often lose sight of the ends of power in the political system under review. It is important to understand that pivotal decisions increasingly are made at the national level, and that this poses genuine difficulties for the maintenance of democratic control. It is also important to understand that a multiplicity of public and private agencies increasingly pressure decision-makers, and that this poses genuine difficulties for the maintenance of effective political leadership. But the fact remains that there have been periods of centralized decision-making and democratic control, multiple constraints on power and effective leadership. There is no simple relationship between the extent to which power is equally distributed and the stability of democratic order. For a democratic order requires strong government as well as public consent by an informed citizenry. Unless current tendencies are measured against both sets of needs, there will be little progress in understanding how either one is frustrated or fulfilled. Finally, in the absence of more disciplined historical and comparative analysis, we shall continue to lack a firm basis for evaluating such widely divergent diagnoses of political malaise as those given us by Mills and Riesman.

VI
CLASS AND RACIAL POWER STRUGGLES

POWER PERSPECTIVES ON STRATIFICATION AND RACE RELATIONS

Marvin E. Olsen

A concern with the exercise of power has not been prevelant in most sociological writings on either social stratification or race relations. Within the past few years, however, a growing number of sociologists have begun to argue that neither phenomenon can be understood fully unless power is seen as the crucial determining factor. *The twin themes that link together stratification and race relations are inequality and conflict, both of which are direct outcomes of power exertion.* This essay will therefore examine first stratification and then race relations from a power perspective, treating both processes as manifestations of the distribution and use of power in societies. Most of the readings in this section are based on the United States, but this represents only the limited nature of the current literature, not a restriction on either theoretical perspective.

The dominant figure in the development of a power perspective on social stratification was of course Karl Marx, whose conception of social classes as based on varying relations the the means of economic production has influenced social scientists—and political activists—for a hundred years. As suggested in a previous essay, however, his "theory of social classes" was perhaps more a sophisticated definitional linkage than an adequate explanation of social stratification. We may therefore reject many aspects of this theory as too narrowly conceived and oversimplified, but nevertheless retain his basic emphasis on power in society as the major determinant of stratification.

Max Weber attempted to broaden Marx's power perspective on stratification, and at the same time relate it more directly to individuals.[1] He argued that the distribution and use of social power typically produces three different kinds of inequality—that is, three distinct yet interrelated dimensions of stratification. These are (a) economic class differences, as determined by individuals' varying "life

---

[1] Max Weber, "Class Status and Party," in *From Max Weber*, edited and translated by H. H. Gerth and C. Wright Mills (New York: Oxford University Press, 1958), Chap. 7.

chances" in the economic marketplace (both productive and consumptive), (b) prestige status distinctions, growing out of common life styles and consequent shared values, and (c) party organization, resulting from efforts of people to exert collective influence on community and societal decision makers. Because of Weber's focus on stratification as a power process, and also because of his recognition that stratification in modern societies is usually multidimensional (rather than unidimensional in the Marxian sense), his essay has become a classic in stratification theory. Unfortunately, however, it gave much more attention to observable expressions of inequality than to underlying causal dynamics, and thus diverted many later sociologists away from the task of formulating a general power theory of stratification.

Two contemporary writers have recently taken up the theoretical challenge laid down by Marx and Weber, however. Ralf Dahrendorf has critically analyzed Marx's theory of social classes, rejecting much of it but retaining its essential concern with power, as exercised in authority structures within industrialized societies.[2] He claims that in goal-oriented (or "imperatively coordinated") associations in modern societies, formal authority becomes the predominant type of power—at least from a sociological perspective. The separation between those who do and those who do not exercise authority in these organizations makes the members socially unequal, thus providing a potential basis for the formation of social classes with conflicting interests. Dahrendorf's thesis can be criticized as too limited on at least four counts: (a) he does not deal at all with other types of power such as force or dominance; (b) he insists that within any organization there can be only two classes, which seems unrealistic; (c) he discusses only formal organizations, and does not expand his theory to the total society; and (d) he fails to account for the origins of formal authority structures within organizations. Hence we must look elsewhere for a general power theory of stratification in society.

For this theory, we turn to the writings of Gerhard Lenski.[3] He has outlined a broad theory of social stratification that treats power as the crucial variable, and has also attempted to evaluate this theory by examining both preindustrialized and industrialized societies. The general theory can be expressed in a number of propositions derived from his writing:

1. The basic components of all social stratification are power, privilege (access to desired goods, services, activities, or social positions—of which wealth is an important but not the only indicator), and prestige (favorable evaluation by others, in such forms as recognition, esteem, and honor). Although in reality all three components are highly interrelated, for analytical purposes they must be at least partially distinguished.

2. *In all societies beyond the bare subsistence level, power determines the distribution of nearly all privileges*, both economic and noneconomic. Altruism may occasionally affect the allocation of some privileges, but for the most part the acquisition of privileges is an outcome of the exercise of power in social life.

---

[2] Ralf Dahrendorf, *Class and Class Conflict in Industrial Societies* (Stanford, Calif.: Stanford University Press, 1957).
[3] Gerhard E. Lenski, *Power and Privilege: A Theory of Social Stratification* (New York: McGraw-Hill Book Co., 1966).

3. In turn, *most prestige is gained directly from the possession of privileges and indirectly from the exertion of power*, at least in postsubsistence societies. Other factors (not specified by the theory) may sometimes increase an actor's prestige, but these are usually quite minor.

4. Cultural and personal values determine which particular kinds of privileges and prestige various persons will seek, but in general all people normally attempt to exercise as much power as possible and to transform this power into valued privileges and prestige.

5. For a variety of social, psychological, and cultural reasons, power—and hence also privileges and prestige—tends to be unequally distributed within any society. Inequality is not a theoretical imperative, but rather an empirical reality.

6. Once the exercise of power has resulted in the acquisition of some amounts of privilege and prestige, these can in turn be employed as resources for exerting additional power and hence gaining more privileges and prestige. Because these factors are so highly interrelated in social life, any one of them can often be transformed into another in a circular process.

7. At any given time, numerous discrepancies may exist among an actor's power, privileges, and prestige, but most actors will try to keep them in at least rough balance as far as possible—that is, to avoid severe status inconsistency. Hence in the long run a major change in any one of the three factors will eventually tend to result in changes in the other two also.

8. Through a variety of means, social actors normally attempt to protect and retain whatever valued power, privileges, and prestige they presently enjoy, and to pass them on to their children or other heirs. The techniques employed in these endeavors range from power conflicts with others to the creation of organizational structures to the formulation of legitimizing ideologies.

9. The resulting patterns of organized and perpetuated social inequality constitute societal systems of stratification.

Lenski has amassed a considerable amount of empirical evidence to illustrate and support this general theory, and makes a compelling argument for its essential validity. At the same time, however, he readily admits that it is far from being a complete explanation of all stratification, and that it requires much additional elaboration and specification. Among the numerous theoretical questions remaining to be answered are these:

1. What sources of power (that is, resources bases) are particularly significant for acquiring privileges and prestige? Lenski gives primary attention to material technology, political authority, and occupational positions, but also notes that economic systems should be given more extensive consideration in future studies.

2. How do force, dominance, and authority differ from one another in producing social stratification, for what reasons do each of these three kinds of power become unequally distributed in a society, and through what specific actions or mechanisms is each type of power transformed into privileges and prestige? Lenski provides extensive descriptive data relevant to these questions, but has not yet attempted to answer them with general theoretical propositions.

3. Under what conditions does the basic process of power → privilege → prestige become either reversed, with prestige and/or privilege being used as resources for power exertion, or else blocked, so that power wielding does not lead to the acquisition of privileges or prestige? The general theory allows for these alternative processes, but does not specify why or when they might occur.

4. What effects do cultural values and similar factors have on the distribution of privilege and prestige in a society? More specifically, as demands increase for greater economic, political, and social equality among all members of a society, will moral values ever override existing power conditions? Very little is presently known about these processes.

5. Finally, in what ways might this power theory of stratification be combined with some form of functional theory, which sees unequal distribution of socio-economic benefits as an outgrowth of the differing contributions made by various occupational and other roles to the welfare of the total society? Lenski has attempted to synthesize the power and functional theories, but his solution is historical rather than theoretical in nature. If functional theory can be stated in terms of demand and supply in the job market, as suggested by Richard Simpson,[4] it might then be seen as one mechanism through which individuals utilize power resources (in this case, job skills) to gain desired privileges and prestige (such as income and occupational status).

Beyond these concerns with the causes of social stratification is the equally challenging question of how and why various social classes exercise power in society. If we define *a social class as a population of people who share roughly similar amounts of power, (and hence also privileges and prestige) on one or more stratification dimensions*, and who are delineated from other classes by some type of social boundary, we are then immediately alerted to look for the ways in which various classes exercise power. In response to Marx, much of the sociological discussion on this topic has centered on the present role and future fate of the "working class" as compared with the "middle class." All observers seem to agree that in Western societies the "working class" has not achieved the organizational unity or capability for exerting power that Marx envisioned, with the result that there have been no major class revolutions in which the "working class" sought to gain control of an entire society. (There have been revolutions, of course, but even in Communist countries these have been primarily conflicts among elite classes, not "workers' revolts.")

Social scientists often disagree, however, concerning current trends and future possibilities in power relationships among classes in contemporary industrialized societies. Perhaps the majority of writers see the "working class" as slowly being absorbed into and merged with the "middle class," to form a vast "middle mass" containing numerous internal status gradations but no divisive class boundaries. Other writers, however, argue that even though the economic standards of living of

---

[4]Richard L. Simpson, "A Modification of the Functional Theory of Stratification," *Social Forces*, December 1956, pp. 132-137.

the "working" and "middle" classes may be constantly improving, both classes are nevertheless being steadily "proletarianized" as they increasingly lose the ability to exercise any significant influence in political processes. These two sets of observations are not entirely incompatible, as long as we conceive of social stratification as multidimensional, so that any particular class might simultaneously be rising on one dimension but declining on another. These are fascinating questions for debate, and they perhaps help us gain greater insight into the dynamics of contemporary class struggles, but at the present time sociology can provide very little empirical evidence with which to resolve the debate.

Directly related to these questions about class conflict is the topic of race relations. In a broad sense, racial inequality is one particular type (or dimension) of social stratification, involving social categorization of people on the basis of minor physical characteristics and discriminatory actions by persons in one such category (or "class" or "caste") toward the members of another less powerful category (or "class" or "caste"). From this perspective, the general power theory of stratification sketched above is fully as applicable to racial stratification as to economic, political, or any other kind of inequality. Thus *differential privileges and prestige enjoyed by various "racial classes" can be seen as direct outcomes of unequal power distribution and use*, whereas racial discrimination and segregation can be viewed as techniques used by members of more powerful racial categories to subordinate and control less powerful racial categories.

There is, however, one crucial difference between socioeconomic and racial classes in modern societies. The boundaries of socioeconomic classes are usually quite vague in definition and variable in practice, so that it is relatively easy for many individuals to move from one class to another—that is, to be socially mobile. To the extent that numerous opportunities for individual mobility do occur in a society, there is little impetus for the members of a subordinate class to organize for collective power exertion and class conflict; it is far easier and less costly for these persons, as they rise in status, to move individually into a higher class. This is not possible with racial classes, though, unless by chance one happens to have mixed ancestry that results in "passable" physical characteristics (e.g., relatively light skin color). For most members of a subordinate racial category there is no possibility of upward individual social mobility into a more desirable racial category, since they cannot change their physical appearance. As a result, class organization, collective power exertion, and class conflict may become prominent social processes in race relations.

Stanely Lieberson has used a power perspective to develop a set of theoretical propositions explaining the broad historical dynamics of racial and ethnic social inequality.[5] He places the roots of racial and ethnic stratification in initial contacts—often resulting from military conquest or voluntary or involuntary migration—between two (or more) populations that differ in physical and/or cultural characteristics. In most cases, one of these populations will be able to exercise more

---

[5]Stanley Lieberson, "A Societal Theory of Race and Ethnic Relations," *American Sociological Review*, Vol. 26, December 1961, pp. 902-910.

power than the other, because of superior technology and wealth or greater numbers or more unified social organization. Depending on the relative power of the migrant population in relation to the indigenous population, differing patterns of racial and ethnic inequality and conflict will then tend to develop.

The history of race relations in the United States fits this theoretical model quite closely. A population of physically identifiable but relatively powerless people was brought to this society and forced by the more powerful indigenous population to become totally subordinate in terms of power, privileges, and prestige. For 250 years the control of blacks by whites was so complete that the prevailing pattern of race relations was largely "paternalistic" in nature. As described by Pierre van den Berghe,[6] a paternalistic pattern of race relations is characterized by rigid racial class barriers with no possibility of upward mobility, extreme social distance but little physical separation between members of these racial populations, relegation of the subordinate population to the lowest occupational and other roles, paternalistic behavior by members of the dominant class, and acquiescence by those in the subordinate racial category to their positions in society. Because of its total control, the dominant racial class has little need to employ formal methods of discrimination or to enforce physical segregation; most members of the subordinate racial population "stay in their place" voluntarily because they have no opportunity to do anything else and because they have been taught since childhood that servitude is their proper role in life.

This paternalistic pattern may give way to a more "competitive" type of race relations, however, as a society becomes more industrialized and urbanized, as slavery is declared illegal, and as members of the subordinate class become more physically mobile and slowly gain education, occupational skills, and wealth.[7] In place of wholly superordinate and wholly subordinate racial populations, two parallel racial categories develop, each having its own organizational structure, division of labor, and socioeconomic status gradations. The formerly dominant population may continue to enjoy numerous advantages in power, privilege, and prestige for a long period of time, but it no longer totally controls the previously subordinate racial population. The old patterns of paternalism and voluntary subservience give way to competition and conflict between the two racial categories, as the subordinate one struggles to increase its share of power, privilege, and prestige in society. Race relations are no longer static and "peaceful"; dynamic conflict and change now prevail.

In an effort to maintain as much of its previous control as possible, the dominant racial class often resorts to elaborate methods of legal and formal discrimination, physical segregation, disenfranchisement, and even violence toward the subordinate racial class. These techniques were not widely used in the United States until the late 1800's, but as many writers have documented, the Civil War, Reconstruction, and expanding industrialization and urbanization largely destroyed the old southern paternalistic pattern of race relations between 1860 and 1890. Formal discrimina-

---

[6]Pierre L. van den Berghe, *Race and Racism: A Comparative Perspective* (New York: John Wiley and Sons, 1967).
[7]*Ibid.*

tion and segregation did not appear immediately, however, since during the Reconstruction period the North forced the South to grant Negroes many rights and benefits. Even after the northern troops withdrew during the 1870's there was less open discrimination and segregation in the South than in the North; the southern landed aristocracy attempted instead to reimpose the old paternalistic pattern that did not require these formal means of social control. But during the period between 1880 and 1910 they gradually lost power to the emerging industrialists and growing urban (white) "middle class."

As these new factions gained economic and political power in the South, and as Negroes began to assert the legal rights given them by the federal government, race relations moved from a paternalistic to a competitive pattern. Paternalism based on stable plantation life no longer provided an adequate means by which whites could control blacks, so formal discrimination and physical segregation were increasingly employed as methods of social control. Almost all southern "Jim Crow" laws and devious restrictions on Negro voting, for instance, were enacted in the South between 1890 and 1910. To those persons who maintain that racial discrimination and segregation cannot be changed through legislation, the obvious rebuttal is that these practices were initiated through political action and hence can be altered in the same manner. The imposition of formal discrimination and segregation against blacks was more protracted in the North than in the South, and did not rely as heavily on legislation, but the basic process and consequent results have been much the same. *As race relations shifted from a paternalistic to a competitive pattern in all parts of the United States during the late 1800's and early 1900's, whites used their superior power resources to force discrimination and segregation upon blacks, in an attempt to retain for themselves as much privilege and prestige in society as possible.*

If racial inequality is in fact largely a consequence of power exertion by whites, it then follows that *blacks seeking to change the situation so as to gain greater equality of privileges and prestige must in turn exercise power against the dominant whites.* This idea may appear to be so self-evident that it hardly needs mentioning, yet not until the late 1950's did large numbers of blacks (and white sympathizers) begin to apply it systematically in an effort to promote widespread social change. Numerous individuals and organizations, both black and white, had of course been trying to combat racism in the United States for many decades prior to that, but for the most part they had relied on an educational rather than an "action" approach. Some of the more blatant aspects of white racism were reduced through extensive educational programs in the schools and through the mass media, but all too frequently the underlying patterns of power exertion did not change significantly; they merely became more covert and subtle.

Part of the reason for this failure was that none of the educational campaigns were ever extensive or intensive enough to reach large numbers of people for sustained periods of time. Perhaps more important, though, is the fact—demonstrated in numerous social psychological experiments—that it is extremely difficult or impossible to alter deep-seated attitudes such as racial prejudice unless the surrounding social environment is also changed. And any major change in the structure of society inevitably requires the exercise of power. When social patterns of discrimination and segregation are eliminated, however, attitudes of racial prejudice often disappear quite rapidly even without purposeful educational pro-grams.[8]

How can a subordinate racial population such as Negroes in the United States effectively wield power to bring about major alterations in patterns of social organization? We cannot here begin to trace the history of the recent civil rights struggle in this society, but we can outline the general process through which successful change efforts frequently occur. Let us call it a "power and conflict" approach to achieving racial equality. This process can be divided into five major stages, though in practice they usually merge and overlap: organization, power exertion, confrontation, social change, and attitude change.

The initial stage of *organization* is necessary to bring together sufficient resources—including participants, finances, leaders, communication channels, and operational procedures—for generating an effective power base from which to act. Isolated individual members of the subordinate racial class can rarely wield enough power to affect significantly the established organizational structures and control mechanisms of the dominant class. But through the collective actions of many individuals, an adequate foundation of power can be created. These organizational activities must center in and be controlled by the black community itself, although they can always utilize support from sympathetic whites as long as these persons do not attempt to control the black organizations.

The second stage of *power exertion* can be opened as soon as sufficient organizational resources have been acquired. These power actions can take innumer-able specific forms—economic, political, legal, physical, and moral—but their goal is always to put pressures on the white community and create tensions and conflicts. If these pressures and conflicts are unfocused (as in many protest parades) or indiscriminate (as in a riot), they will have relatively little effect on the white community, and may invoke retaliation or suppression. To be effective, they must be aimed directly at those persons and organizations that Herbert Blumer calls "key functionaries"—actors in critical positions who are capable of exerting power and effecting change in the white community.[9] They may be elected officials or legislators or business executives or organizational officers or school administrators or police commissioners or religious leaders, depending on the immediate goals of the black movement. These persons may or may not be sympathetic with the goals of the blacks, but that is irrelevant. The important factor is whether the blacks can locate those points at which the key functionaries are vulnerable to outside influences, and then apply sufficient pressures to force the key functionaries to deal with them.

---

[8]A number of social scientific studies supporting this generalization are summarized by Earl Raab and Seymour Martin Lipset in "The Prejudiced Society," in Earl Raab, editor, *American Race Relations Today* (Garden City, N.Y.: Doubleday and Co., 1962), pp. 29-55.

[9]Herbert Blumer, "Social Science and the Desegregation Process," *The Annals of the American Academy of Political and Social Science*, Vol. 304, March 1956, pp. 137-143.

The third stage of *confrontation* is the crucial aspect of this process. The white key functionaries must agree to meet and negotiate with the black leaders, not to build "goodwill" but to resolve the threatening conflicts. Out of this process of give-and-take bargaining between equally powerful antagonists can come, through compromises on both sides, agreements that will produce significant social changes. Lewis Killian and Charles Grigg have described this process of confrontation in a passage that bears repetition:

> The establishing of communication between whites and Negroes in no way means that conflict has been terminated. It does not even mean that a minimum of consensus has been reached on the issue involved. It is more likely to signify that the white men of power have found the conflict so costly that they wish to limit it, moving it from the streets, the stores, and the courtroom into the conference room. In actuality the white and the Negro leaders gathered around the conference table do not constitute a biracial team. They are two "truce teams" representing the still antagonistic parties to a conflict. Realism demands that they concentrate not on their points of agreement but on the issues which underlie the conflict. Limitation of the conflict will result from the strategic use of threats and the reciprocal assessment of the balance of power. . . .[10]

The fourth stage of *social change* begins when the agreements reached through negotiation are put into practice by the key functionaries. This may take the form of new legislation, new organizational policies, new operating rules and regulations, or new behavioral practices. The significant feature here is that these broad social changes are being implemented by those persons in the white community who can exercise sufficient power to ensure their success. As these changes take effect, they will simultaneously (a) open new job, housing, educational, and other opportunities to blacks, and (b) alter the social environments of many whites and stimulate the creation of new kinds of social relationships between blacks and whites.

The final state in this over-all process is widespread *attitude change* among whites, as they discard their old attitudes of racial prejudice. In numerous situations it has been found that when whites enter into cooperative, equal-status relationships with blacks—whether at work, in their neighborhood, in recreation, or in school—prejudicial attitudes very quickly disappear. And the longer and more intense these relationships, the more likely the participants are to develop positive attitudes not only towards each other personally, but towards all members of the other race in all situations.[11]

Awareness and utilization of this "power and conflict" approach to racial struggles have been developing among black leaders in the United States since the late 1950's, and it is the basic theme underlying the "Black Power" movement. Black people are seeking to utilize power to change the society toward greater racial equality and increased privileges and prestige for all members of the black community—which may or may not involve racial integration. To do this, they must create viable social

---

[10]Lewis Killian and Charles Grigg, *Racial Crisis in America: Leadership in Conflict* (Englewood Cliffs, N. J.: Prentice-Hall, 1964), p. 135.

[11]Raab and Lipset, *Ibid.*

organizations that will enable them to exert effective power, both within their own community and throughout the total society. In the words of Stokely Carmichael and Charles Hamilton: "The goal of black self-determination and black self-identify—'Black Power'—is full participation in the decision making processes affecting the lives of black people. . . ."[12]

The readings in this section span the entire scope of ideas on stratification and race relations sketched in this essay. The power conceptions of social stratification advanced by Karl Marx and Ralf Dahrendorf were encountered in previous selections and are not repeated here, but Max Weber's discussion of economic class, prestige status, and party organization dimensions of stratification is included, as well as a statement of Gerhard Lenski's general power theory of social stratification. Articles by C. Wright Mills and T. B. Bottomore both deal with power dynamics among classes in contemporary societies; they agree that class conflict and possibilities for class revolution have diminished, but differ somewhat in their expectations for future trends. In the area of race relations, a general power theory is outlined by Stanley Lieberson, and Charles Silberman briefly describes the enactment of discriminatory legislation by southern states around the turn of the century. Herbert Blumer elaborates some social-psychological aspects of this power perspective, and then introduces the concept of "key functionaries" and discusses their importance in the desegregation process. Several aspects of the "power and conflict" approach to race relations are then cogently presented by Lewis Killian and Charles Grigg, followed by a statement on the nature of "Black Power" by Stokely Carmichael and Charles Hamilton.

------

[12] Stokely Carmichael and Charles Hamilton, *Black Power: The Politics of Liberation in America* (New York: Vintage Books, 1967), p. 47.

CLASS, STATUS, PARTY

Max Weber

Economically Determined Power and the Social Order. Law exists when there is a probability that an order will be upheld by a specific staff of men who will use physical or psychical compulsion with the intention of obtaining conformity with the order, or of inflicting sanctions for infringement of it.[1] The structure of every legal order directly influences the distribution of power, economic or otherwise, within its

------

SOURCE: Abridged from *From Max Weber: Essays in Sociology*, pp. 180-186, edited and translated by H. H. Gerth and C. Wright Mills. Copyright 1946 by Oxford University Press, Inc. Reprinted by permission.

[1] *Wirtschaft und Gesellschaft*, part III, chap. 4, pp. 631-40. The first sentence in paragraph one and the several definitions in this chapter which are in brackets do not appear in the original text. They have been taken from other contexts of *Wirtschaft und Gesellschaft*.

respective community. This is true of all legal orders and not only that of the state. In general, we understand by "power" the chance of a man or of a number of men to realize their own will in a communal action even against the resistance of others who are participating in the action.

"Economically conditioned" power is not, of course, identical with "power" as such. On the contrary, the emergence of economic power may be the consequence of power existing on other grounds. Man does not strive for power only in order to enrich himself economically. Power, including economic power, may be valued "for its own sake." Very frequently the striving for power is also conditioned by the social "honor" it entails. Not all power, however, entails social honor: The typical American Boss, as well as the typical big speculator, deliberately relinquishes social honor. Quite generally, "mere economic" power, and especially "naked" money power, is by no means a recognized basis of social honor. Nor is power the only basis of social honor. Indeed, social honor, or prestige, may even be the basis of political or economic power, and very frequently has been. Power, as well as honor, may be guaranteed by the legal order, but, at least normally, it is not their primary source. The legal order is rather an additional factor that enhances the chance to hold power or honor; but it cannot always secure them.

The way in which social honor is distributed in a community between typical groups participating in this distribution we may call the "social order." The social order and the economic order are, of course, similarly related to the "legal order." However, the social and the economic order are not identical. The economic order is for us merely the way in which economic goods and services are distributed and used. The social order is of course conditioned by the economic order to a high degree, and in its turn reacts upon it.

Now: "classes," "status groups," and "parties" are phenomena of the distribution of power within a community.

Determination of Class-Situation by Market-Situation. In our terminology, "classes" are not communities; they merely represent possible, and frequent, bases for communal action. We may speak of a "class" when (1) a number of people have in common a specific causal component of their life chances, in so far as (2) this component is represented exclusively by economic interests in the possession of goods and opportunities for income, and (3) is represented under the conditions of the commodity or labor markets. [These points refer to "class situation," which we may express more briefly as the typical chance for a supply of goods, external living conditions, and personal life experiences, in so far as this chance is determined by the amount and kind of power, or lack of such, to dispose of goods or skills for the sake of income in a given economic order. The term "class" refers to any group of people that is found in the same class situation.]

It is the most elemental economic fact that the way in which the disposition over material property is distributed among a plurality of people, meeting competitively in the market for the purpose of exchange, in itself creates specific life chances. According to the law of marginal utility this mode of distribution excludes the non-owners from competing for highly valued goods; it favors the owners and, in fact, gives to them a monopoly to acquire such goods. Other things being equal, this mode of distribution monopolizes the opportunities for profitable deals for all those who, provided with goods, do not necessarily have to exchange them. It increases, at least generally, their power in price wars with those who, being propertyless, have nothing to offer but their services in native form or goods in a form constituted through their own labor, and who above all are compelled to get rid of these products in order barely to subsist. . . . All this holds true within the area in which pure market conditions prevail. "Property" and "lack of property" are, therefore, the basic categories of all class situations. It does not matter whether these two categories become effective in price wars or in competitive struggles.

Within these categories, however, class situations are further differentiated: on the one hand, according to the kind of property that is usable for returns; and, on the other hand, according to the kind of services that can be offered in the market. Ownership of domestic buildings; productive establishments; warehouses; stores; agriculturally usable land, large and small holdings . . . ; ownership of mines; cattle; men (slaves); disposition over mobile instruments of production, or capital goods of all sorts, especially money or objects that can be exchanged for money easily and at any time; disposition over products of one's own labor or of others' labor differing according to their various distances from consumability; disposition over transferable monopolies of any kind—all these distinctions differentiate the class situations of the propertied just as does the "meaning" which they can and do give to the utilization of property, especially to property which has money equivalence. Accordingly, the propertied, for instance, may belong to the class of rentiers or to the class of entrepreneurs.

Those who have no property but who offer services are differentiated just as much according to their kinds of services as according to the way in which they make use of these services, in a continuous or discontinuous relation to a recipient. But always this is the generic connotation of the concept of class: that the kind of chance in the *market* is the decisive moment which presents a common condition for the individual's fate. "Class situation" is, in this sense, ultimately "market situation". . . . The creditor-debtor relation becomes the basis of "class situations" only in those cities where a "credit market," however primitive, with rates of interest increasing according to the extent of dearth and a factual monopolization of credits, is developed by a plutocracy. Therewith "class struggles" begin. . . .

Communal Action Flowing from Class Interest. According to our terminology, the factor that creates "class" is unambiguously economic interest, and indeed, only those interests involved in the existence of the "market." Nevertheless, the concept of "class-interest" is an ambiguous one: even as an empirical concept it is ambiguous as soon as one understands by it something other than the factual direction of interests following with a certain probability from the class situation for a certain "average" of those people subjected to the class situation. The class situation and other circumstances remaining the same, the direction in which the individual worker, for instance, is likely to pursue his interests may vary widely, according to whether he is constitutionally qualified for the task at hand to a high, to an average, or to a low degree. In the same way, the direction of interests may vary according to whether or not a *communal* action of a larger or smaller portion of those commonly affected by the "class situation," or even an association among them, e.g. a "trade union," has grown out of the class situation from which the individual may or may not expect promising results. [Communal action refers to that action which is oriented to the feeling of the action that they belong together. Societal action, on the other hand, is oriented to a rationally motivated adjustment of interests.] The rise of societal or even of communal action from a common class situation is by no means a universal phenomenon. . . .

The degree in which "communal action" and possibly "societal action," emerges from the "mass actions" of the members of a class is linked to general cultural conditions, especially to those of an intellectual sort. It is also linked to the extent of the contrasts that have already evolved, and is especially linked to the *transparency* of the connections between the causes and the consequences of the "class situation." For however different life chances may be, this fact in itself, according to all experience, by no means gives birth to "class action" (communal action by the members of a class). The fact of being conditioned and the results of the class situation must be distinctly recognizable. For only then the contrast of life chances can be felt not as an absolutely given fact to be accepted, but as a resultant from either (1) the given distribution of property, or (2) the structure of the concrete economic order. It is only then that people may react against the class structure not only through acts of an intermittent and irrational protest, but in the form of rational association. There have been "class situations" of the first category (1), of a specifically naked and transparent sort, in the urban centers of Antiquity and during the Middle Ages; especially then, when great fortunes were accumulated by factually monopolized trading in industrial products of these localities or in foodstuffs. Furthermore, under certain circumstances, in the rural economy of the most diverse periods, when agriculture was increasingly exploited in a profit-making manner. The most important historical example of the second category (2) is the class situation of the modern "proletariat."

Types of "Class Struggle". Thus every class may be the carrier of any one of the possibly innumerable forms of "class action," but this is not necessarily so. In any case, a class does not in itself constitute a community. To treat "class" conceptually as having the same value as "community" leads to distortion. That men in the same class situation regularly react in mass actions to such tangible situations as economic ones in the direction of those interests that are most adequate to their average number is an important and after all simple fact for the understanding of historical events. . . . Yet, if classes as such are not communities, nevertheless class situations emerge only on the basis of communalization. The communal action that brings forth class situations, however, is not basically action between members of the identical class; it is an action between members of different classes. Communal actions that directly determine the class situation of the worker and the entrepreneur are: the labor market, the commodities market, and the capitalistic enterprise. But, in its turn, the existence of a capitalistic enterprise presupposes that a very specific communal action exists and that it is specifically structured to protect the possession of goods *per se*, and especially the power of individuals to dispose, in principle freely, over the means of production. The existence of a capitalistic enterprise is preconditioned by a specific kind of "legal order." Each kind of class situation, and above all when it rests upon the power of property *per se*, will become most clearly efficacious when all other determinants of reciprocal relations are, as far as possible, eliminated in their significance. It is in this way that the utilization of the power of property in the market obtains its most sovereign importance. . . .

The great shift, which has been going on continuously in the past, and up to our times, may be summarized, although at the cost of some precision: the struggle in which class situations are effective has progressively shifted from consumption credit toward, first, competitive struggles in the commodity market and, then, toward price wars on the labor market. The "class struggles" of antiquity—to the extent that they were genuine class struggles and not struggles between status groups—were initially carried on by indebted peasants, and perhaps also by artisans threatened by debt bondage and struggling against urban creditors. For debt bondage is the normal result of the differentiation of wealth in commercial cities, especially in seaport cities. . . . Along with this, and with an increase in provision of grain for the city by transporting it from the outside, the struggle over the means of sustenance emerged. . . . It lasted throughout antiquity and the entire Middle Ages. The propertyless as such flocked together against those who actually and supposedly were interested in the dearth of bread. This flight spread until it involved all those commodities essential to the way of life and to handicraft production. There were only incipient discussions of wage disputes in antiquity and in the Middle Ages. But they have been slowly increasing up into modern times. In the earlier periods they were completely secondary to slave rebellions as well as to fights in the commodity market.

The propertyless of antiquity and of the Middle Ages protested against monopolies, pre-emption, forestalling, and the withholding of goods from the market in order to raise prices. Today the central issue is the determination of the price of labor.

This transition is represented by the fight for access to the market and for the determination of the price of products. Such fights went on between merchants and workers in the putting-out system of domestic handicraft during the transition to modern times. Since it is quite a general phenomenon we must mention here that the class antagonisms that are conditioned through the market situation are usually most bitter between those who actually and directly participate as opponents in price wars. It is not the rentier, the share-holder, and the banker who suffer the ill will of the worker, but almost exclusively the manufacturer and the business executives who are the direct opponents of workers in price wars. This is so in spite of the fact that it is precisely the cash boxes of the rentier, the share-holder, and the banker into which the more or less "unearned" gains flow, rather than into the pockets of the manufacturers or of the business executives. This simple state of affairs has very frequently been decisive for the role the class situation has played in the varieties of patriarchal socialism and the frequent attempts—formerly, at least—of threatened status groups to form alliances with the proletariat against the "bourgeoisie". . . .

THE DYNAMICS OF DISTRIBUTIVE SYSTEMS

Gerhard E. Lenski

In analyses of social stratification, it is a temptation to turn immediately to the interesting and much debated structural problems, such as those concerning the nature, number, and composition of classes. While such questions must inevitably be a part of any adequate treatment of the subject, they are secondary in importance to questions about the processes which give rise to the structures. Moreover, to attempt to deal with the structural problems without prior attention to these processes, as is sometimes done, is to put the cart before the horse and create confusion. . . .

Two Laws of Distribution. When one seeks to build a theory of distribution on the postulates about the nature of man and society set forth in the last chapter, one soon discovers that these lead to a curious, but important, *dualism*. If those postulates are sound, one would predict that almost all the products of men's labors will be distributed on the basis of two seemingly contradictory principles, *need* and *power*.

In our discussion of the nature of man, it was postulated that where important decisions are involved, most human action is motivated either by self-interest or by partisan group interests. This suggests that power alone governs the distribution of rewards. This cannot be the case, however, since we also postulated that most of these essentially selfish interests can be satisfied only by the establishment of cooperative relations with others. Cooperation is absolutely essential both for survival and for the efficient attainment of most other goals. In other words, men's selfish interests compel them to remain members of society and to share in the division of labor.

If these two postulates are correct, then it follows that *men will share the product of their labors to the extent required to insure the survival and continued productivity of those others whose actions are necessary or beneficial to themselves.* This might well be called the first law of distribution, since the survival of mankind as a species depends on compliance with it.

This first law, however, does not cover the entire problem. It says nothing about how any *surplus*, i.e., goods and services over and above the minimum required to keep producers alive and productive, which men may be able to produce will be distributed. This leads to what may be called the second law of distribtuion. If we assume that in important decisions human action is motivated almost entirely by self-interest or partisan group interests, and if we assume that many of the things men most desire are in short supply, then, as noted before, this surplus will inevitably give rise to conflicts and struggles aimed at its control. If, following Weber, we define power as the probability of persons or groups carrying out their will even when opposed by others,[1] then it follows that *power will determine the distribution of nearly all of the surplus possessed by a society*. The qualification "nearly all" takes account of the very limited influence of altruistic action which our earlier analysis of the nature of man leads us to expect.

This second law points the way to another very important relationship, that between our two chief variables, power and privilege. If privilege is defined as possession or control of a portion of the surplus produced by a society, then it follows that *privilege is largely a function of power, and to a very limited degree, a function of altruism*. This means that to explain most of the distribution of privilege in a society, we have but to determine the distribution of power.

To state the matter this way suggests that the task of explaining the distribution of privilege is simple. Unfortunately, this is not the case since there are many forms of power and they spring from many sources. Nevertheless, the establishment of this key relationship reduces the problem to more manageable proportions, since it concentrates attention on one key variable, power. Thus if we can establish the pattern of its distribution in a given society, we have largely established the pattern for the distribution of privilege, and if we can discover the causes of a given distribution of power we have also discovered the causes of the distribution of privilege linked with it.

To put the matter this way is to invite the question of how the third basic element in every distributive system, *prestige*, is related to power and privilege. It would be nice if one could say that prestige is a simple function of privilege, but unfortunately this does not seem to be the case. Without going into a complex analysis of the matter at this point, the best that can be said is that empirical evidence strongly suggests that *prestige is largely, though not solely, a function of power and privilege, at least in those societies where there is a substantial surplus*. If this is true, it follows that even though the subject of prestige is not often mentioned in this volume, its pattern of distribution and its causes can largely be deduced from discussion of the distribution of power and privilege and their causes in those societies where there is an appreciable surplus.

Graphically, the relationship between these three variables, as set forth in the propositions above, can be depicted in this way:

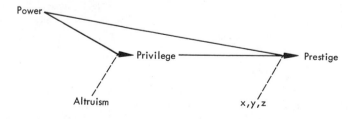

---

[1] See Max Weber, *The Theory of Social and Economic Organization*, translated by A. M. Henderson and Talcott Parsons (New York: Free Press, 1947), p. 152.

The solid lines indicate major sources of influence, the dashed lines secondary sources.

To make this diagram complete, one other dashed line should probably be added, indicating some feedback from prestige to power. Thus a more accurate representation of the relationships would look like this:

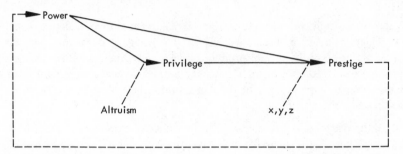

Power is the key variable in the triad from the casual and explanatory standpoint. Hence, it is with this variable that we shall be primarily concerned in the analysis which follows.

The Variable Aspects of Distributive Systems. As the statement of the two laws indicates, the second law does not have any effect on the distributive process until the conditions specified in the first have been satisfied. Until the necessities of life have been made available to enough productive, mutually interdependent members of the group, there is no surplus to be fought over and distributed on the basis of power. Thus, as a first hypothesis we would be led to predict that *in the simplest societies, or those which are technologically most primitive, the goods and services available will be distributed wholly, or largely, on the basis of need.*

As the productivity of societies increases, the possibility of producing a surplus steadily increases, though it should be noted that the existence of a surplus is not a function of technological advance alone. Even though we cannot say that the surplus available to a society increases proportionately with advances in the level of technology, such advances increase the probability that there will be a surplus and also that there will be a sizable surplus. Hence, as a second hypothesis we are led to predict that *with technological advance, an increasing proportion of the goods and services available to a society will be distributed on the basis of power....*

If the first two laws of distribution and the two hypotheses based on them are valid, then *the nature of distributive systems will vary greatly, depending on the degree of technological advance in the societies involved.* The variations should be every bit as great as those which differentiate markets where perfect competition prevails from those where imperfect competition holds sway....

While the foregoing is reason enough to base our special theories on societal types defined in technological terms, there is one other great advantage derived from this approach. Past research has made it clear that technology is never an isolated variable in sociocultural systems. On the contrary, it tends to be linked fairly closely with a whole series of other variables which evidently stand in a dependent relationship to it.[2] This is especially true of many social organizational variables which are linked with distributive systems and tend to define their limits of possible variation, e.g., nature and extent of division of labor, maximum community size, etc. Hence, *by classifying societies on the basis of technology, we are, in effect, simultaneously controlling, wholly or in part, many other relevant variables.* . . .

To say that many other characteristics of human societies vary with technology is not to say that all do. Clearly some do not, and others do so only to a limited degree. Wilbert Moore has suggested that supernatural beliefs and aesthetic forms are not so closely correlated with technology as most forms of social organization.[3] The same may also be true of certain basic aspects of family life. However, while these exceptions deserve recognition and careful consideration, they do not vitiate the basic principle involved.

It should also be noted that classifying societies on the basis of the nature of their technology does not imply that all those in a single category have *identical* distributive systems any more than that all oligopolistic markets function the same way. Obviously there are variations within each societal type just as within each type of market, and an effort will be made to identify and account for the more important of them. However, these may be thought of as *second-order* variations, which are best dealt with after the first-order variations have been established and the internal uniformities associated with them clearly delineated.

In dealing with these second-order variations we shall sometimes have to rely on inductive logic to establish both causal and descriptive generalizations. However, this will not always be the case. Sometimes deductive logic can be employed. For example, if the size of a society's surplus affects the nature of its distributive system, and if the size of the surplus depends to some degree on the nature of the physical environment, then we should predict that *differences in the physical environment will lead to secondary differences in distributive systems.* More specifically, the richer the environment, the larger the surplus and the greater the importance of power in the distributive process.

There are also reasons for predicting that the influence of environmental differences will be greater in primitive societies than in those which are technologically more advanced. To begin with, technological advance makes possible the geographical expansion of societies, and the larger the territory occupied by a society, the less the probability that the total environment will be extremely favorable or unfavorable and the greater the probability that it will include a mixture of favorable and unfavorable land. Hence, environmental variation should be less among the larger, technologically advanced societies than among the smaller, more primitive. In addition, technological advance frequently means the development of alternative solutions to the various problems of production. Technologically advanced societies, therefore, should be less

---

[2]See, for example, L. T. Hobhouse, G. C. Wheeler, and M. Ginsberg, *The Material Culture and Social Institutions of the Simpler Peoples* (London: Chapman & Hall, 1930) and Alvin W. Gouldner and Richard A. Petersen, *Notes on Technology and the Moral Order* (Indianapolis: Bobbs-Merrill, 1962) for broadly comparative studies.

[3]Wilbert E. Moore, *Social Change* (Englewood Cliffs, N. J.: Prentice-Hall, 1963), pp. 72-76.

hampered by environmental limitations than primitive societies are, and thus *environmental variation should have less effect on the level of productivity in advanced societies than in primitive*.

Another important source of secondary variation has been identified by Stanislaw Andrzejewski in his important but neglected book, *Military Organization and Society.*[4] As he has shown, both deductive logic and empirical data indicate that *the degree of inequality in societies of a given level of technological development tends to vary inversely with what he calls "the military participation ratio,"*—that is *the proportion of the adult male population utilized in military operations*. Where most adult males are utilized for such purposes, the degree of inequality tends to be less than in those in which military needs are supplied by a small force of military specialists. Thus, this factor can also be used to explain some of the secondary variations which are found among societies of the same technological type.

A third source of secondary variations which can be anticipated is the technological variation which exists even among societies classified in the same category. No two societies are identical from the technological standpoint, and their classification into technological types is based on similarities (or identity) with respect to certain fundamental characteristics and ignores secondary differences. If primary differences in technology cause major differences in distributive systems, *one would expect these secondary differences in technology to generate lesser differences in distributive systems*. Thus, one would expect considerable differences between a society in the first stages of industrialization and one which is highly industrialized, just as one would expect differences between a hunting and gathering society with no alternative mode of food production and one which has some rudimentary forms of horticulture to supplement its diet.

Finally, as will become evident later in this chapter, *one can expect secondary variations associated with the stage a society occupies in what I shall call "the political cycle"*. . . . In effect, this is a measure of the degree to which the prevailing distributive system is accepted as legitimate. While this is linked somewhat with the level of technological development of societies, it is no simple function of this variable and hence exercises a substantially independent influence.

Force and Its Transformation. Of the two principles which govern the distributive process, need and power, the first is relatively simple and poses few problems of great importance or difficulty. Unhappily, the same cannot be said of the second. Of all the concepts used by sociologists, few are the source of more confusion and misunderstanding than power. Hence it is necessary to spell out in some detail the nature of this concept and how it functions in the distributive process.

As a starting point, it may be well to return briefly to one of the postulates introduced in [a previous] chapter. There it was assumed that survival is the chief goal of the great majority of men. If this is so, then it follows that *the ability to take life is the most effective form of power*. In other words, more men will respond more readily to the threat of the use of *force* than to any other. In effect, it constitutes the final court of appeals in human affairs; there is no appeal from force in a given situation except the exercise of superior force. . . .

---

[4](London: Routledge, 1954), especially Chap. 2.

This principle is. . . . recognized by the leaders of nations, the practical men of affairs. Every sovereign state restricts, and where possible prohibits, the independent exercise of force by its subjects. States may be tolerant of many things, but never of the growth of independent military organizations within their territories. The reason is obvious: any government which cannot suppress each and every forceful challenge to its authority is overthrown. Force is the foundation of sovereignty. . . .

If force is the foundation of political sovereignty, it is also the foundation of the distributive system in every society where there is a surplus to be divided. Where coercive power is weak, challenges inevitably occur, and the system is eventually destroyed and replaced by another based more firmly on force. Men struggling over control of the surplus of a society will not accept defeat so long as there is a higher court of appeals to which they may take their case with some likelihood of success and profit to themselves. . . .

While men will not resort to armed revolution for trivial gains, when control over the entire surplus of a society is involved, the prospect is more enticing. The attractiveness varies directly with the weakness of the current regime.

Nevertheless, as Edmund Burke, the famed English conservative, recognized, "The use of force alone is but temporary. It may subdue for a moment; but it does not remove the necessity of subduing again: and a nation is not governed, which is perpetually to be conquered." Though force is the most effective instrument for seizing power in a society, and though it always remains the foundation of any system of inequality, it is not the most effective instrument for retaining and exploiting a position of power and deriving the maximum benefits from it. Therefore, regardless of the objectives of a new regime, once organized opposition has been destroyed it is to its advantage to make increasing use of other techniques and instruments of control, and to allow force to recede into the background to be used only when other techniques fail.

If the new elite has materialistic goals and is concerned solely with self-aggrandizement, it soon discovers that the rule of might is both inefficient and costly. So long as it relies on force, much of the profit is consumed by the costs of coercion. If the population obeys only out of fear of physical violence, a large portion of the time, energy, and wealth of the elite are invariably consumed in the effort to keep it under control and separate the producers from the product of their labors. Even worse, honor, which normally ranks high in the scale of human values, is denied to those who rule by force alone.[5]

If materialistic elites have strong motives for shifting from the rule of might to the rule of right, ideologically motivated elites have even stronger. If the visions and ideals which led them to undertake the terrible risks and hardships of revolution are ever to be fulfilled, the voluntary cooperation of the population is essential, and this cannot be obtained by force. Force is, at best, the means to an end. That end, the establishment of a new social order, can never by fully attained until most members of society freely accept it as their own. The purpose of the revolution is to destroy the old elite and their institutions, which prevent the fulfillment of this dream. Once they are destroyed, an ideological elite strives to rule by persuasion. Thus *those who seize*

---

[5] For a good discussion of the limitations of rule by force, see Robert Dahl and Charles Lindblom, *Politics, Economics, and Welfare* (New York: Harper & Row, 1953), pp. 107-109.

power by force find it advantageous to legitimize their rule once effective organized opposition is eliminated. Force can no longer continue to play the role it did. It can no longer function as the private resource of a special segment of the population. Rather it must be transformed into a public resource used in the defense of law and order.

This may seem to be the equivalent of saying that those who have at great risk to themselves displaced the old elite must now give up all they have won. Actually, however, this is not at all necessary since, with a limited exercise of intelligence, force can be transformed into authority, and might into right. . . .

The Rule of Right. On first consideration it may seem that the rule of right is merely the rule of might in a new guise, and therefore no real change can be expected in the distributive process. Such a view is as unwarranted as that which denies the role might continues to play in support of vested interests, even under the rule of right. The fact is that, as the basis of power is shifted from might to right, certain subtle but important changes occur which have far-reaching consequences.

To begin with, if the powers of the regime are to be accepted as rightful and legitimate they must be exercised in some degree, at least, in accord with the conceptions of justice and morality held by the majority—conceptions which spring from their self-interest and partisan group interests. Thus, even though the laws promulgated by a new elite may be heavily slanted to favor themselves, there are limits beyond which this cannot be carried if they wish to gain the benefits of the rule of right.

Second, after the shift to the rule of law, the interests of any single member of the elite can no longer safely be equated with the interests of the elite as a whole. For example, if a member of the new elite enters into a contractual arrangement with some member of the nonelite, and this turns out badly for him, it is to his interest to ignore the law and break the contract. However, this is not to the interest of the other members of the elite since most contractual arrangements work to their benefit. Therefore, it is to their interest to enforce the law in support of the claims of the nonelite to preserve respect for the law with all the benefits this provides them.

Vilfredo Pareto, the great Italian scholar who has contributed so much to our understanding of these problems, has pointed out a third change associated with the shift from the rule of might to the rule of right. As he observed, those who have won power by force will, under the rule of right, gradually be replaced by a new kind of person and in time these persons will form a new kind of elite. To describe the nature of this change, Pareto wrote of the passing of governmental power from "the lions" to "the foxes."[6] The lions are skilled in the use of force, the foxes in the use of cunning. In other words, the shift from the rule of might means that new skills become essential, and therefore there is a high probability that many of the elite will be displaced because they lack these skills. This displacement is greatly

---

[6] See Vilfredo Pareto, *The Mind and Society*, translated by A. Bongiorno and Arthur Livingstone and edited by Livingstone (New York: Harcourt, Brace & World, 1935), Vol. III, especially paragraphs 2170-2278.

facilitated by the fact that the interests of the elite as a class are no longer identical with the interests of each individual member, which means that individually they become vulnerable. Even those who hang on are forced to change, so that in time the nature of the elite as a class is substantially altered, provided it is not destroyed first by a new leonine revolution or coup. Though this change means increased reliance on intelligence and less on force, as Pareto's choice of the term "fox" and his emphasis on "cunning" indicate, the shift to the rule of right is not the beginning of the millennium when lambs can lie down safely with lions—or foxes. Nor is it the end of the era in which self-interest and partisan group interests dominate human action.

As Pareto's analysis suggests, the rule of the foxes means not merely the rise and fall of individuals, but also changes in the power position of whole classes. Specifically, it means some decline in the position of the military and a corresponding rise by the commercial class and the class of professional politicians, both of which are traditionally skilled in the use of cunning. To a lesser degree, it means some improvement in the status of most of the nonmanual classes engaged in peaceful, civilian pursuits.

Fourth, and finally, the transition from the rule of might to the rule of right usually means greater decentralization of power. Under the rule of might, all power tends to be concentrated in the hands of an inner circle of the dominant elite and their agents. Independent centers of power are viewed as a threat and hence are destroyed or taken over. Under the rule of right, however, this is not the case. So long as they remain subject to the law, diverse centers of power can develop and compete side by side. This development is not inevitable, but it can, and probably will, happen once the elite no longer has to fear for the survival of the new regime. As many observers have noted, the degree of unity within a group tends to be a function of the degree to which the members perceive their existence as threatened by others.

In view of these changes, it becomes clear that shifts from the rule of might to the rule of right and vice versa constitute one of the more important sources of variation within societal types defined in technological terms. In other words, even among societies at the same level of technological development, we must expect differences along the lines indicated above, reflecting differences in their position on the might-right continuum. . . .

Classes. Stratification is a multi-dimensional phenomenon. Human populations are stratified in various ways, and each of these alternative modes of stratification provides a basis for a different conception of class.[7] Thus, although one may legitimately analyze the population of a given community in terms of prestige classes, this does not exhaust the subject of stratification. The same population can also be analyzed in terms of power classes or privilege classes. Analytically each of these is quite distinct, though empirically there is a substantial measure of overlap. . . .

---

[7]As will be noted later, the concept "class" may actually apply to several adjacent levels of organization, as when we speak of subclasses within classes. However, this does not alter the basic fact that classes are a level of organization standing between individuals and class systems.

The difficulty is further increased since even these three modes of classification are not unidimensional. . . . Power takes many forms and these cannot always be reduced to a meaningful common denominator. An individual may have large property holdings without occupying a correspondingly important and powerful office and vice versa. Similarly, an individual may occupy an important and powerful role in one institutional system but not in others.

In view of this, it is clear that the term "class" should not be defined too narrowly. More can be gained by defining the term broadly and then distinguishing carefully between different kinds of classes. Therefore, we might best define a class as *an aggregation of persons in a society who stand in a similar position with respect to some form of power, privilege, or prestige.*

This is *not* to say that all types of classes are equally important for theoretical and analytical purposes. On the contrary, if our goal is to answer the question of "who gets what and why?" and if our analysis. . . has any validity at all, *power* classes must be our chief concern. The distribution of privilege and prestige seem largely determined by the distribution of power, at least in those societies in which a significant surplus is produced. . . .

Though the definition of class seems relatively simple and straightforward, there are certain ideas implicit in it which are not completely obvious and require examination before moving on to other matters. To begin with, though the classes with which we shall be concerned are defined *in terms* of power, this does not mean that they all *have* power. On the contrary, some have virtually no power, as in the case of the expendables in agrarian societies. . . .

Second, given this definition, a single individual may well be a member of half a dozen power classes. This is inevitable whenever the various forms of power are less than perfectly correlated with one another. To illustrate, in contemporary American society a single individual may be a member of the middle class with respect to property holdings, a member of the working class by virtue of his job in a factory, and a member of the Negro "caste." Each of the major roles he occupies, as well as his status in the property hierarchy, influences his chances of obtaining the things he seeks in life, and thus each places him in a specific class. Since these resources are so imperfectly correlated, he cannot be located in any single class. In this connection, it may be appropriate to note that this tendency seems to become progressively more pronounced as one moves from technologically primitive to technologically advanced societies. In other words, *the necessity of multidimensional analyses seems greatest in modern industrial societies.*

Third, though the definition does not say so explicitly, *the members of every power class share certain common interests with one another, and these shared interests constitute a potential basis for hostility toward other classes.* This follows as a logical corollary of the fact that what unites the members of a class is their common possession, control, or utilization of something which affects their chances of fulfilling their wishes and desires. Given our earlier assumptions about the nature of man, it follows that all members of a given class have a vested interest in protecting or increasing the value of their common resource and in reducing the value of competitive resources which constitute the bases of other classes.

This is not to say that the members of a class always have a conscious awareness of their common interest, much less that they act collectively on the basis of it. Nor are they always consciously or overtly hostile to members of other classes. These are possibilities which may be realized, but there is nothing inevitable about them.

One final feature of the definition deserving note is the somewhat vague and annoying phrase, "a similar position." The critical reader will ask how much similarity is required and will find, unhappily, that there is no definite answer. Whether we like it or not, this kind of phrasing is forced on us by the nature of the reality we seek to analyze. In most cases human populations simply are not stratified into a limited number of clearly differentiated, highly discrete categories. Rather, they tend to be strung out along continua which lack breaks that can be utilized as class boundaries. Furthermore, if we were to insist that members of classes stand in *identical* positions with respect to the distribution of things of value, we should have thousands, possibly millions, of classes in many societies, most with but a handful of members, and some with only one.

To avoid this, we are forced to use less restrictive criteria, but this forces us to use less *precise* ones. In general, students of stratification have found it more advantageous to employ a smaller number of larger and more inclusive classes. Thus, there are frequent references to broad categories such as peasants, merchants, workers, professionals, and so forth. The use of such categories is not meant to deny the existence of internal variation within these classes. Obviously each class can be subdivided into more homogenous subcategories or subclasses, e.g., prosperous peasants and poor peasants or rich merchants and poor merchants. The extent to which this is done depends largely on the nature of the study. . . .

THE NEW MIDDLE CLASS

C. Wright Mills

Ever since the new middle class began numerically to displace the old, its political role has been an object of query and debate. The political question has been closely linked with another—that of the position of new middle-class occupations in modern stratification.

This linkage of politics and stratification was all the more to be expected inasmuch as the white-collar man as a sociological creature was first discovered by Marxian theoreticians in search of recruits for the proletarian movement. They expected that society would be polarized into class-conscious proletariat and

SOURCE: C. Wright Mills, *White Collar* (New York: Oxford University Press, 1953). pp. 289-300. Reprinted by permission.

bourgeoisie, that in their general decline the in-between layers would choose one side or the other—or at least keep out of the way of the major protagonists. Neither of these expectations, however, had been realized when socialist theoreticians and party bureaucrats began at the opening of the present century to tinker with the classic perspective.

In trying to line up the new population into those who could and those who could not be relied upon to support their struggle, party statisticians ran squarely into the numerical upsurge of the white-collar salariat. The rise of these groups as a problem for Marxists signalized a shift from the simple property versus no-property dichotomy to differentiations within the no-property groups. It focused attention upon occupational structure. Moreover, in examining white-collar groups, along with the persistent small entrepreneurs of farm and city, they came upon the further fact that although the new middle class was propertyless, and the smaller entrepreneurs often suffered economic downgrading, members of these strata did not readily take to the socialist ideology. Their political attachments did not coincide with their economic position, and certainly not with their imminently expected position. They represented a numerical upthrust of falsely conscious people, and they were an obstacle to the scheduled course of the revolution.

Theories and Difficulties. To relate in detail all the theories that followed upon these discoveries and speculations would be more monotonous than fruitful; the range of theory had been fairly well laid out by the middle 'twenties, and nothing really new has since been added. Various writers have come upon further detail, some of it crucial, or have variously combined the major positions, some of which have had stronger support than others. But the political directions that can be inferred from the existence of the new middle class may be sorted out into four major possibilities.

1. The new middle class, in whole or in some crucial segment, will continue to grow in numbers and in power; in due course it will develop into a politically independent class. Displacing other classes in performance of the pivotal functions required to run modern society, it is slated to be the next ruling class. The accent will be upon the new middle class; the next epoch will be theirs.

2. The new middle classes will continue to grow in numbers and power, and although they will not become a force that will rise to independent power, they will be a major force for stability in the general balance of the different classes. As important elements in the class balance, they will make for the continuance of liberal capitalist society. Their spread checks the creeping proletarianization; they act as a buffer between labor and capital. Taking over certain functions of the old middle class, but having connections with the wage-workers, they will be able to co-operate with them too; thus they bridge class contrasts and mitigate class conflicts. They are the balance wheel of class interests, the stabilizers, the social harmonizers. They are intermediaries of the new social solidarity that will put an end to class bickering. That is why they are catered to by any camp or movement that is on its way to electoral power, or, for that matter, attempted revolution.

3. Members of the new middle class, by their social character and political outlook, are really bourgeoisie and they will remain that. This is particularly

apparent in the tendency of these groups to become status groups rather than mere economic classes. They will form, as in Nazi Germany, prime human materials for conservative, for reactionary, and even for fascist, movements. They are natural allies and shock troops of the larger capitalist drive.

4. The new middle class will follow the classic Marxian scheme: in due course, it will become homogeneous in all important respects with the proletariat and will come over to their socialist policy. In the meantime, it represents—for various reasons, which will be washed away in crises and decline—a case of delayed reaction. For in historical reality, the "new middle class" is merely a peculiar sort of new proletariat, having the same basic interests. With the intensification of the class struggle between the real classes of capitalist society, it will be swept into the proletarian ranks. A thin, upper layer may go over to the bourgeoisie, but it will not count in numbers or in power.

These various arguments are difficult to compare, first of all because they do not all include the same occupations under the catchword "new middle class." When we consider the vague boundary lines of the white-collar world, we can easily understand why such an occupational salad invites so many conflicting theories and why general images of it are likely to differ. There is no one accepted word for them; white collar, salaried employee, new middle class are used interchangeably. During the historical span covered by different theories, the occupational groups composing these strata have changed; and at given times, different theorists in pursuit of bolstering data have spotlighted one or the other groups composing the total. So contrasting images of the political role of the white-collar people can readily exist side by side (and perhaps even both be correct). Those, for instance, who believe that as the vanguard stratum of modern society they are slated to be the next ruling class do not think of them as ten-cent store clerks, insurance-agents, and stenographers, but rather as higher technicians and staff engineers, as salaried managers of business cartels and big officials of the Federal Government. On the other hand, those who hold that they are being proletarianized do focus upon the mass of clerklings and sales people, while those who see their role as in-between mediators are most likely to include both upper and lower ranges. . . .

Most of the work that has been done on the new middle class and its political role involves more general theories of the course of capitalist development. That is why it is difficult to sort out in a simple and yet systematic way what given writers really think of the white-collar people. Their views are based not on an examination of this stratum as much as on, first, the political program they happen to be following; second, the doctrinal position, as regards the political line-up of classes, they have previously accepted; and third, their judgment in regard to the main course of twentieth-century industrial society.

Proletarian purists would disavow white-collar people; United Fronters would link at least segments of them with workers in a fight over specific issues, while carefully preserving organizational and, above all, doctrinal independence; People's Fronters would cater to them by modifying wage-worker ideology and program in order to unite the two; liberals of "Populist" inclination, in a sort of dogmatic pluralism, would call upon them along with small businessmen, small farmers, and all grades of wage-workers to coalesce. And each camp, if it prevailed long enough for its intellectuals to get into production, would evolve theories about the character of the white-collar people and the role they are capable of playing.

As for political doctrines, the very definition of the white-collar problem has usually assumed as given a more or less rigid framework of fated classes. The belief that in any future struggle between big business and labor, the weight of the white-collar workers will be decisive assumes that there is going to be a future struggle, in the open, between business and labor. The question of whether they will be either proletariat or bourgeoisie, thus in either case giving up whatever identity they may already have, or go their independent way, assumes that there are these other sides and that their struggle will, in fact if not in consciousness, make up the real political arena. Yet, at the same time, the theories to which the rise of the new middle class has given birth distinguish various, independent sectors of the proletariat and of the bourgeoisie, suggesting that the unit of analysis has been overformalized. The problem of the new middle class must now be raised in a context that does not merely assume homogeneous blocs of classes.

The political argument over white-collar workers has gone on over an international scale. Although modern nations do have many trends in common—among them certainly the statistical increase of the white-collar workers—they also have unique features. In posing the question of the political role of white-collar people in the United States, we must learn all we can from discussions of them in other countries, the Weimar Republic especially, but in doing so, we must take everything hypothetically and test it against U.S. facts and trends.

The time-span of various theories and expectations, as we have noted, has in most of the arguments not been closely specified. Those who hold the view that white-collar workers are really only an odd sort of proletariat and will, in due course, begin to behave accordingly, or the view that the new middle class is slated to be the next ruling class have worked with flexible and often conflicting schedules.

What has been at issue in these theories is the objective postion of the new middle classes within and between the various strata of modern society, and the political content and direction of their mentality. Questions concerning either of these issues can be stated in such a way as to allow, and in fact demand, observational answers only if adequate conceptions of stratification and of political mentality are clearly set forth.

Mentalities. It is frequently asserted, in theories of the white-collar people, that there are no classes in the United States because "psychology is of the essence of classes" or, as Alfred Bingham has put it, that "class groupings are always nebulous, and in the last analysis only the vague thing called class-consciousness counts." It is said that people in the United States are not aware of themselves as members of classes, do not identify themselves with their appropriate economic level, do not often organize in terms of these brackets or vote along the lines they provide. America, in this reasoning, is a sandheap of "middle-class individuals."

But this is to confuse psychological feelings with other kinds of social and economic reality. Because men are not "class conscious" at all times and in all places does not mean that "there are no classes" or that "in America everybody is middle class." The economic and social facts are one thing; psychological feelings may or may not be associated with them in expected ways. Both are important, and if psychological feelings and political outlooks do not correspond to economic class, we must try to find out why, rather than throw out the economic baby with the psychological bath, and so fail to understand how either fits into the national tub. No matter what people believe, class structure as an economic arrangement influences their life chances according to their positions in it. If they do not grasp the causes of their conduct this does not mean that the social analyst must ignore or deny them.

If political mentalities are not in line with objectively defined strata, that lack of correspondence is a problem to be explained; in fact, it is the grand problem of the psychology of social strata. The general problem of stratification and political mentality has to do with the extent to which the members of objectively defined strata are homogeneous in their political alertness, outlook, and allegiances, and with the degree to which their political mentality and actions are in line with the interests demanded by the juxtaposition of their objective position and their accepted values.

To understand the occupation, class, and status positions of a set of people is not necessarily to know whether or not they (1) will become class-conscious, feeling that they belong together or that they can best realize their rational interests by combining; (2) will organize themselves, or be open to organization by others, into associations, movements, or political parties; (3) will have "collective attitudes" of any sort, including those toward themselves, their common situation; or (4) will become hostile toward other strata and struggle against them. These social, political, and psychological characteristics may or may not occur on the basis of similar objective situations. In any given case, such possibilities must be explored, and "subjective" attributes must not be used as criteria for class inclusion, but rather, as Max Weber has made clear, stated as probabilities on the basis of objectively defined situations.

Implicit in this way of stating the issues of stratification lies a model of social movements and political dynamics. The important differences among people are differences that shape their biographies and ideas; within any given stratum, of course, individuals differ, but if their stratum has been adequately understood, we can expect certain psychological traits to recur. The probability that people will have a similar mentality and ideology, and that they will join together for action, is increased the more homogeneous they are with respect to class, occupation, and prestige. Other factors do, of course, affect the probability that ideology, organization, and consciousness will occur among those in objectively similar strata. But psychological factors are likely to be associated with *strata*, which consist of people who are characterized by an intersection of the *several* dimensions we have been using: class, occupation, status, and power. The task is to sort out these dimensions of stratification in a systematic way, paying attention to each separately and then to its relation to each of the other dimensions.

The question whether the white-collar workers are a "new middle class," or a "new working class," or what not, is not entirely one of definition, but its empirical solution is made possible only by clarified definitions. The meaning of the term "proletarianized," around which the major theories have revolved, is by no means clear. In the definitions we have used, however, proletarianization might refer to shifts of middle-class occupations toward wage-workers in terms of: income, property, skill, prestige or power, irrespective of whether or not the people involved are aware of these changes. Or, the meaning may be in terms of changes in consciousness, outlook, or organized activity. It would be possible, for example, for a segment of the white-collar people to become virtually identical with wage-workers in income, property, and skill, but to resist being like them in prestige claims and to anchor their whole consciousness upon illusory prestige factors. Only by keeping objective position and ideological consciousness separate in analysis can the problem be stated with precision and without unjustifiable assumptions about wage-workers, white-collar workers, and the general psychology of social classes.

When the Marxist, Anton Pannekoek for example, refuses to include propertyless people of lower income than skilled workers in the proletariat, he refers to ideological and prestige factors. He does not go on to refer to the same factors as they operate among the "proletariat," because he holds to what can only be called a metaphysical belief that the proletariat is *destined* to win through to a certain consciousness. Those who see white-collar groups as composing an independent "class," *sui generis*, often use prestige or status as their defining criterion rather than economic level. The Marxian assertion, for example L. B. Boudin's, that salaried employees "are in reality just as much a part of the proletariat as the merest day-laborer," obviously rests on economic criteria, as is generally recognized when his statement is countered by the assertion that he ignores "important psychological factors."

The Marxist in his expectation assumes, first, that wage-workers, or at least large sections of them, do in fact, or will at any moment, have a socialist consciousness of their revolutionary role in modern history. He assumes, secondly, that the middle classes, or large sections of them, are acquiring this consciousness, and in this respect are becoming like the wage-workers or like what wage-workers are assumed to be. Third, he rests his contention primarily upon the assumption that the economic dimension, especially property, of stratification is the key one, and that it is in this dimension that the middle classes are becoming like wage-workers.

But the fact that propertyless employees (both wage-workers and salaried employees) have not automatically assumed a socialist posture clearly means that propertylessness is not the only factor, or even the crucial one, determining inner-consciousness or political will.

Neither white-collar people nor wage-workers have been or are preoccupied with questions of property. The concentration of property during the last century has been a slow process rather than a sharp break inside the life span of one generation; even the sons and daughters of farmers—among whom the most obvious "expropriation" has gone on—have had their attentions focused on the urban lure rather than on urban propertylessness. As jobholders, moreover, salaried employees have generally, with the rest of the population, experienced a secular rise in standards of living: propertylessness has certainly not necessarily coincided with pauperization. So the centralization of property, with consequent expropriation, has not been widely experienced as "agony" or reacted to by proletarianization, in any psychological sense that may be given these terms.

Objectively, we have seen that the structural position of the white-collar mass is becoming more and more similar to that of the wage-workers. Both are, of course, propertyless, and their incomes draw closer and closer together. All the factors of their status position, which have enabled white-collar workers to set themselves apart from wage-workers, are now subject to definite decline. Increased rationalization is lowering the skill levels and making their work more and more factory-like. As high-school education becomes more universal among wage-workers, and the skills required for many white-collar tasks become simpler, it is clear that the white-collar job market will include more wage-worker children.

In the course of the next generation, a "social class" between lower white-collar and wage-workers will probably be formed, which means, in Weber's terms, that between the two positions there will be a typical job mobility. This will not, of course, involve the professional strata or the higher managerial employees, but it will include the bulk of the workers in salesroom and office. These shifts in the occupational worlds of the propertyless are more important to them than the existing fact of their propertylessness.

Organizations. The assumption that political supremacy follows from functional, economic indispensability underlies all those theories that see the new middle class or any of its sections slated to be the next ruling class. For it is assumed that the class that is indispensable in fulfilling the major functions of the social order will be the next in the sequence of ruling classes. Max Weber in his essay on bureaucracy has made short shrift of this idea: "The ever increasing 'indispensability' of the officialdom, swollen to millions, is no more decisive for this question [of power] than is the view of some representatives of the proletarian movement that the economic indispensability of the proletarians is decisive for the measure of their social and political power position. If 'indispensability' were decisive, then where slave labor prevailed and where freemen usually abhor work as a dishonor, the 'indispensable' slaves ought to have held the positions of power, for they were at least as indispensable as officials and proletarians are today. Whether the power . . . as such increases cannot be decided *a priori* from such reasons."

Yet the assumption that it can runs all through the white-collar literature. Just as Marx, seeing the parasitical nature of the capitalist's endeavor, and the real function of work performed by the workers, predicted the workers' rise to power, so James Burnham (and before him Harold Lasswell, and before him John Corbin) assumes that since the new middle class is the carrier of those skills upon which modern society more and more depends, it will inevitably, in the course of time, assume political power. Technical and managerial indispensability is thus confused with the facts of power struggle, and overrides all other sources of power. The deficiency of such arguments must be realized positively: we need to develop and to use a more open and flexible model of the relations of political power and stratification.

Increasingly, class and status situations have been removed from free market forces and the persistence of tradition, and been subject to more formal rules. A government management of the class structure has become a major means of alleviating inequalities and insuring the risks of those in lower-income classes. Not so much free labor markets as the powers of pressure groups now shape the class positions and privileges of various strata in the United States. Hours and wages, vacations, income security through periods of sickness, accidents, unemployment, and old age—these are now subject to many intentional pressures, and, along with tax policies, transfer payments, tariffs, subsidies, price ceilings, wage freezes, et cetera, make up the content of "class fights" in the objective meaning of the phrase.

The "Welfare State" attempts to manage class chances without modifying basic class structure; in its several meanings and types, it favors economic policies designed to redistribute life-risks and life-chances in favor of those in the more exposed class situations, who have the power or threaten to accumulate the power, to do something about their case.

Labor union, farm bloc, and trade association dominate the political scene of the Welfare State as well as of the permanent war economy; contests within and between these blocs increasingly determine the position of various groups. The state, as a descriptive fact, is at the balanced intersection of such pressures, and increasingly the privileges and securities of various occupational strata depend upon the bold means of organized power.

It is often by these means that the objective position of white-collar and wage-worker becomes similar. The greatest difficulty with the Marxist expectation of proletarianization is that many changes pointing that way have not come about by a lowering of the white-collar position, but often more crucially by a raising of the wage-worker position.

The salary, as contrasted with the wage, has been a traditional hall-mark of white-collar employment. Although still of prestige value to many white-collar positions, the salary must now be taken as a tendency in most white-collar strata rather than a water-tight boundary of the white-collar worlds. The contrast has rested on differences in the time-span of payment, and thus in security of tenure, and in the possibilities to plan because of more secure expectations of income over longer periods of time. But, increasingly, companies put salaried workers, whose salary for some time in many places has been reduced for absences, on an hourly basis. And manual workers, represented by unions, are demanding and getting precisely the type of privileges once granted only white-collar people.

All along the line, it is from the side of the wage-workers that the contrast in privileges has been most obviously breaking down. It was the mass-production union of steel workers, not salaried employees, that precipitated a national economic debate over the issue of regularized employment; and white-collar people must often now fight for what is sometimes assumed to be their inherited privilege: a union of professionals, The Newspaper Guild, has to insist upon dismissal pay as a clause in its contracts.

Whatever past differences between white-collar and wage-workers with respect to income security, sick benefits, paid vacations, and working conditions, the major trend is now for these same advantages to be made available to factory workers. Pensions, especially since World War II, have been a major idea in collective bargaining, and it has been the wage-worker that has had bargaining power. Social insurance to cover work injuries and occupational diseases has gradually been replacing the common law of a century ago, which held the employee at personal fault for work injury and the employer's liability had to be proved in court by a damage suit. In so far as such laws exist, they legally shape the class chances of the manual worker up to a par with or above other strata. Both privileges and income level have been increasingly subject to the power pressures of unions and government, and there is every reason to believe that in the future this will be even more the case.

The accumulation of power by any stratum is dependent on a triangle of factors: will and know-how, objective opportunity, and organization. The opportunity is limited by the group's structural position; the will is dependent upon the group's consciousness of its interests and ways of realizing them. And both structural position and consciousness interplay with organizations, which strengthen consciousness and are made politically relevant by structural position.

SOCIAL CLASS, POLITICS, AND CULTURE

T. B. Bottomore

The egalitarian movement which came to life in socialist clubs, trade unions, co-operative ventures and utopian communities grew stronger throughout the nineteenth century as capitalism developed. In the course of time this movement has taken many different forms—struggles for women's rights and against racial discrimination, and most recently the efforts to close the gap between rich and poor nations—but its driving force has remained the opposition to the hierarchy of social classes. The class system of the capitalist societies is seen as the very fount of inequality, from which arise the chief impediments to individual achievement and enjoyment, the major conflicts within and between nations, and the political dominance of priveleged minorities.

In this movement Marx's analysis of capitalist society acquired—directly or indirectly—a large influence, through the connections which it established between social classes and political institutions. According to Marx, the upper class in society—constituted by the owners of the principal means of production—is necessarily the *ruling* class; that is, it also controls the means of political domination—legislation, the courts, the administration, military force, and the agencies of intellectual persuasion. The other classes in society, which suffer in various ways under this domination, are the source of political opposition, of new social doctrines, and eventually of a new ruling class. Only in the modern capitalist societies, however, does a situation occur in which the contending classes are reduced to two clearly demarcated groups, one of which—the working class—because it contains no significant new social divisions within itself, espouses an egalitarian creed and engages in a political struggle to bring about a classless society.

The appeal of Marx's theory is twofold: it provides a clear and inspiring formulation of the aspirations of the working class, and at the same time it offers an explanation of the development of forms of society and government, and especially of the rise of the modern labor movement itself. There are not lacking, in the present age, governments which are quite plainly the instruments of rule by an upper class, as in those economically backward countries where the landowners dominate an uneducated, unorganized and dispirited peasantry. When Marx undertook his studies the class character of governments was just as apparent in the European countries which had embarked upon industrialization. During much of the nineteenth century only property-owners in these societies enjoyed full political rights; and it was scarcely an exaggeration to conceive the government as "a committee for managing the common affairs of the *bourgeoisie* as a whole." In many European countries it was only during the first two decades of the twentieth century that universal suffrage was finally established.

Since political democracy is such a recent growth Marx can hardly be blamed for having failed to consider all its implications for the association between economic and political power. At least he did not disregard the importance of the suffrage. . . .

The existence of large working-class parties has become a normal feature of the democratic capitalist countries, and this is one of the principal circumstances (another being the political system in the Soviet societies) which raise new problems concerning the relationship between class and politics. In a political system of this kind can the owners of property be regarded any longer as a permanent ruling class? Is the working class still a radical, revolutionary force which seeks to bring about an egalitarian society? Are the relations between classes in the political sphere still the same as they were in the nineteenth-century societies with their restricted franchise? Have new political divisions emerged alongside, or in the place of, those between classes; or have political conflicts lost some of the urgency and importance which they acquired in the period which saw the rise and growth of the labor movement? These questions lie at the heart of present controversies about the changing class structure of industrial societies.

It has become common, for example, to remark upon the great complexity of government in modern societies, and upon the influence which is exerted by the diverse interest groups which are consulted in the course of policy-making; and then to argue that where power is divided among many different groups, whose interests do not always coincide, the notion of a "ruling class" has lost all meaning. But if power is really so widely dispersed, how are we to account for the fact that the owners of property—the upper class in Marx's sense—still predominate so remarkably in government and administration, and in other elite positions; or that there has been so little redistribution of wealth and income, in spite of the strenuous and sustained effort of the labor movement to bring it about? Is it not reasonable to conclude. . .that notwithstanding political democracy, and despite the limited conflicts of interest which occur between elite groups in different spheres, the upper class in the capitalist societies is still a distinctive and largely self-perpetuating social group, and still occupies the vital positions of power? Its power may be less commanding, and it is certainly less arrogantly exercised, than in an earlier period, because it encounters an organized opposition and the test of elections, and because other classes have gained a limited access to the elites; but the power which it has retained enables it to defend successfully its most important economic interests. . . .

It is in any case the changes in the condition of the working class, and especially in its political role, which have most impressed students of class structure in the postwar period. The "new working class," it is claimed, is economically prosperous and aspires to middle-class standards of living:[1] and in consequence it has become less class conscious and less radical in politics. How far are these political inferences warranted? Class consciousness, in a broad sense, may be regarded as one form of the "consciousness of kind" which develops in all enduring social groups; for example, the consciousness of belonging to a particular nation. In this sense, the emergence of class consciousness, the increasing use of the term "class" to describe an individual's position in society, is itself a sign that new social groups have come into existence.[2] But in Marx's usage, which has had a profound influence both upon sociological theories and upon political doctrines, "class consciousness" involves something more than this; namely, the gradual formation of distinctive ideologies and political organizations which have as their object the promotion of particular class interests in a general conflict between classes.[3]

The growing class consciousness of the working class was represented by Marx as showing these characteristics in an exceptional degree; for it was expressed in ideologies and political movements which strongly emphasized the conflict of economic interest between capitalists and workers, and which proposed radical social changes in order to end the system of society based upon classes. The working class was, therefore, a revolutionary element in society; more revolutionary indeed than any earlier oppressed classes, since it aimed consciously at abolishing the whole class system. . . .

This conception of the working class as the animator of a revolutionary movement which is to establish a classless society, appears to many sociologists to be highly

---

[1] See my *Elites and Society* (New York, 1965), pp. 28-31.

[2] There is a good account by Asa Briggs, "The Language of 'Class' in Early Nineteenth Century England" in Asa Briggs and John Saville (eds.), *Essays in Labour History* (New York, 1960).

[3] Writings about the peasantry in *The Eighteenth Brumaire of Louis Bonaparte* Marx observed: "In so far as there is merely a local inter-connection among these smallholding peasants, and the identity of their interests begets no community, no national bond, and no political organization among them, they do not form a class."

questionable in the light of recent investigations. It is not that the prevalence of class consciousness in a broad sense, or the association between class membership and political affiliation, is generally denied. Social surveys have shown plainly that most people are familiar with the class structure of their society, and are aware of their own position within it. Equally, it has been shown that class membership is still the strongest single influence upon a person's social and political attitudes; and that the major political parties in most countries represent pre-eminently class interests. What is brought into question by recent studies is the view that the working class, in the advanced industrial countries, is striving to bring about a revolutionary transformation of society, rather than piecemeal reforms within the existing social structure; or that there is a total incompatibility and opposition between the doctrines and objectives of political parties which draw their main support from different classes. In Marx's theory the working class was revolutionary in two senses: first, that it aimed, or would aim, to produce the most comprehensive and fundamental change in social institutions that had ever been accomplished in the history of mankind, and secondly, that it would do so in the course of a sustained conflict with the *bourgeoisie* which was likely to culminate in a violent struggle for power. The nascent working class of the mid-nineteenth century fitted reasonably well into this scheme, which was constructed largely out of the experiences of the French Revolution. The "new working class" of the mid-twentieth century, it is argued, fits badly. . . .

In all the advanced industrial countries the violence of class conflict has greatly diminished over the past few decades, and the working-class parties which still regard their aims as likely to be achieved by the use of force are few in number and insignificant. The change from the conditions at the end of the nineteenth century has been produced by several factors, among which we may single out the development of political democracy, the more effective power of modern governments, aided by the great advances in military technology, in administration and in communication, and the changes in the nature of working-class aims as well as in the relations between classes. It would be a mistake to dismiss entirely the role of force in political conflicts in the Western industrial societies; for not only did violent class struggles take place as recently as the 1930's, but other types of social conflict—for example, between Negroes and whites in the USA—have often engendered violence during the past decade. Nevertheless, at the present time it is in those countries which have just embarked upon industrialization that violent struggles, especially between classes, are mainly to be found.

Changes in the relations between classes in the capitalist societies have accompanied the changes in the character of the major social classes, influencing and being influenced by the latter. In so far as social mobility has increased, and the middle class has grown in numbers, the image of society as divided between two great contending classes has become blurred by the superimposition of another image, in which society appears as an indefinite and changing hierarchy of status positions, which merge into each other, and between which individuals and families are able to move with much greater facility than in the past. In addition, the everyday economic struggle between workers and employers has been regulated more and more by the state, through the creation of new social institutions for negotiation, arbitration, and joint consultation. It is this situation which leads Ralf Dahrendorf, in his *Class and Class Conflict in Industrial Society*, to write of "post-capitalist societies" in which industrial conflicts have been institutionalized and thereby insulated from the sphere of politics; and although this is an exaggeration, inasmuch as political conflicts are still very largely about class interests, and are widely recognized as such, it contains an element of truth in so far as it points to the moderation of hostility between classes and to the emergence of political issues which are in some measure detached from questions of class interest. There is unquestionably some common ground between the main political parties in the Western industrial countries; and the development of science and technology, economic growth and rising levels of living, urban congestion and crime, are among the issues which have to be dealt with politically along much the same lines in *all* the industrial countries.

The social changes which have produced the "new working class," as well as a political climate in which violent confrontations between the classes are rare, have been interpreted by some sociologists as a crucial phase in a process which is leading to the complete assimilation of the working class into existing society, as a beginning of the "end of ideology" in the precise sense of the decline of socialist doctrines which offer a radical criticism of present-day society and the hope of an alternative form of society. But this interpretation goes beyond the facts which have been discovered by sociological research. It relies, for instance, upon a tacit comparison between the present state of working-class consciousness and its state in some vaguely located and imperfectly known past age, which is seen as a time of heroic resolution and militancy. Against this it should be observed that in the past few decades, in the very period in which the working class is supposed to have become more middle class in its outlook, the support for socialist parties in Europe has been maintained or has substantially increased. It may be objected that this support has been gained by the progressive elimination of distinctively socialist ideas from the programmes of such parties. But this too is doubtful. The language of socialism has changed over the past century, in ways which it would be rewarding to study more closely, but the ends of the labor movement—collectivism and social equality—have not been abandoned or even seriously questioned. . . .

There are several other influences at work in the Western industrial societies which sustain the ideological controversies over the future form of society, and which lend support, in particular, to the socialist doctrines of the working class. One of the most important is the extension, and the more general acceptance of public ownership of industry, public management of the economy, and public provision of a wide range of social and cultural services. The contrast between "private opulence" and "public squalor," to which J. K. Galbraith has pointed, has awakened many people to the fact that in modern societies many of the most valuable private amenities can only be got or preserved through public action. Individuals may be prosperous enough to provide adequately for their personal needs in food, housing, transport, and some kinds of entertainment, but they cannot individually assure what is needed for full enjoyment in the way of roads, facilities for sport and recreation, good working conditions, or a congenial and attractive urban environment. The unrestricted pursuit of private wealth and private enjoyment leads, indeed, to the impoverishment of these vital public services.

In the economic sphere the growth in the size of firms in major branches of industry, and the approach to monopolistic control in some sectors, has reduced the difference between the operations of publicly owned and privately owned enterprises; and if there is, at the present time, no great public excitement over the issue of "nationalization" of industry, this is in part because it is taken for granted that a change of ownership would not affect the economic performance of the industry. In part, also, it is due to recognition of the fact that the economy as a whole, in a modern society, must anyway be increasingly regulated and directed by the political authorities if a consistently high rate of growth is to be achieved, through the systematic application of science to production. Today the entrepreneur has become much less important; while the trained manager (who can perfectly well be a public servant) and the scientist have become much more important.

The increasing provision of social services by the state, which in recent times has been largely brought about by the pressure of the labor movement, has also fortified the socialist conception of a more equal, more collectivist society. Social legislation in the Welfare State may not be preponderantly egalitarian, either in intention or in effect,[4] but as it is extended and comes eventually to include an "incomes policy" so it approaches the conditions in which, as a German social scientist has observed, the task of social policy is to determine the order of priority of claims against the national product.[5] And these are conditions which would accord most fully with the institutions of a classless society.

This discussion of classes and ideologies in the Western societies, if it suggests that the working class may still be considered an independent force in political life, and one which still aims to bring about radical changes in the social structure, also indicates that the development of the working class has diverged in many respects from the course which Marx and the early Marxists expected it to follow. Marx's theory dealt, necessarily, with the first stages in the formation of the working class, and it proposed broad hypotheses rather than settled conclusions based upon intensive research. The Marxist sociologists—in any case few in number—have not greatly advanced the empirical study of social classes. Often they have seemed to be writing about an imaginary society, in which a pure class struggle continues inexorably, unsullied by such events of practical life as the advent of political democracy, the extension of welfare services, the growth of national income, or the increasing governmental regulation of the economy. Marx himself, through his dramatic vision of a revolutionary confrontation between the classes and his initial optimism about the growth of the labor movement, gave some encouragement to an outlook of this kind. There had been bourgeois revolutions, therefore there would be proletarian revolutions.

---

[4] For a discussion of this point see T. H. Marshall, *Social Policy* (New York, 1965), Chapter 13, "Retrospect and Prospect."
[5] Quoted by T. H. Marshall, *Social Policy*, p. 183.

Neither Marx nor his followers examined sufficiently the strengths and weaknesses of the major social classes in capitalist society, many of which, indeed, have only become apparent through the experiences of the past fifty or sixty years. Marx insisted that the ruling ideas in any society are the ideas of the ruling class. But he did not seriously consider how important the ideas themselves might be in sustaining that rule, or how difficult it would be for the working class to oppose them with its own ideas.[6] Doubtless he thought that his own social theory would have a great effect (as it has), and he also counted upon the economic failure of capitalism—the ever-worsening crises—to discredit bourgeois ideas. In fact, bourgeois ideas have only been discredited, for brief periods, in those societies which have suffered defeat in war, and it is in such circumstances that the major revolutions of the twentieth century have occurred. Otherwise it is true to say that the working class in all countries has continued to be profoundly influenced by the dominant ideas of capitalist society; for example, by nationalism and imperialism, by the competitive, acquisitive and possessive conception of human nature and social relations, and in recent times by a view of the overriding purpose of society as being the creation of ever greater material wealth. The attempts to combat these ideas reveal the immense difficulties involved in doing so. The ideal of working-class internationalism, in opposition to national rivalries and war between nations, has never been realized in more than a fragmentary form, in the face of differences of language and culture, and the manifold problems of establishing international associations at any level. On the other side, the idea of competition and of activity as mainly acquisitive easily becomes acceptable when it is associated with equality of opportunity—real or supposed—for which the working class itself has striven; while the idea of uninterrupted economic growth must clearly appeal, with reason, to those who are struggling to escape from cramping poverty.

Yet in spite of these difficulties, egalitarian and collectivist ideas have spread widely during this century. They have done so more slowly than Marx expected, but this might mean no more than that he made a mistake over the time scale while still being right about the general direction of change. The question now is whether these ideas have lost their vigor and have begun to recede, or whether they are still active and effective. A number of sociologists, as we have seen, observe a decline in the enthusiasm of the working class for collective ends, a loss of interest in any social mission, and the gradual erosion of a distinctive working-class culture. . . .

There are several reasons to be cautious about accepting this view that the relative peace on the ideological front, and the apparent decline in the vigor of working-class social ideals, have become permanent features of the capitalist societies; that the final form of industrial society has been reached. First, it is likely that there will be growing discontent as it becomes evident that there is no general trend towards greater economic equality, and that, on the contrary, there are very

---

[6] Among later Marxists, Gramsci was the only one who gave much serious attention to these questions, and I should think that he was influenced in this direction by the work of his compatriot Mosca, who had introduced the term "political formula" to describe the body of doctrine which every ruling class in his view, has to develop and to get accepted by the rest of society if it is to retain power.

powerful movements which tend to produce a more unequal distribution of income and wealth whenever the industrial and political pressure of the working class is relaxed. It is obvious, for example, that in some Western countries there is a great disproportion between the modest wage increases which many industrial workers have claimed in recent years, and the large increases of salary which some groups of professional workers have demanded. Those in the professions have many advantages in pressing their claims, especially where the supply of qualified people is limited by the nature of the educational system; their actions are usually interpreted more sympathetically by the mass media than are the similar actions of industrial workers; and their class consciousness and determination to maintain or improve their established position in society appear to be waxing rather than waning. In society as a whole it is likely that the continued economic growth, which has benefited the working class, has brought even greater gains to those whose incomes are derived wholly or mainly from the ownership of capital. If, therefore, a tranquil and moderate struggle between classes or sectional interests, and ideological peace, depend upon a settled trend towards greater economic equality, they cannot be regarded at present as in any way assured.

A second consideration, which seems to me still more important, is that there is a growing discrepancy between the condition of the working class at work and in leisure time. Security of employment and rising levels of living have brought greater freedom of choice and independence of action for industrial workers outside the workplace, and younger workers in particular have taken advantage of their new opportunities. But one result of this is that the contrast between work and leisure has become more intense: at work there is still constraint, strict subordination, lack of responsibility, absence of means for self-expression. All the studies of the modern working class which I reviewed earlier bring out clearly that workers are profoundly aware of this division in their lives, and that they have a deep hatred of the present system of industrial work. . . .

It is hard to believe that such a division can continue unchanged, but it may be overcome or mitigated in several different ways. Sustained economic growth may result in such a reduction of working hours and expansion of leisure time that the hierarchical and authoritarian structure of industry comes to play a negligible part in the individual's personal and social life, and is no longer a matter for concern. Or, on the other hand, there may be renewed efforts to introduce into the sphere of economic production some of the freedom and independence which exist in leisure time, and these efforts may be helped by changes in the character of production itself, as it becomes increasingly a scientific activity—using both the natural and the social sciences—which needs the services of highly educated and responsible individuals to carry it on. Most probably, there will be some combination of these two movements; but in so far as the second one takes place at all it will be through the actions of working-class organizations seeking to control the labor process, which still appears, as it did to Marx, as the fundamental activity in every social system.

The rise of the working class in modern societies has been a more protracted affair than Marx supposed, and it has only rarely approached that state of decisive struggle with the *bourgeoisie* which he expected. In the future a similar gradual development appears most likely, but the end may still be Marx's ideal society, a classless society. Indeed, it is only now, when the tremendous development of the sciences has created the possibility of truly wealthy societies—but for the uncertainties of population growth and nuclear warfare—that the economic foundations of a classless society can be regarded as assured. What kinds of inequality would remain in the absence of social classes, and in conditions where individuals had independence and responsibility both at work and in leisure, can only be conjectured. There would doubtless be some differences in the prestige of occupations, in incomes, and in the social position of individuals, but there is no reason to suppose that these would be very large, or that they would be incompatible with an awareness of basic human equality and community.

The principal fault in many recent studies of social classes has been that they lack an historical sense. Like the economists of whom Marx said that they believed there had been history, because feudalism had disappeared, but there was no longer any history, because capitalism was a natural and eternal social order, some sociologists have accepted that there was an historical development of classes and of class conflicts in the early period of industrial capitalism, but that this has ceased in the fully evolved industrial societies in which the working class has escaped from poverty and has attained industrial and political citizenship. But this assumption is made without any real study of the evolution of social classes in recent times, or of the social movements at the present time which reveal the possibilities of future social change. An historical analysis of the changing class structure in modern societies, such as I have merely outlined here, remains one of the most important unfulfilled tasks of sociology today.

A SOCIETAL THEORY OF RACE AND ETHNIC RELATIONS

Stanley Lieberson

"In the relations of races there is a cycle of events which tends everywhere to repeat itself." Robert E. Park's assertion served as a prologue to the now classical cycle of competition, conflict, accomodation, and assimilation. A number of other attempts have been made to formulate phases or stages ensuing from the initial contacts between racial and ethnic groups. However, the sharp contrasts between relatively harmonious race relations in Brazil and Hawaii and the current racial turmoil in South Africa and Indonesia serve to illustrate the diffculty in stating—to say nothing of interpreting—an inevitable "natural history" of race and ethnic relations. . . .

This paper seeks to present a rudimentary theory of the development of race and

SOURCE: Stanley Lieberson, "A Societal Theory of Race and Ethnic Relations," *American Sociological Review,* Vol. 26, December 1961, pp. 902-910. Reprinted by permission.

ethnic relations that systematically accounts for differences between societies in such divergent consequences of contact as racial nationalism and warfare, assimilation and fusion, and extinction. It postulates that the critical problem on a societal level in racial or ethnic contact is initially each population's maintenance and development of a social order compatible with its ways of life prior to contact. The crux of any cycle must, therefore, deal with political, social, and economic institutions. The emphasis given in earlier cycles to one group's dominance of another in these areas is therefore hardly surprising.

Although we accept this institutional approach, the thesis presented here is that knowledge of the nature of one group's domination over another in the political, social, and economic spheres is a necessary but insufficient prerequisite for predicting or interpreting the final and intermediate stages of racial and ethnic contact. Rather, institutional factors are considered in terms of a distinction between two major types of contact situations: contacts involving subordination of an indigenous population by a migrant group, for example, Negro-white relations in South Africa; and contacts involving subordination of a migrant population by an indigenous racial or ethnic group, for example, Japanese migrants to the United States.

After considering the societal issues inherent in racial and ethnic contact, the distinction developed between migrant and indigenous superordination will be utilized in examining each of the following dimensions of race relations: political and economic control, multiple ethnic contacts, conflict and assimilation. The terms "race" and "ethnic" are used interchangeably.

Differences Inherent in Contact. Most situations of ethnic contact involve at least one indigenous group and at least one group migrating to the area. The only exception at the initial point in contact would be the settlement of an uninhabited area by two or more groups. By "indigenous" is meant not necessarily the aborigines, but rather a population sufficiently established in an area so as to possess the institutions and demographic capacity for maintaining some minimal form of social order through generations. Thus a given spatial area may have different indigenous groups through time. For example, the indigenous population of Australia is presently largely white and primarily of British origin, although the Tasmanoids and Australoids were once in possession of the area. A similar racial shift may be observed in the populations indigenous to the United States.

Restricting discussion to the simplest of contact situations, i.e., involving one migrant and one established population, we can generally observe sharp differences in their social organization at the time of contact. The indigenous population has an established and presumably stable organization prior to the arrival of migrants, i.e., government, economic activities adapted to the environment and the existing techniques of resource utilization, kinship, stratification, and religious systems. On the basis of a long series of migration studies we may be reasonably certain that the social order of a migrant population's homeland is not wholly transferred to their new settlement. Migrants are required to make at least some institutional adaptations and innovations in view of the presence of an indigenous population, the demographic selectivity of migration, and differences in habitat. . . .

In addition to ... demographic shifts, the new physical and biological conditions of existence require the revision and creation of social institutions if the social order known in the old country is to be approximated and if the migrants are to survive. The migration of eastern and southern European peasants around the turn of the century to urban industrial centers of the United States provides a well-documented case of radical changes in occupational pursuits as well as the creation of a number of institutions in response to the new conditions of urban life, e.g., mutual aid societies, national churches, and financial institutions.

In short, when two populations begin to occupy the same habitat but do not share a single order, each group endeavors to maintain the political and economic conditions that are at least compatible with the institutions existing before contact. These conditions for the maintenance of institutions cannot only differ for the two groups in contact, but are often conflicting. European contacts with the American Indian, for example, led to the decimation of the latter's sources of sustenance and disrupted religious and tribal forms of organization. With respect to a population's efforts to maintain its social institutions, we may therefore assume that the presence of another ethnic group is an important part of the environment. Further, if groups in contact differ in their capacity to impose changes on the other group, then we may expect to find one group "superordinate" and the other population "subordinate" in maintaining or developing a suitable environment.

It is here that efforts at a single cycle of race and ethnic relations must fail. For it is necessary to introduce a distinction in the nature or form of subordination before attempting to predict whether conflict or relatively harmonious assimilation will develop. As we shall shortly show, the race relations cycle in areas where the migrant group is superordinate and the indigenous group subordinate differs sharply from the stages in societies composed of a superordinate indigenous group and subordinate migrants.

Political and Economic Control. Emphasis is placed herein on economic and political dominance since it is assumed that control of these institutions will be instrumental in establishing educational, religious, and kinship, as well as control of such major cultural artifacts as language.

Migrant Superordination. When the population migrating to a new contact situation is superior in technology (particularly weapons) and more tightly organized than the indigenous group, the necessary conditions for maintaining the migrants' political and economic institutions are usually imposed on the indigenous population. Warfare, under such circumstances, often occurs early in the contacts between the two groups as the migrants begin to interfere with the natives' established order. There is frequently conflict even if the initial contact was friendly. Price, for example, has observed the following consequences of white invasion and subordination of the indigenous populations of Australia, Canada, New Zealand, and the United States:

During an opening period of pioneer invasion on moving frontiers the whites decimated the natives with their diseases; occupied their lands by seizure or by pseudo-purchase; slaughtered those who resisted; intensified tribal warfare by supplying white weapons; ridiculed and disrupted native religions, society and culture, and generally reduced the unhappy peoples to a state of despondency under which they neither desired to live, nor to have children to undergo similar conditions.[1]

The numerical decline of indigenous populations after their initial subordination to a migrant group, whether caused by warfare, introduction of veneral and other diseases, or disruption of sustenance activities, has been documented for a number of contact situations in addition to those discussed by Price.

In addition to bringing about these demographic and economic upheavals, the superordinate migrants frequently create political entities that are not at all coterminous with the boundaries existing during the indigenous populations' supremacy prior to contact. For example, the British and Boers in southern Africa carved out political states that included areas previously under the control of separate and often warring groups. Indeed, European alliances with feuding tribes were often used as a fulcrum for the territorial expansion of whites into southern Africa. The bifurcation of tribes into two nations and the migrations of groups across newly created national boundaries are both consequences of the somewhat arbitrary nature of the political entities created in regions of migrant superordination. This incorporation of diverse indigenous populations into a single territorial unit under the dominance of a migrant group has considerable importance for later developments in this type of racial and ethnic contact.

Indigenous Superordination. When a population migrates to a subordinate position considerably less conflict occurs in the early stages. The movements of many European and Oriental populations to political, economic, and social subordination in the United States were not converted into warfare, nationalism, or long-term conflict. Clearly, the occasional labor and racial strife marking the history of immigration of the United States is not on the same level as the efforts to expel or revolutionize the social order. American Negroes, one of the most persistently subordinated migrant groups in the country, never responded in significant numbers to the encouragement of migration to Liberia. The single important large-scale nationalistic effort, Marcus Garvey's Universal Negro Improvement Association, never actually led to mass emigration of Negroes. By contrast, the indigenous American Indians fought long and hard to preserve control over their habitat.

In interpreting differences in the effects of migrant and indigenous subordination, the migrants must be considered in the context of the options available to the group. Irish migrants to the United States in the 1840's, for example, although clearly subordinate to native whites of other origins, fared better economically than if they had remained in their mother country. Further, the option of returning to the homeland often exists for populations migrating to subordinate situations. Harry Jerome reports that net migration to the United States between the midyears of 1907 and 1923 equalled roughly 65 percent of gross immigration. This indicates that immigrant dissatisfaction with subordination or other conditions of contact can

---

[1] A. Grenfell Price, *White Settlers and Native Peoples* (Melbourne: Georgian House, 1950), p. 1.

often be resolved by withdrawal from the area. Recently subordinated indigenous groups, by contrast, are perhaps less apt to leave their habitat so readily.

Finally, when contacts between racial and ethnic groups are under the control of the indigenous population, threats of demographic and institutional imbalance are reduced since the superordinate populations can limit the numbers and groups entering. For example, when Oriental migration to the United States threatened whites, sharp cuts were executed in the quotas. Similar events may be noted with respect to the decline of immigration from the so-called "new" sources of eastern and southern Europe. Whether a group exercises its control over immigration far before it is actually under threat is, of course, not germane to the point that immigrant restriction provides a mechanism whereby potential conflict is prevented.

In summary, groups differ in the conditions necessary for maintaining their respective social orders. In areas where the migrant group is dominant, frequently the indigenous population suffers sharp numerical declines and their economic and political institutions are seriously undermined. Conflict often accompanies the establishment of migrant superordination. Subordinate indigenous populations generally have no alternative location and do not control the numbers of new ethnic populations admitted into their area. By contrast, when the indigenous population dominates the political and economic conditions, the migrant group is introduced into the economy of the indigenous population. Although subordinate in their new habitat, the migrants may fare better than if they remained in their homeland. Hence their subordination occurs without great conflict. In addition, the migrants usually have the option of returning to their homeland and the indigenous population controls the number of new immigrants in the area.

Multiple Ethnic Contacts. Although the introduction of a third major ethnic or racial group frequently occurs in both types of societies distinguished here, there are significant differences between conditions in habitats under indigenous domination and areas where a migrant population is superordinate. Chinese and Indian migrants, for example, were often welcomed by whites in areas where large indigenous populations were suppressed, but these migrants were restricted in the white mother country. Consideration of the causes and consequences of multi-ethnic contacts is therefore made in terms of the two types of racial and ethnic contact.

Migrant Superordination. In societies where the migrant population is superordinate, it is often necessary to introduce new immigrant groups to fill the niches created in the revised economy of the area. The subordinate indigenous population frequently fails, at first, to participate in the new economic and political order introduced by migrants. For example, because of the numerical decline of Fijians after contact with whites and their unsatisfactory work habits, approximately 60,000 persons migrated from India to the sugar plantations of Fiji under the indenture system between 1879 and 1916. For similar reasons, as well as the demise of slavery, large numbers of Indians were also introduced to such areas of indigenous subordination as Mauritius, British Guiana, Trinidad, and Natal. The descendants of these migrants comprise the largest single ethnic group in several of these areas.

McKenzie, after observing the negligible participation of the subordinated indigenous populations of Alaska, Hawaii, and Malaya in contrast to the large numbers of Chinese, Indian, and other Oriental immigrants, offers the following interpretation:

The indigenous peoples of many of the frontier zones of modern industrialism are surrounded by their own web of culture and their own economic structure. Consequently they are slow to take part in the new economy especially as unskilled laborers. It is the individual who is widely removed from his native habitat that is most adaptable to the conditions imposed by capitalism in frontier regions. Imported labor cannot so easily escape to its home village when conditions are distasteful as can the local population.[2]

Similarly, the Indians of the United States played a minor role in the new economic activities introduced by white settlers and, further, were not used successfully as slaves. E. Franklin Frazier reports that Negro slaves were utilized in the West Indies and Brazil after unsuccessful efforts to enslave the indigenous Indian populations. Large numbers of Asiatic Indians were brought to South Africa as indentured laborers to work in the railways, mines, and plantations introduced by whites.

This migration of workers into areas where the indigenous population was either unable or insufficient to work in the newly created economic activities was also marked by a considerable flow back to the home country. For example, nearly 3.5 million Indians left the Madras Presidency for overseas between 1903 and 1912, but close to 3 million returned during this same period. However, as we observed earlier, large numbers remained overseas and formed major ethnic populations in a number of countries. Current difficulties of the 10 million Chinese in Southeast Asia are in large part due to their settlement in societies where the indigenous populations were subordinate.

Indigenous Superordination. We have observed that in situations of indigenous superordination the call for new immigrants from other ethnic and racial population is sufficiently large in number or strength to challenge the supremacy of the indigenous population.

After whites attained dominance in Hawaii, that land provided a classic case of the substitution of one ethnic group after another during a period when large numbers of immigrants were needed for the newly created and expanding plantation economy. According to Andrew W. Lind, the shifts from Chinese to Japanese and Portuguese immigrants and the later shifts to Puerto Rican, Korean, Spanish, Russian, and Philippine sources for the plantation laborers were due to conscious efforts to prevent any single group from obtaining too much power. Similarly, the exclusion of Chinese from the United States mainland stimulated the migration of the Japanese and, in turn, the later exclusion of Japanese led to increased migration from Mexico.

---

[2] R. D. McKenzie, "Cultural and Racial Differences as Bases of Human Symbiosis" in Kimball Young, editor, *Social Attitudes* (New York: Henry Holt, 1931), p. 157.

In brief, groups migrating to situations of multiple ethnic contact are thus subordinate in both types of conflict situations. However, in societies where whites are superordinate but do not settle as an indigenous population, other racial and ethnic groups are admitted in large numbers and largely in accordance with economic needs of the revised economy of the habitat. By contrast, when a dominant migrant group later becomes indigenous, in the sense that the area becomes one of permanent settlement through generations for the group, migrant populations from new racial and ethnic stocks are restricted in number and source.

Conflict and Assimilation. From a comparison of the surge of racial nationalism and open warfare in parts of Africa and Asia or the retreat of superordinate migrants from the former Dutch East Indies and French Indo-China, on the one hand, with the fusion of populations in many nations of western Europe or the "cultural pluralism" of the United States and Switzerland, on the other, one must conclude that neither conflict nor assimilation is an inevitable outcome of racial and ethnic contact. Our distinction, however, between two classes of race and ethnic relations is directly relevant to consideration of which of these alternatives different populations in contact will take. In societies where the indigenous population at the initial contact is subordinate, warfare and nationalism often—although not always—develop later in the cycle of relations. By contrast, relations between migrants and indigenous populations that are subordinate and superordinate, respectively, are generally without long-term conflict.

Migrant Superordination. Through time, the subordinate indigenous population begins to participate in the economy introduced by the migrant group and, frequently, a concomitant disruption of previous forms of soical and economic organization takes place. This, in turn, has significant implications for the development of both nationalism and a greater sense of racial unity. In many African states, where Negroes were subdivided into ethnic groups prior to contact with whites, the racial unity of the African was created by the occupation of their habitat by white invaders. The categorical subordination of Africans by whites as well as the dissolution and decay of previous tribal and ethnic forms of organization are responsible for the creation of racial consciousness among the indigenous populations. As the indigenous group becomes increasingly incorporated within the larger system, both the saliency of their subordinate position and its significance increase. No alternative exists for the bulk of the native population other than the destruction of revision of the institutions of political, economic, and social subordination.

Further, it appears that considerable conflict occurs in those areas where the migrants are not simply superordinate, but where they themselves have also become, in a sense, indigenous by maintaining an established population through generations. . . . Thus, two [Algeria and the Union of South Africa] among the eleven African countries for which such data were available are outstanding with respect to both racial turmoil and the high proportion of whites born in the country. To be sure, other factors operate to influence the nature of racial and ethnic relations. However these data strongly support our suggestions with respect to the significance of differences between indigenous and migrant forms of contact.

Thus where the migrant population becomes established in the new area, it is all the more difficult for the indigenous subordinate group to change the social order.

Additionally, where the formerly subordinate indigenous population has become dominant through the expulsion of the superordinate group, the situation faced by nationalities introduced to the area under earlier conditions of migrant superordination changes radically. For example, as we noted earlier, Chinese were welcomed in many parts of Southeast Asia where the newly subordinated indigenous populations were unable or unwilling to fill the economic niches created by the white invaders. However, after whites were expelled and the indigenous populations obtained political mastery, the gates to further Chinese immigration were fairly well closed and there has been increasing interference with the Chinese already present. In Indonesia, where Chinese immigration had been encouraged under Dutch domain, the newly created indigenous government allows only token immigration and has formulated a series of laws and measures designed to interfere with and reduce Chinese commercial activities. Thompson and Adloff observe that,

Since the war, the Chinese have been subjected to increasingly restrictive measures throughout Southeast Asia, but the severity and effectiveness of these has varied with the degree to which the native nationalists are in control of their countries and feel their national existence threatened by the Chinese.[3]

Indigenous Superordination. By contrast, difficulties between subordinate migrants and an already dominant indigenous population occur within the context of a consensual form of government, economy, and social institutions. However confused and uncertain may be the concept of assimilation and its application in operational terms, it is important to note that assimilation is essentially a very different phenomenon in the two types of societies distinguished here.

Where populations migrate to situations of subordination, the issue has generally been with respect to the migrants' capacity and willingness to become an integral part of the on-going social order. For example, this has largely been the case in the United States where the issue of "new" vs. "old" immigrant groups hinged on the alleged inferiorities of the former. The occasional flurries of violence under this form of contact have been generally initiated by the dominant indigenous group and with respect to such threats against the social order as the cheap labor competition of Orientals in the west coast, the nativist fears of Irish Catholic political domination of Boston in the nineteenth century, or the desecration of sacred principles by Mexican "zoot-suiters" in Los Angeles.

The conditions faced by subordinate migrants in Australia and Canada after the creation of indigenous white societies in these areas are similar to that of the United States; that is, limited and sporadic conflict, and great emphasis on the assimilation of migrants. Striking and significant contrasts to the general pattern of subordinate immigrant assimilation in these societies, however, are provided by the differences

[3] Virginia Thompson and Richard Adloff, *Minority Problems in Southeast Asia* (Stanford, California: Stanford University Press, 1955), p. 3.

between the assimilation of Italian and German immigrants in Australia as well as the position of French Canadians in eastern Canada.

French Canadians have maintained their language and other major cultural and social attributes whereas nineteenth and twentieth century immigrants are in process of merging into the predominantly English-speaking Canadian society. Although broader problems of territorial segregation are involved, the critical difference between French Canadians and later groups is that the former had an established society in the new habitat prior to the British conquest of Canada and were thus largely able to maintain their social and cultural unity without significant additional migration from France.

Similarly, in finding twentieth century Italian immigrants in Australia more prone to cultural assimilation than were German migrants to that nation in the 1800's, Borrie emphasized the fact that Italian migration occurred after Australia had become an independent nation-state. By contrast, Germans settled in what was a pioneer colony without an established general social order and institutions. Thus, for example, Italian children were required to attend Australian schools and learn English, whereas the German immigrants were forced to eastablish their own educational program.

Thus the consequences of racial and ethnic contact may also be examined in terms of the two types of superordinate-subordinate contact situations considered. For the most part, subordinate migrants appear to be more rapidly assimilated than are subordinate indigenous populations. Further, the subordinate migrant group is generally under greater pressure to assimilate, at least in the gross sense of "assimilation" such as language, than are subordinate indigenous populations. In addition, warfare or racial nationalism—when it does occur—tends to be in societies where the indigenous population is subordinate. If the indigenous movement succeeds, the economic and political position of racial and ethnic populations introduced to the area under migrant dominance may become tenuous.

A Final Note. It is suggested that interest be revived in the conditions accounting for societal variations in the process of relations between racial and ethnic groups. A societal theory of race relations, based on the migrant-indigenous and superordinate-subordinate distinctions developed above, has been found to offer an orderly interpretation of differences in the nature of race and ethnic relations in the contact situations considered. Since, however, systematic empirical investigation provides a far more rigorous test of the theory's merits and limitations, comparative cross-societal studies are needed.

CRISIS IN BLACK AND WHITE

Charles E. Silberman

The Negro migration to the city actually began about seventy-five years ago, when the Jim Crow system first began to take shape in the South and white men moved actively and brutally to force the Negro back into his pre-Reconstruction place. Contrary to the popular view that Southern folkways are immutable, the quarter-century following the Civil War had seen a considerable relaxation of the barriers between the races as the South accomodated itself to a new order. Negroes were accepted at the polls, in the courts and legislatures, in the police and militia, and on the trains and trolleys. Col. Thomas Wentworth Higginson of Boston, a noted abolitionist who had been one of John Brown's "Secret Six" before Harper's Ferry, went south in 1878, and reported in *The Atlantic Monthly* his pleasant surprise at how well Negroes were being treated, as compared with his native New England. "How can we ask more of the states formerly in rebellion," he wrote, "than that they should be abreast of New England in granting rights and privileges to the colored race?" In 1885, T. McCants Stewart, a Negro newspaper from Boston, returned to the South for a visit and found traveling "more pleasant than in some parts of New England. . . . I think the whites of the South," he reported, "are really less afraid to [have] contact with colored people than the whites of the North." Negroes were treated particularly well in Virginia. Thus in 1886 the Richmond *Dispatch* took what today would be considered a pro-Negro position:

Our State Constitution requires all State officers in their oath of office to declare that they "recognize and accept the civil and political equality of all men." We repeat that nobody here objects to sitting in political conventions with negroes. Nobody here objects to serving on juries with negroes. No lawyer objects to practicing law in courts where negro lawyers practice. . . . Colored men are allowed to introduce bills into the Virginia Legislature; and in both branches of this body negroes are allowed to sit, as they have a right to sit.

Racism was still widespread, of course, in all its ugliness. But it was held in check by a number of forces: Northern liberal opinion; the prestige and influence of Southern conservatives, with their tradition of *noblesse oblige* and their distaste for the venomous race hatred of the poor whites;[1] and the idealism of Southern radicals, who for a time dreamt of an alliance of all the propertyless against the propertied class. As a result of these competing pressures, Negroes were able to retain the suffrage they had won during Reconstruction. While Negroes were

---

SOURCE: From *Crisis in Black and White*, pp. 20-25, by Charles E. Silberman. © Copyright 1964 by Random House, Inc. Reprinted by permission of Random House, Inc. and Jonathan Cape, Ltd., London.

[1] "It is a great deal pleasanter to travel with respectable and well-behaved colored people than with unmannerly and ruffianly white men," a Charleston, South Carolina, paper observed, suggesting that "the common sense and proper arrangement . . . is to provide first-class cars for first-class passenger, white and colored."

increasingly defrauded and coerced, they did continue to vote in large numbers, and Southern conservatives and radicals competed for their support. "The Southern whites accept them precisely as Northern men in cities accept the ignorant Irish vote," Colonel Higginson wrote, "not cheerfully, but with acquiescence to the inevitable; and when the strict color line is once broken, they are just as ready to conciliate the Negro as the Northern politician to flatter the Irishman. Any powerful body of voters may be cajoled today and intimidated tomorrow and hated always," the abolitionist added, "but it can never be left out of sight."

Beginning around 1890, however, the forces that had kept Southern racism and fanaticism in check rapidly weakened and become discredited. In the North, the desire for sectional reconciliation persuaded liberals to drop their interest in the Negro, who was the symbol of sectional strife; increasingly, liberals and former abolitionists began espousing the shibboleths of the Negroes' innate inferiority in the pages of *The Atlantic Monthly, Harper's, The Nation*, and *The North American Review*; and this, in turn, encouraged the more virulent Southern racists. "Just as the Negro gained his emancipation and new rights through a falling out between white men," wrote historian C. Vann Woodward, "he now stood to lose his rights through the reconciliation of white men."[2] Not only did the Negro serve as a scapegoat to aid the reconciliation of Northern and Southern white men; he served the same purpose in aiding the reconciliation of estranged white classes in the South itself. The battles between the Southern conservatives and radicals had opened wounds that could be healed only by the nostrum of white supremacy.

The first and most fundamental step was the total disfranchisement of the Negro; disfranchisement served both as a symbol of "reform" and as a guarantee that no white faction would ever again seek power by rallying Negro votes against another group of whites. Because of the Federal Constitution, the Southern states had to rob Negroes of their vote through indirection: through the use of the poll tax, the white primary, the "grandfather clause," the "good character clause," the "understanding clause," and other techniques, some of which are still in use in states like Mississippi and Alabama. But while the methods were roundabout, the purpose was not. When the Mississippi Constitution was revised in 1890, for example, the purpose of revision was stated quite baldly: "The policy of crushing out the manhood of the Negro citizens is to be carried on to success." Addressing the Virginia Constitutional Convention eleven years later, the young Carter Glass, then a member of the Virginia State Senate, was no less blunt: "Discrimination? Why that is precisely what we propose; that, exactly, is what this convention was elected for—to discriminate to the very extremity of permissible action under the limitations of the Federal Constitution, with a view to the elimination of every Negro voter who can be gotten rid of, legally, without materially impairing the numerical strength of the white electorate." By the winter of 1902, the Convention had achieved its purpose. By 1910, the Negro was disfranchised in virtually every Southern state. In Louisiana, for example, the number of registered Negro voters dropped abruptly from 130,334 in 1896 to only 1,342 in 1904.

---

[2] Professor Woodward's *The Strange Career of Jim Crow* (New York: Oxford University Press, Galaxy Book, 1957) is a brilliant analysis of the origins of the Jim Crow system.

Disfranchisement was preceded and accomplished by an intensive campaign of race hatred, designed in good measure to allay the supicions of the poor whites that they, too, were in danger of losing the vote. Although the regime of the carpetbaggers had been over for twenty years or more, all the old horror stories were revived and embroidered; the new generation of Southerners (and each succeeding one) was made to feel that it, too, had lived through the trauma of Reconstruction. Newspapers played up stories of Negro crime and "impertinence." The result was a savage outbreak of anti-Negro violence. In Atlanta, white mobs took over the city for four days, looting and lynching at will; in New Orleans, mobs rampaged for three days. And rigid segregation rapidly became the rule. Until 1900, Jim Crow laws had applied only to railroad travel in most Southern states; indeed, South Carolina did not require Jim Crow railroad cars before 1898, North Carolina before 1899, and Virginia before 1900. Until 1899, only three states required separate waiting rooms at railroad terminals. In the next six or eight years, however, Jim Crow laws mushroomed throughout the South, affecting trolleys, theaters, boarding houses, public toilets and water fountains, housing; in Atlanta Jim Crow extended even to the ultimate absurdity of providing separate Jim Crow Bibles for Negro witnesses to swear on in court, and, for a time, to requiring Jim Crow elevators in buildings.

In short, the South, whose leaders today deny the possibility as well as the desirability of rapid change, transformed the pattern of race relations almost overnight. Men's hearts changed as swiftly as their actions. As late as 1898, for example, the Charleston, South Carolina, *News and Courier*, the oldest newspaper in the South, ridiculed the whole idea of segregation of the races. "As we have got on fairly well for a third of a century, including a long period of reconstruction," the editor wrote, "we can probably get on as well hereafter without it, and certainly so extreme a measure [as Jim Crow railroad cars] should not be adopted and enforced without added and urgent cause." The editor went on to discuss the absurd consequences that would follow, once the principles of Jim Crow were accepted. "If there must be Jim Crow cars on the railroads, there should be Jim Crow cars on the street railroads. Also on all passenger boats." Warming to his task, he continued: "If there are to be Jim Crow cars, moreover, there should be Jim Crow waiting saloons at all stations, and Jim Crow eating houses. . . . There should be Jim Crow sections of the jury box, and a separate Jim Crow dock and witness stand in every court—and a Jim Crow Bible for colored witnesses to kiss, and separate Jim Crow sections in government offices so that Negroes and whites would not have to mingle while paying their taxes." "In resorting to the tactics of *reductio ad absurdum*," Professor Woodward has commented, "the editor doubtless believed that he had dealt the Jim Crow principle a telling blow with his heavy irony." But the real irony was unintended: what the *News and Courier* editor regarded as an absurdity in 1898 very rapidly became a reality, down to and including the Jim Crow Bible. So rapidly did the change occur, in fact, that in 1906—only eight years later—the paper had swung completely around. Segregation was no longer ridiculous; it was merely inadequate. Only mass deportation could solve as grave a problem as the presence of Negroes in South Carolina. "There is no room for them here," the paper declared. . . .

SOCIAL SCIENCE AND THE DESEGREGATION PROCESS

Herbert Blumer

Segregation is continuously at work in all human societies as a natural, unguided, and unwitting process. It takes the form of a diverse and chiefly undesigned operation which sets apart groups of people inside of a larger, embracing society. This setting apart may result from practices of exclusion employed by one group against others, or by voluntary withdrawal on the part of given groups, or by the operation of natural forces which place individuals in different localities or different social spheres. The result of this undesigned process is to form disparate groups. Each group is relatively homogeneous. Each constitutes the arena for the bulk of the associations and experiences of its members. Each is limited in access to the life of other groups. Each is denied accordingly, the special privileges granted by other groups to their members. Segregation is a primary means by which a human society develops an inner organization—an allocation of diverse elements into an articulated arrangement.

Nature of Segregation. Sociologists have been concerned with two chief manifestations of this natural process of segregation. These are (1) the formation of diversified areas of residence, chiefly in large cities, and (2) the exclusion exercised by human groups in accepting members and in granting privileges. A brief consideration of these two forms of segregation will be helpful.

Ecological studies of the residential distribution of people, particularly in large cities, show a pattern of distinguishable areas. Each area tends to be distinctive in terms of the people who inhabit it, the kind of local institutions lodged in it, and the general round of life of its people. Such areas are familiar to us in the case of "black belts," "little Italies," and other ethnic areas; they are also noted in the case of slums, working-men areas, homeless-men areas, apartment-house areas, "gold coasts," and rooming-house areas.

The formation of such differentiated areas, while not unaffected by deliberate governmental policy, is primarily a natural and spontaneous process. They are the product roughly of three kinds of forces: (1) neutral forces, such as level of income and accessibility to places of work; (2) forces of attraction, such as wishing to live among people with whom one identifies oneself; and (3) forces of rejection, as when people are found unacceptable or unsuitable as residents in given areas. . . . In our modern complex world this natural process of ecological allocation has become a primary medium and cause of segregation.

The study of human group life reveals clearly another line of segregation in the form of the exclusion exercised by one group against members of other groups. Such exclusion is indigenous in human societies. Every group having a sense of identity and some kind of purpose exercises some measure of control over membership in its body and over access to the privileges which its life affords.

SOURCE: Herbert Blumer, "Social Science and the Desegregation Process," *The Annals of The American Academy of Political and Social Science,* Vol. 304 (March 1956), pp. 137-143. Reprinted by permission of the publisher.

Whether it be a family, a social club, a clique, a group of friends, a business organization, a professional society, a labor union, a church, or a self-conscious neighborhood, the group necessarily recognizes certain criteria of membership and rejects those who are deemed not to meet such criteria. Similarly, it does not grant to outsiders the particular rights and privileges open to its membership. It is only because such group exclusion is so rarely challenged that we fail to realize how basic and extensive it is in the life of human societies. . . . Quite obviously, this process of exclusion has the effect of allocating people into separate groups, of confining them to such groups, and of establishing barriers to their free participation in each other's group life.

These few remarks call attention to the fact that a twofold process of segregation is continuously at work in modern society. This process is natural, spontaneous, and inevitable. It is essential, in the form of group exclusion, to the existence of all human societies; in the form of ecological differentiation it is essential to the existence of modern, urbanized societies. . . .

Segregation as a Social Problem. It is evident, immediately, that when we speak of segregation as a social problem, as a condition to be prevented or overcome, we are not referring to the total process of segregation. We refer instead only to special instances which have been challenged. Such challenges arise in the form of a claim to the right of being accepted into a group or sharing the privileges which the group denies through its act of exclusion. It is evident that the claim arises and has validity only through the application of the standards of a larger inclusive group, such as an embracing political society with legal rights of citizenship or a transcending moral community with a set of ethical expectations. Given lines or instances of group exclusion become suspect only when they contravene political or moral rights. . . .

Every human group may be regarded as having properly an area of private rights—chiefly in the form of deciding whom to allow to become members and to enjoy the privileges which the group life is able to provide. As suggested above, the group possession of such areas of private right is sanctioned in every society irrespective of wide differences in the nature of the rights and in the gratifications which their exercise yields. Discrimination arises when a given line of private right is defined legally or morally as a public right and the group does not accept the definition. The continuing exercise of the private right at the expense of a given group having legal or moral claims to the privileges is what constitutes segregation as a social problem. . . .

The Segregating Group. To understand segregation it is necessary to see its position in the life of the segregating group. Almost always the practices of exclusion or rejection which it involves have grown up naturally in the life experiences of the group. Through these life experiences the group has come to develop a social position, a sense of identity, and a conception of itself in the light of which the practice of exclusion appears natural and proper. As a natural part of the social order the practice comes to be embedded in feelings and convictions and to be justified logically by a set of reasons whose validity is self-evident. Also, the practice is usually legitimated and bulwarked by the endorsement given by institutional authorities within the group; as the spokesmen of the group their official approval places a stamp of truth and virtue on the practice. Further, as a customary practice the exclusion feeds, so to speak, on itself; its continuous routine occurrence becomes an affirmation of its validity. As each member of the group gives expression to the practice in voice and deed, he reinforces in other members the value which all of them are disposed to attach to the practice. Sustained by these various sources of strength and sanction the established practice of group exclusion tends to be a firm part of the way of life.

This general process which imparts toughness and fixity to established practices of group exclusion is usually intensified in cases of racial segregation. The reasons for this are fairly clear. The recognition of racial or physical difference sustains and intensifies the sense of social or status difference which may have happened to develop between racial groups. The observable physical difference reinforces and rivets the feeling of the dominant racial group that the subordinate racial group is alien and not of its kind. Similarly, the feeling of superiority in the dominant group derives a greater measure of natural validity by virtue of the ability to note biological differences between the two groups. Thus, the feeling of racial difference adds tenacity to the practices of exclusion.

We need to note, also, that the range of exclusions between racial groups is likely to be extensive. They meet each other not in a restricted or specialized way, as in the case of the relation of journeymen to apprentices, but over a wide area of diverse association. Where a sense of racial difference has been fused with a sense of status difference, the inevitable tendency will be to extend the practice of exclusion along the array of relations. Since each line of exclusion symbolizes to the dominant group its social position, all its established lines of exclusion hang together and sustain each other. . . .

Desegregation. We can now consider the problem of desegregation. We are interested in considering the general problem of how practices of racial exclusion which are challenged as morally improper or illegal are eliminated through conscious policy and deliberate action. In other words we deal with desegregation not as a natural and unwitting process but as a directed effort to displace an established form of racial exclusion. In this latter form the problem of desegregation is thrown on a different plane. It is not a task of eliminating or reversing the process which led to segregation but rather of arresting or immobilizing its end operation.

To be sure, much—indeed most—of scholarly thought in current psychological and social science presumes that racial desegregation is to be achieved by the elimination or changing of the process which brings segregation into being. This process is usually given a four-step temporal sequence: (1) conditions which implant (2) attitudes of racial prejudice which (3) lead to racial discrimination which (4) results in a condition of segregation. It is thus reasoned that to eliminate segregation one has to eliminate discrimination; to eliminate discrimination one has to change the attitudes which bring it about; and, usually, to change the attitudes one has to correct the conditions that cause them.

Such a formulation is markedly unsuited to success in conscious efforts at racial desegregation. It implies, essentially, a destruction of a tightly interwoven and solid social structure. This can be appreciated by bearing in mind that a given form of racial exclusion is a customary adjustment which has evolved naturally out of given lines of historic experience; that it reflects the actual social positions occupied by the racial groups in their social order; that it expresses the fundamental conception which the dominant racial group has of itself and of the subordinate group; that it carries the virtue and the validity of authoritative endorsement; that it gains continous affirmation through the daily reinforcement which members of the dominant group give to one another's feelings and convictions; and that it is an interlinked part of a system of racial exclusion. To try to eliminate the given practice of racial exclusion by altering the network of conditions which bring it about and sustain it is a task of formidable magnitude. To try to eliminate the practice by changing one phase or part of the network—as in the effort to inculcate attitudes of racial tolerance—is to ignore the complicated structure which sustains the phase or part. The attempt to achieve racial desegregation by a correction of the process which brings segregation about represents a highly unpromising line of action.

The alternative is to block the process from achieving its end result. This is done by controlling the decisions of the main functionaries who carry a given form of racial segregation into actual execution. It is important to recognize that in any given kind of racial segregation there are strategically placed individuals or small groups who set the policies and issue the orders without which the given practice of segregation could not be maintained. School boards, superintendents of education, real estate boards, realtors, hotel owners and managers, medical boards, hospital superintendents, and directors of recreational systems are a very few examples. All work through a system of subordinates who in carrying out orders and understood policies sustain in practice the given form of racial segregation. Thus, control of the decisions of the chief functionaries responsible for the actual operation of the practice of segregation offers a direct means of arresting or immobilizing that practice. To put the point in terms of a theory of social action we can say that it is not essential in efforts to change human conduct to alter, on the part of individuals, the feelings and attitudes behind that conduct, or, on the part of the group, the collective values, claims, and expectations which sustain the conduct. Feelings and attitudes, values and expectations, have to gain expression in conduct; the apparatus essential to such expression is, itself, vulnerable and offers pivotal points for arresting the end expression. Contemporary social and psychological science is backward in coming to see and appreciate this picture.

Role of Functionaries. To exert effective influence on the decisions of centrally placed functionaries in the operating pattern of segregation it is necessary to use the weight of transcending prestige, authority, and power. The functionaries, as members of the dominant racial group, are highly likely to share the feelings and values of that group toward the given form of exclusion, or else to respond to the expectations and pressures of that group. For them to make decisions that are opposed to the feelings and expectations of the dominant group it is necessary for them to be constrained and supported by a transcending group having prestige or power.

Basically, the outcome of the struggle to achieve racial desegregation through conscious effort depends on what influences the central functionaries have to take into account in making their decisions. If the conscious effort takes the form of an educational campaign to change the views of the members of the dominant racial group or a campaign of moral exhortation to change their feelings, the functionaries are essentially well protected. They need merely, so to speak, await the outcome of such effort; they are subjected to no special pressure to change their customary lines of decision and are not forced in juxtaposition to their own group. Parenthetically, this is another reason for the relative ineffectiveness of attempts to achieve racial desegregation through general educational and moral campaigns.

A different setting is formed if the conscious efforts at desegregation are along lines which force functionaries to take cognizance of solicitations, demands, and pressures made on them to carry out a different line of decision. Such influences, if attended by any degree of weight, have the effect, psychologically, of detaching the functionaries from their group and of leading them to weight such influences over against the views and expectations of their racial group. This is the kind of setting that is brought into being by the enactment and application of laws against segregation or by the imposition of regulations and expectations against segregation by leaders of associations and institutions in which the functionaries are in some measure incorporated. The functionaries have to take account of these demands and to form their decisions with some regard to the demands. In a genuine sense the functionary is an exposed target. This is the basic fact which structures the struggle toward deliberate racial desegregation. It also provides the opportunity for adroit advancement even where the dominant racial group is solidly opposed in feeling to a given line of desegregation.

Role of Organizations. Recognizing the pivotal position of the decisions of functionaries, we easily see the important role of organizational pressure and support. The dominant group in a racial community, to a man, may have strong feelings of opposition to a given form of desegregation, yet be lacking in organizations to mobilize such opposition and convert it into action. Under such conditions, even though sharing the feelings of the dominant group the functionary may readily bow to the outside demands and pressures, particularly if these are backed up by weighty organizational support. Conversely, a functionary sympathetic to desegregation may be effectively deterred, not necessarily by the attitudes held by the members of the dominant racial group but by organizations among them that bespeak trouble. There is no need to spell out other possible combinations. The central point is clear. The carrying through as well as the blocking of deliberate desegregation depends on mobilizing and focusing influence and power on central functionaries. This calls, in the case of either side, for the development of organizational strength. The vehicle of procedure is strategical maneuvering, designed to marshal and utilize the potentials of power and prestige available in the given situation. Such potentials are almost certain to vary from situation to situation, thus calling for different tactical operations on local scenes.

It should be observed that in this contest, so to speak, to affect the decisions of the central functionaries, the advantage in the long run is in the hands of the side which is able to capitalize on the prestige and strength of the transcending group. Agencies seeking to achieve racial desegregation have a particularly strong strategic weapon (it is not always seen or used) in focusing on the validity of *applying* the transcending legal or moral standard. This makes it unnecessary to challenge or impugn the feelings and attitudes of the functionary toward the subordinate racial group, or to try to change such feelings and attitudes. It makes it unnecessary, further, to argue the merits or the validity of the legal or moral standard. Instead, the approach to the functionary can appropriately be made in terms of the validity and need of *applying* the standard. This provides the opportunity of shifting the contest from a question of a struggle between the racial groups to a question of obedience to the transcending legal or moral standards. Since such standards carry implicitly the dictates of obedience, one is provided with a line along which to press the case which can largely avoid the issue of racial dispute. It may be added that this line becomes the most effective basis on which to build up organizational strength in acting toward central functionaries, for it offers opportunities of enlisting a support inside the dominant racial group that would be lost on the straight issue of racial struggle.

Conclusions. A few remarks should be made, in closing, on the relation of conscious or designed racial desegregation to natural and unwitting racial desegregation. There can be no question that the former acts back on and abets the latter. Where given programs of racial desegregation succeed, they weaken the support of other established forms of segregation. They interfere with the routine, repetitive affirmation of lines of racial exclusion. Further, in allowing the members of the racial groups to associate as equals in the new situation they lay the groundwork for acting toward one another on a human and personal basis rather than on a basis of membership in racial groups. Deliberate desegregation enters, thus, into a cyclical and reciprocal relation with natural desegregation.

RACIAL CRISIS IN AMERICA

Lewis Killian and Charles Grigg

The prospect is dismal; the need for a solution to the crisis in race relations is desperate.... Americans, particularly white Americans, must soon awake to the fact that the crisis in race relations is second in gravity only to the threat of nuclear war. The conclusions and suggestions advanced below are not intended as the details of a comprehensive, integrated plan for the resolution of the crisis. They are, rather, cautions against false trails.

It is true that tokenism is "too little and too late." But it is also true that token desegregation will be the dominant pattern until the cultural deficit of the Negro

SOURCE: Lewis Killian and Charles Grigg, *Racial Crisis in America: Leadership in Conflict* (pp. 130-144), © 1964. Reprinted by permission of Prentice-Hall, Inc., Englewood Cliffs, N. J. Several footnotes have been omitted.

masses is reduced or the majority of Negroes reject integration as a goal, as the Black Muslims would have it. Although many local laws sustaining compulsory, racial segregation survive pending the day they are specifically challenged, segregation is legally dead. Despite the volume of criticism aimed at the U.S. Supreme Court, there has not been enough unified opposition to lead to nullification by constitutional amendment. And such opposition will never develop as long as the Negro bears the burden of compelling compliance and the white power structure is able to find ways to soften the impact of desegregation through tokenism.

The spatial distribution of the Negro population, the cultural deprivation of the Negro masses, and the social organization of the Negro community make it clear that, in the present circumstances, not many Negroes can benefit directly from the Supreme Court's decisions. Only a minority of "qualified," highly motivated individuals will be willing and able to take advantage of the opportunities provided by the new legal principle. Over and over again it has been demonstrated that plans for "voluntary desegregation" either result in token desegregation or, if more than a token number of Negro volunteers appear, in the eventual "resegregation" of the institution or neighborhood.

To make desegregation compulsory and comprehensive, not voluntary and token, would require major changes in the civil rights laws, in the judicial application of the principle of equity, and in the role of the federal executive. There is little indication that the American electorate to whom the legislative and executive branches are responsive is likely to demand the resolution of the crisis through compulsory desegregation on a massive scale. Ironically, authoritarian methods would be necessary to bring about rapid desegregation and "racial democracy" in the absence of a legislative mandate. But there is great danger that the use of such methods would at once transform the apathy and complacency of the majority of the white populace into active resistance.

Tokenism as a Continuing Objective. In spite of the increasing volume of denunciations of tokenism by Negro leaders, many of these leaders will continue to fight for the symbolic gains which token desegregation brings. Even tokenism shatters the castelike uniformity of traditional patterns of segregation. It provides the basis of hopes for greater gains in the future. Even Negroes who may not be able to take advantage of token desegregation experience a temporary feeling of victory, although they will soon feel frustrated and impatient again. . . . Negroes will continue to fight for such victories as long as they can—and rejoice in them.

More important, for the Negro leader who cannot accept the "racism in reverse" of the Black Muslims, this is the easiest type of victory to achieve. In spite of the costs and the danger, it is still easier to desegregate a few lunch counters than to raise the level of living of millions of Negroes; to gain the admission of a handful of Negro children to a few white schools than to raise the achievement level of thousands of children still attending segregated schools; to compel the employment of a few white-collar workers in "white" stores than to solve the problem of Negro unemployment. Segregation is the symbol of the pervasive inequality of the Negro in American society, and the symbol is a more accessible target than the basic, underlying inequality. Thus either in response to the pricks of conscience or the desire for prestige, many Negro leaders will continue to lead attacks on the surface manifestations of the Negro's inferior status. They will receive support from many lower-class Negroes, who will derive psychic rewards from the struggle even if the victory brings them no direct gains. They will receive even more enthusiastic support from middle-class Negroes, who are able to take advantage of the gains of token desegregation. Because they are "ready" for desegregation, such middle-class Negroes find the arbitrary racial barriers all the more onerous.

Conflict Over Tokenism. But even when Negro leaders accept the limited objective of tokenism, their relationship with white society and its leaders is fundamentally one of conflict. From the legal standpoint, tokenism consists of granting to the individual citizen rights which are his by virtue of his citizenship and which cannot be withheld on the basis of his group membership. They are *his* rights, not the group's. But it is difficult for the white citizen to perceive the Negro pioneer as an individual claimant when he claims rights that have long been enjoyed only by the white group. When the individual is aided and supported by Negro organizations and his legal claim is described as a "class action," it is even more difficult for the white person to see the Negro claimant as anything but a representative and spearhead of the entire Negro community. The Negro pioneer, no matter how exceptional, stands in the shadow of the culturally deprived Negro community. As long as he does, white Americans will react to the threat of having to accept the Negro lower class along with the pioneer. They will not voluntarily sacrifice their status advantage. They will give it up only when confronted with power that threatens other values.

So the prospect is that most of the Negro's gains will continue to come through conflict. White liberals may regard each token step as a gain for which all Americans should be thankful. But in the context of intergroup relations each of these steps will be a victory for Negroes and a defeat for the dominant white group. But such small, symbolic victories will not signify the termination of the power struggle either in the communities in which they occur or in the larger American society. In spite of temporary victories or temporary defeats, the drive of Negroes for identity will continue for a long time. There will be respites following periods of struggle and stress. Token victories will not eliminate the substratum of dissatisfaction which underlies the Negro's struggle, but they will encourage renewal of the struggle.

Realistic and Nonrealistic Conflict. This analysis suggests another reason for expecting recurrent conflict over a long period. That is the fact that much of the conflict will be "nonrealistic." Coser, on the basis of Simmel's analysis of conflict,[1] distinguishes between "realistic" and "nonrealistic" conflict in this way:

Conflicts which arise from frustration of specific demands within the relationship and from estimates of gains of the participants, and which are directed at the presumed frustrating object, can be called *realistic conflicts* insofar as they are means towards a specific result. *Nonrealistic conflicts*, on the other hand, although still involving interaction between two or more persons, are not occasioned by the rival ends of the antagonists but by the need for tension relief of at least one of them.[2]

---

[1] Georg Simmel, *Conflict*, trans. by Kurt H. Wolff (New York: The Free Press of Glencoe, Inc., 1955).

[2] Lewis Coser, *The Functions of Social Conflict* (Glencoe: The Free Press, 1956), p. 49.

The displacement of hostility by members of the dominant group through aggression toward minority groups has been the subject of extensive analysis. In view of the very realistic character of the status struggle, it has been over-emphasized. On the other hand, little research has been directed toward identifying nonrealistic elements in the aggressive acts of the minority group. By definition, the minority group finds in the many forms of discrimination numerous sources of frustration. Ample basis exists, therefore, for realistic conflict initiated by the minority. Nevertheless the most basic and severe frustration which the minority-group member experiences is most diffuse and nonspecific. This is the general status-deprivation and sense of inferiority which he experiences. Although it is relatively easy for him to attack the specific, symbolic manifestations of this status-deprivation, a massive attack on the very structure of the society is necessary for action against the fundamental source of frustration because this source is either too powerful or too inaccessible. For example, one of the greatest deprivations that the Negro minority throughout the United States experiences is the lack of adequate housing. Yet numerous studies of the housing of minority groups show that discrimination in housing is supported by a vast, complex, and sometimes invisible structure ranging from individual realtors, through large home-financing institutions, to some agencies of the federal government itself.

Therefore, in spite of the undeniable existence of a basis for realistic conflicts, the targets of Negro protest activities may be nonrealistic. A second nonrealistic element is introduced, even when conflict has a realistic basis, by the fact that some participants on both sides engage in aggressive action as a means of self-expression rather than of realistic striving toward a goal. Certainly some of the notorious attacks of Negro delinquent gangs on white persons represent such nonrealistic conflict. No matter how realistic the basis for the conflict may be, the presence of such participants maximizes the likelihood of indiscriminate violence. It increases the problem of control by responsible leaders and may change a peaceful demonstration into a bloody riot.

Conflict, Power, and Force. It is evident that the concept of conflict used here implies something broader than merely "violence" or "force." It includes any form of interaction in which the parties attempt to achieve their objectives by demonstrating that they possess superior power. It might be described simply as "a relationship in which somebody has to lose." Submission, not consensus, is the "pay-off." Power may be manifest as force, as Bierstedt has pointed out, or it may consist of the threat of force—"the ability to employ force, not its actual employment, the ability to apply sanctions, not their actual application."[3] Hence the conflict relationship may range from violence, in which physical force is applied (and sometimes resisted) through the invocation of nonviolent forms of force, such as boycotts, demonstrations and legal sanctions to verbal threats of the use of force. James Baldwin reflects the Negro's perception of race relations as power relations when he declares,

---

[3]Robert Bierstedt, "An Analysis of Social Power," *American Sociological Review*, Vol. 15, 1950, p. 733.

The sad truth is that whatever modifications have been effected in the social structure of the South since the Reconstruction, and any alleviations of the Negro's lot within it, are due to great and incessant pressure, very little of it indeed from within the South.[4]

What is different now, of course, is that Negroes in the South, as well as in northern cities, are exerting such pressure themselves. With their own power they are confronting the power which has always sustained the status advantage of the white group.

In such a context as this, the establishing of communication between whites and Negroes in no way means that conflict has been terminated. It does not even mean that a minimum of consensus has been reached on the issues involved. It is more likely to signify that the white men of power have found the conflict so costly that they wish to limit it, moving it from the streets, the stores, and the courtroom into the conference room. In actuality the white and the Negro leaders gathered around the conference table do not constitute a biracial team. They are two "truce teams" representing the still antagonistic parties to a conflict. Realism demands that they concentrate not on their points of agreement but on the issues which underlie the conflict. Limitation of the conflict will result from the strategic use of threats and the reciprocal assessment of the balance of power, not from mutual protestations of goodwill under "the rule of charity."

This suggests that communication and negotiation between white and Negro leaders can be effective only if the relationship is recognized as a conflict relationship. The communicators are antagonists, not partners. When the negotiators are freed from the obligation of playing the dual role of arbitrator and antagonist, each is free to state his position clearly, in a way that will preserve his solidarity with the group which he represents. But each is also free, having stated his position, to retreat strategically in the process of negotiation.

An important corollary of this proposition is that such negotiations can be effective only when the Negro community can muster enough power to require white leaders to negotiate. In some communities Negro leaders have demonstrated the improved power position of the Negro minority by invoking economic or political sanctions. Another significant source of Negro power is intervention from the federal level, either by judicial order or executive action. Appeals to the moral sensibilities of the white community through demonstrations are not likely to be effective unless used in combination with these other sources of power. Demands on the white community, unsupported by power, result only in the display of force to show the superior power of the white community, whether under the guise of law or not.

The effectiveness of the white liberal as a member of the white truce teams is limited. He agrees with representatives of the Negro community to an extent that is not typical of the white power leaders. But it is the ability of a negotiator to influence the people whom he represents that is crucial to his success, not his

---

[4]James Baldwin, *Nobody Knows My Name* (New York: A Delta Book, Dell Publishing Co., 1961), p. 119.

agreement with the opposition. The white liberal is of greatest use in the negotiation process in a role resembling that of an "intelligence officer," who is able to take the role of "the enemy" and interpret the Negroes' position to the other members of the white power structure. He may also be effective as a "liaison agent," who speaks the language of both sides and is trusted by both. In this role he can also be something of a mediator, assessing the relative power positions of the two parties at various stages of the negotiation and summing up the progress that has been made. To play these roles effectively, however, he must remember that he is still a member of the white team and avoid giving the appearance of having "gone over to the enemy."

An Alternate Approach to Negotiation. Can an approach which so frankly recognizes the conflict relationship and deliberately exposes the opposed attitudes of the two sides have any integrative effect? Will it not simply widen the rift between the two racial groups? Coser's theoretical analysis of the integrative functions of conflict suggests that recognition of the inevitability of the conflict nexus may not only limit the conflict but have integrative effects for the community. The authors' actual observation of such a relationship between white and Negro leaders in [a] southern city support this conclusion. The city in which this was observed is...typically "southern...." But, like many other southern cities, it is in the process of shifting from a commercial to an industrial center. Its city officials have explicitly rejected proposals for an official biracial committee, and they have fought a vigorous and highly effective legal delaying action against attempts to desegregate public facilities. Nor has it been able to avoid racial violence. It is one of several southern cities in which nonviolent "sit-ins" were met with violent opposition by segregationist elements in the local population and from surrounding counties.

But it was this violence which provided the impetus for a long process of communication and negotiation. While the Negro demonstrators did not gain an immediate victory, they demonstrated their ability to invoke the sanctions of notoriety upon the community, as national newspapers, radio and television broadcast descriptions of mob violence on the city's main streets. A group of economically powerful white leaders became convinced that this sort of notoriety could be extremely harmful to the city's industrial growth, as the experience of Little Rock had demonstrated. They were also convinced that the Negro community had the power to bring this sort of bad publicity to the city again. As Coser suggests, "Conflict consists in a test of power between antagonistic parties. Accommodation between them is possible only if each is aware of the relative strengths of both parties."[5] In this episode of conflict, these white leaders saw that militant Negroes could be subdued by force but only at a price they did not care to pay.

They did not, however, attempt to form an unofficial biracial committee on which a group of "reasonable" or "moderate" Negro leaders would attempt to speak for the Negro community. Instead, they constituted themselves as a white

---

[5] Coser, *op. cit.*, p. 137.

committee and, through a Negro intergroup relations worker, invited Negro leaders to form a committee of their own. The Negro liaison agent was able to persuade the top officers of a wide range of Negro organizations, including the leaders of the recent demonstrations, to attend an initial meeting with the white leaders. The two groups met in an atmosphere of hostility; no words were minced by either side in condemning the other for its "extremism." But a sufficient number of the white leaders were convinced of the power and determination of the Negro leaders, and a sufficient number of the Negro leaders were impressed by the willingness of even conservative white leaders to listen to them, to allow the negotiations to continue. Within a few months desegregation of some, although not all, of the establishments around which the violence had erupted was accomplished peacefully.

The militant Negro leadership had won. But as so frequently happens in institutional desegregation, it was only a token victory, for only a small proportion of the Negro population profited from the change. One Negro leader declared, "I'm getting ulcers from eating in desegregated restaurants just to prove that they're really desegregated!" The conflict did not end at this point. In fact, many months later a Negro leader would declare to a white leader, "Desegregating eating places is not important—not many Negroes will eat in them; it's creating employment opportunities that is important!" So the negotiations continued.

Token desegregation, creating exceptions to a predominantly segregated pattern, never provides the enduring satisfaction to Negroes that seems in prospect while they are struggling to achieve it. It does not remove the larger, underlying causes of Negro dissatisfaction. Thus each token victory is followed in time by new demands and intensification of the conflict. Moreover, the militant Negro leader cannot long remain a leader if he rests on his laurels after a limited victory. He must define new issues and initiate new struggles.

Negroes demand of protest leaders constant progress. The combination of long-standing discontent and a new-found belief in the possibility of change produces a constant state of tension and aggressiveness in the Negro community. But this discontent is vague and diffuse, not specific; the masses do not define the issues around which action shall revolve. This the leader must do.[6]

So, over a period of two years, Negro leaders in this southern city have selected new issues and marshaled their forces for more demonstrations. During this period, however, they have found the committee of white leaders insisting upon a confrontation over the conference table at the first hint of "trouble." Using the language of the international Cold War, some of the white leaders have described these as "eyeball to eyeball" conferences. The results have varied. The Negroes have sometimes won most of their demands, as in the case of the desegregation of additional eating places. Always agreements reached have been effective because the white leaders are sufficiently high in the power structure to influence business men. Equally important, they represent enough power to cause city officials to be as alert

[6]Lewis M. Killian, "Leadership in the Desegregation Crisis: An Institutional Analysis," in Muzafer Sherif, ed., *Intergroup Relations and Leadership* (New York: John Wiley and Sons, Inc., 1962), p. 159.

in preventing breaches of the peace by white segregationists as in breaking up demonstrations by Negroes. In all of these settlements, the superordinate goal has been "keeping the peace" and avoiding notoriety.

In the case of some demands, such as the insistence that by certain dates Negroes should be employed as sales persons in specific stores, the white leaders have taken the position that they could not or would not accede. They have made it plain that if the Negro leaders carried out their threatened demonstrations, they would use their power to stop the demonstrations through police action and economic reprisals, even at the risk of open conflict. As a result, compromise settlements have been made or the Negroes have shifted their attention to other issues. This has not been merely because the Negro leaders were afraid of arrests and violence. They were even more afraid of losing the concessions they had already won.

It must be emphasized that if this is a committee of white "moderates," they are "moderate segregationists." They have never initiated action to bring about any desegregation except in response to pressure from the Negro community. They make it quite clear that, in their roles as members of the committee, they are only incidentally concerned with segregation as a moral issue. Their primary concern is the image of the community as it affects their economic interests. In meeting with their Negro counterparts, all realize that they are assessing their current power position in a continuing conflict relationship. As a result, there is no resentment of the fact that each group habitually holds a "council of war" before confronting the other. This is expected; in fact, the white leaders urge the Negroes to be sure that all the Negro leaders who might take action with reference to the issue at hand either be represented at the conference or consulted beforehand.

This illustrates another function of conflict which Coser suggests. He proposes,

In view of the advantages of unified organization for purposes of winning the conflict, it might be supposed that each party would strongly desire the absence of unity in the opposing party. Yet this is not always true. If a relative balance of forces exists between the two parties, a unified party prefers a unified opponent.[7]

These white leaders understand that an agreement reached with a segment of a disunited Negro leadership group may be nullified quickly by other segments of the group. The effectiveness of this approach, from the standpoint of the white leaders, was clearly demonstrated when the Negro group pressured one of its most militant members who threatened to violate the terms of agreement accepted by the entire group.

Paradoxically, this interaction within a conflict relationship seems to produce positive changes in the attitudes of the individuals involved. The phenomenon of developing respect for an able antagonist who pursues his objectives with candor, courage, and integrity is not an uncommon one. White Americans may have to learn respect for Negro Americans as opponents before they can accept them as friends and equals.

In a conflict relationship, moreover, stereotypes can be broken down through personal confrontation. Comments of members of these two leadership groups

[7]Coser, *op. cit.*, p. 76.

indicate that they have come to perceive previously unnoticed differences in members of the opposite group. They have developed an awareness of the structural restrictions upon the behavior of each side, so that neither appears quite as unreasonable as before. And even in concentrating on their points of disagreement, they have found areas of agreement and likeness.

In this process, which is still going on, neither whites nor Negroes have achieved dramatic victories. In a very real sense, both have won and both have lost. The white leaders have "given in" to some demands for desegregation, as their critics are quick to charge. But they have achieved their goal of protecting the city from notoriety. The Negroes have achieved only token desegregation, but they have done so without going through the costly and painful process of battling on the streets in order to achieve the same result. Both parties have left the "never-never land" of believing that racial conflict in twentieth-century America is temporary and will disappear with the settlement of any single controversy. They realize that if conflict in their community is not limited by negotiation it will break forth in the streets.

But this is only one level of the conflict relationship. So far these two "truce teams" have concentrated on symbolic manifestations of the Negro's inferior position, not the underlying problems of educational deficiency, lack of job skills, unemployment, and substandard housing. The truce will endure only if drastic action is taken to alleviate these conditions. Otherwise Negro leaders of the type represented here will increasingly find themselves negotiating about token desegregation for the "black bourgeoisie" while the Black Muslims or nationalistic Negro politicians speak for the Negro masses.

The Problem of Inequality. The Black Muslims propose that the Negro in America can solve his problem of identity through segregation, not integration, through becoming fully black and fully proud, not fully American and fully proud. But their program rests also on the assumption that self-imposed segregation must be accompanied by improvement in the material conditions of Negro life. While the Muslim dream of a parallel economy may be unrealistic, there is no doubt that their goal of economic improvement is just as important in attracting and holding followers as are the psychic gratifications of "racism in reverse."

Achievement of identity through the route of desegregation and eventual integration depends, similarly, on raising the level of living of the culturally inferior Negro masses. The white segregationist has long used this cultural inferiority as an excuse for denying even the middle-class Negro full participation. The brutal fact is that it does constitute a real barrier to integration. It limits desegregation to tokenism; it makes the conflict over token desegregation an unending and fruitless one. An assault on segregation unaccompanied by an equally vigorous assault on the cultural deficit can result, at best, in the creation of a three-tiered system of stratification in which the Negro middle class is neither white nor black and is rejected by both the white classes and the black masses.

It has been argued here that the struggle over desegregation will continue, no matter how meaningless it may be. But there needs to be an honest recognition by both white and Negro leaders at all levels that segregation is not the only issue, even while desegregation progresses through tokenism. Unless attacked where it is, inequality will still exist in the segregated institutions of the Negro community. Granted that "separate" cannot be "equal," there could be far less inequality even where obdurate separation persists. Granted that segregation may be the primary source of infection, it cannot be adequately treated until the secondary infections are reduced. This is not to suggest a choice between attacking segregation and attacking inequality. Both must be attacked with equal vigor, and in some cases the choice must be made to attack inequality within the framework of segregation. The fact that James Conant, in *Slums and Suburbs*, suggests an anachronistic vocational emphasis for the *de facto* segregated Negro schools does not vitiate his appeal to improve the quality of education in these schools. Similarly, the drive to develop open-occupancy standards in white neighborhoods should be a supplement to the development of better-quality housing and greater opportunities for home ownership for Negroes, even in segregated neighborhoods. The campaign to eliminate job discrimination against qualified Negroes will have little meaning unless a special effort is made to provide training in the necessary skills.

Since the wealth of the nation is concentrated in the hands of the white population, such a program would demand sacrifice by white Americans. It would require allocation of a disproportionate share of tax money to improve publicly supported institutions for Negroes. It would entail the taking of greater risks by white businessmen who would venture to serve the Negro market. It might even require that more white people serve as teachers to Negroes, like the "Yankee missionaries" of the early days of Negro education in the South. It would require the sort of financial sacrifice that foreign aid programs require; the sort of capitalistic enterprise that expansion into foreign markets demands; and the kind of intensive training that is given Peace Corps members to enable them to work effectively with people of other cultures. It is time for America to face the implications of the fact that it has a "backward nation" within its own boundaries, a nation that requires help from its own fellow citizens if it is to remain psychologically and culturally a part of the greater nation to which it still desperately wants to belong. . . .

The Specter of Conflict. But why should the white American, particularly the segregationist, help the Negro to achieve greater equality when inequality is one of the major bulwarks against integration? Here the American Creed and the dream of government by consensus, not by force, become relevant. It has become painfully evident in the past few years that, unless the nation begins to take longer strides on the first mile of the long road to equality and integration, the Negro revolt will change from a nonviolent to a violent one. The white community will have to fight those Negroes who have too much spirit to submit any longer, and it will have to support with its charity those who are too apathetic to fight. The only other alternative will be increasingly repressive measures which would change the nature of the Republic and destroy the image of American democracy in the eyes of the world. There is no easy way out. The battle has been joined. The question is whether the conflict will rend American society irreparably or draw its racially separated parts together in some yet unforeseeable future.

BLACK POWER

Stokely Carmichael and Charles V. Hamilton

The adoption of the concept of Black Power is one of the most legitimate and healthy developments in American politics and race relations in our time. . . . It is a call for black people in this country to unite, to recognize their heritage, to build a sense of community. It is a call for black people to begin to define their own goals, to lead their own organizations and to support those organizations. It is a call to reject the racist institutions and values of this society.

The concept of Black Power rests on a fundamental premise: *Before a group can enter the open society, it must first close ranks.* By this we mean that group solidarity is necessary before a group can operate effectively from a bargaining position of strength in a pluralistic society. Traditionally, each new ethnic group in this society has found the route to social and political viability through the organization of its own institutions with which to represent its needs within the larger society. Studies in voting behavior specifically, and political behavior generally, have made it clear that politically the American pot has not melted. Italians vote for Rubino over O'Brien; Irish for Murphy over Goldberg, etc. This phenomenon may seem distasteful to some, but it has been and remains today a central fact of the American political system. . . .

The point is obvious: black people must lead and run their own organizations. Only black people can convey the revolutionary idea—and it is a revolutionary idea—that black people are able to do things themselves. Only they can help create in the community an aroused and continuing black consciousness that will provide the basis for political strength. In the past, white allies have often furthered white supremacy without the whites involved realizing it, or even wanting to do so. Black people must come together and do things for themselves. They must achieve self-identity and self-determination in order to have their daily needs met.

Black Power means, for example, that in Lowndes County, Alabama, a black sheriff can end police brutality. A black tax assessor and tax collector and county board of revenue can lay, collect, and channel tax monies for the building of better roads and schools serving black people. In such areas as Lowndes, where black people have a majority, they will attempt to use power to exercise control. This is what they seek: control. When black people lack a majority, Black Power means proper representation and sharing of control. It means the creation of power bases, of strength, from which black people can press to change local or nation-wide patterns of oppression—instead of from weakness.

It does not mean *merely* putting black faces into office. Black visibility is not Black Power. Most of the black politicians around the country today are not

SOURCE: From *Black Power*, pp. 44-48, 50-54, 58-60, 77-81, by Stokely Carmichael and Charles V. Hamilton. © Copyright 1967 by Stokely Carmichael and Charles V. Hamilton. Reprinted by permission of Random House, Inc. and Jonathan Cape, Ltd., London.

examples of Black Power. The power must be that of a community, and emanate from there. The black politicians must start from there. The black politicians must stop being representatives of "downtown" machines, whatever the cost might be in terms of lost patronage and holiday handouts.

Black Power recognizes—it must recognize—the ethnic basis of American politics as well as the power-oriented nature of American politics. Black Power therefore calls for black people to consolidate behind their own, so that they can bargain from a position of strength. But while we endorse the *procedure* of group solidarity and identity for the purpose of attaining certain goals in the body politic, this does not mean that black people should strive for the same kind of rewards (i.e., end results) obtained by the white society. The ultimate values and goals are not domination or exploitation of other groups, but rather an effective share in the total power of the society.

Nevertheless, some observers have labeled those who advocate Black Power as racists; they have said that the call for self-identification and self-determination is "racism in reverse" or "black supremacy." This is a deliberate and absurd lie. There is no analogy—by any stretch of definition or imagination—between the advocates of Black Power and white racists. Racism is not merely exclusion on the basis of race but exclusion for the purpose of subjugating or maintaining subjugation. The goal of the racists is to keep black people on the bottom, arbitrarily and dictatorially, as they have done in this country for over three hundred years. The goal of black self-determination and black self-identity—Black Power—is full participation in the decision-making processes affecting the lives of black people, and recognition of the virtues in themselves as black people. The black people of this country have not lynched whites, bombed their churches, murdered their children, and manipulated laws and institutions to maintain oppression. White racists have. Congressional laws, one after the other, have not been necessary to stop black people from oppressing others and denying others the full enjoyment of their rights. White racists have made such laws necessary. The goal of Black Power is positive and functional to a free and viable society. No white racist can make this claim. . . .

One of the tragedies of the struggle against racism is that up to this point there has been no national organization which could speak to the growing militancy of young black people in the urban ghettos and the black-belt South. There has been only a "civil rights" movement, whose tone of voice was adapted to an audience of middle-class whites. It served as a sort of buffer zone between the audience and angry young blacks. It claimed to speak for the needs of a community, but it did not speak in the tone of that community. None of its so-called leaders could go into a rioting community and be listened to. . . .

We had only the old language of love and suffering. And in most places—that is, from the liberals and middle class—we got back the old language of patience and progress. The civil rights leaders were saying to the country: "Look, you guys are supposed to be nice guys, and we are only going to do what we are supposed to do. Why do you beat us up? Why don't you give us what we ask? Why don't you straighten yourselves out?" For the masses of black people, this language resulted in virtually nothing. In fact, their objective day-to-day condition worsened. The unemployment rate among black people increased while that among whites declined. Housing conditions in the black communities deteriorated. Schools in the black ghettos continued to plod along on outmoded techniques, inadequate curricula, and with all too many tired and indifferent teachers. Meanwhile, the President picked up the refrain of "We Shall Overcome" while the Congress passed civil rights law after civil rights law, only to have them effectively nullified by deliberately weak enforcement. "Progress is being made," we were told.

Such language, along with admonitions to remain nonviolent and fear the white backlash, convinced some that that course was the *only* course to follow. It misled some into believing that a black minority could bow its head and get whipped into a meaningful position of power. The very notion is absurd. The white society devised the language, adopted the rules, and had the black community narcotized into believing that that language and those rules were, in fact, relevant. The black community was told time and again how *other* immigrants finally won *acceptance*: that is, by following the Protestant Ethic of Work and Achievement. They worked hard; therefore, they achieved. We were not told that it was by building Irish Power, Italian Power, Polish Power or Jewish Power that these groups got themselves together and operated from positions of strength. We were not told that "the American dream" wasn't designed for black people. That while today, to whites, the dream may *seem* to include black people, it cannot do so by the very nature of this nation's political and economic system, which imposes institutional racism on the black masses if not upon every individual black. . . .

A key phrase in our buffer-zone days was non-violence. For years it has been thought that black people would not literally fight for their lives. Why this has been so is not entirely clear; neither the larger society nor black people are noted for passivity. The notion apparently stems from the years of marches and demonstrations and sit-ins where black people did not strike back and the violence always came from white mobs. There are many who still sincerely believe in that approach. From our viewpoint, rampaging white mobs and white night-riders must be made to understand that their days of free head-whipping are over. Black people should and must fight back. Nothing more quickly repels someone bent on destroying you than the unequivocal message: "O.K., fool, make your move, and run the same risk I run—of dying."

When the concept of Black Power is set forth, many people immediately conjure up notions of violence. The country's reaction to the Deacons for Defense and Justice, which originated in Louisiana, is instructive. Here is a group which realized that the "law" and law enforcement agencies would not protect people, so they had to do it themselves. If a nation fails to protect its citizens, then that nation cannot condemn those who take up the task themselves. The Deacons and all other blacks who resort to self-defense represent a simple answer to a simple question: what man would not defend his family and home from attack?

But this frightened some white people, because they knew that black people would now fight back. They knew that this was precisely what *they* would have long since done if *they* were subjected to the injustices and oppression heaped on blacks. Those of us who advocate Black Power are quite clear in our own minds that a "non-violent" approach to civil rights is an approach black people cannot afford and a luxury white people do not deserve. It is crystal clear to us—and it must become so with the white society—*that there can be no social order without social justice.* White people must be made to understand that they must stop messing with black people, or the blacks *will* fight back!

Next, we must deal with the term "integration." According to its advocates, social justice will be accomplished by "integrating the Negro into the mainstream institutions of the society from which he has been traditionally excluded." This concept is based on the assumption that there is nothing of value in the black community and that little of value could be created among black people. The thing to do is siphon off the "acceptable" black people into the surrounding middle-class white community.

The goals of integrationists are middle-class goals, articulated primarily by a small group of Negroes with middle-class aspirations or status. Their kind of integration has meant that a few blacks "make it," leaving the black community, sapping it of leadership potential and know-how. . . . Those token Negroes—absorbed into a white mass—are of no value to the remaining black masses. They become meaningless show-pieces for a conscience-soothed white society. Such people will state that they would prefer to be treated "only as individuals, not as Negroes"; that they "are not and should not be preoccupied with race." This is a totally unrealistic position. In the first place, black people have not suffered as individuals but as members of a group; therefore, their liberation lies in group action. This is why SNCC—and the concept of Black Power—affirms that helping *individual* black people to solve their problems on an *individual* basis does little to alleviate the mass of black people. Secondly, while color blindness *may* be a sound goal ultimately, we must realize that race is an overwhelming fact of life in this historical period. There is no black man in this country who can live "simply as a man." His blackness is an ever-present fact of this racist society, whether he recognizes it or not. It is unlikely that this or the next generation will witness the time when race will no longer be relevant in the conduct of public affairs and in public policy decision-making. To realize this and to attempt to deal with it does not make one a racist or overly preoccupied with race; it puts one in the forefront of a significant *struggle.* If there is no intense struggle today, there will be no meaningful results tomorrow. . . .

There is a strongly held view in this society that the best—indeed, perhaps the only—way for black people to win their political and economic rights is by forming coalitions with liberal, labor, church, and other kinds of sympathetic organizations or forces, including the "liberal left" wing of the Democratic Party. With such allies, they could influence national legislation and national social patterns; racism could thus be ended. This school sees the "Black Power Movement" as basically separatist and unwilling to enter alliances. . . .

SNCC has often stated that it does not oppose the formation of political coalitions *per se*; obviously they are necessary in a pluralistic society. But coalitions with whom? On what terms? And for what objectives? All too frequently, coalitions involving black people have been only at the leadership level; dictated by terms set by others; and for objectives not calculated to bring major improvement in the lives of the black masses. . . .

What, then, are the grounds for viable coalitions?

Before one begins to talk coalition, one should establish clearly the premises on which that coalition will be based. All parties to the coalition must perceive a *mutually* beneficial goal based on the conception of *each* party of his *own* self-interest. One party must not blindly assume that what is good for one is automatically—without question—good for the other. Black people must first ask themselves what is good *for them*, and then they can determine if the "liberal" is willing to coalesce. They must recognize that institutions and political organizations have no consciences outside their own special interests.

Secondly, there is a clear need for genuine power bases before black people can enter into coalitions. Civil rights leaders who, in the past or at present, rely essentially on "national sentiment" to obtain passage of civil rights legislation reveal the fact that they are operating from a powerless base. They must appeal to the conscience, the good graces of the society; they are, as noted earlier, cast in a beggar's role, hoping to strike a responsive chord. It is very significant that the two oldest civil rights organizations, the National Association for the Advancement of Colored People and the Urban League, have constitutions which specifically prohibit partisan political activity. (The Congress of Racial Equality once did, but it changed that clause when it changed its orientation in favor of Black Power.) This is perfectly understandable in terms of the strategy and goals of the older organizations, the concept of the civil rights movement as a kind of liaison between the powerful white community and the dependent black community. The dependent status of the black community apparently was unimportant since, if the movement proved successful, that community was going to blend into the white society anyway. No pretense was made of organizing and developing institutions of community power within the black community. No attempt was made to create any base of organized political strength; such activity was even prohibited, in the cases mentioned above. All problems would be solved by forming coalitions with labor, churches, reform clubs, and especially liberal Democrats. . . .

Viable coalitions therefore stem from four preconditions: (a) the recognition by the parties involved of their respective self-interests; (b) the mutual belief that each party stands to benefit in terms of that self-interest from allying with the other or others; (c) the acceptance of the fact that each party has its own independent base of power and does not depend for ultimate decision-making on a force outside itself; and (d) the coalition deals with specific and identifiable—as opposed to general and vague—goals. . . .

Let black people organize themselves *first*, define their interests and goals, and then see what kinds of allies are available. Let any ghetto group contemplating coaltion be so tightly organized, so strong, that—in the words of Saul Alinsky—it is an "indigestible body" which cannot be absorbed or swallowed up.[1] The advocates of Black Power are not opposed to coalitions *per se*. But we are *not* interested in coalitions based on myths. To the extent to which black people can form *viable* coalitions will the end results of those alliances be lasting and meaningful. There will be clearer understanding of what is sought; there will be greater impetus on all

[1] Saul Alinsky speaking at the 1967 Legal Defense Fund Convocation in NYC, May 18, 1967.

sides to deliver, because there will be *mutual* respect of the power of the other to reward or punish; there will be much less likelihood of leaders selling out their followers. Black Power therefore has no connotation of "go it alone." Black Power simply says: enter coalitions only *after* you are able to "stand on your own." Black Power seeks to correct the approach to dependency, to remove that dependency, and to establish a viable psychological, political, and social base upon which the black community can function to meet its needs. . . .

VII
FUTURE TRENDS IN SOCIETAL POWER

POWER TRENDS IN SYSTEMIC SOCIETIES

Marvin E. Olsen

Viewed from a broad perspective, most human history can be seen as a perpetual process of "drifting along and muddling through," with very little purposeful direction. Mankind has for the most part reacted to the conditions in which it found itself, rather than rationally shaping these conditions. In recent years, however, growing numbers of people—including many social scientists—have begun to argue that we can no longer afford the luxury of unplanned social life.

As long as societies and other kinds of social organizations were relatively small and simple, most social activities were limited in scope and affected relatively few people at any one time. The quality of the schools in a community, for instance, was strictly a local concern with little relevance for other communities or the total society. In today's highly complex and interdependent world, in contrast, a "local" decision to exclude Negroes from white schools can have ramifications throughout the society and in international relations. Nor can we continue to assume that poverty is strictly an individual or family concern that will eventually disappear as more and more people climb the "ladder of success" through their own efforts. If these and a thousand other challenges in social life are to be met successfully, it appears that we must begin now to ask such questions as "what social changes are presently occurring?," "what kind of society do we want in the future?," and "what do we have to do to achieve these goals?." No one can predict with certainty the future of mankind's organized social life, but we can investigate current trends in our societies and then use this knowledge rationally to plan and shape future developments.

Our concern in this final essay and the accompanying readings, therefore, is with changes presently occurring in the nature and use of power in contemporary societies, and with possible future outcomes of these trends. Although these writings are partially speculative, the visions of the future they present are all solidly grounded in current trends and hence are relevant for any attempts at social planning. The following essay first briefly examines several long-term alterations in social power

370

that can be discerned at the present time, and then sketches the main outlines of a proposed "systemic model" for possible future societies.

Given the continually expanding rate of technological innovation plus such fundamental social trends as industrialization, urbanization, and bureaucratization, our societies will undoubtedly continue to become ever more complexly organized—hopefully assuming that global warfare, unchecked population growth, or some other major catastrophe does not return us all to the Stone Age. From this we would expect that social power growing out of collective social activities will become increasingly crucial in modernized societies. But on what kinds of resource bases will this power rest? As long as survival in the natural environment is man's chief concern, ecological considerations remain paramount and the economy of a society provides the major resource base for exerting social power. Certainly this condition has characterized most of man's past existence, and still prevails over large portions of the globe today. To this extent, Marx's emphasis on relationships to the major means of economic production—whether it be land or industry—provides a crucial insight into the nature of social power and the organization of societies. Since World War II, however, we have   begun to glimpse—in a few fortunate societies—the possibility of someday achieving universal economic abundance based on high levels of automated industrial production. As this trend slowly emerges, the resource bases for social power also change.

The economy of a society will necessarily always provide a foundation on which other social activities will rest. But should economic production approach the level at which all material needs and wants are supplied with a minimum of human effort, the economy will tend to lose its position of dominant power in society. Paradoxically, universal abundance can eliminate economic dominance arising from scarcity and deprivation—provided that the economy continues to operate smoothly and to satisfy all sustenance requirements. As economic productivity expands in both volume and efficiency, people are freed from basic   subsistence   and other economic concerns, and are then able to direct their attention and efforts toward securing whatever other goals they desire.[1] As a result, mere ownership of wealth no longer provides pervasive social power.

A fully developed "post-industrial society"[2] would undoubtedly contain a wide variety of important new power resources, including administrative and managerial abilities in operating complex organizations, scientific and technological expertise, teaching and mass communication skills, and perhaps even artistic and aesthetic talents. The common element in all these kinds of resources is knowledge, since the fundamental functional requirement in such a society would be expert knowledge and accompanying skills. The scientific-educational-informational network would replace the economy as the major sphere of power in society, and those individuals and organizations who performed such activities would be able—because of their

---

[1] This argument is elaborated by W.W. Rostow in *The Stages of Economic Growth* (New York: Cambridge University Press, 1964), Chaps. 8-10.

[2] Daniel Bell, "Notes on the Post-Industrial Society, I and II," *The Public Interest*, No. 6, Winter 1967, pp. 24-35, and No. 7, Spring 1967, pp. 102-118.

functional dominance—to control numerous resources and exert intensive social power. In addition, the basis of most authority would also tend to shift from occupancy of formal positions to possession of critical knowledge and skills. Thus officials responsible for leading collective activities—in both public and private organizations, from national government to local enterprises—would be granted legitimate authority over others because of their expert abilities, not their formal offices.

In sum, *one crucial trend in post-industrial societies is a shift from economically based power, with its emphasis on the use of force, to authority based on expert knowledge and skills that command functional dominance in society.*

A second important trend is also already becoming evident in all highly industrialized and urbanized societies: *continual growth in the size, complexity, power, and centralization of the national government.* This trend is being produced by such factors as (a) the increasing complexity of these societies and the functional interdependency of all their component parts, so that more and more activities become societal-wide rather than local in scope; (b) modern methods of communication and transportation, which enable a government to know what is happening in all parts of the society and to exert influence on these activities no matter how distant they may be in physical space; (c) growing acceptance of the basic ideal of democratic socialism that the economy (and all other collective activities) should be operated to benefit the general public interest rather than private interests; and (d) slowly increasing pressures for unified national participation in international relationships and organizations.

This tendency toward ever more powerful and centralized national government has alarmed many observers and writers, for if carried far enough it could eventually lead to either a mass or totalitarian type of society—neither of which appear desirable to most people. At the present time both of these are only conceptual models of possible future societies, and no real society fully approximates either type. But the twentieth century has witnessed enough social trends and political movements in these directions to suggest that they could someday become realities.

Both the mass and totalitarian models envision a highly centralized national government that attempts to exert influence throughout its society, but they differ sharply in the extent to which these efforts are successful. In a mass society there would be few or no intermediate organizations between the masses of relatively isolated individuals and the ruling elites, so that individuals would have no effective channels—other than unorganized mass movements—for influencing societal decision-making. But at the same time, the rulers would also lack any reliable means—other than mass meetings and mass communications—for influencing or directing the people in collective activities. Hence the society would consist essentially of a large mass of isolated and powerless individuals, plus a totally centralized but relatively weak and vulnerable set of political rulers.

Such a society would become increasingly unstable as a strong sense of alienation spread among the people and as the government found itself unable to cope with either internal or external demands being made upon it. The outcome might be either a mass popular movement aimed at overthrowing the government or a concerted effort by the ruling elites to strengthen their power and extend their control over the society. In both cases, the society might well tend to move toward the totalitarian model.

The elites in a totalitarian society, in contrast, would be extremely powerful and in complete control of the entire society. In an effort to mobilize and direct the society toward the attainment of some ideal national goals (such as the elimination of deprivation and "class conflict," or perhaps world conquest), the elites would organize themselves into a tightly disciplined political party that pervaded the formal government, so that all major decisions were made within the ranks of the party, not the government. They would also proclaim a highly utopian ideology as a means of gaining popular support and legitimacy. Concurrently, they would utilize sophisticated techniques of organizational proliferation, manipulation, and control to enmesh all individuals throughout the society in a pervasive web of social committments. A totalitarian society would thus be extensively organized, with many layers of intermediate organizations from the lowest to the highest levels, but all such units would be directly and totally controlled by the ruling elites. Because the flow of influence through these organizations would be solely downward, the elites could exert tremendous power over all social activities, while individuals would remain completely powerless. Finally, to enforce their social controls over the people the rulers would not hesitate to employ whatever techniques of surveillance, indoctrination, censorship, coercion, or terror they thought necessary. In the end, totalitarianism would represent centralization of power carried to its ultimate extreme.

Power centralization in the national government need not go as far as either the mass or totalitarian models, however, if two conditions are met: (a) maintenance of a strong network of viable, autonomous intermediate organizations that serve as links for transmitting influence in all directions throughout the society, thus making the pluralistic model truly effective; and (b) separation of coordination, regulation, and planning activities, which must be relatively centralized in a highly complex society, from decision-making and control functions, which need not be centralized in the national government. The systemic societal model to be sketched below attempts to incorporate both these requirements, while at the same time taking into account the functionally necessary and inescapable trend toward organizational complexity and centralization.

A third notable tendency in highly developed societies today is *a gradual merging of "public" and "private" organizations into new forms that might be called "semi-public,"* though perhaps an entirely new name is needed. In the past, there has usually been a fairly clear line between public government (including government-controlled organizations such as public schools and the Post Office) and private organizations such as businesses, churches, and voluntary associations. Public organizations belonged ultimately to all the citizens in a society or community or other geographical area, while private organizations were the property of particular individuals (usually members or stockholders). Private organizations were presumably concerned only with their own interests and goals, and could do more or less as they pleased as long as they remained within the law; they had no broader public responsibilities. In contrast, the function of public government (at least in an ideal sense) was to serve the common interests of all members of the community or society and to perform activities that private organizations could not or would not assume. A major consequence of this distinction has been continual political conflict between "conservatives" seeking to protect private organizations by limiting or reducing governmental activities, and "liberals" or "radicals" seeking to expand these activities.

Today, however, the line between public and private organizations is no longer clear in many cases, and is becoming more blurred all the time. In the United States, for example, many governmental agencies such as the Federal Communications Commission or the Tennessee Valley Authority or the Port of New York Authority are legally public bodies but actually operate as relatively autonomous "private" organizations serving limited clientele. And recently there has even been talk of making the Post Office a quasi-private organization. Substantial portions of most large businesses and industries, meanwhile, are no longer owned by private individuals, but rather by trust funds, insurance companies, mutual funds, and other financial organizations that act as agents for vast numbers of people. Many of these business concerns are also gradually accepting the idea that they have public responsibilities which go far beyond making money for their owners. Or consider universities in this society, some of which are "private" and some "public," but all of which are highly similar in both structure and activities.

The new forms of "semi-public" organizations that seem to be emerging from these changes are simultaneously "public" and "private." They are public in that their basic concern is with serving the interests and welfare of the entire society, while their activities are guided by a strong sense of public responsibility. But they are also private in that they are largely controlled by their members or participants and are relatively autonomous in their activities. The implications of these organizational tendencies for the exercise of power in society—especially functional dominance—are profound. It may become necessary to alter all our thinking, both empirical and valuative, about the distribution and use of social power.

A final current trend in modernized societies concerns the nature of equality and inequality, whether socioeconomic, racial, or political. It is commonplace to read today, in both scholarly and popular writings, of increasing relative equality among large segments of the population, and of the growth of a huge "middle class" that steadily encompasses more and more people. It is certainly true that in the United States and several West European nations the standard of living of many people has risen sharply since World War II, so that there is now less absolute deprivation in these societies than ever before in history—even among disadvantaged persons such as Negroes.[3] And although this trend is far from complete—as the recent "discovery" of extensive poverty in the United States makes abundantly clear—it is quite probable that it will continue and even expand in the future (again barring global war or other catastrophes).

---

[3] This literature is voluminous, but the interested reader might begin with Gerhard E. Lenski, *Power and Privilege: A Theory of Social Stratification* (New York: McGraw-Hill Book Co., 1957) Chaps. 10-12.

Two crucial features of this development must be kept in mind, however: First, even though absolute deprivation may be slowly disappearing this does not necessarily mean that greater relative equality is being achieved. Most of the observable rise in standards of living may be due simply to over-all economic growth, without any major redistribution of wealth. Indeed, there is some evidence that the over-all distribution of socioeconomic benefits has not changed substantially in the United States in many years; more people may live better, but they remain markedly unequal. Second, these discussions of a growing "middle class" are limited almost entirely to socioeconomic status, and do not necessarily apply to other realms of inequality such as race relations. Many racial tensions will undoubtedly be eased as more and more Negroes and other ethnic peoples gain adequate shares of the total national wealth. But racial discrimination involves much more than just economic deprivation, and in fact racial conflict may likely increase in severity as blacks acquire more economic resources with which to oppose whites.[4]

Even if relative socioeconomic and racial equality were someday to be attained, however, this might still leave the realm of politics (or more broadly, collective decision making) completely untouched. The masses of people in modernized societies today may not be losing political power, since if the elitists are at all correct the masses have never had much influence on public decisions or policies. But are they gaining any meaningful political power? Does popular sovereignty as it presently operates contribute significantly to equalizing political power among all citizens, or is voting merely a means whereby elites gain legitimacy? Nor can it be assumed that mass economic affluence is an adequate substitute for participation in collective decision making. Popular voting and rising socioeconomic security may in fact stimulate peoples' demands for more direct and meaningful participation in politics without providing viable means of realizing this goal—thus creating mounting dissatisfaction and conflict. Furthermore, if the trend toward centralization of power in the national government should proceed unchecked, there might well be an absolute decline in whatever little political power the masses of people presently can exert. And compounding all these factors is the emerging emphasis on expert knowledge as the primary basis for exercising legitimate authority, which often transforms debatable political issues into "closed" technical questions and thus entirely excludes the nonexpert from the realm of decision-making.

To summarize this last trend, we might say that while power based on socioeconomic resources may be slowly moving toward at least partial equality, and while it is possible that someday greater racial equality may prevail, there is presently little indication of a substantial shift toward greater equality of political power in developed societies—and *a distinct possibility that the arena of collective decision making may actually shrink at the same time that popular demands for viable participation in politics are multiplying.*

These four contemporary trends—in the major resource bases of social power, centralization of governmental power, merging of "public" and "private" organiza-

---

[4]This possibility is explored by Lewis Killian in *The Impossible Revolution*? (New York: Random House, 1968).

tions, and inequality of power distributions—by no means exhaust all of the major changes now discernible in developed societies. They do indicate, nevertheless, that "post-industrial" societies will be radically different—especially in the realm of social power—from anything presently known. They also suggest that if mankind is to gain some measure of control over organized social life, avoid the drift into mass or totalitarian societal forms, and rationally plan the development of more desirable patterns of social organization, then we must begin now to envision and explore possible future kinds of societies. The systemic societal model provides one step in this direction.

The systemic model is not a precise description of any existing society, but rather a rough sketch of the main characteristics of one type of possible future society. The entire model has never been thoroughly or explicitly formulated, although many of its features have been suggested in a variety of recent social-scientific writings.[5] As described here, the model attempts to take account of all four of the social trends discussed above, as well as the arguments of both elitist and pluralistic theory. Indeed, some sociologists might view the systemic model as merely an extension of pluralism, but there are at least three crucial differences between this model and traditional ideas of pluralism:

First, the systemic model gives serious attention to the elitist argument that as societies become highly developed and complexly organized, the necessity for over-all coordination, regulation, and planning of social activities incessantly accelerates. As more and more activities are organized on a national rather than a local level, societalwide administration becomes imperative. There can be no return to simpler patterns of relatively unrelated communities and small organizations. This does not imply, however, that the national government must assume responsibility for managing and directing the entire society, or that future societies must necessarily be dominated by a small set of immensely powerful elites. As suggested in a previous essay, a society may be organized along functionally distinct lines with separate sets of multitiered elites in each segment, all of which are relatively equal in power.

Second, this model carries the idea of power decentralization much further than does traditional pluralism. As we have already seen, the usual conception of pluralism limits governmental power by imposing an array of intermediate special-interest associations between it and the people, but the polity nevertheless remains the dominant arena of activity on the national level. In practice, this has often resulted in intermediate associations competing with one another in their attempts to influence public decisions and policy, but not directly controlling the national government. In the systemic model, in contrast, power is decentralized along functional lines to the point where the polity becomes only one among many equally powerful functional networks in a society, so that it cannot exercise a preponderance of power.

[5] In addition to the works from which the readings in this section were drawn, three other recent books are particularly pertinent for the systemic model: Peter Drucker, *The Future: Guidelines to Our Changing Society* (New York: Harper and Row, 1968); Amitai Etzioni, *The Active Society* (London: Collier-Macmillan Ltd., 1968); and Piet Thoenes, *The Elite in the Welfare State* (New York: The Free Press, 1966).

The third crucial difference between the two models lies in the earlier mentioned distinction between "competitive" and "countervailing" power. Traditional pluralism is essentially an extension to the total society of the classical economic notion of open competition on the "same side" of the market among many similar, small, and rather weak units, with the government acting as a mediator in these processes. The systemic model relies instead on the idea of countervailing power, in which a few large and quite powerful, but dissimilar, units control each other's activities from "opposite" sides of the market. The model generalizes this conception beyond the economy to all parts of society, so that each broad sphere or network of activity is controlled primarily by other highly organized networks exercising countervailing power against it.

From a structural perspective, *a systemic society would be organized along functional rather than geographic lines. It would be composed of a series of functionally specialized social networks that were relatively autonomous but also interdependent and interrelated.* Each network would in turn consist of a highly complex web of many smaller organizations that carried functional specialization even further. Since each network would normally be concerned with only one particular sphere of activity, there might be separate networks for industry, commerce, agriculture, transportation, communication, education, religion, medicine, science, law, public welfare, housing, recreation, public administration, foreign affairs, and so on. The organizational units comprising any given network would be "private" in their everyday activities and internal control, but "public" in their concern with providing their specialized services for the total society. In addition, because of their functional specialization they would be highly interdependent upon one another, thus giving the entire society considerable functional interrelatedness and unity.

The basic social networks would not be monolithic units that autocratically controlled their component units and activities. They might rather be described as organized administrative linkages and processes for promoting over-all coordination, regulation, and planning within their spheres of competence. Operational responsibility and power would remain largely in the hands of the organizations comprising each network. In a similar manner, each of these organizations would itself contain numerous smaller parts and subparts, each of which operated with considerable autonomy and hence exercised viable power. Thus the total society, its functional networks, and their component organizational units would all be extensively decentralized but also integrated along functional lines. Social unity would be further strengthened by strong common norms of public responsibility, and by codes of professional ethics within each functional realm.

Graphically, each network might be pictured as a large circle. Any individual or group with an interest in the activities of that network could enter it by participating in organizational activities at its periphery. As this actor increased its committment to network functions, gained necessary knowledge and skills, assumed broadening organizational responsibilities and duties, acquired the professional norms of the network, and was granted greater legitimate authority, it would move through organizational structures toward the middle of the circle. Those actors occupying positions at or near the center of the circle—whom we might call "elites" and "subelites"—would have primary responsibility and authority for coordinating, regulating, and planning (but not controlling) activities throughout the network. Their power would be severely checked, moreover, by the many influences exerted on them by all the partially autonomous organizations and smaller units comprising the network. Each of these component parts would in turn constitute smaller circles within the network, operating in much the same manner on a smaller scale.

The major thrust of this systemic societal model is its emphasis on decentralization of power away from the state along functional lines, with each social network exercising strong countervailing power derived from functional dominance and legitimate authority based on its performance of vital services for the total society. The state would thus lose its predominance over other sectors of society and become merely another functional network—or possibly three or four separate networks, Moreover, although the "public administration" network would perform over-all administrative services for the society, it would not necessarily engage in either operational programs (such as highway construction and welfare plans and urban renewal and aviation control) or collective decisions. The hundreds of various kinds of operational programs now being conducted by governmental agencies would be the responsibilities of separate specialized organizations within other functional networks, leaving the administrative network free to concentrate on its particular area of competence. Public decision-making and policy formulation, meanwhile, would be carried out in two different ways:

First, to the extent that any question or problem was essentially technical in nature, so that its solution depended on the application of expert knowledge, it would be handled by one or more specialized organizations within the network (or possibly networks) concerned with that area. Individuals would be selected to handle any given problem on the basis of their technical knowledge and skills, and would operate in as rational a manner as possible. There might be discussion and debate among the experts, but this would not extend to the rest of the people in the society who were not specifically qualified on that topic.

Second, whenever an issue went beyond technical details to involve "valuative" considerations, it would be handled through formal public decision-making procedures. The exact nature of these procedures would undoubtedly vary from one society to another, though two (not incompatible) possibilities might be (a) popular voting on broad issues of policy and goals, and (b) some kind of supreme council or congress comprised of elected representatives of each of the functional networks. The important point, however, is that political leaders and governmental agencies would focus their attentions not on technical questions for which they lacked adequate knowledge and skills, but rather on broad valuative issues such as setting societal goals, formulating long-range policies, evaluating the benefits to society of various operational programs, allocating societal resources among competing activities, resolving serious conflicts between networks, and suggesting guidelines for future societal development. Their nonspecialized, societal-wide orientation and concern would hopefully enable them to transcend vested interests arising from the narrower perspectives of technical specialists and to act in the best interests of the whole society.

Individual citizens, meanwhile, could effectively participate in public decision making in at least three different ways: (1) carrying out their various roles in all of the organizations and networks to which they belonged, at least some of which would involve them as specialized experts (to one degree or another) in technical problems; (2) helping to select members from their particular organizations to represent them as officials of the network (or networks) encompassing these organizations, from among whom would be chosen network representatives to the societal council; and (3) voting as individuals on societal-wide issues involving basic goals and policies.

In summary, it must be reiterated that this speculative model of a systemic society is neither a description of any presently existing social arrangements nor a personal value statement of how all societies should be organized. It is, rather, a rough blueprint of one kind of possible future society that is based on the major organizational power trends discussed above, and which seeks to transform the essential ideas of pluralism into a viable social system that could counter the ever-present possibility of drifting towards extreme centralization of the mass or totalitarian varieties. The fundamental assumption underlying the systemic model is that *operational responsibilities and meaningful power can be decentralized and relatively equalized throughout a society—provided it remains effectively unified—without sacrificing the necessary activities of over-all coordination, regulation, planning, and similar administrative functions.* In such a society all organizational units—and hence ultimately all individuals—would then enjoy as much autonomy of operation, exercise of power, and freedom of action as could be encouraged without infringing on the rights of others.

The following reading selections are representative of the more provocative recent writings by social scientists on future trends in societal power. Robert Lynd sets the tone for this discussion when he describes social power as rooted in the basic structure of society and thus providing a necessary foundation for the attainment of whatever goals a society may seek. John Kenneth Galbraith and Daniel Bell both examine the kinds of social trends discussed in this essay, with emphasis on the shift from ownership of property (or capital) to managerial and technical skills as the primary source of social power. They express considerable agreement on all these issues, even though Galbraith's attention is focused largely on the economy whereas Bell's perspective takes in many different aspects of social life. William Kornhauser then sketches the main features of the mass society model, followed by two descriptions of totalitarian society by Robert Nisbet and Hannah Arendt. Nisbet examines this model in broad analytical and theoretical terms, whereas Arendt is more concerned with the empirical "case examples" of Nazi Germany and the Soviet Union under Stalin. Finally, a fitting climax to this volume is provided by Barrington Moore's argument that the gradual attainment of human freedom is inexorably linked with social change—both evolutionary and revolutionary—and with the exercise of power in the form of "just authority."

POWER IN SOCIETY AS RESOURCE AND PROBLEM

Robert S. Lynd

It is not primarily the desire of some men to constrain others that makes power, in one form or another, so universal a phenomenon in society; rather, it is the necessity in each society—if it is to be a society, not a rabble—to order the relations of men and their institutional ways of achieving needed ends. . . .

Much of the confusion regarding power in contemporary society derives from the transitional identification of power with domination. . . . The identification of power with dominance obscures the fact that power in a genuine democracy may be a human resource which can be used for the enlargement of human freedom. It is my purpose to invite clear recognition of power as a social resource and to consider ways in which it may be used and abused. The traditional identification of power with dominance—riveted home in popular thought by the most widely quoted of all statements about power: Lord Acton's dictum that "power corrupts"—renders public reference to organized power in a society professing democratic values furtive and its use awkward. Liberal democracy has, accordingly, tended to resolve the problem of power by quantitative limitation of its use. And the result of this, as I shall note later, has been the progressive transference of this social resource from use for the ends of democratic society to use by private power agencies for their private purposes. If this tendency is to be reversed, it is necessary to remove the concept of power from the dubious limbo in which it now lives, and ask: Under what conditions may this social resource be used in democratic ways for democratic ends?. . .

Organized thinking about power arose historically in the context of men's political institutions. . . . Man's oldest public preoccupation has been with the burden of tyrants, oligarchies, and other forms of absolute ruling, and with the resulting struggle to establish the rights and freedoms of the citizen under government. The intensity of this preoccupation has deeply prejudiced—right down into the present— consideration of the nature and uses of organized power in society. Under the resulting narrowing of focus to the political model, the tendency has been to view the whole range of reality concerning organized power as equated to, and comprised within, a society's political institutions. In earlier times this often involved exaggeration of the role of leaders and the locating of the "badness" of power in their persons. Latterly, under liberal democracy, the chief villain has been seen as the state.

Political power has historically operated on a scarcity theory. According to this theory, when somebody has power others do not. . . . According to this theory—

SOURCE: Robert S. Lynd, "Power in American Society as Resource and Problem," in Arthur Kornhauser, ed., *Problems of Power in American Democracy* pp. 3-6, 9-14, 20-26, 34-38. With permission of the Wayne State University Press. Copyright 1957 by Wayne State University Press.

which to some extent survives today—every power assumed by the state reduces by precisely that much the power of the people; for whatever is added to the one is assumed necessarily to be taken from the other. Such scarcity versions of power have meant in no uncertain sense that power is power *over* others. The inherited image is one of struggle against others, of winning or losing the right to dominate and to practice against the losers the skills and wiles that go with domination. . . .

The ambiguity I am discussing raises the question whether it is necessary or appropriate to perpetuate in a democratic society this scarcity conception of power conceived in terms of dominance and submission. A thorough-going democracy presumably has a rich resource in the fact that it opens the door to abundance in power by providing opportunity for power *with* others in achieving widely desired ends. . . . Politics in such a society performs the double function of affording full opportunity for men to register their areas of agreement, while also providing occasions for clarifying precisely what it is that is important in the differences among them on concrete issues. It may be that such a democracy is unattainable; but if it is attainable, it will be, not through a politics of dominance and submission, but through a use of power which recognizes the resources inherent in both the common humanity and the diversity in human beings. . . .

Modern mass society is internally highly interdependent. The maintenance of continuous and reliable webs of relation and of flow may no longer be viewed as primarily private concerns, but are matters of basic concern to our whole society. Many things must be done collectively because they can no longer be done so well—or well enough to be socially dependable—individually and piecemeal. But because of the drag I describe upon the positive exercise of thoroughgoing democratic power, the liberal democratic state has no clear warrant for developing an unambiguous, positive theory of the sustained use of democratic power for collective democratic ends. . . .

The suspicion that surrounds state power has not in general extended so acutely to the growth of organized private powers. The growth in size and effective power of private institutions reflects their relative freedom, in fact if not always in visible form, to adapt to changing needs and opportunities. As a result, great corporate industrial blocs, as well as bodies like the American Medical Association, constitute in some very real sense autonomous empires within our liberal democratic society. . . .

As we look at the forms and uses of power in society, it is apparent that power-in-use is very widely distributed: persons may be said to have it in varying degrees in their direct relation with others, in their social roles, and in their participation in the making and application of public opinion; institutions have it; values that motivate social action may be said to have it; and likewise power appears in the structure of society. And there can be no doubt that many factors—such as size, organization, wealth, initiative, and access to professional skills, to channels of communication, and to such subtler resources as secrecy and sophistication, as well as the degree of general dependence of the public on the function performed—may *add to* the power of a given unit, however that power may be generated in any larger senses. In this complex and highly dynamic situation it would appear to be extremely difficult to locate any one generating source from which this pervasive phenomenon may be said to stem. Nevertheless, the fact that certain selected emphases recur again and again in the courses that powers take within a given society, and the persistence these emphases exhibit in penetrating and molding seemingly most unlikely aspects of living, suggest that the least probable hypothesis is the pluralistic one. Rather, it would seem that powers in society do not spring up anywhere and anyhow, nor does each develop thereafter on its own autonomous and idiosyncratic terms. Perhaps some tough, enduring factor may be identified as operating fundamentally and persistently to determine the characteristic functions and intensities of organized powers in each specific society. . . .

Where, then, does one look for the generating source that gives power its characteristic shape, prominence and direction of thrust in a given society? The answer would appear necessarily to lie either at the level of institutions or at the level of the social structure of a society. . . .[1]

Although individual leaders have historically tended to focus the high drama of power in public imagination, it is institutions that have been most widely identified as the place where organized power is and is most truly real. While conditions vary from society to society, the social structure of society has tended to be neither so visible nor so easy to grasp as a whole in its relations to power as have been the institutions that continually exercise control over man's affairs. Reference has already been made to the habit of viewing the state as the great repository of power. From the early Middle Ages to the Reformation and the rise of the nation state, the Church of Rome stood forth as ordering power in Western Europe. More recently attention has focused upon economic institutions as the massive locus of power: Marxism viewed the "mode of production" as determining all other institutions; while liberal capitalism, with its emphasis upon "economic man" in a natural market setting, has factually approached the same end, without directly anticipating it, by largely giving economic institutions their head while reining in the power of the state.

In the United States it has been particularly easy to identify organized power with institutions, rather than with the social structure of American society, because of the absence of an hereditary aristocracy and because of the presence of pronounced individual vertical mobility. Such characteristics, in a setting of formal political democracy preoccupied with its regional differences, have blurred the objective boundaries of classes and thus seemingly emphasized the differentness of American capitalistic democracy from that of the older nations of Europe. This climate of opinion has denied a conspicuous role to our social structure in determining the structure of American power.

---

[1] The term "social structure" refers to the organized relations of groups and categories of people identified within a given society according to kinship, sex, age, division of labor, race, religion, or any other criteria stressed as differentiating people in role, status, access to resources, and authority. This structure establishes durable relations that hold groups of people together for certain purposes and separate them for others. Such a social structure may persist over many generations. Its continuance depends upon its ability to cope with historical changes that involve absorption of new groupings and relations of men without fundamental change in the structure of the society of a kind that involves major transfer of power.

And yet, in our society as elsewhere, one should be warned by the thrust—from somewhere behind or beneath institutions—that appears to impart common directions and common limitations in movement to quite diverse institutions. This apparently active selecting and controlling factor does not operate at random; rather, there is in any given society a pattern in what it is "for" and "against." Certain emphases, as regards both favored and opposed lines of action, repeat themselves again and again. The persistence of these broad types of thrust and resistance is impressive. . . .

This kind of repeated emphasis in diverse institutions, even in cases where the emphasis is incompatible with the professed aims of a given institution, suggests one of two possibilities: either that institutions do not, so to speak, stand on their own feet and are not primary sources of the power they express but, rather, are agents of something else underlying and controlling them; or that some one institution controls all the others, molding their orientation and actions to support its needs.

The first of these explanations leads directly to the general postulate in contemporary sociology and cultural anthropology that the social structure of a given society conditions and controls the structure and uses of the society's institutions. A social structure is, itself, a structure of power. And since one of the pronounced characteristics of organized power is its tendency to extend into, and to maintain itself in, functions relevant to it, it would be the least likely explanation to say that power relations established in the basic social relations of a society would not repeat themselves in the values and institutions by means of which the society lives and maintains itself.

The second explanation, which postulates the "determination" of all other institutions within a society by one dominant institution, is implicit in the historical tendency to accept the power of the state as supreme. But, as noted earlier, each attribution of primary influence to the state confuses the formality of law with the realities of power which secure the enactment of laws. Nor, for the same reason, does the familiar argument from the state's "monopoly over the legitimized use of force" establish the primacy of the state, other than formally, over all other institutions. Accordingly, the case of state power would appear to support the first of the two explanations above, rather than the second.

A clearer warrant for resort to the second explanation would appear to be the dominance of the economic institutions of capitalist societies over other institutions in such societies. But it is important to note that this dominance results not from the inevitable character of economic institutions, but from the special case of capitalism. Capitalism has operated by an ideology that has had no need for the conception of society: economic institutions have been assumed to rest upon free individuals, predominantly economically motivated and devoid of need of, or responsibility to, society because their self-oriented actions had reference only to the natural, i.e., extra-social, ordering mechanism of the market. Under this natural market theory society was invisible and, when it did obtrude into view, it tended to be regarded as an obstructive interruption. This has meant under capitalism that society has been submerged in its economic institutions, while the criteria of "success" in the person and the scope of operation of other institutions has tended to be narrowed to terms of functional serviceability to the economy. But this seeming escape of a single institution into autonomy and dominance overlooks an important factor: though liberal capitalism has theoretically rested upon individuals, it has factually rested upon classes of like-circumstanced individuals—the classes being erected fundamentally on economic interest and power; and it has been the fact that this social structure of classes has been primarily economic—despite the avowed democratic equality in the social structure and the democratic professions of the political institutions—that has made it possible for economic institutions so largely to "determine" the other institutions. Accordingly, one may conclude that here, too, the first of our two explanations is correct, i.e., the power expressed by institutions is not primarily autonomous but derives from the social structure. . . .

The import of the immediately preceeding section is that the generating source of organized power in any society inheres in the social structure of the society; and the locating of this source at the institutional level, however immediately plausible this may seem, tends to confuse both analysis of, and attempts to control the use of, power. This is particularly true where institutional change is at issue. To attempt fundamental change in institutions, of a kind that affects the basic character of organized power in a given society, without changing the social structure of that society is like trying to drive a car forward with the gears set in reverse. . . .

So far I have been concerned with ambiguities regarding power and with identification of sources of these ambiguities. Central to my analysis have been the propositions that power is a term that refers to a continuing process that, in one form or another, society cannot dispense with; that the approach to this process has been historically heavily biased by the identification of power with domination conceived as naturally running to arbitrariness and social irresponsibility; and that this combination of necessary use of power with these traditionally imputed unavoidable but deprecated accompaniments of its concrete use has paralyzed direct approach to power as a major social resource capable of adaptation to the values and institutions of a wide variety of social structures. Clearly, a social system stressing thoroughgoing democratic social relations is a test case likely to burst the seams of the traditional conception of power, since a genuinely democratic social structure and a structure of power operating in terms of arbitary and socially irresponsible dominance are incompatible. . . .

Power is no more necessarily a destructive force that needs to be avoided when possible, and otherwise repressed as much as possible, than is emotion in man. The need is to recognize that organized society and organized power are not two discrete things; but that an organized society is, *ipso facto*, organized power. For a society to exist it must be a system of power. The orderly structure of men's relations as they daily go about institutionally channeled ways of achieving needed things also includes ways of resolving differences among them. It is due in part to the unusual visibility of many of these concrete processes of resolving differences that the incidence of power has been associated so largely with that part of social action that concerns men's differences. Power is, of course, no less present in the massive, habitual routines of living. . . .

The following five propositions are accordingly suggested as a basis for a positive approach to power as a major social resource:

1. Organized power is not an optional factor in society, but an essential component of social living, always and everywhere present in some form.

2. It is neither inherently, and therefore necessarily, "bad" nor "good." The controls it provides establish and maintain the communities by which a given society lives together in the present and lives toward its version of the future. These controls may range in type, depending upon the fundamental structure of a society, from (a) sustained, arbitrary coercion in the presence of which the maintenance of, and resistance to, the manner of its imposition and the results thereof become a major preoccupation in the life of the society; through (b) various mixed types in which arbitrariness is in varying degrees curbed by law but in which coercion remains in intensities that differ according to what is at stake; to (c) voluntary cooperation for commonly desired ends, in which attention tends to concentrate upon the work itself, while concern over the manner of exercise of control is largely limited to the correction of minor excesses and deficiencies in control as they affect the achievement of the ends sought.

3. Organized power may accordingly be conceived as the process by which whatever is the version of *order* and *disorder* in a given society is continually defined, redefined, and maintained. Order in this sense is the way the major routines of a population's daily actions are channeled toward selected goals in the use of available institutional means. It is a relative term that carries no implication of "goodness" or "efficiency" other than that of serviceability to the given society, or to the controlling segments of the society, in respect to how they identify opportunity and insecurity in view of the concrete resources and preoccupations of the given era and location. Disorderly, likewise a relative term, refers to types of action that are recognized as obstructive to, or destructive of, the maintenance of order so defined. What is orderly enough not to be viewed as disorder varies from society to society according to the broad type and concrete detail of its social structure. Order and disorder may vary in detail over time within the same society as a result of change in such factors as size, complexity, technology, and so on.

4. While individual differences in capacities and temperament and the necessarily hierarchical structure of roles in the carrying out of complex social processes will always create some unevenness in ordering society by, for instance, the best conceivable democratic social controls, the issue does not lie at the mercy of such differences among persons and their roles. Different functions, responsibilities and authorities allocated to persons on different levels of a common task need not necessarily create power resentments and antagonisms in a genuinely democratic society.... What does create resentments and antagonisms is capricious authority and irresponsible power, the arbitrary assignment of status, and the resulting institutionalization of unequal life-chances. Nor does the issue inhere in the sheer fact of controls.... Ordering controls that stem from the recognition of widely shared needs and are clearly oriented to commonly sought goals relevant to these needs may establish substantial counter-weights against tendencies to abuse power.

5. The fact of the long historical identification of organized power as a corrupting, disordering factor in society may not be interpreted as precluding the possibility of a society in which positive democratic power would be used in democratic ways for collective ends. There is no fundamental incompatibility between democracy and power. Given a system of social relations that expresses unqualified democracy, the structure of power in that society will tend to express similarly unqualified democracy, and likewise the resulting values and modes of operating institutions.

CAPITAL AND POWER

John Kenneth Galbraith

No subject has been more faithfully explored by economists than the relation between what anciently have been called the factors of production—land, labor, capital and the entrepreneurial talent which brings these together and manages their employment. Until recently, the problem of efficiency in production—that of getting the most from the available productive resources—was envisaged, almost entirely, as one of winning the best combination of these agents. . . .

One aspect of the relationships between the factors of production has, however, been less examined. That is why power is associated with some factors and not with others. Why did ownership of land once convey plenary power over the dominant form of productive enterprise and, therewith, in the community at large? Why under other circumstances has it been assumed that such authority, both over the enterprise and in the society at large, should lie with the owner of capital? Under what circumstances might such power pass to labor. . .?

One reason the question was slighted was that for a long time, in formal economic inquiry, no one associated with economic activity was thought to have any worthwhile exercise of power. In the classical economic tradition—that of Adam Smith, David Ricardo, Thomas Malthus, J. S. Mill and Alfred Marshall—and increasingly as concepts were better defined, the business enterprise . . . was assumed to be small in relation to the market supplied. The price it received was impersonally and competitively determined by the market. So were the prices paid to suppliers. Wages were also set by the market. So was the interest on borrowed funds. Profits reduced themselves to a competitive level. Technology was assumed to be stable. Under these circumstances the ideal volume of production for the firm was externally established by the relation of costs to the market price at various

SOURCE: John Kenneth Galbraith, *The New Industrial State* (Boston: Houghton Mifflin Co., 1967), pp. 46-59, and 392-399. Copyright ©1967 by John Kenneth Galbraith (Hamish Hamilton, London). Reprinted by permission. Footnotes have been omitted.

levels of output. If the man in charge of the firm has no power to influence prices, costs, wages or interest, and if even his best output is externally determined and his profits are subject to the leveling effect of competition, one can rightly be unconcerned about his power. He has none. Until well into the present century the economics of the textbooks assumed a world of such small and competitive firms. The counterpart neglect of the problem of power was both plausible and inevitable. Other traditions of thought, however, were less handicapped.

In particular there was Marx. In the middle of the last century he brought the subject of power into economic discussion with a vehemence which the world has not yet quite ceased to deplore. The notion of a system of competitive and hence passive business firms he dismissed as an exercise in vulgar apologetics. Production is dominated by those who control and supply capital. . . . Their authority in the enterprise is complete. Prices and wages are set in their collective interest. They dominate the society and set its moral tone. They also control the state which becomes an executive committee serving the will and interest of the capitalist class. There is no question of power being associated with any other factor of production. At this stage in historical development it belongs unequivocally and totally with capital.

In the classical tradition there was eventually a measure of agreement with Marx. The notion of the competitive market receded; it survives today in the textbooks as an exceptional case. The business enterprise is routinely assumed to have control over its prices and output—to have the power that is associated with one seller or monopoly, a few sellers or oligopoly, or with some unique feature of its product or service which accords it protection from competition. . . .

And the companion point of Marx is assumed. Such power as may be available naturally and inevitably belongs to capital. Its exercise is the prerogative of ownership. The claims of the other factors of production are inherently subordinate. . . .

Beyond this, the problem of power is still not much discussed. . . .

Yet, over a longer range of time, power over the productive enterprise—and by derivation in the society at large—has shifted radically between the factors of production. The eminence of capital is a relatively recent matter; until about two centuries ago no perceptive man would have doubted that power was decisively associated with land. The comparative wealth, esteem, military position and the sanguinary authority over the lives of the populace that went with land ownership also gave a strong and even controlling direction to history. . . .

This eminence of land, and the incentive to acquire it, were firmly grounded in economics. Until comparatively modern times, agricultural production—the provision of food and fiber—accounted for a large share of all production as it still accounts for seventy to eighty per cent of all output in such economically poor countries as modern India. Ownership or control of land thus accorded one a position in the dominant form of economic activity; to be landless was to be crowed into what was left.

Meanwhile other factors of production had a much less strategic role. Agricultural technology was stable and uncomplicated; accordingly, slaves apart, it offered small scope for capital and, as a broad rule, slaves could only be used in conjunction with land. Non-agricultural activity being relatively unimportant, its demand for capital was small and limited further by simple and stable technology. So—a somewhat neglected point—until two hundred years ago a meager supply of capital was matched by an equally meager opportunity for its use. If a man had land in England or Western Europe he could get the modest supply of capital he needed to till it. Possession of this capital was no guarantee that he could get the land.

Nor was labor difficult to come by. Its well-established tendency was to keep itself in a state of great abundance. . . . That was to say that, given a little time, an unlimited supply would be forthcoming at, or about, a subsistence wage. Enough labor would be used so that, through diminishing returns, the contribution of the marginal worker would be about equal to his subsistence. If he gave up this narrow contest with privation he could easily be replaced. If a man adds little and can easily be replaced, he has small power and small bargaining power.

But no one could doubt the advantage of laying one's hands on an acre, or a hundred acres, or a thousand acres of fertile land. Nor could one doubt the deadly consequences of losing like amounts. This meant that possession of land was strategic and not even the philosophers whose ideas ushered in the Industrial Revolution could quite envisage a society where this was otherwise. Adam Smith, though he was at odds on most points with his Physiocratic precursors in France who had made land the ultimate source of all wealth, attributed a special bounty to real property which was returned, as a special mark of grace, to those who owned it. Forty years later, following the Napoleonic Wars, Ricardo and Malthus made ownership of land even more crucial. Population would grow in accordance with a biological dynamic of its own. This would make an ever more urgent claim on a much more slowly increasing food supply. In consequence the relative price of food and the share of income going to landlords would increase insouciantly and without limit. The decisive factor was the scarcity of land. . . . Not surprisingly, those who owned this rare resource would exercise full authority in the dominant agricultural economy and be men of prestige and power in the community at large.

Ricardo wrote at a moment in history when land was being dethroned. That was partly because the scarcity to which he attributed such importance had set in motion a phenomenal search for a new supply. And the two Americas, South Africa and Australia were all found to have large, unused and highly usable amounts. New land could be obtained or lost land could be replaced by going to the frontier. The need now was for capital to pay the passage for seed, livestock and equipment and to tide a man over until the first harvest. And if a varlet could, on occasion, get more acreage in the New World than the more majestic aristocrat owned in the Old, land was no longer a secure source of distinction.

Meanwhile, mechanical inventions and the growth of metallurgical and engineering knowledge were prodigiously expanding opportunities for the employment of capital. From this greater use of capital in more advanced technology came greater production. From that production came greater income and more saving. . . . Agriculture, with its peculiar dependence on land, contributed a diminishing share of total product. The men who owned or controlled capital could now command the needed labor and land. Control of labor or land accorded no reciprocal power to command capital.

So power over the enterprise passed to capital. And so did prestige in the community and authority in the state. At the beginning of the nineteenth century the British Parliament was still dominated by the great landed families. By the middle of the century they were acceding to industrial pressure to lower the price of food, and therewith the level of factory wages, at the expense of their rents. By the end of the century the premier figure in British politics was the great Birmingham industrialist and pioneer screw manufacturer, Joseph Chamberlain. At the beginning of the century, the United States government was dominated by landed and slave-owning gentlemen of Virginia; by the end of the century by common agreement power had passed, depending on point of view, to the men of enterprise or the malefactors of great wealth. The Senate had become a club of rich businessmen. . . .

It will now be clear what accords power to a factor of production or to those who own or control it. Power goes to the factor which is hardest to obtain or hardest to replace. In precise language it adheres to the one that has the greatest inelasticity of supply at the margin. This inelasticity may be the result of a natural shortage, or an effective control over supply by some human agency, or both.

In its age, if one had land then labor and capital (in the meager amounts required) could be readily obtained. But to have labor and operating capital did not so readily insure that a man could get land. There was an admixture, here, of cause and effect. Because land provided special access to economic and larger power, steps were taken, as through the laws of entail, to confine possession to the privileged or noble caste. And this, in turn, limited the opportunities for acquiring it and further increased the economic power and social authority which, from one generation to the next, land conferred on its owner.

In the age of capital, land was readily available in the minor amounts required for industrial enterprise and increasingly so for agriculture. Labor continued to be plentiful. Now possession of land and labor did not allow one to command capital; but with capital, land and labor could easily be obtained. Capital now accorded power in the enterprise and in consequence in the society.

Should it happen that capital were to become abundant, or redundant, and thus be readily increased or replaced, the power it confers, both in the enterprise and in the society, would be expected to suffer. This would seem especially probable if, at the same time, some other factor of production should prove increasingly difficult to add or replace. . . .

In the industrial system, while capital is used in large amounts, it is, at least in peacetime, even more abundantly supplied. The tendency to an excess of savings, and the need for an offsetting strategy by the state, is an established and well-recognized feature of the Keynesian economy. And savings, we have seen, are supplied by the industrial enterprise to itself as part of its planning. There is high certainty as to their availability, for this is the purpose of the planning.

At the same time the requirements of technology and planning have greatly increased the need of the industrial enterprise for specialized talent and for its organization. The industrial system must rely, in the main, on external sources for this talent. Unlike capital it is not something that the firm can supply to itself. To be effective this talent must also be brought into effective association with itself. It must be in an organization. Given a competent business organization, capital is now ordinarily available. But the mere possession of capital is now no guarantee that the requisite talent can be obtained and organized. One should expect, from past experience, to find a new shift of power in the industrial enterprise, this one from capital to organized intelligence. And one would expect that this shift would be reflected in the deployment of power in the society at large.

This has, indeed, occurred. It is a shift of power as between the factors of production which matches that which occurred from land to capital in the advanced countries beginning two centuries ago. It is an occurrence of the last fifty years and is still going on. A dozen matters of commonplace observation—the loss of power by stockholders in the modern corporation, the impregnable position of the successful corporate management, the dwindling social magnetism of the banker, the air of quaintness that attaches to the suggestion that the United States is run from Wall Street, the increasingly energetic search for industrial talent, the new prestige of education and educators—all attest the point.

This shift of power has been disguised because, as was once true of land, the position of capital is imagined to be immutable. That power should be elsewhere seems unnatural and those who so argue seem to be in search of frivolous novelty. And it has been disguised because power has not gone to another of the established factors as they are celebrated in conventional economic pedagogy. It has not passed to labor. Labor has won limited authority over its pay and working conditions but non over the enterprise. And it still tends to abundance. If overly abundant savings are not used, the first effect is unemployment; if savings are used one consequence is a substitution of machine processes for unskilled labor and standard skills. Thus unskilled labor and workers with conventional skills suffer, along with the capitalist, from an abundance of capital.

Nor has power passed to the classical entrepreneur—the individual who once used his access to capital to bring it into combination with the other factors of production. He is a diminishing figure in the industrial system. Apart from access to capital, his principal qualifications were imagination, capacity for decision and courage in risking money including, not infrequently, his own. None of these qualifications are especially important for organizing intelligence or effective in competing with it.

Power has, in fact, passed to what anyone in search of novelty might be justified in calling a new factor of production. This is the association of men of diverse technical knowledge, experience or other talent which modern industrial technology and planning require. It extends from the leadership of the modern industrial enterprise down to just short of the labor force and embraces a large number of people and a large variety of talent. It is on the effectiveness of this organization, as most business doctrine now implicitly agrees, that the success of the modern business enterprise now depends. Were this organization dismembered or otherwise lost, there is no certainty that it could be put together again. To enlarge it to undertake new tasks is an expensive and sometimes uncertain undertaking. Here one now finds the problem of an uncertainly high supply price at the margin. And here one finds the accompanying power. . . .

Given the deep dependence of the industrial system on the state and the nature of its motivational relationship to the state, i.e., its identification with public goals and the adaptation of these to its needs, the industrial system will not long be regarded as something apart from government. Rather it will increasingly be seen as part of a much larger complex which embraces both the industrial system and the state. Private enterprise was anciently so characterized because it was subordinate to the market and those in command derived their power from ownership of private property. The modern corporation is no longer subordinate to the market; those who run it no longer depend on property ownership for their authority. They must have autonomy within a framework of goals. But this fully allows them to work in association with the bureaucracy and, indeed, to perform for the bureaucracy tasks that it cannot do, or cannot do as well, for itself. In consequence, so we have seen, for tasks of technical sophistication, there is a close fusion of the industrial system with the state. Members of the technostructure work closely with their public counterparts not only in the development and manufacture of products but in advising them of their needs. Were it not so celebrated in ideology, it would long since have been agreed that the line that now divides public from so-called private organization in military procurement, space exploration and atomic energy is so indistinct as to be nearly imperceptible. Men move easily across the line. On retirement, admirals and generals, as well as high civil servants, go more or less automatically to the more closely associated industries. One experienced observer has already called these firms the "semi-nationalized" branch of the economy. . . .

So comprehensive a relationship cannot be denied or ignored indefinitely. Increasingly it will be recognized that the mature corporation, as it develops, becomes part of the larger administrative complex associated with the state. In time the line between the two will disappear. Men will look back in amusement at the pretense that once caused people to refer to General Dynamics and North American Aviation and A.T.&T. as *private* business.

Though this recognition will not be universally welcomed, it will be healthy. There is always a presumption in social matters in favor of reality as opposed to myth. The autonomy of the technostructure is, to repeat yet again, a functional necessity of the industrial system. But the goals this autonomy serves allow some range of choice. If the mature corporation is recognized to be part of the penumbra of the state, it will be more strongly in the service of social goals. It cannot plead its inherently private character or its subordination to the market as cover for the pursuit of different goals of particular interest to itself. The public agency has an unquestioned tendency to pursue goals that reflect its own interest and convenience and to adapt social objective thereto. But it cannot plead this as a superior right. There may well be danger in this association of public and economic power. But it is less if it is recognized. . . .

Most of the individual developments which are leading, if the harshest term may be employed, to the socialization of the mature corporation will be conceded, even by men of the most conservative disposition. The control by the mature corporation over its prices, its influence on consumer behavior, the euthanasia of stockholder power, the regulation by the state of aggregate demand, the effort to stabilize prices and wages, the role of publicly supported research and development, the role of military, space and related procurement, the influence of the firm on these government activities and the modern role of education are, more or less, accepted facts of life.

What is avoided is reflection on the consequences of putting them all together, of seeing them as a system. But it cannot be supposed that the principal beams and buttresses of the industrial system have all been changed and that the structure remains as before. If the parts have changed, so then has the whole. If this associates the mature corporation inextricably with the state, the fact cannot be exorcised by a simple refusal to add. . . .

The two questions most asked about an economic system are whether it serves man's physical needs and whether it is consistent with his liberty. There is little doubt as to the ability of the industrial system to serve man's needs. As we have seen, it is able to manage them only because it serves them abundantly. It requires a mechanism for making men want what it provides. But this mechanism would not work—wants would not be subject to manipulation—had not these wants been dulled by sufficiency.

The prospects for liberty involve far more interesting questions. It has always been imagined, especially by conservatives, that to associate all, or a large part, of economic activity with the state is to endanger freedom. The individual and his preferences, in one way or another, will be sacrificed to the needs and conveniences of the apparatus created ostensibly to serve him. As the industrial system evolves into a penumbra of the state, the question of its relation to liberty thus arises in urgent form. In recent years, in the Soviet-type economies, there has been an ill-concealed conflict between the state and the intellectuals. In essence, this has been a conflict between those for whom the needs of the government, including above all its needs as economic planner and producer of goods, are pre-eminent and those who assert the high but inconvenient claims of uninhibited intellectual and artistic expression. Is this a warning?

The instinct which warns of dangers in this association of economic and public power is sound. It comes close to being the subject of this book. But conservatives have looked in the wrong direction for the danger. They have feared that the state might reach out and destroy the vigorous, money-making entrepreneur. They have not noticed that, all the while, the successors to the entrepreneur were uniting themselves ever more closely with the state and rejoicing in the result. They were also, and with enthusiasm, accepting abridgement of their freedom. Part of this is implicit in the subordination of individual personality to the needs of organization. Some of it is in the exact pattern of the classical business expectation. . . .

The problem, however, is not the freedom of the businessman. Business orators have spoken much about freedom in the past. But it can be laid down as a rule that those who speak most of liberty are least inclined to use it. . . .

The danger to liberty lies in the subordination of belief to the needs of the industrial system. In this the state and the industrial system will be partners. . . .

If we continue to believe that the goals of the industrial system—the expansion of output, the companion increase in consumption, technological advance, the public images that sustain it—are coordinate with life, then all of our lives will be in the service of these goals. What is consistent with these ends we shall have or be allowed; all else will be off limits. Our wants will be managed in accordance with the needs of the industrial system; the policies of the state will be subject to similar influence; education will be adapted to industrial need; the disciplines required by the industrial system will be the conventional morality of the community. All other goals will be made to seem precious, unimportant or antisocial. We will be bound to the ends of the industrial system. The state will add its moral, and perhaps some of its legal, power to their enforcement. What will eventuate, on the whole, will be the benign servitude of the household retainer who is taught to love her mistress and see her interests as her own, and not the compelled servitude of the field hand. But it will not be freedom.

If, on the other hand, the industrial system is only a part, and relatively a diminishing part, of life, there is much less occasion for concern. Aesthetic goals will have pride of place; those who serve them will not be subject to the goals of the industrial system; the industrial system itself will be subordinate to the claims of these dimensions of life. Intellectual preparation will be for its own sake and not for the better service to the industrial system. Men will not be entrapped by the belief that apart from the goals of the industrial system—apart from the production of goods and income by progressively more advanced technical methods—there is nothing important in life.

The foregoing being so, we may, over time, come to see the industrial system in fitting light as an essentially technical arrangement for providing convenient goods and services in adequate volume. Those who rise through its bureaucracy will so see themselves. And the public consequences will be in keeping, for if economic goals are the only goals of the society it is natural that the industrial system should dominate the state and the state should serve its ends. If other goals are strongly asserted, the industrial system will fall into its place as a detached and autonomous arm of the state, but responsive to the larger purposes of the society.

We have seen wherein the chance for salvation lies. The industrial system, in contrast with its economic antecedents, is intellectually demanding. It brings into existence, to serve its intellectual and scientific needs, the community that, hopefully, will reject its monopoly of social purpose.

NOTES ON THE POST-INDUSTRIAL SOCIETY

Daniel Bell

More than a hundred and fifty years ago, the wildly brilliant, almost mono-maniacal technocrat, Claude-Henri de Rouvroy, le Comte de Saint-Simon ("the last gentleman and the first socialist" of France), popularized the word *industrialism* to designate the emergent society, wherein wealth would be created by mechanized production rather than be seized through plunder and war. Past society, said Saint-Simon, had been military society, in which the dominant figures were noblemen, soldiers, and priests, and the leading positions in the society were based either on control of the means of violence or on the manipulation of religious myth. In the new society, the "natural élite" that would organize society in a rational, "positive" fashion would be the industrialists (actually the engineers or technocrats), for the methods of industry were methods of order, precision, and certainty, rather than of metaphysical thought. In this society, ordered by function and capacity, "the real noblemen would be industrial chiefs and the real priests would be scientists."...

If, with the spirit rather than the method of Saint-Simon, one speculates on the shape of society forty or fifty years from now, it becomes clear that the "old" industrial order is passing and that a "new society" is indeed in the making. To speak rashly: if the dominant figures of the past hundred years have been the entrepreneur, the businessman, and the industrial executive, the "new men" are the scientists, the mathematicians, the economists, and the engineers of the new computer technology. And the dominant institutions of the new society—in the sense that they will provide the most creative challenges and enlist the richest talents—will be the intellectual institutions. The leadership of the new society will rest, not with businessmen or corporations as we know them (for a good deal of production will have been routinized), but with the research corporation, the industrial laboratories, the experimental stations, and the universities. In fact, the skeletal structure of the new society is already visible.

The Transformation of Society. We are now, one might say, in the first stages of a post-industrial society. A post-industrial society can be characterized in several ways. We can begin with the fact that ours is no longer primarily a manufacturing economy. The service sector (comprising trade; finance, insurance and real estate; personal, professional, business, and repair services; and general government) now accounts for more than half of the total employment and more than half of the gross national product. We are now, as Victor Fuchs pointed out..., a "service economy"—i.e., the first nation in the history of the world in which more than half

SOURCE: Excerpted from "Notes on the Post Industrial Society" (I) and "Notes on the Post Industrial Society" (II), by Daniel Bell, which will appear in a forthcoming book by Daniel Bell, tentatively entitled *The Transformation of Society*, to be published by Basic Books, Inc., Publishers, New York. Reprinted by permission of the publishers.

of the employed population is not involved in the production of food, clothing, houses, automobiles, and other tangible goods.

Or one can look at a society, not in terms of where people work, but of what kind of work they do—the occupational divisions. In a paper read to the Cambridge Reform Club in 1873, Alfred Marshall, the great figure of neo-classical economics, posed a question that was implicit in the title of his paper, "The Future of the Working Classes." "The question," he said, "is not whether all men will ultimately be equal—that they certainly will not be—but whether progress may not go on steadily, if slowly, till, by occupation at least, every man is a gentleman." And he answered his question thus: "I hold that it may, and that it will."

Marshall's criterion of a gentleman—in a broad, not in the traditional genteel, sense—was that heavy, excessive, and soul-destroying labor would vanish, and the worker would then begin to value education and leisure. Apart from any qualitative assessment of contemporary culture, it is clear that Marshall's question is well on the way to achieving the answer he predicted.

In one respect, 1956 may be taken as the symbolic turning point. For in that year—for the first time in American history, if not in the history of industrial civilization—the number of white-collar workers (professional, managerial, office and sales personnel) outnumbered the blue-collar workers (craftsmen, semi-skilled operatives, and laborers) in the occupational ranks of the American class structure. Since 1956 the ratio has been increasing: today white-collar workers outnumber the blue-collar workers by more than five to four.

Stated in these terms, the change is quite dramatic. Yet it is also somewhat deceptive, for until recently the overwhelming number of white-collar workers have been women, who held minor clerical or sales jobs; and in American society, as in most others, family status is still evaluated on the basis of the job that the man holds. But it is at this point, in the changing nature of the male labor force, that a status upheaval has been taking place. Where in 1900 only 15% of American males wore white collars (and most of these were independent small businessmen), by 1940 the figure had risen to 25%, and by 1970, it is estimated, about 40% of the male labor force, or about 20 million men, will be holding white-collar jobs. Out of this number, 14 million will be in managerial, professional, or technical positions, and it is this group that forms the heart of the upper-middle-class in the United States.

What is most startling in these figures is the growth in professional and technical employment. In 1940, there were 3.9 million professional and technical persons in the society, making up 7.5% of the labor force; by 1962, the number had risen to 8 million, comprising 11.8% of the labor force; it is estimated that by 1975 there will be 12.4 million professional and technical persons, making up 14.2% of the labor force.

A New Principle. In identifying a new and emerging social system, however, it is not only in such portents as the move away from manufacturing (or the rise of "the new property" which Charles Reich has described) that one seeks to understand fundamental social change. It is in the defining characteristics that the nerves of a new system can be located. The ganglion of the post-industrial society is knowledge. But to put it this way is banal. Knowledge is at the basis of every society. But in the post-industrial society, what is crucial is not just a shift from property or political position to knowledge as the new base of power, but a change in the character of knowledge itself.

What has now become decisive for society is the new centrality of *theoretical* knowledge, the primacy of theory over empiricism, and the codification of knowledge into abstract systems of symbols that can be translated into many different and varied circumstances. Every society now lives by innovation and growth; and it is theoretical knowledge that has become the matrix of innovation.

One can see this, first, in the changing relations of science and technology, particularly in the matter of invention. In the 19th and early 20th centuries, the great inventions and the industries that derived from them—steel, electric light, telegraph, telephone, automobile—were the work of inspired and talented tinkerers, many of whom were indifferent to the fundamental laws which underlay their inventions. On the other hand, where principles and fundamental properties were discovered, the practical applications were made only decades later, largely by trial-and-error methods. . . .

In a less direct but equally important way, the changing association of theory and empiricism is reflected in the management of economies. The rise of macro-economics and of governmental intervention in economic matters is possible because new codifications in economic theory allow governments, by direct planning, monetary or fiscal policy, to seek economic growth, to redirect the allocation of resources, to maintain balances between different sectors, and even, as in the case of Great Britain today, to effect a controlled recession, in an effort to shape the direction of the economy by conscious policy.

And, with the growing sophistication of computer-based simulation procedures—simulations of economic systems, of social behavior, of decision problems—we have the possibility, for the first time, of large-scale "controlled experiments" in the social sciences. These, in turn, will allow us to plot "alternative futures," thus greatly increasing the extent to which we can choose and control matters that affect our lives.

In all this, the university, which is the place where theoretical knowledge is sought, tested, and codified in a disinterested way, becomes the primary institution of the new society. Perhaps it is not too much to say that if the business firm was the key institution of the past hundred years, because of its role in organizing production for the mass creation of products, the university will become the central institution of the next hundred years because of its role as the new source of innovation and knowledge.

To say that the primary institutions of the new age will be intellectual is not to say that the majority of persons will be scientists, engineers, technicians, or intellectuals. The majority of individuals in contemporary society are not business-men, yet one can say that this has been a "business civilization." The basic values of society have been focused on business institutions, the largest rewards have been found in business, and the strongest power has been held by the business community, although today that power is to some extent shared within the factory by the trade union, and regulated within the society by the political order. In the most general ways, however, the major decisions affecting the day-to-day life of the citizen—the kinds of work available, the location of plants, investment decisions on new products, the distribution of tax burdens, occupational mobility—have been made by business, and latterly by government, which gives major priority to the welfare of business.

To say that the major institutions of the new society will be intellectual is to say that production and business decisions will be subordinated to, or will derive from, other forces in society; that the crucial decisions regarding the growth of the economy and its balance will come from government, but they will be based on the government's sponsorship of research and development, of cost-effectiveness and cost-benefit analysis; that the making of decisions, because of the intricately linked nature of their consequences, will have an increasingly technical character. The husbanding of talent and the spread of educational and intellectual institutions will become a prime concern for the society; not only the best talents, but eventually the entire complex of social prestige and social status, will be rooted in the intellectual and scientific communities. . . .

Who Holds Power? Decisions are a matter of power, and the crucial questions in any society are: who holds power, and how is power held? Forty-five years ago, as we have noted, Thorstein Veblen foresaw a new society based on technical organization and industrial management, a "society of technicians," as he put it in the striking language he loved to employ in order to scare and mystify the academic world. In making this prediction, Veblen shared the illusion of Saint-Simon that the complexity of the industrial system and the indispensability of the technicians made military and political revolutions a thing of the past. "Revolutions in the 18th century," Veblen wrote, "were military and political; and the Elder Statesmen who now believe themselves to be making history still believe that revolutions can be made and unmade by the same ways and means in the 20th century. But any substantial or effectual overturn in the 20th century will necessarily be an industrial overturn; and by the same token, any 20th-century revolution can be combatted or neutralized only by industrial ways and means."

This syndicalist idea that revolution in the 20th century could only be an "industrial overturn" exemplifies the rationalist fallacy in so much of Veblen's thought. For, as we have learned, though technological and social processes are crescive, the crucial turning points in a society are political events. It is not the technocrat who ultimately holds power, but the politician.

The major changes which have reshaped American society over the past thirty years—the creation of a managed economy, a welfare society, and a mobilized polity—grew out of political responses: in the first instances to accomodate the demands of economically insecure and disadvantaged groups—the farmers, workers, Negroes, and the poor—for protection against the hazards of the market; and, later, as a consequence of the concentration of resources and political objectives following the mobilized postures of the Cold War and the space race.

The result of all this is to enlarge the arena of power, and at the same time to complicate the modes of decision-making. The domestic political process initiated by the New Deal, which continues in the same form in the domestic program of the Johnson administration, was in effect a broadening of the "brokerage" system—the system of political "deals" between constituencies. But there is also a new dimension in the political process which has given the technocrats a new role. Matters of foreign policy are not a reflex of internal political forces, but a judgment about the national interest, involving strategy decisions based on the calculations of an opponent's strength and intentions. Once the fundamental policy decision was made to oppose the Communist power, many technical decisions, based on military technology and strategic assessments, took on the highest importance in the shaping of subsequent policy. And even the reworking of the economic map of the United States followed as well, with Texas and California gaining great importance because of the importance of the electronics and aerospace industries. In these instances, technology and strategy laid down the requirements, and only then could business and local political groups seek to modify, or take advantage of, these decisions so as to protect their own economic interests.

In all this, the technologists are in a double position. To the extent that they have interests in research, and positions in the universities, they become a new constituency—just as the military is a distinct new constituency, since we have never had a permanent military establishment in this country before—seeking money and support for science, for research and development. Thus the technical intelligentsia becomes a claimant, like other groups, for public support (though its influence is felt in the bureaucratic and administrative labyrinth, rather than in the electoral system and through mass pressure). At the same time, the technologists provide an indispensable administrative mechanism for the political office-holder with his public following. As the technical and professional sectors of society expand, the interests of this stratum, of this constituency, exert a greater pressure—in the demands not only for objectives of immediate interest but in the wider social ethos which tends to be associated with the more highly educated: the demands for more amenities, for a more urbane quality of life in our cities, for a more differentiated and better educational system, and an improvement in the character of our culture.

But while the weights of the class system may shift, the nature of the political system, as the arena where interests become mediated, will not. In the next few decades, the political arena will become more decisive, if anything, for three fundamental reasons: we have become, for the first time, a *national society* (though there has always been the idea of the nation) in which crucial decisions, affecting all parts of the society simultaneously (from foreign affairs to fiscal policy) are made by the government, rather than through the market; in addition, we have become a *communal society*, in which many more groups now seek to establish their social rights—their claims on society—through the political order; and third, with our increasing "future orientation," government will necessarily have to do more and more planning. But since all of these involve policy decisions, it cannot be the technocrat alone, but the political figures who can make them. And necessarily, the two roles are distinct, even though they come into complicated interplay with each other. . . .

Social Choices and Individual Values. The irony is that the more planning there is in a society, the more there are open group conflicts. Planning sets up a specific locus of decisions which becomes a visible point at which pressures can be applied. Communal coordination—the effort to create a social choice out of a discordance of individual personal preferences—necessarily *sharpens* value conflicts.

Where a single policy (such as defense) constitutes, in the language of economic theory, a "single-peaked preference curve"—one on whose importance and priority the society, by large, is agreed—there may be little conflict. But what about situations, such as social or welfare policy, where there may be less agreement: how then does one decide? Do we want compensatory education for Negroes at the expense, say, of places for other students when the number of positions is limited? Do we want to keep a redwood forest or provide a going industry to a local community? Will we accept the increased noise of jets in communities near the airports, or force the reduction of weight and payloads—with a consequent increased cost to the industry and the traveler? Should a new highway go through old pleasant sections of a community, or do we route them around such sections with a higher cost to all? These, and thousands more, are issues which cannot be settled on the basis of technical criteria; inevitably they involve value and political choices.

In the "Great Society" more and more goods necessarily have to be purchased communally. The planning of cities and the rationalization of transit, the maintenance of open spaces and the extension of recreational areas, the elimination of air pollution and the cleaning up of the rivers, the underwriting of education and the organization of adequate medical care, all these are now necessarily the concern of "public institutions." Individuals have their own scale of values, which allow them to assess relative satisfactions against costs, and to make their purchases accordingly. But public life lacks such ready measures. We cannot ask for and individually buy in the market place our share of unpolluted air. Regulating the availability of higher education by the market alone would deny many families the possibility of such learning, and also deny the society some of the social benefits which a more educated, and therefore more productive, citizenry might create. But we have no effective social calculus which gives us a true sense of the entire costs and benefits of our public initiatives. . . .

The New Prince. One other item of democratic theory would seem to be in trouble, too, empirically as well as theoretically. This is the theory of interest groups in a pluralistic society.

The theory of representative government reflected a picture of society as a "balance of forces." The legislature, in this conception, was supposed to contain representatives of the various social divisions and class interests in the country, for, as Mill noted in appealing for the right of the working-class to be represented in Parliament, "in the absence of its natural defenders, the interest of the excluded is always in danger of being overlooked." Mill, in fact, was so intent on the idea of the representation of minorities, that he gave enthusiastic endorsement to the proposal of Thomas Hare for proportional representation, "a scheme which has the almost unparalled merit of carrying out a great principle of government in a manner approaching to ideal perfection as regards the special object in view. . . ."

This normative theory was refined by what might be called the "realist" school of political thought, from Arthur F. Bentley on. (Bentley's original formulations in 1908 were ignored for many years, but were restated three decades later by V. O. Key, David Truman, and Earl Latham.) If a "group theory" was lacking in economics, it certainly made its appearance, in full flower, in American political thought in the last few decades. As V. O. Key put it most succinctly:

> At bottom, group interests are the animating forces in the political process. . . . Whatever the bases of group interest may be, the study of politics must rest on an analysis of the objectives and composition of the interest groups within a society. . . . The chief vehicles for the expression of group interest are political parties and pressure groups. Through these formal mechanisms groups of people with like interests make themselves felt in the balancing of political forces.[1]

And, in this conception, the role of the politician was to be a broker:

> The problem of the politician or the statesman in a democracy is to maintain a working balance between the demands of competing interests and values. . . .

Whatever the truth of this "model" as a description of the "nineteenth century inheritance". . . , it is astonishingly out of date for an understanding of politics in the second half of the 20th century, for it fails to take into account the three most decisive characteristics, or shaping elements, of national policy today: the influence of foreign policy, the "future-orientation" of society, and the increasing role of "technical" decision-making.

1. Foreign policy is not formulated primarily in reaction to the needs and pressures of domestic pressure groups (though once decisions are taken, some modifications may be made in response to their demands, e.g., to build airplanes in the Southwest rather than in the Northwest). Foreign policy is shaped in accordance with great power and ideological interests, and as responses to perceived threats from other great powers or ideological forces. But its consequence, under conditions of a cold war, is to force a "mobilized posture" on the society as a whole, to create some sense of national unity, and to centralize decision-making and enormous resources in the hands of a national administration. (Of the $15 billion spent by the Federal government for research and development, 90% goes into three areas: defense, space, and atomic energy.) The social and economic map of the U.S. has been redrawn more in the past 20 years by the influence of defense and defense spending than by any other single factor.

2. The commitment to economic growth, and the new dimensions of social change—its more rapid shock effects on larger and larger sections of the society and the consequent need to anticipate social change and to a considerable extent to direct it—have brought with them a renewed emphasis on planning, on the need to become more conscious of national goals and of the "alternative futures" which a society with a steady increase in productivity (a constant 3 percent growth rate of productivity will double national output in 24 years) can provide.

---

[1] V. O. Key, *Politics, Parties and Pressure Groups* (New York: Alfred A. Knopf, 1942), pp. 23-24.

3. The combination of these two elements brings into play the increasing role of technical decision-making. The shaping of conscious policy, be it in foreign policy, defense, or economics, calls to the fore the men with the skills necessary to outline the constraints ahead, to work out in detail the management and policy procedures, and to assess the consequences of choices. The revolutions in military technology (the introduction of nuclear power, the replacement of manned aircraft by missiles) were initiated by scientists. The development of systems analysis and cost-effectiveness techniques, which have revolutionized both the strategy process as well as the management structure of the Pentagon, was brought about by mathematicians and economists. The management of the national economy, with its close watch on the effects of government spending, requires the services of men skilled in the economic arts, and such crucial policy questions as when to have tax cuts or tax increases, how much to have, and what the wage-price guideposts should be, increasingly become technical decisions.

But the most important political consequence of all this is the passing of effective power, in almost all political systems, from the legislative and parliamentary bodies to the executive, and the re-emergence of what Bertrand de Jouvenal has called, in his elegant fashion, *The Principate*. How could it be otherwise when, in the nature of modern politics, foreign policy is no longer "diplomacy" but an unceasing round of strategic maneuver in which crucial decisions have to be taken speedily, and when, because of the new patterns of social change, the very need to plan policies, rather than lay down laws, gives the initiative to the Executive?

In the United States we have seen, in the past 25 years, the enormous transformation of the Presidency into the Executive Office of the President with the addition of new staff functions—such as the Bureau of the Budget, the Council of Economic Advisors, and the Office of the Science Adviser—directly within that office. For the long run, it is not the growth of the personal powers and prestige of the President that is important, but the *institutionalization* of such crucial control and directing functions.

Although these essential changes—the new role of the Executive, the conflict between technocratic rationality and political bargaining, and the orientation to the future—have been variously described, political theory has, so far, failed to absorb them into a new conceptual structure. . . .

The Public and the Private. The conventional model of the economy concentrates on the private, profit-seeking center. Yet what is public and what is private, and what is profit and what is not-for-profit, is no longer an easy distinction these days. The aerospace companies are private, yet the Federal government purchases 74 percent of their entire output. All profits above a negotiated sum are returned to the government; the government, rather than the competitive market, determines the firms' profitability, and even their survival. The New York Port Authority and the Triborough Bridge Authority are non-profit public corporations, yet they make enormous profits, which are reinvested in new enterprises far beyond the original charter of these corporations. In practical effect, they differ little from private utilities, who pay off a fixed sum of their indebtedness as interest charges and use profits for reinvestment. The Battelle Institute is a not-for-profit research foundation; the Arthur D. Little Company is profit seeking; yet the activities of the two are quite similar. (Battelle did the experimental and development work on xerography and now reaps large royalties; Arthur D. Little does a considerable amount of public service work at no fee.) Mutual insurance companies and mutual savings banks are not-for-profit, yet their dividends, interest rates, salaries, and practices are virtually identical with capital stock insurance companies and savings banks. The University of California at Berkeley is a state university, yet receives large amounts in corporate gifts and other private giving. Columbia University is a private school, yet more than half of its annual $100 million budget comes from Federal contracts and grants. The medical and health service field, the largest "growth industry" in the country, is a commingling of private, profit, non-profit, and government activities.

If one looks at the not-for-profit sector as a whole, taking into account the wide range of government, educational, and health services, the striking fact is that about one-fourth of G.N.P. and "not less than one-third and possibly almost two-fifths of all employment is accounted for by the activities of that sector."[2] In the 1950-1960 decade, in fact, nine out of every ten *new* jobs added to the economy were generated in the not-for-profit sector—i.e., by the vastly enlarged role of the Federal government in connection with the cold war, the expanded activities of state and local governments in providing community services, and the growths of the education and health and welfare fields.

The growth of the not-for-profit sector brings into focus, as employers of significant amounts of manpower, a whole array of organizations whose structure and form differ to a considerable extent from the usual model of "bureaucracy." These are universities, research laboratories, hospitals, community welfare organizations, and the like. The "received" doctrine, as drawn from Max Weber, and accepted by most students of stratification theory, posit a bureaucracy as having a division of labor based on functional specialization, a well-defined hierarchy of authority, impersonal, "bureaucratic" rules of behavior, and the like. This is the "ideal type" model which is often best exemplified in business corporate structure. Yet the variety of new kinds of organizations that are emerging (particularly ones with a high component of technical and research personnel) indicate that the older models, patterned on pyramidal structures, may no longer be applicable, and that in the coming decades the "traditional" bureaucratic form will have given way to organizational modes more adaptive to the needs for initiative, free time, joint consultation, and the like. The emergence of new structural forms of non-bureaucratic organization is one more item on the long agenda of new problems for the post-industrial society.

---

[2]These and subsequent figures are taken from Ginzberg, Hiestand, and Reubens, *The Pluralistic Economy* (New York: McGraw-Hill, 1965).

THE POLITICS OF MASS SOCIETY

William Kornhauser

Two Views of Mass Society. The theory of mass society has two major intellectual sources, one in the nineteenth century reaction to the revolutionary changes in European (especially French) society, and the other in the twentieth century reaction to the rise of totalitarianism, especially in Russia and Germany. The first and major source may be termed the *aristocratic* criticism of mass society; the second, the *democratic* criticism of mass society. The first centers in the intellectual defense of elite values against the rise of mass participation. The second centers in the intellectual defense of democratic values against the rise of elites bent on total domination. . . .

Not all intellectual rejections of revolutionary change have been based on the idea of mass society. Criticisms of nineteenth century trends that may properly be termed theories of mass society found the decisive social process to be *the loss of exclusiveness of elites and the rise of mass participation in cultural and political life.* . . .

Similarly, not all democratic criticisms of totalitarianism are based on a theory of mass society. Those which may properly be termed theories of mass society find the decisive social process to be *the loss of insulation of non-elites and the rise of elites bent on total mobilization of a population.* . . .

Paradoxical as it may appear to be, these democratic critics have come to rely heavily on the intellectual weapons employed by aristocratic thinkers against the rising flood of democratic ideologists during the nineteenth century. The central idea taken over by these democratic theorists from their aristocratic critics is that *the preservation of critical values (especially freedom) requires the social insulation of those segments of society that embody them.* Aristocratic and democratic critics of mass society agree on this, even as they disagree on the content of the values to be preserved—especially the nature of freedom—and, correspondingly, on the segments of society that embody them.

The aristocratic notion of freedom emphasizes the conditions that permit men to act as they *ought* to act, that is, in accordance with standards of right conduct. . . . The traditional order based on moral law insulates aristocratic elites and thereby preserves liberty.

The democratic notion of freedom, on the other hand, implies the minimizing of social control (including that of the traditional order), that is, the removal of as many external constraints on the individual as is consistent with the freedom of his fellows. Freedom so conceived is dependent on *equality of rights.* This value is embodied in the whole community. Therefore, it is the independent group life of

SOURCE: William Kornhauser, *The Politics of Mass Society* (Glencoe: The Free Press, 1959), pp. 21-43, 74-78, 80-84, 90-95, 98-100. Reprinted with permission of The Macmillan Company, and Routledge & Kegan Paul, Ltd., London. © by The Free Press, a Corporation, 1959. Most footnotes have been omitted, and those remaining have been renumbered.

the non-elite which functions to preserve liberty, as independent groups insulate people from domination by elites.

In sum, these two versions of the mass society differ in their conception of freedom and the social foundations of freedom. One sees mass society as a set of conditions under which elites are exposed to mass pressures. The other conceives of mass society as a set of conditions under which non-elites are exposed to elite pressures. Nevertheless, they share a common image of mass society as the *naked society*, where the direct exposure of social units to outside forces makes freedom precarious. We shall attempt to formulate a general theory of mass society that incorporates elements from both the aristocratic and democratic criticism. . . .

Our interest is in analyzing the theoretical basis of each approach, rather than in examining the value orientation typically associated with each of them. The two approaches have been distinguished according to whether the condition of elites or the condition of non-elites is identified as the basic criterion of "mass society." This means that any theory that locates the decisive feature of mass society in the exposure of accessible elites to mass intervention is classified as "aristocratic," while any theory that locates the essential feature of mass society in the exposure of atomized non-elites to elite domination is classified as "democratic." The choice of the terms "aristocratic" and "democratic" to describe these two theories should not obscure the fact that the classification is based on an *analytical* rather than a value distinction. . . .

The Loss of Authority in Mass Society. During the nineteenth century, aristocratic critics of bourgeois society spun a rhetoric of pessimism concerning the value-standards men live by in an age of increasing materialism and equalitarianism. . . .

The conception of mass society contained in such writings as these includes three major terms: (a) growing equalitarianism (loss of traditional authority); (b) widespread readiness to support anti-aristocratic forms of rule (quest for popular authority); (c) rule by the masses (domination by pseudo-authority). In this universe of discourse, "mass society" is the opposite of aristocratic order. Mass society is the condition under which rule by the masses—either directly or through the popularly supported demagogue—displaces aristocratic rule. This condition is equality of voice in the determination of social policy. Therefore, mass society is the equalitarian society, in which the masses seek to raise up leaders in their own image. As a result, it produces rule by the incompetent.

However, the incompetence of the many is not what distinguishes mass society, according to the aristocratic criticism. Mass society is new, whereas there always has been widespread ignorance in society. . . . What has changed is the structural relationship between the many and the few. In the mass society, there is a marked increase in opportunities for the many to intervene in areas previously reserved to the few. These opportunities invite the determination of social policies and cultural standards by large numbers who are not competent to make such decisions.

Mass society from this standpoint is the society in which there is a *loss of exclusiveness of elites*:[1] it is a social structure possessing high access to governing

---

[1] The term "elite" as used in this study refers to a relatively small circle of people who claim and are charged with the responsibility for framing and sustaining fundamental values and policies in their area of competence.

groups. High access to elites results from such procedures as direct popular elections and the shared expectation that public opinion is sovereign. When elites are easily accessible, the masses pressure them to conform to the transitory general will. . . . Therefore, loss of authority on the part of institutional elites results from widespread opportunities to participate in the formation of major social policies.

A system in which there is high access to elites generates popular pressures on the elites that prevent them from performing their creative and value-sustaining functions. People are not expected to have particular qualifications to make different kinds of decisions. Public opinion, viewed as the transitory general will, is regarded as the *immediate* as well as ultimate arbiter of all matters of policy and taste. Therefore, *anyone* is qualified; anyone may feel justified in judging or trying to influence any decision. As a result, the aristocratic critics claim, it is not simply that a large number of individuals is unqualified, but rather, it is the very *system* that is unqualified. For the system makes no provision for separating the qualified from the unqualified; and therefore excellence (whether in governing, in art, or in any other sphere) can neither be discovered, developed, nor protected. It is a situation in which elites cannot be creative nor can they deeply influence society. But only elites can perform these functions. . . .

We must ask the aristocratic critics how *equality* of opportunity to participate leads to *unrestrained* intervention, as in political strikes. We may agree that high access to elites is a permissive condition for recurrent mass behavior of this sort. But it is not a sufficient condition, since *non-elites may be restrained on their side, by means of their own groups and values.* That is, those members of society who identify themselves with the central values of a constitutional order are not likely to exploit opportunities to subvert elites. On the other hand, people who are *alienated* from society may express their resentment by using the most accessible instruments of action to impose their will. In short, the source of mass behavior cannot be located *only* in the structure of elites. It also must be found in the structure of non-elites, in a set of conditions close to the personal environment of the people who engage in mass behavior. Open elites can provide the "pull" for unrestrained participation in the vital centers of society, but not the "push." Since the democratic criticism specifies a set of conditions under which people will be propelled into mass actions, the aristocratic view of mass society may be strengthened by taking these additional conditions into account.

The Loss of Community in Mass Society. From the democratic viewpoint, the threat posed by mass society is less how elites may be protected from the masses and more how non-elites may be shielded from domination by elites. This difference is part of the larger difference dividing the two approaches: concern with opportunities for and functions of the few, on the one hand, versus concern with wide-spread opportunities for large numbers of people to participate in the collective life, on the other hand. The aristocratic position judges the formulation of broad social policy to be the responsibility and capability of the few, whereas the democratic position implies that potentially all members of society share in this responsibility.

Aristocratic critics attribute loss of liberty to the rise of popular participation in areas previously limited to the specially qualified: mass society is a condition under which there is too much control by the many over the few. Democratic critics, in their turn, attribute loss of liberty to the rise of mass manipulation and mobilization in areas previously left to the privacy of the individual and the group: mass society is a condition under which there is too much control by the few over the many. In short, one conception views mass society as unlimited democracy...the other as unlimited tyranny.

Now of course, these two states could be intimately related.... It is the thesis of this study that such an affinity is caught by the concept of mass society; but the fact remains that unlimited democracy is not unlimited tyranny, even though it may become so. Therefore, it remains to be clarified how a theory of mass society may specify this relationship....

What concerns the democratic critics is the possible emergence of another elite modeled after those thrown up by the Nazi and Bolshevik revolutions, with the consequent destruction of political democracy. The core of this imagery is the *atomized society*. Mass society is a situation in which an aggregate of individuals are related to one another only by way of their relation to a common authority, especially the state. That is, individuals are not directly related to one another in a variety of independent groups. A population in this condition is not insulated in any way from the ruling group, nor yet from elements within itself. For insulation requires a multiplicity of independent and often conflicting forms of association, each of which is strong enough to ward off threats to the autonomy of the individual. But it is precisely the weakness or absence of such social groups, *rather than their equality*, which distinguishes the mass society, according to these theorists. In their absence, people lack the resources to restrain their own behavior as well as that of others. Social atomization engenders strong feelings of alienation and anxiety, and therefore the disposition to engage in extreme behavior to escape from these tensions. In a mass society there is a heightened readiness to form hyper-attachments to symbols and leaders.... Total loyalty, in turn, is the psychological basis for total domination, i.e., totalitarianism.

There are three major terms implied in the democratic criticism of mass society: (a) growing atomization (loss of community); (b) widespread readiness to embrace new ideologies (quest for community); (c) totalitarianism (total domination by pseudo-community). In this universe of discourse, mass society is a condition in which elite domination replaces democratic rule. Mass society is objectively the *atomized* society, and subjectively the *alienated* population. Therefore, mass society is a system in which there is *high availability of a population for mobilization by elites.*

People become available for mobilization by elites when they lack or lose an independent group life.... The lack of autonomous relations generates widespread social alienation. Alienation heightens responsiveness to the appeal of mass movements because they provide occasions for expressing resentment against what is, as well as promises of a totally different world. In short, *people who are atomized readily become mobilized.* Since totalitarianism is a state of total mobilization, mass society is highly vulnerable to totalitarian movements and regimes....

We must next inquire whether an available population constitutes by itself a condition sufficient to result in numerous mass movements, as the democratic theorists imply. There are at least three reasons why high access to elites must also be present. In the first place, it is apparent that in order for available masses to become mobilized at all, agents of mobilization—for example, Communist spokesmen and organizations—must have opportunities to contact and appeal to large numbers of people. This requires readily accessible channels of communication. Moreover, if the paths to power were not open, there would be little incentive to mobilize and incite masses. In this sense, an accessible elite can serve as a magnet, both to would-be totalitarian leaders and to discontented masses. People in the mass (i.e., an undifferentiated and amorphous collectivity) are highly susceptible to total mobilization; but unless there is access to the means of communication and power, counter-elites (such as Communist leaders) will not be able to seize the opportunity provided by the mass for the conquest of total power.

Secondly, the success of totalitarian movements is contingent upon the vulnerability of existing elites. An accessible elite should not be equated with a vulnerable elite, for the strength or weakness of elites depends upon a host of factors other than their degree of accessibility. Nevertheless, an accessible elite is more vulnerable than one which is not accessible, other things being equal. When access is low, elites are relatively immune to popular pressures, so that mass movements peter out without overturning elites or infiltrating elite positions. Accessible elites more easily succumb to the attacks of totalitarian movements.

There is yet a third reason for suggesting that an available population does not automatically call forth elite domination. Totalitarian regimes are installed by new elites who have successfully mobilized an available population. But if this were in fact the sole condition required for the seizure of total power by new elites, how is it that the old elites, favored by this very same condition (i.e., an atomized population available for mobilization), have not themselves absorbed total power? Evidently *elites may be restrained on their side by means of their own relations and values.* Old elites generally lack the will and capacity to mobilize a large population. The one major exception is when the very existence of the social order is believed to be threatened, as in war or revolution. That is, mobilized movements led by representatives of existing institutions tend to be military ventures against external or internal enemies. Such mass movements may be developed in response to the mobilization of forces by another nation or by a revolutionary group, or in response to the expectation of such an enemy mobilization. It is under these conditions that a mass society may move toward totalitarianism under the direction of institutional rather than anti-institutional leadership. The model of the "garrison state". . .is precisely such a state of mobilization by established elites in the name of national security.[2]

The "garrison state" undoubtedly is a possible course along which mass society can move. But there are a number of factors which militate against mobilization of large numbers by existing elites (except under conditions of total war). In the first

---

[2] Harold D. Lasswell, "The Garrison State," *The American Journal of Sociology*, Vol. 46, 1941, pp. 455-468.

place, these elites are part of a going concern, and this alone makes for an essentially mundane orientation. Activism entails a readiness to reject routine modes of activity, and therefore tends to be eschewed by groups whose very power is bound to established routines. It usually requires a new elite devoid of the restraints incident upon institutional participation to mobilize widespread activism. . . .

Another reason why existing elites infrequently set in motion a large population is the presence of leadership rivalries. These conflicts between leaders operate as checks on the power of each, including any attempts to expand power by mobilizing masses.

In addition, existing elites may be restrained by their value commitments. They ordinarily have a strong stake in preserving the social order, for their own positions are legitimated by established values. Those who are successful are often more amenable to abiding by the rules of the game. Further, the achievement of high position may reflect or induce a heightened sense of responsibility for and awareness of institutional values.

Thus it is that popular mobilization generally is the work of counter-elites, since they are not inhibited by commitments to the social order, nor by constraints resulting from participation in a balance of power. These counter-elites are pushed towards making allies among the masses, since this is the only way to gain total power in mass society. Finally, established elites in a mass society not only lack the capacity to mobilize a large population; they also are ill-equipped to protect their organizations from penetration by counter-elites bent on destroying an existing order. . . .

Thus, the concept of mass society, in order to be useful for a theory of the transformation of democratic into totalitarian society, *necessarily* presupposes accessible elites. *The democratic criticism of mass society requires for its completion the notion of accessible elites provided by aristocratic critics.* It now may be shown that the negative consequences of accessible elites envisioned by aristocratic critics are greatly increased when non-elites are available by virtue of the loss of community.

Aristocratic theorists assume that whenever people are given the opportunity to participate in the shaping of social policies, they will do so in a destructive manner. But the opportunity for widespread participation in society does not automatically call forth mass action unrestrained by social relations and cultural norms. Not all members of a society, but only *people in the mass* are disposed to seize the opportunity provided by accessible elites to impress mass standards on all spheres of society, and to do so in an unrestrained manner. This is true for two reasons. First, when large numbers of people are interrelated only as members of a mass, they are more likely to pressure elites to provide satisfactions previously supplied by a plurality of more proximate groups. Second, they are likely to do so in a direct and unmediated way, because there is a paucity of intervening groups to channelize and filter popular participation in the larger society. As a result, mass participation tends to be irrational and unrestrained, since there are few points at which it may be checked by personal experience and the experience of others. Where people are not securely related to a plurality of independent groups, they are available for all kinds of adventures and "activist modes of intervention" in the larger society. It is one thing for a population to participate at specified times and in institutional ways for defined interests—for example, through trade associations and trade unions, or in elections. It is quite another to create *ad hoc* methods of direct pressure on critical centers of society, such as the "invasion" of a state legislature, street political gangs, etc. It is the latter form of collective activity that the aristocratic theorists fear, but they err in assuming that equal access to elites is sufficient to produce it: wide-spread availability attendant upon social atomization also must exist.

Thus, each conception of mass society requires the other for its completion. Together they provide the basis for a general theory of mass society.

Conditions of Mass Society. The aristocratic critique of mass society yields the idea of accessible elites, and the democratic critique yields the idea of available non-elites. We have shown that the consequences imputed to each are more likely to follow from a combination of both factors than from either one alone. This suggests a more general conception of mass society than that contained in the aristocratic or democratic version. *Mass society is a social system in which elites are readily accessible to influence by non-elites and non-elites are readily available for mobilization by elites.*

This conception of mass society may be better understood by comparing it with other types of societies. For this purpose, we shall consider communal society, pluralist society, and totalitarian society, insofar as they can be characterized by other combinations of the two variables of (a) accessibility of elites and (b) availability of non-elites. Access and availability vary in kind as well as in degree. For example, access to elites may be institutionalized or it may be direct; access can take the form of membership in elites or of selection of elites. These are some of the main *kinds* of access. There are important differences between social systems in respect to the kinds of access to elites (or the kinds of availability of non-elites) that predominate in each; this aspect of the problem will be explored subsequently. For the moment, we are concerned only with the *degree* of access and availability. As a rough indicator of the degree of access to elites we shall use the extent to which members of the society participate in the selection of elites, and as a comparable measure of the degree of availability of non-elites we may use the extent to which members of the society lack attachments to independent groups. Of each type of society we shall now ask only whether it involves high or low access to elites, high or low availability of non-elites.

		AVAILABILITY OF NON-ELITES	
		Low	High
ACCESSIBILITY OF ELITES	Low	Communal Society	Totalitarian Society
	High	Pluralist Society	Mass Society

Communal society requires inaccessible elites and unavailable non-elites if it is to sustain its traditional structure—as in certain medieval communities. Elites are inaccessible in that elite elements and standards are selected and fixed by traditional ascription. Non-elites are unavailable in that people are firmly bound by kinship and community. Such a population is very difficult to mobilize unless powerful forces have eroded communal ties, as happened in the Late Middle Ages, when the incipient processes of urbanization and industrialization began their destruction of the medieval community, thereby unloosing portions of the population for participation in the various millennial movements that flourished during this period.

Pluralist society requires accessible elites and unavailable non-elites if it is to sustain its freedom and diversity—as in certain liberal democracies. Elites are accessible in that competition among independent groups opens many channels of communication and power. The population is unavailable in that people possess multiple commitments to diverse and autonomous groups. The mobilization of a population bound by multiple commitments would require the breaking up of large numbers of independent organizations, as totalitarian movements have sought to do.

Mass society requires both accessible elites and available non-elites if it is to exhibit a high rate of mass behavior. Elites are accessible and non-elites are available in that there is a paucity of independent groups between the state and the family to protect either elites or non-elites from manipulation and mobilization by the other. In the absence of social autonomy at all levels of society, large numbers of people are pushed and pulled toward activist modes of intervention in vital centers of society; and mass-oriented leaders have the opportunity to mobilize this activism for the capture of power. As a result, freedom is precarious in mass society.

Totalitarian society requires an inaccessible elite and an available population if it is to sustain a system of total control from above—as in certain modern dictatorships. The elite is inaccessible in that elite elements are selected and fixed through co-optation, by virtue of a monopoly over the means of coercion and persuasion in the hands of those at the apex of the structure. The population is available in that its members lack all those independent social formations that could serve as a basis of resistance to the elite. Instead, the population is mobilized by the elite through multiple organizations taken over or created for that purpose.

These are abstract types of society; no large-scale society is purely communal, pluralist, mass, or totalitarian. However, any given society would appear to be like one type more than like other types. For example, large, complex societies always contain some pluralist elements, so that total control is impossible, even under totalitarian regimes. Yet some societies give much greater weight to pluralist elements than do others. They not only exhibit a much greater degree of institutional autonomy, but in addition, "it is acknowledged and guaranteed and finds support in the legal system, the ethos and the distribution of legitimate power."[3]

A weakness of the two theories of mass society may be identified in light of the model of four types of society. Aristocratic critics fasten on popular access to elites

---

[3]Edward A. Shils, *The Torment of Secrecy* (Glencoe: The Free Press, 1956), p. 154.

as the distinguishing characteristic of mass society, and thereby confound pluralist society with mass society. Democratic critics, on the other hand, fasten on the availability of atomized non-elites in their conception of mass society, and thereby confound totalitarian society with mass society. By distinguishing mass society from totalitarian society, on the one side, and pluralist society, on the other, the model presented here would appear to be a more fruitful one for the examination of problems related to social structure and freedom.

Our conception of mass society involves the following major proposition: *a high rate of mass behavior may be expected when both elites and non-elites lack social insulation; that is, when elites are accessible to direct intervention by non-elites, and when non-elites are available for direct mobilization by elites. . . .*

Structure of Mass Society. We can conceive of all but the simplest societies as comprising three levels of social relations. The first level consists of highly personal or primary relations, notably the family. The third level contains relations inclusive of the whole population, notably the state. The second level comprises all intermediate relations, notably the local community, voluntary associations, and occupational groups. These intermediate relations function as links between the individual and his primary relations, on the one hand, and the state and other national relations, on the other hand. It must be emphasized that voluntary associations are not the only kind of intermediate relation; all organized relations that mediate between the family and the nation, such as local government and the local press, are classified as intermediate structures in the present study. . . .

The logic of our model dictates that the structure of mass society must be of such a nature as to support a high rate of mass behavior by fulfilling the two requirements for mass behavior, namely, accessible elites and available non-elites. Such a structure may be shown to be one in which intermediate relations of community, occupation, and association are more or less inoperative, and therefore one in which the individual and primary group are directly related to the state and to nation-wide organizations. The members of mass society, then, are interconnected only by virtue of their common ties to national centers of communication and organization. It is in this sense that we speak of mass society as the *atomized* society.

Mass society lacks intermediate relations, but it is not to be conceived merely as the absence of social relations. The central feature of primary groups in mass society is not so much their internal weakness as it is their external *isolation* from the larger society. The isolation of primary groups means that by themselves they cannot provide the basis for participation in the larger society. Again, mass society is not to be thought of as lacking relations inclusive of the whole population. On the contrary, modern mass society possesses a highly *politicalized* organization. . . . This results in the centralization of the social structure, especially a centralized state. The centralization of communication and decision-making means that to the extent people do participate in the larger society, they must do so through the state, and other inclusive (nation-wide) structures.

We shall elaborate this model of the structure of mass society by examining it on each of its three levels: (1) the weakness of intermediate relations, (2) the isolation of primary relations, and (3) the centralization of national relations.

Weakness of Intermediate Relations. Weak intermediate relations leave elites and non-elites directly exposed to one another, and thereby invite wide-spread mass behavior; for in the absence of intermediate relations, participation in the larger society must be direct rather than filtered through intervening relationships.

The lack of strong independent groups undermines multiple proximate concerns, and thereby increases mass availability.... Unless a variety of forms of association are open to him, the individual is not likely to take an active interest in civic affairs—particularly in the metropolis, where the size of the population and the specialization of activities place a premium on voluntary associations as bases of political participation. Or, in the absence of associations such as the P.T.A. to provide channels of communication and influence between parents and school, the individual is less likely to develop or sustain interest and participation in the education of his children. Examples may be easily multiplied, but these are sufficient to suggest why independent groups are indispensable bases for the maintenance of meaningful proximate concerns.

The lack of a structure of independent groups also removes the basis for self-protection on the part of elites, because it permits direct modes of intervention to replace mediated participation in elites. In the first place, intermediate groups, even though they are independent of top elites, operate to protect these elites from arbitrary and excessive pressures by themselves being responsive to the needs and demands of people. They carry a large share of the burden of seeking to fulfill the interests of people who would otherwise have to rely exclusively on national agencies to minister to their needs. Secondly, the leaders of intermediate groups, irrespective of their particular aims (so long as these aims are not contrary to the integrity of the community), help to shore up the larger system of authority with which their own authority is inextricably bound. Third, intermediate groups help to protect elites by functioning as channels through which popular participation in the larger society (especially in the national elites) may be directed and restrained. In the absence of intermediate groups to act as representatives and guides for popular participation, people must act *directly* in the critical centers of society, and therefore in a manner unrestrained by the values and interests of a variety of social groups.

These reasons why the weakness of intermediate groups characterize mass society are at the same time reasons why the strength of such groups characterizes the pluralist society. A strong intermediate structure consists of stable and independent groups which represent diverse and frequently conflicting interests. The opposition among such groups restrains one another's power, thereby limiting the aggregate intervention in elites; that is, a system of social checks and balances among a plurality of diverse groups operates to protect elites as well as non-elites in ways we have indicated. Furthermore, the separation of the various spheres of society—for example, separation of religion and politics—means that access to elites in one sphere does not directly affect elites in other spheres. The various authorities are more or less autonomous in their own spheres, in that they are not directly determined in their membership or policy by authorities in other spheres. These same factors protect non-elites from elites, since independent groups guard their members from one another, and since overlapping memberships among groups, *each of which concerns only limited aspects of its members' lives*, restrains each group from seeking total domination over its membership.

The state in pluralist society also plays a vital role in support of individual freedom, for it is above all the state which has the capacity to safeguard the individual against domination by particular groups. Durkheim saw more profoundly than most that it is the *combination* of the state and what he called "secondary groups" that engenders individual liberty, rather than one or the other social structure alone. . . .[4]

Where individuals belong to several groups, no one group is *inclusive* of its members' lives. Associations have members with a variety of social characteristics (e.g., class and ethnic identities) and group memberships (e.g., trade unions may possess members who go to various churches, or even belong to church-affiliated trade union associations such as ACTU). . . . Such extensive *cross-cutting solidarities* favor a high level of freedom and consensus: these solidarities help prevent one line of social cleavage from becoming dominant, and they constrain associations to respect the various affiliations of their members lest they alienate them. Socially heterogeneous religious organizations are also important pluralistic agencies; they may be contrasted with situations in which religious and class lines tend to closely correspond, as in France where anti-clericalism is largely a working-class phenomenon. Political parties which draw their support from all major social segments constitute still another kind of cross-cutting solidarity. In this respect, the highly heterogeneous and decentralized American parties may be contrasted with the highly centralized, class-based Socialist parties and religious-based Catholic parties characteristic of European multiparty systems.

Our conception of pluralism includes that of multiple affiliations, which means that medieval society was not pluralist in our use of the term. So long as no association claims or receives hegemony over many aspects of its members' lives, its power over the individual will be limited. This is a vital point, because the authority of a private group can be as oppressive as that of the state.

A plurality of groups that are both independent and non-inclusive not only protects elites and non-elites from one another but does so in a manner that permits liberal democratic control. Liberal democratic control requires that people have *access* to elites, and that they exercise *restraint* in their participation. Independent groups help to maintain access to top-level decision-making by bringing organized pressure to bear on elites to remain responsive to outside influence. Each group has interests of its own in gaining access to elites, and has organized power not available to separate individuals for the implementation of these interests. These interests require not only that elites pay attention to the demands of the group, but also that other groups do not become so strong as to be able to shut off this group's access to the elite. Since independent groups seek to maintain their position by checking one another's power as well as the power of higher-level elites, the

---

[4]Emile Durkheim, *Professional Ethics and Civic Morals* (Glencoe: The Free Press, 1958), pp. 62-63.

interaction of these groups helps to sustain access to decision-making processes in the larger society.

A plurality of independent groups also helps to regulate popular participation by integrating people into a wide range of proximate concerns. Where people possess multiple interests and commitments, attachments to remote objects, such as loyalty to the nation-state, are mediated by proximate relations. Therefore, people in pluralist society engage in relatively little *direct* participation in national decisions, not because elites prevent them from doing so, but because they can influence decisions more effectively through their own groups. Furthermore, people tend to be *selective* in their participation, limiting their direct involvement in the larger society to matters that appear to them of particular concern in light of their values and interests. Since pluralist society engenders a variety of values and interests, self-selective involvement in national politics tends to limit the number of people who are vitally concerned with any given issue.

The intermediate structure of pluralist society helps to maintain access to elites by virtue of its *independence* from elites. The intermediate structure of totalitarian society, on the other hand, helps to prevent access to the elite by virtue of its *domination* by the elite. By means of intermediate groups instituted and controlled from above, the totalitarian regime is able to keep the population in a state of mobilization. Such organizations as Soviet trade unions have the primary function of activating and channelizing the energies of workers in directions determined by the regime. If there were no controlled intermediate organizations in all spheres of society, people would be free to regroup along lines independent of the regime. That is why it is of the utmost importance to totalitarian regimes to keep the population active in these controlled groups. Totalitarian regimes search out all independent forms of organizations in order to transform them or destroy them. . . .

The intermediate structure corresponding to each of our four types of society has been analyzed along two dimensions: (a) the strength of intermediate social organizations, especially their capacity to operate as autonomous centers of power; and (b) the inclusiveness of intermediate organizations, that is, the extent to which they encompass all aspects of their members' lives. The results of our analysis may be summarized in the form of a diagram. . . .

| | | INTERMEDIATE GROUPS ARE: | |
		Strong	Weak
	Inclusive	Communal Society	Totalitarian Society
INTERMEDIATE GROUPS ARE:	Non-inclusive	Pluralist Society	Mass Society

Isolation of Personal Relations. Personal as well as intermediate relations become increasingly peripheral to the central operations of the mass society. This is shown by the change in social position of the family from an extended kinship system to an *isolated* conjugal unit following upon the loss of many social functions. The family gives up its educational role to a public school system, its mutual aid role to a social security system, and so on. The loss of functions sharply limits the public meaning of the family, though not necessarily its private meaning, and diminishes its capacity for relating the individual to the larger society. Kinship units may be too narrow in scope and too far removed from the public realm to be able to provide an effective basis for developing interest and participation in it.

With this argument in mind, many students of mass society imply that mass society lacks family ties as well as intermediate social relations. This view is open to serious question. In the first place, since the family by itself is inherently incapable of linking the individual to large-scale society, it is theoretically unnecessary to assume that such relations are absent in order to have a mass society. In other words, it is entirely possible to have a society in which there are family ties but which is still a mass society due to the lack of intermediate relations. Furthermore, since the individual who is *totally* isolated (that is, without even family ties) for long periods is not likely to possess that minimum of personal organization required by collective activity, the loss of all family life leads to personal deviance—in the extreme case, mental disorders and suicides—rather than to mass behavior. But it is mass behavior which marks the mass society.

Data showing that extreme personal deviance and extreme political behavior do not vary together lend support to this view, for they indicate that different social conditions may give rise to each. . . .

Thus, there are good theoretical and empirical reasons (although the data are far from conclusive) for not assuming that the loss of family life is a necessary condition underlying mass tendencies. Rather, we contend that it is the *isolation* of the family and other primary groups which marks the mass society.

Since social isolation, as the term will be used herein, refers to the lack of social relations to the larger society, individuals may be isolated even though they possess family ties—so long as the family groups in turn are not linked to the larger society in any firm way. For isolated families (or other kinds of primary associations, such as friendship groups) cannot by themselves provide the basis for understanding or managing the impersonal environment with which the individual also must grapple. Therefore, whereas the isolation of a small group does not entail the isolation of its members from one another, the individual member of such a group may nevertheless be isolated from the common life of the "great society." A central proposition of this study states that meaningful and effective participation in the larger society requires a structure of groups intermediate between the family and the nation; and the weakness of such a structure creates a vulnerability to mass movements. Participation in small but isolated groups such as the family is no substitute for participation in intermediate groups and may even be favorable to participation in mass movements, since the individual is more likely to engage in new ventures when he receives support from his close associates, and because the member of even a small group is a more accessible target for mass agitation than is a completely unattached person. In other words, the totally isolated individual (that is, the person without *any* social ties) will be unable to maintain his personal organization sufficiently to engage in cooperative ventures of any kind, whereas the individual who has personal ties but no broader ties in the society is more likely to be available for mass movements.

Centralization of National Relations. The organizing principle of large-scale mass society centers on the national level. This is indicated by the proliferation of governmental functions in previously autonomous spheres of activity, by the growth of national organizations, and by the concomitant shift in power from local to national centers. Structures on the national level develop in response to the size and complexity of society; they expropriate functions formerly reserved to intermediate groups and the family. Modern mass society is characterized by the great degree to which this transference has taken place, so that the state and national organization assume the central role in the direction of all kinds of collective activity. Mass society finds a major basis of integration in large-scale organization. Therefore, we would be misconstruing mass society if we were to describe it as a state of social disorganization.

National organization that is centralized at the expense of smaller forms of association helps to create amorphous masses. People are more easily manipulated and mobilized when they become directly and exclusively dependent on the national organization for the satisfaction of interests otherwise also met in proximate relations. When the national organization is atomized, its members find it increasingly difficult to orient themselves to the larger society. They cannot understand the workings of the overall system. . . . Furthermore, increasing distance between centers of decision and daily life make it more difficult for people to grasp the meaning of issues at stake. Faced with the impersonality and incomprehensibility of national relations, and at the same time lacking an independent group life, the individual may withdraw from participation in the larger society. Or he may act in spite of the lack of group relations. Certain spheres of mass society are based on such unmediated participation of large numbers of individuals. . . .

In general, formal organizations are to be identified as mass organizations, not by their size, but when they lack intermediate units which have some autonomy from the central leadership. In the absence of a structure of smaller groups, formal organizations themselves become remote from their members. That is, they get beyond the reach of their members, and as a result cannot deeply influence them nor command their allegiance in the face of competition for member loyalties. Consequently, members of excessively bureaucratized organizations may become mobilized by totalitarian elites. This is illustrated by the Nazi success in capturing many youth groups in Germany during the 1920's. . . .

Large-scale organizations that fail to develop or sustain independent subgroups tend to be characterized by low levels of membership participation. Because they are not close enough to their members to allow for effective participation, mass organizations engender widespread apathy. Furthermore, the lack of a pluralist structure within organizations, like its absence in the larger society, not only discourages membership participation. It also discourages the formation of an informed membership, the development of new leadership, and the spread of responsibility and authority, so that the wide gap between the top and the bottom of mass organizations tends to be bridged by manipulation.

At the same time that mass relations permit extensive manipulation of people by elites, they also encourage manipulation of elites by non-elites. Elites are more directly influenced by non-elites in the absence of intermediate groups because they are less insulated. Elites lose their insulation since demands and impulses of large numbers of people that formerly were sublimated and fulfilled by intermediate groups now are focused directly on the national level. Higher elites absorb functions formerly reserved to intermediate elites and therefore no longer can depend on these groups to siphon off popular pressures and to regulate participation. Furthermore, popular participation in the higher elites is all the stronger and less restrained for being in part a substitute for diversified participation in intermediate groups—especially in times of crisis.

In conclusion, the growth of centralized organizations at the expense of intermediate groups constrains both elites and non-elites to engage in efforts to directly manipulate the other. Media of communication that command the attention of millions of people simultaneously are major instruments of this manipulation by those who command them, but also by the audience upon which their success or failure directly is dependent. Centralized decision-making also may cut two ways: if the populace can make its voice felt more easily when it can influence directly one master decision, rather than having to influence many smaller decisions to achieve the same result, then by the same token elites also may grasp one major lever of power more readily than many smaller ones. Centralization of decision-making functions does not preclude direct intervention either by the mass or the elite, although it certainly does prevent people from expressing and implementing individual views on public matters. When centralized national relations are combined with weak intermediate relations and isolated family relations, elites are unprotected from mass pressures and masses are unprotected from elite pressures. The structure of mass society thus provides extensive opportunity for mass movements. . . .

THE TOTAL COMMUNITY

Robert A. Nisbet

We must recognize that there is no single intellectual image intrinsic to the totalitarian design. There is no single spiritual or cultural value inherently incapable of being made into the central image of a totalitarian society. It can as well be racial equality as inequality, godly piety as atheism, labor as capital, Christian brotherhood as the toiling masses. What is central is not the specific image held up to the masses but, rather, the sterilization and destruction of all other images and the subordination of all human relationships to the central power that contains this image.

SOURCE: Abridged from *Community and Power (The Quest for Community)* pp. 192-209, by Robert A. Nisbet. Copyright 1953 by Oxford University Press, Inc. Used by permission of the publisher and author. Most footnotes have been omitted.

Nor are poverty and economic distress, as such, the crucial factors leading to the rise of totalitarianism. Such analyses too are undiscriminating efforts to make the larger evil simply the sum of lesser evils. Poverty may, in certain circumstances, be a powerful basis of appeal for the totalitarian leader. It may be used as a piece of concrete symbolism for all the real and imaginary deprivations and frustrations of a population. But mere poverty itself does not automatically impel men to the acceptance of totalitarian power. What is decisive is the social context, the sensations of disinheritance and exclusion from rightful membership in a social and moral order. These may or may not accompany poverty.

Nor can the effective source of totalitarianism be confined to any one class or section of the population. For a long time, Marxism had the regrettable effect of convincing even well-informed observers that all the massive changes which took place in Germany after 1933 were simply "reactionary" efforts of a group of men known as capitalists to maintain an existing economy. Because in its early phases some highly placed industrialists contributed financially to the Nazi Party, and learned too late that rootless men always betray, the legend arose that totalitarianism is indistinguishable from predatory efforts of capitalists.

But we must recognize that totalitarianism can as easily be the work of industrial managers, who are themselves revolting against the capitalists, or of labor leaders, scientists, church leaders, or any group of intellectuals who may find themselves strategically placed to accomplish through revolution or bureaucracy the transition from free society to totalitarianism.

Least of all can totalitarianism—in whatever form it has taken, Nazi or Fascist included—be regarded seriously as a "reactionary" movement. Totalitarianism may not be revolutionary in the sense the word possessed in the nineteenth century, but in none of its forms can it be placed in the conservative category of reaction. To describe totalitarianism as simply the effort of a minority to maintain, through force, existing institutions of society misses grotesquely the sweeping dislocations and atomizations actually involved in such a movement as Nazism. Far from being, as it is sometimes absurdly argued, a lineal product of nineteenth-century Conservatism, totalitarianism is, in fact, the very opposite of it.

Nor can totalitarianism be reduced to the operation of force and terror. That these exist, and horribly, in every totalitarian country is beside the point. The essence of totalitarianism lies in its relation to the masses, and to the masses the leaders never bring the satanic arts of the torture chamber and the exterminations of the concentration camp. The totalitarian order will use force and terror, where necessary, to destroy organized *minorities*—refractory labor unions, churches, ethnic groups—but to the masses of individuals who are left when these social relationships are destroyed, a totally different approach is employed. It is an approach based upon the arts of psychological manipulation—cajolery, flattery, bribery, mass identification with new images, and all the modern techniques of indoctrination.

We merely delude ourselves if we suppose that there is always necessary conflict between totalitarian governments and the desires and aspirations of the masses. Here the recent words of Hannah Arendt are illuminating. "In view of the unparalleled misery which totalitarian regimes have meant to their people—horror to many and unhappiness to all—it is painful to realize that they are always preceded by mass movements and that they 'command and rest upon mass support' up to the end. Hitler's rise to power was legal in terms of majority rule and neither he nor Stalin could have maintained the leadership of large populations, survived so many interior and exterior crises, and braved the numerous dangers of the relentless intra-party struggles, if they had not had the confidence of the masses."[1]

The totalitarian leader is never loath to identify himself with the "will and wisdom" of the masses. No intellectual defense against totalitarianism could be more futile than that which sees the States of Hitler and Stalin as operating in open contempt and hatred of the people. Such States may plead with, flatter, and persuade, but they never openly insult the people. It was this dependence upon popular support that permitted Mussolini to call his Fascism "an organized, centralized, authoritarian democracy," and Hitler to refer to the Third Reich as "Teutonic democracy based upon the free choice of the leader." We do not have to be reminded of the ceaseless efforts of the Soviet leaders to identify their policies and actions with the tradition of democracy in the West and of their incessant attempts to maintain popular support of these policies.

There are two other misconceptions, greater than any of the foregoing, each of which precludes an understanding of totalitarianism. The first consists of the view of totalitarianism as some sort of vast irrationality, a kind of collective derangement. Here we are victims of the supine optimism that has characterized so much of Western thought during the past two centuries. We insist upon making the irrational and the evil interpenetrating essences of one another. Because totalitarianism is manifestly evil we suppose that it is also fundamentally irrational. And because we have thus proved it to be irrational we comfort ourselves with the belief that it must be destroyed by its own departure from reason.

The total State is evil, but we merely delude ourselves if we do not recognize in it elements of almost overpowering rationality. In terms of basic organization it is at least as rational as the huge industrial corporation, the mass political party, or the mammoth bureaucracies of all modern governments. Indeed the total State would be inconceivable without a background, in some degree, composed of these and related elements. We might as well conceive of selling the Rotary Creed to savages on the banks of the Amazon as disseminating Nazi or Communist creeds to populations unfamiliar with the basic and overt manifestations of economic and political rationalism.

The total State is rational in that it recognizes in human personality certain basic needs for security and recognition and strives through every art and technique to satisfy those needs in calculated political terms. It is rational in that it seeks to eliminate from culture all of those ceremonial, ritualistic, or symbolic features inherited from the past that constitute by their existence obstructions to the achievement of a perfect mobilization of popular will. New ceremonies and symbols will be created by totalitarian rulers, but these will be made to fit as closely into the total design of political power as manipulative intelligence can contrive. Old

---

[1] *The Origins of Totalitarianism* (New York: Harcourt, Brace and Co., 1951), p. 301.

complexities of language and syntax will be removed, where necessary, in the interests of a more rational structure of communication readily assimilable by all members of the population; ancient legal procedures will be abolished or stream-lined in the interests of a more rational and remorseless legal code; superfluous or irrelevant forms of recreation will be outlawed, subtly or forcibly as circumstances may require, and replaced by new forms harmonious with the purposes of the State. Horrible as were the Nazi concentration and extermination camps, in moral terms, we cannot miss the essential rationality of their operation. They were rational not merely in the ruthless efficiency of their techniques but in their calculated separation of victim and overseer alike from all the emotional and spiritual aspects of personality.

To start out with the assumption that totalitarianism is irrational, and hence doomed to self-destruction, is to start out with an extremely unintelligent view of a form of society that has used all the rational arts of modern public administration, economic management, and social psychology to maintain itself and to make its identity ever more emphatic in the minds of its people.

Equally fatal to our understanding of totalitarianism is the assumption, drawn from the philosophy of Progress, that this form of society represents some kind of historical abnormality or deflection from the appointed course of history. Here also we are in the presence of the typical confusion between the morally good and the historically inevitable. Because we, for so long, saw in political freedom, rights, and justice the basic elements not merely of moral goodness but also of historical necessity, there are many who persist in regarding such movements as Nazism and Soviet Communism as deviations from the normal development of civilization.

Related to this view are the efforts to place totalitarianism in the category of primitivism, of antique tribalism. Such efforts are a part of the larger perspective of moral philosophy that makes all evil a mere reversion to the past, as though there were some inevitable link between time and moral states. The total State, it is said, is nothing more than a reversion to the infancy of civilization. It is the product of certain dark forces, buried beneath the superego man has acquired through centuries of moral progress, now manifesting themselves in Nazism and Communism. This view may be gratifying to sensibilities nourished by the idea of Progress, but it is as delusive as the idea that totalitarianism is a vast collective irrationality. To explain all evil as simply a reversion to the past is, as Reinhold Niebuhr once observed, like describing individual insanity as simply a reversion to childhood.

What is most dangerous in this whole view is the supposition that totalitarianism is a kind of monstrous accident, an interruption of the normal, a deflection that must be set right by the operation of the so-called laws of historical progress. But if there are any laws of unilinear progress, we have not discovered them, and there is no more justification in purely historical terms for regarding totalitarianism as an abnormal development than there is for so regarding democracy, or liberalism.

II. There are two central elements of totalitarianism: the first is the existence of the masses; the second is the ideology, in its most extreme form, of the political community. Neither can be fully described apart from its relation to the other, for the two exist always, in modern society, in sensitive interaction with each other.

What works toward the creation of the masses works also toward the establishment of the omnicompetent, absolute State. And everything that augments the power and influence of the State in its relation to the individual serves also to increase the scope of the masses. . . .

The essence of the masses, however, does not lie in the mere fact of numbers. It is not the quantitative but the qualitative aspect that is essential. A population may be vast, as is that of India, and yet, by reason of the stability of its social organization, be far removed from the condition of massdom. What is crucial in the formation of the masses is the atomization of all social and cultural relationships within which human beings gain their normal sense of membership in society. The mass is an aggregate of individuals who are insecure, basically lonely, and ground down, either through decree or historical circumstance, into mere particles of social dust. Within the mass all ordinary relationships and authorities seem devoid of institutional function and psychological meaning. Worse, such relationships and authorities come to seem positively hostile; in them the individual can find not security but despair. . . .

When the masses, in considerable number, already exist, as the consequence of historical forces, half the work of the totalitarian leader has been done for him. What remains but to complete, where necessary, the work of history, and to grind down into atomic particles all remaining evidences of association and social authority? What remains, then, but to rescue the masses from their loneliness, their hopelessness and despair, by leading them into the Promised Land of the absolute, redemptive State? The process is not too difficult, or even too violent, providing the masses have already been created in significant size by processes that have destroyed or diminished the social relationships and cultural values by which human beings normally live and in which they gain not merely their sense of order but their desire for freedom.

But where the masses do not already exist in great numbers, and where, through the accident of quick seizure of power, the totalitarian mentality comes into ascendancy, then it becomes necessary to *create* the masses: to do through the most ruthless force and in the shortest possible time the work that has been done in other areas by the operation of past processes.

Here is where the most shocking acts of totalitarianism become manifest—not in its attitude toward the already existing masses, but toward those human beings, still closely related by village, church, or family, or labor union, and whose very relationships separate them from the indispensable condition of massdom. Such relationships must be ruthlessly destroyed. If they cannot be destroyed easily and inexpensively by propaganda and intimidation, they must be destroyed by all the techniques of the torture chamber, by enforced separation of loved ones, by the systematic obliteration of legal identities, by killing, and by the removal of large segments of a population to labor camps.

The violence and the horrors of Soviet Russia, in many ways greater perhaps even than those of Nazi Germany, have arisen from the fact that in Russia, down to the beginnings of the First World War, the masses scarcely existed. The ancient relationships of class, family, village, and association were nearly as strong as they had been in medieval times. Only in small areas of Russia were these relationships dissolving and the masses beginning to emerge. . . .

Hence, beginning in the nineteen-twenties, the destruction of all traditional associations, the liquidation of old statuses. Hence also the conversion of professional and occupational associations into administrative arms of the government. The hopes of older Russian intellectuals, who had supposed that socialism in Russia might be founded upon the communal institutions of the peasantry, supplemented by the emerging workers' organizations in the cities, were proved fatuous. For the new rulers of Russia realized that the kind of power requisite to the establishment of the Marxian order could not long exist if any competing associations and authorities were allowed to remain. The vast association of the nation, which Marx had prophesied, could come into being only through the most absolute and extensive central political power. And, for the establishment and maintenance of this power, the creation of the undifferentiated, unattached, atomized mass was indispensable.

III. We may regard totalitarianism as a process of the annihilation of individuality, but, in more fundamental terms, it is the annihilation, first, of those social relationships within which individuality develops. It is not the extermination of individuals that is ultimately desired by totalitarian rulers, for individuals in the largest number are needed by the new order. What is desired is the extermination of those social relationships which, by their autonomous existence, must always constitute a barrier to the achievement of the absolute political community.

The individual alone is powerless. Individual will and memory, apart from the reinforcement of associative tradition, are weak and ephemeral. How well the totalitarian rulers know this. Even constitutional guarantees and organic laws dim to popular vision when the social and cultural identities of persons become atomized, when the reality of freedom and order in the *small areas* of society becomes obscure.

The prime object of totalitarian government thus becomes the incessant destruction of all evidences of spontaneous, autonomous association. For, with this social atomization, must go also a diminution of intensity and a final flickering out of political values that interpose themselves between freedom and despotism.

To destroy or diminish the reality of the smaller areas of society, to abolish or restrict the range of cultural alternatives offered individuals by economic endeavor, religion, and kinship, is to destroy in time the roots of the will to resist despotism in its large forms. In its negative aspects totalitarianism is thus a ceaseless process of cultural nihilism. How else can the individual be separated from the traditions and values which, if allowed to remain intact, would remind him constantly of his cultural past? A sense of the past is far more basic to the maintenance of freedom than hope for the future. The former is concrete and real; the latter is necessarily amorphous and more easily guided by those who can manipulate human actions and beliefs. Hence the relentless effort by totalitarian governments to destroy memory. And hence the ingenious techniques for abolishing the social allegiances within which individual memory is given strength and power of resistance.

Totalitarianism is thus made possible only through the obliteration of all the intermediate layers of value and association that commonly nourish personality and serve to protect it from external power and caprice. Totalitarianism has been well described as the ultimate invasion of human privacy. But this invasion of privacy is possible only after the social contexts of privacy—family, church, association—have been atomized. The political *enslavement* of man requires the *emancipation* of man from all the authorities and memberships (obstructions to popular will, as the Nazis and Communists describe them) that serve, in one degree or another, to insulate the individual from external political power.

The destruction of the independent labor unions in Nazi Germany was followed by the prohibition of independent economic organizations of every kind. It was not the fact of labor that was central; it was the social fact of *union*. All autonomous organizations were destroyed and made illegal: professions, service clubs, voluntary mutual aid groups, fraternal associations, even philatelist and musical societies. Such organizations were regarded, and correctly, by the totalitarian government as potential sources of future resistance, if only because in them people were brought together for purposes, however innocent, that did not reflect those of the central government. As organizations they interposed themselves between the people as a society and the people as the masses.

Despite the fact that the early Nazis used the symbolism of family and religion for its possible sentimental appeal, the actual realities of family and religion were as remorselessly attacked by the government and Party as were the labor unions. The shrewd totalitarian mentality knows well the powers of intimate kinship and religious devotion for keeping alive in a population values and incentives which might well, in the future, serve as the basis of resistance. Thus to emancipate each member, and especially the younger members, from the family was an absolute necessity. And this planned spiritual alienation from kinship was accomplished, not only through the negative processes of spying and informing but through the sapping of the functional foundations of family membership and through the substitution of new and attractive political roles for each of the social roles embodied in the family structure. The techniques varied. But what was essential was the atomization of the family and of every other type of grouping that intervened between the people as society and the people as a mindless, soulless, traditionless mass. What the totalitarian must have for the realization of his design is a spiritual and cultural vacuum.

IV. Totalitarianism is an ideology of nihilism. But nihilism is not enough. No powerful social movement can be explained in negative terms alone. There is always the positive goal and absorptive association for which all the destructive and desolative actions are but a preparation, a clearing of the way. We should miss the essence of the total State if we did not see in it elements that are profoundly affirmative. The extraordinary accomplishments of totalitarianism in the twentieth century would be inexplicable were it not for the immense, burning appeal it exerts upon masses of individuals who have lost, or had taken away, their accustomed roots of membership and belief.

The atomization of old values and associations does not leave for long an associational vacuum. The genius of totalitarian leadership lies in its profound awareness that human personality cannot tolerate moral isolation. It lies, further, in its knowledge that absolute and relentless power will be acceptable only when it comes to seem the only available form of community and membership.

Here we have the clue to that fatal affinity of power and individual loneliness.... Knowing the basic psychological truth that life apart from some sense of membership in a larger order is intolerable for most people, the leaders of the total State thus direct their energies not just to the destruction of the old order but to the manufacture of the new.

This new order is the absolute, the total, political community. As a community it is made absolute by the removal of all forms of membership and identification which might, by their existence, compete with the new order. It is, further, made absolute by the insistence that all thought, belief, worship, and membership be within the structure of the State. What gives historical identity to the totalitarian State is not the absolutism of one man or of a clique or a class; rather, it is the absolute extension of the structure of the administrative State into the social and psychological realm previously occupied by a plurality of associations. Totalitarianism involves the demolishment of autonomous social ties in a population, but it involves, no less, their replacement by new ones, each deriving its meaning and sanction from the central structure of the State.

The total State is monolithic. It is not convincing to argue, as have some of even the best students, that the power of the Party in the total State, paralleling at every point the powers of the formal bureaucracy, is proof of the contrary. In the first place, the totalitarian Party is regarded as but a necessary transitional step in the attainment of a formal governmental structure that will be, ultimately, free of any distractive allegiance, Party included. The Party may hold heavy powers over the actual bureaucracy, but its essential function is catalytic. It is designed to bring not only the people as a whole but the bureaucracy itself into line with the basic purposes of totalitarian society. In the second place, with all allowance for the so-called "dual state" created by the powers of the Party, what is crucial is the fact that the Party is dedicated to the same ends which are sovereign over the whole population and the official bureaucracy. The Party may be outside the formal sphere of governmental administration, but it is never outside the range of ends that are absolute and exclusive in the whole society.

Nor is any other form of association. The monolithic cast of the totalitarian State arises from the sterilization or destruction of all groups and statuses that, in any way, rival or detract from the allegiance of the masses to State.

It is characteristic of the total State, as Peter Drucker has pointed out, that the distinction between ordinary civil society and the army is obliterated. The natural diversity of society is swept away, and the centralization and omnicompetence native to the war band become the organizing principles of human life.... Every decision is converted into a military decision, dependent for its meaning upon the strategies and tactics of war. Every difficulty, every obstacle, is translated by totalitarian leadership into the imagery of war against evil, of defense against aggression. Every significant deviation from official policy—in art and in politics, in science and economy—is ruthlessly exterminated in the name of unity and preparedness. All relationships are conceived eventually in the likeness of those of the garrison.

To convert the whole of society into the ordered regularity of the army may seem a fair estimate of the objectives of Communist and Nazi totalitarianism. But, basically, there is little choice between these objectives and those that seek to convert society into the ordered regularity of the factory, the bureau, or the asylum. We must not be led astray by the analogy of the army. It is not war, anymore than it is race or economic class, that is central. What is central is simply the absolute substitution of the State for all the diversified associations of which society is normally composed.

In the totalitarian order the political tie becomes the all-in-all. It needs the masses as the masses need it. It integrates even where it dissolves, unifies where it separates, inspires where it suffocates. The rulers of the total community devise their own symbolism to replace the symbolism that has been destroyed in the creation of the masses.

The communal likeness of power is indispensable, for power that seems remote and inaccessible will be, no matter how ruthlessly it is imposed, unavailing and ineffectual. At every stage the power of the government must seem to proceed from the basic will of the people. The government thus chooses to bend, soften, and corrode the will to resistance in preference to forcible and brutal breaking of the will. For in the latter lie dread possibilities of overt resistance which might serve to dramatize opposition and create the potent symbolism of martyrdom.

New meanings must therefore be created for popular assimilation. Even new "memories" must be fabricated to replace the memories which, by their continual reminder of a past form of society, would ceaselessly militate against the new form. New conceptions of good and evil, of truth and falsehood, of freedom and tyranny, of the sacred and the secular, must be established in the popular mind to replace those lost or destroyed. History, art, science, and morality, all of these must be redesigned, placed in a new context, in order to make of a power a seamless web of certainty and conformity. Totalitarian power is insupportable unless it is clothed in the garments of deep spiritual belief.

But the spiritual transformation of a people, the creation of new meanings and symbols, cannot proceed apart from the creation of new social contexts of belief and meaning. Here is where the real genius of the totalitarian order becomes manifest.

The atomization of old groups and associations is accompanied by the establishment of new forms of association, each designed to meet the needs and to carry on the functions that were embedded in the old forms of social grouping. To these new associations, each based upon some clear and positive function, inevitably go the allegiances of the masses. In these groups, reaching down to the most primary levels of relationship, lies escape from the intolerable emptiness and demonic nature of mass society. Such groups, in time, come to seem the very difference between membership and isolation, between hope and despair, between existence and non-existence. From them come, for constantly widening aggregates, the anesthetic release from sensations of alienation, hostility, and irrationality. These associations are not only the context of personal identification and belonging; they are also the indispensable contexts of totalitarian indoctrination.

As old cultural values and spiritual meanings become dim and unremembered through the destruction or erosion of social relationships that once made them vivid, so, in the totalitarian order which replaces the old, new meanings and values are given root and solidity in new associations and memberships. With new social status comes in time a new set of allegiances, new values, even new perceptions.

Powerful and unprecedented as it is, totalitarian domination of the individual will is not a mysterious process, not a form of sorcery based upon some vast and unknowable irrationalism. It arises and proceeds rationally and relentlessly through the creation of new functions, statuses, and allegiances, which, by conferring community, makes the manipulation of the human will scarcely more than an exercise in scientific social psychology.

The superficial evidences of the old political structure may be left intact. There may well be a parliament or legislature. Old civil service positions, old titles of office may be left undisturbed. There may be periodic elections or plebiscites, and the terminology of freedom may be broadcast unabatedly. There may be left even the appearance of individual freedom, provided it is *only* individual freedom. All of this is unimportant, always subject to guidance and control, if the primary social contexts of belief and opinion are properly organized and managed. What is central is the creation of a network of functions and loyalties reaching down into the most intimate recesses of human life where ideas and beliefs will germinate and develop.

All the rational skills of modern social manipulation, borrowed from every quarter of modern, large-scale economic and political society, go into the process of reassimilation. New organizations based upon place, work, and interest are created. The same force that seeks constantly to destroy the social substance of the old family is concerned with the establishment of new organizations designed to assimilate each sex and each age group of the family. Labor unions are either remade into agencies of the State, or new labor organizations are created to replace the old. New professional, scientific, and artistic groups are created—even new associations for the varied hobbies of a people.

As the totalitarian psychologist well knows, within these new formal associations based upon clear function and meaning, there will inevitably arise over a period of time the vastly more important network of new *informal* relationships, new interpersonal allegiances and affections, and with them a new sense of personal status, which will reach like a chain from the lowliest individual to the highest center of government.

But the new groups, associations, and formal statuses are without exception agencies of the State itself. They are plural only in number, not in ultimate allegiance or purpose. What we must recognize is that each association is but a social and psychological extension of the central administration of the State. Each exists as a primary context of the political re-personalization of man that follows the nihilistic process of social depersonalization. Each is the instrument, ultimately, of the central government, the psychological setting that alone makes possible the massive remaking of the human consciousness. All such groups, with their profound properties of status, are the means of implementing whatever image—race, proletariat, or mankind—surmounts the structure of the absolute, monolithic, political community. . . .

THE SO-CALLED TOTALITARIAN STATE

Hannah Arendt

What strikes the observer of the totalitarian state is certainly not its monolithic structure. On the contrary, all serious students of the subject agree at least on the co-existence (or the conflict) of a dual authority, the party and the state. Many, moreover, have stressed the peculiar "shapelessness" of the old totalitarian government. Thomas Masaryk saw early that "the so-called Bolshevik system has never been anything but a complete absence of system"[1]; and it is perfectly true that "even an expert would be driven mad if he tired to unravel the relationships between Party and State" in the Third Reich.[2] It has also been frequently observed that the relationship between the two sources of authority, between state and party, is one of ostensible and real authority, so that the government machine is usually pictured as the powerless facade which hides and protects the real power of the party.

All levels of the administrative machine in the Third Reich were subject to a curious duplication of offices. With a fantastic thoroughness, the Nazis made sure that every function of the state administration would be duplicated by some party organ[3]: the Weimar division of Germany into states and provinces was duplicated by the Nazi division into *Gaue* whose borderlines, however, did not coincide, so that every given locality belonged, even geographically, to two altogether different administrative units. Nor was the duplication of functions abandoned when, after 1933, outstanding Nazis occupied the official ministries of the state; when Frick, for instance, became Minister of the Interior or Guerthner Minister of Justice. These old and trusted party members, once they had embarked upon official nonparty

SOURCE: Hannah Arendt, *The Origins of Totalitarianism* (Cleveland: The World Publishing Co., 1958), pp. 395-404, 408-409, 417-418. Reprinted by permission. Several footnotes have been omitted and those remaining have been renumbered.

[1] Quoted from Boris Souvarine, *Stalin: A Critical Survey of Bolshevism* (New York, 1939), p. 695.

[2] Stephen H. Roberts, *The House that Hitler Built* (London, 1939), p. 72.

[3] "For those positions of state power which the National Socialists could not occupy with their own people, they created corresponding 'shadow offices' in their own party organization, in this way setting up a second state beside the state. . . ." (Konrad Heiden, Der Fuehrer: *Hitler's Rise to Power* (Boston, 1944), p. 616.

careers, lost their power and became as uninfluential as other civil servants. Both came under the factual authority of Himmler, the rising chief of the police, who normally would have been subordinate to the Minister of the Interior. . . . Finally, in addition to these party institutions, the Foreign Office received another duplication in the form of an SS Office, which was responsible "for negotiations with all racially Germanic groups in Denmark, Norway, Belgium and the Netherlands." These examples prove that for the Nazis the duplication of offices was a matter of principle and not just an expedient for providing jobs for party members.

The same division between a real and an ostensible government developed from very different beginnings in Soviet Russia.[4] The ostensible government originally sprang from the All-Russian Soviet Congress, which during the civil war lost its influence and power to the Bolshevik party. This process started when the Red Army was made autonomous and the secret political police re-established as an organ of the party, and not of the Soviet Congress[5]; it was completed in 1923, during the first year of Stalin's General Secretaryship. From then on, the Soviets became the shadow government in whose midst, through cells formed by Bolshevik party members, functioned the representatives of real power who were appointed and responsible to the Central Committee in Moscow. The crucial point in the later development was not the conquest of the Soviets by the party, but the fact that "although it would have presented no difficulties, the Bolsheviks did not abolish the Soviets and used them as the decorative outward symbol of their authority."[6]

Duplication of offices and division of authority, the co-existence of real and ostensible power, are sufficient to create confusion but not to explain the "shapelessness" of the whole structure. One should not forget that only a building can have a structure, but that a movement—if the word is to be taken as seriously and as literally as the Nazis meant it—can have only a direction, and that any form of legal or governmental structure can be only a handicap to a movement which is being propelled with increasing speed in a certain direction. Even in the prepower stage the totalitarian movements represented those masses that were no longer willing to live in any kind of structure, regardless of its nature; masses that had started to move in order to flood the legal and geographical borders securely determined by the government. Therefore, judged by our conceptions of government and state structure, these movements, so long as they find themselves physically still limited to a specific territory, necessarily must try to destroy all structure, and for this willful destruction a mere duplication of all offices into party and state institutions would not be sufficient. Since duplication involves a relationship between the facade of the state and the inner core of the party, it, too, would eventually result in some kind of structure, where the relationship between party

---

[4]"Behind the ostensible government was a real government," which Victor Kravchenko [*I Chose Freedom: The Personal Life of a Soviet Official* (New York, 1946), p. 111] saw in the "secret police system."

[5]See Arthur Rosenberg, *A History of Bolshevism* (London, 1934), chapter 6. "There are in reality two political edifices in Russia that rise parallel to one another: the shadow government of the Soviets and the *de facto* government of the Bolshevik Party."

[6]*Ibid.*

and state would automatically end in a legal regulation which restricts and stabilizes their respective authority.

As a matter of fact, duplication of offices, seemingly the result of the party-state problem in all one-party dictatorships, is only the most conspicuous sign of a more complicated phenomenon that is better defined as multiplication of offices than duplication. The Nazis were not content to establish *Gaue* in addition to the old provinces, but also introduced a great many other geographical divisions in accordance with the different party organizations; the territorial units of the SA were neither co-extensive with the *Gaue* nor with the provinces; they differed, moreover, from those of the SS and none of them corresponded to the zones dividing the Hitler Youth. To this geographical confusion must be added the fact that the original relationship between real and ostensible power repeated itself throughout, albeit in an ever-changing way. The inhabitant of Hitler's Third Reich lived not only under the simultaneous and often conflicting authorities of competing powers, such as the civil services, the party, the SA, and the SS; he could never be sure and was never explicitly told whose authority he was supposed to place above all others. He had to develop a kind of sixth sense to know at a given moment whom to obey and whom to disregard.

Those, on the other hand, who had to execute the orders which the leadership, in the interest of the movement, regarded as genuinely necessary—in contradistinction to governmental measures, such orders were of course entrusted only to the party's elite formations—were not much better off. Mostly such orders were "intentionally vague, and given in the expectation that their recipient would recognize the intent of the order giver, and act accordingly"[7]; for the elite formations were by no means merely obligated to obey the orders of the Fuehrer (this was mandatory for all existing organizations anyway), but "to execute the *will* of the leadership." And, as can be gathered from the lengthy proceedings concerning "excesses" before the party courts, this was by no means one and the same thing. The only difference was that the elite formations, thanks to their special indoctrination for such purposes, had been trained to understand that certain "hints meant more than their mere verbal contents."

Technically speaking, the movement within the apparatus of totalitarian domination derives its mobility from the fact that the leadership constantly shifts the actual center of power, often to other organizations, but without dissolving or even publicly exposing the groups that have thus been deprived of their power. In the early period of the Nazi regime, immediately after the Reichstag fire, the SA was the real authority and the party the ostensible one; power then shifted from the SA to the SS and finally from the SS to the Security Service. The point is that none of the organs of power was ever deprived of its right to pretend that it embodied the will of the Leader. But not only was the will of the Leader so unstable that compared with it the whims of Oriental despots are a shining example of steadfastness; the consistent and ever-changing division between real secret authority and ostensible open representation made the actual seat of power a mystery by

---

[7]Nuremberg Documents, PS 3063 in the Centre de Documentation Juive in Paris.

definition, and this to such an extent that the members of the ruling clique themselves could never be absolutely sure of their own position in the secret power hierarchy. . . .

In other words, since knowledge of whom to obey and a comparatively permanent settlement of hierarchy would introduce an element of stability which is essentially absent from totalitarian rule, the Nazis constantly disavowed real authority whenever it had come into the open and created new instances of government compared with which the former became a shadow government—a game which obviously could go on indefinitely. One of the most important technical differences between the Soviet and the National Socialist system is that Stalin, whenever he shifted the power emphasis within his own movement from one apparatus to another, had the tendency to liquidate the apparatus together with its staff, while Hitler, in spite of his comtemptuous comments on people who "are unable to leap across their own shadows,"[8] was perfectly willing to continue using these shadows even though in another function.

The multiplication of offices was extremely useful for the constant shifting of power; the longer, moreover, a totalitarian regime stays in power, the greater becomes the number of offices and the possibility of jobs exclusively dependent upon the movement, since no office is abolished when its authority is liquidated. The Nazi regime started this multiplication with an initial co-ordination of all existing associations, societies, and institutions. The interesting thing in this nation-wide manipulation was that co-ordination did not signify incorporation into the already existing respective party organizations. The result was that up to the end of the regime, there were not one, but two National Socialist student organizations, two Nazi women's organizations, two Nazi organizations for university professors, lawyers, physicians, and so forth. It was by no means sure, however, that in all cases the original party organizations would be more powerful than its co-ordinated counterpart. Nor could anybody predict with any assurance which party organ would rise in the ranks of the internal party hierarchy. . . .

The facade of the Soviet government, despite its written constitution, is even less impressive, erected even more exclusively for foreign observation than the state administration which the Nazis inherited and retained from the Weimar Republic. Lacking the Nazis' original accumulation of offices in the period of co-ordination, the Soviet regime relies even more on constant creation of new offices to put the former centers of power in the shadow. The gigantic increase of the bureaucratic apparatus, inherent in this method, is checked by repeated liquidation through purges. Nevertheless, in Russia, too, we can distinguish at least three strictly separate organizations: the Soviet or state apparatus, the party apparatus, and the NKVD apparatus, each of which has its own independent department of economy, a political department, a ministry of education and culture, a military department, etc.

In Russia, the ostensible power of the party bureaucracy as against the real power of the secret police corresponds to the original duplication of party and state as

---

[8] *Hitlers Tischgespräche* (Bonn, 1951), p. 213.

known in Nazi Germany, and the multiplication becomes evident only in the secret police itself, with its extremely complicated, widely ramified network of agents, in which one department is always assigned to supervising and spying on another. Every enterprise in the Soviet Union has its special department of the secret police, which spies on party members and ordinary personnel alike. Co-existent with this department is another police division of the party itself, which again watches everybody, including the agents of the NKVD, and whose members are not known to the rival body. Added to these two espionage organizations must be the unions in the factories, which must see to it that the workers fulfill their prescribed quotas. Far more important than these apparatuses, however, is "the special department" of the NKVD which represents "an NKVD within the NKVD," *i.e.*, a secret police within the secret police. All reports of these competing police agencies ultimately end up in the Moscow Central Committee and the Politburo. Here it is decided which of the reports is decisive and which of the police divisions shall be entitled to carry out the respective police measures. Neither the average inhabitant of the country nor any one of the police departments knows, of course, what decision will be made; today it may be the special division of the NKVD, tomorrow the party's network of agents; the day after, it may be the local committees or one of the regional bodies. Among all these departments there exists no legally rooted hierarchy of power or authority; the only certainty is that eventually one of them will be chosen to embody "the will of the leadership."

The only rule of which everybody in a totalitarian state may be sure is that the more visible government agencies are, the less power they carry, and the less is known of the existence of an institution, the more powerful it will ultimately turn out to be. According to this rule, the Soviets, recognized by a written constitution as the highest authority of the state, have less power than the Bolshevik party; the Bolshevik party, which recruits its members openly and is recognized as the ruling class, has less power than the secret police. Real power begins where secrecy begins. In this respect the Nazi and the Bolshevik states were very much alike; their difference lay chiefly in the monopolization and centralization of secret police services in Himmler on one hand, and the maze of apparently unrelated and unconnected police activities in Russia on the other.

If we consider the totalitarian state solely as an instrument of power and leave aside questions of administrative efficiency, industrial capacity, and economic productivity, then its shapelessness turns out to be an ideally suited instrument for the realization of the so-called Leader principle. A continuous competition between offices, whose functions not only overlap but which are charged with identical tasks, gives opposition or sabotage almost no chance to become effective; a swift change of emphasis which relegates one office to the shadow and elevates another to authority can solve all problems without anybody's becoming aware of the change or of the fact that opposition had existed, the additional advantage of the system being that the opposing office is likely never to learn of its defeat, since it is either not abolished at all (as in the case of the Nazi regime) or it is liquidated much later and without any apparent connection with the specific matter. This can be done all the more easily since nobody, except these few initiated, knows the exact relationship between the authorities. . . .

As techniques of government, the totalitarian devices appear simple and ingeniously effective. They assure not only an absolute power monopoly, but unparalleled certainty that all commands will always be carried out; the multiplicity of the transmission belts, the confusion of the hierarchy, secure the dictator's complete independence of all his inferiors and make possible the swift and surprising changes in policy for which totalitarianism has become famous. The body politic of the country is shock-proof because of its shapelessness. . . .

The trouble with totalitarian regimes is not that they play power politics in an especially ruthless way, but that behind their politics is hidden an entirely new and unprecedented concept of power, just as behind their *Realpolitik* lies an entirely new and unprecedented concept of reality. Supreme disregard for immediate consequences rather than ruthlessness; rootlessness and neglect of national interests rather than nationalism; contempt for utilitarian motives rather than unconsidered pursuit of self-interest; "idealism," *i.e.*, their unwavering faith in an ideological fictitious world, rather than just for power—these have all introduced into international politics a new and more disturbing factor than mere aggressiveness would have been able to do.

Power, as conceived by totalitarianism, lies exclusively in the force produced through organization. . . .

PROGRESS, REVOLUTION, AND FREEDOM

Barrington Moore, Jr.

I. For quite some time there has been a concerted effort to bar the terms "progressive" and "reactionary" from any discussion of human affairs that claimed to be objective or scientific. In the academic disciplines of political science, sociology, and history the attempt has enjoyed a large measure of success, though one can still come upon unreconstructed thinkers who continue to use these terms. The main argument against their use is that the terms carry with them ethical and factually incorrect judgments to the effect that the course of history has been, in general, an advance toward greater freedom of the individual.

Anyone with a sharp ear can detect the muffled sounds of a grinding axe on both sides of this discussion. Those who seek to outlaw the terms "progressive" and "reactionary" are trying to strike the main weapons from the hands of certain social critics: those who use historical theories of human society to criticize the existing

SOURCE: Reprinted by permission of the publishers from Barrington Moore, Jr., *Political Power and Social Theory* (Cambridge, Mass.: Harvard University Press). Copyright 1958, 1962, by the President and Fellows of Harvard College.

social order. Hegel and Marx are, of course, the most important figures here, though they are no more than the culmination of a long train of thought. One of the more disagreeable conclusions that can be drawn from these theories is that any society, including our own, is destined to become antiquated and replaced by something better.[1]

The experience of the past fifty years has of course been very hard on theories of progress. Two world wars, the retreat of parliamentary democracy, the rise of totalitarian governments, concentration camps, and the perfection of the means of mass destruction are facts difficult to square with any theory of progress. Yet they are not the only facts. During the same period the material condition of the masses has almost certainly improved in large areas of the world, and promises to rise further. Future historians of freedom might find this to be the most significant fact of all. Such considerations, together with the obvious political partisanship, in effect if not by intention, of those who reject the concept of progress, make it appear worthwhile to have a fresh look at the problem. The following remarks do not pretend to be more than observations, set down, I hope, in a fairly satisfactory logical order, that have occurred to me in the course of other research.

It is appropriate to begin with the question: Do the terms "progressive" and "reactionary" have any objective meaning—that is, any meaning independent of the political hopes and dislikes of thinkers who use these words? Do they refer to any real facts?[2]

"Progress" in ordinary speech means movement in a single direction toward an approved goal. Then the question becomes in part: Is it possible to discern any unidirectional movement in human history? Now there is at least one area, technology, in which there is overwhelming factual evidence of continual advance from the earliest record of *homo sapiens* down to the present day. Even the most confirmed opponent of theories of cultural evolution must concede this point in the face of the evidence accumulated by now.[3] To be sure, there are occasional setbacks. But there can be no doubt about the general trend.

As soon as one concedes the fact of technical advance, one must make other concessions as well. There is no need to be a technological determinist to realize that changes in technology are accompanied by changes in social structure. Here I do not propose to discuss what the main phases of human history have been. All that is necessary for the argument is that *some* notion of phases is bound to make

---

[1] In both Hegel and Marx the movement of history comes to a stop at a definite point, when their particular social ideal has been reached. This seems to me a device to bar criticism of their ideal. Thus they adopt the same technique as their critics. Others, such as Condorcet, adopt the dubious assumption of endless perfectibility to get around this difficulty. To be consistent one would have to hold that the history of humanity is but one stage in the course of progress and that some other form of life may take over the torch after human history has reached its upper limit. But here we have already passed the bounds of profitable speculation, as is often the case in pushing a theory to its logical conclusion.

[2] Progress might have a perfectly unambiguous meaning even if it did not refer to any historical facts. It might simply be an ideal for the future.

[3] For the present state of the question see the papers in Betty J. Meggers ed., *Evolution and Anthropology* (Washington, 1959).

sense. In a civilization, for example, that uses electricity and internal combustion engines as its main sources of energy, we are unlikely to find the gathering of shellfish as the chief way of obtaining food, or the tribe as the main form of social organization. Thus it seems clear that we must grant the objective existence of some form of advance as part of an overall historical process.

At this point, however, it is quite legitimate to deny that technological advance with all its consequences implies movement toward freedom.[4] It is doubtful that there has been any trend toward greater freedom in the course of human history. The most that the facts allow us to assert with any confidence is an advance in important prerequisites of freedom, through the elimination of the necessity for hunger, disease, and toil. (Need one add that we have not yet reached the end of this road?) And the same advance in the prerequisites of freedom has simultaneously provided the prerequisites for dynamic and terrifying despotism. Without modern weapons and methods of mass communication twentieth-century totalitarian states could not exist, even though these technological advances cannot by themselves be regarded as the fundamental cause of these horrors.

Despite these objections, the advance in the prerequisites of freedom seems clear enough and important enough to justify the use of the term "progress." That will be its meaning in this essay. What the facts demand is that we separate progress, so defined, from movement toward freedom itself. If we regard progress as distinct from advance toward freedom, it becomes possible to ask what relationship there may be between the two.

II. Marxists also distinguish between progress in the prerequisites of freedom and the advance of freedom itself. At the same time they frequently identify the advocates of liberty with political progress and the enemies of liberty with reaction.

There are certain reasons for doubting this connection as well as some that Marxists can advance to support it. The opposing arguments differ in their logical structure and the way they represent social reality. Both points of view shed

---

[4] As used here, the term "freedom" has simultaneously (1) the negative meaning of the absence of constraint on concrete human beings and (2) the positive meaning of opportunities to make important choices among real alternatives, at least one of which is desirable according to an objective standard. Thus a young man who can choose whether he will become a doctor or a lawyer is more free than one who must choose whether he will remain a poor peasant or become a coolie.

As far as I can tell, any definition of freedom is open to objection on some ground. Even though this consideration calls for charity, I would reject as too subjective the definition recently proposed by Robert A. Dahl and Charles E. Lindblom in *Politics, Economics, and Welfare* (New York, 1953), p. 31, where the authors define freedom as the "absence of obstacles to the realization of desires." What desires, one may reasonably ask? By such a definition any brainwashed, goose-stepping fanatic becomes a free man. Any notion limited to "felt freedom" flings open the door to all the irrational self-deceptions that are among the main enemies of freedom today. At times these self-deceptions may be more dangerous in formally democratic countries than in totalitarian ones. Under a totalitarian regime official doctrine exists as something crudely external and hostile to many individuals who reject it as a matter of course. In a formally democratic country the same type of moderately intelligent citizen may accept official lies because they are defined for him as the "impartial" outcome of free discussion.

valuable light on the problems of despotism and liberty. By using each to reveal the shortcomings of the other it may be possible to perceive the real situation more clearly, or at least to raise important yet neglected questions.

As a matter of historical fact, by no means every reactionary movement has advocated despotism. Nor have progressive movements always been the upholders of liberty. Hence it may be worthwhile to glance at the possible combinations and some of their concrete historical manifestations. Logically these are four: Authoritarian-reactionary, Libertarian-reactionary, Libertarian-progressive, Authoritarian-progressive. This scheme is no magic formula to order all political phenomena. As the analysis proceeds, we shall see its limitations. The value of any classificatory scheme lies merely in the way it calls attention to relationships we might otherwise overlook.

The authoritarian-reactionary type of regime is a familiar one. Sparta might be cited as a Western example, the Legalist movement in ancient China as an Oriental one. Both were despotic; both were backward-looking in that they involved strong attempts to prevent technical progress. More specifically both were efforts to prevent the undermining of an agrarian elite through commercial relationships and a money economy.

It is somewhat more difficult to find concrete examples of the libertarian-reactionary combination. At least I am unable to think of any large community where such a movement has held power for a substantial period of time. But it is not too difficult to come upon important political currents that match the specifications. Certain forms of nineteenth-century and even twentieth-century agrarian populism and anarchism show a strong inclination to reject the technical advances of modern life. Gandhi's movement in India is perhaps the most widely known example. Their positive goal is a return to some form of simple community where, they argue, the freedom of the individual can be achieved. Though they share with some authoritarian-reactionary movements a marked hostility toward the intrusion of commercial influences and motivations into social life, they differ from the preceding variety in their strong hostility to the agrarian elite (nobility, plantation owners, and the like).

The third combination is the libertarian-progressive one. At least in theory it is familiar to us as the basic ideal of Western democracy. In the present context its most important feature is the belief that political conflicts can be resolved through rational argument and compromise among free men, together with the institutional arrangements that give effect to this belief. Some of the difficulties inherent in this viewpoint will come up in the course of further discussion.

The notion of an authoritarian-progressive movement is familiar from the phrase "dictatorship of the proletariat." The essence of the notion is of course that the dictatorship—the use of force and terror—is a necessary but temporary phase to sweep aside the weakened remnants of the *ancien régime*. In Marxist theory, then, it is the necessary historical prelude to a regime of greater human freedom. Though the facts are open to debate, perhaps one can point to Robespierre's dictatorship as fulfilling this function for the bourgeois revolution. On the other hand, in Russia, as matters worked out in practice, the "dictatorship of the proletariat"—in which the proletariat played almost no role—served not only to sweep away the *ancien régime*, but far more significantly to *create* the economic and social basis for a new social order. Shortly we shall have to come back to the problems raised by this form. But I do not think it is too much to grant that the authoritarian-progressive movement is a recognizable political species.

As already stated, this rough classification makes no claim to exhaust all the varied forms of political reality. No concrete political movement fits absolutely exactly into the scheme. What the scheme does help to bring out, I believe, is, first of all, that the terms "progressive" and "reactionary" have recognizable counterparts in historical and social reality. The overtones of approval or disapproval in these terms need not obscure their objective meaning. Indeed, as pointed out above, it is perfectly possible to approve of reactionary movements and disapprove of progressive ones. What nearly always happens, however, is that the political philosopher approves of *only one* of these four combinations. He may like libertarian-progressive movements and disapprove of authoritarian-progressive ones, as well as both authoritarian- and libertarian-reactionary ones. That would seem to be still the dominant philosophy in American academic circles today. There is no need to mention the other forms of approval and disapproval.

III. There are certain objections that a Marxist might legitimately make to the preceding conclusions and the reasoning upon which they are based. First, such thinkers might hold that in the analysis of any political movement it is necessary to distinguish between what the movement advocates and the objective historical consequences that flow from the appearance of such a movement. In the same vein they might argue that any formal scheme such as this one does violence to reality by tearing facts from their historical context. To a Marxist the most important fact about any form of social structure is its relationship to what precedes it and what follows it. Any valid system of classification must have this element of change built into it from the start, or it will produce grotesque distortions, just as a snapshot of a person walking often grotesquely distorts the realities of movement.

More specifically a Marxist might assert that the agrarian populist and anarchist movements, classified above as libertarian-reactionary, are merely attempts to put back the clock of history. Unless they ally themselves or come under the leadership of urban movements of revolt they will either be doomed to failure or else they will, in their consequences, serve the cause of despotic reaction, turning into such phenomena as anti-Semitic pogroms. . . . (cf. the Black Hundreds in Russia). Thus the libertarian-reactionary is an unstable, even protean, transitional form that arises as more advanced economic relationships penetrate the countryside.

The authoritarian-progressive category, to continue the Marxist argument, also describes a transitional phase. A revolutionary dictatorship, exercised on behalf of an oppressed class as it emerges to power, is often an indispensable step toward freedom.

Here we encounter the most important problems of all. Can a revolutionary dictatorship be merely a transitional phase? Will it necessarily seek to perpetuate itself? Is violence a necessary feature of humanity's hesitating steps toward freedom? Such questions cannot be answered in general formulas abstracted from concrete historical situations. Nevertheless it may be possible to make certain general suggestions that are helpful in assessing concrete circumstances, those of the future as well as of the past. What the Marxists are trying to tell us is that a rough calculus of revolutionary violence is not only possible but indispensable if the forces of freedom are not to paralyze themselves by refusing to use their strength. Let us look at the argument as carefully and dispassionately as we can.

IV. When, then, is violence justified and why? First of all, the Marxists tell us, it must be used on behalf of freedom. The enemies of freedom can be counted on to have few scruples about the resort to force. If the friends of freedom tie their own hands by abstract scruples, they will merely guarantee the triumph of the status quo. From this standpoint too one must draw some sharp distinctions according to the uses to which force may be put. For a Hitler, violence was almost an end in itself; at the most an instrument to maintain the hegemony of one group over another. Its purpose was frankly and strictly repressive. For a Stalin, violence was a means to catapult an agrarian country into the modern world, eliminating disease, famine, and illiteracy. This is not to say that all of Stalin's victims were somehow "historically necessary." It would be hard to find any Marxists willing to defend such a position today. It does mean that one cannot merely equate Hitler and Stalin as some contemporary liberals are inclined to do.

Probably no one but the most doctrinaire pacifist would object to the view that violence can be justified on behalf of freedom. Still, when is *revolutionary* violence justified? Essentially the Marxist answer, as I understand it, asserts, "when the prevailing social order is unnecessarily repressive." It is possible to assert, in principle at any rate, that a given type of social order is unnecessarily repressive on strictly factual grounds. Where scientific and technological advance has made certain kinds of suffering (such as extreme toil, hunger, disease and ignorance) obsolete and unnecessary, there is a justification for designating any society in which they still occur an unduly repressive one. A society that destroys food when people are starving, the Marxists declared thirty years ago, is unnecessarily repressive and ripe for upheaval. Nowadays this argument has a rather anachronistic ring, a point to which I will return later. When we have some reasonable assurance that another system will work more satisfactorily, to continue the Marxist view, it is time to support revolutionary action.

As part of this argument the Marxists make one point that I think deserves to be stressed. Those of us who are skeptical of revolutionary changes at once point to the Reign of Terror as part of the terrible price of revolution. But the mere continuation of the existing social order exacts its tragic price too. How many children die in India each year as part of the price of a "reasonable" rate of economic advance? How many adults died in two world wars as part of the price of a system of "free and independent" states? The calculus of suffering likely to result from revolutionary violence[5] must include that which will come from prolonging the present state of affairs.

Thus the failure to seize a revolutionary opportunity and to exercise it resolutely may throw victory to the reactionary forces and be the cause of prolonged disaster for the forces of freedom. Under these circumstances the appearance of such slogans as "free speech for all" merely reveals a lack of conviction and the absence of intelligent political realism on the part of groups that advance them. More than that, such slogans are really hypocritical, since they sound liberal but actually serve the cause of bloody reaction. The behavior of the democratic socialists in Germany at the close of the First World War, when their adherence to "democracy" and "law and order" opened the door to the reactionaries and, in the long run, to Hitler, can be cited as one recent example of what happens when liberal slogans substitute for vigorous action. Many others are available from the history of revolutionary movements. By these justifications for the use of violence the Marxists might seek to reestablish the fundamental link between progress and freedom.

At the very least one must confess that the Marxist argument is a powerful and disturbing one. To repeat complacent clichés about the virtues of democratic discussion and the vices of despotic dictatorship may reassure the readers of so-called intelligent magazines. It cannot substitute for real discussion.

V. Obviously then one cannot reject violence merely as a matter of principle. This rejection is the weak point in the armor of those who oppose communism on the ground that Communists "won't obey the rules of the game" and seek their objectives by violence. The game itself may be unfair, and the rules enforced by those who have something to lose by change. Nor are free elections in and by themselves any guarantee of a free society. The Nazis in Germany came to power under reasonably free elections. People can be taught in both subtle and brutal ways to prefer repression to freedom. Repressive vested interests in a democracy can dominate the press, radio, television, set standards for "sound" appointments in academic life, and influence the climate of opinion to the point where "free elections" become meaningless, or even a reactionary slogan. The notion of free choice makes no sense where the person making the choice has been systematically deprived of insight into the meaning of his action. Totalitarian dictatorships try to accomplish this by terror and propaganda. Modern democracies may get the same results more effectively by presenting the citizens with pseudo-alternatives.

Yet, even if we cannot reject violence on principle, or use-its application to distinguish tyranny from freedom, we do not have to endorse it either. The ideal glimpsed by John Stuart Mill, where men can discuss their differences both passionately and reasonably in order to reach rational conclusions about the ordering of social affairs, is in my opinion both more realistic and more attractive than the

---

[5]By far the largest proportion of the victims in the French and Russian revolutionary dictatorships were the revolutionists themselves. As each section of society gains it objectives, it detaches itself from the revolution. Therefore, as the social base of the revolution shrinks, the remaining radical group resorts more and more to terror, mainly against its former allies. The Marxist notion of a temporary revolutionary dictatorship directed mainly against the *ancien régime* fails to bring out these important facts.

secular utopia of the Marxists. Mill's argument is more realistic insofar as it does not assume that history will come to a stop when men have solved some of their most important problems. His standpoint allows for permanent change and permanent dissent. He is more attractive in that, unlike both secular and religious utopians, he refrains from positing any form of eternal bliss suitable to only a few temperaments, that of their convinced advocates.[6]

At the same time it is necessary to confess that the conditions under which rational yet passionate discussion will work are very rare and have only been approximated at a few points in human history. What are these conditions? To spell them out in detail would be too much of an undertaking here. One may suggest that at the psychological level they require a certain maturity and balance in the human personality. At the level of history and sociology they may boil down to a rate of "progress" slow enough not to frighten unduly the defenders of the status quo and rapid enough to satisfy at least moderately those who suffer under the prevailing system. England in Mill's day roughly approximated this situation. Still speaking in rather general terms, at first glance it might seem possible to reconcile the two standpoints by holding that modern society may have to pass through the revolutionary fires prescribed by Marx in order to attain the situation hoped for by Mill. If the type of freedom envisaged by Mill were to grow out of a successful revolution, the society in which the revolution occurred would have to be relatively "advanced." The material base for the elimination of toil, disease, and starvation would have to exist. The society would have to have reached a point where sweeping aside the remnants of an outmoded social order would not be so bloody and difficult a process as to make subsequent reconciliation and the operation of a free society impossible. That is roughly the situation Marx envisaged—and which failed to materialize.

"Through Marx to Mill" seems unpromising enough as a slogan the moment it is uttered. Is there something wrong with it beyond its superficial appearance of paradox? I suggest that there is, but not at the level of paradox. The ideas we associate with these names may not be as much of an oil-and-water mixture as commonly supposed. The point is more important: both the Marxist and the liberal intellectual framework may now be inadequate to cope with the problem of freedom and progress. Both may be the prisoners of their own past history and the circumstances under which they arose, and may mislead us seriously when we apply them uncritically to contemporary problems.

Marx wrote at a time when concrete material poverty and brutal physical oppression contrasted with scientific and technical progress that in his view rendered such suffering unnecessary. Since his day the problem has changed its character. The "success" of capitalism and socialism is known to every newspaper reader. Professional intellectuals in both systems devote much energy to demonstrating that the achievements of their own system have been due to the virtues of its philosophy and the integrity of its leaders, while the shortcomings of the opposite system are

---

[6]Marx of course did allow for considerable variety under the new dispensation (*see German Ideology*). This relatively minor current in Marxism largely disappeared later.

due to the inadequacy of its philosophy and the moral depravity of its leaders. There may be some truth in these statements but, in the words of H. L. Mencken, precious little. The main factor in the success of both systems has been the existence of a powerful enemy.[7]

It was not Keynesian economics that saved Western capitalism, but a war boom. For the past twenty years we have had nothing else. Economists may tell us that they know enough about the mechanics of our economy to prevent a collapse if the war boom stopped tomorrow. I am willing to accept the strictly technical aspects of the argument. But I am highly skeptical about the political side, which economists generally refrain from discussing. In the United States war prosperity reaches into every street and hamlet, not to mention every university campus. What an outcry its removal would produce! Do we really have anything that could replace it as the motor that keeps so much of our society going?

The role of the foreign enemy in creating the Soviet regime is too familiar to require more than passing comment. Soviet bureaucracy came into being as a repressive organization to hold down living standards and crush any manifestation of opinion that ran counter to the objectives of the revolutionary elite. There are those who maintain that the Soviet government, unlike the American, could withstand the shock of losing its enemy, because the Soviet bureaucracy could then devote its full resources to raising living standards. Granted that such questions cannot receive definitive answers, I hold that this view is part of Marxist mythology. It is highly unlikely that a state created in the fire of liquidating whole social classes could transform itself, without another revolutionary upheaval, into the "administration of things" or, let us say, into an efficient agency to produce and distribute frozen foods.

At a more general level it is possible to agree that a socialist state may not have *all* or even necessarily the same aggressive and repressive features that appear, at least in some countries, in the late stages of capitalist society. But there have been wars and despotic regimes before capitalism. On the record so far, socialism seems quite capable of developing and intensifying its own historical variety of these plagues.[8] Socialism may be especially vulnerable to the abuses of power because the anarchist streak in socialist theory blinds socialists to real problems. To be sure, the Russian Communists have come a long way since the day when Lenin asserted that any cook could run the country. But their abundant practical experience and lore have never really amalgamated with the idealistic theory. The arts of casuistry paper over the gap for ceremonial occasions. While the practical man of affairs resents the theory as a nuisance, at the same time he organizes much of his experience in terms of its categories.[9]

---

[7] It is hardly necessary to add that the enemy need not have a radically different social system.

[8] Socialists blame the "distortions" of socialism on the existence of capitalism, just as liberals in the West see the defects of liberal capitalism as the consequence of the Soviet threat. Both views are equally onesided.

[9] The same tension between ideals and practices exists on both sides of the Cold War. Meanwhile each antagonist interprets the behavior of the other as a form of simple-minded yet Machiavellian hypocrisy.

Least of all have socialists been able to answer the question: Who is to control the planners? How does one get the enormous benefits of a centralized coordination without its turning into despotism? Is it indeed possible to get the kind of co-ordination necessary to operate a huge economic network without a strong dose of compulsion? Transferring the means of production to "the workers" or "the people" tells us practically nothing about how "the workers" will have to organize themselves to carry on the tasks of production and distribution. Advances in automation can be expected to lighten the purely physical labor of the task. At the same time the general process of technological advance can be expected to multiply the tasks of allocation and coordination and to make the various parts of the world increasingly strategic to one another. The notion of freely organized socialist communities living peacefully with one another does seem to be a utopian image carried into the modern world from a pretechnological age.

Thus powerful forces in favor of a repressive and stultifying form of society continue to arise from the internal dynamics of the socialist camp as well as from the relationship between this camp and its antagonists. If this reasoning is correct, the Soviet leaders would very likely be as horrified by the sudden disappearance of the United States as Wall Street might be by the disappearance of the Soviet Union. What this amounts to is that the continuing success of both systems rests on a fundamentally destructive base. While there are important differences in the character of this base, in both cases the essential element is fear of the enemy.

Thus there has been a fundamental change in the character of the revolutionary task since Marx's day. What remains valid is his insight that modern society rests on the threat of destruction. At the same time in "advanced" countries only tiny and ineffective minorities are interested in changing the situation radically enough to make any difference. At a moment in history when, from the standpoint of a commitment to freedom, there may be the greatest need for revolution there is the least desire for it. These two facts are of course intimately connected with one another, a form of dialectical change that Marx did not foresee.

One obvious implication is that crucial aspects of the Marxist analysis are indeed obsolete. The opposition to revolutionary change in the United States is no mere reflection of capitalist vested interests. To a very limited extent Marxists can "save the appearances" for their theory by pointing to the conflict between former colonial areas and a declining capitalist imperialism. But it seems that the backward countries are mainly anxious to create the situation that already prevails in the advanced ones. They want to go through Russia to reach America. At least such is the attitude of the articulate and the influential in many areas. So far there are few grounds for anticipating that revolutionary contagion will spread to industrially advanced areas. At the most it may gradually undermine further the capitalist position, in any case very much on the defensive since the end of World War II. That freedom will advance from this decline (again as distinct from the material bases for freedom) would be much harder to demonstrate.

The liberal position is equally obsolete, and not merely because the Cold War poisons all serious discussion by narrowing the range of alternatives. More important is the fact that the fundamental preconditions of free discussion—some degree of equality among the participants and some opportunity to change the situation through rational persuasion—no longer exist. Present-day liberals will probably take violent exception to this interpretation. Can they, however, point to any significant area of human affairs in which liberal methods have solved a problem and won a clear victory over the forces of blood and iron, *without* calling on these forces and becoming in great measure their prisoner?

To sum up, neither the conditions of orderly progress as envisaged by nineteenth-century liberalism nor those of revolutionary progress as seen by their Marxist contemporaries prevail today.

At the moment we live in an age of obsolete political dinosaurs, who are still very dangerous. Nor does there seem to be any realistic prospect that they will become either smaller or less dangerous. What makes it worse is that most people cannot bear to think of them as dangerous, but insist on regarding them as somehow mainly benign, if occasionally stern and irascible, father figures. Like Job, we simply cannot conceive of the possibility that Yahweh is an arbitrary brute.

VI. This brief essay is not the place to undertake a "solution." If it has succeeded in demonstrating the existence of some misconceptions that bar the way to solutions, it will have solved its purpose. Nevertheless it may be appropriate to close with a few suggestions about the direction in which the solution may lie and the possibilities of progress toward it.

If the analysis in the preceding pages is near the mark, a "plague on both your houses" would seem to be the only starting point consistent with a commitment to freedom today. Naturally this stand is not limited to support for purely technical schemes for achieving world government, which are, in Halévy's vivid phrase, no more than aspirin for an earthquake. Here I can only point at some of the problems involved. But the objective is reasonably clear: to maintain as much of the scientific and technical achievements of modern civilization, as well as its social organization, as is, or will be, necessary to meet biological needs and those civilized ones that are not imposed by repressive vested interests. The rest we can junk. We can keep good medicine and dispense with expensively advertised pills for tired blood. We can keep bravery, intelligence, and a sense of humor in coping with the many tragedies inevitable in any society at any time. But we can do without brainwashing and super-patriotism.

Conceivably humanity may have to pass through another major war, even a series of them. If a world state emerges from the slaughter and destruction, one could still call it progress. Naturally there is nothing inevitable about such an outcome, and there is a very strong possibility that all civilization, indeed all life, may be destroyed first. On the other hand, all experience seems to be against the possibility of peaceful federation in the absence of an external enemy. Even the threat of universal destruction is unlikely to make the people of any major country force its government to give in to the demands of a major opponent to the point where it involves the loss of sovereignty and the reorganization of their own society.

If a world state ever does emerge from conquest, will it necessarily be a super-tyranny? Will we not have the world of Tacitus and Suetonius amplifed a thousand-fold by the power of modern technology? Did we not assert a moment ago that a state created with violence could scarely transform itself without further revolutionary upheaval into the "administration of things"?

I admit and would even wish to emphasize the force of these arguments. There are compelling grounds for the belief that humanity is subject to the fate of Sisyphus: forever creating the prerequisites of freedom and in this very way destroying the possibility of freedom. Such does seem to be the tale of "progress" from our present vantage point.

Yet these arguments do not constitute the whole story, and our present vantage point may obscure real if distant possibilities. That a world state would be a super-tyranny at least for a time seems highly likely. Nevertheless such an achievement could conceivably destroy some of the main bases and sources of contemporary forms of tyranny. It would mean the overcoming of our present situation in which the success of each of the main social and political systems depends upon the threat of a foreign enemy.

Nor is it absolutely inevitable that any form of centralized authority has to be tyrannical. This widespread notion owes much of its force to the eloquence and insight of De Tocqueville. One may summarize his message fairly accurately in these terms. Centralized authority tends to be tyrannical because it destroys those niches and resting places in an old and tradition-dominated society where independent and cantankerous minds may find a refuge. Equality can lead to a similar result. De Tocqueville performed a most valuable service in calling attention to real dangers. His point is valid, though not the whole truth. To limit our conception of freedom and its sources to this view alone is to narrow our vision unnecessarily and to bar any change whatever in the organization of society. To take De Tocqueville this literally would be to hold that only a decaying *ancien régime* contains the possibility of freedom. The injustices of such regimes give the lie to this vulgarized version of his thesis. Franco and Salazar, not to mention restoration France with which De Tocqueville had little sympathy, provide enough evidence to discard this argument.

Even today non-tyrannical forms of centralized authority are more pervasive than we sometimes realize. There is a whole fund of very prosaic experience from the operation of a post office to the authority of a ship's commander that bears witness to the possibility of its existence. Often enough its consequences are vexations, as in the case of the orders of a traffic policeman, or even painful, as in the case of a doctor's. The common features in all these humble examples are the competence of the person holding this authority and widespread agreement on objectives for which authority is granted. Where these features are present and where the objectives themselves are not destructive, we generally regard authority as just, no matter how centralized.

Very many knotty factual problems require convincing answers before it becomes possible to apply this criterion in practice. Those who benefit by a social institution are likely to claim that its repressive features are essential to its virtues, while those who suffer often see little but a mass of injustices. Modern and ancient imperialisms provide only the more striking examples of these familiar rationalizations. It is extremely difficult, probably impossible, to determine how much brutality was part of the necessary historical ingredients for the creation of Roman law. About contemporary problems the evidence for making such judgments is more abundant, but detachment and a capacity for objective appraisal seem harder to achieve.

All these difficulties are obvious enough; so obvious that we must beware of those who use them to bludgeon us into refusing to ask embarrassing questions about our own and other societies. And for the present argument no more than a general principle is at stake: that freedom requires just authority. Difficult as they are to reconcile in practice, the tradition that they are compatible is a sound one.

It is much more difficult to establish justified authority in the political sphere than in the humbler areas discussed a moment ago. In politics there is often, though not always, disagreement about ends as well as means, conflict over what a decent society should be. Articulate spokesmen for various interest groups are continually putting forth explicitly or implicitly new notions on this score. They will appear periodically unless humanity destroys itself or decides to live like ants. Even in politics, on the other hand, one cannot claim that it is totally beyond the wit of man to establish an orderly and reasonably just government that still permits shifts in the influence, prestige, and power of the social groups that make up the society, without breaking down into periodic civil wars. England has managed the problem reasonably well since the seventeenth century. The combination of liberty with progress does have some basis in actual experience.

Any such world state would change rapidly enough—and slowly enough—to leave plenty of niches for the cantankerous. A commitment to freedom is emphatically not a commitment to a society that is perfect once and for all. Nor is it a commitment to some variety of intellectual egalitarianism. There is no reason to shrink at this bogey. The notion of turning every housewife into a Sappho and every businessman into a Socrates *is* utopian. Under present circumstances these ideas have conservative and reactionary consequences, since they are efforts to reconcile people to a fundamentally destructive and irrational society. The logical conclusion of this trend, if it continues, would be discussions of the meaning of freedom in Plato and Aristotle, conducted by well-dressed men and women in air-conditioned bomb shelters hundreds of feet beneath the surface of the earth. It is both more honest and more realistic to accept the conclusion that even in a free society the vast majority of the citizens would be neither professional intellectuals nor the holders of political power. What ordinary people might do with the time liberated from work by advancing technology in a society *also* liberated from the threat of destruction is indeed a problem. Certainly there would be room—and there is room even today—for vastly more participation by the intelligent amateur in the life of the intellect. But that problem can wait.

Today the real question is whether a free society can some day emerge from this age of obsolete political dinosaurs. The conception of freedom upon which this discussion has been based is a preindustrial one. May not the experience of industrial society obliterate this tradition, the critique of modern society made possible through it, and the very desire for a different kind of world?

Perhaps. No one knows. But once before, long ago, at a time too when the clouds were darkening on the prospect of a free society, a famous historian expressed its ideals in a speech he attributed to a famous statesman:

Just as our political life is free and open, so is our day-to-day life in our relations with each other. We do not lose our temper at our neighbor if he enjoys himself in his own way, nor do we give him the kind of black looks, which, though they do no real harm, still do hurt people's feelings. We are free and tolerant in our private lives; but in public affairs we keep to the law since it commands our deep respect. . . .

When our work is over, we are in a position to enjoy all kinds of recreation for our spirits. . . . In our own homes we find a beauty and good taste to delight us every day and drive away our cares. . . . We love beauty without extravagance; things of the mind without effeminacy. Wealth we regard as something to be used properly, rather than as something to boast about. . . .

We are capable at the time of taking risks and of estimating them beforehand. Others are brave out of ignorance; and when they stop to think, they begin to fear. But the man who truly deserves to be judged brave is he who best knows the meaning of what is sweet in life and of what is terrible, and then goes out undeterred to meet what is come.[10]

Athens fell short of this ideal and succumbed soon after its expression by Pericles. Yet the triumphs and defeats of twenty-five centuries have failed to erase it from men's minds. Not even the victory of Christianity, which did so much to change men's spirits, destroyed this proud standard. Later phases of Western civilization have at times come closer to meeting it than did Athens itself. Is it then so much to hope that it will withstand the present onslaught too?

---

[10]Thucydides, *Peloponnesian War*, Vol. II, pp. 27-40, trans. by Rex Warner (Penguin Classics, 1954), pp. 117–19. I have taken the liberty of attempting a few minor improvements on Warner's version.

INDEX

447